Computer Algorithms

Computer Algorithms

Introduction to Design and Analysis

THIRD EDITION

Sara Baase
San Diego State University

Allen Van Gelder
University of California at Santa Cruz

An imprint of Addison Wesley Longman, Inc.

Reading, Massachusetts • Menlo Park, California • New York
Harlow, England • Don Mills, Ontario • Sydney • Mexico City
Madrid • Amsterdam

Acquisitions Editor: Maite Suarez-Rivas
Assistant Editor: Jason Miranda
Composition/Art: Paul C. Anagnostopoulos, Windfall Software
Copy Editor: Joan Flaherty
Proofreader: Brooke Albright
Cover Illustration: Janetmarie Colby
Cover Design: Lynne Reed
Manufacturing Coordinator: Timothy McDonald

Access the latest information about Addison-Wesley titles from our World Wide Web site: www.awlonline.com

This book was typeset in ZzTEX on a PC. The font families used were Times, Optima, Lucida Sans, and MathTime. It was printed on New Era Matte.

Library of Congress Cataloging-in-Publication Data

Baase, Sara.
    Computer algorithms / Sara Baase, Allen Van Gelder. — 3rd ed.
      p. cm.
    ISBN 0-201-61244-5
    1. Computer algorithms.   I. Van Gelder, Allen.   II. Title.
  QA76.9.A43B33   2000
  519.7—dc21   99-14185
                                         CIP

Reprinted with corrections, April 2000

To Keith—always part of what I do   S.B.

To Jane—for her patience   A.V.G.

Preface

Purpose

This book is intended for an upper-division or graduate course in algorithms. It has sufficient material to allow several choices of topics.

The purpose of the book is threefold. It is intended to teach algorithms for solving real problems that arise frequently in computer applications, to teach basic principles and techniques of computational complexity (worst-case and average behavior, space usage, and lower bounds on the complexity of a problem), and to introduce the areas of $\mathcal{NP}$-completeness and parallel algorithms.

Another of the book's aims, which is at least as important as teaching the subject matter, is to develop in the reader the habit of always responding to a new algorithm with the questions: How good is it? Is there a better way? Therefore, instead of presenting a series of complete, "pulled-out-of-a-hat" algorithms with analysis, the text often discusses a problem first, considers one or more approaches to solving it (as a reader who sees the problem for the first time might), and then begins to develop an algorithm, analyzes it, and modifies or rejects it until a satisfactory result is produced. (Alternative approaches that are ultimately rejected are also considered in the exercises; it is useful for the reader to know why they were rejected.)

Questions such as: How can this be done more efficiently? What data structure would be useful here? Which operations should we focus on to analyze this algorithm? How must this variable (or data structure) be initialized? appear frequently throughout the text. Answers generally follow the questions, but we suggest readers pause before reading the ensuing text and think up their own answers. Learning is not a passive process.

We hope readers will also learn to be aware of how an algorithm actually behaves on various inputs—that is, Which branches are followed? What is the pattern of growth and shrinkage of stacks? How does presenting the input in different ways (e.g., listing the vertices or edges of a graph in a different order) affect the behavior? Such questions are raised in some of the exercises, but are not emphasized in the text because they require carefully going through the details of many examples.

Most of the algorithms presented are of practical use; we have chosen not to emphasize those with good asymptotic behavior that are poor for inputs of useful sizes (though some important ones are included). Specific algorithms were chosen for a variety of reasons

including the importance of the problem, illustrating analysis techniques, illustrating techniques (e.g., depth-first search) that give rise to numerous algorithms, and illustrating the development and improvement of techniques and algorithms (e.g., Union-Find programs).

Prerequisites

The book assumes familiarity with data structures such as linked lists, stacks, and trees, and prior exposure to recursion. However, we include a review, with specifications, for the standard data structures and some specialized ones. We have also added a student-friendly review of recursion.

Analysis of algorithms uses simple properties of logarithms and some calculus (differentiation to determine the asymptotic order of a function and integration to approximate summations), though virtually no calculus is used beyond Chapter 4. We find many students intimidated when they see the first log or integral sign because a year or more has passed since they had a calculus course. Readers will need only a few properties of logs and a few integrals from first-semester calculus. Section 1.3 reviews some of the necessary mathematics, and Section 1.5.4 provides a practical guide.

Algorithm Design Techniques

Several important algorithm design techniques reappear in many algorithms. These include divide-and-conquer, greedy methods, depth-first search (for graphs), and dynamic programming. This edition puts more emphasis on algorithm design techniques than did the second edition. Dynamic programming, as before, has its own chapter and depth-first search is presented with many applications in the chapter on graph traversals (Chapter 7). Most chapters are organized by application area, rather than by design technique, so we provide here a list of places where you will find algorithms using divide-and-conquer and greedy techniques.

The divide-and-conquer technique is described in Section 4.3. It is used in Binary Search (Section 1.6), most sorting methods (Chapter 4), median finding and the general selection problem (Section 5.4), binary search trees (Section 6.4), polynomial evaluation (Section 12.2), matrix multiplication (Section 12.3), the Fast Fourier Transform (Section 12.4), approximate graph coloring (Section 13.7), and, in a slightly different form, for parallel computation in Section 14.5.

Greedy algorithms are used for finding minimum spanning trees and shortest paths in Chapter 8, and for various approximation algorithms for $\mathcal{NP}$-hard optimization problems, such as bin packing, knapsack, graph coloring, and traveling salesperson (Sections 13.4 through 13.8).

Changes from the Second Edition

This edition has three new chapters and many new topics. Throughout the book, numerous sections have been extensively rewritten. A few topics from the second edition have been moved to different chapters where we think they fit better. We added more than 100 new exercises, many bibliographic entries, and an appendix with Java examples. Chapters 2, 3, and 6 are virtually all new.

Chapter 2 reviews abstract data types (ADTs) and includes specifications for several standard ADTs. The role of abstract data types in algorithm design is emphasized throughout the book.

Chapter 3 reviews recursion and induction, emphasizing the connection between the two and their usefulness in designing and proving correctness of programs. The chapter also develops recursion trees, which provide a visual and intuitive representation of recurrence equations that arise in the analysis of recursive algorithms. Solutions for commonly occurring patterns are summarized so they are available for use in later chapters.

Chapter 6 covers hashing, red-black trees for balanced binary trees, advanced priority queues, and dynamic equivalence relations (Union-Find). The latter topic was moved from a different chapter in the second edition.

We rewrote all algorithms in a Java-based pseudocode. Familiarity with Java is not required; the algorithms can be read easily by anyone familiar with C or C++. Chapter 1 has an introduction to the Java-based pseudocode.

We significantly expanded the section on mathematical tools for algorithm analysis in Chapter 1 to provide a better review and reference for some of the mathematics used in the book. The discussion of the asymptotic order of functions in Section 1.5 was designed to help students gain a better mastery of the concepts and techniques for dealing with asymptotic order. We added rules, in informal language, that summarize the most common cases (Section 1.5.4).

Chapter 4 contains an accelerated version of Heapsort in which the number of key comparisons is cut nearly in half. For Quicksort, we use the Hoare partition algorithm in the main text. Lomuto's method is introduced in an exercise. (This is reversed from the second edition.)

We split the old graph chapter into two chapters, and changed the order of some topics. Chapter 7 concentrates on (linear time) traversal algorithms. The presentation of depth-first search has been thoroughly revised to emphasize the general structure of the technique and show more applications. We added topological sorting and critical path analysis as applications and because of their intrinsic value and their connection to dynamic programming. Sharir's algorithm, rather than Tarjan's, is presented for strongly connected components.

Chapter 8 covers greedy algorithms for graph problems. The presentations of the Prim algorithm for minimum spanning trees and the Dijkstra algorithm for shortest paths were rewritten to emphasize the roles of priority queues and to illustrate how the use of abstract data types can lead the designer to efficient implementations. The asymptotically optimal $\Theta(m + n \log n)$ implementation is mentioned, but is not covered in depth. We moved Kruskal's algorithm for minimum spanning trees to this chapter.

The presentation of dynamic programming (Chapter 10) was substantially revised to emphasize a general approach to finding dynamic programming solutions. We added a new application, a text-formatting problem, to reinforce the point that not all applications call for a two-dimensional array. We moved the approximate string matching application (which was in this chapter in the second edition) to the string matching chapter (Section 11.5). The exercises include some other new applications.

Our teaching experience has pinpointed particular areas where students had difficulties with concepts related to $\mathcal{P}$ and $\mathcal{NP}$ (Chapter 13), particularly nondeterministic algorithms and polynomial transformations. We rewrote some definitions and examples to make the concepts clearer. We added a short section on approximation algorithms for the traveling salesperson problem and a section on DNA computing.

Instructors who used the second edition may particularly want to note that we changed some conventions and terminology (usually to conform to common usage). Array indexes now often begin at 0 instead of 1. (In some cases, where numbering from 1 was clearer, we left it that way.) We now use the term *depth* rather than *level* for the depth of a node in a tree. We use *height* instead of *depth* for the maximum depth of any node in a tree. In the second edition, a *path* in a graph was defined to be what is commonly called a *simple path*; we use the more general definition for *path* in this edition and define *simple path* separately. A directed graph may now contain a self-edge.

Exercises and Programs

Some exercises are somewhat open-ended. For example, one might ask for a good lower bound for the complexity of a problem, rather than asking students to show that a given function is a lower bound. We did this for two reasons. One is to make the form of the question more realistic; a solution must be discovered as well as verified. The other is that it may be hard for some students to prove the best known lower bound (or find the most efficient algorithm for a problem), but there is still a range of solutions they can offer to show their mastery of the techniques studied.

Some topics and interesting problems are introduced only in exercises. For example, the maximum independent set problem for a tree is an exercise in Chapter 3, the maximum subsequence sum problem is an exercise in Chapter 4, and the sink finding problem for a graph is an exercise in Chapter 7. Several $\mathcal{NP}$-complete problems are introduced in exercises in Chapter 13.

The abilities, background, and mathematical sophistication of students at different universities vary considerably, making it difficult to decide exactly which exercises should be marked ("starred") as "hard." We starred exercises that use more than minimal mathematics, require substantial creativity, or require a long chain of reasoning. A few exercises have two stars. Some starred exercises have hints.

The algorithms presented in this book are not programs; that is, many details not important to the method or the analysis are omitted. Of course, students should know how to implement efficient algorithms in efficient, debugged programs. Many instructors may teach this course as a pure "theory" course without programming. For those who want to assign programming projects, most chapters include a list of programming assignments. These are brief suggestions that may need amplification by instructors who choose to use them.

Selecting Topics for Your Course

Clearly the amount of material and the particular selection of topics to cover depend on the particular course and student population. We present sample outlines for two undergraduate courses and one graduate course.

This outline corresponds approximately to the senior-level course Sara Baase teaches at San Diego State University in a 15-week semester with 3 hours per week of lecture.

Chapter 1: The whole chapter is assigned as reading but I concentrate on Sections 1.4 and 1.5 in class.

Chapter 2: Sections 2.1 through 2.4 assigned as reading.

Chapter 3: Sections 3.1 through 3.4, 3.6, and 3.7 assigned as reading with light coverage in class.

Chapter 4: Sections 4.1 through 4.9.

Chapter 5: Sections 5.1 through 5.2, 5.6, and some of 5.4.

Chapter 7: Sections 7.1 through 7.4 and either 7.5 or 7.6 and 7.7.

Chapter 8: Sections 8.1 through 8.3 and brief mention of 8.4.

Chapter 11: Sections 11.1 through 11.4.

Chapter 13: Sections 13.1 through 13.5, 13.8, and 13.9.

The next outline is the junior-level course Allen Van Gelder teaches at the University of California, Santa Cruz, in a 10-week quarter with 3.5 hours per week of lecture.

Chapter 1: Sections 1.3 and 1.5, and remaining sections as reading.

Chapter 2: Sections 2.1 through 2.3, and remaining sections as reading.

Chapter 3: All sections are touched on; a lot is left for reading.

Chapter 4: Sections 4.1 through 4.9.

Chapter 5: Possibly Section 5.4, the average linear time algorithm only.

Chapter 6: Sections 6.4 through 6.6.

Chapter 7: Sections 7.1 through 7.6.

Chapter 8: The entire chapter.

Chapter 9: Sections 9.1 through 9.4.

Chapter 10: Possibly Sections 10.1 through 10.3, but usually no time.

For the first-year graduate course at the University of California, Santa Cruz (also 10 weeks, 3.5 hours of lecture), the above material is compressed and the following additional topics are covered.

Chapter 5: The entire chapter.

Chapter 6: The remainder of the chapter, with emphasis on amortized analysis.

Chapter 10: The entire chapter.

Chapter 13: Sections 13.1 through 13.3, and possibly Section 13.9.

The primary dependencies among chapters are shown in the following diagram with solid lines; some secondary dependencies are indicated with dashed lines. A secondary dependency means that only a few topics in the earlier chapter are needed in the later chapter, or that only the more advanced sections of the later chapter require the earlier one.

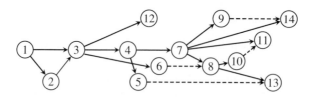

While material in Chapters 2 and 6 is important to have seen, a lot of it might have been covered in an earlier course. Some sections in Chapter 6 are important for the more advanced parts of Chapter 8.

We like to remind readers of common themes or techniques, so we often refer back to earlier sections; many of these references can be ignored if the earlier sections were not covered. Several chapters have a section on lower bounds, which benefits from the ideas and examples in Chapter 5, but the diagram does not show that dependency because many instructors do not cover lower bounds.

We marked ("starred") sections that contain more complicated mathematics or more complex or sophisticated arguments than most others, but only where the material is not central to the book. We also starred one or two sections that contain optional digressions. We have not starred a few sections that we consider essential to a course for which the book is used, even though they contain a lot of mathematics. For example, at least some of the material in Section 1.5 on the asymptotic growth rate of functions and in Section 3.7 on solutions of recurrence equations should be covered.

Acknowledgments

We are happy to take this opportunity to thank the people who helped in big and small ways in the preparation of the third edition of this book.

Sara Baase acknowledges the influence and inspiration of Dick Karp, who made the subject of computational complexity exciting and beautiful in his superb lectures. Allen Van Gelder acknowledges the insights gained from Bob Floyd, Don Knuth, Ernst Mayr, Vaughan Pratt, and Jeff Ullman; they all teach more than is "in the book." Allen also wishes to acknowledge colleagues David Helmbold for many discussions on how to present algorithms effectively and on fine points of many algorithms, and Charlie McDowell for help on many of the aspects of Java that are covered in this book's appendix. We thank Lila Kari for reading an early draft of the section on DNA computing and answering our questions.

Of course, we'd have nothing to write about without the many people who did the original research that provided the material we enjoy learning and passing on to new generations of students. We thank them for their work.

In the years since the second edition appeared, several students and instructors who used the book sent in lists of errors, typos, and suggestions for changes. We don't have a complete list of names, but we appreciate the time and thought that went into their letters.

The surveys and manuscript reviews obtained by Addison-Wesley were especially helpful. Our thanks to Iliana Bjorling-Sachs (Lafayette College), Mohammad B. Dadfar (Bowling Green State University), Daniel Hirschberg (University of California at Irvine),

Mitsunori Ogihara (University of Rochester), R. W. Robinson (University of Georgia), Yaakov L. Varol (University of Nevada, Reno), William W. White (Southern Illinois University at Edwardsville), Dawn Wilkins (University of Mississippi), and Abdou Youssef (George Washington University).

We thank our editors at Addison-Wesley, Maite Suarez-Rivas and Karen Wernholm, for their confidence and patience in working with us on this project that often departed from standard production procedures and schedules. We thank Joan Flaherty for her painstakingly careful copy editing and valuable suggestions for improving the presentation. Brooke Albright's careful proofreading detected many errors that had survived earlier scrutiny; of course, any that remain are the fault of the authors.

We thank Keith Mayers for assisting us in various ways. Sara thanks him for not reminding her too often that she broke her wedding vow to work less than seven days a week.

Sara Baase, *San Diego, California*
http://www-rohan.sdsu.edu/faculty/baase

Allen Van Gelder, *Santa Cruz, California*
http://www.cse.ucsc.edu/personnel/faculty/avg.html

June, 1999

Contents

7 Graphs and Graph Traversals   313

8 Graph Optimization Problems and Greedy Algorithms   387

9 Transitive Closure, All-Pairs Shortest Paths   425

10 Dynamic Programming   451

11   String Matching   483

12   Polynomials and Matrices   515

13 $\mathcal{NP}$-Complete Problems   547

1

Analyzing Algorithms and Problems: Principles and Examples

1.1   Introduction

To say that a problem is solvable algorithmically means, informally, that a computer program can be written that will produce the correct answer for any input if we let it run long enough and allow it as much storage space as it needs. In the 1930s, before the advent of computers, mathematicians worked very actively to formalize and study the notion of an algorithm, which was then interpreted informally to mean a clearly specified set of simple instructions to be followed to solve a problem or compute a function. Various formal models of computation were devised and investigated. Much of the emphasis in the early work in this field, called *computability theory*, was on describing or characterizing those problems that could be solved algorithmically and on exhibiting some problems that could not be. One of the important negative results, established by Alan Turing, was the proof of the unsolvability of the "halting problem." The halting problem is to determine whether an arbitrary given algorithm (or computer program) will eventually halt (rather than, say, get into an infinite loop) while working on a given input. There cannot exist a computer program that solves this problem.

Although computability theory has obvious and fundamental implications for computer science, the knowledge that a problem can theoretically be solved on a computer is not sufficient to tell us whether it is practical to do so. For example, a perfect chess-playing program could be written. This would not be a very difficult task; there are only a finite number of ways to arrange the chess pieces on the board, and under certain rules a game must terminate after a finite number of moves. The program could consider each of the computer's possible moves, each of its opponent's possible responses, each of its possible responses to those moves, and so on until each sequence of possible moves reaches an end. Then since it knows the ultimate result of each move, the computer can choose the best one. The number of distinct arrangements of pieces on the board that it is reasonable to consider (much less the number of sequences of moves) is roughly 10^{50} by some estimates. A program that examined them all would take several thousand years to run. Thus such a program has not been run.

Numerous problems with practical applications can be solved—that is, programs can be written for them—but the time and storage requirements are much too great for these programs to be of practical use. Clearly the time and space requirements of a program are of practical importance. They have become, therefore, the subject of theoretical study in the area of computer science called *computational complexity*. One branch of this study, which is not covered in this book, is concerned with setting up a formal and somewhat abstract theory of the complexity of computable functions. (Solving a problem is equivalent to computing a function from the set of inputs to the set of outputs.) Axioms for measures of complexity have been formulated; they are basic and general enough so that either the number of instructions executed or the number of storage bits used by a program can be taken as a complexity measure. Using these axioms, we can prove the existence of arbitrarily complex problems and of problems for which there is no best program.

The branch of computational complexity studied in this book is concerned with analyzing specific problems and specific algorithms. This book is intended to help readers build a repertoire of classic algorithms to solve common problems, some general design techniques, tools and principles for analyzing algorithms and problems, and methods of proving correctness. We will present, study, and analyze algorithms to solve a variety of problems for which computer programs are frequently used. We will analyze the amount of time the algorithms take to execute, and we will also often analyze the amount of space used by the algorithms. In the course of describing algorithms for a variety of problems, we will see that several algorithm design techniques often prove useful. Thus we will pause now and then to talk about some general techniques, such as divide-and-conquer, greedy algorithms, depth-first search, and dynamic programming. We will also study the computational complexity of the problems themselves, that is, the time and space inherently required to solve the problem no matter what algorithm is used. We will study the class of $\mathcal{NP}$-complete problems—problems for which no efficient algorithms are known—and consider some heuristics for getting useful results. We will also describe an approach for solving these problems using DNA instead of electronic computers. Finally, we will introduce the subject of algorithms for parallel computers.

In the following sections we outline the algorithm language, review some background and tools that will be used throughout the book, and illustrate the main concepts involved in analyzing an algorithm.

1.2 Java as an Algorithm Language

We chose Java as the algorithm language for this book by balancing several criteria. The algorithms should be easy to read. We want to focus on the strategy and techniques of an algorithm, not declarations and syntax details of concern to a compiler. The language should support data abstraction and problem decomposition, to make it easy to express algorithmic ideas clearly. The language should provide a practical pathway to implementation. It should be widely available and provide support for program development. Actually implementing and running algorithms can enhance the student's understanding greatly, and should not turn into a frustrating battle with the compiler and debugger. Finally, because this book is teaching algorithms, not a programming language, it should be reasonably easy to translate an algorithm to a variety of languages that readers might wish to use, and specialized language features should be minimized.

Java showed up well by several of our criteria, although we would not claim it is ideal. It supports data abstraction naturally. It is type-safe, meaning that objects of one type cannot be used in operations intended for a different type; arbitrary type conversions (called "casts") are not permitted, either. There is an explicit **boolean** type, so if one types "=" (the assignment operator) when "==" (the equality operator) was intended, the compiler catches it.

Java does not permit pointer manipulations, which are a frequent source of obscure errors; in fact, pointers are hidden from the programmer and handled automatically behind the scenes. At run time, Java checks for out-of-range array subscripts, and other inconsistencies that might be other sources of obscure errors. It performs "garbage collection," which means that it recycles the storage space of objects that are no longer referenced; this takes a big burden of space management off the programmer.

On the downside, Java has many of the same terse, cryptic syntax features of C. The object structure may force inefficiencies in time and space. Many Java constructs require greater verbosity than other languages, such as C, for instance.

Although Java has many specialized features, the algorithms presented in this book avoid most of them, in the interest of being language-independent. In fact, some steps within an algorithm may be stated in pseudocode for easier readability. This section describes a small subset of Java that we use for the book, and the pseudocode conventions that we use to improve readability of the algorithms. The Java-specific Appendix A gives some additional implementation details for readers who want to get a Java program running, but these details are not pertinent to understanding the main text.

1.2.1   A Usable Subset of Java

A thorough acquaintance with Java is not important to understand the algorithms in this text. This section gives a brief overview of the Java features that do appear, for those readers who wish to follow the implementation issues closely. In some cases we point out object-oriented features of Java that might be used, but which we avoid so that the text can be fairly language-independent; this is mainly for the benefit of readers who are familiar with some other object-oriented language, such as C++, but who are not completely familiar with Java. A sample Java "main program" appears in Appendix A. Many books are available for in-depth coverage of the Java language.

Readers who are well acquainted with Java will undoubtedly notice many instances in which some nice Java feature could have been used. However, the *concepts* behind the algorithms do not require any special features, and we want these concepts to be easy to grasp and apply in a variety of languages, so we leave it to the readers, once they have grasped the concepts, to tailor the implementations to their favorite language.

Readers familiar with C syntax will recognize many similarities in Java syntax: Blocks are delimited by curly braces, "{" and "}"; square brackets, "[" and "]", enclose array indexes. As in C and C++, a two-dimensional array is really a one-dimensional array whose elements are themselves one-dimensional arrays, so two pairs of square brackets are needed to access an element, as in "matrix[i][j]". Operators "==", "!=", "<=", and ">=" are the keyboard versions of the mathematical relational operators "=", "$\neq$", "$\leq$", and "$\geq$", respectively. In pseudocode the text usually prefers the mathematical versions. Text examples use the "++" and "−−" operators to increment and decrement, but never use them embedded in other expressions. There are also the operators "+=", "−=", "*=", and "/=" adopted from C. For example,

```
p += q;  /* Add q to p. */
y −= x;  // Subtract x from y.
```

As just illustrated, comments extend from "//" to end-of-line, or from "/*" to "*/", as in C++.

Function headers normally look the same in Java as in C. The function header specifies the *parameter type signature* in parentheses after the function name; it specifies the *return type* before the function name. The combination of return type and parameter type signature is called the function's *full type signature*, or *prototype*. Thus

    int getMin(PriorityQ pq)

tells us that getMin takes one parameter of type (or **class**) PriorityQ and returns type **int**.

    Java has a few *primitive types* and all remaining types are called *classes*. The primitive types are logical (**boolean**) and numerical (**byte, char, short, int, long, float,** and **double**) types. All classes (nonprimitive types) in Java are *reference* classes. Behind the scenes, variables declared in classes are "pointers"; their values are addresses. Instances of classes are called *objects*. Declaring a variable does not create an object. Generally, objects are created with a "**new**" operator, which returns a reference to the new object.

    The data fields of an object are called *instance fields* in object-oriented terminology. The binary dot operator is used to access instance fields of an object.

Example 1.1   Creating and accessing Java objects

For this example, let's assume that date information has the following nested logical structure:

- year
  - number
  - isLeap
- month
- day

That is, using informal terminology, year is a compound attribute that consists of the boolean attribute isLeap and the integer attribute number, while month and day are simple integer attributes. To reflect this nested structure, we have to define two classes in Java, one for the whole date and another for the year field. Assume we choose the names Date and Year, respectively, for these classes. Then we would declare number and isLeap as instance fields in the Year class and declare year, month, and day as instance fields in the Date class. Moreover, we would most likely define Year as an inner class of Date. The syntax is shown in Figure 1.1.

```
class Date
    {
    public Year year;
    public int month;
    public int day;

    public static class Year
        {
        public int number;
        public boolean isLeap;
        }
    }
```

       Figure 1.1   Java syntax for the Date class with an inner Year class

Without the **public** keyword, the instance fields would not be accessible outside of the Date and Year classes; for simplicity, we make them **public** here. The reason for declaring the inner class, Year, to be **static** is so we can create an instance of Year that is not associated with any particular Date object. All inner classes will be **static** in this book.

Suppose we have created a Date object that is referenced by variable dueDate. To access the instance field year in this object, the dot operator is used, as in "dueDate.year." If the instance field is in a class (as opposed to being in a primitive type), then further dot operators access its instance fields, as in "dueDate.year.isLeap."

The assignment statement copies only the *reference*, or *address*, of an object in a class; it does not make a copy of the instance fields. For example, "noticeDate = dueDate" causes variable noticeDate to *refer to the same object as* variable dueDate. Therefore the following code fragment would probably be a logical error:

```
noticeDate = dueDate;
noticeDate.day = dueDate.day − 7;
```

See Section 1.2.2 for additional discussion.   ■

Control statements **if**, **else**, **while**, **for**, and **break** have the same meanings in Java as in C (and C++) and are used in this book. Several other control statements exist, but are not used. The syntax for **while** and **for** are

while (continuation condition **)** body
for (initializer **;** continuation condition **;** incrementer **)** body

where "initializer" and "incrementer" are simple statements (without "{, }"), "body" is an arbitrary statement, and "continuation condition" is a **boolean** expression. The **break** statement causes an immediate exit from the closest enclosing **for** or **while** loop.[1]

All classes form a tree (also called a hierarchy), with the **Object** class being the root. When declaring a new class, it is possible to say it *extends* a previously defined class, and the new class becomes a child of the previously defined class in the class tree. We will not create such structures in this text, to keep the code as language-independent as possible; however, a few examples are given in Appendix A. When the new class is not declared to extend any class, then it extends **Object** by default. Complex class structures are not needed for the algorithms studied in this text.

Operations on objects are called *methods* in object-oriented terminology; however, we will restrict ourselves to the use of *static methods*, which are simply procedures and functions. In our terminology a *procedure* is a named sequence of computation steps that may be called (with parameters); a *function* is a procedure that also returns a value to the caller. In Java a procedure that returns no value is declared as having return type **void**; C and C++ are similar in this respect. The term *static* is technical Java terminology, which means that the method can be applied to any object or objects of the appropriate types (an object's type is its class) according to the method's type signature (often called

---

[1] It also exits from **switch**, but **switch** is not used in this book.

its prototype). A static method is not "attached" to any particular object. Static methods behave like the usual functions and procedures of programming languages like C, Pascal, and so on. However, their names must be prefixed by the class in which they are defined, as in "List.first(x)" to apply method first defined in class List to parameter x.

In Java, instance fields of an object are private by default, which means that they can be accessed only by methods (functions and procedures) that are defined within the class. This is consistent with the theme of abstract data type (ADT) design that objects should be accessed only through the operations defined for the ADT. The code that implements these ADT operations (or static methods, or functions and procedures) exists within the class and is aware of the private instance fields and their types. Methods are also private by default, but usually are specified as "public," so that methods defined in other classes may call them. However, "low-level" methods that should be called only by other methods in the same class may also be private.

The *clients* of the ADT (procedures and functions that call the ADT) are implemented outside the class in which the ADT "lives," so they have access only to the *public* parts of the ADT class. The maintenance of private data is called *encapsulation*, or *information hiding*.

Instance fields of an object retain the values that are assigned to them for the lifetime of the object, or until overwritten by a subsequent assignment. Here we can see the advantage of having them private to the class in which they are defined. A public instance field could be assigned an arbitrary value by any part of the overall program. A private instance field can be assigned a value only by going through a method for the ADT class that is designed for the purpose. This method can perform other computations and tests to be sure that the value assigned to an instance field is consistent with the ADT specifications, and is consistent with values stored in other instance fields of the same object.

A new object is created by the phrase "**new** className()," for example:

Date dueDate = **new** Date();

This statement causes Java to invoke a default *constructor* for the Date class. A constructor reserves storage for a new object (or instance) of the class and returns a reference (probably an address) for accessing this object. The instance fields of this new object might not be initialized.

Java sidelight: The programmer may write additional constructor functions for a class, the bodies of which may initialize various instance fields and perform other computations. In the interest of language-independence, this text does not use such constructors, so details are omitted.

Arrays are declared somewhat differently in Java than in C and C++, and their properties are also slightly different. The Java syntax to declare an array of integers (more precisely, to declare a variable whose type is "array of integers") is "**int**[] x," whereas C might use "**int** x[]." This statement does not initialize x; that is accomplished with

x = **new int**[howMany];

where howMany is either a constant or a variable whose value denotes the desired length of the array. Declarations of arrays for classes are similar. The declaration and initialization may be, and usually should be, combined into one statement:

```
int[] x = new int[howMany];
Date[] dates = new Date[howMany];
```

While these statements initialize x and dates in the sense of reserving storage for the arrays, they only initialize the *elements* to default values, which are unlikely to be useful. Therefore individual elements dates[0], dates[1], . . . , must be assigned values (possibly using the **new** operator) before they are used. The syntax, outside the Date class, is

```
dates[0] = new Date();
dates[0].month = 1;
dates[0].day = 1;
dates[0].year = new Date.Year();
dates[0].year.number = 2000;
dates[0].year.isLeap = true;
```

Notice that field names come after the index that selects a specific array element. Also notice that the inner class name, Year, is qualified by the outer class name, Date, in the second **new** statement, because the statement is outside the Date class. As mentioned, Java programmers can write constructors that take parameters to accomplish such initialization of newly constructed objects, but this text does not use such constructors in the interest of language independence.

Once array x is initialized with a **new** statement, as shown a few paragraphs above, the length of the array it references cannot change. Java provides a way to query this length, which is x.length. That is, the *instance field* length is automatically "attached" to the array object as part of the **new** operation, and can be accessed through x, as shown, as long as x refers to this object.

The valid indexes (or subscripts) for elements of this array are 0 through (x.length − 1). Java will stop the program (technically, throw an exception) if the program attempts to access an element with an index outside this range. We will often wish to use indexes in the range 1 through n, and therefore will initialize arrays with "**new** int[n+1]" in these cases.

Java permits *overloading* and *overriding* of methods. A method is said to be *overloaded* if it has multiple definitions with varying parameter types, but the same return type. Many arithmetic operators are overloaded. *Overriding* means there are multiple definitions of a single method in the class hierarchy with the same parameter types, and Java applies the "closest" definition. (Again, for compatibility with other languages and because this capability is not central for understanding the algorithms, we avoid these features and refer interested readers to books on the Java language.) The same names for methods may be used in different classes, but this is not really overloading because the class name (or object name) appears as a qualifier when the names are used outside the class in which they are defined. Later examples will make this clear.

For readers acquainted with C++, it is worth pointing out that Java does not permit the programmer to define new meanings for *operators*. This text uses such operators for readability in pseudocode (e.g., $x < y$, where x and y are in some nonnumeric class, such as **String**). However, if you define a class and you develop an actual Java program with it, you must write named functions (e.g., less()) and call them to compare objects in your class.

1.2.2 Organizer Classes

We coin the term *organizer class*, which is not a standard Java term, to describe a very simple class that merely groups several instance fields. This construct fulfills a role somewhat analogous to the C *struct* and the Pascal or Modula *record*; analogous constructs exist in Lisp, ML, and most other programming languages. Organizer classes are diametrically opposite from abstract data types in their purpose; they merely organize some storage, but do not limit access to it and do not provide any customized operations on it. It is often convenient to define an organizer class within some other class; in this case, the organizer class is called an *inner class* in Java terminology.

An organizer class has just one method, called copy. Since variables are *references* to objects in Java, the assignment statement copies only the reference, not the fields of the object, as was illustrated in Example 1.1 with dueDate and noticeDate. If these variables are declared in an organizer class named Date, then we could use the statements

```
noticeDate = Date.copy(dueDate);
noticeDate.day = dueDate.day − 7;
```

to copy the fields of dueDate into a new object referenced by noticeDate, then modify the day field of noticeDate only.

Definition 1.1   The copy function for organizer classes

The general rule for how the copy function (or method) in an organizer class should assign values to the instance fields of the new object (illustrated by assuming object d is being copied into a new object d2) is as follows:

1. If the instance field (say year) is in another *organizer* class, then the copy method for that class is invoked, as in d2.year = Year.copy(d.year).
2. If the instance field (say day) is *not* in an *organizer* class, a simple assignment is used, as in d2.day = d.day.

The complete example is given in Figure 1.2.   ∎

The programmer must ensure that cycles do not occur in the definitions of organizer classes, or else copy might not terminate. Of course, a new object in an organizer class can also be created in the usual way:

```
Date someDate = new Date();
```

Java sidelight: Java provides a facility for making a one-level copy of an object without having to write out each assignment statement, based on the **clone** method, but this will not handle nested structures such as Date automatically; you will still need to write some code for these cases. Appendix A gives the code for a "generic" copy1 level function.

```
class Date
    {
    public Year year;
    public int month;
    public int day;

    public static class Year
        {
        public int number;
        public boolean isLeap;

        public static Year copy(Year y)
            { Year y2 = new Year();
              y2.number = y.number;
              y2.isLeap = y.isLeap;
              return y2;
            }
        }

    public static Date copy(Date d)
        { Date d2 = new Date();
          d2.year = Year.copy(d.year); // organizer class
          d2.month = d.month;
          d2.day = d.day;
          return d2;
        }

    public static int defaultCentury;
    }
```

Figure 1.2   An organizer class Date with an inner organizer class Year

An organizer class contains only **public** instance fields. If the **static** keyword also appears in the field declaration, the field is not associated with any particular object, but is essentially a global variable.

Example 1.2   Typical organizer classes

In Figure 1.2 the classes of Example 1.1 are embellished with copy functions, so they will qualify as organizer classes. As we see, the definition of copy is mechanical, though tedious. Its details will be omitted from future examples. For completeness, we included defaultCentury as an example of a "global variable," although most organizer classes will not contain global variables.   ■

To summarize, we invented the term *organizer class* to denote a class that simply groups together some instance fields and defines a function to make copies of them.

1.2.3 Java-Based Pseudocode Conventions

Most algorithms in this book use Java-based pseudocode, rather than strict Java, for easier readability. The following conventions are used (except in the Java-specific Appendix A).

1. Block delimiters ("{" and "}") are omitted. Block boundaries are indicated by indentation.

2. The keyword **static** is omitted from method (function and procedure) declarations. All methods declared in the text are **static**. (Nonstatic built-in Java methods appear occasionally; in particular, s.length() is used to obtain the length of strings.) The keyword **static** *does* appear where needed for instance fields and inner classes.

3. Class name qualifiers are omitted from method (function and procedure) calls. For example, x = cons(z, x) might be written when the Java syntax requires x = IntList. cons(z, x). (The IntList class is described in Section 2.3.2.) Class name qualifiers are required in Java whenever static methods are called from outside the class in which they are defined.

4. Keywords to control visibility, **public**, **private**, and **protected**, are omitted. Placing all files related to one Java program in the same directory eliminates the need to deal with visibility issues.

5. Mathematical relational operators "$\neq$," "$\leq$," and "$\geq$" are usually written, instead of their keyboard versions. Relational operators are used on types where the meaning is clear, such as **String**, even though this would be invalid syntax in Java.

6. Keywords, which are either reserved words or standard parts of Java, are set in this font: **int**, **String**. *Comments are set in this font.* Code statements and program variable names are set in this font. However, pseudocode statements are set in the regular font of the text, like this sentence.

Occasional departures from this scheme occur when we are making a specific point about the Java language.

1.3 Mathematical Background

We use a variety of mathematical concepts, tools, and techniques in this book. Most should already be familiar to you, although a few might be new. This section collects them to provide a ready reference, as well as a brief review. Proof concepts are covered in greater depth in Chapter 3.

1.3.1 Sets, Tuples, and Relations

This section provides informal definitions and a few elementary properties of sets and related concepts. A set is a collection of distinct elements that we wish to treat as a single object. Usually the elements are of the same "type" and have some additional common properties that make it useful to think of them as one object. The notation $e \in S$ is read "element e is a member of set S" or, briefly, "e is in S." Notice that e and S are different types in this case. For example, if e is an integer, S is a *set of* integers, which is different from being an integer.

A particular set is defined by listing or describing its elements between a pair of curly braces. Examples of this notation are

$$S_1 = \{a, b, c\}, \qquad S_2 = \{x \mid x \text{ is an integer power of 2}\}, \qquad S_3 = \{1, \ldots, n\}.$$

The expression for S_2 is read "the set of *all* elements x *such that* x is an integer power of 2." The "$\mid$" symbol is read "such that" in this context. Sometimes a colon ("$:$") is used in this place. The ellipsis "$\ldots$" may be used when the implicit elements are clear.

If all elements of one set, S_1, are also in another set, S_2, then S_1 is said to be a *subset* of S_2 and S_2 is said to be a *superset* of S_1. The notations are $S_1 \subseteq S_2$ and $S_2 \supseteq S_1$. To denote that S_1 is a subset of S_2 *and is not equal to* S_2, we write $S_1 \subset S_2$ or $S_2 \supset S_1$. It is important not to confuse "$\in$" with "$\subset$." The former means "is an element in" and the latter means "is a set of elements contained within." The *empty set*, denoted by $\emptyset$, has no elements, so it is a subset of every set.

A set has no inherent order. Thus, in the above examples, S_1 could have been defined as $\{b, c, a\}$ and S_3 could have been defined as $\{i \mid 1 \leq i \leq n\}$ when it is understood that i is an integer.

A group of elements *in a specified order* is called a *sequence*. Besides order, another important difference between sets and sequences is that sequences can have repeated elements. Sequences are denoted by listing their elements in order, enclosed in parentheses. Thus (a, b, c), (b, c, a), and (a, b, c, a) are distinct sequences. The ellipsis can also be used for sequences, as in $(1, \ldots, n)$.

A set S is *finite* if there is an integer n such that the elements of S can be placed in a one-to-one correspondence with $\{1, \ldots, n\}$; in this case we write $|S| = n$. In general, $|S|$ denotes the number of elements in set S, also called the *cardinality* of S. A sequence is *finite* if there is an integer n such that the elements of the sequence can be placed in a one-to-one correspondence with $(1, \ldots, n)$. A set or sequence that is not finite is *infinite*. If all the elements of a finite sequence are distinct, that sequence is said to be a *permutation* of the finite *set* consisting of the same elements. This again underscores the difference between a set and a sequence. One set of n elements has $n!$ distinct permutations (see Section 1.3.2).

How many distinct subsets does a finite set of n elements have? Keep in mind that the empty set and the entire set are subsets. To construct any subset we have n binary choices: to include or exclude each element of the given set. There are 2^n distinct ways to make these choices, so there are 2^n subsets.

How many distinct subsets *of cardinality* k does a finite set of n elements have? There is a special notation for this quantity: $\binom{n}{k}$, read "n choose k" or, more verbosely, "number of combinations of n items taken k at a time." The notation $C(n, k)$ is also used, and these quantities are called *binomial coefficients*.

To find an expression for $\binom{n}{k}$, or $C(n, k)$, we focus on choices in the subset of k instead of choices in the original set, say S. We can make a *sequence* of k distinct elements of S as follows: The first element of the sequence can be chosen from any element of S, so there are n choices. Then the second element of the sequence can be chosen from any remaining element of S, so there are $(n - 1)$ choices for this, and so on until k elements are chosen. (If $k > n$ it is impossible to make k distinct choices, so the result is 0.) Therefore there are $n(n - 1) \cdots (n - k + 1)$ distinct sequences of k distinct elements. But we saw that a specific set of k elements can be represented as $k!$ sequences. So the number of distinct subsets of k, drawn from a set of n, is

$$C(n, k) \equiv \binom{n}{k} = \frac{n(n - 1) \cdots (n - k + 1)}{k!} = \frac{n!}{(n - k)! \, k!} \quad \text{for } n \geq k \geq 0. \quad (1.1)$$

Since every subset must have *some* size from 0 through n, we arrive at the identity

$$\sum_{k=0}^{n} \binom{n}{k} = 2^n. \quad (1.2)$$

Tuples and the Cross Product

A *tuple* is a finite sequence whose elements often do not have the same type. For example, in a two-dimensional plane, a point can be represented by the ordered pair (x, y). If it is a geometric plane, x and y are both "length." But if it is a plot of running time vs. problem size, then y might be seconds and x might be an integer. Short tuples have special names: pair, triple, quadruple, quintuple, and so on. In the context of "tuple" these are understood to be ordered; in other contexts "pair" might mean "set of two" instead of "sequence of two," and so on. A k-tuple is a tuple of k elements.

The *cross product* of two sets, say S and T, is the set of pairs that can be formed by choosing an element of S as the first element of the tuple and an element of T as the second. In mathematical notation we have

$$S \times T = \{(x, y) \mid x \in S, y \in T\}. \quad (1.3)$$

Therefore $|S \times T| = |S| \, |T|$. It often happens that S and T are the same set, but this is not necessary. We can define the iterated cross product to produce longer tuples. For example, $S \times T \times U$ is the set of all triples formed by taking an element of S, followed by an element of T, followed by an element of U.

Relations and Functions

A *relation* is simply some subset of a (possibly iterated) cross product. This subset might be finite or infinite, and can be empty or the entire cross product. The most important case is a *binary* relation, which is simply some subset of a simple cross product. We are all familiar with many examples of binary relations, such as "less than" on the reals. Letting $\mathbf{R}$ denote the set of all reals, the "less than" relation can be defined formally as $\{(x, y) \mid x \in \mathbf{R}, y \in \mathbf{R}, x < y\}$. As we see, this is a subset of $\mathbf{R} \times \mathbf{R}$. As another example, if P is the set of all people, then $P \times P$ is the set of all pairs of people. We can define "parent of" as (x, y) such that x is a parent of y, "ancestor of" as (x, y) such that x is an ancestor of y, and these are subsets of $P \times P$.

Although many relations are pairs in which both elements are the same type, this is not required by the definition. A set of pairs $\{(x, y) \mid x \in S, y \in T\}$ is a binary relation. Going back to our earlier example of a tuple in a plot, such a relation might represent the relationship between problem size and running time for some program. For another example, we might let F be the set of all female people, and then "x is mother of y" would be a subset of $F \times P$.

Although relations may be arbitrary subsets, there are certain common properties of interest that a relation R might have when both elements are drawn from the same underlying set, say S. Also, in these cases, because many standard relations have an infix notation (such as $x < y$), the notation $x R y$ is often used to mean $(x, y) \in R$.

Definition 1.2   Important properties of relations

Let $R \subseteq S \times S$. Note the meanings of the following terms:

reflexive	for all $x \in S$, $(x, x) \in R$.
symmetric	whenever $(x, y) \in R$, (y, x) is also in R.
antisymmetric	whenever $(x, y) \in R$, (y, x) is *not* in R.
transitive	whenever $(x, y) \in R$ and $(y, z) \in R$, then $(x, z) \in R$.

A relation that is reflexive, symmetric, and transitive is called an *equivalence relation*, often denoted with "$\equiv$".   ■

Note that "less than" is transitive and antisymmetric, while "less than or equal" is transitive and reflexive, but not antisymmetric (because $x \leq x$).

Equivalence relations are important in many problems because such a relation *partitions* the underlying set S; that is, it divides S into a collection of disjoint subsets (called *equivalence classes*) $S_1, S_2, \ldots$, such that all elements in S_1 are "equivalent" to each other, all elements in S_2 are equivalent to each other, and so on. For example, if S is some set of nonnegative integers and R is defined as $\{(x, y) \mid x \in S, y \in S, (x - y) \text{ is divisible by } 3\}$, then R is an equivalence relation on S. Clearly, $(x - x)$ is divisible by 3. If $(x - y)$ is divisible by 3, so is $(y - x)$. Finally, if $(x - y)$ and $(y - z)$ are divisible by 3, so is $(x - z)$. So R satisfies the properties that define an equivalence relation. How does R partition S? There are three groups, each with a different nonnegative remainder when divided by 3. All elements with the same remainder are equivalent to each other.

Since a binary relation is a set whose elements are ordered pairs, it is often convenient to think of the relation as a two-column table in which each row contains one tuple. A *function* is simply a relation in which no element of the first column is repeated within the relation.

Many problems that involve binary relations can be cast as problems on graphs. Graph problems constitute a rich class of challenging algorithmic problems. For example, in a big project involving many interdependent tasks, we might have many facts of the form "task x depends on task y having been completed." With a fixed set of people to perform the tasks, how should they be scheduled to minimize the elapsed time? We will study many problems like this in later chapters.

1.3.2 Algebra and Calculus Tools

This section provides some definitions and elementary properties about logarithms, proba-bility, permutations, summation formulas, and common mathematical sequences and se-ries. (A series is the sum of a sequence in this context.) We will introduce additional mathematical tools for recurrence equations in Chapter 3. You can find formulas not de-rived here by consulting the sources in Notes and References at the end of the chapter.

Floor and Ceiling Functions

For any real number x, $\lfloor x \rfloor$ (read "floor of x") is the largest integer less than or equal to x. $\lceil x \rceil$ (read "ceiling of x") is the smallest integer greater than or equal to x. For example, $\lfloor 2.9 \rfloor = 2$, and $\lceil 6.1 \rceil = 7$.

Logarithms

The logarithm function, usually to the base 2, is the mathematical tool used most exten-sively in this book. Although logarithms do not occur very frequently in natural sciences, they are prevalent in computer science.

Definition 1.3   Logarithm function and logarithmic base

For $b > 1$ and $x > 0$, $\log_b x$ (read "log to the base b of x") is that real number L such that $b^L = x$; that is, $\log_b x$ is the power to which b must be raised to get x.   ∎

The following properties of logarithms follow easily from the definition.

Lemma 1.1   Let x and y be arbitrary positive real numbers, let a be any real number, and let $b > 1$ and $c > 1$ be real numbers.

1. $\log_b$ is a strictly increasing function, that is, if $x > y$, then $\log_b x > \log_b y$.
2. $\log_b$ is a one-to-one function, that is, if $\log_b x = \log_b y$, then $x = y$.
3. $\log_b 1 = 0$.
4. $\log_b b^a = a$.
5. $\log_b(xy) = \log_b x + \log_b y$.
6. $\log_b(x^a) = a \log_b x$.
7. $x^{\log_b y} = y^{\log_b x}$.
8. To convert from one base to another: $\log_c x = (\log_b x)/(\log_b c)$.   □

Since the log to the base 2 is used most often in computational complexity, there is a special notation for it: "lg"; that is, $\lg x = \log_2 x$. The natural logarithm (log to the base e) is denoted by "ln"; that is, $\ln x = \log_e x$. When $\log(x)$ is used without any base being mentioned, it means the statement is true for any base.

Sometimes the logarithm function is applied to itself. The notation $\lg \lg(x)$ means $\lg(\lg(x))$. The notation $\lg^{(p)}(x)$ means p applications, so $\lg^{(2)}(x)$ is the same as $\lg \lg(x)$. Note that $\lg^{(3)}(65536) = 2$, which is quite different from $(\lg(65536))^3 = 4096$.

Throughout the text we almost always take logs of integers, not arbitrary positive numbers, and we often need an integer value close to the log rather than its exact value. Let n be a positive integer. If n is a power of 2, say $n = 2^k$, for some integer k, then $\lg n = k$. If n is not a power of 2, then there is an integer k such that $2^k < n < 2^{k+1}$. In this case, $\lfloor \lg n \rfloor = k$ and $\lceil \lg n \rceil = k + 1$. The expressions $\lfloor \lg n \rfloor$ and $\lceil \lg n \rceil$ are used often. You should verify these inequalities:

$$n \le 2^{\lceil \lg n \rceil} < 2n.$$

$$\tfrac{n}{2} < 2^{\lfloor \lg n \rfloor} \le n.$$

Finally, here are a few more useful facts: $\lg e \approx 1.443$ and $\lg 10 \approx 3.32$. The derivative of $\ln(x)$ is $1/x$. Using part 8 of Lemma 1.1, the derivative of $\lg(x)$ is $\lg(e)/x$.

Permutations

A permutation of n distinct objects is a sequence that contains each object once. Let $S = \{s_1, s_2, \ldots, s_n\}$. Note that the elements of S are ordered by their indexes; that is, s_1 is the first element, s_2 the second, and so on. A permutation of S is a one-to-one function π from the set $\{1, 2, \ldots, n\}$ onto itself. We think of π as rearranging S by moving the ith element, s_i, to the $\pi(i)$th position. We may describe π simply by listing its values, that is, $(\pi(1), \pi(2), \ldots, \pi(n))$. For example, for $n = 5$, $\pi = (4, 3, 1, 5, 2)$ rearranges the elements of S as follows: s_3, s_5, s_2, s_1, s_4.

The number of permutations of n distinct objects is $n!$. To see this, observe that the first element can be moved to any of the n positions; then that position is filled and the second element can be moved to any of the $n - 1$ remaining positions; the third element can be moved to any of the remaining $n - 2$ positions, and so on. So the total number of possible rearrangements is $n \times (n - 1) \times (n - 2) \times \ldots \times 2 \times 1 = n!$.

Probability

Suppose that in a given situation an event, or experiment, may have any one, and only one, of k outcomes, $s_1, s_2, \ldots, s_k$. These outcomes are called *elementary events*. The set of all elementary events is called the *universe* and is denoted U. With each outcome s_i we associate a real number $Pr(s_i)$, called the probability of s_i, such that

$$0 \le Pr(s_i) \le 1 \qquad \text{for } 1 \le i \le k;$$

$$Pr(s_1) + Pr(s_2) + \cdots + Pr(s_k) = 1.$$

It is natural to interpret $Pr(s_i)$ as the ratio of the number of times s_i is expected to occur to the total number of times the experiment is repeated. (Note, however, that the definition does not require that the probabilities correspond to anything in the real world.) The events $s_1, \ldots, s_k$ are said to be *mutually exclusive* because at most one of them can occur.

The examples most frequently used to illustrate the meaning of probability are flipping coins, throwing dice, and various events with playing cards. In fact the origin of probability theory is thought to be in the study of gambling games by Blaise Pascal, a French mathematician. If the "experiment" is the flip of a coin, then the coin may land with "heads" facing up or with "tails" facing up. We let $s_1 = $ 'heads' and $s_2 = $ 'tails' and assign $Pr(s_1) = 1/2$ and $Pr(s_2) = 1/2$. (If someone objects because the coin could land on its edge, we may let $s_3 = $ 'edge' and define $Pr(s_3) = 0$. However, with a finite number of events, an event of probability zero can be ignored, so such elementary events are not usually defined.) If a six-sided die is thrown, there are six possible outcomes: for $1 \leq i \leq 6$, $s_i = $ "the die lands with side number i facing up," and $Pr(s_i) = 1/6$. In general, if there are k possible outcomes and each is considered equally likely, then we let $Pr(s_i) = 1/k$ for each i. Often, there is no reason to assume all outcomes are equally likely; primarily, this is an assumption used in examples or used because there is no data to support a better assumption.

If the experiment involves several objects, then an elementary event must take into account what is observed about all of them. For example, if two dice, A and B, are thrown, then the event "A lands with side 1 facing up" is not an elementary event because there are several outcomes associated with B. In this case, the elementary events would be $s_{ij} = $ "die A lands with side i facing up and die B lands with side j facing up," for $1 \leq i, j \leq 6$. We will abbreviate this description to "A shows i and B shows j" from here on. There are 36 elementary events, and it is customary to assign a probability of 1/36 to each.

We often need to consider the probability of any one of several specified outcomes occurring or the probability that the outcome has a particular property. Let S be a subset of the elementary events $\{s_1, \ldots, s_k\}$. Then S is called an *event*, and $Pr(S) = \sum_{s_i \in S} Pr(s_i)$. For example, suppose one die is thrown, and define the event S to be "the number appearing is divisible by 3." Then, the probability of S is $Pr(S) = Pr(\{s_3, s_6\}) = Pr(s_3) + Pr(s_6) = 1/3$. Elementary events are also events.

Two special events are the *sure event*, $U = \{s_1, \ldots, s_k\}$, which has probability 1, and the *impossible event*, $\emptyset$, which has probability 0. (Recall that $\emptyset$ denotes the empty set.) Also, for any event S, there is the complement event "not S," consisting of all the elementary events that are not in S, that is, $U - S$. Clearly, $Pr(\text{not } S) = 1 - Pr(S)$.

Events can be defined in terms of other events by using the logical connectives "and" and "or." The event "S_1 and S_2" is $(S_1 \cap S_2)$, the intersection of S_1 and S_2. The event "S_1 or S_2" is $(S_1 \cup S_2)$, the union of S_1 and S_2.

We often need to analyze probabilities based on some degree of partial knowledge about the experiment. These are called *conditional probabilities*.

Definition 1.4   Conditional probability

The *conditional probability of an event S given an event T* is defined as

$$Pr(S \mid T) = \frac{Pr(S \text{ and } T)}{Pr(T)} = \frac{\sum\limits_{s_i \in S \cap T} Pr(s_i)}{\sum\limits_{s_j \in T} Pr(s_j)}, \qquad (1.4)$$

where s_i and s_j range over elementary events.   ■

Example 1.3   Conditional probability with two dice

Suppose two dice, A and B, are thrown in the experiment. Let us define three events:

S_1: "A shows 1,"

S_2: "B shows 6,"

S_3: "The sum of the numbers showing is 4 or less."

To get a feel for what the conditional probability means, let's consider the simple case in which all the elementary events have the same probability. For our example, the 36 elementary events are of the form "A shows i and B shows j," for $1 \le i, j \le 6$. Then the conditional probability $Pr(S_1 \mid S_3)$ can be interpreted as the answer to the question, "Out of all the elementary events in S_3, what fraction of those elementary events are also in S_1?"

Let us list all the elementary events in S_3:

"A shows 1 and B shows 1,"   "A shows 2 and B shows 1,"

"A shows 1 and B shows 2,"   "A shows 2 and B shows 2,"

"A shows 1 and B shows 3,"   "A shows 3 and B shows 1."

The event S_1 consists of 6 elementary events in which A shows 1, and B shows each of its six possible values. Three of the elementary events in S_3 are also in S_1, so the answer to the question is $3/6 = 1/2$. By an exact calculation from the formula in Equation (1.4), the probability of S_1 given S_3 is

$$Pr(S_1 \mid S_3) = \frac{3/36}{6/36} = 1/2.$$

Notice that the conditional probability of S_2 given S_3 is 0; that is, $Pr(S_2 \mid S_3) = 0$.   ∎

In general, the procedure for calculating conditional probabilities given some specified event S is to eliminate all the elementary events that are not in S, then rescale the probabilities of all the remaining elementary events by the same factor so that the rescaled probabilities sum to 1. The required factor is $1/Pr(S)$.

The conditional probability of an event may be either larger or smaller than the unconditional probability of that event. In Example 1.3 the unconditional probability of S_1 is $1/6$ and the conditional probability of S_1 given S_3 is $1/2$. On the other hand, the unconditional probability that "the number shown by A is divisible by 3" is $1/3$. But in Example 1.3 we see that the conditional probability that "the number shown by A is divisible by 3" given S_3 is $1/6$.

Definition 1.5   Stochastic independence

Given two events S and T, if

$$Pr(S \text{ and } T) = Pr(S)Pr(T)$$

then S and T are *stochastically independent*, or simply *independent*.   ∎

If S is stochastically independent of T, then $Pr(S \mid T) = Pr(S)$ (see Exercise 1.8). That is, knowing that event T has occurred does not influence the probability that event S occurs, one way or the other. The property of independence is extremely useful when it exists, because it permits probabilities of different events to be analyzed separately. However, many errors in analysis are made by unjustified assumptions of independence.

Example 1.4   Stochastic independence

Continuing with the events defined in Example 1.3, events S_1 and S_2 are independent because the probability of each is 1/6, and (S_1 and S_2) consists of one elementary event, whose probability is 1/36. Notice also that $Pr(S_1 \mid S_2) = (1/36)/(6/36) = 1/6 = Pr(S_1)$.

From the discussion in Example 1.3, we see that S_1 and S_3 are not independent, and that S_2 and S_3 are not independent.   ■

Random variables and their expected values are important for many situations that involve probabilities. A random variable is a real valued variable that depends on which elementary event has occurred; in other words, it is a function defined for elementary events. For example, if the number of operations done by an algorithm depends on the input, and each possible input is an elementary event, then the number of operations is a random variable.

Definition 1.6   Expectation and conditional expectation

Let $f(e)$ be a random variable defined on a set of elementary events $e \in U$. The *expectation* of f, denoted as $E(f)$, is defined as

$$E(f) = \sum_{e \in U} f(e)Pr(e).$$

This is often called the *average value* of f, also. The *conditional expectation* of f given an event S, denoted as $E(f \mid S)$, is defined as

$$E(f \mid S) = \sum_{e \in U} f(e)Pr(e \mid S) = \sum_{e \in S} f(e)Pr(e \mid S)$$

since the conditional probability of any event not in S is 0.   ■

Expectations are often easier to manipulate than the random variables themselves, particularly when several interrelated random variables are involved, due to the following important laws, which are easily proven from the definitions.

Lemma 1.2 (Laws of expectations)   For random variables $f(e)$ and $g(e)$ defined on a set of elementary events $e \in U$, and any event S:

$$E(f + g) = E(f) + E(g),$$
$$E(f) = Pr(S)E(f \mid S) + Pr(\text{not } S)\, E(f \mid \text{not } S). \quad \square$$

Example 1.5   Conditional probability and order

In Chapter 4 we will consider probabilities in connection with order information gained by doing comparisons. Let's look at an example of that type involving four elements A,

B, C, D, which have distinct numerical values, but initially we know nothing about their values or relative values. We will write the letters in order to denote the elementary event that this is their relative order; that is, $CBDA$ is the event that $C < B < D < A$. There are 24 possible permutations:

$$
\begin{array}{cccccc}
ABCD & ACBD & CABD & ACDB & CADB & CDAB \\
ABDC & ADBC & DABC & ADCB & DACB & DCAB \\
BACD & BCAD & CBAD & BCDA & CBDA & CDBA \\
BADC & BDAC & DBAC & BDCA & DBCA & DCBA
\end{array}
$$

We begin by assuming all input permutations are equally likely, so the probability of each one is 1/24. What is the probability that $A < B$? In other words, defining $A < B$ as an event, what is its probability? Intuitively we expect it to be 1/2, and we can verify that by counting the number of permutations in which A apears before B in the sequence. Similarly, for any pair of elements, the probability that one is less than another is 1/2. For example, the event $B < D$ has probability 1/2.

Now suppose the program *compares* A and B and discovers that $A < B$. How does this "affect" the probabilities? To make this question more rigorous, we phrase it as, "What are the probabilities conditioned on the event $A < B$?" We see by inspection that the event $A < B$ consists of all the elementary events in the first two rows of the table. Therefore the conditional probabilities of these elementary events given $A < B$ are twice their original probabilities, 2/24 = 1/12, while the conditional probabilities of the elementary events given $A < B$ in the last two rows are 0.

Recall that before any comparisons, the probability of the event $B < D$ was 1/2. We have not compared B and D. Is the conditional probability of $B < D$ given $A < B$ still 1/2? To answer the question, we check how many sequences in the first two rows have B preceding D. In fact, there are only four cases in which B precedes D in the first two rows. So $Pr(B < D \mid A < B) = 1/3$.

Now consider the event $C < D$. Is its conditional probability different from 1/2? Again checking the first two rows of the table, we see that C precedes D in six cases, so $Pr(C < D \mid A < B) = 1/2$. Therefore the events $A < B$ and $C < D$ are stochastically independent. This is what we would expect: The relative order of A and B should not "have any influence" on the order of C and D.

Finally, suppose the program does another comparison and discovers $D < C$ (it already discovered $A < B$). Let's look at the conditional probabilities given both of these events (which is also the single event "$A < B$ and $D < C$"). We see by inspection that the event "$A < B$ and $D < C$" consists of all the elementary events in the second row of the table. To make the conditional probabilities sum to 1, all of these elementary events must have a conditional probability of 1/6. The program has not compared A or B to either of C or D. Does this mean that the conditional probabilities of the events $A < C$, $A < D$, $B < C$, and $B < D$ are unchanged from their original probabilities, which were all 1/2? The answer is worked out in Exercise 1.10. ■

Example 1.6   Expected number of inversions

Consider the same probability space as Example 1.5. Let us define the random variable $I(e)$ to be the number of pairs of elements whose relative key order is opposite their alphabetical order. This is called the number of *inversions* in the permutation. For example, $I(ABCD) = 0$, $I(ABDC) = 1$ because $D < C$ but C precedes D in alphabetical order, $I(DCBA) = 6$, and so on. By inspection we see that $E(I) = 3$. Now consider $E(I \mid A < B)$ and $E(I \mid B < A)$. Again, by direct count we find they are 2.5 and 3.5, respectively. Since $Pr(A < B) = Pr(B < A) = \frac{1}{2}$, Lemma 1.2 tells us that $E(I) = \frac{1}{2}(2.5 + 3.5)$, which is true. ∎

To summarize, conditional probabilities reflect the uncertainties of a situation when we have some partial knowledge. They can be calculated by discarding all the elementary events that are known not to be possible in the current situation, then scaling up the remaining probabilities of elementary events so that they again sum to 1. Any event whose probability does *not* change as a result of this calculation is (stochastically) independent of the known event. Independent events often involve objects that do not influence each other (like multiple coins or multiple dice).

Summations and Series

There are several summations that occur frequently when analyzing algorithms. Formulas for some of them are listed here and in the next section, with brief hints that may help you to remember them. A note on terminology: A *series* is the sum of a *sequence*.

Arithmetic Series: The sum of consecutive integers:

$$\sum_{i=1}^{n} i = \frac{n(n+1)}{2}. \tag{1.5}$$

How to remember it: Write out the integers from 1 to n. Pair up the first and last, that is, 1 and n; pair up the second and next to last, 2 and $n - 1$, and so on. Each pair adds up to $(n + 1)$ and there are $n/2$ pairs, giving the result. (If n is odd the central element counts as "half a pair.") The same trick works for limits other than 1 and n.

Polynomial Series: First, we consider the sum of squares.

$$\sum_{i=1}^{n} i^2 = \frac{2n^3 + 3n^2 + n}{6}. \tag{1.6}$$

This can be proved by induction on n. The main thing to remember is that the sum of the first n squares is roughly $n^3/3$. Equation (1.6) is not used in the text, but you may need it for some of the exercises.

The general case is

$$\sum_{i=1}^{n} i^k \approx \frac{1}{k+1} n^{k+1}, \tag{1.7}$$

which is justified by approximation by an integral, as described in the next section. (For any specific k an exact formula can be proved by induction.) Compare this kind of series carefully with "geometric series," which follow.

Powers of 2:   This is a frequently occurring case of a *geometric series*.

$$\sum_{i=0}^{k} 2^i = 2^{k+1} - 1. \tag{1.8}$$

How to remember it: Think of each term 2^i as a 1-bit in a binary number; then:

$$\sum_{i=0}^{k} 2^i = 11 \ldots 1.$$

There are $k + 1$ 1-bits. If 1 is added to this number the result is

$$100 \ldots 0 = 2^{k+1}.$$

(This result can also be obtained by using the following formula for the geometric series.)

Geometric Series:

$$\sum_{i=0}^{k} a\, r^i = a\left(\frac{r^{k+1} - 1}{r - 1}\right). \tag{1.9}$$

To verify this, divide out the right-hand side. As a special case, with $r = \frac{1}{2}$, we have

$$\sum_{i=0}^{k} \frac{1}{2^i} = 2 - \frac{1}{2^k}. \tag{1.10}$$

A geometric series is distinguished by having a constant in the base and a variable in the exponent. A polynomial series has a variable in the base and a constant exponent. The behaviors are quite different.

Harmonic Series:

$$\sum_{i=1}^{n} \frac{1}{i} \approx \ln(n) + \gamma, \qquad \text{where } \gamma \approx .577. \tag{1.11}$$

The sum is called the nth Harmonic number. The constant γ is called *Euler's constant*. See also Example 1.7.

Arithmetic-Geometric Series: In the next sum, the i term would give us an arithmetic series and the 2^i term would give us a geometric series, hence the name.

$$\sum_{i=1}^{k} i\, 2^i = (k - 1)2^{k+1} + 2. \tag{1.12}$$

The derivation is an example of "summation by parts," which is analogous to "integration by parts." The sum is rearranged into a difference of two sums that cancel except for their first and last terms, minus a third sum of a simpler form:

$$\sum_{i=1}^{k} i\, 2^i = \sum_{i=1}^{k} i\,(2^{i+1} - 2^i)$$

$$= \sum_{i=1}^{k} i\, 2^{i+1} - \sum_{i=0}^{k-1} (i+1)2^{i+1}$$

$$= \sum_{i=1}^{k} i\, 2^{i+1} - \sum_{i=0}^{k-1} i\, 2^{i+1} - \sum_{i=0}^{k-1} 2^{i+1}$$

$$= k\, 2^{k+1} - 0 - (2^{k+1} - 2) = (k-1)2^{k+1} + 2.$$

Fibonacci Numbers: The Fibonacci sequence is defined recursively as:

$$F_n = F_{n-1} + F_{n-2} \qquad \text{for } n \geq 2,$$
$$F_0 = 0, \quad F_1 = 1. \tag{1.13}$$

Although this is not a summation, the series occurs frequently in analysis of algorithms.

Monotonic and Convex Functions

Sometimes very general properties are enough for us to draw some useful conclusions about the behavior of functions. Two such properties are *monotonicity* and *convexity*. Throughout the discussion of monotonicity and convexity in this section, we assume some interval $a \leq x < \infty$ is understood, where a is usually 0, but might be 1 if logs are involved. All points mentioned are in this interval, and f is defined in this interval. The domain may be either reals or integers.

Definition 1.7   Monotonic and antimonotonic functions

A function $f(x)$ is said to be *monotonic*, or *nondecreasing*, if $x \leq y$ always implies that $f(x) \leq f(y)$. A function $f(x)$ is *antimonotonic*, or *nonincreasing*, if $-f(x)$ is monotonic.
■

Examples of familiar monotonic functions are x, x^2 for $x \geq 0$, $\log(x)$ for $x > 0$, and e^x. Less familiar monotonic functions are $\lfloor x \rfloor$ and $\lceil x \rceil$, showing that monotonic functions need not be continuous. An antimonotonic example is $1/x$ for $x > 0$.

Definition 1.8   Linear interpolation function

The *linear interpolation* of a given function $f(x)$ between two points u and v, $u < v$, is the function defined by

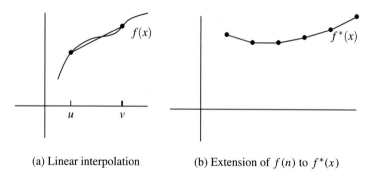

(a) Linear interpolation   (b) Extension of $f(n)$ to $f^*(x)$

Figure 1.3 Illustrations for convexity discussion: The function f is different in parts (a) and (b). In part (b), $f^*(x)$ is convex.

$$L_{f,u,v}(x) = \frac{(v-x)f(u) + (x-u)f(v)}{(v-u)}$$

$$= f(u) + (x-u)\frac{f(v)-f(u)}{v-u} = f(v) - (v-x)\frac{f(v)-f(u)}{v-u}, \quad (1.14)$$

that is, the straight-line segment joining $f(u)$ and $f(v)$ (see Figure 1.3a). ■

Definition 1.9   Convex functions

A function $f(x)$ is said to be *convex* if for all $u < v$, $f(x) \le L_{f,u,v}(x)$ in the interval (u, v). Informally, $f(x)$ is convex if it never curves downward. ■

Thus functions like x, x^2, $1/x$, and e^x are convex. The function in Figure 1.3(b) is convex (but not monotonic), whether interpreted on the reals or just on the integers; the function in Figure 1.3(a) is monotonic, but not convex. Also, $\log(x)$ and $\sqrt{x}$ are not convex. What about $x \log(x)$? The following lemmas develop some practical tests for convexity. It is easy to see (and possible to prove) that a discontinuous function cannot be convex. Lemma 1.3 states that it is sufficient to consider equally spaced points to test for convexity, which simplifies things considerably. The proof is Exercise 1.16.

Lemma 1.3

1. Let $f(x)$ be a continuous function defined on the reals. Then $f(x)$ is convex if and only if, for any points x, y,

$$f(\tfrac{1}{2}(x + y)) \le \tfrac{1}{2}(f(x) + f(y)).$$

In words, f evaluated at the midpoint between x and y lies on or below the midpoint of the linear interpolation of f between x and y. Note that the midpoint of the linear interpolation is just the average of $f(x)$ and $f(y)$.

2. A function $f(n)$ defined on integers is convex if and only if, for any $n, n+1, n+2$,

$$f(n+1) \le \tfrac{1}{2}(f(n) + f(n+2)).$$

In words, $f(n+1)$ is at most the average of $f(n)$ and $f(n+2)$. $\square$

Lemma 1.4 summarizes several useful properties of monotonicity and convexity. It states that functions defined only on the integers can be extended to the reals by linear interpolation, preserving properties of monotonicity and convexity. Also, some properties involving derivatives are stated. The proofs are in Exercises 1.17 through 1.19.

Lemma 1.4

1. Let $f(n)$ be defined only on integers. Let $f^*(x)$ be the extension of f to the reals by linear interpolation between consecutive integers (see Figure 1.3b).

   a. $f(n)$ is monotonic if and only if $f^*(x)$ is monotonic.
   b. $f(n)$ is convex if and only if $f^*(x)$ is convex.

2. If the first derivative of $f(x)$ exists and is nonnegative, then $f(x)$ is monotonic.
3. If the first derivative of $f(x)$ exists and is monotonic, then $f(x)$ is convex.
4. If the second derivative of $f(x)$ exists and is nonnegative, then $f(x)$ is convex. (This follows from parts 2 and 3.) $\square$

Summations Using Integration

Several summations that arise often in the analysis of algorithms can be approximated (or bounded from above or below) using integration. First, let us review some useful integration formulas:

$$\int_0^n x^k \, dx = \frac{1}{k+1}n^{k+1}. \qquad \int_0^n e^{ax} \, dx = \frac{1}{a}\left(e^{an} - 1\right).$$

$$\int_1^n x^k \ln(x) \, dx = \frac{1}{k+1}n^{k+1}\ln(n) - \frac{1}{(k+1)^2}n^{k+1}.$$

(1.15)

If $f(x)$ is monotonic (or nondecreasing), then

$$\int_{a-1}^b f(x)dx \le \sum_{i=a}^b f(i) \le \int_a^{b+1} f(x)dx.$$

(1.16)

Similarly, if $f(x)$ is antimonotonic (or nonincreasing), then

$$\int_a^{b+1} f(x)dx \le \sum_{i=a}^b f(i) \le \int_{a-1}^b f(x)dx.$$

(1.17)

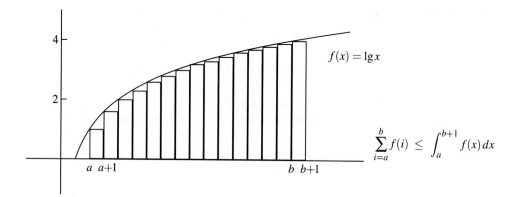

(a) Overapproximation

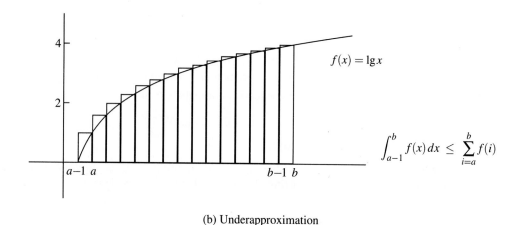

(b) Underapproximation

Figure 1.4   Approximating a sum of values of a monotonic (or nondecreasing) function

This situation for monotonic $f(x)$ is illustrated in Figure 1.4. Here are two examples that are used later in the text.

Example 1.7   An estimate for $\displaystyle\sum_{i=1}^{n} \frac{1}{i}$

$$\sum_{i=1}^{n} \frac{1}{i} \leq 1 + \int_{1}^{n} \frac{dx}{x} = 1 + \ln x\Big|_{1}^{n} = 1 + \ln n - \ln 1 = \ln(n) + 1.$$

by using Equation (1.17). Notice that we split off the first term of the sum and applied the integral approximation to the rest, to avoid a divide-by-zero at the lower limit of integration. Similarly,

$$\sum_{i=1}^{n} \frac{1}{i} \geq \ln(n+1).$$

See Equation (1.11) for a closer approximation. ∎

Example 1.8   A lower bound for $\displaystyle\sum_{i=1}^{n} \lg i$

$$\sum_{i=1}^{n} \lg i = 0 + \sum_{i=2}^{n} \lg i \geq \int_{1}^{n} \lg x \, dx$$

by Equation (1.16) (see Figure 1.4b). Now

$$\int_{1}^{n} \lg x \, dx = \int_{1}^{n} (\lg e) \ln x \, dx = (\lg e) \int_{1}^{n} \ln x \, dx$$

$$= (\lg e)(x \ln x - x)\big|_{1}^{n} = (\lg e)(n \ln n - n + 1)$$

$$= n \lg n - n \lg e + \lg e \geq n \lg n - n \lg e.$$

Since $\lg e < 1.443$,

$$\sum_{i=1}^{n} \lg i \geq n \lg n - 1.443n. \tag{1.18}$$

∎

Using the ideas of the previous example, but with more precise mathemathics, it is possible to derive *Stirling's formula* giving bounds for $n!$:

$$\left(\frac{n}{e}\right)^{n} \sqrt{2\pi n} < n! < \left(\frac{n}{e}\right)^{n} \sqrt{2\pi n} \left(1 + \frac{1}{11n}\right) \qquad \text{for } n \geq 1. \tag{1.19}$$

Manipulating Inequalities

These rules for combining inequalities are frequently useful.

Transitivity	*Addition*	*Positive Scaling*	
If $\quad A \leq B$	If $\quad A \leq B$	If $\quad A \leq B$	
and $\quad B \leq C$	and $\quad C \leq D$	and $\quad \alpha > 0$	(1.20)
then $\quad A \leq C$	then $\quad A + C \leq B + D$	then $\quad \alpha A \leq \alpha B$	

1.3.3   Elements of Logic

Logic is a system for formalizing natural language statements so that we can reason more accurately. The simplest statements are called *atomic formulas*. More complex statements can be built up through the use of *logical connectives*. Examples of atomic formulas are "$4 > 3$," "4.2 is an integer," and "$x + 1 > x$." Notice that a logical statement need not be true. The objective of a proof is to show that a logical statement is true.

The most familiar logical connectives are "$\wedge$" (and), "$\vee$" (or), and "$\neg$" (not), which are also called Boolean operators. The truth value of a complex statement is derived from the truth values of its atomic formulas, according to rules for the connectives. Let A and B be logical statements. Then,

1. $A \wedge B$ is true if and only if A is true and B is true;
2. $A \vee B$ is true if and only if A is true or B is true, or both;
3. $\neg A$ is true if and only if A is false.

Another important connective for reasoning is called "implies," which we denote with the symbol "$\Rightarrow$". (The symbol "$\rightarrow$" is also seen.) The statement $A \Rightarrow B$ is read as "A implies B," or "if A then B." (Notice that this statement has no "else" clause.) The "implies" operator can be represented with a combination of other operators, according to the following identity:

$$A \Rightarrow B \quad \text{is logically equivalent to} \quad \neg A \vee B. \tag{1.21}$$

This can be verified by checking all combinations of truth assignments to A and B.

Another useful set of identities are called *DeMorgan's laws*:

$$\neg(A \wedge B) \quad \text{is logically equivalent to} \quad \neg A \vee \neg B, \tag{1.22}$$

$$\neg(A \vee B) \quad \text{is logically equivalent to} \quad \neg A \wedge \neg B. \tag{1.23}$$

Quantifiers

Another important kind of logical connective is the *quantifier*. The symbol $\forall x$ is called the *universal quantifier* and is read "for all x," while the symbol $\exists x$ is called the *existential quantifier* and is read "there exists x." These connectives can be applied to statements that contain the variable x. The statement $\forall x\, P(x)$ is true if and only if $P(x)$ is true for all x. The statement $\exists x\, P(x)$ is true if and only if $P(x)$ is true for *some* value of x. Most frequently, a universally quantified statement is conditional: $\forall x(A(x) \Rightarrow B(x))$. This can be read "For all x such that $A(x)$ holds, $B(x)$ holds."

Quantified statements obey a variation on DeMorgan's laws:

$$\forall x\, A(x) \quad \text{is logically equivalent to} \quad \neg \exists x(\neg A(x)), \tag{1.24}$$

$$\exists x\, A(x) \quad \text{is logically equivalent to} \quad \neg \forall x(\neg A(x)). \tag{1.25}$$

Sometimes the translation from natural language into a quantified statement is troublesome. People don't speak in the stilted language of logic, usually. We need to realize that "for any x" usually means "for all x," although "any" and "some" are often interchangeable in normal speech. The best guideline is to try rephrasing a sentence in natural language to be more like the logical form, and then ask yourself if it means the same thing in natural language. For example, "Any person must breathe to live" might be the sentence you start with. Possible rephrasings are "For all people x, x must breathe to live" and "For some person x, x must breathe to live." Which means the same as the original sentence?

Negating a Quantified Statement, Counterexamples

What is necessary to prove that a general statement, say $\forall x(A(x) \Rightarrow B(x))$, is false? We can use the foregoing identities to clarify the goal. The first thing to realize is that it is *not* necessary to prove $\forall x(A(x) \Rightarrow \neg B(x))$. This is too strong a statement. The negation of $\forall x(A(x) \Rightarrow B(x))$ is $\neg(\forall x(A(x) \Rightarrow B(x)))$, which can be put through a series of transformations:

$$\neg(\forall x(A(x) \Rightarrow B(x))) \quad \text{is logically equivalent to} \quad \exists x \neg(A(x) \Rightarrow B(x))$$
$$\text{is logically equivalent to} \quad \exists x \neg(\neg A(x) \vee B(x)) \quad (1.26)$$
$$\text{is logically equivalent to} \quad \exists x(A(x) \wedge \neg B(x)).$$

In words, if we can exhibit *some* object x for which $A(x)$ is true and $B(x)$ is false, then we have proven that $\forall x(A(x) \Rightarrow B(x))$ is false. Such an object (x) is called a *counterexample*.

Contrapositives

When trying to prove a statement, it is often convenient to manipulate it into a logically equivalent form. One such form is the *contrapositive*. The *contrapositive* of $A \Rightarrow B$ is $(\neg B) \Rightarrow (\neg A)$. Equation (1.21) allows us to verify that the *contrapositive* of an implication is true exactly when the implication itself is true:

$$A \Rightarrow B \quad \text{is logically equivalent to} \quad (\neg B) \Rightarrow (\neg A). \quad (1.27)$$

Sometimes, proving the contrapositive of a statement is called "proof by contradiction," but "proof by contraposition" is a more accurate description. The genuine "proof by contradiction" is described next.

Proof by Contradiction

Suppose the goal is to prove a statement of the form $A \Rightarrow B$. A genuine *proof by contradiction* adds an additional hypothesis of $\neg B$, and then proves B itself. That is, $(A \wedge \neg B) \Rightarrow B$ is the full statement that is proved. The following identity justifies this method:

$$A \Rightarrow B \quad \text{is logically equivalent to} \quad (A \wedge \neg B) \Rightarrow B. \quad (1.28)$$

A genuine proof by contradiction is rare in algorithm analysis. However, Exercise 1.21 calls for one. Most so-called proofs by contradiction are actually proofs by contraposition.

Rules of Inference

So far we have seen numerous pairs of *logically equivalent* statements, or *logical identities*: One statement is true if and only if the second statement is true. Identities are "reversible."

Most proofs are directed at "irreversible" combinations of statements, however. The complete statement to be proved is of the form "if *hypotheses*, then *conclusion*." The reversal, "if conclusion, then hypotheses" is often *not* true. Logical identities are not flexible enough to prove such "if–then" statements. In these situations, we need *rules of inference.*

A rule of inference is a general pattern that allows us to draw some *new* conclusion from a set of given statements. It can be stated, "If we know $B_1, \ldots, B_k$, then we can conclude C," where $B_1, \ldots, B_k$, and C are logical statements in their own right. Here are a few well-known rules:

If we know			*then we can conclude*	
B	and	$B \Rightarrow C$	C	(1.29)
$A \Rightarrow B$	and	$B \Rightarrow C$	$A \Rightarrow C$	(1.30)
$B \Rightarrow C$	and	$\neg B \Rightarrow C$	C	(1.31)

Some of the these rules are known by their Greek or Latin names. Equation (1.29) is *modus ponens*, Equation (1.30) is *syllogism*, and Equation (1.31) is the *rule of cases*. These rules are not independent; in Exercise 1.21 you will prove the rule of cases using other rules of inference and logical identities.

1.4 Analyzing Algorithms and Problems

We analyze algorithms with the intention of improving them, if possible, and for choosing among several available for a problem. We will use the following criteria:

1. Correctness
2. Amount of work done
3. Amount of space used
4. Simplicity, clarity
5. Optimality

We will discuss each of these criteria at length and give several examples of their application. When considering the optimality of algorithms, we will introduce techniques for establishing lower bounds on the complexity of problems.

1.4.1 Correctness

There are three major steps involved in establishing the correctness of an algorithm. First, before we can even attempt to determine whether an algorithm is correct, we must have a clear understanding of what "correct" means. We need a precise statement about the characteristics of the inputs it is expected to work on (called the *preconditions*), and what result it is to produce for each input (called the *postconditions*). Then we can try to prove statements about the relationships between the input and the output, that is, that if the preconditions are satisfied, the postconditions will be true when the algorithm terminates.

There are two aspects to an algorithm: the solution method and the sequence of instructions for carrying it out, that is, its implementation. Establishing the correctness of the method and/or formulas used may be easy or may require a long sequence of lemmas and theorems about the objects on which the algorithm works (e.g., graphs, permutations, matrices). For example, the validity of the Gauss elimination method for solving systems of linear equations depends on a number of theorems in linear algebra. Some of the methods used in algorithms in this book are not obviously correct; they must be justified by theorems.

Once the method is established, we implement it in a program. If an algorithm is fairly short and straightforward, we generally use some informal means of convincing ourselves that the various parts do what we expect them to do. We may check some details carefully (e.g., initial and final values of loop counters), and hand-simulate the algorithm on a few small examples. None of this proves that it is correct, but informal techniques may suffice for small programs. More formal techniques, such as loop invariants, may be used to verify correctness of parts of programs. Section 3.3 expands upon this topic.

Most programs written outside of classes are very large and very complex. To prove the correctness of a large program, we can try to break the program down into smaller modules; show that, if all of the smaller modules do their jobs properly, then the whole program is correct; and then prove that each of the modules is correct. This task is made easier if (it may be more accurate to say, "This task is possible only if") algorithms and programs are written in modules that are largely independent and can be verified separately. This is one of the many strong arguments for structured, modular programming. Most of the algorithms presented in this book are the small segments from which large programs are built, so we will not deal with the difficulties of proving the correctness of very long algorithms or programs.

We will not always do formal proofs of correctness in this book, though we will give arguments or explanations to justify complex or tricky parts of algorithms. Correctness *can be proved*, though indeed for long and complex programs it is a formidable task. In Chapter 3 we will introduce some techniques to help make proofs more manageable.

1.4.2 Amount of Work Done

How shall we measure the amount of work done by an algorithm? The measure we choose should aid in comparing two algorithms for the same problem so that we can determine whether one is more efficient than the other. It would be handy if our measure of work gave some indication of how the actual execution times of the two algorithms compare, but we will not use execution time as a measure of work for a number of reasons. First, of course, it varies with the computer used, and we don't want to develop a theory for one particular computer. We may instead count all the instructions or statements executed by a program, but this measure still has several of the other faults of execution time. It is highly dependent on the programming language used and on the programmer's style. It would also require that we spend time and effort writing and debugging programs for each algorithm to be studied. We want a measure of work that tells us something about the efficiency of the *method* used by an algorithm independent of not only the computer, programming language, and programmer, but also of the many implementation details, overhead (or "bookkeeping" operations) such as incrementing loop indexes, computing array indexes, and setting pointers in data structures. Our measure of work should be both precise enough and general enough to develop a rich theory that is useful for many algorithms and applications.

A simple algorithm may consist of some initialization instructions and a loop. The number of passes made through the body of the loop is a fairly good indication of the work done by such an algorithm. Of course, the amount of work done in one pass through a loop may be much more than the amount done in another pass, and one algorithm may have longer loop bodies than another algorithm, but we are narrowing in on a good measure of work. Though some loops may have, say, five steps and some nine, for large inputs the number of passes through the loops will generally be large compared to the loop sizes. Thus counting the passes through all the loops in the algorithm is a good idea.

In many cases, to analyze an algorithm we can isolate a particular operation fundamental to the problem under study (or to the types of algorithms being considered), ignore initialization, loop control, and other bookkeeping, and just count the chosen, or basic, operations performed by the algorithm. For many algorithms, exactly one of these operations is performed on each pass through the main loops of the algorithm, so this measure is similar to the one described in the previous paragraph.

Here are some examples of reasonable choices of basic operations for several problems:

Problem	Operation
Find x in an array of names.	Comparison of x with an entry in the array
Multiply two matrices with real entries.	Multiplication of two real numbers (or multiplication and addition of real numbers)
Sort an array of numbers.	Comparison of two array entries
Traverse a binary tree (see Section 2.3.3).	Traversing an edge
Any noniterative procedure, including recursive	Procedure invocation

So long as the basic operation(s) are chosen well and the total number of operations performed is roughly proportional to the number of basic operations, we have a good measure of the work done by an algorithm and a good criterion for comparing several algorithms. This is the measure we use in this chapter and in several other chapters in this book. You may not yet be entirely convinced that this is a good choice; we will add more justification for it in the next section. For now, we simply make a few points.

First, in some situations, we may be intrinsically interested in the basic operation: It might be a very expensive operation compared to the others, or it might be of some theoretical interest.

Second, we are often interested in the rate of growth of the time required for the algorithm as the inputs get larger. So long as the total number of operations is roughly proportional to the number of basic operations, just counting the latter can give us a pretty clear idea of how feasible it is to use the algorithm on large inputs.

Finally, this choice of the measure of work allows a great deal of flexibility. Though we will often try to choose one, or at most two, specific operations to count, we could include some overhead operations, and, in the extreme, we could choose as the basic operations the set of machine instructions for a particular computer. At the other extreme, we could consider "one pass through a loop" as the basic operation. Thus by varying the choice of basic operations, we can vary the degree of precision and abstraction in our analysis to fit our needs.

What if we choose a basic operation for a problem and then find that the total number of operations performed by an algorithm is not proportional to the number of basic operations? What if it is substantially higher? In the extreme case, we might choose a basic operation for a certain problem and then discover that some algorithms for the problem use such different methods that they do not do *any* of the operations we are counting. In such a situation, we have two choices. We could abandon our focus on the particular operation and revert to counting passes through loops. Or, if we are especially interested in the particular operation chosen, we could restrict our study to a particular *class of algorithms*, one for which the chosen operation is appropriate. Algorithms that use other techniques for which a different choice of basic operation is appropriate could be studied separately. A class of algorithms for a problem is usually defined by specifying the operations that may be performed on the data. (The degree of formality of the specifications will vary; usually informal descriptions will suffice in this book.)

Throughout this section, we have often used the phrase "the amount of work done by an algorithm." It could be replaced by the term "the complexity of an algorithm." *Complexity* means the amount of work done, measured by some specified *complexity measure*, which in many of our examples is the number of specified basic operations performed. Note that, in this sense, complexity has nothing to do with how complicated or tricky an algorithm is; a very complicated algorithm may have low complexity. We will use the terms "complexity," "amount of work done," and "number of basic operations done" almost interchangeably in this book.

1.4.3 Average and Worst-Case Analysis

Now that we have a general approach to analyzing the amount of work done by an algorithm, we need a way to present the results of the analysis concisely. The amount of work done cannot be described by a single number because the number of steps performed is not the same for all inputs. We observe first that the amount of work done usually depends on the size of the input. For example, alphabetizing an array of 1000 names usually requires more operations than alphabetizing an array of 100 names, using the same algorithm. Solving a system of 12 linear equations in 12 unknowns generally takes more work than solving a system of 2 linear equations in 2 unknowns. We observe, secondly, that even if we consider inputs of only one size, the number of operations performed by an algorithm may depend on the particular input. An algorithm for alphabetizing an array of names may do very little work if only a few of the names are out of order, but it may have to do much more work on an array that is very scrambled. Solving a system of 12 linear equations may not require much work if most of the coefficients are zero.

The first observation indicates that we need a measure of the size of the input for a problem. It is usually easy to choose a reasonable measure of size. Here are some examples:

Problem	Size of input
Find x in an array of names.	The number of names in the array
Multiply two matrices.	The dimensions of the matrices
Sort an array of numbers.	The number of entries in the array
Traverse a binary tree.	The number of nodes in the tree
Solve a system of linear equations.	The number of equations, or the number of unknowns, or both
Solve a problem concerning a graph.	The number of nodes in the graph, or the number of edges, or both

Even if the input size is fixed at, say, n, the number of operations performed may depend on the particular input. How, then, are the results of the analysis of an algorithm to be expressed? Most often we describe the behavior of an algorithm by stating its *worst-case complexity*.

Definition 1.10   Worst-case complexity

Let D_n be the set of inputs of size n for the problem under consideration, and let I be an element of D_n. Let $t(I)$ be the number of basic operations performed by the algorithm on input I. We define the function W by

$$W(n) = \max \{t(I) \mid I \in D_n\}.$$

The function $W(n)$ is called the *worst-case complexity* of the algorithm. $W(n)$ is the maximum number of basic operations performed by the algorithm on any input of size n.
■

It is often not very difficult to compute $W(n)$. Section 1.5 introduces techniques for cases where an exact computation would be difficult. The worst-case complexity is valuable because it gives an upper bound on the work done by the algorithm. The worst-case analysis could be used to help form an estimate for a time limit for a particular implementation of an algorithm. We will do worst-case analysis for most of the algorithms presented in this book. Unless otherwise stated, whenever we refer to the amount of work done by an algorithm, we mean the amount of work done in the worst case.

It may seem that a more useful and natural way to describe the behavior of an algorithm is to tell how much work it does on the average; that is, to compute the number of operations performed for each input of size n and then take the average. In practice some inputs might occur much more frequently than others so a weighted average is more meaningful.

Definition 1.11   Average complexity

Let $Pr(I)$ be the probability that input I occurs. Then the average behavior of the algorithm is defined as

$$A(n) = \sum_{I \in D_n} Pr(I)t(I). \quad \blacksquare$$

We determine $t(I)$ by analyzing the algorithm, but $Pr(I)$ cannot be computed analytically. The function $Pr(I)$ is determined from experience and/or special information about the application for which the algorithm is to be used, or by making some simplifying assumption (e.g., that all inputs of size n are equally likely to occur). If $Pr(I)$ is complicated, the computation of average behavior is difficult. Also, of course, if $Pr(I)$ depends on a particular application of the algorithm, the function A describes the average behavior of the algorithm for only that application.

The following examples illustrate worst-case and average analysis.

Example 1.9   Search in an unordered array

Problem: Let E be an array containing n entries (called keys), E[0], ..., E[n−1], in no particular order. Find an index of a specified key K, if K is in the array; return -1 as the answer if K is not in the array. (The problem in which the array entries are in order is studied in Section 1.6.)

Strategy: Compare K to each entry in turn until a match is found or the array is exhausted. If K is not in the array, the algorithm returns -1 as its answer.

There is a large class of procedures similar to this one, and we call these procedures *generalized searching routines*. Often they occur as subroutines of more complex procedures.

Definition 1.12   Generalized searching routine

A *generalized searching routine* is a procedure that processes an indefinite amount of data until it either exhausts the data or achieves its goal. It follows this high-level outline:

> If there is no more data to examine:
> > *Fail.*
>
> else
> > Examine one datum.
> > If this datum is what we want:
> > > *Succeed.*
> >
> > else
> > > *Keep searching* in remaining data.

The scheme is called *generalized* searching because the routine often performs some other simple operations as it searches, such as moving data elements, adding to or deleting from a data structure, and so on. $\blacksquare$

Algorithm 1.1   Sequential Search, Unordered

Input: E, n, K, where E is an array with n entries (indexed $0, \ldots, n - 1$), and K is the item sought. For simplicity, we assume that K and the entries of E are integers, as is n.

Output: Returns ans, the location of K in E (-1 if K is not found).

```
int seqSearch(int[] E, int n, int K)
1.  int ans, index;
2.  ans = -1;  // Assume failure.
3.  for (index = 0; index < n; index ++)
4.      if (K == E[index])
5.          ans = index;  // Success!
6.          break;  // Take the rest of the afternoon off.
        // Continue loop.
7.  return ans;
```

Basic Operation: Comparison of x with an array entry.

Worst-Case Analysis: Clearly $W(n) = n$. The worst cases occur when K appears only in the last position in the array and when K is not in the array at all. In both of these cases K is compared to all n entries.

Average-Behavior Analysis: We will make several simplifying assumptions first to do an easy example, then do a slightly more complicated analysis with different assumptions. We assume that the elements in the array are distinct, and that if K is in the array, then it is equally likely to be in any particular position.

For our first case, we assume that K is in the array, and we denote this event by "*succ*," in accordance with the terminology of probabilities (Section 1.3.2). The inputs can be categorized according to where in the array K appears, so there are n inputs to consider. For $0 \leq i < n$, let I_i represent the event that K appears in the ith position in the array. Then, let $t(I)$ be the number of comparisons done (the number of times the condition in line 4 is tested) by the algorithm on input I. Clearly, for $0 \leq i < n, t(I_i) = i + 1$. Thus

$$A_{succ}(n) = \sum_{i=0}^{n-1} Pr(I_i \mid succ)t(I_i)$$

$$= \sum_{i=0}^{n-1} \left(\frac{1}{n}\right)(i+1) = \left(\frac{1}{n}\right)\frac{n(n+1)}{2} = \frac{n+1}{2}.$$

The subscript "*succ*" denotes that we are assuming a successful search in this computation. The result should satisfy our intuition that on the average, about half the array will be searched.

Now, let us consider the event that K is not in the array at all, which we call "*fail*." There is only one input for this case, which we call I_{fail}. The number of comparisons in this case is $t(I_{fail}) = n$, so $A_{fail} = n$.

Finally, we combine the cases in which K is in the array and is not in the array. Let q be the probability that K is in the array. By the law of conditional expectations (Lemma 1.2):

$$A(n) = Pr(succ)A_{succ}(n) + Pr(fail)A_{fail}(n)$$

$$= q\left(\tfrac{1}{2}(n+1)\right) + (1-q)n = n(1 - \tfrac{1}{2}q) + \tfrac{1}{2}q.$$

If $q = 1$, that is, if K is always in the array, then $A(n) = (n+1)/2$, as before. If $q = 1/2$, that is, if there is a 50-50 chance that K is not in the array, then $A(n) = 3n/4 + 1/4$; roughly three-fourths of the entries are examined. This concludes Example 1.9. ∎

Example 1.9 illustrates how we should interpret D_n, the set of inputs of size n. Rather than consider all possible arrays of names, numbers, or whatever, that could occur as inputs, we identify the properties of the inputs that affect the behavior of the algorithm; in this case, whether K is in the array at all and, if so, where it appears. An element I in D_n may be thought of as a set (or equivalence class) of all arrays and values for K such that K occurs in the specified place in the array (or not at all). Then $t(I)$ is the number of operations done for any one of the inputs in I.

Observe also that the input for which an algorithm behaves worst depends on the particular algorithm, not on the problem. For Algorithm 1.1 a worst case occurs when the only position in the array containing K is the last. For an algorithm that searched the array backwards (i.e., beginning with index $= n - 1$), a worst case would occur if K appeared only in position 0. (Another worst case would again be when K is not in the array at all.)

Finally, Example 1.9 illustrates an assumption we often make when doing average analysis of sorting and searching algorithms: that the elements are distinct. The average analysis for the case of distinct elements gives a fair approximation for the average behavior in cases with few duplicates. If there might be many duplicates, it is harder to make reasonable assumptions about the probability that K's first appearance in the array occurs at any particular position.

Example 1.10   Matrix multiplication

Problem: Let $A = (a_{ij})$ be an $m \times n$ matrix and $B = (b_{ij})$ be an $n \times p$ matrix, both with real entries. Compute the product matrix $C = AB$. (This problem is discussed much more thoroughly in Chapter 12. In many cases we assume the matrices are square, that is, $m = n$ and $p = n$.)

Strategy: Use the algorithm implied by the definition of the matrix product:

$$c_{ij} = \sum_{k=0}^{n-1} a_{ik}b_{kj} \qquad \text{for } 0 \le i < m, \ 0 \le j < p.$$

Algorithm 1.2   Matrix Multiplication

Input: Matrices A and B, and integers m, n, p, designating that A is an $m \times n$ matrix and B is an $n \times p$ matrix.

Output: Matrix C, an $m \times p$ matrix. C is passed in; the algorithm fills it.

```
matMult(A, B, C, m, n, p)
    for (i = 0; i < m; i ++)
        for (j = 0; j < p; j ++)
            cᵢⱼ = 0;
            for (k = 0; k < n; k ++)
                cᵢⱼ += aᵢₖbₖⱼ
```

Basic operation: Multiplication of matrix entries.

Analysis: To compute each entry of C, n multiplications are done. C has mp entries so

$$A(m, n, p) = W(m, n, p) = mnp.$$

For the common case that $m = n = p$, $A(n) = W(n) = n^3$. This concludes Example 1.10.
■

Example 1.10 illustrates that for some algorithms the instructions performed, hence the amount of work done, are independent of the details of the input; they depend only on the size of the input. In such cases the average and worst cases are equal. In other algorithms for the same problem, this may not be true.

The concepts of worst-case and average-behavior analysis would be useful even if we had chosen a different measure of work (say, execution time) The observation that the amount of work done often depends on the size and properties of the input would lead to the study of average behavior and worst-case behavior, no matter what measures were used.

1.4.4   Space Usage

The number of memory cells used by a program, like the number of seconds required to execute a program, depends on the particular implementation. However, some conclusions about space usage can be made just by examining an algorithm. A program will require storage space for the instructions, the constants and variables used by the program, and the input data. It may also use some workspace for manipulating the data and storing information needed to carry out its computations. The input data itself may be representable in several forms, some of which require more space than others.

If the input data have one natural form (say, an array of numbers or a matrix), then we analyze the amount of *extra* space used, aside from the program and the input. If the amount of extra space is constant with respect to the input size, the algorithm is said to work *in place*. This term is used especially in reference to sorting algorithms. (A relaxed definition of *in place* is often used when the extra space is not constant, but is only a logarithmic function of the input size, because the log function grows so slowly; we will clarify any cases in which we use the relaxed definition.)

If the input can be represented in various forms, then we will consider the space required for the input itself as well as any extra space used. In general, we will refer to the number of "cells" used without precisely defining cells. You may think of a cell as being large enough to hold one number or one object. If the amount of space used depends on the particular input, worst-case and average-case analysis can be done.

1.4.5 Simplicity

It is often, though not always, the case that the simplest and most straightforward way to solve a problem is not the most efficient. Yet simplicity in an algorithm is a desirable feature. It may make verifying the correctness of the algorithm easier, and it makes writing, debugging, and modifying a program easier. The time needed to produce a debugged program should be considered when choosing an algorithm, but if the program is to be used very often, its efficiency will probably be the determining factor in the choice.

1.4.6 Optimality

No matter how clever we are, we can't improve an algorithm for a problem beyond a certain point. Each problem has inherent complexity; that is, there is some minimum amount of work required to solve it. To analyze the complexity of a problem, as opposed to that of a specific algorithm, we choose a class of algorithms (often by specifying the types of operations the algorithms will be permitted to perform) and a measure of complexity, for example, the basic operation(s) to be counted. Then we may ask how many operations are actually *needed* to solve the problem. We say that an algorithm is *optimal* (in the worst case) if there is no algorithm in the class under study that performs fewer basic operations (in the worst case). Note that when we speak of algorithms in the class under study, we don't mean only those algorithms that people have thought of. We mean all possible algorithms, including those not yet discovered. "Optimal" doesn't mean "the best known"; it means "the best possible."

1.4.7 Lower Bounds and the Complexity of Problems

Then how can we show that an algorithm is optimal? Do we have to analyze individually every other possible algorithm (including the ones we have not even thought of)? Fortunately, no; we can prove theorems that establish a lower bound on the number of operations needed to solve a problem. Then any algorithm that performs that number of operations would be optimal. Thus there are two tasks to be carried out in order to find a good algorithm, or, from another point of view, to answer the question: How much work is necessary and sufficient to solve the problem?

1. Devise what seems to be an efficient algorithm; call it **A**. Analyze **A** and find a function W_A such that, for inputs of size n, **A** does at most $W_A(n)$ steps in the worst case.

2. For some function F, prove a theorem stating that, for any algorithm in the class under consideration, there is some input of size n for which the algorithm must perform at least $F(n)$ steps.

If the functions W_A and F are equal, then the algorithm **A** is optimal (for the worst case). If not, it may be that there is a better algorithm or that there is a better lower bound. Observe that analysis of a specific algorithm gives an *upper bound* on the number of steps necessary to solve a problem, and a theorem of the type described in item 2 above gives a *lower bound* on the number of steps necessary (in the worst case). In this book, we will see problems for which optimal algorithms are known and other problems for which there is still a gap between the best known lower bound and the best known algorithm. Simple examples of each case follow.

The concept of a lower bound for the worst-case behavior of algorithms is very important in computational complexity. Example 1.11 and the problems studied in Section 1.6 and Chapters 4 and 5 will help to clarify the meaning of lower bounds and illustrate techniques for establishing them. You should keep in mind that the definition "F is a lower bound for a class of algorithms" means that for *any* algorithm in the class, and any input size n, there is *some* input of size n for which the algorithm must perform *at least* $F(n)$ basic operations.

Example 1.11   Finding the largest entry in an array

Problem: Find the largest entry in an array of n numbers. (Say the type is **float** to be specific; any numeric type will do.)

Class of Algorithms: Algorithms that can compare and copy numbers of type **float**, but do no other operations on them.

Basic Operation: Comparison of an array entry with any object of type **float**. It could be another array entry or a stored variable.

Upper Bound: Suppose the numbers are in an array E. The following algorithm finds the maximum.

Algorithm 1.3   FindMax

Input: E, an array of numbers, defined for indexes $0, \ldots, n - 1$; $n \geq 1$, the number of entries.

Output: Returns max, the largest entry in E.

```
int findMax(E, n)
 1.  max = E[0];
 2.  for (index = 1; index < n; index ++)
 3.      if (max < E[index])
 4.          max = E[index];
 5.  return max;
```

Comparisons of array entries are done in line 3, which is executed exactly $n - 1$ times. Thus $n - 1$ is an upper bound on the number of comparisons necessary to find the maximum in the worst case. Is there an algorithm that does fewer?

Lower Bound: To establish a lower bound we can assume that the entries in the array are all distinct. This assumption is permissible because, if we can establish a lower bound on worst-case behavior for some subset of inputs (arrays with distinct entries), it is a lower bound on worst-case behavior when all valid inputs are considered.

In an array with n distinct entries, $n - 1$ entries are *not* the maximum. We can conclude that a particular entry is not the maximum only if it is smaller than at least one other entry in the array. Hence, $n - 1$ entries must be "losers" in comparisons done by the algorithm. Each comparison has only one loser, so at least $n - 1$ comparisons must be done. That is, if there are two or more nonlosers left when the algorithm terminates, it cannot be sure it has identified the maximum. Thus $F(n) = n - 1$ is a lower bound on the number of comparisons needed.

Conclusion: Algorithm 1.3 is optimal. This concludes Example 1.11.   ∎

We could take a slightly different point of view to establish the lower bound in Example 1.11. If we are given an algorithm and an array of n numbers such that the algorithm halts and produces an answer after doing fewer than $n - 1$ comparisons, then we can prove that the algorithm gives the *wrong* answer for some set of input data. If no more than $n - 2$ comparisons are done, two entries are never losers; that is, they are not known to be smaller than any other entries. The algorithm can specify at most one of them as the maximum. We can simply replace the other with a larger number (if necessary). Since the results of all comparisons done will be the same as before, the algorithm will give the same answer as before and it will be wrong.

This argument is a proof by contraposition (see Section 1.3.3). We proved "if **A** does fewer than $n - 1$ comparisons in any case, then **A** is not correct." By contraposition, we can conclude "if **A** is correct, then **A** does at least $n - 1$ comparisons in all cases." It illustrates a useful technique for establishing lower bounds, namely, to show that, if an algorithm does not do enough work, one can arrange the input so that the algorithm gives the wrong answer.

Example 1.12   Matrix multiplication

Problem: Let $A = (a_{ij})$ and $B = (b_{ij})$ be two $n \times n$ matrices with real entries. Compute the product matrix $C = AB$.

Class of Algorithms: Algorithms that can perform multiplications, divisions, additions, and subtractions on the matrix entries and on the intermediate results obtained by performing these operations on the entries.

Basic Operation: Multiplication.

Upper Bound: The usual algorithm (see Example 1.10) does n^3 multiplications; hence at most n^3 multiplications are necessary.

Lower Bound: It has been proven in the literature that at least n^2 multiplications are necessary.

Conclusions: There is no way to tell from the information available whether or not the usual algorithm is optimal. Some researchers have been trying to improve the lower bound, that is, to prove that more than n^2 multiplications are necessary, while others have looked for better algorithms. To date it has been shown that the usual algorithm is *not* optimal;

there is a method that does approximately $n^{2.376}$ multiplications. Is this method optimal? The lower bound has not yet been improved, so we don't know if there are algorithms that do substantially fewer multiplications.   ■

Up until now we have been discussing lower bounds and optimality of worst-case behavior. What about average behavior? We can use the same approach that we use with worst-case behavior. Choose what seems to be a good algorithm and figure out the function $A(n)$ such that the algorithm does $A(n)$ operations, on the average, for inputs of size n. Then prove a theorem stating that any algorithm in the class being studied must perform at least $G(n)$ operations on the average for inputs of size n. If $A = G$, we can say that the average behavior of the algorithm is optimal. If not, look for a better algorithm or a better lower bound (or both).

For many problems analyzing the number of operations exactly is too difficult. It is customary to regard an algorithm as optimal if the number of operations it does is within a constant factor of the exact optimum (which itself is often known only within a constant factor). In Section 1.5 we will develop a methodology for analyzing many problems within a constant factor, although we are unable to perform an exact analysis.

We can use the same approach to investigate space usage as we used for time analysis. Analyze a particular algorithm to get an upper bound on the amount of space needed, and prove a theorem to establish a lower bound. Can we find one algorithm for a given problem that is optimal with respect to both the amount of work done and the amount of space used? The answer to this question is: sometimes. For some problems, there is a trade-off between time and space.

1.4.8 Implementation and Programming

Implementation is the task of turning an algorithm into a computer program. Algorithms may be described by detailed computer-language–like instructions for manipulating variables and data structures, or by very abstract, high-level explanations in English of solution methods for abstract problems, making no mention of computer representations of the objects involved. Thus the implementation of an algorithm may be a fairly straightforward translating job or it may be a very lengthy and difficult job requiring a number of important decisions on the part of the programmer, particularly concerning the choice of data structures. Where appropriate, we will discuss implementation in the general sense of choosing data structures and describing ways to carry out instructions given in an English description of an algorithm. Such discussion is included for two reasons. One, it is a natural and important part of the process of producing a (good) working program. Two, consideration of implementation details is often necessary for analyzing an algorithm; the amount of time required to perform various operations on abstract objects such as sets and graphs depends on how these objects are represented. For example, forming the union of two sets may require only one or two operations if the sets are represented as linked lists, but would require a large number of operations, proportional to the number of elements in one of the sets, if they are represented as arrays and one must be copied into the other.

In the narrow sense, implementation, or simply programming, means converting a fairly detailed description of an algorithm and the data structures it uses into a program for a particular computer. Our analysis will be implementation-independent in this sense; in other words, it will be independent of the computer and programming language used and of many minor details of the algorithm or program.

A programmer can refine the analysis of algorithms under consideration using information about the particular computer to be used. For example, if more than one operation is counted, the operations can be weighted according to their execution times; or estimates of the actual number of seconds a program will use (in the worst or average case) can be made. Sometimes knowledge of the computer used will lead to a new analysis. For example, if the computer has any unusual, powerful instructions that can be used effectively in the problem at hand, then one can study the class of algorithms that make use of those instructions and count them as the basic operations. If the computer has a very limited instruction set that makes implementation of the basic operation awkward, a different class of algorithms may be considered. Generally, however, if the implementation-independent analysis has been done well, then the program-dependent analysis should serve mainly to add detail.

A detailed analysis of the amount of space used by the algorithms being studied is, of course, also appropriate when particular implementations are being considered.

Any special knowledge about the inputs to the problem for which an algorithm is sought can be used to refine the analysis. If, for example, the inputs will be restricted to a certain subset of all possible inputs, a worst-case analysis can be done for that subset. As we have noted, a good average-behavior analysis depends on knowing the probability of the various inputs occurring.

1.5 Classifying Functions by Their Asymptotic Growth Rates

Just how good is our measure of work done by an algorithm? How precise a comparison can we make between two algorithms? Because we are not counting every step executed by an algorithm, our analysis necessarily has some imprecision. We have said that we will be content if the total number of steps is roughly proportional to the number of basic operations counted. This is good enough for separating algorithms that do drastically different amounts of work for large inputs.

Suppose one algorithm for a problem does $2n$ basic operations, hence roughly $2cn$ operations in total, for some constant c, and another algorithm does $4.5n$ basic operations, or $4.5c'n$ in total. Which one runs faster? We really don't know. The first algorithm may do many more overhead operations; that is, its constant of proportionality may be a lot higher. Thus if the functions describing the behavior of two algorithms differ by a constant factor, it may be pointless to try to distinguish between them (unless we do a more refined analysis). We consider such algorithms to be in the same complexity class.

Suppose one algorithm for a problem does $n^3/2$ multiplications and another algorithm does $5n^2$. Which algorithm will run faster? For small values of n the first does fewer multiplications, but for large values of n, the second is better—even if it does more overhead operations. The rate of growth of a cubic function is so much greater than that of a quadratic function that the constant of proportionality doesn't matter when n gets large.

As these examples suggest, we want a way to compare or classify functions that ignores constant factors and small inputs. We get just such a classification by studying what is called the *asymptotic growth rate*, *asymptotic order* or, simply, the *order* of functions.

Is it reasonable to ignore constants and small input values? Here is a completely nontechnical, nonmathematical analogy that may help you understand our use of asymptotic order. Suppose you are choosing a city to live in and your main criterion is that it have a very hot climate. The choices are El Paso, Texas, and Yuma, Arizona. There's not much difference in temperature between them, is there? But suppose you are choosing between three cities: El Paso, Yuma, and Anchorage, Alaska. You'd rule out Anchorage immediately. This is analogous to saying two functions are of the same order, and a third one is of a different order. Knowing the order lets us make broad distinctions; we can eliminate those that are poor by our criterion.

Now, how will you choose between El Paso and Yuma (or two algorithms whose running time is of the same order)? We could look up temperature records to find out that temperatures in one city average a few degrees higher than the other. This might be analogous to looking at the constant on two functions of the same order; for algorithms it might mean counting all operations, including overhead to get a more precise estimate of running time. Another approach would be to consider other criteria, perhaps availability of jobs and cultural amenities when choosing a city, or the amount of extra space used when choosing an algorithm.

Is there ever a day when it is warmer in Anchorage than in El Paso? Sure; there might be a beautiful, unusually warm spring day in Anchorage when a cold front is passing through El Paso. This doesn't make it wrong to say, in general, that Anchorage is much colder than El Paso. In the definitions we will give for big oh, big theta, and the other "order sets," the behavior of the functions being compared is ignored for small values of n. Ignoring some small arguments (input sizes, for algorithms) is analogous to ignoring the few days when Anchorage might be warmer than El Paso or Yuma.

1.5.1   Definitions and Asymptotic Notation

We will use the usual notation for natural numbers and real numbers.

Definition 1.13   Notation for natural numbers and reals

1. The set of *natural numbers* is denoted as $\mathbf{N} = \{0, 1, 2, 3, \ldots\}$.
2. The set of positive integers is denoted as $\mathbf{N}^+ = \{1, 2, 3, \ldots\}$.
3. The set of real numbers is denoted as $\mathbf{R}$.
4. The set of positive reals is denoted as $\mathbf{R}^+$.
5. The set of *nonnegative* reals is denoted as $\mathbf{R}^*$.   ■

Let f and g be functions from $\mathbf{N}$ to $\mathbf{R}^*$. Figure 1.5 informally describes the sets we use to show the relationships between the orders of functions. Keeping the picture and

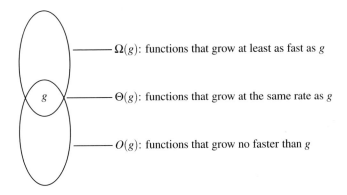

$\Omega(g)$: functions that grow at least as fast as g

$\Theta(g)$: functions that grow at the same rate as g

$O(g)$: functions that grow no faster than g

Figure 1.5   Big omega (Ω), big theta (Θ), and big oh (O)

the informal definitions in mind will help clarify the following formal definitions and properties.

Definition 1.14   The set $O(g)$

Let g be a function from the nonnegative integers into the positive real numbers. Then $O(g)$ is the set of functions f, also from the nonnegative integers into the positive real numbers, such that for some real constant $c > 0$ and some nonnegative integer constant n_0, $f(n) \leq c\, g(n)$ for all $n \geq n_0$.   ■

It is often useful to think of g as some *given* function, and f as the function we are analyzing. Notice that a function f may be in $O(g)$ even if $f(n) > g(n)$ for all n. The important point is that f is bounded above by some *constant multiple* of g. Also, the relation between f and g for small values of n is not considered. Figure 1.6 shows the order relations for a few functions. (Note that the functions in Figure 1.6 are drawn as continuous functions defined on $\mathbf{R}^+$ or $\mathbf{R}^*$. The functions that describe the behavior of most of the algorithms we will study have such natural extensions.)

The set $O(g)$ is usually called "big oh of g" or just "oh of g" although the "oh" is actually the Greek letter omicron. And, although we have defined $O(g)$ as a set, it is common practice to say "f is oh of g," rather than "f is a member of oh of g."

There is an alternative technique for showing that f is in $O(g)$:

Lemma 1.5   A function $f \in O(g)$ if $\lim\limits_{n \to \infty} \dfrac{f(n)}{g(n)} = c < \infty$, including the case in which the limit is 0.   □

That is, if the limit of the ratio of f to g exists and is not ∞, then f grows no faster than g. If the limit is ∞, then f does grow faster than g.

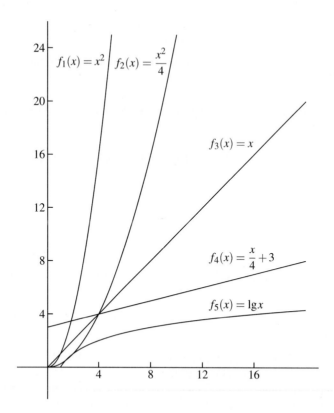

Figure 1.6   The orders of functions: $f_3 \in O(f_4)$, even though $f_3(x) > f_4(x)$ for $x > 4$, since both are linear. f_1 and f_2 are of the same order. They grow faster than the other three functions. f_5 is of the lowest order among the functions shown.

Example 1.13   Functions of different asymptotic orders

Let $f(n) = n^3/2$ and $g(n) = 37n^2 + 120n + 17$. We will show that $g \in O(f)$, but $f \notin O(g)$.

Since for $n \geq 78$, $g(n) < 1\ f(n)$, it follows that $g \in O(f)$. We could have come to the same conclusion from:

$$\lim_{n\to\infty} \frac{g(n)}{f(n)} = \lim_{n\to\infty} \frac{37n^2 + 120n + 17}{n^3/2} = \lim_{n\to\infty} (74/n + 240/n^2 + 34/n^3) = 0.$$

We can show that $f \notin O(g)$ by observing that the limit of $f/g = \infty$. Here is an alternative method. We assume $f \in O(g)$ and derive a contradiction. If $f \in O(g)$, then there exist constants c and n_0 such that for all $n \geq n_0$,

$$\frac{n^3}{2} \leq 37cn^2 + 120cn + 17c.$$

So

$$\frac{n}{2} \le 37c + \frac{120c}{n} + \frac{17c}{n^2} \le 174c.$$

Since c is a constant and n may be arbitrarily large, it is impossible to have $n/2 \le 174c$ for all $n \ge n_0$.   ■

The following theorem is useful for computing limits when f and g extend to continuous, differentiable functions on the reals.

Theorem 1.6 (L'Hôpital's Rule)   Let f and g be differentiable functions, with derivatives f' and g', respectively, such that

$$\lim_{n \to \infty} f(n) = \lim_{n \to \infty} g(n) = \infty.$$

Then

$$\lim_{n \to \infty} \frac{f(n)}{g(n)} = \lim_{n \to \infty} \frac{f'(n)}{g'(n)}. \quad \square$$

Example 1.14   Use of L'Hôpital's Rule

Let $f(n) = n^2$ and $g(n) = n \lg n$. We will show that $f \notin O(g)$, but $g \in O(f)$. First, we simplify.

$$\lim_{n \to \infty} \frac{f(n)}{g(n)} = \lim_{n \to \infty} \frac{n^2}{n \lg n} = \lim_{n \to \infty} \frac{n}{\lg n}.$$

Now we note (see Lemma 1.1) that $\lg n = \ln(n)/\ln(2)$ in preparation for using L'Hôpital's Rule:

$$\lim_{n \to \infty} \frac{n \ln(2)}{\ln n} = \lim_{n \to \infty} \frac{\ln(2)}{1/n} = \lim_{n \to \infty} n \ln(2) = \infty.$$

Therefore $f \notin O(g)$. However, $g \in O(f)$ since the inverse ratio goes to 0.   ■

The definition of $\Omega(g)$, the set of functions that grow at least as fast as g, is the dual of the definition of $O(g)$.[2]

Definition 1.15   The set $\Omega(g)$

Let g be a function from the nonnegative integers into the positive real numbers. Then $\Omega(g)$ is the set of functions f, also from the nonnegative integers into the positive real numbers, such that for some real constant $c > 0$ and some nonnegative integer constant n_0, $f(n) \ge c\, g(n)$ for all $n \ge n_0$.   ■

The alternative technique for showing that f is in $\Omega(g)$ is as follows:

---

[2] Readers who plan to consult other books and papers should be aware that the definition of Ω may vary slightly: The phrase "for all" may be weakened to "for infinitely many." The definition of Θ shifts accordingly.

Lemma 1.7 Function $f \in \Omega(g)$ if $\lim\limits_{n \to \infty} \dfrac{f(n)}{g(n)} > 0$, including the case in which the limit is ∞. ☐

Definition 1.16 The set $\Theta(g)$, asymptotic order of g

Let g be a function from the nonnegative integers into the positive real numbers. Then $\Theta(g) = O(g) \cap \Omega(g)$, that is, the set of functions that are in both $O(g)$ and $\Omega(g)$. The most common way of reading "$f \in \Theta(g)$" is "f is order g." We often use the phrase "asymptotic order" for definiteness, and the term "asymptotic complexity" is also seen. ■

We also have:

Lemma 1.8 Function $f \in \Theta(g)$ if $\lim\limits_{n \to \infty} \dfrac{f(n)}{g(n)} = c$ for some constant c such that $0 < c < \infty$. ☐

Example 1.15 Asymptotic order of some algorithms

The worst-case complexities of Algorithm 1.1 (sequential search, unordered) and Algorithm 1.3 (finding the maximum element) are both in $\Theta(n)$. The complexity (worst case or average) of Algorithm 1.2 for matrix multiplication in the case $m = n = p$ is in $\Theta(n^3)$. ■

The terminology commonly used in talking about the order sets is imprecise. For example: "This is an order n^2 algorithm" really means that the function describing the behavior of the algorithm is in $\Theta(n^2)$. The exercises establish several facts about commonly encountered order sets, and relationships among them, such as the fact that $n(n-1)/2 \in \Theta(n^2)$.

Sometimes we wish to indicate that one function has strictly smaller, or strictly greater, asymptotic order than another. We can use the following definitions.

Definition 1.17 The sets $o(g)$ and $\omega(g)$

Let g be a function from the nonnegative integers into the positive real numbers.

1. $o(g)$ is the set of functions f, also from the nonnegative integers into the positive real numbers, such that $\lim\limits_{n \to \infty} \dfrac{f(n)}{g(n)} = 0$.

2. $\omega(g)$ is the set of functions f, also from the nonnegative integers into the positive real numbers, such that $\lim\limits_{n \to \infty} \dfrac{f(n)}{g(n)} = \infty$. ■

Usually, "$o(g)$" and "$\omega(g)$" are read "little oh of g" and "little omega of g." It is easy to remember that functions in $o(g)$ are the "smaller" functions in $O(g)$. However, $\omega(g)$ is not seen very often, probably because it is hard to remember that functions in $\omega(g)$ are the *larger* functions of $\Omega(g)$! For more properties of $o(g)$, see Exercises 1.33 and 1.34.

Algorithm	1	2	3	4	
Time function (microsec.)	$33n$	$46n \lg n$	$13n^2$	$3.4n^3$	2^n

Input size (n)	Solution time				
10	.00033 sec.	.0015 sec.	.0013 sec.	.0034 sec.	.001 sec.
100	.003 sec.	.03 sec.	.13 sec.	3.4 sec.	$4 \cdot 10^{16}$ yr.
1,000	.033 sec.	.45 sec.	13 sec.	.94 hr.	
10,000	.33 sec.	6.1 sec.	22 min.	39 days	
100,000	3.3 sec.	1.3 min.	1.5 days	108 yr.	

Time allowed	Maximum solvable input size (approx.)				
1 second	30,000	2,000	280	67	20
1 minute	1,800,000	82,000	2,200	260	26

Table 1.1   How functions grow

1.5.2   How Important Is Asymptotic Order?

Table 1.1[3] shows the running times for several actual algorithms for the same problem. (The last column does not correspond to an algorithm for the problem; it is included to demonstrate how fast exponential functions grow, and hence how bad exponential algorithms are.) Look over the entries in the table to see how fast the running time increases with input size for the algorithms of higher complexities. One of the important lessons in the table is that the high constant factors on the $\Theta(n)$ and $\Theta(n \log n)$ algorithms do not make them slower than the other algorithms except for very small inputs.

The second part of the table looks at the effect of asymptotic growth rate on the increase in the size of the input that can be handled with more computer time (or by using a faster computer). It is *not* true in general that if we multiply the time (or speed) by 60 we can handle an input 60 times as large; that is true only for algorithms whose complexity is in $O(n)$. The $\Theta(n^2)$ algorithm, for example, can handle an input only $\sqrt{60}$ times as large.

To further drive home the point that the asymptotic order of the running time of an algorithm is more important than a constant factor (for large inputs), look at Table 1.2. A program for the cubic algorithm from Table 1.1 was written for the Cray-1 supercomputer; it ran in $3n^3$ nanoseconds for input of size n. The linear algorithm was programmed on a TRS-80 (an inexpensive 1980s personal computer); it ran in $19.5\,n$ milliseconds (which is $19,500,000\,n$ nanoseconds). Even though the constant on the linear algorithm is 6.5 million times as big as the constant on the cubic algorithm, the linear algorithm is faster

---

[3] This table (except the last column) and Table 1.2 are adapted from *Programming Pearls* by Jon Bentley (Addison-Wesley, Reading, Mass., 1986) and are reproduced here with permission.

n	Cray-1 Fortran [a] $3n^3$ nanoseconds	TRS-80 Basic [b] $19,500,000n$ nanoseconds
10	3 microseconds	.2 seconds
100	3 milliseconds	2.0 seconds
1,000	3 seconds	20.0 seconds
2,500	50 seconds	50.0 seconds
10,000	49 minutes	3.2 minutes
1,000,000	95 years	5.4 hours

[a] Cray-1 is a trademark of Cray Research, Inc.
[b] TRS-80 is a trademark of Tandy Corporation.

Table 1.2   Asymptotic order wins out.

Number of steps performed on input of size n $f(n)$	Maximum feasible input size s	Maximum feasible input size in t times as much time s_{new}
$\lg n$	s_1	s_1^t
n	s_2	$t\, s_2$
n^2	s_3	$\sqrt{t}\, s_3$
2^n	s_4	$s_4 + \lg t$

Table 1.3   The effect of increased computer speed on maximum input size

for input sizes $n \geq 2500$. (Whether one considers this a large or small input size would depend on the context of the problem.)

If we focus on the asymptotic order of functions (thus including, say, n and $1,000,000\,n$ in the same class), then when we can show that two functions are *not* of the same order, we are making a strong statement about the difference between the algorithms described by those functions. If two functions *are* of the same order, they may differ by a large constant factor. However, the value of the constant is irrelevant in determining the effect of a faster computer on the maximum input size an algorithm can handle in a given amount of time. That is, the value of the constant is irrelevant to the increase between the last two rows of Table 1.1. Let's look a little more closely at the meaning of those numbers.

Suppose we fix on a certain amount of time (one second, one minute—the specific choice is unimportant). Let s be the maximum input size a particular algorithm can handle within that amount of time. Now suppose we allow t times as much time (or our computer speed increases by a factor of t, either because technology has improved, or simply because we went out and bought a more expensive machine). Table 1.3 shows the effect of the speedup for several complexities.

The values in the third column are computed by observing that

$$f(s_{new}) = \text{number of steps after speedup}$$
$$= t \cdot (\text{number of steps before the speedup}) = tf(s)$$

and solving

$$f(s_{new}) = tf(s)$$

for s_{new}.

Now, if we multiply the functions in the first column by some constant c, the entries in the third column will not change! This is what we meant by saying that the constant is irrelevant to the effect of increased computer time (or speed) on the maximum input size an algorithm can handle.

1.5.3   Properties of O, Ω, and Θ

The order sets have a number of useful properties. Most of the proofs are left as exercises; they follow easily from the definitions. For all the properties, assume that $f, g, h : \mathbf{N} \rightarrow \mathbf{R}^*$. That is, the functions map nonnegative integers into nonnegative reals.

Lemma 1.9   If $f \in O(g)$ and $g \in O(h)$, then $f \in O(h)$; that is, O is transitive. Also, Ω, Θ, o, and ω are transitive.

Proof   Let c_1 and n_1 be such that $f(n) \leq c_1 g(n)$ for all $n \geq n_1$, and let c_2 and n_2 be such that $g(n) \leq c_2 h(n)$ for all $n \geq n_2$. Then for all $n \geq \max(n_1, n_2)$, $f(n) \leq c_1 c_2 h(n)$. So $f \in O(h)$. The proofs for Ω, Θ, o, and ω are similar.   □

Lemma 1.10

1. $f \in O(g)$ if and only if $g \in \Omega(f)$.
2. If $f \in \Theta(g)$, then $g \in \Theta(f)$.
3. Θ defines an equivalence relation on the functions. (See Section 1.3.1 for what needs to be shown.) Each set $\Theta(f)$ is an equivalence class, which we call a complexity class.
4. $O(f + g) = O(\max(f, g))$. Similar equations hold for Ω and Θ. (They are useful when analyzing complex algorithms, where f and g may describe the work done by different parts of the algorithm.)   □

Since Θ defines an equivalence relation, we can indicate the complexity class of an algorithm by specifying any function in the class. We usually choose the simplest representative. Thus if the number of steps carried out by an algorithm is described by the function $f(n) = n^3/6 + n^2 + 2 \lg n + 12$, we say simply that the complexity of the algorithm is in $\Theta(n^3)$. If $f \in \Theta(n)$, we say that f is linear; if $f \in \Theta(n^2)$, we say f is quadratic; and if $f \in \Theta(n^3)$, f is cubic.[4] $O(1)$ denotes the set of functions bounded by a constant (for large n).

Here are two useful theorems. The proofs use the techniques presented in Section 1.5.1, especially L'Hôpital's rule; they are left for exercises.

Theorem 1.11 $\lg n$ is in $o(n^\alpha)$ for any $\alpha > 0$. That is, the log function grows more slowly than any positive power of n (including fractional powers).   □

Theorem 1.12 n^k is in $o(2^n)$ for any $k > 0$. That is, powers of n grow more slowly than the exponential function 2^n. (In fact, powers of n grow more slowly than any exponential function c^n where $c > 1$.)   □

1.5.4   The Asymptotic Order of Commonly Occurring Sums

Order notation makes it easy to derive and remember the asymptotic order of many sums that come up over and over in the analysis of algorithms. Some of these summations were defined in Section 1.3.2.

Theorem 1.13   Let d be a nonnegative constant and let r be a positive constant not equal to 1.

1. The sum of a *polynomial series* increases the exponent by 1.

    Recall that a *polynomial series* of degree d is a sum of the form $\sum_{i=1}^{n} i^d$. The rule is that this kind of sum is in $\Theta\left(n^{d+1}\right)$.

2. The sum of a *geometric series* is in Θ of its largest term.

    Recall that a *geometric series* is a sum of the form $\sum_{i=a}^{b} r^i$.

    The rule applies whether $0 < r < 1$ or $r > 1$, but clearly not when $r = 1$. The limits a and b are not both constants; typically, the upper limit b is some function of n and the lower limit a is a constant.

3. The sum of a *logarithmic series* is in Θ(the number of terms times the log of the largest term).

    A *logarithmic series* is a sum of the form $\sum_{i=1}^{n} \log(i)$. The rule states that this kind of sum is in $\Theta\left(n \log(n)\right)$. Recall that, for statements about asymptotic order, the base of the logarithm does not matter.

---

[4] Note that the terms *linear*, *quadratic*, and *cubic* are used somewhat more loosely here than they usually are used by mathematicians.

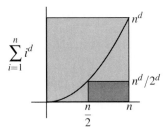
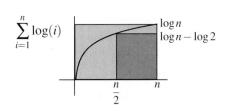

Figure 1.7   Rectangles provide upper and lower bounds for many kinds of sums. When the areas of both rectangles have the same asymptotic order, that must be the order of the sum.

4.   The sum of a *polynomial-logarithmic series*, which is a sum of the form $\sum\limits_{i=1}^{n} i^d \log(i)$,

is in $\Theta\left(n^{d+1} \log(n)\right)$.

Proof   Look at Figure 1.7. Since all the series in the theorem are of the form $\sum\limits_{i=1}^{n} f(i)$,
where $f(i)$ is monotonic, it is clear that the larger rectangle, of height $f(n)$ and width n, is
an upper bound on the sum. Also, as seen in Figure 1.4(b), the area under the graph of $f(i)$
between $i = 0$ and $i = n$ is a lower bound on the sum. For the cases of polynomial series
and logarithmic series, that area can easily be bounded below by the area of the smaller,
darkly shaded, rectangle. In the left picture, the area of the larger rectangle is n^{d+1}, while
the area of the smaller rectangle is $n^{d+1}/2^{d+1}$. Since the areas of both rectangles have the
same asymptotic order, the sum must have that order also. In the right picture, the two
areas are $n \log n$ and $(n/2)(\log n - \log 2)$. Polynomial-logarithmic series are similar, but
this technique does not work for geometric series. The rule for the geometric series follows
directly from Equation (1.9) in Section 1.3.2.   □

1.6   Searching an Ordered Array

To illustrate the ideas presented in the previous sections, we will study a familiar problem.

Problem 1.1   Ordered array search

Given an array E containing n entries sorted in nondecreasing order, and given a value K,
find an index for which $K = E[index]$ or, if K is not in the array, return -1 as the answer.
∎

In practice, K is usually the *key* for an entry and the entries are in some class with other
instance fields beside the key, so a more precise requirement might be $K = E[index].key$.
To simplify the discussion, we assume the entire array entry is the key and it is some
numeric type.

Let's pretend for the moment that we don't know the Binary Search algorithm; we approach the problem as if for the first time. We will consider various algorithms, analyze worst-case and average behavior, and finally consider Binary Search and show that it is optimal by establishing a lower bound on the number of key comparisons needed.

1.6.1   Some Solutions

Observe that the sequential search algorithm (Algorithm 1.1) solves the problem, but it makes no use of the fact that we now have an array in which the entries are in order. Can we modify that algorithm so that it uses the added information and does less work?

The first improvement is prompted by the observation that, since the array is in non-decreasing order, as soon as an entry larger than K is encountered, the algorithm can terminate with the answer -1. (How should the test on line 4 of that algorithm be changed to avoid doing two comparisons on each pass through the loop?) How does this change affect the analysis? Clearly, the modified algorithm is better in some cases; it will terminate sooner for some inputs. The worst-case complexity, however, remains unchanged. If K is the last entry in the array or if K is larger than all the entries, then the algorithm will do n comparisons.

For the average analysis of the modified algorithm, we must know how likely it is that K is *between* any two array entries. Suppose we define a *gap*, g_i, to be the set of values y such that $E[i-1] < y < E[i]$ for $i = 1, \ldots, n - 1$. Also, let g_0 be all values less than $E[0]$ and g_n be all values greater than $E[n-1]$. We will assume, as we did in Example 1.9, that there is a probability q that K is in the array. If K is in E we assume that all positions in the array are equally likely (i.e., have a conditional probability $1/n$). If K is not in the array, we assume that all gaps are equally likely (i.e., have a conditional probability $1/(n + 1)$). For $0 \le i < n$, it takes $i + 1$ comparisons to determine that $K = E[i]$ or that K is in g_i, and it takes n comparisons to determine that K is in g_n. So we compute the average number of comparisons, conditioned on success (A_{succ}) and conditioned on failure (A_{fail}), as follows:

$$A_{succ}(n) = \sum_{i=0}^{n-1} \left(\frac{1}{n}\right)(i + 1) = \frac{n + 1}{2},$$

$$A_{fail}(n) = \sum_{i=0}^{n-1} \left(\frac{1}{n + 1}\right)(i + 1) + \left(\frac{1}{n + 1}\right)n.$$

The first equation corresponds to cases in which K is in the array, and is the same as in Example 1.9. The second equation corresponds to cases in which K is not in the array. Evaluating the sum is easy and left as an exercise. As in Example 1.9, the results are combined by the equation $A(n) = qA_{succ}(n) + (1 - q)A_{fail}(n)$. The result is that $A(n)$ is roughly $n/2$, regardless of q. Algorithm 1.1 did $3n/4$ comparisons on the average when $q = \frac{1}{2}$, so the modified algorithm is an improvement, although its average behavior is still linear.

Let's try again. Can we find an algorithm that does substantially fewer than n comparisons in the worst case? Suppose we compare K to, say, every fourth entry in the array. If there is a match, we are done. If K is larger than the entry to which it is compared, say E[i], then the three entries preceding E[i] need not be explicitly examined. If $K < $ E[i], then K is between the last two entries to which it was compared. A few more comparisons (how many?) will suffice to determine the position of K if it is in the array or to determine that it is not there. The details of the algorithm and the analysis are left for readers to work out, but it is easy to see that only about one-fourth of the entries in the array are examined. Thus in the worst case approximately $n/4$ comparisons are done.

We could pursue the same scheme, choosing a large value for j and designing an algorithm that compares K to every jth entry, hence allowing us to eliminate from consideration $j - 1$ keys at each comparison as we proceed through the array. Thus we do roughly n/j comparisons to locate a small section of E that may contain K. Then we follow up with about j comparisons to explore the small section. For any fixed j the algorithm will still be linear, but if we choose j to minimize $(n/j + j)$, we find by calculus that j should be chosen as $\sqrt{n}$. Then the total search cost is only $2\sqrt{n}$. We have broken the linear-time barrier!

But can we do still better? Notice that we switched strategy after locating the small section. That section has about j elements, and we paid j to explore it, which is a linear cost. But now we know that a linear cost is too high. This suggests that we should recursively use our "master strategy" on the small section, instead of switching strategies.

The idea of the well-known Binary Search algorithm takes the "every jth entry" to its logical extreme, by jumping across half of the entries in one step. Instead of choosing a particular integer j and comparing K to every jth entry, we compare K first to the entry in the middle of the array. This eliminates half the keys with one comparison.

Once we have determined which half might contain K, we apply the same strategy recursively. Until the section that might contain K has shrunk to zero size, or K has been found in the array, we continue to compare K to the middle entry in the section of the array under consideration. After each comparison, the size of the section of the array that may contain K is cut in half. Notice that this is another example of a generalized searching routine (Definition 1.12). The procedure *fails* when the section that might contain K has shrunk to zero size; it *succeeds* if it locates K; and it *keeps searching* if neither of those events occurs.

This procedure is a prime example of the *divide-and-conquer* paradigm, which we will discuss at greater length in Chapters 3 and 4. The problem of finding K among n sorted elements is divided into two subproblems by comparing K with the middle element (assuming the middle element is not K). We will see through analysis that solving the two subproblems separately is easier (in the worst case and in the average case) than solving the original problem without dividing it up. Actually, one of the subproblems is solved with zero work because we know that K can't be in that part of the array.

Algorithm 1.4   Binary Search

Input: E, first, last, and K, where E is an ordered array in the range first, ..., last, and K is the key sought. For simplicity, we assume that k and the entries of E are integers, as are first and last.

Output: index such that E[index] = K if K is in E within the range first, . . ., last, and index = -1 if K is not in this range of E.

```
int binarySearch(int[] E, int first, int last, int K)
 1.     if (last < first)
 2.          index = -1;
 3.     else
 4.          int mid = (first + last) / 2;
 5.          if (K == E[mid])
 6.               index = mid;
 7.          else if (K < E[mid])
 8.               index = binarySearch(E, first, mid-1, K);
 9.          else
10.               index = binarySearch(E, mid+1, last, K);
11.     return index;
```

Correctness of Algorithm 1.4 is proved in detail in Section 3.5.7 as an illustration of a formal proof of correctness, after some needed material has been introduced. The kind of informal reasoning that is more often done was discussed just before the algorithm.

1.6.2   Worst-Case Analysis of Binary Search

Let us define the problem size for binarySearch as $n =$ last $-$ first $+ 1$, the number of entries in the range of E to be searched. A reasonable choice of basic operation for the Binary Search algorithm is a comparison of K to an array entry. (A "comparison" for this discussion always means a comparison with an entry of E, not an index comparison as in line 1.) Let $W(n)$ be the number of such comparisons performed by the algorithm in the worst case on arrays with n entries in the range to be searched.

It is usual to assume that one comparison with a three-way branch is done for the tests on K in lines 5 and 7. (Even without three-way comparisons, about the same bound can be achieved with binary comparisons; see Exercise 1.42.) Thus $W(n)$ is also the number of invocations of the binarySearch function, other than the one that reaches line 2 and exits without a comparison.

Java sidelight: Many Java classes, including **String**, support three-way comparisons with the Comparable interface; user-defined classes can implement this feature also; see Appendix A.

Suppose $n > 0$. The task of the algorithm is to find K in a range of n entries indexed from first through last. It proceeds to line 5 and compares K to E[mid], where mid $= \lfloor$(first + last)/2$\rfloor$. In the worst case these keys are not equal and either line 8 or line 10 is reached, depending on whether the left or right section of the range (relative to mid) might contain K. How many entries are there in these sections? If n is even, there are $n/2$ entries in the right section of the array and $(n/2) - 1$ entries in the left section. If n is odd, there are $(n - 1)/2$ entries in both sections. Hence, there are at most $\lfloor n/2 \rfloor$ entries in the section of the array that is specified to the recursive call. Therefore it is a conservative estimate that the size of the range is divided by 2 with each recursive call.

How many times can we divide n by 2 without getting a result less than 1? In other words, what is the largest d for which $n/2^d \geq 1$? We solve for d: $2^d \leq n$ and $d \leq \lg(n)$. Therefore we can do $\lfloor \lg(n) \rfloor$ comparisons following recursive calls, and one comparison before any recursive calls, for at most $W(n) = \lfloor \lg(n) \rfloor + 1$ comparisons in all. Exercise 1.5 gives us a slightly more convenient form for this expression, which is well defined for $n = 0$; it is $\lceil \lg(n + 1) \rceil$. Thus we have shown that:

Theorem 1.14   The Binary Search algorithm does $W(n) = \lceil \lg(n + 1) \rceil$ comparisons of K with array entries in the worst case (where $n \geq 0$ is the number of array entries). Since one comparison is done on each function invocation, the running time is in $\Theta(\log n)$.   □

Binary Search does fewer comparisons in the worst case than a sequential search does on the average.

1.6.3   Average-Behavior Analysis

To simplify the analysis a little, we will assume that K appears in at most one place in the array. As we observed at the beginning of this section, there are $2n + 1$ positions that K might occupy: the n positions in E, which we call *success positions*, and the $n + 1$ gaps, or *failure positions*. For $0 \leq i < n$, let I_i represent all inputs for which $K = E[i]$. For $1 \leq i < n$, let I_{n+i} represent inputs for which $E[i-1] < x < E[i]$. I_n and I_{2n} represent inputs where $K < E[0]$ and $K > E[n-1]$, respectively. Let $t(I_i)$ be the number of comparisons of K with array entries done by Algorithm 1.4 on input I_i. Table 1.4 shows the values of t

i	$t(I_i)$		i	$t(I_i)$
0	4		13	4
1	5		14	5
2	3		15	3
3	4		16	4
4	5		17	5
5	2		18	2
6	4		19	4
7	5		20	5
8	3		21	3
9	5		22	5
10	4		23	4
11	5		24	5
12	1		gaps 25, 28, 31, 38, 41, 44	4
			all other gaps	5

Table 1.4   The number of comparisons done by Binary Search, depending on the location of K, for $n = 25$

for $n = 25$. Observe that most successes and all gaps are within one of the worst case; that is, it takes 4 to 5 comparisons to find K most of the time. (For $n = 31$ we would find that most successes and all gaps are exactly the worst case.) So if we assume that all success positions are equally likely, it is not unreasonable to expect the number of comparisons done on the average to be close to $\lg n$. Computation of the average assuming each position has probability $1/51$ yields $223/51$, or approximately 4.37, and $\lg 25 \approx 4.65$.

Since the average number of comparisons may depend on the probability that the search is successful, let us denote that probability by q, and define $A_q(n)$ to be the average number of comparisons when the probability of success is q. We have, by the law of conditional expectations (Lemma 1.2), that

$$A_q(n) = q\, A_1(n) + (1 - q)\, A_0(n).$$

Therefore we can solve the special cases $A_1(n)$ (success is certain) and $A_0(n)$ (failure is certain) separately, and combine them to get a solution for any q. Notice that A_1 is the same as A_{succ} and A_0 is the same as A_{fail}, in the nomenclature used for the sequential search.

We will derive approximate formulas for $A_0(n)$ and $A_1(n)$, given these assumptions:

1. All success positions are equally likely: $Pr(I_i \mid succ) = 1/n$ for $1 \le i \le n$.
2. $n = 2^k - 1$, for some integer $k \ge 0$.

The last assumption is made to simplify the analysis. The result for all values of n is very close to the result that we will obtain.

For $n = 2^k - 1$ it is easily seen that every failing search will use exactly k comparisons, no matter which gap K falls in. Therefore $A_0(n) = \lg(n + 1)$.

The key to analyzing the average behavior for successful searches is to switch from thinking about how many comparisons are done on a particular input I_i, to thinking about: How many inputs do a *specific number* of comparisons, say t comparisons? For $1 \le t \le k$, let s_t be the number of inputs for which the algorithm does t comparisons.

For example, for $n = 25$, $s_3 = 4$ because three comparisons would be done for each of the four inputs I_2, I_8, I_{15}, and I_{21}.

It is easy to see that $s_1 = 1 = 2^0$, $s_2 = 2 = 2^1$, $s_3 = 4 = 2^2$, and in general, $s_t = 2^{t-1}$. Since each input has probability $1/n$, the probability that the algorithm does t comparisons is just s_t/n, and the average is

$$A_1(n) = \sum_{t=1}^{k} t\left(\frac{s_t}{n}\right) = \frac{1}{n}\sum_{t=1}^{k} t\, 2^{k-1} = \frac{(k-1)2^k + 1}{n}$$

by using Equation (1.12). (If we did not assume $n = 2^k - 1$, the value of s_k would not follow the pattern, and some failures would use only $k - 1$ comparisons as in Table 1.4 for $n = 25$.) Now, since $n + 1 = 2^k$,

$$A_1(n) = \frac{(k-1)(n+1) + 1}{n} = \lg(n + 1) - 1 + O\left(\frac{\log n}{n}\right).$$

As mentioned, $A_0(n) = \lg(n + 1)$ holds for the assumption that K is not in the array. Thus we have proved the following theorem.

Theorem 1.15   Binary Search (Algorithm 1.4) does approximately $\lg(n + 1) - q$ comparisons on the average for arrays with n entries, where q is the probability that the search is successful, and all success positions are equally likely.   □

1.6.4   Optimality

In the previous section we began with a $\Theta(n)$ algorithm, improved it to $\Theta(\sqrt{n})$, and then to $\Theta(\log n)$. Are more improvements possible? Even if we can't improve the asymptotic order, can we improve the constant factor? The role of lower bounds analysis is to tell us when one or both of these questions can be answered negatively. A "tight" lower bound, one that matches the upper bound for our algorithm, assures us that further improvements cannot be found.

We will show that the binary search algorithm is optimal in the class of algorithms that can do no other operations on the array entries except comparisons. We will establish a lower bound on the number of comparisons needed by examining *decision trees* for search algorithms in this class.[5] Let **A** be such an algorithm. A decision tree for **A** and a given input size n is a binary tree whose nodes are labeled with numbers between 0 and $n - 1$ and are arranged according to the following rules:

1.   The root of the tree is labeled with the index of the first entry in the array to which the algorithm **A** compares K.

2.   Suppose the label on a particular node is i. Then the label on the left child of that node is the index of the entry to which the algorithm will compare K next if $K < E[i]$. The label on the right child is the index of the entry to which the algorithm will compare K next if $K > E[i]$. The node does not have a left (or right) child if the algorithm halts after comparing K to $E[i]$ and discovering that $K < E[i]$ (or $K > E[i]$). There is no branch for the case $K = E[i]$. A reasonable algorithm would do no more comparisons in that case.

The class of algorithms that can be modeled by such decision trees is very broad; it includes sequential search and the variations considered at the beginning of this section. (Notice that the algorithm is permitted to compare two keys in the array, but this does not provide any information, because the array is already sorted, so we don't make a node in the decision tree for this.) Figure 1.8 shows the decision tree for the Binary Search algorithm with $n = 10$.

Given a particular input, algorithm **A** will perform the comparisons indicated along one path beginning at the root of its decision tree. The number of key comparisons performed is the number of nodes on the path. The number of comparisons performed in the worst case is the number of nodes on a longest path from the root to a leaf; call this number p. Suppose the decision tree has N nodes. Each node has at most two children, so the number of nodes at a particular distance (counting each edge as one) from the root is at

---

[5] We assume readers are acquainted with the terminology of binary trees, including terms such as *root*, *leaf*, and *path*; if not, please look ahead to Section 2.3.3 before proceeding.

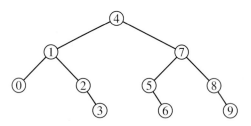

Figure 1.8   Decision tree for the Binary Search algorithm with $n = 10$

most twice the number at the previous distance. Since the maximum distance of any node from the root is $p - 1$, we have

$$N \le 1 + 2 + 4 + \cdots + 2^{p-1}.$$

By Equation (1.8) the right-hand side is $2^p - 1$, so we have $2^p \ge (N + 1)$.

We have a relationship between p and N, but we want to relate p to n, the number of elements in the array to be searched. The key claim is that $N \ge n$ if the algorithm **A** works correctly in all cases. In particular, we claim that there is some node in the decision tree labeled i for each i from 0 through $n - 1$.

Suppose, to the contrary, that there is no node labeled i, for some i in the range 0 through $n - 1$. We can make up two input arrays E1 and E2 such that E1$[i] = K$ but E2$[i] = K' > K$. For all indexes j less than i we make E1$[j] = $ E2$[j]$ using some key values less than K, in sorted order; for all indexes j greater than i we make E1$[j] = $ E2$[j]$ using some key values greater than K', in sorted order. Since no node in the decision tree is labeled i, the algorithm **A** never compares K to E1$[i]$ or E2$[i]$. It behaves the same way on both inputs since their other entries are identical, and it must give the same output for both. Thus **A** gives the wrong output for at least one of the arrays and it is not a correct algorithm. We conclude that the decision tree has at least n nodes.

So $2^p \ge (N + 1) \ge (n + 1)$, where p is the number of comparisons on the longest path in the decision tree. Now we take logs, and get $p \ge \lg(n + 1)$. Since **A** was an arbitrary algorithm from the class of algorithms considered, we have proved the following theorem.

Theorem 1.16   Any algorithm to find K in an array of n entries (by comparing K to array entries) must do at least $\lceil \lg(n + 1) \rceil$ comparisons for some input.   □

Corollary 1.17   Since Algorithm 1.4 does $\lceil \lg(n + 1) \rceil$ comparisons in the worst case, it is optimal.   □

Exercises

Section 1.2 Java as an Algorithm Language

1.1 Define an organizer class for personal information consisting of name, address, telephone number, and e-mail address, making reasonable assumptions about how these items would need to be broken down.

Section 1.3 Mathematical Background

1.2 For all $n > 0$ and $k > 0$, show that

$$\binom{n}{k} = \binom{n-1}{k} + \binom{n-1}{k-1} \tag{1.32}$$

where the notation of Equation (1.1) is being used. Using the alternative notation of that equation, Equation (1.32) becomes $C(n,k) = C(n-1,k) + C(n-1,k-1)$. You will need the fact that $0! = 1$ for some boundary cases.

1.3 Prove part 7 of Lemma 1.1, about logarithms. *Hint*: Take logs on both sides of the equation and use part 2 of that lemma.

1.4 Prove part 8 of Lemma 1.1, about logarithms.

1.5 Show that $\lceil \lg(n+1) \rceil = \lfloor \lg n \rfloor + 1$ for integers $n \geq 1$. *Hint*: Group values of n into ranges of the form $2^k \leq n \leq 2^{k+1} - 1$.

1.6 Write a function (pseudocode is fine) to find $\lceil \lg(n+1) \rceil$, where n is a nonnegative integer, by repeatedly dividing n by 2. Assume your programming language truncates the result of integer division, dropping any remainder, as most languages do. Hand calculate a table of the first ten values to check your function.

1.7

a. How many different arrangements are there for an ordinary deck of 52 cards? (This should be easy.)

b. Scientists estimate that approximately 10^{18} seconds have passed since the "Big Bang," the beginning of the universe. Give an (easy) lower bound for your answer to part (a) in the form of a power of 10. How does it compare to the number of seconds since the Big Bang?

1.8 Show that if S and T are stochastically independent, then

$$Pr(S \mid T) = Pr(S) \quad \text{and} \quad Pr(T \mid S) = Pr(T).$$

1.9 Show from the definitions that $Pr(S) = Pr(S \mid T)Pr(T) + Pr(S \mid \text{not } T)Pr(\text{not } T)$.

1.10   What are the conditional probabilities of these four events given that $A < B$ and $D < C$, in the situation of Example 1.5: $A < C$, $A < D$, $B < C$, $B < D$?

1.11   With the situation described in Example 1.6, what are $E(I \mid A < D)$ and $E(I \mid D < A)$?

1.12   Suppose three coins are lying on a table. One coin is chosen at random and flipped. We want to find the probability that after the flip the majority of the coins (that is, two or three of them) will have "heads" up, starting from various initial configurations. For each initial configuration given below, give the coins names, define the elementary events, and give their probabilities. State any assumptions you are making in assigning the probabilities. Which set of events is defined by the property that a majority of the coins have "heads" up after the flip, and what is the probability of this event? Suppose the sides facing up initially are

a.   heads, tails, tails.

b.   tails, tails, tails.

c.   heads, heads, tails.

1.13   Consider four dice containing the numbers indicated below. For each pair of dice, say D_i and D_j with $1 \le i, j \le 4$ and $i \ne j$, compute the probability that on a fair toss of the two dice, the top face of D_i will show a higher number than the top face of D_j. (Show the results in a 4×4 matrix.)

$$
\begin{array}{llllllll}
D_1: & 1, & 2, & 3, & 9, & 10, & 11 \\
D_2: & 0, & 1, & 7, & 8, & 8, & 9 \\
D_3: & 5, & 5, & 6, & 6, & 7, & 7 \\
D_4: & 3, & 4, & 4, & 5, & 11, & 12
\end{array}
$$

(If you do the computation correctly and study the results carefully, you will discover that these dice have a surprising property. If you and another player were gambling on who throws the higher number, and you chose your die first, the other player could always choose a die with a high probability of beating yours. These dice are discussed in Gardner (1983) where their discovery is attributed to B. Efron.)

1.14   Give a formula for $\displaystyle\sum_{i=a}^{n} i$ where a is an integer between 1 and n.

1.15   Prove Equation (1.6).

★ **1.16**   Prove Lemma 1.3. *Hint*: Suppose $f(x)$ is above the linear interpolation line at *some* point between u and v, for some choice, $u < v$. Then, let w be the point between u and v such that $f(w)$ is *farthest* above the line, in that interval. (Such a w must exist for continuous functions.)

⋆ **1.17** Prove part 1 of Lemma 1.4.

1.18 Prove part 2 of Lemma 1.4.

⋆ **1.19** Prove part 3 of Lemma 1.4. *Hint*: You may find Lemma 1.3 helpful.

1.20 Prove Equation (1.26); that is, cite the precise identities needed to justify each line in the derivation.

⋆ **1.21** This exercise is an opportunity to make a genuine proof by contradiction. Prove the rule of cases, Equation (1.31), which can be stated as follows:

Proposition 1.18 (Rule of cases) If $(B \Rightarrow C)$ and $(\neg B \Rightarrow C)$, then C. □

Begin by assuming $\neg C$, and eventually derive C, using the hypotheses of the proposition, Equation (1.27), and *modus ponens*, Equation (1.29).

Section 1.4 Analyzing Algorithms and Problems

1.22 Give a formula for the total number of operations done by the Sequential Search algorithm (Algorithm 1.1) in the worst case for an array with n entries. Count comparisons of K with array entries, comparisons with the variable index, additions, and assignments to index.

1.23 The *median* of an ordered set is an element such that the number of elements less than the median is within one of the number that are greater, assuming no ties.

   a.   Write an algorithm to find the median of three distinct integers a, b, and c.
   b.   Describe D, the set of inputs for your algorithm, in light of the discussion in Section 1.4.3 following Example 1.9.
   c.   How many comparisons does your algorithm do in the worst case? On the average?
   d.   How many comparisons are necessary in the worst case to find the median of three numbers? Justify your answer.

1.24 Write an algorithm to find the second largest element in a set containing n entries. How many comparisons of elements does your algorithm do in the worst case? (It is possible to do better than $2n - 3$; we will consider this problem again.)

1.25 Write an algorithm to find both the smallest and largest elements in a set of n entries. Try to find a method that does roughly $1.5n$ comparisons of elements in the worst case.

1.26 Given the polynomial $p(x) = a_n x^n + a_{n-1} x^{n-1} + \cdots + a_1 x + a_0$, suppose the following algorithm is used to evaluate it.

```
p = a₀;
xpower = 1;
for (i = 1; i ≤ n; i ++)
    xpower = x * xpower;
    p = p + aᵢ * xpower;
```

a. How many multiplications are done in the worst case? How many additions?

b. How many multiplications are done on the average?

c. Can you improve on this algorithm? (We will consider this problem again.)

Section 1.5   Classifying Functions by Their Asymptotic Growth Rates

1.27 Suppose Algorithm 1 does $f(n) = n^2 + 4n$ steps in the worst case, and Algorithm 2 does $g(n) = 29n + 3$ steps in the worst case, for inputs of size n. For what input sizes is Algorithm 1 faster than Algorithm 2 (in the worst case)?

1.28 Let $p(n) = a_k n^k + a_{k-1} n^{k-1} + \cdots + a_1 n + a_0$ be a polynomial in n of degree k with $a_k > 0$. Prove that $p(n)$ is in $\Theta(n^k)$.

1.29 Add a row to Table 1.1 showing the approximate maximum input size that can be solved in one day, for each column.

1.30 Let α and β be real numbers such that $0 < \alpha < \beta$. Show that n^α is in $O(n^\beta)$ but n^β is not in $O(n^\alpha)$.

1.31 List the functions below from lowest asymptotic order to highest asymptotic order. If any two (or more) are of the same asymptotic order, indicate which.

a. Start with these basic functions:

$$n \qquad 2^n \qquad n \lg n \qquad \qquad n^3$$
$$n^2 \qquad \lg n \qquad n - n^3 + 7n^5 \qquad n^2 + \lg n$$

★ **b.** Combine the following functions into your answer for part (a). Assume $0 < \epsilon < 1$.

$$e^n \qquad \sqrt{n} \qquad 2^{n-1} \qquad \lg \lg n$$
$$\ln n \qquad (\lg n)^2 \qquad n! \qquad n^{1+\epsilon}$$

★ **1.32** Prove or give a counterexample: For every positive constant c and every function f from nonnegative integers into nonnegative reals, $f(cn) \in \Theta(f(n))$. *Hint*: Consider some of the fast-growing functions listed in the preceding problem.

★ **1.33** Prove or give a counterexample: For every function f from nonnegative integers into nonnegative reals, $o(f) = O(f) - \Theta(f)$. (Here, "$-$" denotes set difference: $A - B$ consists of elements in A that are not in B.)

★ **1.34** Prove or give a counterexample: For every function f from nonnegative integers into nonnegative reals, no function g is in both $\Theta(f)$ and $o(f)$, that is, $\Theta(f) \cap o(f) = \emptyset$.

⋆ **1.35** Prove Lemma 1.10.

1.36 Prove Theorem 1.11.

⋆ **1.37** Prove Theorem 1.12.

⋆ **1.38** Show that the values in the third column of the speedup table (Table 1.3) are unchanged when we replace any function $f(n)$ in the first column by $cf(n)$, for any positive constant c.

1.39 Give an example of two functions $f, g: \mathbf{N} \rightarrow \mathbf{R}^*$, such that $f \notin O(g)$ and $g \notin O(f)$.

1.40 Prove or disprove:

$$\sum_{i=1}^{n} i^2 \in \Theta(n^2).$$

Section 1.6   Searching an Ordered Array

1.41 Write out the algorithm to find K in an ordered array by the method suggested in the text that compares K to every fourth entry until K itself or an entry larger than K is found, and then, in the latter case, searches for K among the preceding three. How many comparisons does your algorithm do in the worst case?

1.42 Design a variation of Binary Search (Algorithm 1.4) that performs only one *binary* comparison (that is, the comparison returns a Boolean result) of K with an array entry, per function invocation. You may add additional comparisons on range variables. Analyze the correctness of your procedure. *Hint*: When should your one comparison be equality (==)?

1.43 Draw a decision tree for the Binary Search algorithm (Algorithm 1.4) with $n = 17$.

1.44 Describe the decision tree for the Sequential Search algorithm (Algorithm 1.1) in Section 1.4 for an arbitrary n.

1.45 How can you modify Binary Search (Algorithm 1.4) to eliminate unnecessary work if you are certain that K is in the array? Draw a decision tree for the modified algorithm for $n = 7$. Do worst-case and average-behavior analyses. (For the average, you may assume $n = 2^k - 1$ for some k.)

⋆ **1.46** Let S be a set of m integers. Let E be an array of n distinct integers $(n \leq m)$, randomly chosen from the set S. Assume that the entries in E are sorted in ascending order. Let K be an element randomly chosen from S. On the average, how many comparisons will be done by Binary Search (Algorithm 1.4) given $E, 0, n - 1$, and K as input? Express your answer as a function of n and m.

⋆ **1.47** The first n cells of the array E contain integers sorted in increasing order. The remaining cells all contain some very large integer that we may think of as infinity (call it *maxint*). The array may be arbitrarily large (you may think of it as infinite), and *you don't know n*. Give an algorithm to find the position of a given integer x ($x < maxint$) in the array in $O(\log n)$ time. (The technique used here is useful for certain arguments about $\mathcal{NP}$-complete problems that we will see in Chapter 13.)

Additional Problems

⋆ **1.48** The expression $x \ln(x)$ often needs to be evaluated at $x = 0$, but $\ln(0) = -\infty$, so it is not clear what the value should be. Note that $-x \ln(x)$ is positive for $0 < x < 1$. Show that $-x \ln(x)$ approaches 0 as x approaches 0 through positive values.

⋆ **1.49** We are given a probability space with elementary events $U = \{s_1, \ldots, s_k\}$ and some conditional event E. The event E defines conditional probabilities $p_i(E) = Pr(s_i \mid E)$. (If $E = U$, then $p_i(U) = Pr(s_i)$.)

Define the *entropy of E* as the function

$$H(E) = - \sum_{i=1}^{k} p_i(E) \lg(p_i(E)). \tag{1.33}$$

Exercise 1.48 justifies considering only events of nonzero probability when computing entropy.

Intuitively, the entropy measures the amount of *ignorance* about the events: The larger the value, the less we know. If one event is certain and the rest are impossible, the entropy is 0. Entropy can also be viewed as a measure of randomness.

a. Suppose $Pr(s_i) = 1/k$ for $1 \le i \le k$. What is $H(U)$?

b. Consider the situation of Example 1.5 for this and remaining parts of the exercise. For simplicity, use 1.6 as the value of $\lg(3)$.

What is the entropy before any comparisons are made? (See part a.)

c. What is the entropy after $A < B$ is discovered? That is, what is $H(E)$, where E is the event $A < B$? Would it be different if $B < A$ were discovered?

d. What is the entropy after $A < B$ and $D < C$ are discovered? That is, what is $H(E)$, where E is the event "$A < B$ and $D < C$"? Would it be different if any of these inequalities were reversed?

e. Suppose the program first compares A and B and finds out that $A < B$, then compares B and C. What are the entropies after each possible outcome of this comparison?

f. Suppose two programs, P and Q, are trying to find out the order among the elements. Both start by comparing A and B. Suppose P next compares the maximum of A and B with C, as in part (e), and suppose Q next compares C and D, as in part (d). Assume that both programs make optimal choices of comparisons after the first two; you do *not* need to work out what the optimal choices are.

Based on this much information, which program would you *expect* to use the smaller number of comparisons to find the complete order, in the worst case? What about the best case? Only an informed guess and reasonable explanation are needed, not a proof.

1.50   You have 70 coins that are all supposed to be gold coins of the same weight, but you know that one coin is fake and weighs less than the others. You have a balance scale; you can put any number of coins on each side of the scale at one time, and it will tell you if the two sides weigh the same, or which side is lighter if they don't weigh the same. Outline an algorithm for finding the fake coin. How many weighings will you do?

Notes and References

Several other texts on design and analysis of algorithms are listed in the Bibliography.

James Gosling is the main designer of Java. Gosling, Joy, and Steele (1996) and later editions give the specification of the Java language.

Many of the references that follow are more advanced than this chapter; they would be useful and interesting to consult throughout the reading of this book.

The ACM's Alan M. Turing Award has been given to several people who have done important work in computational complexity. The Turing Award Lectures by Richard M. Karp (1986), Stephen A. Cook (1983), and Michael O. Rabin (1977) give very nice overviews of questions, techniques, and points of view of computational complexity.

Graham, Knuth, and Patashnik (1994) cover many useful advanced mathematical techniques. Equations (1.11) and (1.19) are given there. Grassmann and Tremblay (1996) provide a good introduction to logic and proofs.

Knuth (1976) discusses the meaning and history of the notations $O(f)$ and $\Theta(f)$. Brassard (1985) presents arguments for the variation of the definitions used in this book.

Bentley (1982 and 1986) and his past columns "Programming Pearls" in the *Communications of the ACM* contain beautifully written discussions of algorithm design and techniques for making programs more efficient in practice.

Readers who wish to browse through research articles will find a lot of material in the *Journal of the ACM*, *SIGACT News*, the *SIAM Journal on Computing*, *Transactions on Mathematical Software*, and *IEEE Transactions on Computers*, to name a few sources. Many annual conferences present research on algorithms.

Knuth (1984), a paper about the space complexity of songs, is very highly recommended for when the going gets rough.

2

Data Abstraction and Basic Data Structures

2.1 Introduction

Data abstraction is a technique that allows us to focus on the important properties of a data structure, while leaving less important aspects unspecified. An *abstract data type* (*ADT*) consists of a data structure declaration, plus a set of operations involving the data structure. The *client*, or user, of an ADT calls these operations to create, destroy, manipulate, and interrogate *objects* (or *instances*) of the abstract data type. In this context, a *client* is just some procedure or function that is defined outside the ADT.

This chapter describes a technique for specifying the required behavior of abstract data types, shows how to apply this technique to several widely used data structures, and also reviews some of the important properties of standard data structures that will play a part in later algorithm development.

The specification technique is based on the pioneering work of David Parnas (see Notes and References at the end of the chapter). The key idea is called *information hiding*, or *data encapsulation*. ADT modules maintain private data that is accessible outside the module only through well-defined operations. Parnas's goal was to provide a software design technique that would permit many parts of a large project to be worked on independently, yet still fit together and function correctly.

In algorithm design and analysis, ADTs have another important role. The main design can be carried out using the ADT operations, without deciding how to implement these operations. After the algorithm is designed at this level, we can undertake an analysis to count how many of each ADT operation the algorithm uses. Armed with this information, we may be able to steer the implementation of the ADT operations in a direction that makes the more frequently used operations the least expensive.

In other words, we may reason about the *correctness* of the algorithm considering only the logical properties of the ADTs used, which are independent of the implementation. However, the *performance analysis* depends upon the implementation. Designing with ADTs permits us to separate these two concerns.

A programming language *supports* data abstraction to the extent that it permits the programmer to restrict clients' access to an abstract data type; access is restricted to the defined operations and other *public* parts of the ADT class. The maintenance of private data is called *encapsulation*, or *information hiding*. This provides a tool for the programmer to ensure that certain *invariants* of the ADT object are preserved. That is, if the only access by clients to an instance of the ADT is through a small set of operations defined as the interface for that ADT, then the programmer who implements the operations can (at least in theory) make sure that the relationships among different parts of the data structure always satisfy the specifications of the ADT. The scenario is suggested in Figure 2.1. These considerations explain why ADTs are important in software engineering.

We chose Java as the language in which to present algorithms mainly because of its simple and natural support for data abstraction. In Java an ADT is identified as a *class*. (However, not every class is an ADT; for example, see Section 1.2.2.) The program may create *objects* in this class; these objects are simply elements of the abstract data type.

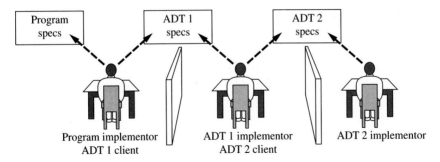

Figure 2.1 ADT specifications provide the interface between client and implementor. In this example ADT 1 is implemented by using some services of ADT 2.

2.2 ADT Specification and Design Techniques

The *specifications* of an ADT describe how the operations behave, in terms that are meaningful to the clients of the ADT. That is, specifications should avoid reference to private instance fields, because the clients are unaware of the private instance fields. The specifications describe the *logical relationships* among the public parts of the ADT, which are usually operations and constants. (Examples of specifications in later sections of this chapter will clarify these generalities.) ADT operations (functions and procedures) are called "methods" in Java terminology.

A significant advantage of designing with ADTs is that the client can develop a *logically correct* algorithm knowing only the ADT specifications, without committing to a specific implementation (or even a specific language) for the ADT. This is the chief motivation for presenting ADT methodology in this book.

2.2.1 ADT Specifications

Specifications can usually be broken down into *preconditions* and *postconditions*. The *preconditions* of a particular operation are statements that are assumed to be true when the operation is called. If the operation has parameters it is important that the preconditions be stated in terms of these parameter names, for clarity. It is the client's responsibility to meet the preconditions before calling any operation (or static method, or function, or procedure) of the ADT class. The *postconditions* of a particular operation are statements that the client may assume to be true when the operation returns. Again, if the operation has parameters it is important that the postconditions be stated in terms of these parameter names. The postconditions are also called the *objectives* of the operation.

Java provides a special comment format for the documentation of a class, including the preconditions and postconditions of its methods. Comments beginning with "/**" begin a javadoc comment. We use the javadoc commenting convention in the text to signal that a comment relates to the *specifications* for a procedure or block of code, as opposed to a remark about the implementation.

What Goes into an ADT

For our purposes an ADT is a coherent set of procedures and functions whose specifications interact to provide a certain capability. We adopt a minimalist view, by including only the necessary operations in the ADT itself; these are the operations that "need to know" how the objects are implemented. Thus an ADT is not a library of procedures that might be convenient; such a library might be supplied as an additional class, if desired.

The necessary operations fall into three categories, *constructors*, *access functions*, and *manipulation procedures*. Destructors, which deallocate an object and make its storage space available for a new use, are not crucial because Java performs "garbage collection" automatically. Garbage collection locates unreferenced objects and recycles their space.

Definition 2.1   Types of ADT operation

Three categories of operation for ADTs follow:

Constructors	create a new object and return a reference to it.
Access functions	return information about an object, but do not modify it.
Manipulation procedures	modify an object, but do not return information.

Thus, after an object is created, an operation may either modify the state of the object or return information about its state, but not both.   ■

Let us note here that an ADT constructor is not a constructor in the Java sense, and, like the other categories of ADT operations, is independent of the programming language. In Java it should *not* be preceded by the **new** keyword; it is used with the same syntax as any other function (or static method).

Because of our rule that access functions do not modify the state of any objects, ADT specifications can usually be organized in a special way. It is normally unnecessary to give postconditions for access functions. Moreover, when stating the specifications of manipulation procedures and ADT constructors, their effects should be described in terms of the access functions of the ADT, as far as possible. Sometimes the specification needs to state the combined effect of several operations. It may seem illogical at first to look at the postcondition of an ADT constructor or manipulation procedure to find out what an access function "does." However, if we view the access functions collectively as a sort of generalized "value" of an object, then it makes good sense: Whenever an operation initializes or changes the state of an object, the postcondition of that operation should tell us (whatever is relevant) about the new generalized "value" of the object.

In choosing a set of operations for an ADT, it is important to be sure the set of access functions is sufficient to check the preconditions for all operations. This gives the client the capability to be sure no operation is ever called erroneously.

For practical software development, it is convenient to have a library of frequently needed operations on the ADT. The distinction between the library and the ADT is that the operations in the library can be implemented by using the ADT operations; they do not need to "look under the hood" to see how the objects are implemented. (However, in some cases, "looking under the hood" would permit a faster version of a library function.)

2.2.2 ADT Design Techniques

Definitions of several important ADTs that we use in the development of algorithms are given in later sections of this chapter. Readers can see by example how Java is used to define and implement some of these ADTs. It should also be easy to see how to implement them in other programming languages with which readers may be familiar.

For simple and very standard ADTs, like linked lists, trees, stacks, and FIFO queues, the ADT used during design can be carried right through to the final implementation. In some cases other ADTs may be clients of these standard ADTs, and use them as building blocks.

For more complex or nonstandard ADTs, such as the Dictionary, Priority Queue, and Union-Find, the ADT can be used during design for its logical advantages (such as simplifying the analysis of correctness), but then for the final implementation it may be more convenient to "unwrap" the ADT and implement a special case for the algorithm that uses it.

Remaining sections of this chapter present several standard data structures and their associated abstract data types, proceeding generally from the simple to the complex. Various issues concerning specification techniques are addressed as they arise along the way. In this chapter, except for linked lists, implementations are discussed only in some of the exercises. We include a few examples for linked lists to provide some sample Java code to serve as a guide in other situations. In general, implementations are discussed in the algorithms that use the ADTs, so the implementation can be tailored to the usage pattern of that algorithm.

2.3 Elementary ADTs—Lists and Trees

The abstract data types for lists and trees are simple, but very versatile, and their operations can all be implemented easily in constant time. We will specify these ADTs to have constructors and some access functions, but no manipulation procedures. The absence of manipulation procedures makes the specifications particularly simple. Other reasons for omitting manipulation procedures are explained in Section 2.3.2. Lists and trees are most naturally defined recursively.

2.3.1 Recursive ADTs

An ADT is recursive if any of its *access functions* returns the same class as the ADT. In other words, some part of the object (as returned by the access function) is of the same type as the object itself. In such cases the ADT usually also has a constructor that has a parameter of the same class as the ADT. Such an ADT necessarily has a nonrecursive constructor as well. However, the "nonrecursive constructor" is often simply a constant (which can be thought of as a function that takes *no* parameters). Linked lists and trees are common data structures that are most naturally defined recursively. As we shall see in Sections 2.3.2 through 2.3.5, their specifications are extremely simple and concise.

The best way to think of an object in a recursive data type is as a structure that includes not only the fields that are immediately accessible, but also the fields that are *indirectly*

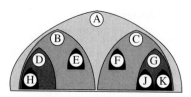

Figure 2.2 Objects in a recursive ADT should be viewed as all elements that are transitively part of the structure, not just the immediately accessible element.

accessible through access functions in the ADT, some of which return objects of the same type as the ADT. For example, in Figure 2.2, the best way to view binary tree rooted at *A* is as the entire shaded structure, even though the root *A* is the only immediately accessible element.

2.3.2 The List ADT

Lists are a fundamental data structure in computer science, with theoretical, as well as practical, significance. Many of the algorithms developed in this text, although presented using arrays, have efficient versions in which lists are the principal, or only, data structure. The programming language *Lisp* was originally built upon lists as the only data structure in the language; Lisp is an acronym for "list processing." Several other programming languages, among them ML and Prolog, incorporate lists as built-in features. The list ADT presented here corresponds to list facilities offered by these languages, and the operation names are adopted from Common Lisp.

In this text the term *list* always refers to what is often called a *linked list* in data-structure contexts. (For general ordered sets with no particular data structure in mind, we use the term *sequence*.) The shorter term *list* is a more suitable name for the ADT because no term "link" appears in the ADT specifications; if "links" are used in the implementation, that fact is concealed from the List clients.

The kind of list needed most often in algorithms, particularly algorithms on graphs, is a list of integers. Therefore, this variety of list is used for illustrative purposes in this section.

Java sidelight: Experienced Java users will be tempted to define IntList, and lists of other specific element types, as subclasses of the very general List. We did not choose this route because it introduces complications when the elements are of a primitive type, and it requires a close understanding of how inheritance decisions are made behind the scenes. These topics are not relevant to the study of algorithms. There are numerous texts on the Java language that delve into these possibilities.

The specifications for the IntList ADT are shown in Figure 2.3. As indicated in the caption, transformations for lists of some other type are straightforward. This remark applies to code, as well as to specification statements. No name confusion results from having cons, first, rest, and nil in several classes because the language requires the expression IntList.cons to access the version in the IntList class, etc.

IntList cons(int newElement, IntList oldList)

Precondition: none.

Postconditions: If x = cons(newElement, oldList), then:

1. x refers to a newly created object;
2. $x \neq$ nil;
3. first(x) = newElement;
4. rest(x) = oldList;

int first(IntList aList)

Precondition: aList $\neq$ nil.

IntList rest(IntList aList)

Precondition: aList $\neq$ nil.

IntList nil

Constant denoting the empty list.

Figure 2.3   Specifications of the IntList ADT. The function cons is the constructor; first and rest are access functions. The List ADT is the same except that all occurrences of **int** become **Object**, and all occurrences of IntList become List. Transformations for other element types are similar.

The procedure header, enclosed in a box, shows the type signature of the function or procedure in Java and C syntax. Each parameter name is preceded by its type. Thus the first parameter of cons is an **int** and the second is an IntList. The type (or class) appearing before the procedure name is its return type.

The rest of the specifications state preconditions and postconditions. It is unnecessary to state that parameters are of the appropriate types in the preconditions, because this is given in the prototype. In keeping with the methodology of Section 2.2.1, the behaviors of the access functions, first and rest, are described under the postcondition of cons.

It is worth taking a moment to reflect about the simplicity of the List ADT. It is rather amazing, when you stop to think about it, that every computable function can be computed using lists as the only data structure. There is one constant for the empty list, and one function (whose standard name is cons, so we adopt that name) for building up a list by putting one new element at the front of a previous list (which might be the empty list). The other functions simply return information about a (nonempty) list. What is its first element? What list represents the rest of the elements? It is clear that all List operations can be implemented in constant time. (We are assuming that memory can be allocated for a new object in constant time, which is a common assumption.)

The specifications for IntList can be implemented in several ways without changing the code in the *clients* of the ADT. Figure 2.4 shows a typical (and minimal) implementation. Notice that this implementation does not test for satisfaction of the preconditions of first

```
import java.lang.*;

public class IntList
    {
    int element;
    IntList next;

    /** The constant nil denotes the empty list. */
    public static final
    IntList  nil = null;

    /** Precondition: L is not nil.
     * Returns: first element of L. */
    public static
    int  first(IntList L)
        { return L.element; }

    /** Precondition: L is not nil.
     * Returns: list of all elements of L, except 1st. */
    public static
    IntList  rest(IntList L)
        { return L.next; }

    /** Precondition: None.
     * Postcondition: Let newL be the return value of cons.
     * Then: newL refers to a new object, newL is not nil,
     * first(newL) = newElement, rest(newL) = oldList. */
    public static
    IntList  cons(int newElement, IntList oldList)
        {
        List  newL = new IntList();

        newL.element = newElement;
        newL.next = oldList;
        return newL;
        }
```

Figure 2.4   A typical implementation of the IntList ADT as a Java class. Each object has private instance fields element and next; the public field nil is a constant due to the keyword **final**; remaining parts of the class are methods. The javadoc utility associates a comment of the form "/** . . . */" with the program element *following* the comment, and formats the documentation for Web browsers.

and rest. It is the caller's responsibility to see that preconditions of any called function are satisfied. We show the IntList implementation completely (Figure 2.4) as a guide for readers who want to get started on Java, and as a model that other ADTs can follow. In general, this book does not give complete code. Readers will have to fill in some details.

For software engineering purposes we may want to create a class named IntListLib. (This class would have no constructor specified.) Methods in this library might well include length, copy, equals, reverse, sum, max, and min.

Java sidelight: From a debugging point of view, it might be helpful to include the Java *error* or *exception* feature, but this complicates writing a complete set of specifications for both the ADT and the clients of the ADT. Throughout the text we adopt the approach that algorithmic code will concentrate on solving the problem. We remind readers that software engineering considerations will often suggest embellishments.

Partial Rebuilding and Nondestructive Operations

Attentive readers may be wondering how we ever *modify* a list under the IntList ADT regimen. The answer is simple: We don't! There are no *manipulation procedures*. This ADT is called *nondestructive* for the reason that once an object is created it cannot be updated. (The term *immutable* is also seen.) There are three choices for tasks that require "updating" a list:

1. In an object-oriented language, such as Java, define a subclass of IntList with the added update capability (making the subclass a *destructive*, or *mutable*, class), or

2. Modify the class IntList itself with the added update capability (making it a *destructive*, or *mutable*, class), or

3. Leave the definition of IntList intact. To accomplish an "update," partially rebuild the original list, yielding a new list, and reassign the list variable to *refer to* the new list instead of the original list.

The idea of partial rebuilding is illustrated conceptually in Figure 2.5. The goal is to insert a new element, 22, between existing elements, 13 and 44, in the list represented by the object w in the top portion of the diagram. (Per the earlier discussion of recursive ADTs, we think of w as the whole list, not just the first element.) The parts of the list containing elements 10 and 13, prior to the point of insertion, are "rebuilt," as shown in the lower portion of the diagram. Of course, a new object is created for the new element 22. But new objects x', to

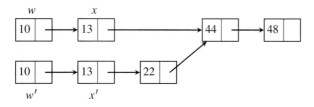

Figure 2.5 Partial rebuilding technique for insertion of 22 into a sorted list of 10, 13, 44, 48

contain a new copy of 13, and w', to contain a new copy of 10, are also created. Objects x and w thus remain intact.

In general, partial rebuilding means that, for any object x that has a field we need to modify, we create a new object x' with identical values for other fields and the new value for the field to be modified. Objects referenced by both x and x' do not need to be modified, which is why the rebuilding is partial. But now, if an object w that also cannot be updated referred to x and we want the "update" to affect w, we need to recursively rebuild by creating w' from w, except that w' refers to x' instead of x. As we see in the next example, it is normally no trouble to locate w because we already used w to locate x, and the function invocation using w is still active. Thus, after the function invocation that creates x' returns, we will be back in a context where w is known.

Example 2.1   Insertion into a sorted list with partial rebuilding

Figure 2.6 shows the Java code to insert an integer into an existing sorted list of integers by the method of partial rebuilding. As with almost all recursive procedures, we begin with a test for a base case: Is oldList empty? Remember, the empty list is sorted! Then we test another base case: Can newElement simply be inserted in front of oldList? In either case, oldList need not be modified, and we insert the new element "in front" of it with cons.

If neither base case applies, a recursive call is made, which returns a rebuilt list (stored in newRest) with the new element in place somewhere within it. Our task now is to include oldFirst "in front of" newRest. Since we can't modify the object oldList, we "rebuild" by calling cons to create a new object (stored in newList). Note that newList and oldList have the same first element in this recursive case, but rest(newList) differs from rest(oldList) by containing newElement somewhere within it.

This procedure is an example of a *generalized searching routine* (see Definition 1.12). We are "searching" for the element in front of which to put the new element, that is, an element with a larger key. The "fail" event is the empty list, because there clearly is no larger element. The "succeed" event is finding the larger element as the first element of the list being examined. If neither event occurs we "keep searching" in the rest of the list. One rebuilding operation occurs for each unsuccessful search step.

The frequent use of local variables assists both in debugging and in proving correctness. Note that local variables may be defined in "inner blocks" and need not be at the beginning of the function. Also note that, throughout these code examples, local variables are assigned a value only once per function invocation; the practice of assigning one value, then overwriting it with another value makes correctness arguments more complicated. This subject is discussed at greater length in Section 3.3.

Consider the example in Figure 2.5 where 22 is inserted into a list containing 10, 13, 44, 48. The initial list is w, with 10 as its first element and x as the rest of its elements. Since $22 > 10$, 22 has to be inserted into x, creating a new list x'. A recursive call to IntList.insert is made. Since $22 > 13$, a second recursive call is made, and this call creates and returns a reference to the new object with 22 as its first element. Objects whose first elements are 44 and 48 did not need rebuilding.

Back in the first recursive call, a new object x' is created whose rest is the list just returned, beginning with the new element 22, and whose first is copied from x. This new

```
/** Precondition: oldList is in ascending order.
 * Returns: a list that is in ascending order
 * consisting of newElement and all elements of oldList.
 */
public static
IntList  insert1(int newElement, IntList oldList)
    {
    IntList  newList;

    if (oldList == IntList.nil)
        // newElement belongs in front of oldList.
        newList = IntList.cons(newElement, oldList);
    else
        {
        int  oldFirst = IntList.first(oldList);

        if (newElement <= oldFirst)
            // newElement belongs in front of oldList.
            newList = IntList.cons(newElement, oldList);
        else
            {
            IntList  oldRest = IntList.rest(oldList);
            IntList  newRest = insert1(newElement, oldRest);

            // Partially rebuild oldList into newList.
            newList = IntList.cons(oldFirst, newRest);
            }
        }
    return newList;
    }
```

Figure 2.6 Function (or Java method) for insertion into a sorted list of integers, using partial rebuilding technique. Note the use of class-name qualifiers on members (methods and fields) of the IntList class. They are needed because insert1 is not in that class.

object x' is returned (that is, a reference to it is returned) to the initial call, which knows w as the initial list. The initial call creates w', whose rest is x' and whose first is copied from w, and returns a reference to w' to conclude the sorted insert operation. Thus objects x' and w' are rebuilt from x and w as we "back out of" the recursion.

Now that the insertion is completed, does the overall program still need w? Clearly, this is a question that the List ADT cannot answer. If the answer is "no," the overall program will (most likely) not contain any reference to w, because any fields or variables that referred to w earlier now refer to w'. If the answer is "yes," there is still an important reference to w somewhere in the program. Programmer decisions about when to deallocate and recycle storage are known to be frequent sources of obscure bugs in practice, but an automatic garbage collector relieves programmers of these decisions.   ■

Java sidelight: Readers familiar with C++ are again reminded that Java does not permit the programmer to define a new meaning for "<=", so this operator must be replaced with a method call before the code can be transformed to operate on nonnumerical classes. Java (beginning with release 1.2) provides an *interface* facility with the name **Comparable** for working with ordered classes in a general way, as sketched in Appendix A.

Several other ADTs can be implemented using a List ADT as a building block. Some examples are general trees (Section 2.3.4) and stacks (Section 2.4.1). Others would require a List ADT with updatable lists, such as in-trees (Section 2.3.5) and queues (Section 2.4.2).

2.3.3 Binary Tree ADT

We can think of binary trees as the simplest nonlinear generalization of lists; instead of having one way to continue to another element, there are two alternatives that lead to two different elements. Binary trees have many applications in algorithms.

Definitions and Basic Properties of Binary Trees

Mathematically, a *binary tree T* is a set of elements, called nodes, that is empty or else satisfies the following:

1. There is a distinguished node r called the *root*.
2. The remaining nodes are divided into two disjoint subsets, L and R, each of which is a binary tree. L is called the *left subtree* of T and R is called the *right subtree* of T.

Binary trees are represented on paper by diagrams such as the one in Figure 2.7. If a node v is the root of binary tree T and a node w is the root of the left (right) subtree of T, then w is called the *left (right) child* of v and v is called the *parent* of w; there is a directed edge from v to w in the diagram. (The direction is downward in the absence of an arrowhead.)

The *degree* of a tree node is the number of nonempty subtrees it has. A node with degree zero is a *leaf*. Nodes with a positive degree are *internal nodes*.

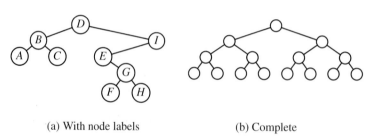

(a) With node labels   (b) Complete

Figure 2.7   Binary trees

BinTree buildTree(**Object** newRoot, BinTree oldLT, BinTree oldRT)

Precondition: none.

Postconditions: If x = buildTree(newRoot, oldLT, oldRT), then:

1. x refers to a newly created object;
2. $x \neq$ nil;
3. root(x) = newRoot;
4. leftSubtree(x) = oldLT;
5. rightSubtree(x) = oldRT;

Object root(BinTree t)

Precondition: t $\neq$ nil.

BinTree leftSubtree(BinTree t)

Precondition: t $\neq$ nil.

BinTree rightSubtree(BinTree t)

Precondition: t $\neq$ nil.

BinTree nil

Constant denoting the empty tree.

Figure 2.8 Specifications of the BinTree ADT. The function buildTree is the constructor; root, leftSubtree, and rightSubtree are access functions. Specializations in which the nodes are in a class more specific than **Object** are defined analogously.

The *depth* of the root is 0 and the depth of any other node is one plus the depth of its parent.[1] A *complete binary tree* is a binary tree in which all internal nodes have degree 2 and all leaves are at the same depth. The binary tree on the right in Figure 2.7 is complete.

The *height* of a binary tree (sometimes called its *depth*) is the maximum of the depths of its leaves. The *height* of any node in a binary tree is the height of the subtree of which it is the root. In Figure 2.7 (a) the depth of I is 1 and the height of I is 3; the depth of D is zero and its height is 4.

The following facts are used often in the text. The proofs are easy and are omitted.

Lemma 2.1   There are at most 2^d nodes at depth d of a binary tree.   □

Lemma 2.2   A binary tree with height h has at most $2^{h+1} - 1$ nodes.   □

Lemma 2.3   A binary tree with n nodes has height at least $\lceil \lg(n + 1) \rceil - 1$.   □

Figure 2.8 gives the specifications for the BinTree ADT. Analogies with the List ADT of Section 2.3.2 are obvious. The root access function is analogous to List.first;

---

[1] Beware: Some authors define *depth* so that the depth of the root is 1.

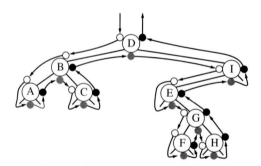

Figure 2.9   Binary tree traversal as a journey around the tree

it accesses the immediately available data. However, in place of List.rest there are two
access functions, leftSubtree and rightSubtree, enabling the client to access only part of
the remainder of the tree.[2]

Binary Tree Traversal

We can visualize a standard traversal of a binary tree as a boat journey around the tree,
starting at the root, as suggested in Figure 2.9. We imagine each node as an island and
each edge as a bridge that is too low for the boat to pass under. (For the image to work
correctly we also imagine a pier jutting out wherever an empty tree occurs.) The boat starts
at the root node and sails along edges, visiting nodes along the way. The first time a node
is visited (white dot) is called its *preorder* time, the second time it is visited (gray dot,
returning from the left child) is called its *inorder* time, and the last time it is visited (black
dot, after returning from the right child) is called its *postorder* time. Tree traversal can be
expressed elegantly as a recursive procedure, with the following skeleton:

```
void  traverse(BinTree T)
    if (T is not empty)
        Preorder-process root(T);
        traverse(leftSubtree(T));
        Inorder-process root(T);
        traverse(rightSubtree(T));
        Postorder-process root(T);
    return;
```

The return type for traverse will vary according to the application, and it may also take
additional parameters. The above procedure shows the common skeleton.

---

[2] These names are not standard, and some other literature uses the names "leftChild" and "rightChild." However,
in the ADT context, it is best to think of the object as the whole subtree, not just its root node. In our terminology
the left and right children are the *roots of* the left and right subtrees, respectively.

For the binary tree in Figure 2.9, the traversal node orderings are the following:

Preorder (white dots):	D	B	A	C	I	E	G	F	H
Inorder (gray dots):	A	B	C	D	E	F	G	H	I
Postorder (black dots):	A	C	B	F	H	G	E	I	D

2.3.4 The Tree ADT

A *general tree* (more precisely, *general out-tree*) is a nonempty structure with nodes and directed edges such that one node, called the *root*, has no incoming edges and all other nodes have exactly one incoming edge. Furthermore, there is a path from the root to all other nodes. There is no restriction on the number of outgoing edges from any node. A *forest* is a collection of separate trees.

Every node in a tree is the root of its own *subtree*, consisting of all the nodes it can reach, including itself. Each edge is said to go from the parent to the child. If node v is parent of node w in a tree, then the tree rooted at w is called a *principal subtree* of the tree rooted at v. Each principal subtree of a tree has fewer nodes than the whole tree. It is not feasible to name each principal subtree individually, so the Tree ADT is somewhat more complex than the BinTree ADT.

For a general tree, the subtrees do not necessarily have an inherent order, whereas they are ordered "left" and "right" for a binary tree. (If the subtrees of a general tree *are* considered to be ordered, the structure is called an "ordered tree.") Another difference from binary trees is that there is no representation for an empty general tree.

If all the edges are oriented toward the root instead of away from the root, then the structure is an *in-tree*, and edges go from child to parent (see Figure 2.10). Different data structures and operations are appropriate for this variety of trees, as discussed in Section 2.3.5.

The Tree ADT (again, a minimal collection of operations) is described by the specifications in Figure 2.11. Similarities to the BinTree ADT are evident. However, instead of two named subtrees, we have an indefinite number of *principal subtrees*, so List is the natural structure for these objects. Unless the tree is considered to be an ordered tree, the order imparted by the list is incidental, and the subtrees are considered as a set, rather than as a sequence.

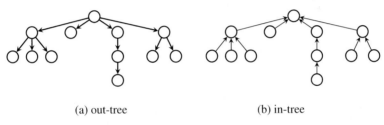

(a) out-tree   (b) in-tree

Figure 2.10 A general out-tree and the corresponding in-tree

Tree buildTree(**Object** newRoot, TreeList oldTrees)

Precondition: none.

Postconditions: If x = buildTree(newRoot, oldTrees), then:

1. x refers to a newly created object;
2. root(x) = newRoot;
3. subtrees(x) = oldTrees;

Object root(Tree t)

Precondition: none.

TreeList subtrees(Tree t)

Precondition: none.

The TreeList ADT is the analog of IntList with class Tree in place of class **int** for the element type. The prototypes follow.

$$\text{TreeList cons(Tree t, TreeList rSiblings)}$$

$$\text{Tree first(TreeList siblings)}$$

$$\text{TreeList rest(TreeList siblings)}$$

$$\text{TreeList nil}$$

Figure 2.11   Specifications of the (general) Tree ADT. Specializations in which the nodes are in a class more specific than **Object** are defined analogously.

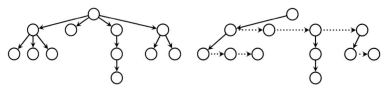

(a) logical structure   (b) list-based structure

Figure 2.12   (a) The logical, or conceptual, structure of a general out-tree and (b) the corresponding representation in which principal subtrees are in a list: Downward, solid arrows go to leftmost subtrees and sideways, dotted arrows go to right sibling subtrees.

The first principal subtree, say t_0, is called the *leftmost subtree*; the root of t_0 is called the *leftmost child*. For any principal subtree, t_i, the next principal subtree in sequence, t_{i+1}, is called the *right sibling subtree* of t_i, if it exists. The root of t_{i+1} is called the *right sibling* of the root of t_i. See Figure 2.12 for an example. In spite of this nomenclature for the data structure, we reiterate that the relative order of subtrees in the list is considered to be

```
void  traverse(Tree T)
    TreeList  remainSubs;
    Preorder-process Tree.root(T);
    remainSubtrees = Tree.subtrees(T);
    while (remainSubtrees ≠ TreeList.nil);
        Tree  subtree = TreeList.first(remainSubtrees);
        traverse(subtree);
        Inorder-process Tree.root(T) and subtree;
        remainSubtrees = TreeList.rest(remainSubtrees);
    Postorder-process Tree.root(T);
    return;
```

Figure 2.13   The general tree traversal skeleton

incidental for the abstract tree. The ADT constructor buildTree combines a root node and a list of trees, creating a larger tree.

Java sidelight: To define these interrelated ADTs in Java with the ideal control of visibility, Java's *package* feature should be used. Two files in the same directory are required, and they must be named Tree.java and TreeList.java. The details are not difficult, but they are beyond the scope of this book. Putting clients and ADTs in the same directory avoids the need to deal with packages.

Tree traversal can be expressed by a logical extension of binary-tree traversal (Section 2.3.3), with the skeleton shown in Figure 2.13. The subtrees are traversed within a **while** loop because their number is indefinite, and there are an indeterminate number of inorder times. (Class name qualifiers are included here, because two classes are involved.) The return type for traverse will vary according to the application, and it may take additional parameters, also. Figure 2.13 shows the common skeleton.

2.3.5 In-Tree ADT

It is a wise father that knows his own child.
  —Shakespeare, *The Merchant of Venice*

Usually, the access pattern in a tree proceeds from the root toward the leaves, commonly depicted in a downward direction. However, there are cases when it is desirable (or sufficient) for the access to be oriented from the leaves toward the root (upward, see Figure 2.10 b), and downward access is unnecessary. An *in-tree* is a tree with *only* this kind of access: A node does not "know" its children.

An important concept for in-trees is that of *ancestor*. This can be defined recursively, as follows.

Definition 2.2

Node v is itself an *ancestor* of v. If p is the parent of v, then every ancestor of p is also an *ancestor* of v. The inverse of ancestor is *descendant*.   ■

In an in-tree, a node can access its ancestors, but not its descendants. Unlike the usual *Tree* ADT, where the object is an entire tree, an object of an in-tree is a node and its ancestors, so the class is named InTreeNode, and the ADT constructor is makeNode.

Let v be an object in the class InTreeNode. What access functions do we need to navigate? The first access function needed is isRoot(v), a Boolean function that returns **true** if v has no parent. The second access function is parent(v), which has as its precondition that isRoot(v) is **false**. In other words, whenever isRoot(v) is **true**, it is an error to call parent(v).

Figure 2.14 contains the specifications for the InTreeNode ADT. When a node is constructed with makeNode, it is the only node of its tree, so isRoot is **true**. Clearly we need to have some way to construct bigger trees. Unlike earlier ADTs, this one uses a *manipulation procedure* to achieve functionality. Recall that manipulation procedures are always type **void**; they return no value. The manipulation procedure is setParent(v, p), which sets the parent of v to be p. It has the precondition that v must not be an ancestor of p (otherwise a cycle would be created). The postconditions are that isRoot(v) is **false**, and parent(v) returns p.

Depending on the application, it is often necessary to maintain some kind of data at the nodes. Since this has no bearing on the structure of the tree, we can define a simple pair of operations, setNodeData and nodeData, to allow the client to store and retrieve such data. Although node data might be a variety of types, depending on the application, we define it as **int**, because that is the type most frequently encountered. For example, even though a node does not know its descendants, it is possible to keep track of how *many* descendants each node has (Exercise 2.12).

In-trees usually occur embedded in some other data structure, rather than as an ADT in their own right. This is almost necessary since there is no node from which the whole tree is accessible. We will encounter in-trees in algorithms for minimum spanning trees, shortest paths in graphs, and in the implementation of the Union-Find ADT. The Union-Find ADT is used in turn in various algorithms, including one for minimum spanning forests.

2.4   Stacks and Queues

Stacks and Queues illustrate the next level of complexity in abstract data type specifications. Their ADTs include manipulation procedures, so objects in these classes can change their "state." The specifications now need to describe what state changes can occur. However, all operations on these versatile ADTs can be implemented in constant time without too much difficulty. Stacks and Queues are good for keeping track of tasks that need to be done in situations where one task might generate an unpredictable number of other tasks.

2.4.1   Stack ADT

A *stack* is a linear structure in which insertions and deletions are always made at one end, called the *top*. This updating policy is called *last in, first out (LIFO)*. The top item in a stack is the one most recently inserted, and only this element can be inspected. To push an item on a stack means to insert the item in the stack. To pop the stack means to delete the

InTreeNode makeNode(**int** d)

Precondition: none.

Postconditions: If x = makeNode(d), then:

1. x refers to a newly created object;
2. nodeData(x) = d;
3. isRoot(x) = **true**;

boolean isRoot(InTreeNode v)

Precondition: none.

InTreeNode parent(InTreeNode v)

Precondition: isRoot(v) = **false**.

int nodeData(InTreeNode v)

Precondition: none.

void setParent(InTreeNode v, InTreeNode p)

Precondition: Node v is not an ancestor of p.

Postconditions:

1. nodeData(v) remains unchanged;
2. parent(v) = p;
3. isRoot(v) = **false**;

void setNodeData(InTreeNode v, **int** d)

Precondition: none.

Postconditions:

1. nodeData(v) = d;
2. parent(v) = remains unchanged;
3. isRoot(v) = remains unchanged;

Figure 2.14 Specifications of the InTreeNode ADT. The function makeNode is the constructor; isRoot, parent, and nodeData are access functions; setParent and setNodeData are manipulation procedures. Specializations in which node data is in a class different from **int** are defined analogously.

top entry. The top element of a nonempty stack can be accessed with top. Modern practice is not to combine the functions of top and pop into one operation. Figure 2.15 gives the Stack ADT specifications.

Unlike the previous ADT specifications, it is not possible to state explicitly what values will be returned by the access functions isEmpty and top after a pop. Therefore, a section called *Explanation* is needed to provide information about *sequences* of pushes and

Stack create()

Precondition: none.

Postconditions: If s = create(), then:

1. s refers to a newly created object;
2. isEmpty(s) = **true**;

boolean isEmpty(Stack s)

Precondition: none.

Object top(Stack s)

Precondition: isEmpty(s) = **false**.

void push(Stack s, **Object** e)

Precondition: none.

Postconditions:

1. top(s) = e;
2. isEmpty(s) = **false**;

void pop(Stack s)

Precondition: isEmpty(s) = **false**.

Postconditions: See Explanation below.

Explanation: Following create, any legal sequence of push and pop operations (i.e., there are never more pops than pushes, cumulatively) yields the same stack state as a certain sequence consisting only of push operations. To obtain this sequence, repeatedly find any pop that is immediately preceded by a push and delete this pair of operations from the sequence. This uses the *Stack Axiom*: A push followed by a pop has no net effect on the stack.

Figure 2.15   Specifications of the Stack ADT. The constructor is create; isEmpty and top are access functions; push and pop are manipulation procedures. Specializations in which the element is in a class more specific than **Object** are defined analogously.

pops. See Exercise 2.13 for an example. The Explanation section indirectly describes the postconditions of pop. The technique of specifying properties, or invariants, of sequences of operations permits the ADT to be specified logically, still without referring to aspects of the implementation that are not accessible to the client. This technique is often needed for more complex ADTs.

Most needs for the stack as an explicit structure are obviated by recursive procedures, because the "run-time" system implements a stack of local variables for each function call. A stack can be implemented in an array or built upon the List ADT. Either way, all operations can be implemented in $\Theta(1)$ time. If the maximum size to which the stack might grow is not known in advance, an array-doubling technique can be used to expand its size (see Section 6.2). This implementation detail can be hidden from the clients of the Stack ADT.

2.4.2 Queue ADT

A *queue* is a linear structure in which all insertions are done at one end, called the *rear* or *back*, and all deletions are done at the other end, called the *front*. Only the front element can be inspected. This updating policy is called *first in, first out* (*FIFO*). The manipulation procedures are *enqueue* to insert and *dequeue* to delete. We have access functions isEmpty and front to test if the queue is empty, and if not, to access its front element. Figure 2.16 gives the Queue ADT specifications.

As with the Stack ADT, it is not possible to state explicitly what values will be returned by the access functions after a dequeue. Therefore, a section called *Explanation* is needed to provide information about *sequences* of enqueues and dequeues. See Exercise 2.13 for an example.

A queue may be implemented efficiently (all operations in $\Theta(1)$) using an array. If the maximum size to which the queue might grow is not known in advance, an array-doubling technique can be used to expand its size (see Section 6.2). This implementation detail can be hidden from the clients of the Queue ADT. Also, you can define an updatable variant of the List ADT, in which the value of rest can be updated to append some list to the back end of an existing list (see Appendix A). Then enqueue appends a list consisting only of the new element to the end of the current queue. For this to be in $\Theta(1)$ it is necessary to keep a reference to the last element in the queue, as well as a reference to the whole queue.

2.5 ADTs for Dynamic Sets

A *dynamic set* is a set whose elements change during the course of the algorithm using the set. Often, the objective of the algorithm is to build up this set itself. But to do so, it needs to access the set as it is being constructed to determine how to continue the construction. The appropriate set of operations for a dynamic set ADT varies widely, depending on the needs of the algorithm or application that is using it. Some standard examples are priority queues, collections of disjoint sets requiring union and find operations, and dictionaries. These are described in this section.

Dynamic sets impose the most rigorous requirements on their data structures. For each of the ADTs in this section it is not possible to implement all the needed operations in constant time. Trade-offs must be made, and different implementations will prove most efficient for different applications. The search for efficiency has led to some very advanced and complex implementations, some of which are touched upon in Chapter 6.

Queue create()

Precondition: none.

Postconditions: If q = create(), then:

1. q refers to a newly created object;
2. isEmpty(q) = **true**;

boolean isEmpty(Queue q)

Precondition: none.

Object front(Queue q)

Precondition: isEmpty(q) = **false**.

void enqueue(Queue q, **Object** e)

Precondition: none.

Postconditions: Let $/q/$ denote the state of q before the operation.

1. If isEmpty($/q/$) = **true**, front(q) = e,
2. If isEmpty($/q/$) = **false**, front(q) = front($/q/$).
3. isEmpty(q) = **false**;

void dequeue(Queue q)

Precondition: isEmpty(q) = **false**.

Postconditions: See Explanation below.

Explanation: Following create, any legal sequence of enqueue and dequeue operations (i.e., there are never more dequeues than enqueues, cumulatively) yields the same queue state as a certain sequence consisting only of enqueue operations. To obtain this sequence repeatedly find the first (earliest) dequeue and the first enqueue and delete this pair of operations from the sequence. The access functions front(q) and isEmpty(q) take on the same values as they would after this equivalent sequence, consisting entirely of enqueue operations.

Figure 2.16 Specifications of the Queue ADT. The constructor is create; isEmpty and front are access functions; enqueue and dequeue are manipulation procedures. Specializations in which the element is in a class more specific than **Object** are defined analogously.

2.5.1 Priority Queue ADT

A *priority queue* is a structure with some aspects of a FIFO queue (Section 2.4.2), but in which element order is related to each element's *priority*, rather than its chronological arrival time. Element priority (also called "key") is a parameter supplied to the insert operation, not some innate property known to the ADT. We will assume it is type **float** for definiteness. We will also assume that elements are of type **int** because this is the type seen in most optimization applications. In practice, elements have an *identifier* that is an **int** and have other associated data fields; this identifier should not be confused with the "key," which is the traditional name for the priority field.

As each element is inserted into a priority queue, *conceptually* it is inserted in order of its priority. The one element that can be inspected and removed is the *most important* element currently in the priority queue. Actually, what occurs behind the scenes is up to the implementation, as long as all outward *appearances* are consistent with this view.

The notion of priority can be either that the most important element has the smallest priority (a cost viewpoint) or that it has the largest priority (a profit viewpoint). In optimization problems, the cost viewpoint prevails, and so the historical names of certain priority-queue operations reflect this viewpoint: getMin, deleteMin, and decreaseKey.

One important application of the priority queue is the sorting method known as *Heapsort* (Section 4.8), named after the *heap* implementation of the priority queue. In the case of *Heapsort*, the *largest* key is considered the most important, so the proper names are getMax and deleteMax in this context.

Unlike FIFO queues, priority queues cannot be implemented in such a way that all operations are in $\Theta(1)$. Trade-offs among competing implementation methods must be considered in conjunction with the needs of a particular algorithm or application to arrive at a choice that provides the best overall efficiency. These issues will be studied in conjunction with the various algorithms that use priority queues. Besides *Heapsort* (Section 4.8), there is a family of algorithms called *greedy algorithms*, which typically use a priority queue, including Prim's and Kruskal's minimum-spanning-tree algorithms (Sections 8.2 and 8.4), Dijkstra's single-source-shortest-path algorithm (Section 8.3), and certain approximation algorithms for *NP*-hard problems (Chapter 13). The *greedy method* is a major paradigm of algorithm design.

Now let us turn to the specifications of the priority queue ADT, which are shown in Figures 2.17 and 2.18. Similarities to the (FIFO) queue ADT are evident. One major departure is that the deletion operation is deleteMin, which, as its name implies, deletes the element with the minimum priority field (minimum "key"), rather than the oldest element.

Another major change is that priority order can be rearranged by means of the decreaseKey operation. But this operation and the getPriority function can be omitted from implementations intended for *Heapsort* and other applications that do not need these capabilities; they add considerable complications to both specification and implementation (as we will see in Section 6.7.1). We call the ADT without decreaseKey and getPriority an *elementary* priority queue.

PriorityQ create()

Precondition: none.

Postconditions: If pq = create(), then, pq refers to a newly created object and isEmpty(pq) = **true**.

boolean isEmpty(PriorityQ pq)

Precondition: none.

int getMin(PriorityQ pq)

Precondition: isEmpty(pq) = **false**.

void insert(PriorityQ pq, **int** id, **float** w)

Precondition: If decreaseKey is implemented (see Figure 2.18), then id must not already be in pq.

Postconditions: The identifier of the element to be inserted is id and the priority is w.

1. isEmpty(pq) = **false**;
2. If getPriority is implemented (see Figure 2.18), then getPriority(pq, id) = w.
3. See Explanation below for value of getMin(pq).

void deleteMin(PriorityQ pq)

Precondition: isEmpty(pq) = **false**.

Postconditions:

1. If the number of deleteMins is less than the number of inserts since create(pq), then isEmpty(pq) = **false**, else it is **true**.
2. See Explanation below for value of getMin(pq).

Explanation: Think of /pq/ (the state of pq before the operation in question) abstractly as a sequence of pairs $((id_1, w_1), (id_2, w_2), \ldots, (id_k, w_k))$, in nondecreasing order of the values of w_i, which represent the priorities of the elements id_i. Then insert(pq, id, w) effectively inserts (id, w) into this sequence in order, extending pq to $k + 1$ elements in all. Also, deleteMin(pq) effectively deletes the first element of the sequence /pq/, leaving pq with $k - 1$ elements. Finally, getMin(pq) returns id_1.

Figure 2.17 Specifications of the *elementary* Priority Queue (PriorityQ) ADT. The constructor is create; isEmpty and getMin are access functions; insert and deleteMin are manipulation procedures. Additional operations for a *full* Priority Queue ADT are specified in Figure 2.18. Specializations in which the element is in a class different from **int** are defined analogously.

float getPriority(PriorityQ pq, **int** id)

Precondition: id is "in" pq.

void decreaseKey(PriorityQ pq, **int** id, **float** w)

Precondition: id is "in" pq and $w <$ getPriority(pq, id). That is, the new priority w is required to be less than the existing priority of the same element.

Postconditions: isEmpty(pq) remains **false**. getPriority(pq, id) = w. See Explanation below for value of getMin(pq).

Explanation: As in the explanation in Figure 2.17, think of /pq/ abstractly as a sequence of pairs $((id_1, w_1), (id_2, w_2), \ldots, (id_k, w_k))$, ordered by the values of w_i. Also, all ids are unique. Then, decreaseKey(pq, id, w) requires that id $= id_i$ for some $1 \le i \le k$, and effectively removes (id_i, w_i) from the sequence /pq/, then inserts (id_i, w) into the sequence in order by w. The final sequence still has k elements. As before, getMin(pq) returns id_1.

Figure 2.18 Specifications for additional operations that are defined only for a *full* Priority Queue (PriorityQ) ADT. See Figure 2.17 for the other operations. Here, getPriority is an access function, and decreaseKey is a manipulation procedure.

2.5.2   Union-Find ADT for Disjoint Sets

The *Union-Find* ADT is named after its two main operations, but is sometimes called the *Disjoint Sets* ADT. Initially, all elements of interest are placed in separate singleton sets with the constructor operation create or they are added individually with the manipulation procedure makeSet. The find access function returns the current *set id* of an element. Through a union operation, two sets can be combined, after which they no longer exist as separate entities. Therefore, no element can ever be in more than one set. Often, in practice, elements are integers, and the set id is some particular element in the set, called the *leader*. However, in theory, elements can be any type and set ids need not be the same type as elements.

There is no way to "traverse" through all the elements of one set. Notice the similarity to in-trees (Section 2.3.5), in which there is no way to traverse an entire in-tree. In fact, in-trees can be used effectively to implement the Union-Find ADT. Implementations of the Union-Find ADT are described in detail in Section 6.6. The specifications of UnionFind are stated in Figure 2.19.

2.5.3   Dictionary ADT

A dictionary is a general associative storage structure. That is, items have an identifier of some kind and have certain information that needs to be stored and retrieved. The information is *associated with* the identifier. The name "Dictionary" for this ADT comes from the analogy with an ordinary dictionary, in which words are their own identifiers, and definitions, pronunciations, and so forth, are the associated information. However, the analogy should not be stretched too far, because there is no order implied for identifiers in

UnionFind create(**int** n)

Precondition: none.

Postconditions: If sets = create(n), then sets refers to a newly created object; find(sets, e) = e for $1 \leq e \leq n$, and is undefined for other values of e.

int find(UnionFind sets, int e)

Precondition: Set {e} has been created in the past, either by makeSet(sets, e) or create.

void makeSet(UnionFind sets, **int** e)

Precondition: find(sets, e) is undefined.

Postconditions: find(sets, e) = e; that is, e is the set id of a singleton set containing e.

void union(UnionFind sets, **int** s, **int** t)

Preconditions: find(sets, s) = s and find(sets, t) = t, that is, both s and t are set ids, or "leaders." Also, $s \neq t$.

Postconditions: Let /sets/ refer to the state of sets before the operation. Then for all x such that find(/sets/, x) = s, or find(/sets/, x) = t, we now have find(sets, x) = u. The value of u will be either s or t. All other find calls return the same value as before the union operation.

Figure 2.19   Specifications of the UnionFind ADT. The constructor is create; find is an access function; makeSet and union are manipulation procedures.

a Dictionary ADT. The important aspect of a dictionary is that any stored information can be retrieved at any time.

The Dictionary specifications are given in Figure 2.20. These specifications are "preliminary" until the type (or class) DictId is specified. This is the type or class of the *identifier* for dictionary entries. Usually it will be either the built-in class **String**, or the primitive type **int**, or an organizer class grouping several of these types. One of the advantages of designing with the Dictionary ADT is that this decision can be postponed until the algorithm that uses this Dictionary has been designed. We can create an empty dictionary, then store pairs (id, info) in it. We can query whether any id is a member of the Dictionary, and if it is, we can retrieve the associated information. For applications in this book, no deletion is needed, but for other applications, a delete operation might be appropriate.

The Dictionary ADT is very useful in the design of dynamic programming algorithms (Chapter 10). Dictionaries are also handy for recording external names (usually strings read from input) so that a program can determine when it has seen a name before and when it is seeing a name for the first time. For example, compilers need to keep track of what data names and procedure names have occurred.

`Dict create()`

Precondition: none.

Postconditions: If d = create(), then:

1. d refers to a newly created object;
2. member(d, id) = **false** for all id.

`boolean member(Dict d, DictId id)`

Precondition: none.

`Object retrieve(Dict d, DictId id)`

Precondition: member(d) = **true**.

`void store(Dict d, DictId id, Object info)`

Precondition: none.

Postconditions:

1. retrieve(d, id) = info;
2. member(d, id) = **true**;

Figure 2.20 Specifications of the Dict ADT, which are preliminary until DictId is changed into an existing type or class. The constructor is create; member and retrieve are access functions; store is a manipulation procedure. Specializations in which informational data is in a class more specific than **Object** are defined analogously.

Exercises

Section 2.2   ADT Specification and Design Techniques

2.1 Consider some ADT operations with the type signatures shown below. The name of the ADT class is Gorp. Based on Definition 2.1, what are the possible categories for each operation? Explain your answers briefly.

a. **void** warp(Gorp g).
b. Gorp harp().
c. **int** pork(Gorp g).
d. **void** work(Gorp g, **int** i).
e. **int** perk(Gorp g1, Gorp g2).
f. Gorp park(Gorp g1, Gorp g2, Gorp g3, **int** i).

2.2 You need to write some code that uses an abstract data type Gorp that has been in use for a while by other people, but which you have not seen before. In addition to the documentation available, you can look at Gorp.java, the source file for the ADT and

GorpTester.java, a program that uses the ADT. Which file is preferable as a source of additional information on how best to use the operations of the Gorp ADT, and why?

Section 2.3   Elementary ADTs—Lists and Trees

2.3   Use the IntList ADT operations (see the specifications in Figure 2.3) to implement the following list utilities, as a *client* of the ADT. That is, your procedures are outside the IntList class, so they do not know how the lists are implemented. This exercise is a good warm-up for the kinds of list manipulation that are needed by algorithms in later chapters.

For tasks that involve traversing a list, try to develop a common skeleton with variations for the different tasks, rather than having a different approach to each task. Clear pseudocode is acceptable, and even preferred, rather than strict syntax; however, it should be clear how the ADT operations are used, and what value, if any, your procedure returns.

If your procedure doesn't work on all lists of integers, be sure to state the appropriate preconditions that it requires to work correctly. (Don't worry about overflowing the size of the **int** type.) Don't forget about empty lists.

a.   Count the number of elements in a list (list length).

b.   Sum the elements in a list.

c.   Multiply the elements in a list.

d.   Return the maximum element in a list.

e.   Return the minimum element in a list.

f.   Return a new list consisting of the elements of the original list in reverse order.

g.   Build (and return) a list of integers read from "input." So that you do not need to worry about what "input" means, exactly, assume there are methods named moreData and readInt available, and that the input has nothing except integers in it. The function moreData is **boolean** and returns **true** if and only if there is another integer to read. The function readInt returns an integer that it has read from "input," and has the precondition that moreData returns **true**. After readInt returns an integer, that integer is no longer in the "input."

h.   Distribute the integers in a list according to their sizes, creating an array of lists, named bucket. The array bucket has 10 entries. List elements in the range 0 through 99 should go into the list bucket[0], elements in the range 100 through 199 should go into the list bucket[1], and so on, and all elements that are 900 or over should go into the list bucket[9]. Assume your procedure takes two parameters, the list of elements to distribute and the array bucket (so your procedure does not need to create the array, but needs to initialize it and fill it).

2.4   Prove Lemma 2.1.

2.5   Prove Lemma 2.2.

2.6   Prove Lemma 2.3.

2.7 Give a sequence of BinTree ADT operations to build each of the binary trees shown. Declare a separate variable for each node, to be the subtree rooted at that node, and let the value of the root (as returned by the access function root) be the node's name, as a **String**. For example, the variable named q stores the subtree rooted at q in the diagram, and root(q) == "q" after q is constructed.

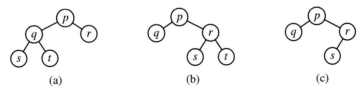

(a)   (b)   (c)

2.8 Implement the List ADT (with elements of type **Object**) by using the operations of the BinTree ADT (see Figures 2.3 and 2.8). That is, treat the List class as a client of the BinTree class. (Pseudocode is okay; exact Java would require Appendix A.6.)

★ **2.9** Implement the BinTree ADT by using the operations of the List ADT (with elements of type **Object**) (see Figures 2.3 and 2.8). That is, treat the BinTree class as a client of the List class. (Pseudocode is okay; exact Java would require Appendix A.6.)

2.10 Give a sequence of Tree and/or TreeList ADT operations to build the general (out-) tree shown below. Declare a separate variable for each node, to be the subtree rooted at that node, and let the value of the root be the node's name, as a **String**. For example, the variable named s stores the subtree rooted at s in the diagram, and that subtree has "s" as the value of its root.

2.11 Give a sequence of InTreeNode ADT operations to build the in-tree shown below. Assume the nodes are in an array named inNode and that each node's nodeData is its own index in that array. A node's index is the number that appears in the diagram. For example, inNode[3] stores the root node.

2.12 Write library procedures makeSizedNode and setSizedParent to keep track of how many nodes are in each subtree of an in-tree as well as performing the operations of makeNode and setParent. By interfacing with the InTreeNode ADT operations of Figure 2.14, they should cause nodeData(v) to return the number of nodes in the subtree rooted at v. The function makeSizedNode should take no parameters and should return an InTreeNode. (What value should nodeData return for the node returned by make-SizedNode?) The procedure setSizedParent has the same type signature as setParent. *Hint*: Think carefully about which tree sizes change and by how much as a result of a setParent operation. There are several cases to consider.

Section 2.4   Stacks and Queues

2.13   Consider the sequence of operations: add(1), add(2), del, add(3), add(4), add(5), add(6), del, del, add(7), del, del.

a.   Interpreting add and del as Stack operations, push and pop, give an equivalent sequence with no del operations. What would be returned by top after the sequence?

b.   Do the same, interpreting add and del as Queue operations, enqueue and dequeue. What would be returned by front after the sequence?

2.14   Outline an implementation of the Stack ADT, as specified in Figure 2.15, using the List ADT, as specified in Figure 2.3. That is, treat the Stack class as a client of the List class. Assuming each List operation runs in $O(1)$ (constant time), how long does each Stack operation take, for your implementation?

2.15   Consider a variant of the Stack ADT in which the constructor has an integer parameter n with the intended meaning that the stack will never contain more than n elements. That is, the signature is Stack create(**int** n). However, due to combinations of push and pop, there might be many more than n push operations over the life of the stack.

a.   How should the specifications be modified to take into account this new parameter? Avoid major changes. *Hint*: Consider preconditions.

b.   Outline an implementation based on storing the stack elements in an array, which is constructed by create. (Each operation can be performed in constant time with a good implementation.)

c.   Now consider the even stronger restriction that a total of at most n push operations will be done over the life of the stack. Can you simplify your implementation? Explain.

2.16   Consider a variant of the Queue ADT in which the constructor has an integer parameter n with the intended meaning that the queue will never contain more than n elements. That is, the signature is Queue create(**int** n). However, due to combinations of enqueue and dequeue, there might be many more than n enqueue operations over the life of the queue.

a.   How should the specifications be modified to take into account this new parameter? Avoid major changes. *Hint*: Consider preconditions.

b.   Outline an implementation based on storing the queue elements in an array, which is constructed by create. Be sure to consider where enqueue places new elements, especially when there are more than n enqueue operations. How do front and de-queue work? How do you detect an empty queue? Can you distinguish an empty queue from a queue containing n elements? (Each operation can be performed in constant time with a good implementation.)

c. Now consider the even stronger restriction that a total of at most n enqueue operations will be done over the life of the queue. (Later we will encounter algorithms for which this is a practical restriction.) Can you simplify your implementation? Explain.

Section 2.5 ADTs for Dynamic Sets

2.17 For each part of this exercise, outline a straightforward implementation of the elementary Priority Queue ADT, as specified in Figure 2.17, using the List ADT, as specified in Figure 2.3. That is, treat the PriorityQ class as a client of the List class. Your class may include some other instance fields, but the List should be the main data structure for storing elements of the priority queue. Describe the main ideas; it is not necessary to write the code.

a. Arrange for the insert operation to run in $O(1)$ (constant time). How long do the other operations run, in the worst case, when the priority queue contains n elements?

b. Arrange for the deleteMin operation to run in $O(1)$. How long do the other operations run, in the worst case, when the priority queue contains n elements?

c. Suppose you are able to use an array instead of a linked list to store the elements. (Don't worry about it overflowing—assume it can be made long enough, somehow.) *Using the same general ideas* as you used in parts (a) and (b), will any of the operations have a better asymptotic order for their running times? Explain. (In later chapters we will see some sophisticated implementations of priority queues, and they will need arrays.)

Additional Problems

⋆ **2.18** You are given a set of in-tree nodes, stored in an array named inNode in positions $1, \ldots, n$. The value of nodeData for each node is the node's index in the inNode array. In other words, for $1 \le v \le n$, nodeData(inNode[v]) = v. You may assume that the nodes actually form one in-tree; that is, isRoot is true for exactly one node, every other node's parent is in the same array, and there are no cycles involving sequences of parents.

Design an algorithm to build the corresponding out-tree, using the InTreeNode and Tree ADTs as a client; your algorithm does not know how these ADTs are implemented. Ideally, your algorithm will run in linear time, $\Theta(n)$. You may want to use a few work arrays, and a Stack object can also be useful.

Hint: Because the Tree ADT has no manipulation procedures, the out-tree must be built from the leaves to the root. The following outline uses a general technique called *source pruning* and similar names.

Initialize an array of counters, called remaining to record how many children each node has that still need to have their Tree objects created. Initialize another array of type TreeList, called subtrees, to empty lists. If a node's remaining counter is 0, it becomes a *source*, and its Tree object can be created. A stack is a good way to keep track of sources. When a Tree object is created for node v (v being the index in the inNode, an integer), it can be inserted into the subtrees list of the parent of v, and that parent's remaining counter can be reduced by 1.

Notes and References

The foundations for the style of abstract data type specification and design presented in this chapter were laid by Parnas (1972). Parnas was one of the earlier researchers to stress the need for data encapsulation, which strongly influenced the development of Object-Oriented Programming (OOP).

There are numerous texts on data structures that may be used for review and reference, for example, Roberts (1995), Kruse, Tondo, and Leung (1997), and Weiss (1998).

3

Recursion and Induction

3.1   Introduction

Professor John McCarthy of Massachusetts Institute of Technology, and later Stanford University, is credited with being the first to realize the importance of recursion in programming languages. He strongly advocated its inclusion in the design of *Algol60* (a precursor of Pascal, PL/I, and C) and he developed the language *Lisp*, which introduced recursive data structures, along with recursive procedures and functions. Lists in this text are modeled after Lisp. The value of recursion became appreciated during the period of intense algorithm development in the 1970s, and today nearly all popular programming languages support recursion.

Recursion and induction are very closely related. The presentation of induction in this chapter is formulated to make the relationship clear. In a quite literal sense, a proof by induction can be considered a recursive proof. Proving properties of recursive procedures by induction is greatly simplified by their similarity of structure. (In this chapter, as in the previous, we include "function" in the general meaning of "procedure"; the Java terminology is "method.")

Recursion trees are introduced in Section 3.7 to provide a general framework for analyzing the time requirements of recursive procedures. Several commonly occurring patterns of recursion are solved, and the results are summarized in theorems.

3.2   Recursive Procedures

A clear understanding of how recursion actually works in the computer is very helpful for thinking recursively, for executing recursive code by hand, and for analyzing the running time of recursive procedures. We begin with a brief review of how procedure calls are implemented with *activation frames*, and how this supports recursion. However, for most activities involving design and analysis of recursive procedures we want to think at a higher level than activation frames. To help readers in this respect, we introduce Method 99, which is really a mental trick, for designing recursive solutions.

3.2.1   Activation Frames and Recursive Procedure Calls

This section gives a brief and somewhat abstract description of how procedure calls are implemented in such a way that recursion works. For a more thorough description, refer to the sources in Notes and References at the end of the chapter.

The basic unit of storage for an individual procedure invocation at run time is called an *activation frame*. This frame provides storage space for the procedure's local variables, actual parameters, and compiler "temporary variables," including the return value, if the procedure returns a value. It also provides storage space for other bookkeeping needs, such as the return address, which tells what instruction the program should execute after this procedure exits. Thus it provides a "frame of reference" in which the procedure executes *for this invocation only*.

The compiler generates code to allocate space in a region of storage called the *frame stack* (often abbreviated to "stack") as part of the code that implements a procedure call.

This space is referenced by a special register called the *frame pointer*, so that as this procedure invocation executes, it knows where its local variables, input parameters, and return value are stored. Each procedure invocation that is active has a unique activation frame. A procedure invocation is active from the time it is entered until it exits. If recursion occurs, all invocations of the recursive procedure that are active simultaneously have distinct frames. As a procedure invocation (recursive or not) exits, its activation frame is automatically deallocated so that the space can be used by some future function invocation. A hand execution of code that depicts the states of activation frames is called an *activation trace*.

Example 3.1   Activation frames for Fibonacci function

Figure 3.1 shows several points during an activation trace for the Fibonacci function, where main executes x = fib(3). The pseudocode for fib is

```
int  fib(int n)
     int  f, f1, f2;
1.  if (n < 2)
2.      f = n;
3.  else
4.      f1 = fib(n − 1);
5.      f2 = fib(n − 2);
6.      f = f1 + f2;
7.  return f;
```

This code declares several local variables that would usually be compiler-generated temporaries, so we can see the activation frame in more detail. In fact, the fib function, like many recursively defined functions, can be written in one "monster" statement, as follows:

```
return n < 2 ? n : fib(n−1) + fib(n−2);
```

but this form is hardly amenable to activation tracing.

The top row, left column, in Figure 3.1 shows the frame stack just before fib(3) is called, and the next row shows it immediately after fib has been entered. The line indicated under each frame shows the line about to be executed, or in the middle of execution if that frame is not on top of the frame stack. Program execution is always "in" the top activation frame, so the lines shown in other frames indicate where execution was when a procedure call shifted execution to a new stack frame. The value of each local variable is shown following the colon. Variables with no values have not been initialized yet.

Subsequent rows show execution proceeding to line 4, when another function invocation occurs. (That it is a recursive call does not matter.) To save space, the next row omits the progression from lines 1 to 4 and just shows line 4 after the next function invocation. This invocation proceeds to lines 2, then 7, because a base case has occurred; f has received its value and this invocation is about to return. The last line in the column shows the situation after the previous invocation has returned the value 1; the return value has been stored as f1, and line 5 is about to be executed.

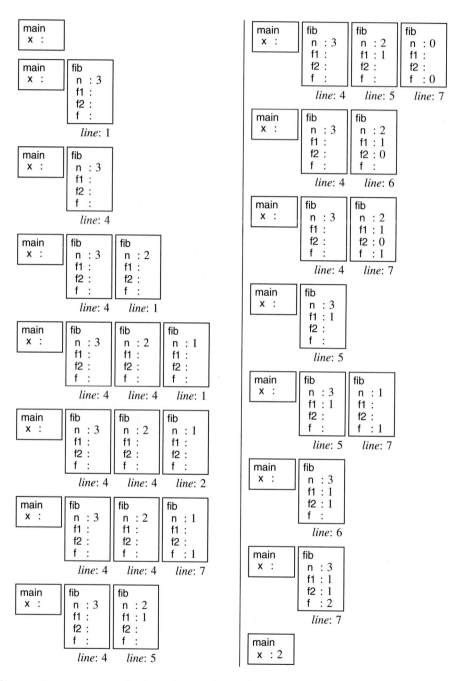

Figure 3.1   An activation trace for the fib function: The top of the stack is at the right. The sequence of snapshots runs down the left column, then down the right column.

The top of the right column shows the situation after the invocation of fib(0) has reached line 7; it is about to return. The space for the activation frame released upon the completion of the invocation of fib(1) is now reused. The subsequent three rows show the completion of the call fib(2). Its return value is stored in the copy of f1 in the activation frame for fib(3). This activation frame progresses to line 5. The next function call expands the stack again. Then the stack contracts as earlier invocations complete their processing and return. ∎

Let us say that a *simple statement* in a procedure is any statement that does not make a procedure call. As the fib code above illustrated, it is possible to write out the procedure as a sequence of lines with at most one procedure call or simple statement per line. It is reasonable to assume that each simple statement takes constant time and that the bookkeeping surrounding a procedure call (setting up the next activation frame, etc.) is also constant. Therefore it follows that:

Lemma 3.1   In a computation without **while** or **for** loops, but possibly with recursive procedure calls, the time that any particular activation frame is on the top of the frame stack is $O(L)$, where L is the number of lines in the procedure that contain either a simple statement or a procedure call.   □

But the size L of any procedure is itself constant; that is, it does not change with different inputs. In any fixed algorithm there is some maximum L over all procedures in that algorithm. The total time taken by any particular run of the algorithm is certainly the sum of the times that various activation frames are on the top of the frame stack. It is also reasonable to assume that any activation frame that is put on the stack is there for at least some minimum time, due to bookkeeping, even if it returns "instantly." This gives us a powerful tool for analyzing the running time of a recursive computation.

Theorem 3.2   In a computation without **while** or **for** loops, but possibly with recursive procedure calls, the total computation time is $\Theta(C)$, where C is the total number of procedure calls (including function calls as procedure calls) that occur during the computation.   □

To take this idea one step further, we can define an *activation tree* to make a permanent record of all procedure invocations that occurred during one run of an algorithm. Each node corresponds to a different procedure invocation, just at the point when it is about to return. The root is the top-level call to that algorithm. The parent of each other node is just the node whose activation frame was on top of the frame stack at the time this one was created. The children of each node appear left to right in the order in which their activation frames were created. See Figure 3.2 for an example.

A preorder traversal of the activation tree visits each activation frame in order of its creation, and the number of nodes in the tree is proportional to the total execution time. Any snapshot of the frame stack during execution corresponds to some path in this tree, starting at the root. (We return to this correspondence in connection with depth-first search

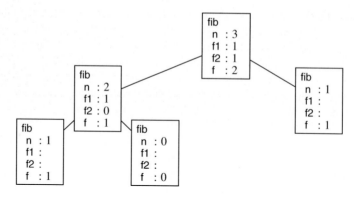

Figure 3.2 Activation tree for fib(3)

in Section 7.4.1.) In Section 3.7.3 we examine a relationship between activation trees and analysis of recurrence equations. It is very helpful for analyzing recursive algorithms.

3.2.2 Hints for Recursion—Method 99

For advanced algorithm development, recursion is an essential design technique. An in-depth discussion of recursive design is beyond the scope of this book, but here are a few hints. See Notes and References at the end of the chapter for further reading.

Identify to yourself some "unit of measure" for the size of the problem your function or procedure will work on. Then pretend that your task is to write a procedure, say p, that will work on problems of *all sizes 0 through 100*. This means that, while designing the solution, you may *assume* the problem has a size at most 100—that is your "fantasy precondition."

Also, pretend that you are allowed to call a *given subroutine*, named p99, that does exactly what your procedure is supposed to do, and has the same type signature, except that *its* "fantasy precondition" is that its problem has a size of 0 through 99. You are allowed to use this subroutine (provided you call it with parameters that meet its preconditions) and you don't have to write its code.

A second hint is to identify clearly the nonrecursive case of your problem. Make it as small as possible. Your procedure will nearly always begin by testing for this nonrecursive case, also called the *base case*.

A final stipulation is that it is "too expensive" to determine whether the input problem for p has a size of exactly 100. (We could have made the fantasy size limit 1,000,000,000, but "method 999,999,999" is too hard to say.) However, it is feasible to determine if its size is 0, or any small constant.

Now *Method 99* is to figure out a way to write p by calling p99 when needed. (You don't need to write p99, so don't even think about it.) Of course, if p detects an easy case, then it does not *need* to call p99. The key idea is that, when p detects a case that is not solvable immediately, then it needs to create a subproblem for p99 to solve, which satisfies three conditions:

1. The subproblem size is less than p's problem size.
2. The subproblem size is not below the minimum (0, for this discussion).
3. The subproblem satisfies all other preconditions of p99 (which are the same as the preconditions of p).

The subproblem is guaranteed (in our fantasy) to satisfy the size restrictions of p99 (Why?).

If you can break the solution up in this way, you are almost finished. Just write the code for p, calling p99 when necessary.

Let us practice with the task of writing delete(L, x), which is supposed to delete element x from an IntList L, returning a new IntList that contains all elements of L except the first occurrence of x. Possibly x does not occur in L. The size of the problem is the number of elements in list L. (Section 2.3.2 described the IntList ADT, in which cons is the constructor, first and rest are the access functions, and the constant nil denotes the empty list.)

To apply Method 99, we pretend we only need to worry about lists up to (and including) 100 elements, and that we are given delete99 to use. Clearly, if we can eliminate one element (say, the first) from L, then we can let delete99 take over with rest(L). We don't know how many elements rest(L) has, but we take a hard-nosed attitude: If there are at most 100 elements in L, then the call to delete99 is okay, and if there are more, it doesn't matter what happens because (in our fantasy) we were only supposed to make delete work for lists of 100 elements or less.

Following the second hint, we need to test for the base case. What is the base case? Since it is permitted that x is not in the list, an empty list is possible. Besides the empty list, there is another case we can recognize and solve instantly, without needing delete99: if x is the first element of L. In this case, we accomplish the objective of delete by simply returning rest(L).

So now we have arrived at the following Method 99 procedure to implement delete.

```
IntList  delete(IntList L, int x)
    IntList newL, fixedL;
    if (L == nil)
        newL = L;
    else if (x == first(L))
        newL = rest(L);
    else
        fixedL = delete99(rest(L), x);
        newL = cons(first(L), fixedL);
    return newL;
```

Oh, yes. To finish the job, just remove the "99" from the name of the called subroutine, turning it into a recursive call of your own procedure.

The delete procedure again fits the pattern of *generalized searching routines* (see Definition 1.12): If there is no more data, fail; if this datum is what we are searching for, succeed (by deleting it, in this case); otherwise continue the search in the remaining data.

3.2.3   Wrappers for Recursive Procedures

Frequently a task has parts that should be done only once at the beginning or the end. In such cases, you need a nonrecursive procedure that sets things up and then calls the recursive procedure, and possibly finishes up after that procedure returns. ("Procedure" includes functions.) We call such a nonrecursive procedure a *wrapper* for the recursive procedure. Sometimes it is as simple as initializing an extra argument for the recursive procedure. For example, Binary Search (Algorithm 1.4) needs a wrapper to make the first call with the entire array as the range. The wrapper can simply be

```
int orderedSearch(int[] E, int n, int K)
    return binarySearch(E, 0, n-1, K);
```

3.3   What Is a Proof?

Before launching into induction proofs, let's take a moment to review what a proof is. As mentioned in Section 1.3.3, logic is a system for formalizing natural language statements so that we can reason more accurately. Proofs are the *result* of reasoning with logical statements. This section describes detailed proofs. In practice, people often omit many details, leaving them for the reader to fill in; such writings are more accurately called *proof sketches*.

Theorems, lemmas, and corollaries are all statements that can be proved, and the differences are not sharply defined. In general, a lemma is a statement that is not very interesting by itself, but is important because it helps to prove something that *is* interesting, which is usually called a theorem. A corollary is usually an easy consequence of a theorem, but not necessarily less important. It does not matter whether the statement to be proved is called a "proposition," "theorem," "lemma," "corollary," or other term, the proof process is the same. We will use "proposition" as the generic term.

A proof is a sequence of *statements* that form a logical argument. Each statement is a *complete sentence* in the normal grammatical sense: It has a subject, a verb, and so on. Although mathematical notation provides a shorthand, the statement should still correspond to a complete sentence. For example, "$x = y + 1$" corresponds to "x equals $y + 1$," which is a full sentence, whereas "$y + 1$" by itself is not a sentence.

While the precise *inference rules* for combining logical statements into a proof can be listed exhaustively, we will take a more informal approach. The most important rules are given in Section 1.3.3, Equations 1.29 through 1.31. Each statement should draw a new conclusion from facts that are

- well known, and not what you are trying to prove (e.g., mathematical identities), or
- assumptions (premises) of the theorem you are proving, or
- statements established earlier in the proof (intermediate conclusions), or
- instances of the *inductive hypothesis*, discussed in Section 3.4.1.

The last statement of a proof must be the conclusion of the proposition being proven. When a proof branches into cases, each case should follow the above structure.

Each sentence should state not only the new conclusion, but how it is supported—what facts it depends on. The statements that immediately support the new conclusion are called its *justifications*. Vague justifications are the cause of most logical errors.

Format of the Theorem or Proposition

The proposition you need to prove has two parts, the *assumptions* (also called *premises* or *hypotheses*) and the *conclusion*. Let us call the conclusion the *goal statement*. Usually the proposition has a phrase of the form "for all x in set W," and the goal statement is something about x. (There may be several variables like x in the statements.) In practice, the set W (for "world") is some familiar set, such as the natural numbers, the reals, or a family of data structures, such as lists, trees, or graphs. Let us abstractly represent the proposition to be proven as

$$\forall x \in W \ \left[A(x) \Rightarrow C(x)\right]. \tag{3.1}$$

Here $A(x)$ represents the assumptions and $C(x)$ represents the conclusion, or goal statement. The symbol "$\Rightarrow$" is read as "implies." The square brackets are just for readability; they group like parentheses. In natural language the proposition statement is often in the form "for all x in W, if $A(x)$, then $C(x)$." Many variations of wording are possible. Frequently, we need to "massage" the most natural statement into a sort of standard form like the above examples before we are sure what we are trying to prove, and which parts correspond to x, W, $A(x)$, and $C(x)$.

Example 3.2

A proposition might be stated as:

Proposition 3.3 For constants $\alpha < \beta$, $2^{\alpha n} \in o(2^{\beta n})$.   □

Reworded into the general format of Equation (3.1), it becomes

Proposition 3.4 For all $\alpha \in \mathbf{R}$, for all $\beta \in \mathbf{R}$, if α and β are constants and $\alpha < \beta$, then $2^{\alpha n} \in o(2^{\beta n})$.   □

Let's check the correspondences. We see that the pair (α, β) plays the role of x and $\mathbf{R} \times \mathbf{R}$ is in the role of W. The hypotheses of the theorem, $A(\alpha, \beta)$, are the three statements: "α is constant," "β is constant," and "$\alpha < \beta$." The conclusion, $C(\alpha, \beta)$, is "$2^{\alpha n} \in o(2^{\beta n})$."

Two-Column Proof Format

We now describe a two-column format for proof presentation. The purpose of this format is to clarify the role of justifications in the proof; the right column contains all justifications. Each proof statement occupies a numbered proof line. Each *new conclusion* in the left column is paired with its justifications in the right column. Reference to earlier statements in the proof is accomplished by giving their line numbers.

Example 3.3

The statement from Example 3.2 is proved in the two-column format. Both the theorem and the proof are written very verbosely, as an illustration of how justifications fit into the proof. We include all the parts that authors usually expect readers to fill in for themselves. Additional remarks follow the proof.

Theorem 3.5 For all $\alpha \in \mathbf{R}$, for all $\beta \in \mathbf{R}$, if α and β are constants, with $\alpha < \beta$, then $2^{\alpha n} \in o(2^{\beta n})$.

Proof

	Statement	Justification
1.	First we want to show that $\lim\limits_{n \to \infty} \dfrac{2^{\beta n}}{2^{\alpha n}} = \infty$.	
2.	$\dfrac{2^{\beta n}}{2^{\alpha n}} = 2^{(\beta - \alpha)n}$.	Math identity.
3.	$\beta - \alpha > 0$ and is constant.	Theorem hypotheses + math identity.
4.	$\lim\limits_{n \to \infty} 2^{(\beta - \alpha)n} = \infty$.	(3) + known math property.
5.	$\lim\limits_{n \to \infty} \dfrac{2^{\beta n}}{2^{\alpha n}} = \infty$.	(2) + (4) and substitution.
6.	$2^{\alpha n} \in o(2^{\beta n})$.	(5) + definition of o sets (Definition 1.17). $\square$

Some additional remarks:

1. Besides the statements that comprise the substance of the proof, it is common to include some "road map" or "plan" statements saying what a section of the proof is intended to show, or what general methodology will be employed, or what remains to be proven to complete a section of the proof, and so on.

    Line 1 is clearly phrased as a *plan* statement, not as a conclusion. Hence it cannot be referenced later, and it requires no justification. It tells the reader the intermediate goal of the succeeding proof lines. That goal is completed on line 5.

2. The new conclusion on the last line is exactly the goal statement of the theorem.

3. All other lines *are* referenced as justifications; there is nothing wasted. ∎

To become familiar with and fluent in proofs, it is a good idea to write some out in detail, following the two-column format. It is often instructive to complete the details of proof sketches, to be sure you understand how each new statement is concluded.

3.4 Induction Proofs

Induction proofs are a mechanism, often the *only* mechanism, for proving a statement about an infinite set of objects. The method of induction that we describe here is often called *strong* induction. Strong induction is the easiest form to use for most proofs about algorithms and data structures. Even when its full power is not needed, it is no harder to use than its weaker variants. Therefore we adopt a "one-size-fits-all" approach, and use this method exclusively.

We will see later that recursion and induction (the strong variety) fit hand-in-glove. By and large, proofs are difficult, and we need all the help we can get to make them comprehensible and reliably accurate. The similarity of structure between induction proofs and recursive procedures is a significant aid for reasoning about sophisticated algorithms.

In many cases induction is done over the set of natural numbers (nonnegative integers, Section 1.5.1) or the set of positive integers. However, the induction method is valid over more general sets, provided that they have two properties:

1. The set is partially ordered; that is, an order relationship is defined between some pairs of elements, but perhaps not between all pairs.
2. There is no infinite chain of decreasing elements in the set.

For example, induction cannot be used on the set of *all* integers (with the usual order).

Trees provide an example of a partially ordered set that is often used for induction. The usual partial order is defined as: $t_1 < t_2$ if t_1 is a *proper subtree* of t_2 (see Figure 3.3). Later we will see that graphs can be similarly partially ordered. Induction over such sets is often called *structural induction*.

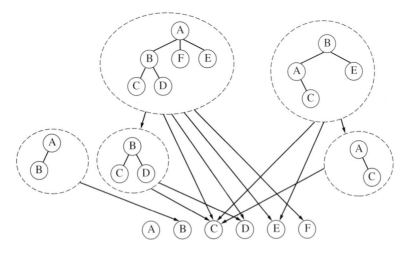

Figure 3.3 The *subtree* partial order among the set of trees shown

Typical theorems that need induction proofs are theorems about a mathematical formula, theorems about a property of a procedure, theorems about a property of data structures, and theorems about recurrence equations, which arise frequently in the analysis of the running time of a recursive procedure. Section 3.5 covers the kinds of lemmas that are needed to prove that a procedure accomplishes its objectives and terminates. Section 3.6 covers typical recurrence equations.

3.4.1   Induction Proof Schema

The first thing to realize about an induction proof is

There is no such thing as "$n + 1$" in an induction proof.

Unfortunately, many readers learned otherwise. Why are we adopting this dogmatic position?

The answer lies in the motivation we gave earlier—to connect induction proofs to recursive procedures. We know that a recursive procedure works by *creating and solving smaller subproblems*, then combining the smaller solutions to solve the main problem. We want our induction proof to follow this plan. For the proof, the "main problem" is the stated theorem, and the "subproblems" are smaller instances of the stated theorem that can be combined to prove the main instance. In practice, these are likely to correspond directly to the exact subproblems the recursive procedure created.

All induction proofs follow a common pattern, which we call the *induction schema*. The most critical part of the schema is the correct introduction of the *inductive hypothesis*. First, we give an example proof, then we describe the general schema, and follow with more examples.

Example 3.4

The proof of the following proposition illustrates the induction schema to be described in general form after this example. The phrases in **boldface** are elements that appear practically verbatim in any detailed induction proof. Detailed remarks follow the proof, which uses the two-column format for clarity.

Proposition 3.6   For all $n \geq 0$, $\displaystyle\sum_{i=1}^{n} \frac{i(i+1)}{2} = \frac{n(n+1)(n+2)}{6}$.

Proof

Statement	Justification
1. **The proof is by induction on** n, the upper limit of the sum.	
2. **The base case is** $n = 0$.	
3. In this case both sides of the equation are 0.	Math.

4. **For n greater than 0, assume that**

$$\sum_{i=0}^{k} \frac{i(i+1)}{2} = \frac{k(k+1)(k+2)}{6}$$

holds for all $k \geq 0$ such that $k < n$.

5. $\displaystyle\sum_{i=0}^{n-1} \frac{i(i+1)}{2} = \frac{(n-1)(n)(n+1)}{6}.$ Ind. Hyp. with $k = n - 1$.

6. $\displaystyle\sum_{i=1}^{n} \frac{i(i+1)}{2} = \sum_{i=1}^{n-1} \frac{i(i+1)}{2} + \frac{n(n+1)}{2}.$ Math.

7. $\displaystyle\sum_{i=1}^{n} \frac{i(i+1)}{2} = \frac{(n-1)(n)(n+1)}{6} + \frac{n(n+1)}{2}.$ (5) + (6).

8. $\dfrac{(n-1)(n)(n+1)}{6} + \dfrac{n(n+1)}{2} = \dfrac{n(n+1)(n+2)}{6}.$ Math.

9. $\displaystyle\sum_{i=1}^{n} \frac{i(i+1)}{2} = \frac{n(n+1)(n+2)}{6}.$ (7) + (8). □

Line-by-line remarks follow.

1. Announce that n is the main induction variable. Note that the proposition is in the form $\forall n \in \mathbf{N}\,[A(n) \Rightarrow C(n)]$. Here $A(n)$ is simply the Boolean *true*, and $C(n)$ is the equation.
2. An induction proof always has two main cases, called the *base case* and the *inductive case*. Identify the base case(s).
3. *Prove* the base case(s).
4. Introduce the auxiliary variable k and state the inductive hypothesis. Notice that the inductive hypothesis takes the form $A(k) \Rightarrow C(k)$, recalling that for this proposition $A(k)$ is just the Boolean *true*.
    Notice that the range of k includes the base cases.
    Notice that k is restricted to be strictly less than n; otherwise we would be assuming what we are trying to prove.
    The statement of the inductive hypothesis signals that the proof of the inductive case is beginning.
5. *Use* the inductive hypothesis. (Notice that we are "pulling up to" n.) The auxiliary variable k is *locally* instantiated to $n - 1$. Since we are proving the case $n > 0$, this value of k satisfies $0 \leq k < n$, as required on line 4.
    The auxiliary variable k may be instantiated to other values in its range on other lines, if needed for the proof. This is one strength of "strong" induction. In this simple proof it happens that other instantiations of k are not needed.

6. The justification is a standard mathematical identity, presumably known to the reader.

7. The justification indicates which two earlier lines support this new conclusion, but does not state what *rule of inference* was used, assuming the reader can figure this out. Here the rule of inference is known as "substitution of equals for equals," or just "substitution." Line 9 is similar.

8. Another mathematical identity is applied. In practice, lines 6 through 9 would be condensed to one line, assuming the reader can figure out the steps. However, such condensations contribute to or cause many erroneous "proofs." The proof writer should be careful that a precise set of steps *could be* written.

9. This conclusion is exactly the goal statement, $C(n)$. ■

The preceding proof follows a pattern that can be generalized into the following schema. Note that the generic term *proposition* may be *theorem, lemma, corollary*, or some other term without changing the proof process.

Definition 3.1   Induction proof schema

First we explain the notation used in the schema below. The **boldface** text appears essentially verbatim. Terms between angle brackets, "⟨, ⟩", are replaced by substitution, according to the proposition to be proved. Similarly, the variables x and y take on names according to the proposition. They range over the set W (for "world"). The logical statement $C(x)$ is called the *goal statement*. The logical statement $A(x)$ is called the *hypothesis of the proposition* (hypotheses if it is a conjunction). The variable x is called the *main induction variable* (or simply *induction variable*). The variable y is called the *auxiliary variable*.

An induction proof for a proposition in the form

$$\forall x \in W \ [A(x) \Rightarrow C(x)]$$

consists of the following parts, in the order given.

1. **The proof is by induction on** x, ⟨description of x⟩.
2. **The base case is (cases are)** ⟨base-case⟩.
3. ⟨*Proof* of goal statement with base-case substituted into it, that is, C(base-case).⟩.
4. **For** ⟨x⟩ **greater than** ⟨base-case⟩, **assume that** $[A(y) \Rightarrow C(y)]$ **holds for all** $y \in W$ **such that** $y < x$.
5. ⟨*Proof* of the goal statement, $C(x)$, exactly as it appears in the proposition⟩. ■

An induction proof has two main cases: the base case and the inductive case. Part (2) of the schema defines the base case; part (3) proves the theorem for the base case, which may actually be several cases. Part (4) defines the inductive case, and states the inductive hypothesis. Part (5) proves the theorem for the inductive case, and is usually the main substance of the proof. This proof of $C(x)$ may be supported by:

1. the fact that x is greater than ⟨base-case⟩ in this case of the proof;
2. the hypotheses of the proposition, $A(x)$ (but *not* $A(y)$);

3. any number of instances of the inductive hypothesis, which is $[A(y) \Rightarrow C(y)]$, with elements of W that are *strictly smaller than* x substituted for the auxiliary variable y.

As usual, preceding conclusions in the proof, external identities, theorems, and the like, may be used.

Three "boilerplate" statements are permitted without giving a justification because they draw no conclusion; they simply explain the scheme of the proof and define some notation. They are

- "The proof is by induction on x, . . . "
- "The base case is . . . "
- "For $x > \langle$base case$\rangle$, assume that $[A(y) \Rightarrow C(y)]$ holds for all $y < x$."

The latter two statements divide the proof into two cases: x is a base case, and x is greater than any base case. These two cases must cover the entire set W over which x ranges.

Variations on the Induction Schema

1. If the assumptions $A(x)$ do not actually depend on x, then the inductive hypothesis simplifies to: **Assume** $C(y)$ **holds for all** $y \in W$ **less than** x. You should be able to explain why this simplification is justified by referring back to the justifications for proof statements.

2. There may be two or more base cases if the inductive case requires more than one smaller case, as in Fibonacci numbers, Equation (1.13). However, it is best to put as many elements as possible into the inductive case, because each base case requires its own proof.

3. There may be many base-case elements when the induction is over data structures, such as lists, trees, or graphs, or other sets W that have only a partial order. In Figure 3.3 the six singleton trees are base cases.

3.4.2 Induction Proof on a Recursive Procedure

The next example shows how induction and recursion work together. The lemma we will prove, about a procedure to compute external path length of 2-trees, is useful in lower bounds analysis (see Section 4.7.3). External path lengths arise naturally in several other problems. First we need some definitions.

Definition 3.2 External nodes and 2-trees

In certain types of binary trees the base case, instead of being an empty tree, is a tree with a single node of a different type from the rest of the tree. This type of node is called an *external node*. A tree that consists of an external node is called a *leaf*, and it does not have any subtrees. The other type of node is called an *internal node*, and it must have two children. Such binary trees are called *2-trees* because each node has two children or no children. ∎

Notice that, if we replace all external nodes in a 2-tree by empty trees, what remains is a normal, unrestricted, binary tree. In a 2-tree it is usually possible to recognize a leaf without checking to see if it has children because its node is a different type from that of internal nodes. Exercise 3.1 shows that a 2-tree must have one more external node than internal node.

Definition 3.3   External path length

In a 2-tree t, the *external path length* of t is the sum of the lengths of all the paths from the root of t to any external node in t. The length of a path is the number of its edges.

Alternatively, the *external path length* of a 2-tree can be defined inductively as follows:

1. The external path length of a leaf is 0.
2. Let t be a nonleaf, with left subtree L and right subtree R (either may be a leaf). The external path length of t is the external path length of L plus the number of external nodes in L plus the external path length of R plus the number of external nodes in R. (The number of external nodes in t is the sum of the numbers of external nodes in L and R.)

The equivalence of the two definitions is clear because every path from the root of t to an external node in L is one longer than a corresponding path from the root of L to the same external node, and similarly for R.   ∎

The binary-tree traversal skeleton of Section 2.3.3 can easily be annotated to calculate external path lengths. The class of the parameter is TwoTree, which is defined analogously to BinTree, except that the smallest tree is a leaf, rather than an empty tree. The base case is changed accordingly. The function needs to return two values, so we assume an organizer class (see Section 1.2.2) has been defined, named EplReturn, with two integer fields, epl and extNum, to represent external path length and the number of external nodes, respectively. The result is shown in Figure 3.4. We see that the function simply implements the inductive version of the definition. We can now prove the following lemma about calcEpl.

Lemma 3.7   Let t be any 2-tree. Let *epl* and m be the values of the fields epl and extNum, respectively, as returned by calcEpl(t). Then:

1. *epl* is the external path length of t.
2. m is the number of external nodes in t.
3. $epl \geq m \lg(m)$.

Proof   Before proving the lemma, let's correlate the statement of the lemma with our pattern for propositions to be proved, Equation (3.1). Note that it is split into several sentences, for easier reading, but the parts are all there. Thus t is the main induction variable and W is the set of all 2-trees. The second sentence states the hypotheses, so corresponds to $A(t)$. Finally the three conclusions comprise $C(t)$. As in previous examples, **boldface** text appears essentially verbatim in any induction proof.

```
EplReturn  calcEpl(TwoTree t)
    EplReturn  ansL, ansR;  // returned from subtrees
    EplReturn  ans = new EplReturn();  // to return

1.  if (t is a leaf)
2.       ans.epl = 0; ans.extNum = 1;
3.  else
4.       ansL = calcEpl(leftSubtree(t));
5.       ansR = calcEpl(rightSubtree(t));
6.       ans.epl = ansL.epl+ansR.epl + ansL.extNum+ansR.extNum;
7.       ans.extNum = ansL.extNum + ansR.extNum;
8.  return ans;
```

Figure 3.4 Function to calculate external path length of a 2-tree. The return type EplReturn is used so that the function can return two quantities, epl and extNum.

The proof is by induction on t, the parameter of calcEpl, with the "subtree" partial order. **The base case is** that t is a leaf. Line 2 of calcEpl is reached, so $epl = 0$ and $m = 1$, which are correct for parts (1) and (2), and $0 \geq 0$ holds for part (3).

For t not a leaf, **assume that the lemma holds for all** s, **where** s is a proper subtree of t. That is, if epl_s and m_s are returned by calcEpl(s), then m_s is the number of external nodes in s, epl_s is the external path length of s, and $epl_s \geq m_s \lg(m_s)$. Let L and R denote the left and right subtrees of t, respectively. These are proper subtrees of t, so the inductive hypothesis applies. Because t is not a leaf, lines 4 through 7 are executed, from which it follows that

$$epl = epl_L + epl_R + m_L + m_R,$$
$$m = m_L + m_R.$$

By the inductive hypothesis and the inductive definition of external path length, epl is the external path length of t. Every external node of t occurs in either L or R so m is the number of external nodes in t.

It remains to show that $epl \geq m \lg(m)$. We note (see Exercise 3.2) that the function $x \lg(x)$ is convex for $x > 0$, so we can use Lemma 1.3. By the inductive hypothesis we have

$$epl \geq m_L \lg(m_L) + m_R \lg(m_R) + m$$
$$m_L \lg(m_L) + m_R \lg(m_R) \geq 2 \left(\frac{m_L + m_R}{2} \right) \lg \left(\frac{m_L + m_R}{2} \right).$$

Therefore, by transitivity of "$\geq$",

$$epl \geq m \left(\lg(m) - 1 \right) + m = m \lg(m). \quad \square$$

Corollary 3.8   The external path length *epl* of a 2-tree with *n* internal nodes has the lower bound: $epl \geq (n + 1) \lg(n + 1)$.

Proof   Every 2-tree with *n* internal nodes has $(n + 1)$ external nodes (see Exercise 3.1). Apply Lemma 3.7.   □

It often happens that a recursive procedure benefits from returning multiple quantities in an organizer class, even though only one quantity is eventually needed. In this example, extNum was not asked for, but returning it from recursive calls greatly simplified the rest of the computation. For another example, see Exercise 3.13, which asks you to design a function to compute the maximum weight of an independent set of tree vertices.

3.5   Proving Correctness of Procedures

Things should be made as simple as possible—but not simpler.
    —Albert Einstein

It is generally acknowledged that proving correctness of programs is a hopelessly difficult task, *in general*. Nevertheless, proving correctness can be a valuable activity for solving problems and producing correctly working programs. The trick is to *program in a style for which proving correctness is practical*. We call this a *proof-friendly style*. We want proofs to help us, not to be an additional burden. The way to let proofs help is to write algorithms in a proof-friendly style, or at least be able to convert back and forth between a proof-friendly style and an efficient style.

In this section we build up a collection of proof methods, starting with simple constructs, and eventually getting more complex, but remaining manageable. The style we develop is used for the algorithms in this book. The foundations are the single-assignment paradigm and recursion. The single-assignment paradigm is introduced in Section 3.5.3.

3.5.1   Definitions and Terminology

A *block* is a section of code with one entry point and one exit point. Blocks are the main subdivisions of program code and procedure code. A *procedure* is a block with a name, so it can be called. It usually has *parameters*, which, for our purposes, are designated either as *input* or *output*. For simplicity, we assume no parameter is both input and output; one can designate two parameters to achieve the same effects. Also, we will assume input parameters are *not modified* during execution of the procedure. They may be copied into local data (see below) if modification is desired. This convention permits us to state postconditions in terms of input parameters without having to specify that we are referring to the values at the time of entry.

A *function* is a procedure with some output parameters; if there are multiple output parameters, we may assume they are collected in an object of an *organizer class* (Section 1.2.2), and thereby they can all be returned with a return statement. There is only one exit point, so the return statement must be at that point. This formalism permits us to handle functions as a special case of procedures.

A procedure often refers to *nonlocal data*, which is any data defined outside the header and body of the procedure. Indeed, if a procedure has no output parameters, the only effects of calling it are its effects on nonlocal data. Also, a procedure can define *local data*. The parameters of the procedure may also be considered to be local data during the execution of the procedure.

A block within a procedure also can refer to *nonlocal data*, which is any data defined outside the block. This is often called *global data*. This could be data in a higher level, enclosing block, or it could be outside the procedure, in which case visibility rules for the particular language being used apply.

The treatment of arrays is worth clarifying. If an array is passed as a parameter, the *reference* to the array is considered to be local data, while the *contents* of the array are considered to be nonlocal data. Similarly, in Java, the *reference* to an object is local, while the *instance fields* of the object are nonlocal. Updating nonlocal data is very important for the efficiency of some algorithms, but introduces great difficulties in proofs of correctness.

3.5.2 Elementary Control Structures

Control structures are mechanisms for causing various blocks to be executed. To begin with, we will consider just three control structures (see Figure 3.5): *sequence* (block 1, then block 2), *alternation* (if *condition* then true-block, else false-block), and *procedure call*. The omission of **for** and **while** loops from our basic proof methodology is intentional. We discuss adaptations for these constructs after the basic methodology has been developed (in Section 3.5.4).

Can we write anything worthwhile without loops? The surprising answer is "yes." With recursion, it is possible, and often simpler, to write any computation that was originally written using a loop.

"Proving correctness" means proving certain logical statements about a procedure. Like a "limited warranty," the statements are phrased carefully, so that they are not so sweeping that a proof would be hopelessly difficult. Now we describe the form these statements take.

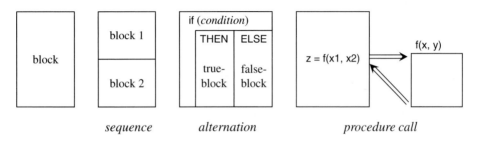

Figure 3.5 Elementary procedural control structures

Definition 3.4   Precondition, postcondition, and specification

A *precondition* is a logical statement about the input parameters and nonlocal data of a block (including a procedure or function) that is intended to be true at the time the block is entered. A *postcondition* is a logical statement about the input parameters, output parameters, and nonlocal data of a block that is intended to be true at the time the block exits. The *specifications* of a block are the preconditions and postconditions that describe the correct behavior of the block.   ■

Every block (including procedures and functions) should have specifications if we are attempting to prove correctness.

To prove correct behavior, it is sufficient to prove a lemma of the following form.

Proposition 3.9 (General correctness lemma form)   If all *preconditions* hold when the block is entered, then all *postconditions* hold when the block exits.   □

Suppose a block is subdivided by the *sequence* construct: block 1, then block 2. To prove correctness of the block, it suffices to prove a lemma of this form:

Proposition 3.10 (Sequence correctness lemma form)

1. The preconditions of the block imply the preconditions of block 1.
2. The postconditions of block 1 imply the preconditions of block 2.
3. The postconditions of block 2 imply the postconditions of the block.   □

Suppose a block is subdivided by the *alternation* construct: if (*condition*) then true-block, else false-block. To prove correctness of the block, it suffices to prove a lemma of this form:

Proposition 3.11 (Alternation correctness lemma form)

1. The preconditions of the block *and* the truth of *condition* imply the preconditions of true-block.
2. The postconditions of true-block *and* the truth of *condition* (at the time true-block is entered) imply the postconditions of the block.
3. The preconditions of the block *and* the falsity of *condition* imply the preconditions of false-block.
4. The postconditions of false-block *and* the falsity of *condition* (at the time false-block is entered) imply the postconditions of the block.   □

Figure 3.6 shows how the parts of each lemma in Propositions 3.10 and 3.11 combine to make a proof of the form of Proposition 3.9

Suppose a block consists of a procedure call. To prove correctness of the block, it suffices to prove a lemma of this form:

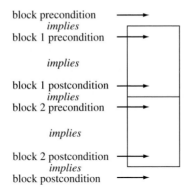

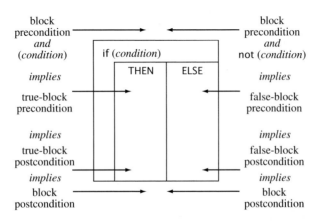

Figure 3.6   The chains of inferences to prove that the block's preconditions imply its postconditions, for *sequence* and *alternation*.

Proposition 3.12 (Procedure-Call Correctness Lemma Form)

1. The preconditions of the block imply the preconditions of the called procedure with its actual parameters.
2. The postconditions of the called procedure with its actual parameters imply the postconditions of the block.   □

It is important to notice that we are *not* required to prove the correctness of the called procedure in order to prove correctness of the block containing the call; correctness of the called procedure is a separate issue.

We have described the structure of proofs that enable us to prove correct behavior of a block, but have not gone into the details of how to prove specific facts about specific program statements. This is a highly technical and complex subject.

For example, suppose we see a statement in Java, "x=y+1." What logical statement do we know is true after that statement (i.e., what is the statement's postcondition)? It is tempting to say the postcondition is the equation $x = y + 1$. But now suppose the statement is "y=y+1;"? Or suppose we have the *sequence* of statements "x=y+1; y=z;"?

In practice, people rely on "common sense" arguments, rather than formal proof methods. Rather than try to figure out what logical statements are implied by the procedure code, we concentrate on whether the desired postconditions are achieved, and try to come up with *ad hoc* arguments for that conclusion. The next topic describes a better approach.

3.5.3   The Single-Assignment Paradigm

Early in the investigation of proof-friendly programming styles, researchers identified two constructs that caused major difficulties in proving correctness: the *go to* statement and the *assignment* statement. It was considered impractical to eliminate assignment statements, so they worked on eliminating the need for the *go to* statement, and the field of structured programming developed. Unfortunately, even with no *go to* statements, proofs are usually too involved to be practical.

More recently, the question of eliminating assignment statements has been re-examined. The emerging methodology is to eliminate *overwriting* assignments. That is, after a variable is created, it may receive only one assignment; the value assigned cannot subsequently be overwritten. Since its value can never change for its lifetime, reasoning about this variable is much simplified. This is the *single-assignment paradigm*.

Several programming languages have been developed that incorporate the single-assignment restriction, such as Prolog, ML, Haskell, Sisal (for *S*treams and *i*teration in a *s*ingle *a*ssignment *l*anguage) and SAC (for *S*ingle *A*ssignment *C*).

It has also been shown that programs in other languages, including C, Fortran, and Java, can be transformed into a single-assignment form without changing the computation they perform. Such transformations are used for compiler optimization and for detection of parallelizable code. It has been found that program analysis can be carried out to a much greater depth after the program is in single-assignment form. (See Notes and References at the end of the chapter.) Can we take advantage of the single-assignment paradigm in everyday programming?

The *single-assignment paradigm* cannot be applied universally, but can be applied to local variables of loop-free code very easily. Loop-free code includes code with recursive procedure calls, so this limitation is not so severe that the paradigm is useless. In fact, the compiler for Sisal transforms **for** and **while** loops into recursive procedure calls behind the scenes, so that it can employ the single-assignment paradigm in the transformed program. Then, with the single-assignment paradigm in force, the Sisal compiler is able to reason automatically about which sections of code can be executed in parallel. However, a limited form of single assignments can also be used with **while** and **for** loops.

Recall the assignment statements that made reasoning difficult, earlier in this section. Within the single-assignment paradigm "x=y+1;" *does* imply the equation $x = y + 1$ for the entire time x has a value. The troublesome statements "y=y+1;" and "x=y+1; y=z;" both violate the paradigm by assigning a value to y a second time.

In a loop-free procedure with x and y being local variables, we can always do the computation we want by defining a few additional local variables.

Example 3.5

To fix the statement "y=y+1;" we write "y1=y+1;" instead and we get the valid *equation* $y1 = y + 1$. To fix the statement "x=y+1; y=z;" we write "x=y+1; y1=z;" and we get two valid equations, $x = y + 1$ and $y1 = z$. In both cases, all later references to y in this branch of the procedure get changed to y1 so they reference the updated value. ∎

Let's look at one more common difficulty: A variable is updated in only one branch of an alternation, but is used after the branches of the alternation have merged back together.

Example 3.6

Consider the code fragment:

```
1.  if (y < 0)
2.      y = 0;
3.  x = 2 * y;
```

According to what we said earlier, we should define a new local variable y1 and replace line 2 with "y1 = 0." But what about line 3? We apparently do not know whether to use y or y1. The solution is to follow the rule that if a local variable is assigned its value in one branch of an alternation, then assign it an appropriate value in all branches. In this case multiple assignment statements appear in the code but only one can be executed in any pass through the procedure. The revised code that fits the single-assignment paradigm is

```
1.  if (y < 0)
2.      y1 = 0;
3.  else
4.      y1 = y;
5.  x = 2 * y1;
```

Now we have the very clean logical relationships among the variables involved (recalling that "⇒" is "implies" and "∧" is conjunction):

$$(y < 0 \Rightarrow y1 = 0) \land (y \geq 0 \Rightarrow y1 = y) \land (x = 2\,y1).$$

Efficiency buffs may wince at the idea of creating extra variables, but actually an optimizing compiler can easily determine if the original y will not be referenced again and use its space for y1. ∎

However, let's remember that the single-assignment paradigm, while very useful for local variables, is not so practical for programming with arrays. It is very common that array elements need to be updated, and we obviously can't afford to define a whole new array each time we update one element. Even if we did, we would encounter difficulties in trying to derive any logical statement describing the array state. The same problems arise with objects that have instance fields that need to be updated.

Conversion into a Loop-Free Procedure

If we want to apply the reasoning tools of this section to a procedure with a **while** or **for** loop, and the procedure is reasonably compact, the easiest method is probably to convert the loop into a recursive procedure.

Example 3.7

An iterative procedure for Sequential Search was given in Algorithm 1.1. The code below gives the recursive version and uses the single-assignment paradigm. Propositions 3.9 through 3.12 are applied to prove its correctness. (We did not prove correctness of Algorithm 1.1 because of the complications arising from variables having multiple values.)

Recall the pattern of *generalized searching routines* (see Definition 1.12): If there is no more data, fail; else look at one datum; if it is what we are looking for, succeed; else search the remaining data. This pattern is clearly followed in the procedure below.

Algorithm 3.1   Sequential Search, Recursive

Input: E, m, num, K, where E is an array with num entries (indexed $0, \ldots,$ num-1), K is the item sought, and $m \geq 0$ is the least index in the array segment to be searched. For simplicity, we assume that K and the entries of E are integers, as is num.

Output: ans, a location of K in E, in the range $m \leq$ ans $<$ num, or -1 if K is not found in that range.

Remark: The top-level call should be ans = seqSearchRec(E, 0, num, K).

```
int seqSearchRec(int[] E, int m, int num, int K)
      int ans;
  1.  if (m ≥ num)
  2.      ans = -1;
  3.  else if (E[m] == K)
  4.      ans = m;
  5.  else
  6.      ans = seqSearchRec(E, m+1, num, K);
  7.  return ans;
```

Notice that ans appears in three assignment statements, but they are all in different branches of the code, so this fits the single-assignment paradigm. Let's see what is involved in applying the propositions to verify correctness of the procedure.

First, we need to formulate the preconditions for seqSearchRec:

1. $m \geq 0$.
2. For $m \leq i <$ num, E[i] is initialized.

Now we state the objective, or postcondition, which should be true at line 7.

1. If ans $= -1$, then for $m \leq i <$ num, E[i] $\neq K$.
2. If ans $\neq -1$, then $m \leq$ ans $<$ num and E[ans] $= K$.

Now, following Proposition 3.9, we show that if the preconditions hold when seqSearch-Rec is entered, then the postconditions hold when it is done. We see that the procedure splits into three alternative cases, lines 2, 4, and 6, which converge at line 7, the **return** statement. Proposition 3.11 is used on each alternative. For each alternative, the conditions that led to that alternative are additional facts that can be used to prove that the postcondition holds for that alternative.

If line 2 is reached, the condition of line 1 is true ($m \geq$ num). After line 2, ans $= -1$, and the flow drops to line 7. At this point, the truth of the condition in line 1 implies that there are no indexes in the range $m \leq i <$ num, so postcondition 1 holds. Postcondition 2 is true due to its hypothesis being false (recall Section 1.3.3).

Similarly, if line 4 is reached, the condition of line 1 is false (so $m <$ num), and the condition of line 3 is true (E[m] $= K$). Line 4 itself establishes the equation (ans $= m$). Combining these yields that postcondition 2 is true. The equation (ans $= m$) and precondition 1 imply that the hypothesis of postcondition 1 is false; therefore postcondition 1 is true.

Finally, if line 6 is reached, the conditions of lines 1 and 3 are false (so $m <$ num and E[m] $\neq K$). First, we need to show that we "have the right to call" seqSearchRec with the actual parameters used on line 6. That is, we need to verify that the preconditions of seqSearchRec hold when instantiated with these actual parameters:

1. If $m \geq 0$, then $m + 1 \geq 0$.
2. The range $m + 1, \ldots,$ num-1 is contained within $m, \ldots,$ num-1, so E[i] is initialized there.

Now, by Proposition 3.12, *we may conclude that the procedure call on line 6 meets its postconditions.* Since the value of ans assigned on line 6 is just the value returned by the call on line 6, it satisfies the postconditions for that call (with the actual parameter of $m + 1$). These postconditions and the statement E[m] $\neq K$ imply the postconditions of the current call (with actual parameter m). For example, if -1 is returned, that implies that none of E[m+1], $\ldots,$ E[num-1] contains K, and so none of E[m], $\ldots,$ E[num-1] contains K. Otherwise, ans $\geq m + 1$, so ans $\geq m$ also.

Thus we have shown that whenever line 7 is reached, the required postconditions hold. The only remaining question is whether it is possible that line 7 is never reached, due to an endless recursion. Section 3.5.6 addresses this question. ■

Exercise 3.6 asks you to prove the correctness of Euclid's algorithm for finding the greatest common divisor of two integers, using the techniques of this section.

3.5.4 Procedures with Loops

Propositions 3.9 through 3.12 give us a framework for proving correctness in the absence of **for** and **while** loops. Within loops, single assignment is normally impossible, so it becomes necessary to define indexed variable names, indexed both by line number in the procedure *and* by number of passes through the loop to keep track of all the values taken on by the same program variable. Then it is necessary to trace the history carefully for each change in value. Rather than try to formalize and carry out this procedure, we believe that it is easier in practice to transform the loop into a recursive procedure, for which the proof tools are much simpler. This section describes how to go about this in a fairly mechanical fashion.

In fact, once we understand the relationship between the loop and the recursive version, it is usually unnecessary to actually carry out the transformation. As a preprocessing step, we should do the following.

1. Declare local variables within the loop body to the extent possible, and follow the single-assignment paradigm on these. That is, give the variable only one value in any one pass.
2. For variables that must be updated (and are necessarily declared outside the loop), do all the updates at the end of the loop body.

These rules minimize the number of different cases that must be considered.

The general rules for re-expressing a **while** loop with recursion are

1. Variables updated in the loop become procedure input parameters. Their initial values at loop entry correspond to the actual parameters in the top-level call of the recursive procedure. We call these *active parameters*.
2. Variables referenced in the loop but defined earlier and not updated in the loop are also likely to become parameters, because otherwise they would be inaccessible in the new recursive procedure. But they are just "passed through," from call to call, so we call these *passive parameters*. For analysis purposes (if we are not actually converting the code), we can treat passive parameters as global variables.
3. The recursive procedure begins by mimicking the **while** condition and returns (i.e., drops to the **return** statement of the new recursive procedure) if the **while** condition is false.
4. A **break** also corresponds to a procedure return.
5. If the end of the **while** body is reached, a recursive call occurs. The actual parameters of the recursive call are the *updated* values of variables used in the loop body. These are concentrated at the end of the loop body if we did the suggested preprocessing.

The rules for **for** loops are similar.

This transformation is illustrated with the factorial function in Figure 3.7. Note that n is a passive parameter.

Except for line 7, the loop body in factLoop follows the single-assignment paradigm. Thus we can reason about the loop body using Propositions 3.9 through 3.12 and using equations among the variables, without getting involved in the complicated indexing or tagging that is usually needed when one variable takes on many different values during the procedure execution. At least, we can do this up to line 7, where variable values "roll over" in preparation for the next pass. Furthermore, if we can visualize this "rolling over" as a new procedure invocation with new actual parameters, *and a smaller problem size*, we can try to prove something about it using induction. In this limited sense, the single-assignment paradigm can be used in procedures with loops.

```
int  factLoop(int n)              int  fact(int n)
    int  k, f;                    9.  return factRec(n, 1, 1);
1.  k = 1;
2.  f = 1;                        int  factRec(int n, int k, int f)
3.  while (k ≤ n)                     int  ans;
4.      {                         3a.  if (k > n)
5.          int  fnew = f * k;    3b.      ans = f;
6.          int  knew = k + 1;    4.  else
7.          k = knew; f = fnew;   5.      int  fnew = f * k;
8.      }                         6.      int  knew = k + 1;
9.  return f;                     7.      ans = factRec(n, knew, fnew);
                                      return ans;
```

Figure 3.7 Transformation of **while** loop into recursive function. Curly braces unrelated to the transformation are omitted.

3.5.5 Correctness Proofs as a Debugging Tool

One of the great practical values of proofs of correctness—even very informal "mental" proofs—is that they often pinpoint bugs in a procedure before coding and testing even begin. Partly it is just the discipline of thinking through the procedure's preconditions and postconditions, and *writing them down as comments in the code*. (Even if your proof will be "mental" you should not shirk from this documentation step.)

Many program bugs are simple and obvious mismatches between a procedure's preconditions and the actual conditions that exist when it is called. A great many others are due to the corresponding postcondition mismatch. These mismatches usually become evident as soon as Proposition 3.12 is considered.

When the problem is subtler, and everything "looks okay," you should try to construct the proof using the Propositions to get from block to block in reasonably sized chunks. This involves asking, for each chunk that you are treating as one block, "What is this chunk supposed to accomplish?", then "What does it need to be true to accomplish that?" Now do the prior chunks make those things true?

If there is a bug in the code, and you are careful about your reasoning, *the point where the proof breaks down tells you where the bug is*. That is, the bug is likely to be in one of the two blocks on either side of the boundary across which you found a mismatch of postconditions and preconditions.

For example, in the recursive sequential search (Algorithm 3.1), if the condition on line 1 were mistakenly written as (m ≥ num−1), then postcondition 1 would not be implied after line 2, and the bug would be localized.

For another example, suppose Algorithm 3.1 is revised to interchange lines 1–2 with lines 3–4, that is, line 1 becomes "if (E[m] == K)." All the statements mentioned in the proof we gave can be repeated with a change in line number, but the procedure has a bug. To catch that bug during a verification check, we have to realize that a precondition for *any* statement that evaluates an expression is that all data elements in the expression have been given values, that we are not accessing any uninitialized variables or instance fields. If m might be greater than num−1, we can't be sure of this. Again, the proof attempt exposes the bug, but only if we are checking very carefully. It is always a good idea to ask, as we are reviewing our code, "Has this data element been initialized?"

3.5.6   Termination of Recursive Procedures

In the presence of recursive procedures, Propositions 3.9 through 3.12, the lemmas described in Section 3.5.2, demonstrate what is called *partial* correctness, because they do not address the question of whether the procedure terminates. To complete the proof of *total* correctness, it is necessary to demonstrate that each recursive procedure call is working on a problem that is smaller than the problem being solved by the calling procedure.

At the point where one needs to prove that the preconditions for the recursive call are satisfied, one also argues that the structure or "problem size" being passed to the recursive call is smaller than that of the caller. As with other correctness issues, in practice people use reasonableness arguments that appeal to common sense, rather than formal proofs with axioms and rules of inference.

In many cases the size of the problem is a nonnegative integer, such as the number of elements in a subrange, the number of elements in a linked list, and so on. For example, in Algorithm 3.1 in Section 3.5.2 "problem size" is conveniently defined as $n = (\text{num} - m)$, the number of unexamined elements. This difference decreases by one from the current call to the recursive call, and the recursion ends if it becomes zero.

In some cases, one can use directly a partial order defined on the structure being passed as an input parameter, such as the *subtree* partial order (see Figure 3.3). For example, in a binary-tree-traversal procedure, such as Figure 3.4 if the input parameter to the procedure is tree T, and T is not a base case, then each subtree of T is "less than" T in this partial order. Therefore the recursive procedure terminates on any correctly formed binary tree structure.

To be technically accurate, a procedure that does recursion on a binary tree should have a precondition that its input parameter T is a correctly formed binary tree structure—in particular, that it has no cycles. One motivation for specifying the Binary Tree abstract data type nondestructively (as we did in Section 2.3.3) is that this condition holds automatically.

3.5.7   Correctness of Binary Search

We now prove the correctness of the recursive procedure binarySearch in some detail (see Algorithm 1.4, Binary Search). This serves as an illustration of the use of induction to prove correctness of a recursive procedure. An induction proof establishes total correctness of a loop-free recursive procedure; that is, it establishes that the procedure terminates, as well as establishing that its preconditions imply its postconditions. (If the recursive procedure calls subroutines, then correctness of the subroutines is added as a *hypothesis* to the theorem of correctness for the recursive procedure being proven.)

```
    int binarySearch(int[] E, int first, int last, int K)
1.      if (last < first)
2.          index = −1;
3.      else
4.          int  mid = (first + last) / 2;
5.          if (K == E[mid])
6.              index = mid;
7.          else if (K < E[mid])
8.              index = binarySearch(E, first, mid−1, K);
9.          else
10.             index = binarySearch(E, mid+1, last, K);
11.     return index;
```

Figure 3.8　Procedure for binarySearch, repeated from Algorithm 1.4.

We define the problem size for binarySearch as $n = $ last $-$ first $+ 1$, the number of entries in the range of E to be searched. The procedure is repeated in Figure 3.8 for convenience.

Lemma 3.13　For all $n \geq 0$, if binarySearch(E, first, last, K) is called, and the problem size is (last $-$ first $+ 1$) $= n$, and E[first], . . ., E[last] are in nondecreasing order, then it returns -1 if K does not occur in E within the range first, . . ., last, and it returns index such that $K = E$[index] otherwise.

Proof　The proof is by induction on n, the problem size. The base case is $n = 0$. In this case, line 1 is true, line 2 is reached, and -1 is returned.

For $n > 0$, assume that binarySearch(E, f, ℓ, K) satisfies the lemma on problems of size k such that $0 \leq k < n$, and f and ℓ are any indexes such that $k = \ell - f + 1$. Because $n > 0$, line 1 is false, first $\leq$ last, and control reaches line 4, then line 5. From the preceding inequality and the equation mid $= \lfloor$(first $+$ last)/2$\rfloor$, we see that first $\leq$ mid $\leq$ last. Therefore mid is within the search range. If line 5 is true, the procedure accomplishes its objective on line 6.

For the remainder of the proof, assume line 5 is false. From the previous pair of inequalities and the definition of n, we have (by transitivity of $\leq$)

$$(\text{mid} - 1) - \text{first} + 1 \leq (n - 1),$$

$$\text{last} - (\text{mid} + 1) + 1 \leq (n - 1),$$

so the inductive hypothesis applies for both recursive calls, on lines 8 and 10.

Now, if line 7 is true, then line 8 is executed. It is straightforward to check that the preconditions of binarySearch are satisfied with the actual parameters of line 8 (only the third parameter changed, and it decreased). Therefore we can assume that the call accomplishes the objective of binarySearch. If the call on line 8 returns a positive index, this solves the current problem. If the call on line 8 returns -1, this implies that K is not in E in the range first, . . ., mid $- 1$. But the truth of line 7 implies that K is not in E in the range mid, . . ., last, so returning -1 from the current procedure invocation is correct. If line 7 is false, then line 10 is executed, and the argument is similar.   □

A point worth emphasizing about the proof is that, before we could (justifiably) assume that the calls on lines 8 and 10 accomplish their objectives, we needed to verify that the preconditions for the calls were met. Since many logical errors are caused by calling procedures without meeting their preconditions, this kind of check can uncover many bugs.

3.6   Recurrence Equations

A recurrence equation defines a function over the natural numbers, say $T(n)$, in terms of its own value at one or more integers smaller than n. In other words, $T(n)$ is defined inductively. As with all inductions, there are base cases to be defined separately, and the recurrence equation only applies for n larger than the base cases. Although we will be interested mainly in recurrence equations for functions that describe the resources used by algorithms (usually the running time, number of key comparisons, or the count of some other important operation), this is not a requirement to have a recurrence equation. Many interesting mathematical functions can be defined by recurrence equations, such as the well-known Fibonacci numbers, Equation (1.13).

Recurrence equations arise very naturally to express the resources used by recursive procedures. The purposes of this section are to show how to derive such recurrence equations from the procedure code, and to describe some commonly occurring patterns from algorithms. Section 3.7 explores how to solve some of the typical recurrence equations that arise this way. Because a number of different resources might be measured (time, space, number of key comparisons, etc.), we will use the general term *cost* for the quantity being described by, or bounded by the recurrence equation.

We first need to specify some way of measuring the size of the problem the recursive procedure is solving: Let's call that size n. The left side of the recurrence equation will be $T(n)$. To make up the right side of the equation we need to estimate how much the various blocks in the procedure will cost as a function of n. Often the cost for some block will be a constant. We can just call all constants 1 if we are satisfied with an answer that is within a constant factor.

In our terminology, a *subroutine* is any procedure that is not recursive with the one we are analyzing; that is, no sequence of calls from the subroutine can lead back to this procedure. Quantities related to subroutines usually carry the subscript S. Quantities related to recursive calls usually carry the subscript R.

Combining the costs of blocks for worst-case analysis is simple if the procedure has no loops.

1. For a *sequence* of blocks, *add* the individual costs.
2. For an *alternation* of blocks, where neither is a base case, take the *maximum* of the alternatives.

3. If a block contains a subroutine call, figure out how big its actual parameters are, as a function of n. For simplicity assume only one parameter size is needed, and call it $n_S(n)$. We need to know the cost function, say T_S, for the subroutine. Then the cost of this call is specified as $T_S(n_S(n))$.

4. If a block contains a recursive procedure call, figure out how big its actual parameter size is, as a function of n, and call it $n_R(n)$. Then the cost of this recursive call is $T(n_R(n))$. This is the same T that is on the left side of the recurrence equation.

The terms that occur on the right side of the equation, other than those containing the function T (which appears on the left side), are called the *nonrecursive cost* of the procedure call. This is to distinguish this cost from the total cost of the procedure call, which includes the T terms as well.

Combining the costs of blocks for average-case analysis requires a different treatment of the *alternation* construct. The cost of each alternative is weighted by its probability of occurring, and the weighted costs are summed, to yield the *expected*, or *average* cost for this block. Also, if the sizes of subproblems ($n_S(n)$ and $n_R(n)$) can vary for different inputs, the costs of subroutine calls and recursive calls need to be averaged. For this reason, average-case analysis is often considerably more difficult than worst-case analysis.

Example 3.8

For a simple application of these rules, consider the recursive function

    seqSearchRec(E, m, num, K)

from Algorithm 3.1, whose procedure body is repeated here for convenience:

```
1.  if (m ≥ num)
2.      ans = -1;
3.  else if (E[m] == K)
4.      ans = m;
5.  else
6.      ans = seqSearchRec(E, m+1, num, K);
7.  return ans;
```

We specify as our measure of problem size the number of elements in the array E that might contain the key K being searched for. Thus $n = num - m$, where m and num are the second and third actual parameters of the current call. Let's decompose the procedure into blocks, so the rules can be applied. Blocks can be described by their range of line numbers. The whole procedure is 1–7. It is decomposed as suggested in this diagram, in which "OR" denotes *alternation* and ";" denotes *sequence*.

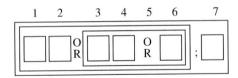

The base case is block 2–2 and is excluded from the recurrence equation, which only applies to nonbase cases. All innermost blocks are simple statements, except for 6–6. When the cost is running time, we will assume simple statements require constant cost and use 1 to represent any constant (so 1+1=1 in this context). When the cost is the number of some specified operation, then the operations are counted. We will assume, for definiteness, that the cost is the number of comparisons with an array element. Thus line 3 incurs a cost of 1 and the other simple statements are free in this cost model.

Looking at the call on line 6 in Algorithm 3.1, we see the actual second and third parameters are $m + 1$ and num, so its problem size is $\text{num} - (m + 1) = n - 1$. Therefore the cost of 6–6 is $T(n - 1)$. The cost for the whole block is built up from the costs of the statements using max to combine alternatives and $+$ to combine sequential blocks. Block 2–2 is excluded as an alternative here. Note that 1–7 is the sum of 1–6 and 7–7, and gives us the expression on the right side of the recurrence equation for seqSearchRec:

$$\bigl(0 + (1 + \max(0, T(n - 1)))\bigr) + 0.$$

Simplifying, we see that the recurrence equation is $T(n) = T(n - 1) + 1$. The nonrecursive cost is 1 in this case.

Base cases are always small problems, so we assume they are always unit cost when time is the cost. But here we are counting comparisons, so $T(0) = 0$. ■

Example 3.9

For another example, consider the Binary Search procedure, Algorithm 1.4, repeated in Section 3.5.7. The problem size is $n = \text{last} - \text{first} + 1$. The cost measure is again key comparisons, so line 5 costs 1. On lines 8 and 10 the recursive calls are on problems of size $n/2$ or $(n - 1)/2$, but these are alternatives, so the combination cost is the maximum, not the sum. None of the remaining statements does a key comparison so the recurrence equation is found to be

$$T(n) = T(n/2) + 1.$$

In this procedure only one recursive call is actually made although two appear in the procedure. In Chapter 4 we will encounter sorting procedures that actually make both recursive calls, and their recurrence equations have terms on the right-hand side for each recursive call. ■

Problems arise if the sizes $n_S(n)$ or $n_R(n)$ are not known very accurately. For example, in a binary-tree traversal on a tree with n nodes (Section 2.3.3), we know that the left and right subtrees add up to $n - 1$ nodes, but we don't know how the sum is divided between them. Suppose we introduce an extra variable r to represent the size of the right subtree. Then we arrive at the recurrence equation

$$T(n) = T(n - 1 - r) + T(r) + 1, \qquad T(0) = 1.$$

Fortuitously, we can determine by substitution that the function $T(n) = 2n + 1$ solves this recurrence without knowing any values for r. In general, we are not so lucky, and behavior is different for different values of r. This problem has to be addressed in Quicksort (Section 4.4.3).

Common Recurrence Equations

We can describe several categories of recurrence equation that occur frequently and can be solved (to some degree) by standard methods. In all cases "subproblem" refers to a smaller instance of the main problem, to be solved by a recursive call. Symbols b and c are constants.

Divide and Conquer: In many cases of the *divide-and-conquer* paradigm, the sizes of subproblems are known to be $n/2$ or some other fixed fraction of n, the size of the current problem. Examples of this behavior are Binary Search (Section 1.6), which we have seen, and algorithms we study in Chapter 4: Mergesort (Section 4.6) and heap operations (Section 4.8.3). For example, in Section 4.6 we derive this recurrence equation for T_{MS}, the number of comparisons done by Mergesort:

$$T_{MS}(n) = T_{MS}\left(\frac{n}{2}\right) + T_{MS}\left(\frac{n}{2}\right) + M(n), \qquad T_{MS}(1) = 0. \tag{3.2}$$

The cost $M(n)$ arises from a subroutine call. We need to know what that function is before we can make progress on solving for $T_{MS}(n)$.

In general, for problems of the divide-and-conquer type, the main problem of size n can be divided into b subproblems ($b \geq 1$) of size n/c ($c > 1$). There is also some nonrecursive cost $f(n)$ (to split up the problem into subproblems and/or to combine the solutions of the subproblems into a solution of the main problem).

$$T(n) = b\,T\left(\frac{n}{c}\right) + f(n). \tag{3.3}$$

We call b the *branching factor*.

Chip and Conquer: The main problem of size n can be "chipped down" to one subproblem of size $n - c$, where $c > 0$, with nonrecursive cost $f(n)$ (to create the subproblem and/or to extend the solution of the subproblem into a solution of the overall problem).

$$T(n) = T(n - c) + f(n). \tag{3.4}$$

Chip and Be Conquered: The main problem of size n can be "chipped down" to b subproblems ($b > 1$), each of size $n - c$, where $c > 0$, with nonrecursive cost $f(n)$ (to split up the problem into subproblems and/or to combine the solutions of the subproblems into a solution of the main problem). We call b the *branching factor*.

$$T(n) = b\,T(n - c) + f(n). \tag{3.5}$$

If the subproblems have various sizes, but all are within some constant range $n - c_{max}$ to $n - c_{min}$, then upper and lower bounds can be obtained by using c_{min} and c_{max}, respectively, in place of c in the equation. This case is also considered in Exercise 3.11.

In the next section we look at a methodical approach to analyzing these typical recurrence equations.

3.7 Recursion Trees

Recursion trees provide a tool for analyzing the cost (running time, number of key comparisons, or other measure) of recursive procedures for which we have developed recurrence equations. First we will show how to develop a recursion tree from a recurrence equation with an example, then we will describe the general procedure. From the general procedure we will be able to derive several general solutions (Lemma 3.14, Lemma 3.15, Theorem 3.16, Theorem 3.17, Equations 3.12 and 3.13). These solutions cover many of the recurrence equations that arise in practice from analysis of algorithms, and they serve as a rough guide even when the recurrence equations are not exactly in one of the standard forms. It is not necessary to follow all of the technical details in this section to be able to apply the general solutions mentioned.

Each node in the recursion tree has two fields, the *size* field and the *nonrecursive cost* field. A node is represented as follows:

$$\boxed{T(size) \mid nonrec.\ cost}$$

The size field states the actual parameter of T for this node. We include the recurrence name T to remind us that the size field is not a cost.

Example 3.10   Simple divide-and-conquer recursion tree

Consider the recurrence equation:

$$T(n) = T\left(\frac{n}{2}\right) + T\left(\frac{n}{2}\right) + n.$$

This is a special case of the form in Equation (3.3), with $b = 2$ and $c = 2$. This is a slightly simplified form of the recurrence equation for Mergesort, and it comes up in many situations. We will go through the steps to develop the corresponding recursion tree. The first step, which helps to avoid substitution errors, is to rewrite the equation with an auxiliary variable (there is an analogy with the auxiliary variable in an induction hypothesis). We call this our *work copy* of the recurrence equation.

$$T(k) = T\left(\frac{k}{2}\right) + T\left(\frac{k}{2}\right) + k. \tag{3.6}$$

A node can be created as soon as its size field is known; later we can use the size field to calculate a value for the nonrecursive cost field. We are ready to create the root node of the recursion tree for $T(n)$; here $size = n$.

$$\boxed{T(n) \mid }$$

The process of determining the nonrecursive cost field and the children of an incomplete node is called *expansion* of that node. We take the size field in the node to be expanded, n in this case, and substitute it for k in our work copy, Equation (3.6). We look at the resulting right side, which is $T(n/2) + T(n/2) + n$. All the terms with T become children of the node we are expanding and all the remaining terms become that node's nonrecursive cost, as follows:

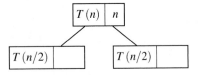

Since all nodes at the same depth look the same we can generate them in batches. In general, each incomplete node must be generated according to its own size field. Here all the size fields are $n/2$, so this time we substitute $n/2$ for k in Equation (3.6), and we see that the right side looks like: $T(n/4) + T(n/4) + n/2$. So now we have

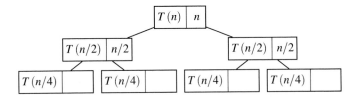

We continue several levels until we can see what pattern the tree is following. Figure 3.9 shows the tree after expanding another level; there are eight incomplete children for which details are not shown. Here we can see that at depth d the size parameter is $n/2^d$ and the nonrecursive cost also happens to be $n/2^d$. (Recall that the depth of the root is zero in our convention.) In this simple example all nodes at the same tree depth are identical, but this is not always the case. ∎

We summarize the rules for developing a recursion tree on the next page.

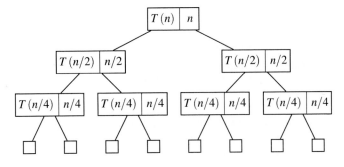

Figure 3.9 Three top levels of a recursion tree. The size fields of the eight incomplete children are not shown.

Definition 3.5   Recursion tree rules

1. The *work copy* of the recurrence equation uses a different variable from the original copy; it is called the *auxiliary variable*. Let k be the auxiliary variable for purposes of this discussion. The left side of the original copy of the recurrence equation (let's assume it is $T(n)$) becomes the size field of the root node for the recursion tree.

2. An incomplete node has a value for its size field, but not for its nonrecursive cost.

3. The process of determining the nonrecursive cost field and the children of an incomplete node is called *expansion* of that node. We take the size field in the node to be expanded and substitute it for the auxiliary variable k in our work copy of the recurrence equation. The resulting terms containing T on the right side of that equation become children of the node being expanded; all the remaining terms become that node's nonrecursive cost.

4. Expanding a base-case size gives a nonrecursive cost field and no children.

    To simplify the presentation, we assume that the recurrence equation is defined in such a way that no base case has cost zero. If the equation is presented with base cases costing zero, we can just compute the smallest cases that have nonzero cost and use them as the base cases, instead.

    In fact, we will usually assume the base case costs 1, for definiteness. Variations can be worked out if necessary. ∎

In any subtree of the recursion tree, the following equation holds:

$$\text{size field of root} = \sum \text{nonrec. costs of expanded nodes}$$
$$+ \sum \text{size fields of incomplete nodes.} \tag{3.7}$$

This is easy to prove by induction. In the base case, $T(n) = T(n)$. After one expansion, the root node has been expanded and the children are incomplete, so Equation (3.7) gives exactly the original recurrence equation, and so on.

Example 3.11   Recursion tree interpretation

In the seven-node tree in Example 3.10 (with four incomplete nodes), Equation (3.7) states that $T(n) = n + 2(n/2) + 4\,T(n/4) = 2n + 4\,T(n/4)$. ∎

The technique to evaluate the recursion tree is this: First sum the nonrecursive costs of all nodes at the same depth; this is called the *row-sum* for that tree depth. Then sum those row-sums over all depths. Continuing the example of Figure 3.9, some row-sums are shown in Figure 3.10.

To evaluate the sum of row-sums, it is necessary (usually) to know the maximum depth of the recursion tree. This is the depth at which the size parameter reduces to a base case.

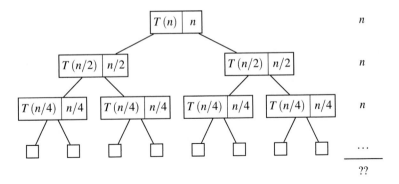

Figure 3.10 Summing nonrecursive costs in a recursion tree. The row sum for each of the first three rows is shown at the right.

Example 3.12   Recursion tree evaluation

For the tree of Example 3.10 (see Figure 3.10) we observe that the size as a function of node depth d is $n/2^d$, so the base cases occur about at $d = \lg(n)$. Since each row-sum is n, the total for the tree, which gives the value of $T(n)$, is about $n \lg(n)$. ■

3.7.1 Divide-and-Conquer, General Case

Following the same steps as in Examples 3.10 through 3.12, we can evaluate the general divide-and-conquer recurrence equation (Equation (3.3), repeated here for convenience), to get the asymptotic order of $T(n)$.

$$T(n) = b\,T\left(\frac{n}{c}\right) + f(n). \tag{3.8}$$

This section gets technical, but the lemmas and theorems can be understood and used without following all the steps of the derivations.

First, we can see that the size parameter decreases by a factor of c each time the depth increases (we had $c = 2$ in the example). Therefore the base cases (leaves of the tree) occur about when $(n/c^D) = 1$, where D is the node depth of base-case nodes. We solve and get $D = \lg(n)/\lg(c) \in \Theta(\log(n))$. However, we should not jump to the conclusion that row-sums are the same at all depths.

It is useful to know how *many* leaves the tree has. The branching factor is b so the number of nodes at depth D is $L = b^D$. To get this into a more convenient form we take logs: $\lg(L) = D \lg(b) = (\lg(b)/\lg(c)) \lg(n)$. The coefficient of $\lg(n)$ is very significant, so we give it a name.

Definition 3.6   Critical exponent

For b and c in Equation (3.3) (or Equation 3.8) we define the *critical exponent* as

$$E = \frac{\lg(b)}{\lg(c)}. \quad ■$$

By Lemma 1.1, part 8, any convenient base can be used for the logarithms in the formula for E, as long as it is the same in the numerator and denominator. With this notation, the paragraph before the definition has shown that:

Lemma 3.14   The number of leaves in the recursion tree for Equation (3.8) is approximately $L = n^E$, where E is the critical exponent defined in Definition 3.6.   □

Assuming the nonrecursive cost is 1 in the leaves, this tells us that the cost of the tree is *at least* n^E. Even if the nonrecursive costs in the leaves are zero, there will be nonzero costs in the level above the leaves (or some constant number of levels above the leaves in an extreme case). But there are still $\Theta(n^E)$ nodes at this level, so a lower bound of $\Omega(n^E)$ still holds.

Let's summarize what we know.

Lemma 3.15   With the notation of the foregoing discussion, we have, approximately:

1. The recursion tree has depth $D = \lg(n)/\lg(c)$, so there are about that many row-sums.
2. The zeroth row-sum is $f(n)$, the nonrecursive cost of the root.
3. The Dth row-sum is n^E, assuming base cases cost 1, or $\Theta(n^E)$ in any event.
4. The value of $T(n)$, that is, the solution of Equation (3.8), is the sum of the nonrecursive costs of all nodes in the tree, which is the sum of the row-sums.   □

In many practical cases the row-sums form a geometric series (or can be well approximated from above and below by two geometric series). Recall that a geometric series has the form $\sum_{d=0}^{D} ar^d$ (Section 1.3.2). The constant r is called the *ratio*. Quite a few simplifications occur in practice that are based on the principle of Theorem 1.13, part 2, which stated that, for a geometric series whose ratio is not 1, the sum is in Θ of its largest term. By this theorem and Lemma 3.15, we can conclude the following:

Theorem 3.16 (Little Master Theorem)   With the notation of the foregoing discussion, and $T(n)$ defined by Equation (3.8):

1. If the row-sums form an increasing geometric series (starting from row 0 at the top of the tree), then $T(n) \in \Theta(n^E)$, where E is the *critical exponent* defined in Definition 3.6. That is, the cost is proportional to the number of leaves in the recursion tree.
2. If the row-sums remain about constant, $T(n) \in \Theta(f(n)\log(n))$.
3. If the row-sums form a decreasing geometric series, then $T(n) \in \Theta(f(n))$, which is proportional to the cost of the root.

Proof   In case 1 the sum is dominated by the last term. In case 2 there are $\Theta(\log(n))$ equal terms. In case 3 the sum is dominated by the first term.   □

By going into greater technical depth it is possible to generalize this theorem considerably. The generalization is often useful when the function $f(n)$ in Equation (3.8) involves logarithms, because then the row-sums may not behave very neatly. (For an even more general version, see Exercise 3.9.)

Theorem 3.17 (Master Theorem) With the terminology of the preceding discussion, the solution of the recurrence equation

$$T(n) = b \, T\left(\frac{n}{c}\right) + f(n) \tag{3.9}$$

(restated from Equations 3.3 and 3.8) has forms of solution as follows, where $E = \lg(b)/\lg(c)$ is the *critical exponent* defined in Definition 3.6.

1. If $f(n) \in O(n^{E-\epsilon})$ for some positive ϵ, then $T(n) \in \Theta(n^E)$, which is proportional to the number of leaves in the recursion tree.
2. If $f(n) \in \Theta(n^E)$, then $T(n) \in \Theta(f(n) \, \log(n))$, as all node depths contribute about equally.
3. If $f(n) \in \Omega(n^{E+\epsilon})$ for some positive ϵ, and $f(n) \in O(n^{E+\delta})$ for some $\delta \geq \epsilon$, then $T(n) \in \Theta(f(n))$, which is proportional to the nonrecursive cost at the root of the recursion tree.

(Possibly none of these cases applies.)

Proof At node depth d there are b^d nodes, and each contributes a nonrecursive cost of $f(n/c^d)$. Therefore we have the following general expression for the solution of Equation (3.8):

$$T(n) = \sum_{d=0}^{\lg(n)/\lg(c)} b^d \, f\left(\frac{n}{c^d}\right). \tag{3.10}$$

We will just sketch the proof, which follows the lines of the reasoning for Theorem 3.16. (See Notes and References for sources with a complete proof.) Consider case 3. Ignoring coefficients, $f(n)$ is about $n^{E+\epsilon}$, for some positive ϵ. So

$$f\left(\frac{n}{c^d}\right) \approx \frac{n^{E+\epsilon}}{\left(c^d\right)^{E+\epsilon}} \approx \frac{f(n)}{c^{Ed+\epsilon d}}.$$

Then $b^d \, f\left(n/c^d\right)$ is about $f(n) \, b^d / \left(c^{Ed} \, c^{\epsilon d}\right)$. But $c^E = b$ through standard identities, so c^{Ed} in the denominator cancels b^d in the numerator. We finally have $f(n)/c^{\epsilon d}$, which gives a decreasing geometric series in d. Analysis of other cases is similar. $\quad\square$

3.7.2 Chip and Conquer, or Be Conquered

A different picture emerges for Equations (3.4) and (3.5). If the branching factor is greater than 1, we have Equation (3.5), repeated here for convenience:

$$T(n) = b \, T(n - c) + f(n). \tag{3.11}$$

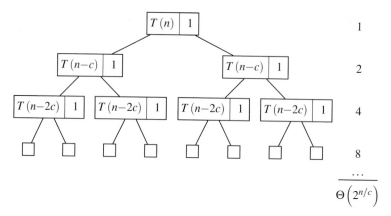

Figure 3.11   Summing nonrecursive costs in a chip-and-be-conquered recursion tree

Figure 3.11 shows the recursion tree for an example of Equation (3.11) with $f(k) = 1$. Since the size decreases by c with each depth increase of 1, the base cases occur at about $d = n/c$.

As illustrated in Figure 3.11, the total for the tree is exponential in n, the problem size. This holds even with the most favorable assumption that $f(n) = 1$. The following general expression can be found by inspection of the recursion tree for Equation (3.11):

$$T(n) = \sum_{d=0}^{n/c} b^d \, f(n - cd) = b^{n/c} \sum_{h=0}^{n/c} \frac{f(c\,h)}{b^h} \quad \text{(solution of Eq. 3.11)} \quad (3.12)$$

where the second sum uses $h = (n/c) - d$, so h is zero at the leaves and increases toward the root. In most practical cases, the last sum is $\Theta(1)$, giving $T(n) \in \Theta\left(b^{n/c}\right)$. This function grows exponentially in n. A more general case of chip-and-be-conquered is considered in Exercise 3.11. As we saw in Section 1.5, algorithms with exponential growth rates will not be able to solve the worst cases of problems of any significant size.

However, if the branching factor b is 1 in Equation (3.11) (giving Equation 3.4), then the general expression of Equation (3.12) becomes much friendlier:

$$T(n) = \sum_{d=0}^{n/c} f(n - cd) = \sum_{h=0}^{n/c} f(c\,h) \approx \frac{1}{c} \int_0^n f(x) \, dx \quad \text{(solution of Eq. 3.4)} \quad (3.13)$$

For example, if $f(n)$ is a polynomial n^α, then $T(n) \in \Theta(n^{\alpha+1})$. Alternatively, if $f(n) = \log(n)$, then $T(n) \in \Theta(n \log(n))$. (See Section 1.3.2.)

In summary, we have two tools for evaluating the cost of a recursive procedure: the recursion tree and the recurrence equation. They are different representations of the same information. Several techniques have been developed to evaluate commonly occurring forms of these trees and equations. Even if a situation arises that does not fit a standard form, the recursion tree still expresses the correct solution of the recurrence equation; it just may be difficult to evaluate.

⋆ 3.7.3 Why Recursion Trees Work

This section explains the connection between the recursion tree for a given recurrence equation and a programmed function to calculate the solution by recursion. It can be omitted without loss of continuity.

One way to visualize the recursion tree is to imagine that we actually programmed a simple recursive function (call it evalT(k)) to evaluate some recurrence equation, such as Equations 3.2 through 3.5. The activation tree for the programmed function corresponds very exactly to the recursion tree. The recurrence equation looks like $T(k) = f(k) + \ldots$ (terms with T). We assume our recursive function evalT has one parameter, k, that represents problem size, and a local variable nonrecCost to store the computed value of nonrecursive cost (i.e., $f(k)$). Ignoring the base case, the code of evalT(k) is assumed to be

> nonrecCost = $f(k)$;
> **return** nonrecCost + ... (terms with evalT);

where the terms with evalT just mimic the terms with T on the right side of the recurrence equation.

The *recursion tree* for that recurrence equation, with $T(n)$ at the root, would be the *activation tree* for evalT(n). (This assumes that the nonrecursive cost function, $f(k)$, can be evaluated with simple statements.)

The essential insight is that the sum of all nonrecCost values throughout the tree is exactly the value returned to top level. We assume the top-level call is evalT(n), to compute the value of $T(n)$ for the recurrence equation.

Exercises

Section 3.2   Recursive Procedures

3.1   Show that every 2-tree (Definition 3.2) with n internal nodes has $n + 1$ external nodes.

3.2   In Lemma 3.7 we used the fact that $x \lg(x)$ is convex. Prove this.

3.3   Show that the external path length *epl* in a 2-tree with m external nodes satisfies $epl \leq \frac{1}{2}(m^2 + m - 2)$. Conclude that $epl \leq \frac{1}{2}n(n + 3)$ for a 2-tree with n internal nodes.

3.4   Equation (1.13) defined the Fibonacci sequence as $F(n) = F(n - 1) + F(n - 2)$ for $n \geq 2$, $F(0) = 0$, and $F(1) = 1$. Prove (by induction) the correct statement between the following:

1. For $n \geq 1$, $F(n) \leq 100 \left(\frac{3}{2}\right)^n$.

2. For $n \geq 1$, $F(n) \geq .01 \left(\frac{3}{2}\right)^n$.

The constants have been chosen to make it hard to guess which statement is correct—you will have to rely on your proof.

Section 3.5   Proving Correctness of Procedures

3.5   Consider this procedure, which takes two arrays as parameters:

```
shiftAdd(int[] A, int[] B)
    A[0] = B[0];
    B[0] ++;
    return;
```

Assuming no integer overflow occurs, is it necessarily true that $A[0] < B[0]$?

3.6   In this exercise all integers are considered to be nonnegative, for simplicity. A *divisor* of an integer k is any integer $d \neq 0$ such that k/d has no remainder. A *common divisor* for a set of integers is an integer that is a divisor for each integer in the set. Euclid's algorithm for finding the greatest common divisor (GCD) of two nonnegative integers, m and n, can be written without using division, as follows:

```
int  gcd(int m, int n)
        int  ans;
1.  if (m == 0)
2.      ans = n;
3.  else if (m > n)
4.      ans = gcd(n, m)
5.  else
6.      nLess = n−m;
7.      ans = gcd(m, nLess);
8.  return ans;
```

The preconditions for gcd(m, n) are that $m \geq 0$, $n \geq 0$, and at least one of m and n is positive. You will need a few (not too many) facts about arithmetic for the following proofs.

1. If $a > b$, then $a - c > b - c$. (See Equation (1.20) for other variations.)
2. If d is a divisor of k, then d is a divisor of $k - d$ and $k + d$. (However, you have to check separately whether $k - d < 0$.)
3. If d is a divisor of k, then $d \leq k$ or $k = 0$.

Prove the following using induction and the lemmas of Section 3.5.2, as needed.

a.   If the preconditions of gcd(m, n) are satisfied, then the value that the function returns is *some* common divisor of m and n.

★ **b.**   If the preconditions of gcd(m, n) are satisfied, then the value that the function returns is the *greatest* common divisor of m and n.

Section 3.6 Recurrence Equations

3.7 Suppose that the function M is defined for all powers of 2 and is described by the following recurrence equation and base case:

$$M(n) = n - 1 + 2\,M(n/2)$$
$$M(1) = 0.$$

a. What is the asymptotic order of $M(n)$?

b. Find an exact solution for M when n is a power of 2.

3.8 Suppose W satisfies the following recurrence equation and base case (where c is a constant):

$$W(n) = cn + W(\lfloor n/2 \rfloor)$$
$$W(1) = 1.$$

What is the asymptotic order of $W(n)$?

$\star$ **3.9** Another approach to solving divide-and-conquer recurrence equations involves changes of variables and function transformations. This is a long exercise involving some complicated mathematics; its last part gives a generalization of the Master Theorem.

The starting equation, as in Theorem 3.17, is

$$T(n) = b\,T\left(\frac{n}{c}\right) + f(n).$$

First, we will limit ourselves to n of the form $n = c^k$, and assume that $T(1) = f(1)$. The variable k will be a nonnegative integer throughout this exercise. We perform a change of variables by defining $U(k) = T(c^k)$ for all k. Then we perform a function transformation by defining $V(k) = U(k)/b^k$ for all k.

a. Derive the recurrence equation for $U(k)$, and determine the value of $U(0)$. The variable n should be completely eliminated.

b. Derive a recurrence equation for $V(k)$, and determine the value of $V(0)$. The left-hand side of the equation should be $V(k)$, and the right-hand side should be reasonably simplified.

c. Re-express the recurrence equation for V as $V(i)$, introducing i as an auxiliary variable. Then express $V(k)$ as a certain sum from $i = 0$ to k.

d. Let $E = \lg(b)/\lg(c)$, as in Theorem 3.17, for the rest of this exercise. Show that if $m = c^i$, then $m^E = b^i$.

e. Suppose $f(m) \in \Theta(m^E)$. Note that this is case 2 of the Master Theorem. (We have introduced m as an auxiliary variable to avoid confusion with n, which we want in the final answer.) Find the asymptotic order of $V(k)$.

f. Convert your expression for $V(k)$ in part (e) into an expression for $U(k)$, and then for $T(n)$. (It should agree with case 2 of the Master Theorem. Part (d) can help.)

g. Now suppose $f(m) \in \Theta(m^E \log^a(m))$, where E is defined as in Theorem 3.17, for some positive constant a. (Note that $\log^a(m) = (\log m)^a$.) Find the asymptotic order of $V(k)$.

h. Convert your expression for $V(k)$ in part (g) into an expression for $U(k)$, and then for $T(n)$. Conclude that when $f(m) \in \Theta(m^E \log^a(m))$, the solution for the divide-and-conquer recurrence is

$$T(n) \in \Theta\left(n^E \log^{a+1}(n)\right). \tag{3.14}$$

This is the generalization of case 2 of the Master Theorem. (Which special case of Equation (3.14) gives case 2 of the Master Theorem?)

3.10 Find the asymptotic order of the solutions for the following recurrence equations. You may assume $T(1) = 1$, the recurrence is for $n > 1$, and c is some positive constant. For some of these, Equation (3.14) is needed, and it may be used without proving it.

a. $T(n) = T(n/2) + c \lg n$.

b. $T(n) = T(n/2) + cn$.

c. $T(n) = 2T(n/2) + cn$.

d. $T(n) = 2T(n/2) + cn \lg n$.

e. $T(n) = 2T(n/2) + cn^2$.

$\star$ **3.11** Consider the chip-and-be-conquered recurrence equation

$$T(n) = b_1 T(n-1) + b_2 T(n-2) + \cdots + b_k T(n-k) + f(n) \quad \text{for } n \geq k \tag{3.15}$$

for some constant $k \geq 2$. The coefficients b_i are nonnegative; some may be zero. For example, the Fibonacci recurrence, Equation (1.13), corresponds to $k = 2$, $b_1 = b_2 = 1$, and $f(n) = 0$.

The *characteristic equation* for the above recurrence equation is

$$x^k - b_1 x^{k-1} - b_2 x^{k-2} - \cdots - b_k = 0. \tag{3.16}$$

$\star$ **a.** (This part requires advanced calculus and some theory of polynomials.) Show that Equation (3.16) has exactly one positive real root, and that root is greater than 1 if and only if $(b_1 + \cdots + b_k) > 1$. Also, show that the magnitude of any root is at most the size of the positive root.

b. Suppose r is a solution of Equation (3.16). Show that $T(n) = r^n$ is a solution of Equation (3.16) if $f(n) = 0$ and the base cases are $T(i) = r^i$ for $0 \leq i < k$.

c. Let r be the positive solution of Equation (3.16). Conclude that if $(b_1 + \cdots + b_k) > 1$ and $T(i) \geq 1$ for $0 \leq i < k$ and $f(n) \geq 0$, then $T(n) \in \Omega(r^n)$. You can use earlier parts of this exercise even if you did not prove them.

d. Define $\phi = \frac{1}{2}(1 + \sqrt{5})$; this is known as the *Golden Ratio* and is about 1.618. Show that the solution of the Fibonacci recurrence, Equation (1.13), is in $\Theta(\phi^n)$. You can use earlier parts of this exercise even if you did not prove them.

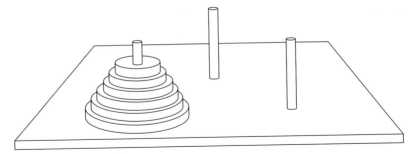

Figure 3.12 Towers of Hanoi

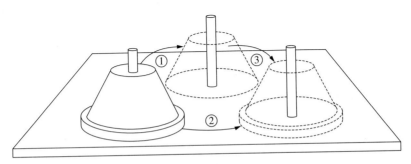

Figure 3.13 Moving the disks

Additional Problems

3.12 The Towers of Hanoi problem is often used as an example when teaching recursion. Six disks of different sizes are piled on a peg in order by size, with the largest at the bottom, as shown in Figure 3.12. There are two empty pegs. The problem is to move all the disks to the third peg by moving only one at a time and never placing a disk on top of a smaller one. The second peg may be used for intermediate moves. The usual solution recursively moves all but the last disk from the starting peg to the spare peg, then moves the remaining disk on the start peg to the destination peg, and then recursively moves all the others from the spare peg to the destination peg. The three steps are illustrated in Figure 3.13 and described in the following procedure.

```
hanoi(numberOfDisks, start, destination, spare)
/** Objective: move numberOfDisks from top of start peg
 * to top of destination peg, using spare peg as buffer. */
    if (numberOfDisks > 0)
        hanoi(numberOfDisks−1, start, spare, destination);
        Move top disk from peg start to peg destination.
        hanoi(numberOfDisks−1, spare, destination, start);
    return
```

Write a recurrence equation for the number of moves done. Then solve it.

3.13 Consider a general tree T (Section 2.3.4) in which each vertex v has a *weight*, v.wgt, associated with it. An *independent set* of vertices is a set I such that there is no edge in T between any two vertices in I; in other words, if vertex $v \in I$ then neither the parent of v nor any of the children of v are in I. The *weight* of a set of vertices is the sum of their individual weights. The goal of this exercise is to design a function that computes the maximum weight of any independent set of vertices in the tree T. (Although your function does not need to identify an independent set that has this maximum weight, it will be easy to modify it to do so.)

The key to an efficient design is to consider two restricted collections of independent sets for T: those that *include* the root of T and those that *exclude* the root of T. Let takeWgt denote the maximum weight of any independent set in T that *includes* the root of T, and let dropWgt denote the maximum weight of any independent set in T that *excludes* the root of T.

a. Give a recursive definition for takeWgt for T in terms of root(T).wgt and the values of takeWgt and dropWgt for the principal subtrees of T.

b. Give a recursive definition for dropWgt for T in terms of the values of takeWgt and dropWgt for the principal subtrees of T.

c. Design a function (clear pseudocode is okay, even preferred) based on the tree traversal skeleton of Figure 2.13 that computes takeWgt and dropWgt. Use an organizer class with those two fields so that your function can return both quantities. If you are careful, you won't need any arrays or global variables.

d. Analyze the time and space requirements of your function.

Notes and References

Perlis (1978) credits McCarthy with advocating that the design of Algol 60 should include recursion. The importance of recursion in program design is stressed in Roberts (1997), where the topic is treated thoroughly.

Gries (1981) is concerned with proving correctness of programs and techniques for writing programs that make them more likely to be correct. Hantler and King (1976) is a survey of both formal and informal techniques for proving program correctness. Sethi (1996) describes proof rules for partial correctness in some detail. Kingston (1997) considers proof techniques for algorithms. Practical difficulties in proving correctness are discussed by De Millo, Lipton, and Perlis (1979). Grassmann and Tremblay (1996) discuss induction on numerous sets other than the natural numbers.

There are numerous articles on Sisal, a single-assignment language for parallel programming, one of the earlier ones being Oldehoeft, Cann, and Allan (1986). Cytron, Ferrante, Rosen, Wegman, and Zadeck (1991) discuss the advantages of single-assignment form for program analysis, and describe an algorithm for converting a procedure into static single-assignment form. This form is now a popular tool for compiler optimization and automatic code parallelization.

The use of recursion trees and the Master Theorem (Theorem 3.17) for evaluating recurrence equations are based on Cormen, Leiserson, and Rivest (1990). Aho, Hopcroft, and Ullman (1983) contains an excellent discussion of the structure of solutions for recurrence equations. For more advanced mathematical tools for analysis of algorithms, see Purdom and Brown (1985), Lueker (1980), and Greene and Knuth (1990).

4

Sorting

4.1   Introduction

In this chapter we will study several algorithms for sorting, that is, for arranging the elements of a set into order. The problem of sorting a set of objects was one of the first intensely studied computer science problems. Many of the best-known applications of the Divide-and-Conquer algorithm design paradigm are sorting algorithms. During the 1960s, when commercial data processing became automated on a large scale, the sort program was the most frequently run program at many computer installations. One software company stayed in business for years on the strength of its better sort program. With today's hardware, the performance issues of sorting have shifted somewhat. In the 1960s, transferring data between slow storage (tape or disk) and main memory was a major performance bottleneck. Main memory was in the neighborhood of 100,000 bytes, and files to be sorted were orders of magnitude larger. Algorithms to perform this kind of sorting were the main focus of attention. Today, main memories 1,000 times that size (i.e., 100 megabytes) are commonplace, and 10,000 times that size (a few gigabytes) are available. So most files can fit in main memory.

There are several good reasons for studying sorting algorithms. First, they are of practical use because sorting is done often. Just as having the entries in telephone books and dictionaries in alphabetical order makes them easy to use, working with large sets of data in computers is facilitated when the data are sorted. Second, quite a lot of sorting algorithms have been devised (more than will be covered here), and studying a number of them should impress upon you the fact that you can take many different points of view toward the same problem. The discussion of the algorithms in this chapter should provide some insights on the questions of how to improve a given algorithm and how to choose among several. Third, sorting is one of few problems for which we can easily derive strong lower bounds for worst case and average behavior. The bounds are strong in the sense that there are algorithms that do approximately the minimum amount of work specified. Thus we have essentially optimal sorting algorithms.

In the descriptions of most of the algorithms, we assume the set to be sorted is stored as an array, so that the element at any position can be accessed at any time; this is called *random access*. However, some of the algorithms are useful for sorting files and linked lists, as well. When the set is only accessed in a sequential fashion, we use the term *sequence*, to emphasize that the structure might be a linked list or sequential file, as well as an array. If an array is defined over the range of indexes $0, \ldots, n-1$, then a *range* or *subrange* of that array is a contiguous sequence of entries between two specified indexes, first and last, such that $0 \leq$ first and last $\leq n-1$. If last $<$ first, the range is said to be *empty*.

We assume that each element in the set to be sorted contains an identifier, called a *key*, which is an element of some linearly ordered set, and that two keys can be compared to determine which is larger or that they are equal. We always sort keys into nondecreasing order. Each element in the set might contain other information aside from the key. When keys are rearranged during the sorting process, the associated information is also rearranged as appropriate, but sometimes we refer only to the keys and make no explicit mention of the rest of the entry.

The algorithms considered in Sections 4.2 through 4.10 are all from the class of sorting algorithms that may compare keys (and copy them) but must not do other operations on the keys. We call these "algorithms that sort by comparison of keys," or "comparison-based algorithms," for short. The measure of work primarily used for analyzing algorithms in this class is the number of comparisons of keys. In Section 4.7, lower bounds on the number of comparisons performed by such algorithms are established. Section 4.11 discusses sorting algorithms for which operations other than comparisons of keys are available, and for which different measures of work are appropriate.

The algorithms in this chapter are called *internal sorts* because the data are assumed to be in the computer's high-speed, random-access memory. Different performance issues arise for sorting data sets that are too large to fit in memory. Algorithms for sorting large sets of data stored on external, slower storage devices with restrictions on the way data are accessed are called *external sorts*. See Notes and References at the end of the chapter for sources on such algorithms.

When analyzing sorting algorithms, we will consider how much extra space they use (in addition to the input). If the amount of extra space is constant with respect to the input size, the algorithm is said to work *in place*.

To help make the algorithms as clear as possible, we use Element and Key as type identifiers, but treat Key as a numeric type in that we use the relational operators "$=, \neq, <$," and so on. When the book has a key-comparison expression like "E[i].key < x," if the actual types are nonnumeric (**String**, for example), a Java program requires syntax involving a method call, such as "less(E[i].key, x)." This holds for many languages besides Java.

Java sidelight: By means of the **Comparable** interface in Java, it is possible to write one procedure that is able to compare a wide variety of key types. The type name Key would be replaced by the key word **Comparable**. Some details are given in Appendix A. Recall that an array with entries of type Element is declared as

```
Element[] arrayName;
```

in Java.

4.2 Insertion Sort

Insertion Sort is a good sorting algorithm to begin with because the idea behind it is a natural and general one, and its worst-case and average-behavior analyses are easy. It is also used as part of a faster sorting algorithm that we describe in Section 4.10.

4.2.1 The Strategy

We begin with a sequence E of n elements in arbitrary order, as illustrated by Figure 4.1. (Insertion Sort can be used on keys from any linearly ordered set, but for the stick figure illustrations, think of the keys as the heights of the sticks, which are the elements.)

Suppose we have sorted some initial segment of the sequence. Figure 4.2 shows a snapshot of the sequence after the five elements on the left end have been sorted. The

Figure 4.1 Unsorted elements

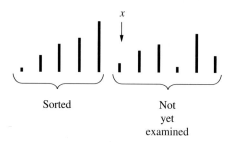

Sorted

Not
yet
examined

Figure 4.2 Partially sorted elements

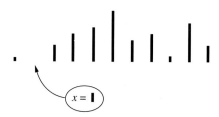

$x = $

Figure 4.3 Insertion of x in proper order

general step is to increase the length of the sorted segment by inserting the next element in its proper place.

Let x be the next element to be inserted in the sorted segment, that is, x is the leftmost element in the unexamined segment. First we pull x "out of the way" (that is, copy it to a local variable), leaving a *vacancy* in its former position. Then we repeatedly compare x to the element just to the left of the vacancy, and as long as x is smaller, we move the that element *into* the vacancy, thereby leaving a vacancy where it was. That is, the vacancy shifts one place to the left. This process stops when we run out of elements to the left of the current vacancy, or when the element to the left of the current vacancy is smaller than or equal to x. Then x is inserted in the vacancy, as shown in Figure 4.3. To get the algorithm started, we need only observe that the first element alone can be considered a sorted segment. As we formalize this into a procedure, we assume the sequence is an array; however, the idea works with lists and other sequential structures.

int shiftVac(Element[] E, **int** vacant, Key x)

Precondition: vacant is nonnegative.

Postconditions: Let xLoc be the value returned to the caller. Then:

1. Elements in E at indexes less than xLoc are in their original positions and have keys less than or equal to x.

2. Elements in E at positions xLoc $+ 1, \ldots,$ vacant are greater than x and were shifted up by one position from their positions when shiftVac was invoked.

Figure 4.4   Specifications for shiftVac

4.2.2   The Algorithm and Analysis

We now spell out the sorting procedure in more detail. Let the subroutine shiftVac(E, vacant, x) have the job of shifting elements until the vacancy is at the correct position in which to place x among the sorted elements. The procedure returns the index of the vacancy, say xLoc, to the caller. The preconditions and postconditions are stated in Figure 4.4. In other words, shiftVac makes the transition from Figure 4.2 to Figure 4.3. Now insertionSort can just keep calling shiftVac, making a longer and longer sorted segment at the left end, until all elements are in the sorted segment.

The shiftVac procedure takes a typical form for *generalized searching routines* (Definition 1.12). If there is no more data to look at, fail; else look at one data item, and if it is what we are looking for, succeed; otherwise continue with the unexamined data. Because there are two terminating cases, this can be awkward for a **while** loop, unless a **break** is used for one or more of the terminating cases. The recursive formulation is straightforward.

```
int shiftVacRec(Element[] E, int vacant, Key x)
      int xLoc;
 1.  if (vacant == 0)
 2.      xLoc = vacant;
 3.  else if (E[vacant−1].key ≤ x)
 4.      xLoc = vacant;
 5.  else
 6.      E[vacant] = E[vacant−1];
 7.      xLoc = shiftVacRec(E, vacant−1, x);
 8.  return xLoc;
```

To verify that we are using recursion properly on line 7, we note that the recursive call is working on a smaller range, and its second argument is nonnegative, so the precondition (stated in Figure 4.4) is satisfied. (You should check the chain of reasoning for why vacant $- 1$ is nonnegative—why can't it be negative?) Correctness is now straightforward if we remember that we can *assume* that the recursive call on line 7 accomplishes its objective.

Although the procedure for shiftVacRec is very simple, if we visualize the activation trace for the nth element of E to be inserted, we realize that the depth of recursion, or the frame stack, could grow to size n. This could be undesirable for large n. Therefore this is a case where the recursion should be changed into an iteration, after we are sure everything is working correctly. (Trying to optimize a nonworking program is surely an exercise in futility.) The purpose is not so much to save time as to conserve space. Actually, many compilers, if told to optimize shiftVacRec, will perform this transformation automatically. The full algorithm below includes the iteratively coded version of shiftVac.

Algorithm 4.1   Insertion Sort

Input: E, an array of elements, and $n \geq 0$, the number of elements. The range of indexes is $0, \ldots, n - 1$.

Output: E, with elements in nondecreasing order of their keys.

Remark: The specifications for the shiftVac subroutine are given in Figure 4.4.

```
void  insertionSort(Element[] E, int n)
    int  xindex;
    for (xindex = 1; xindex < n; xindex ++)
        Element  current = E[xindex];
        Key  x = current.key;
        int  xLoc = shiftVac(E, xindex, x);
        E[xLoc] = current;
    return;

int  shiftVac(Element[] E, int xindex, Key x)
    int  vacant, xLoc;
    vacant = xindex;
    xLoc = 0;  // Assume failure.
    while (vacant > 0)
        if (E[vacant−1].key ≤ x)
            xLoc = vacant;  // Succeed.
            break;
        E[vacant] = E[vacant−1];
        vacant −−;  // Keep looking.
    return xLoc;
```

Worst-Case Complexity

For the analysis, we use i for xindex. For each value of i, the maximum number of key comparisons possible (in one call to the iterative shiftVac, or one top-level call of the recursive shiftVacRec) is i. Thus the total is

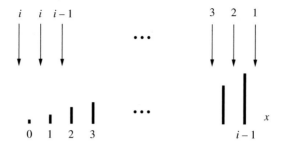

Figure 4.5 Number of comparisons needed to determine the position for x

$$W(n) \le \sum_{i=1}^{n-1} i = \frac{n(n-1)}{2}.$$

Note that we have established an upper bound on the worst-case behavior; it takes a moment of thought to verify that there are indeed inputs for which $n(n-1)/2$ comparisons are done. One such worst case is when the keys are in reverse (i.e., decreasing) order. So

$$W(n) = \frac{n(n-1)}{2} \in \Theta(n^2).$$

Average Behavior

We assume that all permutations of the keys are equally likely as input. We will first determine how many key comparisons are done on the average to insert one new element into the sorted segment, that is, one call of shiftVac, for any particular value of i (used for xindex). To simplify the analysis, we assume that the keys are distinct. (The analysis is very similar to that done for the Sequential Search algorithm in Chapter 1.)

There are $i + 1$ positions where x may go. Figure 4.5 shows how many comparisons are done depending on the position.

The probability that x belongs in any one specific position is $1/(i + 1)$. (This depends on the fact that x has not been examined earlier by the algorithm. If the algorithm had made any earlier decisions based on the value of x, we could not necessarily assume that x is uniformly random with respect to the first i keys.) Thus the average number of comparisons in shiftVac to find the location for the ith element is

$$\frac{1}{i+1} \sum_{j=1}^{i} j + \frac{1}{i+1}(i) = \frac{i}{2} + \frac{i}{i+1} = \frac{i}{2} + 1 - \frac{1}{i+1}.$$

Now, adding for all $n - 1$ insertions,

$$A(n) = \sum_{i=1}^{n-1} \left(\frac{i}{2} + 1 - \frac{1}{i+1} \right) = \frac{n(n-1)}{4} + n - 1 - \sum_{j=2}^{n} \frac{1}{j},$$

where we substituted $j = i + 1$ to get the last sum. We saw from Equation (1.16) that $\sum_{j=1}^{n}(1/j) \approx \ln n$, and we can incorporate the 1 preceding the sum to make the lower limit $j = 1$. Ignoring lower-order terms, we have

$$A(n) \approx \frac{n^2}{4} \in \Theta(n^2).$$

Space

Clearly, Insertion Sort is an in-place sort with the iterative version of shiftVac. With the recursive version the frame stack can grow to $\Theta(n)$.

4.2.3   Lower Bounds on the Behavior of Certain Sorting Algorithms

Think of the element whose key is x as occupying the "vacant" position in the array while Insertion Sort compares x to the key to its left. Then after each comparison, Insertion Sort either moves no elements or simply interchanges two adjacent elements. We will show that all sorting algorithms that do such limited, "local" moving of elements after each comparison must do about the same amount of work as Insertion Sort.

A permutation on n elements can be described by a one-to-one function from the set $N = \{1, 2, \ldots, n\}$ onto itself. There are $n!$ distinct permutations on n elements. Let the elements in the unsorted sequence E be $x_1, x_2, \ldots, x_n$. To simplify the notation in this discussion, let's assume that the elements to be sorted are stored in positions $1, \ldots, n$ of E, rather than in $0, \ldots, n - 1$. There is a permutation π such that, for $1 \leq i \leq n$, $\pi(i)$ is the correct position of x_i when the sequence is sorted. Without loss of generality, we can assume that the keys are the integers $1, 2, \ldots, n$ since we can substitute 1 for the smallest key, 2 for the next smallest, and so on, without causing any changes in the instructions carried out by the algorithm. Then the unsorted input is $\pi(1), \pi(2), \ldots, \pi(n)$. For example, consider the input sequence 2, 4, 1, 5, 3. $\pi(1) = 2$ means that the first key, 2, belongs in the second position, which it clearly does. $\pi(2) = 4$ because the second key, 4, belongs in the fourth position, and so on. We will identify the permutation π with the sequence $\pi(1), \pi(2), \ldots, \pi(n)$.

An *inversion* of the permutation π is a pair $(\pi(i), \pi(j))$ such that $i < j$ and $\pi(i) > \pi(j)$. If $(\pi(i), \pi(j))$ is an inversion, the ith and jth keys in the sequence are out of order relative to each other. For example, the permutation 2, 4, 1, 5, 3 has four inversions (2, 1), (4, 1), (4, 3), and (5, 3). If a sorting algorithm removes at most one inversion after each key comparison (say, by interchanging adjacent elements, as Insertion Sort does), then the number of comparisons performed on the input $\pi(1), \pi(2), \ldots, \pi(n)$ is at least the number of inversions of π. So we investigate inversions.

It is easy to show that there is a permutation that has $n(n - 1)/2$ inversions. (Which permutation?) Thus the worst-case behavior of any sorting algorithm that removes at most one inversion per key comparison must be in $\Omega(n^2)$.

To get a lower bound on the average number of comparisons done by such sorting algorithms, we compute the average number of inversions in permutations. Each permutation π can be paired off with its *transpose permutation* $\pi(n), \pi(n - 1), \ldots, \pi(1)$. For example, the transpose of 2, 4, 1, 5, 3 is 3, 5, 1, 4, 2. Each permutation has a unique transpose and is distinct from its transpose (for $n > 1$). Let i and j be integers between 1 and n, and suppose $j < i$. Then (i, j) is an inversion in exactly one of the permutations π and transpose of π. There are $n(n - 1)/2$ such pairs of integers. Hence each pair of permutations has $n(n - 1)/2$ inversions between them, and therefore an average of $n(n - 1)/4$. Thus, overall, the average number of inversions in a permutation is $n(n - 1)/4$, and we have proved the following theorem.

Theorem 4.1   Any algorithm that sorts by comparison of keys and removes at most one inversion after each comparison must do at least $n(n - 1)/2$ comparisons in the worst case and at least $n(n - 1)/4$ comparisons on the average (for n elements).   □

Since Insertion Sort does $n(n - 1)/2$ key comparisons in the worst case and approximately $n^2/4$ on the average, it is about the best we can do with any algorithm that works "locally," for example, interchanging only adjacent elements. It is, of course, not obvious at this point that any other strategy can do better, but if there are significantly faster algorithms they must move elements more than one position at a time.

4.3 Divide and Conquer

The principle behind the Divide-and-Conquer algorithm design paradigm is that it is (often) easier to solve several small instances of a problem than one large one. Algorithms in Sections 4.4 through 4.8 use the Divide-and-Conquer approach. They *divide* the problem into smaller instances of the same problem (in this case into smaller sets to be sorted), then solve (*conquer*) the smaller instances recursively (i.e., by the same method), and finally *combine* the solutions to obtain the solution for the original input. To escape from the recursion, we solve some small instances of the problem directly. In contrast, Insertion Sort just "chipped off" one element and created one subproblem.

We have already seen one prime example of Divide and Conquer—Binary Search (Section 1.6). The main problem was divided into two subproblems, one of which did not even have to be solved.

In general, we can describe Divide and Conquer by the skeleton procedure in Figure 4.6.

To design a specific Divide-and-Conquer algorithm, we must specify the subroutines directlySolve, divide, and combine. The number of smaller instances into which the input is divided is k. For an input of size n, let $B(n)$ be the number of steps done by directlySolve, let $D(n)$ be the number of steps done by divide, and let $C(n)$ be the number of steps done by combine. Then the general form of the recurrence equation that describes the amount of work done by the algorithm is

$$T(n) = D(n) + \sum_{i=1}^{k} T(size(I_i)) + C(n) \qquad \text{for } n > \text{smallSize}$$

```
solve(I)
    n = size(I);
    if (n ≤ smallSize)
        solution = directlySolve(I);
    else
        divide I into I₁, . . . , Iₖ.
        for each i ∈ {1, . . . , k}:
            Sᵢ = solve(Iᵢ);
        solution = combine(S₁, . . . , Sₖ);
    return solution;
```

Figure 4.6   The Divide-and-Conquer skeleton.

with base cases $T(n) = B(n)$ for $n \leq$ smallSize. For many Divide-and-Conquer algorithms, either the divide step or the combine step is very simple, and the recurrence equation for T is simpler than the general form. The Master Theorem (Theorem 3.17) gives solutions for a wide range of Divide-and-Conquer recurrence equations.

Quicksort and Mergesort, the sorting algorithms presented in the next few sections, differ in the ways they divide the problem and later combine the solutions, or sorted subsets. Quicksort is characterized as "hard division, easy combination," while Mergesort is characterized as "easy division, hard combination." Aside from the bookkeeping of procedure calls, we will see that all the "real work" is done in the "hard" section. Both sorting procedures have subroutines to do their "hard" section, and these subroutines are useful in their own rights. For Quicksort, the workhorse is partition, and it is the divide step in the general framework; the combine step does nothing. For Mergesort, the workhorse is merge, and it is the combine step; the divide step does one simple calculation. Both algorithms divide the problem into two subproblems. However, with Mergesort, those two subproblems are of equal size (within a margin of one element), whereas with Quicksort, an even subdivision is not assured. This difference leads to markedly different performance characteristics, which will be discovered during analysis of the respective algorithms.

At the top level, HeapSort (Section 4.8) is not a Divide-and-Conquer algorithm, but uses heap operations that are in the Divide-and-Conquer category. The accelerated form of Heapsort uses a more sophisticated Divide-and-Conquer algorithm.

In later chapters, the Divide-and-Conquer strategy will come up in numerous problems. In Chapter 5, it is applied to the problem of finding the median element of a set. (The general problem is called the selection problem.) In Chapter 6, we will use Divide and Conquer in the form of binary search trees, and their balanced versions, red-black trees. In Chapter 9, we will apply it to problems of paths in graphs, such as transitive closure. In Chapter 12, we will use it on several matrix and vector problems. In Chapter 13, we will apply it to approximate graph coloring. In Chapter 14, it reappears in a slightly different form for parallel computation.

4.4   Quicksort

Quicksort is one of the earlier Divide-and-Conquer algorithms to be discovered; it was published by C. A. R. Hoare in 1962. It is still one of the fastest in practice.

4.4.1   The Quicksort Strategy

Quicksort's strategy is to rearrange the elements to be sorted so that all the "small" keys precede the "large" keys in the array (the "hard division" part). Then Quicksort sorts the two subranges of "small" and "large" keys recursively, with the result that the entire array is sorted. For an array implementation there is nothing to do in the "combination" step, but Quicksort can also work on lists (see Exercise 4.22), in which case the "combination" step concatenates the two lists. We describe the array implementation for simplicity.

Let E be the array of elements and let first and last be the indexes of the first and last entries, respectively, in the subrange Quicksort is currently sorting. At the top level first $= 0$ and last $= n - 1$, where n is the number of elements.

The Quicksort algorithm chooses an element, called the *pivot element*, whose key is called the pivot, from the subrange that it must sort, and "pulls it out of the way"; that is, it moves the pivot element to a local variable, leaving a *vacancy* in the array. For the moment we assume that the leftmost element in the subrange is chosen as the pivot element.

Quicksort passes the pivot (the key field only) to the Partition subroutine, which rearranges the *other* elements, finding an index splitPoint such that:

1.   for first $\leq$ i < splitPoint, E[i].key < pivot;
2.   and for splitPoint < i $\leq$ last, E[i].key $\geq$ pivot.

Notice that there is now a *vacancy* at splitPoint.

Then Quicksort deposits the pivot element in E[splitPoint], which is its correct position, and the pivot element is ignored in the subsequent sorting. (See Figure 4.7.) This completes the "divide" process, and Quicksort continues by calling itself recursively to solve the two subproblems created by Partition.

The Quicksort procedure may choose to partition around any key in the array between E[first] and E[last], as a preprocessing step. Whatever element is chosen is moved to a local variable named pivot, and if it is *not* E[first], then E[first] is moved into its position, ensuring that there is a vacancy at E[first] when Partition is called. Other strategies for choosing a pivot are explored in Section 4.4.4.

Algorithm 4.2   Quicksort

Input: Array E and indexes first, and last, such that elements E[i] are defined for first $\leq$ i $\leq$ last.

Output: E[first], . . ., E[last] is a sorted rearrangement of the same elements.

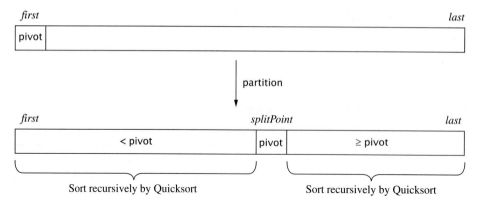

Figure 4.7   Quicksort

```
void quickSort(Element[] E, int first, int last)
    if (first < last)
        Element  pivotElement = E[first];
        Key  pivot = pivotElement.key;
        int  splitPoint = partition(E, pivot, first, last);
        E[splitPoint] = pivotElement;
        quickSort (E, first, splitPoint − 1);
        quickSort (E, splitPoint + 1, last);
    return;
```

4.4.2 The Partition Subroutine

All the work of comparing keys and moving elements is done in the Partition subroutine. There are several different strategies that may be used by Partition; they yield algorithms with different advantages and disadvantages. We present one here and consider another in the exercises. The strategy hinges on how to carry out the rearrangement of elements. A very simple solution is to move elements into a temporary array, but the challenge is to rearrange them in place.

The partitioning method we now describe is essentially the method originally described by Hoare. As motivation, remember that the lower bound argument in Section 4.2.3 showed that, to improve on Insertion Sort, it is necessary to be able to move an element many positions after one compare. Here the vacancy is initially at E[first]. Given that we want small elements at the left end of the range, and that we want to move elements long distances whenever possible, it is very logical to start searching backward from E[last] for a small element, that is, an element less than pivot. When we find one, we move that element into the vacancy (which was at first). That leaves a new vacancy where the small element used to be; we call it highVac. The situation is illustrated in the first two array diagrams in Figure 4.8.

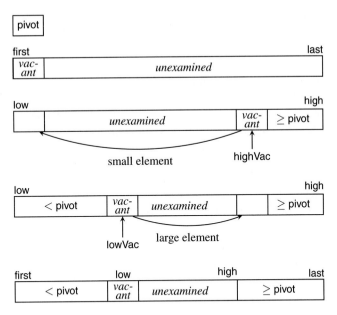

Figure 4.8 The progression of Partition through its first cycle

We know all the elements with indexes greater than highVac (through last) are greater than or equal to pivot. If possible, some other large element should be moved into highVac. Again, we want to move elements long distances, so it is logical to search forward for a *large* element this time, starting at first + 1. When we find one, we move that element into the vacancy (which was at highVac), and that leaves a new vacancy, which we call lowVac. We know all the elements with indexes less than lowVac (down to first) are less than pivot.

Finally, we update the variables low and high as indicated in the last row of Figure 4.8 to prepare for another cycle. As at the beginning of the first cycle, the elements in the range low+1 through high have not been examined yet, and E[low] is vacant. We can repeat the cycle just described, searching backward from high for a small element, moving it to the low vacancy, then searching forward from low+1 for a large element, and moving it to highVac, creating a vacancy at lowVac, the position from which the large element was moved. Eventually lowVac and highVac meet, meaning all elements have been compared with the pivot.

The Partition procedure is implemented as a repetition of the cycle just described, using subroutines to organize the code. The subroutine extendLargeRegion scans backward from the right end, passing over large elements until it either finds a small element and moves it into the vacancy at the left end, or runs into that vacancy without finding any small element. In the latter case, the partitioning is completed. In the former case, the new vacant position is returned, and the second subroutine is invoked. The subroutine extendSmallRegion is similar, except that it scans forward from the left end, passing over small elements, until it finds and moves a large element into the vacancy at the right end, or runs out of data.

Initially, the small-key region (left of low) and large-key region (right of high) are both empty, and the vacancy is at the left end of the middle region (which is the whole range at this point). Each call to a subroutine, extendLargeRegion or extendSmallRegion, shrinks the middle region by at least one, and shifts the vacancy to the other end of the middle region. The subroutines also ensure that only small elements go into the small-key region and only large elements go into the large-key region. This can be seen from their postconditions. When the middle region shrinks to one position, that position is the vacancy, and it is returned as splitPoint. It is left as an exercise to determine, line by line in the **while** loop of partition, what the boundaries are for the middle region and at which end the vacancy is located. Although the procedure for Partition can "make do" with fewer variables, each variable we define has its own meaning, and simplifies the answer for the exercise.

Algorithm 4.3   Partition

Input: Array E, pivot, the key around which to partition, and indexes first, and last, such that elements E[i] are defined for first $+ 1 \leq i \leq$ last and E[first] is vacant. It is assumed that first < last.

Output: Let splitPoint be the returned value. The elements originally in first+1, . . ., last are rearranged into two subranges, such that

1. the keys of E[first], . . ., E[splitPoint−1] are less than pivot, and
2. the keys of E[splitPoint+1], . . ., E[last] are greater than or equal to pivot.

Also, first $\leq$ splitPoint $\leq$ last, and E[splitPoint] is vacant.

Procedure: See Figure 4.9.   ■

To avoid extra comparisons inside the **while** loop in partition, there is no test for high−Vac = lowVac before line 5, which would indicate that all elements have been partitioned. Consequently, high might be one less than low when the loop terminates, when logically it should be equal. However, high is not accessed after the loop terminates, so this difference is harmless.

A small example is shown in Figure 4.10. The detailed operation of Partition is shown only the first time it is called. Notice that the smaller elements accumulate to the left of low and the larger elements accumulate to the right of high.

4.4.3   Analysis of Quicksort

Worst case

Partition compares each key to pivot, so if there are k positions in the range of the array it is working on, it does $k - 1$ key comparisons. (The first position is vacant.) If E[first] has the smallest key in the range being split then splitPoint = first, and all that has been accomplished is splitting the range into an empty subrange (keys smaller than pivot) and

```
int  partition(Element[] E, Key pivot, int first, int last)
     int  low, high;
1.   low = first; high = last;
2.   while (low < high)
3.        int  highVac = extendLargeRegion(E, pivot, low, high);
4.        int  lowVac = extendSmallRegion(E, pivot, low+1, highVac);
5.        low = lowVac; high = highVac − 1;
6.   return low;  // This is the splitPoint.
```

/** *Postcondition for extendLargeRegion:*
  * *The rightmost element in E[lowVac+1], . . . , E[high]*
  * *whose key is < pivot is moved to E[lowVac] and*
  * *the index from which it was moved is returned.*
  * *If there is no such element, lowVac is returned.*
  */

```
int  extendLargeRegion(Element[] E, Key pivot, int lowVac, int high)
     int  highVac, curr;
     highVac = lowVac;  // In case no key < pivot.
     curr = high;
     while (curr > lowVac)
        if (E[curr].key < pivot)
            E[lowVac] = E[curr];
            highVac = curr;
            break;
        curr −−;  // Keep looking.
     return highVac;
```

/** *Postcondition for extendSmallRegion:* (Exercise) */
```
int  extendSmallRegion(Element[] E, Key pivot, int low, int highVac)
     int  lowVac, curr;
     lowVac = highVac;  // In case no key ≥ pivot.
     curr = low;
     while (curr < highVac)
        if (E[curr].key ≥ pivot)
            E[highVac] = E[curr];
            lowVac = curr;
            break;
        curr ++;  // Keep looking.
     return lowVac;
```

Figure 4.9 Procedure for Algorithm 4.3

The keys

45	14	62	51	75	96	33	84	20

"Pulling out" the pivot

45 ⟵ pivot

___	14	62	51	75	96	33	84	20

The first execution of Partition

___	14	62	51	75	96	33	84	20	
↕low							high↕		beginning of **while** loop
20	14	62	51	75	96	33	84	___	
							hVac↕		after extendLargeRegion
20	14	___	51	75	96	33	84	62	
	lVac						hVac		after extendSmallRegion
20	14	___	51	75	96	33	84	62	
		↕low				↕high			beginning of **while** loop
20	14	33	51	75	96	___	84	62	
						↕hVac			after extendLargeRegion
20	14	33	___	75	96	51	84	62	
			lVac			hVac			after extendSmallRegion
20	14	33	___	75	96	51	84	62	
			↕low		↕high				beginning of **while** loop
20	14	33	___	75	96	51	84	62	
			↕hVac						after extendLargeRegion
20	14	33	___	75	96	51	84	62	
			lVac hVac						after extendSmallRegion
20	14	33	___	75	96	51	84	62	
		high	↕low						**while** loop exits
20	14	33	45	75	96	51	84	62	Place pivot in final position

Partition first section (details not shown)

14	20	33

Partition second section (details not shown)

75 ⟵ pivot

___	96	51	84	62
62	51	75	84	96

Partition left subsection

51	62

Partition right subsection

84	96

Final sequence

14	20	33	45	51	62	75	84	96

Figure 4.10 Example of Quicksort

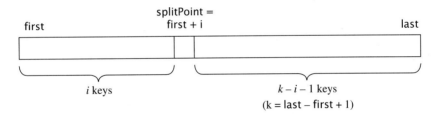

Figure 4.11   Average behavior of Quicksort.

a subrange with $k - 1$ elements. Thus, if pivot is the smallest key each time Partition is called, then the total number of key comparisons done is

$$\sum_{k=2}^{n}(k - 1) = \frac{n(n - 1)}{2}.$$

This is as bad as Insertion Sort and Maxsort (Exercise 4.1). And, strangely enough, the worst case occurs when the keys are already sorted in ascending order! Is the name Quicksort just a bit of false advertising?

Average Behavior

In Section 4.2.3 we showed that if a sorting algorithm removes at most one inversion from the permutation of the keys after each comparison, then it must do at least $(n^2 - n)/4$ comparisons on the average (Theorem 4.1). Quicksort, however, does not have this restriction. The Partition algorithm can move an element across a large section of the array, eliminating up to $n - 1$ inversions with one move. Quicksort deserves its name because of its average behavior.

We assume that the keys are distinct and that all permutations of the keys are equally likely. Let k be the number of elements in the range of the array being sorted, and let $A(k)$ be the average number of key comparisons done for ranges of this size. Suppose the next time Partition is executed pivot gets put in the ith position in this subrange (Figure 4.11), counting from 0. Partition does $k - 1$ key comparisons, and the subranges to be sorted next have i elements and $k - 1 - i$ elements, respectively.

It is important for our analysis that after Partition finishes, no two keys within the subrange (first, . . . , splitPoint − 1) have been compared to each other, so all permutations of keys in this subrange are still equally likely. The same holds for the subrange (splitPoint + 1, . . . , last). This justifies the following recurrence.

Each possible position for the split point i is equally likely (has probability $1/k$) so, letting $k = n$, we have the recurrence equation

$$A(n) = n - 1 + \sum_{i=0}^{n-1}\frac{1}{n}(A(i) + A(n - 1 - i)) \qquad \text{for } n \geq 2$$

$$A(1) = A(0) = 0.$$

Inspection of the terms in the sum lets us simplify the recurrence equation. The terms of the form $A(n-1-i)$ run from $A(n-1)$ down to $A(0)$, so their sum is the same as the sum of the $A(i)$ terms. Then we can drop the $A(0)$ terms, giving

$$A(n) = n - 1 + \frac{2}{n} \sum_{i=1}^{n-1} A(i) \qquad \text{for } n \geq 1. \tag{4.1}$$

This is a more complicated recurrence equation than the ones we saw earlier, because the value of $A(n)$ depends on all earlier values. We can try to use some ingenuity to solve the recurrence, or we can make a guess at the solution and prove it by induction. The latter technique is especially suitable for recursive algorithms. It is instructive to see both methods, so we will do both.

To form a guess for $A(n)$, let's consider a case in which Quicksort works quite well. Suppose that each time Partition is executed, it partitions the range into two equal subranges. Since we're just making an estimate to help guess how fast Quicksort is on the average, we will estimate the size of the two subranges at $n/2$ and not worry about whether this is an integer. The number of comparisons done is described by the recurrence equation

$$Q(n) \approx n + 2Q(n/2).$$

The Master Theorem (Theorem 3.17) can be applied: $b = 2$, $c = 2$, so $E = 1$, and $f(n) = n^1$. Therefore $Q(n) \in \Theta(n \log n)$. Thus if E[first] were close to the median each time the range is split, the number of comparisons done by Quicksort would be in $\Theta(n \log n)$. This is significantly better than $\Theta(n^2)$. But if all permutations of the keys are equally likely, are there enough "good" cases to affect the average? We prove that there are.

Theorem 4.2   Let $A(n)$ be defined by the recurrence equation Equation (4.1). Then, for $n \geq 1$, $A(n) \leq cn \ln n$ for some constant c. (*Note*: We have switched to the natural logarithm to simplify some of the computation in the proof. The value for c will be found in the proof.)

Proof   The proof is by induction on n, the number of elements to be sorted. The base case is $n = 1$. We have $A(1) = 0$ and $c1 \ln 1 = 0$.

For $n > 1$, assume that $A(i) \leq ci \ln(i)$ for $1 \leq i < n$, for the same constant c stated in the theorem. By Equation (4.1) and the induction hypothesis,

$$A(n) = n - 1 + \frac{2}{n} \sum_{i=1}^{n-1} A(i) \leq n - 1 + \frac{2}{n} \sum_{i=1}^{n-1} ci \ln(i).$$

We can bound the sum by integrating (see Equation 1.16):

$$\sum_{i=1}^{n-1} ci \ln(i) \leq c \int_{1}^{n} x \ln x \, dx.$$

Using Equation (1.15) from Section 1.3.2 gives

$$\int_1^n x \ln x \, dx = \tfrac{1}{2}n^2 \ln(n) - \frac{1}{4}n^2$$

so

$$A(n) \le n - 1 + \frac{2c}{n} \left(\tfrac{1}{2}n^2 \ln(n) - \frac{1}{4}n^2 \right)$$

$$= cn \ln n + n(1 - \frac{c}{2}) - 1.$$

To show that $A(n) \le cn \ln n$, it suffices to show that the second and third terms are negative or zero. The second term is less than or equal to zero for $c \ge 2$. So we can let $c = 2$ and conclude that $A(n) \le 2n \ln n$. $\square$

A similar analysis shows that $A(n) > cn \ln n$ for any $c < 2$. Since $\ln n \approx 0.693 \lg n$, we therefore have:

Corollary 4.3 On average, assuming all input permutations are equally likely, the number of comparisons done by Quicksort (Algorithm 4.2) on sets of size n is approximately $1.386 \, n \lg n$, for large n. $\square$

⋆ Average Behavior, More Exactly

Although we have established the average behavior of Quicksort, it is still instructive to return to the recurrence equation (Equation 4.1) and try to solve it directly, getting more than the leading term. This section uses some sophisticated mathematics, and can be omitted without loss of continuity.

We have, by Equation (4.1),

$$A(n) = n - 1 + \frac{2}{n} \sum_{i=1}^{n-1} A(i). \tag{4.2}$$

$$A(n - 1) = n - 2 + \frac{2}{n-1} \sum_{i=1}^{n-2} A(i). \tag{4.3}$$

If we subtract the summation in Equation (4.3) from the summation in Equation (4.2), most of the terms drop out. Since the summations are multiplied by different factors, we need a slightly more complicated bit of algebra. Informally, we compute

$$n \times \text{ Equation (4.2)} - (n-1) \times \text{ Equation (4.3)}.$$

So

$$nA(n) - (n-1)A(n-1) = n(n-1) + 2 \sum_{i=1}^{n-1} A(i) - (n-1)(n-2) - 2 \sum_{i=1}^{n-2} A(i)$$

$$= 2A(n-1) + 2(n-1).$$

So

$$\frac{A(n)}{n+1} = \frac{A(n-1)}{n} + \frac{2(n-1)}{n(n+1)}.$$

Now let

$$B(n) = \frac{A(n)}{n+1}.$$

The recurrence equation for B is

$$B(n) = B(n-1) + \frac{2(n-1)}{n(n+1)} \qquad B(1) = 0.$$

With the aid of Equation (1.11), we leave it for readers to verify that

$$B(n) = \sum_{i=1}^{n} \frac{2(i-1)}{i(i+1)} = 2\sum_{i=1}^{n} \frac{1}{i} - 4\sum_{i=1}^{n} \frac{1}{i(i+1)}$$

$$\approx 2(\ln n + 0.577) - 4n/(n+1).$$

Therefore

$$A(n) \approx 1.386\, n \lg n - 2.846\, n.$$

Space usage

At first glance it may seem that Quicksort is an in-place sort. It is not. While the algorithm is working on one subrange, the beginning and ending indexes (call them the borders) of all the other subranges yet to be sorted are saved on the frame stack, and the size of the stack depends on the number of subranges into which the range will be split. This, of course, depends on n. In the worst case, Partition splits off one entry at a time; the depth of the recursion is n. Thus the worst-case amount of space used by the stack is in $\Theta(n)$. One of the modifications to the algorithm described next can significantly reduce the maximum stack size.

4.4.4 Improvements on the Basic Quicksort Algorithm

Choice of Pivot

We have seen that Quicksort works well if the pivot key used by Partition to partition a segment belongs near the middle of the segment. (Its position is the value, splitPoint, returned by Partition.) Choosing E[first] as the pivot element causes Quicksort to do poorly in cases where sorting should be easy (for example, when the array is already sorted). There are several other strategies for choosing the pivot element. One is to choose a random integer q between first and last and let pivot = E[q].key. Another is to let pivot be the median key of the entries E[first], E[(first+last)/2], and E[last]. (In either case, the element in E[first] would be swapped with the pivot element before proceeding with the Partition algorithm.) Both of these strategies require some extra work to choose pivot, but they pay off by improving the average running time of a Quicksort program.

Alternative Partition Strategy

The version of Partition presented in the text does the fewest element movements, on average, compared to other partitioning strategies. It is shown with subroutines for clarity, and coding these in-line would save some overhead; however, some optimizing compilers can make this change automatically. Other optimization considerations are mentioned in Notes and References at the end of the chapter. There is an alternative version in the exercises that is easy to understand and program, but somewhat slower.

Small Sort

Quicksort is not particularly good for small sets, due to the overhead of procedure calls. But, by the nature of the algorithm, for large n Quicksort will break the set up into small subsets and recursively sort them. Thus whenever the size of a subset is small, the algorithm becomes inefficient. This problem can be remedied by choosing a small smallSize and sorting subsets of size less than or equal to smallSize by some simple, nonrecursive sort, called smallSort in the modified algorithm. (Insertion Sort is a good choice.)

```
quickSort(E, first, last)
    if (last − first ≥ smallSize)
        pivotElement = E[first];
        pivot = pivotElement.key;
        int  splitPoint = partition(E, pivot, first, last);
        E[splitPoint] = pivotElement;
        quickSort(E, first, splitPoint − 1);
        quickSort(E, splitPoint + 1, last);
    else
        smallSort(E, first, last);
```

A variation on this theme is to skip calling smallSort. Then when Quicksort exits, the array is not sorted, but no element needs to move more than smallSize places to reach its correct sorted position. (Why not?) Therefore one postprocessing run of Insertion Sort will be very efficient, and will do about the same comparisons as all the calls to it in its role as smallSort.

What value should smallSize have? The best choice depends on the particular implementation of the algorithm (that is, the computer being used and the details of the program), since we are making some trade-offs between overhead and key comparisons. A value close to 10 may do reasonably well.

Stack Space Optimization

We observed that the depth of recursion for Quicksort can grow quite large, proportional to n in the worst case (when Partition splits off only one element each time). Much of the pushing and popping of the frame stack that will be done is unnecessary. After Partition, the program starts sorting the subrange E[first], . . ., E[splitPoint − 1]; later it must sort the subrange E[splitPoint+1], . . ., E[last].

The second recursive call is the last statement in the procedure, so it can be converted into iteration in the manner we have seen earlier for shiftVac in Insertion Sort. The first recursive call remains, so the recursion is only partially eliminated.

With only one recursive call left in the procedure, we still need to be concerned about excessive depth of recursion. This can occur through a succession of recursive calls that each work on a subrange only slightly smaller than the preceding one. So the second trick we use is to avoid making the recursive call on the *larger* subrange. By ensuring that each recursive call is on at most half as many elements as its "parent" call, the depth of recursion is guaranteed to remain within about lg n. The two ideas are combined in the following version, in which "TRO" stands for "tail recursion optimization." The idea is that after each partition, the next recursive call will work on the smaller subrange, and the larger subrange will be handled directly in the **while** loop.

```
quickSortTRO(E, first, last)
    int  first1, last1, first2, last2;

    first2 = first; last2 = last;
    while (last2 − first2 ≥ 1)
        pivotElement = E[first2];
        pivot = pivotElement.key;
        int  splitPoint = partition(E, pivot, first2, last2);
        E[splitPoint] = pivotElement;
        if (splitPoint ≤ (first2 + last2) / 2)
            first1 = first2; last1 = splitPoint − 1;
            first2 = splitPoint + 1; last2 = last2;
        else
            first1 = splitPoint + 1; last1 = last2;
            first2 = first2; last2 = splitPoint − 1;
        quickSortTRO(E, first1, last1);
        // Continue loop for first2, last2.
    return;
```

Combined Improvements

We discussed the preceding modifications independently, but they are compatible and can be combined in one program.

Remarks

In practice, Quicksort programs run quite fast on the average for large n, and they are widely used. In the worst case, though, Quicksort behaves poorly. Like Insertion Sort (Section 4.2), Maxsort and Bubble Sort (Exercises 4.1 and 4.2), Quicksort's worst-case time is in $\Theta(n^2)$, but unlike the others, Quicksort's average behavior is in $\Theta(n \log n)$. Are there sorting algorithms whose worst-case time is in $\Theta(n \log n)$, or can we establish a worst-case lower bound of $\Theta(n^2)$? The Divide-and-Conquer approach gave us the improvement in average behavior. Let's examine the general technique again and see how to use it to improve on the worst-case behavior.

4.5 Merging Sorted Sequences

In this section we review a straightforward solution to the following problem: Given two sequences A and B sorted in nondecreasing order, merge them to create one sorted sequence C. Merging sorted subsequences is essential to the strategy of Mergesort. It also has numerous applications in its own right, some of which are covered in the exercises. The measure of work done by a merge algorithm will be the number of comparisons of keys performed by the algorithm.

Let k and m be the number of items in sequences A and B, respectively. Let $n = k + m$ be the "problem size." Assuming neither A nor B is empty, we can immediately determine the first item in C: It is the minimum between the first items of A and B. What about the rest of C? Suppose the first element of A was the minimum. Then the remainder of C must be the result of merging all elements of A *after* the first with all elements of B. But this is just a smaller version of the same problem we started with. The situation is symmetrical if the first element of B was the minimum. In either case the problem size for the remaining problem (of constructing the rest of C) is $n - 1$. Method 99 (Section 3.2.2) comes to mind.

If we assume that we only need to merge problems of size up to 100, and we can call upon merge99 to merge problems of size up to 99, then the problem is already solved. The pseudocode follows:

```
merge(A, B, C)
    if (A is empty)
        rest of C = rest of B
    else if (B is empty)
        rest of C = rest of A
    else
        if (first of A ≤ first of B)
            first of C = first of A
            merge99(rest of A, B, rest of C)
        else
            first of C = first of B
            merge99(A, rest of B, rest of C)
    return
```

Now just change merge99 to merge for the general recursive solution.

Once the solution idea is seen, we can also see how to formulate an iterative solution. The idea works for all sequential data structures, but we state the algorithm in terms of arrays, for definiteness. We introduce three indexes to keep track of where "rest of A," "rest of B," and "rest of C" begin at any stage in the iteration. (These indexes would be parameters in the recursive version.)

Algorithm 4.4   Merge

Input: Arrays A with k elements and B with m elements, each in nondecreasing order of their keys.

Output: C, an array containing $n = k + m$ elements from A and B in nondecreasing order. C is passed in and the algorithm fills it.

```
void  merge(Element[] A, int k, Element[] B, int m, Element[] C)
    int  n = k + m;
    int  indexA = 0; indexB = 0; indexC = 0;
    // indexA is the beginning of rest of A; same for B, C.

    while (indexA < k && indexB < m)
        if (A[indexA].key ≤ B[indexB].key)
            C[indexC] = A[indexA];
            indexA ++;
            indexC ++;
        else
            C[indexC] = B[indexB];
            indexB ++;
            indexC ++;
        // Continue loop
    if (indexA ≥ k)
        Copy B[indexB, . . ., m–1] to C[indexC, . . ., n–1].
    else
        Copy A[indexA, . . ., k–1] to C[indexC, . . ., n–1].
```

4.5.1 Worst Case

Whenever a comparison of keys from A and B is done, at least one element is moved to C and never examined again. After the last comparison, at least two elements—the two just compared—have not yet been moved to C. The smaller one is moved immediately, but now C has at most $n - 1$ elements, and no more comparisons will be done. Those that remain in the other array are moved to C without any further comparisons. So at most $n - 1$ comparisons are done. The worst case, using all $n - 1$ comparisons, occurs when $A[k - 1]$ and $B[m - 1]$ belong in the last two positions in C.

4.5.2 Optimality of Merge

We show next that Algorithm 4.4 is optimal in the worst case among comparison-based algorithms when $k = m = n/2$. That is, for any comparison-based algorithm that merges correctly on all inputs for which $k = m = n/2$ there must be *some* input for which it requires $n - 1$ comparisons. (This is not to say that for a *particular* input no algorithm could do better than Algorithm 4.4.) After considering $k = m = n/2$, we look at some other relationships between k and m.

Theorem 4.4 Any algorithm to merge two sorted arrays, each containing $k = m = n/2$ entries, by comparison of keys, does at least $n - 1$ such comparisons in the worst case.

Proof Suppose we are given an arbitrary merge algorithm. Let a_i and b_i be the ith entries of A and B, respectively. We show that keys can be chosen so that the algorithm must compare a_i with b_i, for $0 \leq i < m$, and a_i with b_{i+1}, for $0 \leq i < m - 1$. Specifically, choose keys so that, whenever the algorithm compares a_i and b_j, if $i < j$, the result is that $a_i < b_j$, and if $i \geq j$, the result is that $b_j < a_i$. Choosing the keys so that

$$b_0 < a_0 < b_1 < a_1 < \cdots < b_i < a_i < b_{i+1} < \cdots < b_{m-1} < a_{m-1} \qquad (4.4)$$

will satisfy these conditions. However, if for some i, the algorithm never compares a_i and b_i, then choosing keys in the same order as in Equation (4.4), except that $a_i < b_i$, will also satisfy these conditions and the algorithm would not be able to determine the correct ordering.

Similarly, if for some i, it never compares a_i and b_{i+1}, the arrangement of Equation (4.4), except that $b_{i+1} < a_i$ would be consistent with the results of the comparisons done, and again the algorithm could not determine the correct ordering. $\square$

Can we generalize this conclusion? Suppose k and m differ slightly (as we will see they might in Mergesort)?

Corollary 4.5 Any algorithm to merge two sorted arrays by comparison of keys, where the inputs contain k and m entries, respectively, k and m differ by one, and $n = k + m$, does at least $n - 1$ such comparisons in the worst case.

Proof The same proof as in Theorem 4.4 applies, except there is no a_{m-1}. $\square$

Can we generalize this conclusion still further? If we find one kind of behavior at one extreme, it is often a good idea to check the other extreme. Here the first "extreme" was $k = m$, so the other extreme makes k and m as different as possible. Let's look at an extreme case, where $k = 1$ and m is large, so $n = m + 1$. We can devise an algorithm that uses at most $\lceil \lg(m + 1) \rceil$ comparisons. (What is it?) So clearly $n - 1$ is not a lower bound in this case. The improvement for $k = 1$ can be generalized to other cases where k is much less than n (see Exercise 4.24). Therefore the lower bound arguments of Theorem 4.4 and Corollary 4.5 cannot be extended to all combinations of k and m. For further possibilities, look at Exercise 4.33 after reading Section 4.7.

4.5.3 Space Usage

It might appear from the way in which Algorithm 4.4 is written that merging sequences with a total of n entries requires enough memory locations for $2n$ entries, since all entries

Before the merge

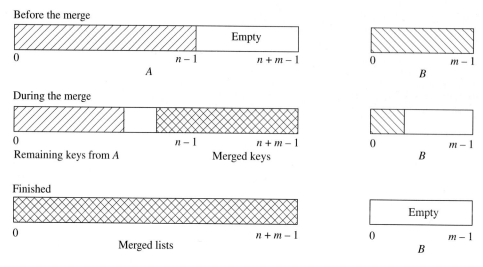

Figure 4.12   Overlapping arrays for Merge

are copied to C. In some cases, however, the amount of extra space needed can be decreased. One case is that the sequences are linked lists, and A and B are not needed (as lists) after the merge is completed. Then the list nodes of A and B can be recycled as C is created.

Suppose the input sequences are stored in arrays and suppose $k \geq m$. If A has enough room for $n = k + m$ elements, then only the extra m locations in A are needed. Simply identify C with A, and do the merging from the right ends (larger keys) of A and B, as indicated in Figure 4.12. The first m entries moved to "C" will fill the extra locations of A. From then on the vacated locations in A are used. There will always be a gap (i.e., some empty locations) between the end of the merged portion of the array and the remaining entries of A until all of the entries have been merged. Observe that if this space-saving storage layout is used, the last lines in the merge algorithm (**else** Copy A[indexA], . . ., A[k−1] to C[indexC], . . ., C[n−1]) can be eliminated because, if B empties before A, the remaining items in A are in their correct position and do not have to be moved.

Whether or not C overlaps one of the input arrays, the extra space used by the Merge algorithm when $k = m = n/2$ is in $\Theta(n)$.

4.6 Mergesort

The problem with Quicksort is that Partition doesn't always decompose the array into two equal subranges. Mergesort just slices the array in two halves and sorts the halves separately (and of course, recursively). Then it merges the sorted halves (see Figure 4.13).

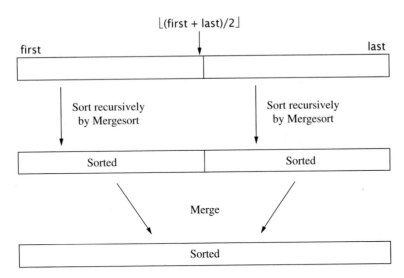

Figure 4.13 Mergesort strategy

Thus, using the divide-and-conquer terminology of Section 4.3, divide merely computes the middle index of the subrange and does no key comparisons; combine does the merging.

We assume that Merge is modified to merge adjacent subranges of one array, putting the resulting merged array back into the cells originally occupied by the elements being merged. Its parameters now are the array name E, and the first, mid, and last indexes of the subranges it is to merge; that is, the sorted subranges are E[first], . . ., E[mid] and E[mid+1], . . ., E[last], and the final sorted range is to be E[first], . . ., E[last]. In this modification, the merge subroutine is also responsible for allocating additional workspace needed. Some of the issues were discussed in Section 4.5.3.

Algorithm 4.5 Mergesort

Input: Array E and indexes first, and last, such that the elements of E[i] are defined for first $\leq i \leq$ last.

Output: E[first], . . ., E[last] is a sorted rearrangement of the same elements.

```
void  mergeSort(Element[] E, int first, int last)
    if (first < last)
        int  mid = (first+last) / 2;
        mergeSort(E, first, mid);
        mergeSort(E, mid + 1, last);
        merge(E, first, mid, last);
    return;
```

We have observed that students often confuse the Merge and Mergesort algorithms. Remember that Merge*sort* is a sorting algorithm. It begins with *one* scrambled array and sorts it. Merge begins with *two* arrays that are already sorted; it combines them into one sorted array.

Mergesort Analysis

First, we find the asymptotic order of the worst-case number of key comparisons for Mergesort. As usual, we define the problem size as $n = \mathsf{last} - \mathsf{first} + 1$, the number of elements in the range to be sorted. The recurrence equation for the worst-case behavior of Mergesort is

$$W(n) = W(\lfloor n/2 \rfloor) + W(\lceil n/2 \rceil) + n - 1 \qquad (4.5)$$
$$W(1) = 0.$$

The Master Theorem tells us immediately that $W(n) \in \Theta(n \log n)$. So we finally have a sorting algorithm whose worst-case behavior is in $\Theta(n \log n)$. Rather than carry out a separate analysis of the average complexity of Mergesort, we will defer this question until we have developed the very general Theorem 4.11, concerning average behavior, in Section 4.7, just ahead.

A possible disadvantage of Mergesort is its requirement for auxiliary workspace. Because of the extra space used for the merging, which is in $\Theta(n)$, Mergesort is not an in-place sort.

⋆ Mergesort Analysis, More Exactly

It is of some interest to obtain a more exact estimate of the worst-case number of comparisons, in light of lower bounds to be developed in the next section (Section 4.7). We will see that Mergesort is very close to the lower bound. Readers may skip the details of this section without loss of continuity and proceed to its main conclusion, Theorem 4.6.

In the recursion tree for Equation (4.5) (see Figure 4.14), we observe that the nonrecursive costs of nodes at depth d sum to $n - 2^d$ (for all node depths not containing any base cases). We can determine that all base cases (for which $W(1) = 0$) occur at depths $\lceil \lg(n + 1) \rceil - 1$ or $\lceil \lg(n + 1) \rceil$. There are exactly n base-case nodes. Let the maximum depth be D (that is, $D = \lceil \lg(n + 1) \rceil$) and let B be the number of base cases at depth $D - 1$. Then there are $n - B$ base cases at depth D (and no other nodes at depth D). Each nonbase node at depth $D - 1$ has two children, so there are $(n - B)/2$ nonbase cases at depth $D - 1$. Using this information, we compute the sum of nonrecursive costs for the last few depths as follows:

1. Depth $D - 2$ has 2^{D-2} nodes, none of which are base cases. The sum of nonrecursive costs for this level is $n - 2^{D-2}$.

2. Depth $D - 1$ has $(n - B)/2$ nonbase cases. Each has problem size 2 (with cost 1), so the sum of the nonrecursive costs for this level is $(n - B)/2$.

3. Depth D has $n - B$ base cases, cost 0.

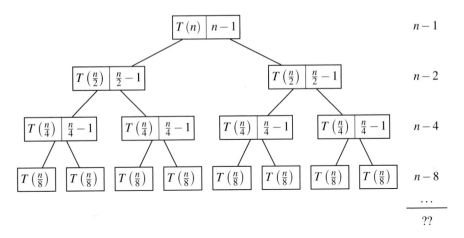

Figure 4.14 Recursion tree for Mergesort. Wherever a node size parameter is odd, the left child size is rounded up and the right child size is rounded down.

You can verify that $B = 2^D - n$ (Exercise 4.29). Therefore

$$
\begin{aligned}
W(n) &= \sum_{d=0}^{D-2} \left(n - 2^d\right) + (n - B)/2 \\
&= n(D - 1) - 2^{D-1} + 1 + (n - B)/2 \\
&= n\, D - 2^D + 1.
\end{aligned}
\tag{4.6}
$$

Because D is rounded up to an integer and occurs in the exponent, it is hard to tell how Equation (4.6) behaves between powers of 2. We prove the following theorem, which removes the ceiling function from the exponent.

Theorem 4.6 The number of comparisons done by Mergesort in the worst case is between $\lceil n \lg(n) - n + 1 \rceil$ and $\lceil n \lg(n) - .914\, n \rceil$.

Proof If we define $\alpha = 2^D/n$, then $1 \le \alpha < 2$, and D can be replaced throughout Equation (4.6) by $(\lg(n) + \lg(\alpha))$. This leads to $W(n) = n \lg(n) - (\alpha - \lg \alpha)n + 1$. The minimum value of $(\alpha - \lg \alpha)$ is about .914 (see Exercise 4.30) and the maximum in the range under consideration is 1. ☐

Thus Mergesort does about 30 percent fewer comparisons in the worst case than Quicksort does in the average case. However, Mergesort does more element movement than Quicksort does on average, so its time may not be faster (see Exercises 4.21 and 4.27).

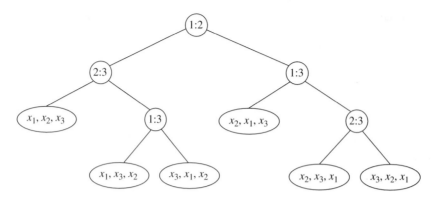

Figure 4.15   Decision tree for a sorting algorithm, $n = 3$.

4.7   Lower Bounds for Sorting by Comparison of Keys

The number of key comparisons done by Insertion Sort and Quicksort in the worst case is in $\Theta(n^2)$. We were able to improve on this with Mergesort, whose worst case is in $\Theta(n \log n)$. Can we do even better?

In this section we derive lower bounds for the number of comparisons that must be done in the worst case and on the average by any algorithm that sorts by comparison of keys. These results tell us when we can stop looking for a better algorithm. To derive the lower bounds we assume that the keys in the array to be sorted are distinct.

4.7.1   Decision Trees for Sorting Algorithms

Let n be fixed and suppose that the keys are $x_1, x_2, \ldots, x_n$. We will associate with each algorithm and positive integer n, a (binary) decision tree that describes the sequence of comparisons carried out by the algorithm on any input of size n. Let Sort be any algorithm that sorts by comparison of keys. Each comparison has a two-way branch (since the keys are distinct), and we assume that Sort has an output instruction that outputs the rearranged array of keys. The decision tree for Sort is defined inductively by associating a tree with each comparison and each output instruction as follows. The tree associated with an output instruction consists of one node labeled with the rearrangement of the keys. The tree associated with an instruction that compares keys x_i and x_j consists of a root labeled $(i : j)$, a left subtree that is the tree associated with the (comparison or output) instruction executed next if $x_i < x_j$, and a right subtree that is the tree associated with the (comparison or output) instruction executed next if $x_i > x_j$. The decision tree for Sort is the tree associated with the first comparison instruction it executes. Figure 4.15 shows an example of a decision tree for $n = 3$.

The action of Sort on a particular input corresponds to following one path in its decision tree from the root to a leaf. The tree must have at least $n!$ leaves because there are $n!$ ways in which the keys can be permuted. Since the unique path followed for each input depends only on the ordering of the keys and not on their particular values, exactly

$n!$ leaves can be reached from the root by actually executing Sort. We will assume that any paths in the tree that are never followed are removed. We also assume that comparison nodes with only one child are removed and replaced by the child, and that this "pruning" is repeated until all internal nodes have degree 2. The pruned tree represents an algorithm that is at least as efficient as the original one, so the lower bounds we derive using trees with exactly $n!$ leaves and all internal nodes of degree 2 will be valid lower bounds for all algorithms that sort by comparison of keys. From now on we assume Sort is described by such a tree.

The number of comparisons done by Sort on a particular input is the number of internal nodes on the path followed for that input. Thus the number of comparisons done in the worst case is the number of internal nodes on the longest path, and that is the height of the tree. The average number of comparisons done is the average of the lengths of all paths from the root to a leaf. (For example, for $n = 3$, the algorithm whose decision tree is shown in Figure 4.15 does three comparisons in the worst case and two and two-thirds on the average.)

4.7.2 Lower Bound for Worst Case

To get a worst-case lower bound for sorting by comparison, we derive a lower bound for the height of a binary tree in terms of the number of leaves, since the only quantitative information we have about the decision trees is the number of leaves.

Lemma 4.7   Let L be the number of leaves in a binary tree and let h be its height. Then $L \leq 2^h$.

Proof   A straightforward induction on h.   □

Lemma 4.8   Let L and h be as in Lemma 4.7. Then $h \geq \lceil \lg L \rceil$.

Proof   Taking logs of both sides of the inequality in Lemma 4.7 gives $\lg L \leq h$. Since h is an integer, $h \geq \lceil \lg L \rceil$.   □

Lemma 4.9   For a given n, the decision tree for any algorithm that sorts by comparison of keys has height at least $\lceil \lg n! \rceil$.

Proof   Let $L = n!$ in Lemma 4.8.   □

So the number of comparisons needed to sort in the worst case is at least $\lceil \lg n! \rceil$. Our best sort so far is Mergesort, but how close is $\lceil \lg n! \rceil$ to $n \lg n$? To find the answer, we need to put $\lg n!$ into a more convenient form, and get a lower bound on its value. There are several ways to do this. Perhaps the simplest, but not very exact, way is to observe that

$$n! \geq n(n-1) \cdots (\lceil n/2 \rceil) \geq \left(\frac{n}{2} \right)^{\frac{n}{2}},$$

so

$$\lg n! \geq \frac{n}{2} \lg \frac{n}{2},$$

which is in $\Theta(n \log n)$. Thus we see already that Mergesort is of optimal asymptotic order. To get a closer lower bound, we use the fact that

$$\lg n! = \sum_{j=1}^{n} \lg(j).$$

Using Equation (1.18) we get

$$\lg n! \geq n \lg n - (\lg e)n,$$

where e denotes the base of natural logarithms, and $\lg(e)$ is about 1.443. Thus the height of the decision tree is at least $\lceil n \lg n - 1.443n \rceil$.

Theorem 4.10   Any algorithm to sort n items by comparisons of keys must do at least $\lceil \lg n! \rceil$, or approximately $\lceil n \lg n - 1.443n \rceil$, key comparisons in the worst case.   □

So Mergesort is very close to optimal. There is some difference between the exact behavior of Mergesort and the lower bound. Consider the case where $n = 5$. Insertion sort does 10 comparisons in the worst case, and Mergesort does 8, but the lower bound is $\lceil \lg 5! \rceil$ = $\lceil \lg 120 \rceil$ = 7. Is the lower bound simply not good enough, or can we do better than Mergesort? We encourage you to try to find a way to sort five elements with only seven key comparisons in the worst case (Exercise 4.32).

4.7.3   Lower Bound for Average Behavior

We need a lower bound on the average of the lengths of all paths from the root to a leaf in a decision tree. Recall from Definition 3.2 that a binary tree in which every node has degree 0 or 2 is called a *2-tree*. Leaves in such a tree may be *external nodes*, which are of a different type from the internal nodes. Our decision trees are 2-trees, and all of their leaves are output instructions, whereas all of the internal nodes are comparison instructions.

Recall from Definition 3.3 that the *external path length* of a tree is the sum of the lengths of all paths from the root to an external node (i.e., output instruction); it will be denoted by *epl*. If a decision tree has L leaves, the average path length from the root to a leaf is *epl/L*.

We are looking for a lower bound on *epl* among all decision trees (2-trees) with L leaves, thinking of L as fixed, for the moment. We can argue that the trees (with L leaves) that minimize *epl* are as balanced as possible. Suppose we have a 2-tree with height h that has a leaf X at depth k, where k is two or more less than h. See Figure 4.16(a) for an illustration. Figure 4.16(b) shows a 2-tree with the same number of leaves and lower *epl*. We choose a node Y at depth $h - 1$ that is not a leaf, remove its two children, and attach those two children to X. The total number of leaves has not changed but the *epl* has. Three paths in the original tree, with lengths totaling $h + h + k$, are no longer counted

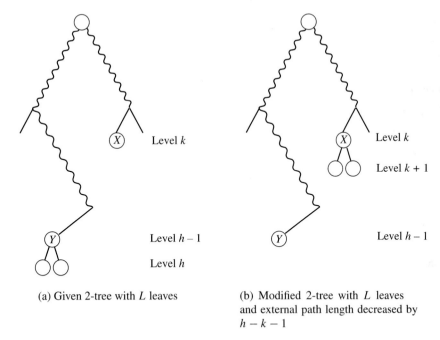

(a) Given 2-tree with L leaves

(b) Modified 2-tree with L leaves and external path length decreased by $h - k - 1$

Figure 4.16 Reducing external path length

(the paths to the children of Y and to X). There are three new paths (to Y and to X's new children), with lengths totaling $h - 1 + 2(k + 1)$. The net change in *epl* is $k + 1 - h$, which is negative, so *epl* has decreased. Therefore if a 2-tree has minimum *epl* among all 2-trees with L leaves, its external path length is about $L \lg(L)$.

Lemma 3.7 makes this bound more precise; it states (in our context) that any decision tree with L leaves has $epl \geq L \lg(L)$, and so the average path length to an output-instruction node is at least $\lg(L)$. This immediately implies the following theorem:

Theorem 4.11 The average number of comparisons done by an algorithm to sort n items by comparison of keys is at least $\lg(n!)$, which is about $n \lg n - 1.443\, n$. □

The only difference from the worst-case lower bound is that there is no rounding up to an integer—the average need not be an integer, but the worst case must be. Although we never analyzed the average behavior of Mergesort, this general bound allows us to conclude that it cannot be much lower than its worst case; the leading terms must agree and there is only a gap of about $0.5\, n$ in the second-order term. Also, the average case for Quicksort can be improved only by about 30 percent at the most by any enhancements, such as choosing the splitting element more carefully.

4.8   Heapsort

Quicksort rearranges elements in the original array, but cannot be sure of making an even subdivision of the problem, and so it has a bad worst case. Mergesort can guarantee an even subdivision, and has a nearly optimal worst case, but cannot rearrange the elements in the original array; it needs sizable auxiliary workspace. Heapsort rearranges elements in the original array, and its worst case is in $\Theta(n \log n)$, which is optimal in terms of growth rate, so in a sense it combines the advantages of Quicksort and Mergesort. The disadvantage of Heapsort is a higher constant factor than the other two. However, a newer version of Heapsort reduces this constant factor to a level that is competitive with Quicksort and Mergesort. We call this newer version *Accelerated Heapsort*. Thus Accelerated Heapsort may become the sorting method of choice.

4.8.1   Heaps

The Heapsort algorithm uses a data structure called a *heap*, which is a binary tree with some special properties. The definition of a heap includes a description of the structure and a condition on the data in the nodes, called the *partial order tree property*. Informally, a heap *structure* is a complete binary tree with some of the rightmost leaves removed. (See Figure 4.17 for illustrations.) A heap provides an efficient implementation of the *priority queue* abstract data type (Section 2.5.1). In a heap the element of "highest" priority is kept in the root of the binary tree. Depending on the notion of priority, this might be the minimum key (for a minimizing heap) or the maximum key (for a maximizing heap). For Heapsort to sort in ascending order, a maximizing heap is used, so we will describe heaps in these terms. Elsewhere we will encounter uses for minimizing heaps.

We will use the terminology that S is a set of elements with keys that have a linear ordering, and T is a binary tree with height h whose nodes contain elements of S.

Definition 4.1   Heap structure

A binary tree T is a heap *structure* if and only if it satisfies the following conditions:

1. T is complete at least through depth $h - 1$.
2. All leaves are at depth h or $h - 1$.
3. All paths to a leaf of depth h are to the left of all paths to a leaf of depth $h - 1$.

The rightmost internal node at depth $h - 1$ of a heap structure may have a left child and no right child (but not vice versa). All other internal nodes have two children. Another name for a heap structure is a *left-complete* binary tree.   ■

Definition 4.2   Partial order tree property

A tree T is a (maximizing) *partial order tree* if and only if the key at any node is greater than or equal to the keys at each of its children (if it has any).   ■

Observe that a complete binary tree is a heap structure. When new nodes are added to a heap, they must be added left to right at the bottom level, and if a node is removed, it

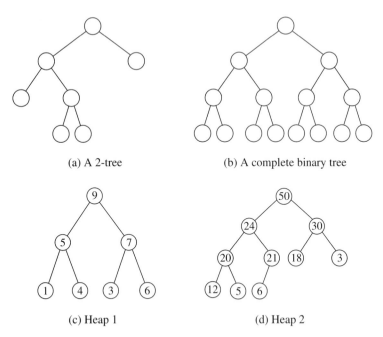

(a) A 2-tree   (b) A complete binary tree

(c) Heap 1   (d) Heap 2

Figure 4.17   2-trees, complete binary trees, and heaps

must be the rightmost node at the bottom level if the resulting structure is still to be a heap. Note that the root must contain the largest key in the heap.

4.8.2   The Heapsort Strategy

If the elements to be sorted are arranged in a heap, then we can build a sorted sequence in reverse order by repeatedly removing the element from the root (the largest remaining key), and rearranging the elements still in the heap to reestablish the partial order tree property, thus bringing the next largest key to the root. This operation is just deleteMax for the priority queue ADT. (We could build the sorted sequence in ascending order with a minimizing heap; the reason for using a maximizing heap becomes clear when we study a particularly efficient implementation in Section 4.8.5.)

Since this approach requires constructing a heap in the first place, and then repeatedly doing deleteMax, which involves some rearranging of the elements in the heap, it does not look like a promising strategy for getting an efficient sorting algorithm. However, it turns out to do quite well. Thus we outline the strategy here, and then proceed to work out the details. As usual, we assume the n elements are stored in an array E, but this time we assume the range of indexes is $1, \ldots, n$, for reasons that will become clear when we look at the implementation of the heap. For the moment we assume the heap (named H) is elsewhere.

```
heapSort(E, n)  // OUTLINE
    Construct H from E, the set of n elements to be sorted;
    for (i = n; i ≥ 1; i --)
        curMax = getMax(H);
        deleteMax(H);
        E[i] = curMax;
```

The first and last pictures in Figure 4.18 show an example before and after one iteration of the **for** loop. The intervening pictures show steps in the rearrangements that are carried out by deleteMax and the subroutine fixHeap, which is called by deleteMax.

```
deleteMax(H)  // OUTLINE
    Copy the rightmost element on the lowest level of H into K.
    Delete the rightmost element on the lowest level of H.
    fixHeap(H, K);
```

As we see, almost all the work is done by fixHeap.

We now need an algorithm to construct a heap and an algorithm for fixHeap. Since fixHeap can be used to solve the heap construction problem as well, we consider it next.

4.8.3   FixHeap

The fixHeap procedure restores the partial order tree property in a heap structure for which that property already exists everywhere except possibly at the root. Specifically, when fixHeap begins, we have a heap structure with a "vacant" root. The two subtrees are partial order trees, and we have an extra element, say K, to be inserted. Since the root is vacant, we begin there and let K (and the vacant node) filter down to its correct position. At its final position, K (more precisely, K's key) must be greater than or equal to each of its children, so at each step K is compared to the larger of the children of the currently vacant node. If K is larger (or equal) it can be inserted at the currently vacant node. Otherwise, the larger child is moved up to the vacant node and the process is repeated.

Example 4.1   FixHeap in action

The action of fixHeap is illustrated in the second through fifth pictures of Figure 4.18. To back up a little, the first picture shows the initial configuration, at the beginning of the **for** loop in the heapSort outline in Section 4.8.2. First, heapSort copies the key 50 from the root of H into curMax, making the root of the tree effectively vacant; then it calls deleteMax, which copies the key 6 from the rightmost node on the bottom level of the tree into K, and actually deletes that node.

This brings us to the second picture and that is where fixHeap(H, K) begins. The larger child of the vacant node is 30, and this is also larger than K, which is 6, so 30 moves up into the vacant position and the vacant node filters down, leading to the third picture. Again, the larger child of the vacant node is larger than K, so the vacant node filters down again. The next time, the vacant node is a leaf, so K can be inserted there, and the partial order tree property of H is restored.   ∎

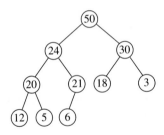

(a) The heap

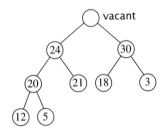

(b) The key at the root has been removed; the rightmost leaf at the bottom level has been removed. $K = 6$ must be reinserted.

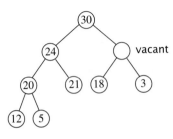

(c) The larger child of vacant, 30, is greater than K, so it moves up and vacant moves down.

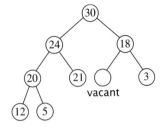

(d) The larger child of vacant, 18, is greater than K, so it moves up and vacant moves down.

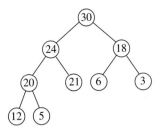

(e) Finally, since vacant is a leaf, $K = 6$ is inserted.

Figure 4.18 Deleting the element at the root and reestablishing the partial order tree property

Although the tree structure of the heap is essential to motivating and understanding Heapsort, we will see later that we will be able to represent heaps and subheaps without any explicit edges.

Algorithm 4.6 FixHeap (Outline)

Input: A nonempty binary tree H with a "vacant" root, such that its left and right subtrees are partial order trees, and an element K to be inserted. The type of H is called Heap for this outline. Nodes of H are assumed to be type Element.

Output: A binary tree H consisting of K and the original elements of H, satisfying the partial order tree property.

Remark: The structure of H is not altered, but the contents of its nodes are changed.

```
fixHeap(H, K)  // OUTLINE
    if (H is a leaf)
        insert K in root(H);
    else
        Set largerSubHeap to leftSubtree(H) or rightSubtree(H), whichever
        has larger key at its root. This involves one key comparison, unless
        rightSubtree is empty.
        if (K.key ≥ root(largerSubHeap).key)
            insert K in root(H);
        else
            insert root(largerSubHeap) in root(H);
            fixHeap(largerSubHeap, K);
    return;
```

Lemma 4.12 The fixHeap procedure does $2h$ comparisons of keys in the worst case on a heap with height h.

Proof At most two comparisons of keys are done in each procedure activation, and the tree height decreases by one in the recursive call. (One comparison is implicit in the determination of largerSubHeap.) ☐

4.8.4 Heap Construction

Suppose we start by putting all the elements in a heap structure in arbitrary order; that is, the partial order tree property is not necessarily satisfied in any subheap. The fixHeap algorithm suggests a Divide-and-Conquer approach to establishing the partial order tree property. The two subtrees can be turned into heaps recursively, then fixHeap can be used to filter the element at the root down to its proper place, thus combining the two smaller heaps and the root into one large heap. The base case is a tree consisting of one node (i.e., a leaf); it is already a heap. The following algorithm implements this idea.

Algorithm 4.7 Construct Heap

Input: A heap structure H that does not necessarily have the partial order tree property.

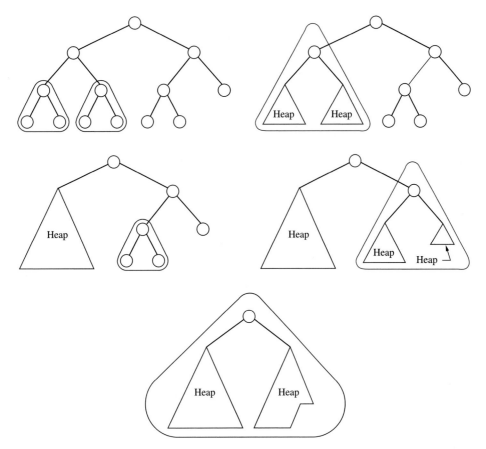

Figure 4.19 Constructing the heap: The leaves are heaps. The fixHeap procedure is called for each circled subtree.

Output: *H* with the same nodes rearranged to satisfy the partial order tree property.

```
void constructHeap(H) // OUTLINE
    if (H is not a leaf)
        constructHeap(left subtree of H);
        constructHeap(right subtree of H);
        Element K = root(H);
        fixHeap(H, K);
    return;
```

If we unravel the work done by this Divide-and-Conquer algorithm, we see that it really starts rearranging elements near the leaves first, and works its way up the tree. (It is a sort of postorder traversal.) See Figure 4.19 for an illustration. Exercise 4.38 asks you to write an iterative version of constructHeap.

Correctness

Theorem 4.13 Procedure constructHeap establishes the partial order tree property in its parameter, H.

Proof The proof is by induction on heap structures. The base case is a heap of one node, which has the partial order tree property vacuously.

For heaps H of more than one node, assume the theorem holds for proper subheaps of H. The recursive calls to constructHeap are on such subheaps. There is no problem about meeting the preconditions for the recursive calls, because subtrees of a heap structure are also heap structures. Therefore, by the inductive hypothesis, *we can assume they accomplish their objectives*; it is not necessary to burrow into the recursion.

The final point concerning correctness is whether the preconditions for the subroutine fixHeap are satisfied at the point it is called. But those preconditions are just the postconditions of the two recursive calls to constructHeap. So we can assume fixHeap accomplishes its objective, which is just the objective of the current invocation of constructHeap: to make H satisfy the partial order tree property. $\square$

Worst-Case Analysis

A recurrence equation for constructHeap depends on the cost of fixHeap. Defining the problem size as n, the number of nodes in the heap structure H, we saw that fixHeap requires about $2 \lg(n)$ key comparisons. Let r denote the number of nodes in the right subheap of H. We then have

$$W(n) = W(n - r - 1) + W(r) + 2 \lg(n) \qquad \text{for } n > 1.$$

Although heaps are as balanced as possible, r can be as little as $n/3$. Therefore, while constructHeap is a Divide-and-Conquer algorithm, its two subproblems are not necessarily equal. With some difficult mathematics the recurrence can be solved for arbitrary n, but we will take a shortcut. We first solve it for $N = 2^d - 1$, that is, for complete binary trees, then note that for n between $\frac{1}{2}N$ and N, $W(N)$ is an upper bound on $W(n)$.

For $N = 2^d - 1$, the numbers of nodes in the right and left subtrees are equal, so the recurrence equation becomes

$$W(N) = 2W(\tfrac{1}{2}(N - 1)) + 2 \lg(N) \qquad \text{for } N > 1.$$

Now apply the Master Theorem (Theorem 3.17). We have $b = 2$, $c = 2$ (the difference between $N/2$ and $(N - 1)/2$ is unimportant), $E = 1$, and $f(N) = 2 \lg(N)$. Now choosing $\epsilon = 0.1$ (or any fraction less than one) shows that case 1 of that theorem applies: $2 \lg(N) \in O\left(n^{0.9}\right)$. It follows that $W(N) \in \Theta(N)$.

Now, returning to general n, since $N \le 2n$, $W(n) \le W(N) \in \Theta(2n) = \Theta(n)$. Thus the heap is constructed in linear time! (An alternative counting argument is given in Exercise 4.39.)

It is not yet clear that Heapsort is a good algorithm; it seems to require extra space. It is time to consider the implementation of a heap.

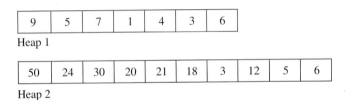

9	5	7	1	4	3	6

Heap 1

50	24	30	20	21	18	3	12	5	6

Heap 2

Figure 4.20   Storage of the heaps in Figure 4.17

4.8.5   Implementation of a Heap and the Heapsort Algorithm

Binary trees are usually implemented as linked structures with each node containing pointers (or some other kind of references) to the roots of its subtrees. Setting up and using such a structure requires extra time and extra space for the pointers. However, we can store and use a heap efficiently without any pointers at all. In a heap there are no nodes at, say, depth d unless depth $d - 1$ is completely filled, so a heap can be stored in an array level by level (beginning with the root), left to right within each level. Figure 4.20 shows the storage arrangement for the heaps in Figure 4.17. For this scheme to be useful we must be able to find the children of a node quickly and determine if a node is a leaf quickly. It is important that the root be stored at index 1, not 0, in the array, for the specific formulas that we are about to describe.

Suppose the index i of a node is given. Then we can use a counting argument to show that its left child has index $2i$ and that its right child has index $2i + 1$; similarly, the parent is $\lfloor i/2 \rfloor$. (The proof is left for an exercise.) It is to keep these formulas simple that we use indexes beginning at 1 for heaps.

The startling feature of Heapsort is that the whole sorting procedure can be carried out in place; the small heaps built during the construction phase and, later the heap and the deleted elements, can occupy the array E that originally contained the unsorted set of elements. During the deletion phase, when the heap contains, say, k elements, it will occupy the first k locations in the array. Thus just one variable is needed to mark the end of the heap. Figure 4.21 illustrates the sharing of the array between the heap and the sorted elements. (Note that the fixHeap outline in Algorithm 4.6 had only two parameters. The more detailed implementation below has four.)

Algorithm 4.8   Heapsort

Input: E, an unsorted array, and $n \geq 1$, the number of elements. The range of indexes is $1, \dots, n$.

Output: E, with elements in nondecreasing order of their keys.

Remark: E[0] is not used. Remember to allocate $n + 1$ positions for E.

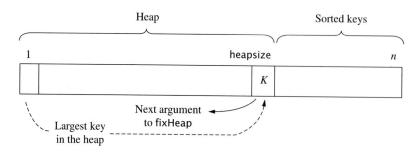

Figure 4.21 The heap and sorted elements in the array

```
void  heapSort(Element[] E, int n)
    int  heapsize;

    constructHeap(E, n);
    // Repeatedly remove root element and rearrange heap.
    for (heapsize = n; heapsize ≥ 2; heapsize −−)
        Element  curMax = E[1];
        Element  K = E[heapsize];
        fixHeap(E, heapsize−1, 1, K);
        E[heapsize] = curMax;
    return;
```

The fixHeap algorithm (Algorithm 4.6), revised for the array implementation, is given next. The revisions for constructHeap (Algorithm 4.7) follow the same pattern and are omitted.

Algorithm 4.9 FixHeap

Input: An array E representing a heap structure; heapSize, the number of elements in the heap; root, the root of the subheap to fix, a vacant position; K, the element to be inserted into the subheap in a way that restores the partial order tree property. The precondition is that the subheaps rooted at the left and right children of root have the partial order tree property.

Output: The subheap rooted at root has K inserted and has the partial order tree property.

Procedure: See Figure 4.22. ∎

Heapsort Analysis

We can now see clearly that Heapsort is an in-place sort in terms of work space for the elements to be sorted. Although some subroutines use recursion, the depth of recursion is limited to about lg n, which is usually not a cause for concern. However, we can recode these subroutines to eliminate recursion and work in place (see Exercise 4.38).

```
void fixHeap(Element[] E, int heapSize, int root, Element K)
    int left = 2 * root, right = 2 * root + 1;
    if (left > heapSize)
        E[root] = K;  // Root is a leaf.
    else
        // Determine largerSubHeap.
        int largerSubHeap;
        if (left == heapSize)
            largerSubHeap = left;  // No right SubHeap.
        else if (E[left].key > E[right].key)
            largerSubHeap = left;
        else
            largerSubHeap = right;
        // Decide whether to filter K down.
        if (K.key ≥ E[largerSubHeap].key)
            E[root] = K;
        else
            E[root] = E[largerSubHeap];
            fixHeap(E, heapSize, largerSubHeap, K);
    return;
```

Figure 4.22 Procedure for Algorithm 4.9

We have seen in Section 4.8.4 that the number of comparisons done by constructHeap is in $\Theta(n)$. Now consider the main loop of Algorithm 4.8. By Lemma 4.12 the number of comparisons done by fixHeap on a heap with k nodes is at most $2\lfloor \lg k \rfloor$, so the total for all the deletions is at most $2 \sum_{k=1}^{n-1} \lfloor \lg k \rfloor$. This sum can be bounded by an integral, which takes the form of Equation (1.15),

$$2 \sum_{k=1}^{n-1} \lfloor \lg k \rfloor \leq 2 \int_1^n (\lg e) \ln x \, dx$$

$$= 2 \, (\lg e)(n \ln n - n) = 2(n \lg(n) - 1.443 \, n).$$

The following theorem sums up our results.

Theorem 4.14   The number of comparisons of keys done by Heapsort in the worst case is $2 \, n \lg n + O(n)$. Heapsort is an $\Theta(n \log n)$ sorting algorithm.

Proof   The heap construction phase does at most $O(n)$ comparisons, and the deletions do at most $2n \lg(n)$.   □

Heapsort does $\Theta(n \log n)$ comparisons on the average as well as in the worst case. (How do we know this?)

4.8.6   Accelerated Heapsort

Recall that fixHeap handles the case that the root of a heap is vacant, but all other elements satisfy the partial order tree property. A new element is to be inserted, but it may be too small to belong in the root. The element is "filtered down" to either the left or the right, until it is in the correct relation to its children.

Suppose a key happens to be too low in the partial order tree, that is, too large for its current position? A dual procedure suggests itself for "bubbling" that element *up* the tree (i.e., toward the root), in analogy with an air bubble rising through water. In fact, "bubbling up" is simpler, because the element in question has only one parent—there is no "left or right" decision to make. The bubbleUpHeap procedure is a natural complement to fixHeap (Algorithm 4.9). After working out the details of bubbleUpHeap, we will see how to use the expanded repertoire to speed up Heapsort by about a factor of two.

We continue to assume a maximizing heap, because that is the kind used by Heapsort. More exactly, bubbleUpHeap is given an element K and a "vacant" position, such that placing the element in that vacant position may place it too low in the heap; that is, K may be bigger than its parent.

The procedure lets small elements on the path from vacant to the root migrate down, as vacant bubbles up, until the proper place for the new element is found. (For an index i, parent$(i) = \lfloor i/2 \rfloor$.) The operation is similar to the action of Insertion Sort as it inserts a new element into the sorted portion of the array.

Algorithm 4.10   Bubble-Up Heap

Input: An array E representing a heap structure; integers root and vacant, and an element K to be inserted at vacant or some ancestor node of vacant, up to root, in such a way as to maintain the partial order tree property in E. As a precondition, E has the partial order tree property if the node vacant is disregarded.

Output: The subheap rooted at root has K inserted and has the partial order tree property.

Remark: The structure of E is not altered, but the contents of its nodes are changed.

```
void  bubbleUpHeap(Element[] E, int root, Element K, int vacant)
    if (vacant == root)
        E[vacant] = K;
    else
        int  parent = vacant / 2;
        if (K.key ≤ E[parent].key)
            E[vacant] = K;
        else
            E[vacant] = E[parent];
            bubbleUpHeap(E, root, K, parent);
```

Bubbling an element up through the heap using bubbleUpHeap requires only one comparison per level. Algorithm 4.10 can be used to support insertion into a heap (see Exercise 4.41).

Combining bubbleUpHeap with a slightly modified fixHeap allows us to cut the number of comparisons done by Heapsort by about a factor of two. This makes Heapsort very competitive with Mergesort in terms of the number of comparisons—their worst-case leading terms now have the same coefficient (one). The number of element movements is not reduced further, but that measure was already comparable to Mergesort. Heapsort has the advantage of not requiring an auxiliary array, as Mergesort does.

The main idea is simple. Filtering an element down with fixHeap requires two comparisons per level. But we can avoid one of these comparisons—the one with K, the element being filtered down—without upsetting the partial order tree property. That is, compare the left child of vacant with the right child of vacant and move the larger element up to vacant (assuming a maximizing heap). Now vacant moves down to the former position of the child that moved up. This costs only one comparison per level, instead of two. We will call this variant *risky* fixHeap, for the moment.

By not comparing the larger child with K, we risk going too far down the tree and "promoting" elements that are smaller than K. However, if this kind of overshooting occurs, we can use bubbleUpHeap to move K *up* to its correct position, at a cost of one compare per level. Since bubbling K back up the tree at most pays back the comparisons we saved on the way down, we can't really lose. Let h be the height of the heap with n nodes. The normal fixHeap costs $2h$ comparisons in the worst case. Running the risky fixHeap all the way down the tree costs only h comparisons. Now bubbleUpHeap requires at most h comparisons, and might require a lot fewer.

Recall how deleteMax works. After removing the element at the root, we reinsert an element K taken from the bottom of the heap. So K is likely to be a rather small node, and probably will not bubble very far up the tree. In fact, on average, this modified method saves a factor of two in the number of comparisons needed for deleteMax. However, in the worst case, K will bubble almost all the way back up to the root of the heap, and wipe out almost all the savings. Is there a way to do better in the worst case, also? We invite you to think about this problem before continuing.

■   ■   ■

The solution is a surprising application of Divide and Conquer. Let's call "risky fix–Heap" by the more descriptive name: promote. Use promote to filter the vacant position *halfway* down the tree—that is, $\frac{1}{2}h$ levels. See Figure 4.23 for an illustration. Then test whether K is bigger than the parent of vacant. If it is, then start bubbleUpHeap from this level, and the cost is at most another $\frac{1}{2}h$ compares, for a total of h. If not, then recursively find the correct position for K in the subheap rooted at vacant; this subheap has height of only $\frac{1}{2}h$. That is, run promote to filter the vacant position down another $h/4$ levels and test K against the parent of vacant. If K is bigger, then start bubbleUpHeap from this level (depth $(3/4)h$). But now bubbleUpHeap can bubble K up *at most* to depth $\frac{1}{2}h$, because we already found out that K was smaller than (or equal to) the parent of the node at depth $\frac{1}{2}h$. If K is again smaller, then promote is run down another $h/8$ levels, and so on.

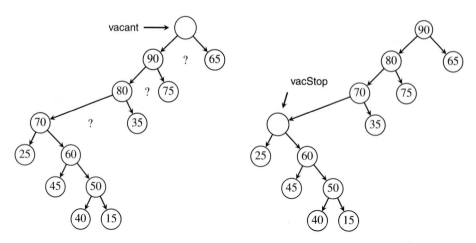

Figure 4.23 Calling promote on the heap at the left (nodes not near the path are not shown) with $h = 6$ and hStop $= 3$ leads to the heap at right.

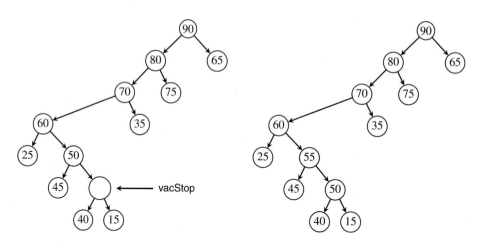

Figure 4.24 Continuing from Figure 4.23, with $K = 55$ to be reinserted. Since $K < 70$, promote is called with $h = 3$ and hStop $= 1$ leading to the heap at the left. Then bubbleUpHeap is called, leading to the final configuration on the right.

Example 4.2 Accelerated fixHeap in action

Suppose the element to be reinserted into the heap is $K = 55$, beginning with the heap that is partially shown at the left of Figure 4.23. As mentioned, promote does three comparisons and promotes 90, 80, and 70 without ever inspecting K, leading to the situation on the right.

Now K is compared with 70, the parent of the current vacStop, and is found to be smaller. Therefore promote is invoked again to lower the vacant node from height 3 to height 1; that is, $60 > 25$, so 60 is promoted, then $50 > 45$, so 50 is promoted, leading to the situation on the left of Figure 4.24.

Now K (55) is compared with 50, and is larger, so it needs to bubble up somewhere higher in the tree, but no higher than height 3, due to the earlier comparison with 70. The fixHeap operation is concluded by using bubbleUpHeap to bubble K (55) back up the path, leading to the final heap shown on the right of Figure 4.24. ∎

Algorithm 4.11   Accelerated FixHeap

Input: E, an array storing a heap structure, E[1] being the root of the entire heap; n, the number of elements in E; K, an element for which a correct location in the heap must be found; vacant, an index in E that is a candidate location for K and currently has no element in it; h, the maximum possible height of the subheap rooted at vacant (due to incomplete last level, the height may vary by 1).

The precondition is that the partial order tree property is satisfied in proper subheaps of the subheap rooted at vacant.

Output: E with K inserted in the subheap rooted at vacant so that the partial order tree property holds for this subheap.

Remark: Procedure deleteMax would call fixHeapFast with the parameters vacant = 1 and $h = \lceil \lg(n + 1) \rceil - 1$.

Procedure: See Figure 4.25. ∎

Analysis

Essentially, there is one comparison each time vacant changes a level due to the action of either bubbleUpHeap or promote. The first promote moves vacant down $\frac{1}{2}h$ levels. If bubbleUpHeap is called now, it moves vacant up by at most $\frac{1}{2}h$ levels, completing the work of fixHeapFast. Otherwise, K has been found to be smaller than the element at the parent of vacant, and promote is called again and moves vacant down by another $h/4$ levels. But in this case, if bubbleUpHeap is called next, it will move vacant up by at most $h/4$ levels, because we already found out that K was smaller than (or equal to) the parent of the node at depth $\frac{1}{2}h$. Therefore the total cost is still limited to about h in this case. This pattern continues, going down another $h/8$ levels, then $h/16$ levels, and so on. So the total number of comparisons done by all calls to promote and possibly one call to bubbleUpHeap is $h + 1$ (allowing for rounding if h is odd).

Assume bubbleUpHeap is never called, so fixHeapFast reaches its base case (and possibly needs two more comparisons in the base case). Then, eventually, fixHeapFast has made $\lg(h)$ checks to see whether to reverse direction. Adding these to the comparisons made by promote and bubbleUpHeap gives approximately $h + \lg(h)$ comparisons altogether.

Proceeding more formally, the recurrence equation is

$$T(h) = \lceil \tfrac{1}{2}h \rceil + \max\left(\lceil \tfrac{1}{2}h \rceil, 1 + T(\lfloor \tfrac{1}{2}h \rfloor)\right) \qquad T(1) = 2.$$

```
void  fixHeapFast(Element[] E, int n, Element K, int vacant, int h)
    if (h ≤ 1)
        Process heap of height 0 or 1.
    else
        int  hStop = h / 2;
        int  vacStop = promote(E, hStop, vacant, h);
        // vacStop is new vacant location, at height hStop.
        int  vacParent = vacStop / 2;
        if (E[vacParent].key ≤ K.key)
            E[vacStop] = E[vacParent];
            bubbleUpHeap(E, vacant, K, vacParent);
        else
            fixHeapFast(E, n, K, vacStop, hStop);

int  promote(Element [] E, int hStop, int vacant, int h)
    int  vacStop;
    if (h ≤ hStop)
        vacStop = vacant;
    else if (E[2*vacant].key ≤ E[2*vacant+1].key)
        E[vacant] = E[2*vacant+1];
        vacStop = promote(E, hStop, 2*vacant+1, h - 1);
    else
        E[vacant] = E[2*vacant];
        vacStop = promote(E, hStop, 2*vacant, h - 1);
    return vacStop;
```

Figure 4.25   Procedure for Algorithm 4.11

If we assume $T(h) \geq h$, as it is for the base case, the recurrence simplifies to

$$T(h) = \lceil \tfrac{1}{2}h \rceil + 1 + T(\lfloor \tfrac{1}{2}h \rfloor) \qquad T(1) = 2.$$

We can obtain the solution from the recursion tree (see Section 3.7). We might also guess the solution by computing a few small cases, then verify it by induction. (See Exercise 4.44 for the key identity.)

$$T(h) = h + \lceil \lg(h + 1) \rceil.$$

Thus deleteMax on a heap of n elements can be carried out with $\lg(n + 1) + \lg \lg(n + 1)$ comparisons, roughly, instead of about $2 \lg(n + 1)$. The following theorem summarizes the result.

Theorem 4.15   The number of comparisons for the accelerated Heapsort using the fix–HeapFast subroutine is $n \lg(n) + \Theta(n \log \log(n))$, in the worst case.   □

Algorithm	Worst case	Average	Space usage
Insertion sort	$n^2/2$	$\Theta(n^2)$	In place
Quicksort	$n^2/2$	$\Theta(n \log n)$	Extra space proportional to $\log n$
Mergesort	$n \lg n$	$\Theta(n \log n)$	Extra space proportional to n for merging
Heapsort	$2n \lg n$	$\Theta(n \log n)$	In place
Accel. Heapsort	$n \lg n$	$\Theta(n \log n)$	In place

Table 4.1   Results of analysis of four sorting algorithms. Entries are number of comparisons and include the leading terms only.

4.9   Comparison of Four Sorting Algorithms

Table 4.1 sums up the results of the analysis of the behavior of the four sorting algorithms that have been discussed so far. Although Mergesort is close to optimal in the worst case, there are algorithms that do fewer comparisons. The lower bound obtained in Section 4.7 is quite good. It is known to be exact for some values of n; that is, $\lceil \lg n! \rceil$ comparisons are sufficient to sort, for some values of n. It is also known that $\lceil \lg n! \rceil$ comparisons are not sufficient for all n. For example, $\lceil \lg 12! \rceil = 29$, but it has been proved that 30 comparisons are necessary (and sufficient) to sort 12 items in the worst case. See Notes and References at the end of the chapter for references on sorting algorithms whose worst-case behavior is close to the lower bound.

4.10   Shellsort

The technique used by Shellsort (named for its inventor Donald Shell) is interesting, and the algorithm is easy to program and runs fairly quickly. Its analysis, however, is very difficult and incomplete.

4.10.1   The Algorithm

Shellsort sorts an array E with n elements by successively sorting subsequences whose entries are intermingled in the whole array. The subsequences to be sorted are determined by a sequence, $h_t, h_{t-1}, \ldots, h_1$, of parameters called *increments*. Suppose, for example, that the first increment, h_t, is 6. Then the array is divided into six subsequences, as follows:

1. E[0], E[6], E[12], . . .
2. E[1], E[7], E[13], . . .
3. E[2], E[8], E[14], . . .
4. E[3], E[9], E[15], . . .
5. E[4], E[10], E[16], . . .
6. E[5], E[11], E[17], . . .

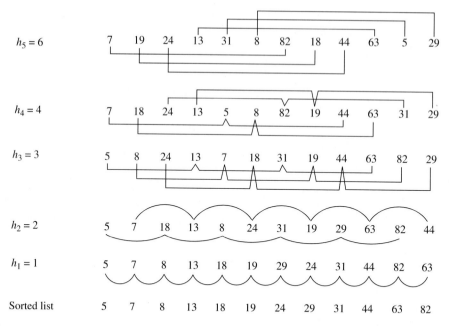

Figure 4.26   Shellsort: Note that only two pairs of elements are interchanged on the final pass.

As we see, the subsequences skip through the array at intervals of 6, in this example, and at intervals of h_t, in general.

After these subsequences are sorted, the next increment h_{t-1} is used to separate the array again into subsequences, this time with entries h_{t-1} elements apart, and again subsequences are sorted. The process is repeated for each increment. The final increment, h_1, is always 1, so at the end, the entire array will be sorted. Figure 4.26 illustrates the action of this method on a small array.

The informal description of Shellsort should prompt a number of questions. What algorithm should be used to sort the subsequences? Considering that the last increment is 1 and the entire array is sorted on the last pass, is Shellsort any more efficient than the algorithm used to sort the subsequences? Can the algorithm be written to minimize all the bookkeeping that seems to be needed to control the sorting of all the subsequences? What increments should be used?

We tackle the first two questions first. As the example in Figure 4.26 shows, when the last few passes are made using small increments, few elements will be out of order because of all the work that was done in earlier passes. So Shellsort may be efficient if, and indeed would be efficient only if, the method used to sort subsequences is one that does very little work if the array is already sorted or nearly sorted. Insertion Sort (Section 4.2) has this property. It does only $n - 1$ comparisons if the array is completely sorted, it is simple to program, and it has very little overhead.

Now suppose Shellsort is using an increment h and is to sort h subsequences, each containing approximately n/h entries. If each subsequence is to be completely sorted before any work is begun on the next, the algorithm would need to keep track of which subsequences have been sorted and which remain to be done. We avoid this bookkeeping by having the algorithm make one pass through the entire array (for each increment) intermingling its work on all the subsequences. Consecutive elements of a subsequence are h cells apart rather than one apart. Recall Insertion Sort (Algorithm 4.1) and its iterative subroutine shiftVac. Generally, "1" in shiftVac is replaced by "h" in shiftVacH, the subroutine used by Shellsort.

Algorithm 4.12   Shellsort

Input: E, an unsorted array of elements, $n \geq 0$, the number of elements, a sequence of diminishing increments $h_t, h_{t-1}, \ldots, h_1$, where $h_1 = 1$, and t, the number of increments. The range of indexes of the array E is $0, \ldots, n - 1$.

Output: E, with elements in nondecreasing order of their keys.

Remark: The sequence of increments might be computed rather than input.

```
void  shellSort(Element[] E, int n, int[] h, int t);
    int  xindex, s;

    for (s = t; s ≥ 1; s --)
        for (xindex = h[s]; xindex < n; xindex ++)
        // xindex begins at second element of subsequence 0.
            Element  current = E[xindex];
            Key  x = current.key;
            int  xLoc = shiftVacH(E, h[s], xindex, x);
            E[xLoc] = current;
    return;


// Shellsort version of shiftVac, uses increment h.
int  shiftVacH(Element[] E, int h, int xindex, Key x)
    int  vacant, xLoc;
    vacant = xindex;
    xLoc = 0;  // Assume failure.
    while (vacant ≥ h)
        // vacant-h is preceding index in current subsequence.
        if (E[vacant-h].key ≤ x)
            xLoc = vacant;  // Succeed.
            break;
        E[vacant] = E[vacant-h];
        vacant -= h;  // Keep looking.
    return xLoc;
```

Recall that Insertion Sort was slow because shiftVac removed at most one inversion after each comparison. Although after each comparison in Shellsort, shiftVacH removes at most one inversion from the subsequence it is sorting, it has the chance of eliminating up to h inversions from the whole array for each comparison because it causes elements to be moved across many others. Thus there is a possibility that the average behavior of Shellsort is in $o(n^2)$. The efficiency of Shellsort stems from the fact that sorting with one increment, say k, will not undo any of the work done previously when a different increment, say h, was used. More precisely, we say that a list is h-ordered if $E[i] \le E[i + h]$ for $0 \le i < n - h$, in other words, if all the subsequences consisting of every hth element are sorted. To h-sort an array means to sort subsequences using increment h.

Theorem 4.16   If an h-ordered array is k-sorted, the array will still be h-ordered.

Proof   See Notes and References at the end of the chapter. It is worthwhile to examine Figure 4.26 to see that the theorem is true for the example given there.   □

4.10.2   Analysis and Remarks

The number of comparisons done by Shellsort is a function of the sequence of increments used. A complete analysis is extremely difficult and requires answers to some mathematical problems that have not yet been solved. Therefore the best possible sequence of increments has not been determined, but some specific cases have been thoroughly studied. One of these is the case where $t = 2$, that is, where exactly two increments, h and 1, are used. It has been shown that the best choice for h is approximately $1.72 \sqrt[3]{n}$, and with this choice the average running time is proportional to $n^{5/3}$. This may seem surprising since using the increment 1 is the same as doing Insertion Sort, which has $\Theta(n^2)$ average behavior; just doing one preliminary pass through the array with increment h lowers the asymptotic order of the running time. By using more than two increments, the running time can be improved even more.

It is known that if the increments are $h_k = 2^k - 1$ for $1 \le k \le \lfloor \lg n \rfloor$, the number of comparisons done in the worst case is in $O(n^{3/2})$. Empirical studies (with values of n as high as 250,000) have shown that another set of increments gives rise to very fast-running programs. These are defined by $h_i = (3^i - 1)/2$ for $1 \le i \le t$, where t is chosen as the smallest integer such that $h_{t+2} \ge n$. These increments are easy to compute iteratively. We can find h_t at the beginning of the sort by using the relation $h_{s+1} = 3h_s + 1$ and comparing the results to n. Instead of storing all the increments, we can recompute them in reverse order during the sort using the formula $h_s = (h_{s+1} - 1)/3$.

It has been proven that, if the increments consist of all integers of the form $2^i 3^j$ that are less than n (used in decreasing order), then the number of comparisons done is in $O(n(\log n)^2)$. The worst-case running times for the other sets of increments are known or expected to be of higher asymptotic order. However, because of the large number of integers of the form $2^i 3^j$, there will be more passes through the array, hence more overhead, with these increments than with others. Therefore they are not particularly useful unless n is fairly large.

Shellsort is clearly an in-place sort. Although the analysis of the algorithm is far from complete, and it is not known which increments are best, its speed and simplicity make it a good choice in practice.

4.11 Radix Sorting

For the sorting algorithms in Sections 4.2 through 4.10, only one assumption was made about the keys: They are elements of a linearly ordered set. The basic operation of the algorithms is a comparison of two keys. If we make more assumptions about the keys, we can consider algorithms that perform other operations on them. This section studies a few such algorithms, called "bucket sorts," "radix sorts," and "distribution sorts."

4.11.1 Using Properties of the Keys

Suppose the keys are names and are printed on cards, one name per card. To alphabetize the cards by hand we might first separate them into 26 piles according to the first letter of the name, or fewer piles with several letters in each; alphabetize the cards in each pile by some other method, perhaps similar to Insertion Sort; and finally combine the sorted piles. If the keys are all five-digit decimal integers, we might separate them into 10 piles according to the first digit. If they are integers between 1 and m, for some m, we might make a pile for each of the k intervals $[1, m/k]$, $[m/k + 1, 2m/k]$, and so on. In each of these examples the keys are distributed into different piles as a result of examining individual letters or digits in a key or by comparing keys to predetermined values. Then the piles are sorted individually and recombined. Algorithms that sort by such methods are not in the class of algorithms previously considered because to use them we must know something about either the structure or the range of the keys.

We will present one *radix sort* algorithm in detail later. To distinguish the specific algorithm from others of the same type, we use the term "bucket sorts" for the general class of algorithms.

How Fast Are Bucket Sorts?

A bucket sort has three phases:

1. distribute keys,
2. sort buckets individually,
3. combine buckets.

The type of work done in each phase is different, so our usual approach of choosing one basic operation to count will not work well here. Suppose there are k buckets.

During the distribution phase, the algorithm examines each key once (either examining a particular field of bits or comparing the key to some constant number of preset values). Then it does some work to indicate in which bucket the key belongs. This might involve copying the element or setting some indexes or pointers. The number of operations performed by a reasonable implementation of the first phase should be in $\Theta(n)$.

To sort the buckets, suppose that we use an algorithm that sorts by comparison of keys doing, say, $S(m)$ comparisons for a bucket with m elements. Let n_i be the number of elements in the ith bucket. The algorithm does $\sum_{i=1}^{k} S(n_i)$ comparisons during the second phase.

The third phase, combining buckets, may require, at worst, that all of the elements be copied from the buckets into one list; the amount of work done is in $O(n)$.

Thus most of the work is done while sorting buckets. Suppose $S(m)$ is in $\Theta(m \log m)$. Then if the keys are uniformly distributed among the buckets, the algorithm does roughly $ck(n/k) \lg(n/k) = cn \lg(n/k)$ comparisons of keys in the second phase, where c is a constant that depends on the sorting algorithm used in the buckets. Increasing k, the number of buckets, decreases the number of comparisons done. If we choose $k = n/10$, then $n \lg 10$ comparisons would be done and the running time of the bucket sort would be linear in n, assuming that the keys are evenly distributed and that the running time for the first phase does not depend on k. (As a caveat, the fewer elements per bucket, the less likely it is that the distribution will be even.) However, in the worst case, all of the elements will go into one bucket and the entire list will be sorted in the second phase, turning all of the work of the first and last phases into wasteful overhead. Thus, in the worst case, a bucket sort would be very inefficient. If the distribution of the keys is known in advance, the range of keys to go into each bucket can be adjusted so that all buckets receive an approximately equal number of elements.

The amount of space needed by a bucket sort depends on how the buckets are stored. If every bucket is to consist of a set of sequential locations (e.g., an array), then each must be allocated enough space to hold the maximum number of elements that might belong in one bucket, and that is n. Thus kn locations would be used to sort n elements. As the number of buckets increases, the speed of the algorithm increases but so does the amount of space used. Linked lists would be better; only $\Theta(n + k)$ space (for n elements plus links and a list head for each bucket) would be used. Distributing keys among the buckets would require constructing list nodes. But then how would the elements in each bucket be sorted? Quicksort and Mergesort, two of the faster algorithms discussed, can easily be implemented to sort linked lists (see Exercises 4.22 and 4.28). If the number of buckets is large, the number of elements in each will generally be small and a slower algorithm could be used. Insertion Sort can also be modified easily to sort elements in a linked list (see Exercise 4.11). With approximately n/k elements per bucket, Mergesort will do approximately $(n/k)(\lg(n) - \lg(k))$ comparisons on the average for each bucket, or $n(\lg(n) - \lg(k))$ comparisons in all. Here again, as k increases, so does the speed, but so also does the amount of space used.

You might wonder why we don't use a bucket sort algorithm recursively to create smaller and smaller buckets. There are several reasons. The bookkeeping would quickly get out of hand; pointers indicating where the various buckets begin and information needed to recombine the elements into one list would have to be stacked and unstacked often. Due to the amount of bookkeeping necessary for each recursive call, the algorithm should not count on ultimately having only one element per bucket, so another sorting algorithm will be used anyway to sort small buckets. Thus if a fairly large number of buckets is used in the first place, there is little to gain and a lot to lose by bucket sorting recursively. However,

Unsorted file	First bkt	First Pass	Second bkt	Second Pass	Third bkt	Third Pass	Fourth bkt	Fourth Pass	Fifth bkt	Fifth Pass	Sorted file
48081	1	48081	0	48001	0	48001	0	90283	0	00972	00972
97342		48001		53202		48081		90287			38107
90287	2	97342		38107	1	38107		90583	3	38107	41983
90583		53202	1	65215	2	53202		00972	4	41983	48001
53202		00972		65315		65215	1	81664		48001	48081
65215	3	90583				90283		41983		48081	53202
78397		41983	4	97342		90287	3	53202	5	53202	65215
48001		90283	6	81664	3	65315	5	65215	6	65215	65315
00972	4	81664	7	00972		97342		65315		65315	78397
65315	5	65215	8	48081		78397	7	97342	7	78397	81664
41983		65315		90583	5	90583	8	48001	8	81664	90283
90283	7	90287		41983	6	81664		48081	9	90283	90287
81664		78397		90283				38107		90287	90583
38107		38107		90287	9	00972		78397		90583	97342
			9	78397		41983				97342	

Figure 4.27 Radix Sort

although recursively distributing keys into buckets is not efficient, something quite useful can be salvaged from this idea.

4.11.2 Radix Sort

Suppose that the keys are five-digit numbers. A recursive algorithm, as just suggested, could first distribute the keys among 10 buckets according to the leftmost, or most significant, digit and then distribute the keys in each bucket among 10 more buckets according to the next most significant digit, and so on. The buckets could not be combined until they were completely sorted, hence the large amount of messy bookkeeping. It is startling that if the keys are distributed into buckets first according to their *least significant* digits (or bits, letters, or fields), then the buckets can be combined in order before distributing on the next digit. The problem of sorting the buckets has been completely eliminated. If there are, say, five digits in a key, then the algorithm distributes keys into buckets and combines the buckets five times. It distributes keys on each digit position in turn, right to left, as illustrated in Figure 4.27.

Does this always work? On the final pass when two keys are put into the same bucket because they both start with, say, 9, what ensures that they are in the proper order relative to each other? In Figure 4.27, the keys 90283 and 90583 differ in the third digit only and are put in the same bucket in each pass except the third. After the third pass, so long as the buckets are combined in order and the relative order of two keys placed in the same bucket is not changed, these keys remain in proper order relative to each other. In general, if the leftmost digit position in which two keys differ is the ith position (from the right), they will be in the proper order relative to each other after the ith pass. This statement can be proved by straightforward induction.

This sorting method is used by card-sorting machines. On old machines, the machine did the distribution step; the operator collected the piles after each pass and combined them into one for the next pass.

The distribution into piles, or buckets, may be controlled by a column on a card, a digit position, or a bit field in the key. The algorithm is called *Radix Sort* because it treats the keys as numbers in a particular radix, or base. In the example in Figure 4.27, the radix is 10. If the keys are 32-bit positive integers, the algorithm could use, say, four-bit fields, implicitly treating the keys as numbers in radix 16. It would distribute them among 16 buckets. Thus the radix is also the number of buckets. In the Radix Sort algorithm that follows, we assume that distribution is done on bit fields. The fields are extracted from the keys beginning with the low-order bits. If possible, the number of fields is held constant and does not depend on n, the number of elements in the input. In general, this requires that the radix (number of buckets) increases with n. A versatile choice is the largest $2^w \leq n$, where w is an integer. Then each field is w bits wide. If the keys are densely distributed (i.e., in a range proportional to some polynomial in n), this strategy yields a constant number of fields.

The data structure is illustrated in Figure 4.28 for the third pass of the example in Figure 4.27. Note that each buckets list is in reverse order because new elements are attached to the beginning of the prior list. However, the combine procedure reverses them again as it combines them, so the final combined list is in the correct order.

Algorithm 4.13   Radix Sort

Input: An unsorted list L, radix the number of buckets for distribution, and numFields, the number of fields in a key on which the distribution is done.

Output: The sorted list, newL.

Remark: The procedure distribute reverses lists going into buckets and combine reverses them again coming out (and has its loop in reverse order), so the combination preserves the desired order. Operations of the List ADT are used to manipulate linked lists (see Figure 2.3).

```
List radixSort(List L, int radix, int numFields)
    List[] buckets = new List[radix];
    int field;  // field number within the key.
    List newL;

    newL = L;
    for (field = 0; field < numFields; field ++)
        Initialize buckets array to empty lists.
        distribute(newL, buckets, radix, field);
        newL = combine(buckets, radix);
    return newL;
```

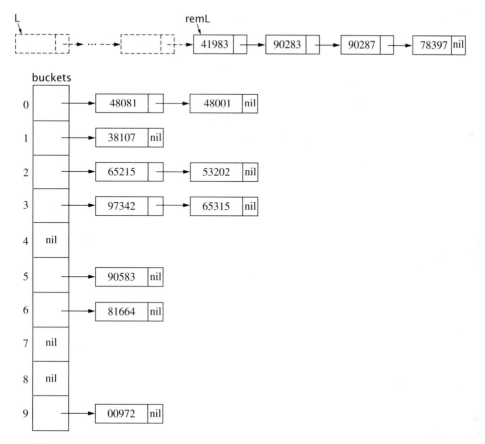

Figure 4.28   The data structure for Radix Sort during distribution on the third digit

```
void  distribute(List L, List[] buckets, int radix, int field)
    // Distribute keys into buckets.
    List remL;

    remL = L;
    while (remL ≠ nil)
        Element  K = first(remL);
        int  b = maskShift(field, radix, K.key);
        // maskShift(f, r, key) selects field f (counting
        // from the right) of key, based on radix r.
        // The result, b, is the range 0 ... radix−1,
        // and is the bucket number for K.
        buckets[b] = cons(K, buckets[b]);
        remL = rest(remL);
    return;
```

```
List  combine(List[] buckets, int radix)
    // Combine linked lists in all buckets into one list L.
    int  b;  // bucket number
    List  L, remBucket;

    L = nil;
    for (b = radix−1; b ≥ 0; b −−)
        remBucket = buckets[b];
        while (remBucket ≠ nil)
            Key  K = first(remBucket);
            L = cons(K, L);
            remBucket = rest(remBucket);
    return L;
```

Analysis and Remarks

Distributing one key requires extracting a field and doing a few link operations; the number of steps is bounded by a constant. So, for all keys, distribute does $\Theta(n)$ steps. Similarly, combine does $\Theta(n)$ steps. The number of distribution and combination passes is num-Fields, the number of fields used for distribution. If this can be held constant, the total number of steps done by Radix Sort is linear in n.

Our implementation of Radix Sort used $\Theta(n)$ extra space for the link fields, provided the radix is bounded by n. Other implementations that do not use links also use extra space in $\Theta(n)$.

Exercises

Section 4.1   Introduction

4.1   One of the easiest sorting algorithms to understand is one that we call Maxsort. It works as follows: Find the largest key, say max, in the unsorted section of the array (initially the whole array) and then interchange max with the element in the last position in the unsorted section. Now max is considered part of the sorted section consisting of larger keys at the end of the array; it is no longer in the unsorted section. Repeat this procedure until the whole array is sorted.

a.   Write an algorithm for Maxsort assuming an array E contains n elements to be sorted, with indexes $0, \ldots, n - 1$.

b.   How many comparisons of keys does Maxsort do in the worst case? On the average?

4.2   The next few exercises are about a sorting method called Bubble Sort. It sorts by making several passes through the array, comparing pairs of keys in adjacent locations, and interchanging their elements if they are out of order. That is, the first and second keys are compared and interchanged if the first is larger than the second; then the (new) second and the third keys are compared and interchanged if necessary, and so on. It is easy to see that the largest key will bubble up to the end of the array; on subsequent passes it will be ignored. If on any pass no entries are interchanged, the array is completely sorted and the algorithm can halt. The following algorithm makes this informal description of the method precise.

Algorithm 4.14   Bubble Sort

Input: E, an array of elements, and $n \geq 0$, the number of elements.

Output: E with elements in nondecreasing order of their keys.

```
void  bubbleSort(Element[] E, int n)
    int  numPairs; // the number of pairs to be compared
    boolean  didSwitch; // true if an interchange is done
    int  j;

    numPairs = n − 1;
    didSwitch = true;
    while (didSwitch)
        didSwitch = false;
        for (j = 0; j < numPairs; j ++)
            if (E[j] > E[j + 1])
                Interchange E[j] and E[j + 1].
                didSwitch = true;
            // Continue for loop.
        numPairs −−;
    return;
```

The example in Figure 4.29 illustrates how Bubble Sort works.

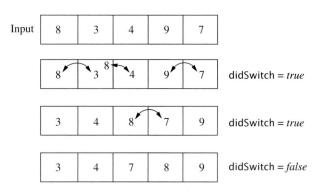

Figure 4.29   Bubble Sort

a. How many key comparisons does Bubble Sort do in the worst case? What arrangement of keys is a worst case?

b. What arrangement of keys is a best case for Bubble Sort, that is, for what input does it do the fewest comparisons? How many comparisons does it do in the best case?

4.3   The correctness of Bubble Sort (Exercise 4.2) depends on several facts. These are easy to verify but worth doing in order to consciously recognize the mathematical properties involved.

a. Prove that, after one pass through the array, the largest entry will be at the end.

b. Prove that, if there is no pair of consecutive entries out of order, then the entire array is sorted.

4.4   We can modify Bubble Sort (Exercise 4.2) to avoid unnecessary comparisons in the tail of the array by keeping track of where the last interchange occurred in the **for** loop.

a. Prove that if the last exchange made in some pass occurs at the jth and $(j + 1)$st positions, then all entries from the $(j + 1)$st through the $(n - 1)$th are in their correct position. (Note that this is stronger than saying simply that these items are in order.)

b. Modify the algorithm so that if the last exchange made in a pass occurs at the jth and $(j + 1)$st positions, the next pass will not examine any entries from the $(j + 1)$st position to the end of the array.

c. Does this change affect the worst-case behavior of the algorithm? If so, how?

4.5   Can something similar to the improvement in the preceding exercise be done to avoid unnecessary comparisons when the keys at the beginning of the array are already in order? If so, write the modifications to the algorithm. If not, explain why not.

Section 4.2   Insertion Sort

4.6   We observed that a worst case for Insertion Sort occurs when the keys are initially in decreasing order. Describe at least two other initial arrangements of the keys that are also worst cases. Show inputs for which the *exact* number of key comparisons (not just the *asymptotic order*) is the worst possible.

4.7   What is a best case for Insertion Sort? Describe how the elements in the list would be arranged, and tell how many comparisons of list elements would be done in that case.

4.8   Consider the following variation of Insertion Sort: For $1 \leq i < n$, to insert the element $E[i]$ among $E[0] \leq E[1] \leq \cdots \leq E[i - 1]$, do a Binary Search to find the correct position for $E[i]$.

a. How many key comparisons would be done in the worst case?

b. How many times are elements moved in the worst case?

c. What is the asymptotic order of the worst-case running time?

d. Can the number of moves be reduced by putting the elements in a linked list instead of an array? Explain.

4.9 In the average analysis of Insertion Sort we assumed that the keys were distinct. Would the average for all possible inputs, including cases with duplicate keys, be higher or lower? Why?

4.10 Show that a permutation on n items has at most $n(n-1)/2$ inversions. Which permutation(s) have exactly $n(n-1)/2$ inversions?

4.11 Give an algorithm to perform Insertion Sort on a linked list of integers, using the operations of the IntList abstract data type, in Section 2.3.2. Analyze its time and space requirements. Does the space usage depend on whether the language has "garbage collection" (see Example 2.1)?

Section 4.3   Divide and Conquer

4.12 Suppose we have a straightforward algorithm for a problem that does $\Theta(n^2)$ steps for inputs of size n. Suppose we devise a Divide-and-Conquer algorithm that divides an input into two inputs half as big, and does $D(n) = n \lg n$ steps to divide the problem and $C(n) = n \lg n$ steps to combine the solutions to get a solution for the original input. Is the Divide-and-Conquer algorithm more or less efficient than the straightforward scheme? Justify your answer. *Hint*: See Equation (3.14) and Exercise 3.10.

Section 4.4   Quicksort

4.13 Complete the postconditions of extendSmallRegion in Algorithm 4.3.

4.14 In Algorithm 4.3, define the *middle region* to be the range of indexes containing the unexamined elements and the vacancy. For each of the lines 2 through 5 in the partition procedure, which variables or variable expressions (some plus or minus 1's might be needed) specify the left and right ends of the middle region? For each of the lines 2 through 5, which end of the middle region contains the vacancy? Answer for the situation immediately *before* each line is executed.

4.15 How many key comparisons does Quicksort (Algorithms 4.2 and 4.3) do if the array is already sorted? How many element movements does it do?

4.16 Prove that if the "stack space optimization" improvement in Section 4.4.4 is used in Algorithm 4.2, then the maximum stack size is in $O(\log n)$.

4.17 Suppose that, instead of choosing E[first] as pivot, Quicksort lets pivot be the median of E[first], E[(first+last)/2], and E[last]. How many key comparisons will Quicksort do in the worst case to sort n elements? (Remember to count the comparisons done in choosing pivot.)

4.18   This exercise examines an alternative algorithm for Partition, with simple and elegant code. This method is due to Lomuto; we call it partitionL. The idea, as illustrated in Figure 4.30, is to collect small elements to the left of the vacancy, large elements immediately to the right of the vacancy, with unknown (i.e., unexamined) elements being at the far right of the range. Initially, all the elements are in the unknown group. "Small" and "large" are determined with respect to pivot. When partitionL finds a small element in the unknown group, it moves the small element to the vacancy, then creates a new vacancy one place to the right by moving a large element from that place to the end of the "large" range.

```
int  partitionL(Element[] E, Key pivot, int first, int last)
     int vacant, unknown;

1.  vacant = first;
2.  for (unknown = first+1; unknown ≤ last; unknown ++)
3.        if (E[unknown] < pivot)
4.             E[vacant] = E[unknown];
5.             E[unknown] = E[vacant+1];
6.             vacant ++;
7.  return vacant;
```

At each iteration of its loop partitionL compares the next unknown element, which is E[unknown], to pivot. Finally, after all the elements have been compared to pivot, vacant is returned as the splitPoint.

a.   At the beginning of each of the lines 2 through 6, what are the boundaries of the small-key region and the large-key region? Express your answer using unknown and other index variables.

b.   At the beginning of line 7, what are the boundaries of the small-key region and the large-key region? Express your answer *without* using unknown.

c.   How many key comparisons does partitionL do on a subrange of E with k elements? If Quicksort uses partitionL instead of partition, what is the impact on the total number of key comparisons done in the worst case?

4.19   Suppose the array E contains the keys 10, 9, 8, . . ., 2, 1, and is to be sorted using Quicksort.

a.   Show how the keys would be arranged after each of the first two calls to the partition procedure in Algorithm 4.3. Tell how many element movements are done by each of these two calls to partition. From this example, estimate the total number of element movements that would be done to sort n elements initially in decreasing order.

b.   Do the same for partitionL described in the preceding exercise.

c.   List some of the relative advantages and disadvantages of the two partition algorithms.

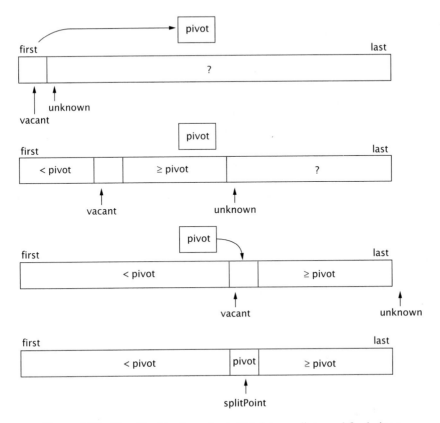

Figure 4.30 How PartitionL works: initial, intermediate, and final views

4.20 Suppose all *n* elements in the array to be sorted by Quicksort are equal. How many key comparisons will Quicksort do to sort the array (using partition in Algorithm 4.3)? Justify your answer.

4.21 This exercise explores the average number of element movements done by Quicksort using different versions of Partition. *Hint for parts* (a) *and* (b): When an element is compared with the pivot, what is the probability that it has to be moved?

a. How many element movements does Quicksort do on the average, using the partitionL subroutine of Exercise 4.18?

b. How many element movements does Quicksort do on the average, using the partition subroutine of Algorithm 4.3?

c. How do these results compare to Mergesort (see Exercise 4.27)?

4.22 Write a version of Quicksort and Partition for linked lists of integers, using the operations of the IntList abstract data type, in Section 2.3.2. Analyze its time and space requirements. Does the space usage depend on whether the language has "garbage collection" (see Example 2.1)?

Section 4.5   Merging Sorted Sequences

4.23   Give an algorithm to merge two sorted linked list of integers, using the operations of the IntList abstract data type, in Section 2.3.2.

★ **4.24**   Suppose the array subranges to be merged are of lengths k and m, where k is much less than m. Describe a merging algorithm that takes advantage of this to do at most (say) $(k + m)/2$ comparisons, provided k is sufficiently small in relation to m. How small does k have to be to achieve this bound in the worst case? Is there a range of k for which the bound $\sqrt{k + m}$ can be achieved? What can you say about the amount of element movement that is needed in these cases?

4.25   Show that the number of permutations that can be formed by merging two sorted segments A and B of lengths k and m, where $k + m = n$, is $\binom{n}{k} = \binom{n}{m}$. (Recall this notation from Equation 1.1.) Assume $k \leq m$ for definiteness, and assume no duplicate keys. *Hint*: Formulate a recurrence based on the relationship of A[0] and B[0], then look at Exercise 1.2. There are several other ways of looking at this problem that also work.

Section 4.6   Mergesort

4.26   How many key comparisons are done by Mergesort if the keys are already in order when the sort begins?

4.27   Mergesort (Algorithm 4.5) was described assuming that Merge developed its output in a work array, then copied the contents of the work array back to the input array when it was done.

a.   Work out a strategy for "toggling" between the input array and the work array to avoid this extra copying. That is, at alternate levels of the recursion either the original input array has the data to be merged or the work array has it.

b.   With the above optimization, how many element movements does Mergesort do on the average? How does this compare to Quicksort (see Exercise 4.21)?

4.28   Write a version of Mergesort for linked lists of integers, using the operations of the IntList abstract data type, in Section 2.3.2. Analyze its time and space requirements. Does the space usage depend on whether the language has "garbage collection" (see Example 2.1)?

4.29   For the Mergesort analysis using the recursion tree (Section 4.6), where D is the maximum depth of the tree and B is the number of base cases at depth $D - 1$, verify that $B = 2^D - n$.

4.30   Derive the minimum value of the expression $(\alpha - \lg \alpha)$ in the interval $(1,2)$, which was used in the proof of Theorem 4.6. Show that it is $(1 + \ln \ln 2)/\ln 2$.

Section 4.7   Lower Bounds for Sorting by Comparison of Keys

4.31   Draw the decision tree for Quicksort with $n = 3$. (You will have to modify the conventions a bit. Some branches should be labeled "$\leq$" or "$\geq$.")

4.32

a.   Give an algorithm to sort four elements using only five key comparisons in the worst case.

⋆ **b.**   Give an algorithm to sort five elements that is optimal in the worst case. (This problem will be revisited in Chapter 5 after some new techniques have been introduced.)

⋆ **4.33**   Using the result of Exercise 4.25, give a lower bound based on decision trees for the number of comparisons needed to merge two sorted segments of lengths k and m, where $k + m = n$. Assume $k \leq m$ for definiteness, and assume no duplicate keys. Your expression will involve both k and m, since they are not assumed to be equal; n might also be used for convenience, but it can be replaced by $k + m$.

a.   First, derive an expression that may involve sums, but is exact.

b.   For $k = m = n/2$, find an approximation in closed form that is close to, but guaranteed to be less than, your expression from part (a). ("Closed form" means that the expression should not contain sums or integrals.) How does your expression compare with Theorem 4.4?

⋆⋆ **c.**   This part may require some involved mathematics. Find an approximation in closed form for the case when $k < m$. As in part (b), it should be close to, but guaranteed to be less than, your expression from part (a). To get good results, you might wish to consider several ranges for the relationship between k and n.

Section 4.8   Heapsort

4.34   Suppose the elements in an array are (starting at index 1) 25, 19, 15, 5, 12, 4, 13, 3, 7, 10. Does this array represent a heap? Justify your answer.

4.35   Suppose the array to be sorted (into alphabetical order) by Heapsort initially contains the following sequence of letters:

C O M P L E X I T Y

Show how they would be arranged in the array after the heap construction phase (Algorithm 4.7). How many key comparisons are done to construct the heap with these keys?

4.36   The nodes of a heap are stored in an array E level by level beginning with the root and left to right within each level. Prove that the left child of the node in the ith cell is in the $2i$th cell. (Recall that a heap is stored with the root in E[1]. E[0] is not used.)

4.37   An array of distinct keys in decreasing order is to be sorted (into increasing order) by Heapsort (not Accelerated Heapsort).

a. How many comparisons of keys are done in the heap construction phase (Algorithm 4.7) if there are 10 elements?

b. How many are done if there are n elements? Show how you derive your answer.

c. Is an array in decreasing order a best case, worst case, or intermediate case for Algorithm 4.7? Justify your answer.

4.38   Heapsort, as described in the text, is not quite an in-place sort because recursion uses space on the activation-frame stack.

a. How much space is used on the activation-frame stack?

b. Convert fixHeap to an iterative procedure.

c. Convert fixHeapFast to an iterative procedure.

d. Convert constructHeap to an iterative procedure by calling fixHeapFast (or fixHeap) in a **for** loop starting at E[n/2] and going backwards to E[1], the root of the heap.

e. How many comparisons does the iterative version of constructHeap do in the worst case (what asymptotic order)?

4.39   This exercise gives an alternative argument for the worst-case analysis of the heap construction phase of Heapsort. The constructHeap procedure calls fixHeap once for each node in the heap, and we know that the number of key comparisons done by fixHeap in the worst case is twice the height of the node. (Recall that the *height* of a node in a binary tree is the height of the subtree rooted at that node.) Thus the number of key comparisons done in the worst case is at most twice the sum of the heights of all the nodes. Prove that the sum of the heights of the nodes in a heap of n nodes is at most $n - 1$. *Hint*: Use a marking strategy, systematically marking off one branch in the tree for each unit of height in the sum.

4.40   We could eliminate one call to fixHeap in Heapsort (Algorithm 4.8) by changing the **for** loop control to

    for (heapsize = n; heapsize $\geq$ 3; heapsize −−;)

What statement, if any, must be added after the **for** loop to take care of the case when two elements remain in the heap? How many comparisons, if any, are eliminated?

4.41   Suppose we have a heap with heapSize elements stored in an array H, and we want to add a new element, K. Using bubbleUpHeap from Section 4.8.6, the procedure is simply

```
int heapInsert(Element[] H, Element K, int heapSize)
    int newSize = heapSize + 1;
    bubbleUpHeap(H, 1, K, newSize);
    return newSize;
```

a. How many comparisons of keys does heapInsert do in the worst case on a heap that contains n elements after the insertion?

b. An earlier version of Heapsort used heapInsert to construct a heap from the elements to be sorted by inserting the elements, one at a time, into a heap that was initially empty. How many comparisons are done by this method in the worst case to construct a heap of n elements?

c. How many comparisons would be done in the worst case by Heapsort if heapInsert were used, as described in part (b), to construct the heap?

4.42 A heap contains 100 elements, which happen to be in decreasing order in the array, with keys 100, 99, . . ., 1.

a. Show how deleteMax will work on this heap (to delete key 100 only) if it is implemented with fixHeapFast. Show specifically what comparisons and element movements occur.

b. How many comparisons are done?

c. How does this compare with the implementation using fixHeap?

4.43 An array of distinct keys in decreasing order is to be sorted (into increasing order) by Accelerated Heapsort. Assume fixHeapFast is used instead of fixHeap.

a. How many comparisons of keys are done in the heap construction phase (Algorithm 4.7) if there are 31 elements?

b. How many are done if there are n elements? Show how you derive your answer.

c. Is an array in decreasing order a best case, worst case, or intermediate case for Algorithm 4.7, using fixHeapFast? Justify your answer.

★ **4.44** Show that $\lceil \lg(\lfloor \frac{1}{2}h \rfloor + 1) \rceil + 1 = \lceil \lg(h + 1) \rceil$ for all integers $h \geq 1$.

Section 4.10   Shellsort

4.45 Suppose five increments are used in Shellsort and they are all constant (independent of n, the number of elements being sorted). Show that, although the number of comparisons done in the worst case may be somewhat smaller than the number done by Insertion Sort, it will still be in $\Theta(n^2)$.

Section 4.11   Radix Sorting

4.46 Suppose Radix Sort does m distribution passes on keys with w bits (where m is a divisor of w) and there is one bucket for each pattern of w/m bits, hence radix $= 2^{w/m}$. Since mn key distributions are done, it may seem advantageous to decrease m. How large must the new radix be if m is halved?

Additional Problems

4.47 Suppose an algorithm does m^2 steps on an array of m elements (for any $m \geq 1$). The algorithm is to be used on two arrays A_1 and A_2 (separately). The arrays contain a total of n elements. A_1 has k elements and A_2 has $n - k$ elements ($0 \leq k \leq n$).

For what value(s) of k will the most work be done? For what value(s) of k will the least work be done? Justify your answers. (Remember that an example is not a proof. There is a good solution for this problem using some simple calculus.)

4.48   To sort or not to sort: Outline a reasonable method of solving each of the following problems. Give the order of the worst-case complexity of your methods.

a.   You are given a pile of thousands of telephone bills and thousands of checks sent in to pay the bills. (Assume telephone numbers are on the checks.) Find out who didn't pay.

b.   You are given an array in which each entry contains the title, author, call number, and publisher of all the books in a school library and another array of 30 publishers. Find out how many of the books were published by each of those 30 companies.

c.   You are given an array containing checkout records of all the books checked out of the campus library during the past year. Determine how many distinct people checked out at least one book.

★ **4.49**   Solve the following recurrence equation:

$$T(n) = \sqrt{n}\,T(\sqrt{n}) + cn \qquad \text{for } n > 2 \qquad T(2) = 1$$

where c is some positive constant.

4.50   Give an efficient in-place algorithm to rearrange an array of n elements so that all the negative keys precede all the nonnegative keys. How fast is your algorithm?

4.51   A sorting method is *stable* if equal keys remain in the same relative order in the sorted sequence as they were in the original sequence. (That is, a sort is stable if for any $i < j$ such that initially $E[i] = E[j]$, the sort moves $E[i]$ to $E[k]$ and moves $E[j]$ to $E[m]$ for some k and m such that $k < m$.) Which of the following algorithms are stable? For each that is not, give an example in which the relative order of two equal keys is changed.

a.   Insertion Sort.
b.   Maxsort (Exercise 4.1).
c.   Bubble Sort (Exercise 4.2).
d.   Quicksort.
e.   Heapsort.
f.   Mergesort.
g.   Shellsort.
h.   Radix Sort.

4.52   Suppose you have an array of 1000 records in which only a few are out of order and they are not very far from their correct positions. Which sorting algorithm would you use to put the whole array in order? Justify your choice.

4.53   What sorting algorithm described in this chapter would be difficult to adapt to sort elements stored in a linked list (without changing the worst-case asymptotic order)?

4.54 Throughout most of this chapter we have assumed that the keys in the set to be sorted were distinct. Often, there are duplicate keys. Such duplication could make sorting easier, but algorithms that were designed for distinct (or mostly distinct) keys may not take advantage of the duplication. Let's consider the extreme case where there are only two possible key values, say, 0 and 1.

   a. What is the asymptotic order of the number of key comparisons done by Insertion Sort in the worst case? (Describe a worst-case input.)

   b. What is the order of the number of key comparisons done by Quicksort in the worst case? (Describe a worst-case input.)

   c. Give an efficient algorithm for sorting a set of n elements whose keys may each be either 0 or 1. What is the order of the worst-case running time of your algorithm?

★ **4.55** Each of n elements in an array may have one of the key values *red*, *white*, or *blue*. Give an efficient algorithm for rearranging the elements so that all the *red*s come before all the *white*s, and all the *white*s come before all the *blue*s. (It may happen that there are no elements of one or two of the colors.) The only operations permitted on the elements are examination of a key to find out what color it is, and a swap, or interchange, of two elements (specified by their indexes). What is the asymptotic order of the worst-case running time of your algorithm? (There is a linear solution.)

4.56 Suppose that you have a computer with n memory locations, numbered 1 through n, and one instruction CEX, called "compare-exchange." For $1 \leq i, j \leq n$, CEX i, j compares the keys in memory cells i and j and interchanges them if necessary so that the smaller key is in the cell with the smaller index. The CEX instruction can be used to sort. For example, the following program sorts for $n = 3$:

```
CEX 1,2
CEX 2,3
CEX 1,2
```

   a. Write an efficient program using only CEX instructions to sort six elements. (*Suggestion:* Write programs for $n = 4$ and $n = 5$ first. It is easy to write programs for $n = 4$, 5, and 6 using 6, 10, and 15 instructions, respectively. However, none of these is optimal.)

   b. Write a CEX program to sort n elements in n cells for a fixed but arbitrary n. Use as few instructions as you can. Describe the strategy your program uses and include comments where appropriate. Since there are no loop and test instructions, you may use ellipses to indicate repetition of instructions of a certain form; for example:

```
CEX 1,2
CEX 2,3
  ⋮
CEX n − 1, n
```

c. How many CEX instructions does your program for part (b) have?

d. Give a lower bound on the number of CEX instructions needed to sort n elements.

4.57

a. Suppose CEX instructions (described in the preceding exercise) can be carried out simultaneously if they are working on keys in different memory cells. For example CEX 1,2, CEX 3,4, CEX 5,6, and so on, can all be carried out at the same time. Give an algorithm to sort four elements in only three time units. (Recall that sorting four elements requires five comparisons.)

★ **b.** Give an algorithm using (simultaneous) CEX instructions to sort n elements in $o(\log(n!))$ time units.

★ **4.58** M is an $n \times n$ integer matrix in which the entries of each row are in increasing order (reading left to right) and the entries in each column are in increasing order (reading top to bottom). Give an efficient algorithm to find the position of an integer x in M, or determine that x is not there. Tell how many comparisons of x with matrix entries your algorithm does in the worst case. You may use three-way comparisons; that is, a comparison of x with M[i][j] tells if $x <$ M[i][j], $x =$ M[i][j], or $x >$ M[i][j].

★ **4.59** E is an array containing n integers, and we want to find the maximum sum for a contiguous subsequence of elements of E. (If all elements of a sequence are negative, we define the maximum contiguous subsequence to be the empty sequence with sum equal to zero.) For example, consider the sequence with elements

$$38, -62, 47, -33, 28, 13, -18, -46, 8, 21, 12, -53, 25.$$

The *maximum subsequence sum* for this array is 55. The maximum contiguous subsequence occurs in positions 3 through 6 (inclusive).

a. Give an algorithm that finds the maximum subsequence sum in an array. What is the asymptotic order of the running time of your algorithm? (The data in Tables 1.1 and 1.2 come from various algorithms for this problem. As those tables indicate, there are many solutions of varying complexity, including a linear one.)

b. Show that any algorithm for this problem must examine all elements in the array in the worst case. (So any algorithm does $\Omega(n)$ steps in the worst case.)

★ **4.60**   Instead of rearranging an array E of large records during sorting, it is easy to change to code to work with an array of *indexes* of these records, and rearrange the indexes, instead. When the sorting is finished, the array of indexes defines the correct permutation, π, of the original array, E, to bring those records into sorted order. That is, $E[\pi[0]]$ is the minimum record, $E[\pi[1]]$ is the next smallest, and so on. This exercise studies the problem of rearranging the records themselves, after the correct permutation has been determined.

Your algorithm is given E, an array of records, and integer n, such that entries of E are defined for indexes $0, 1, \ldots, n - 1$. Your algorithm is also given another array, π, that stores a permutation of the numbers $0, 1, \ldots, n - 1$.

a. Write an algorithm that rearranges the records of E in the order $\pi[0]$, $\pi[1]$, ..., $\pi[n-1]$. That is, the record originally in $E[\pi[0]]$ should wind up in $E[0]$, the record originally in $E[\pi[1]]$ should wind up in $E[1]$, and so forth. Assume that the records in E are large; in particular, they will not fit in the π array. Your algorithm may destroy π, and you may store values outside of the range $0, ..., n-1$ in π entries. If you use extra space, state how much.

b. What is the total number of times records are moved by your algorithm in the worst case? Is the running time of your algorithm proportional to the number of moves? If so, explain why. If not, what is the asymptotic order of the running time?

4.61   What sorting method would you use for each of the following problems? Explain your choice.

a. A university in Southern California has about 30,000 full-time students and about 10,000 part-time students. (There is a cap of 50,000 students allowed to enroll in the university at one time, due to parking limitations.) Each student record contains the student's name, nine-digit identification number, address, grades, and so forth. A name is stored as a string of 41 characters, 20 characters each for the first and last name, and one character for the middle initial.

   The problem is to produce an alphabetized class list for each of approximately 5000 courses at the beginning of each semester. These lists are given to the instructors before the first day of class. The maximum class size is about 200. Most of the classes have about 30 students. The input for each class is an unsorted array with at most 200 records. These records contain a student's name, identification number, and university standing (freshman, sophomore, junior, senior, grad), and the address of the student's full record on disk.

b. The problem is to sort 500 exam papers alphabetically by student's last name. The sorting will be done by one person in an office with two desktops temporarily cleared of all other papers, books, and coffee cups. It is 1:00 A.M., and the person would like to go home as soon as possible.

4.62   Is it always true that an array that is already sorted is a best-case input for sorting algorithms? Give an argument or a counterexample.

4.63   Suppose we have an unsorted array A of n elements and we want to know if the array contains any duplicate elements.

a. Outline (clearly) an efficient method for solving this problem.

b. What is the asymptotic order of the running time of your method in the worst case? Justify your answer.

c. Suppose we know the n elements are integers from the range $1, ..., 2n$, so other operations besides comparing keys may be done. Give an algorithm for the same problem that is specialized to use this information. Tell the asymptotic order of the worst-case running time for this solution. It should be of lower order than your solution for part (a).

4.64   Suppose a large array is maintained with the following policy. The list is initially sorted. When new elements are added, they are inserted at the end of the array and counted. Whenever the number of new elements reaches 10, the array is resorted and the counter is cleared. What strategy would be good to use for the resorting of the array? Why?

4.65   You are given a sorted array E1 with k elements and an unsorted array E2 with $\lg k$ elements. The problem is to combine the arrays into one sorted array (with n elements, where $n = k + \lg k$). You may assume that the first array has space for all n elements if you wish.

One way to solve the problem is simply to sort the combined array, doing $\Theta(n \log n)$ key comparisons in the worst case. We want to do better. Describe two other algorithms for this problem. (You don't have to write any code.) Clearly describe the main steps for each method (in enough detail so that it is easy to estimate the number of key comparisons done). Tell the asymptotic order of the number of key comparisons for each method as a function of n (preferred) or as a function of k (if it is difficult to express as a function of n).

For at least one of the methods you describe, the number of key comparisons should be in $o(n \log n)$.

4.66   At a large university, each semester, a program must be run to detect student computer accounts that are to be deleted. Any enrolled student may have an account, and they have a "grace period" of one semester after they leave. So an account is to be deleted if the student is not currently enrolled and was not enrolled in the previous semester.

a.   Outline an algorithm to make a list of accounts to be deleted. The next two paragraphs describe the files you have to work with. You don't have to give code, but be clear about what you are doing.[1]

  The Account File is sorted by username. Each entry contains the username, real name, ID number, creation date, expiration date, major code, and other fields. The expiration date is set as Dec. 31, 2030 when a student account is established because the true expiration date is unknown at that time. For faculty accounts and other nonstudent accounts, the ID number field contains zero. There are approximately 12,000 accounts in the file.

  The Student Master File, maintained by the administration, contains a record for each student currently enrolled, approximately 30,000 entries. It is sorted alphabetically by real name. Each record includes the student ID number and other information. There are duplicate names; that is, sometimes different students have the same name. The Student Master File for the previous semester is available.

b.   Let n be the number of accounts and let s be the number of students. Express the asymptotic order of the running time of your method in terms of n and s. (Give some justification for your answer.)

c.   Real-world problems often have complications. Describe at least one situation that can occur (and is reasonably likely) but is not covered clearly in the specifications.

---

[1] The system manager at a real university reported that two people wrote programs for this problem. One took 45 minutes to run; the other took 2 minutes.

Programs

For each program include a counter that counts comparisons of keys. Include among your test data files in which the keys are in decreasing order, increasing order, and random order. Use files with various numbers of elements. Output should include the number of elements and the number of comparisons done.

1. Quicksort. Use the improvements described in Section 4.4.4.
2. Accelerated Heapsort. Show the full heap after all the elements have been inserted.
3. Radix Sort.
4. Mergesort: Implement the improvement suggested in Exercise 4.27.

Notes and References

Much of the material in this chapter is based on Knuth (1998), without a doubt the major reference on sorting and related problems. Interested readers are strongly encouraged to consult this book for more algorithms, analyses, exercises, and references. Some of the original sources of the algorithms are: Hoare (1962) for Quicksort, including variations and applications; Williams (1964) for Heapsort (with an early improvement by Floyd (1964)); and Shell (1959) for Shellsort.

The version of Partition given in Algorithm 4.3 is very close to that published by Hoare. Recent empirical evidence (unpublished) has shown that "optimizations" that reduce the number of instructions in the inner loop, at the expense of extra instructions elsewhere, are actually counterproductive on modern workstations. The reason seems to be that the eliminated instruction, a comparison of two indexes, is performed in machine registers, so is very fast anyway, whereas the extra instructions entail memory accesses and take relatively longer.

The version of the Partition procedure in Exercise 4.18 appears in Bentley (1986) where it is attributed to N. Lomuto.

Carlsson (1987) seems to be the first paper to describe a version of Heapsort that uses about $n \lg(n)$ comparisons instead of about $2n \lg(n)$, in the worst case. Several other researchers rediscovered the idea since then.

The concise argument given in Section 4.2 for the average number of inversions in a permutation was pointed out by Sampath Kannan. At the end of Section 4.8 we commented that there are algorithms that do fewer comparisons than Mergesort in the worst case. The Ford-Johnson algorithm, called Merge Insertion, is one such algorithm. It is known to be optimal for small values of n. Binary Insertion is another algorithm that does approximately $n \lg n$ comparisons in the worst case. See Knuth (1998) for descriptions of these algorithms, a discussion of various choices of increments for Shellsort, a proof of Theorem 4.16, and discussion of external sorting.

The sorting problem in Exercise 4.55 is solved in Dijkstra (1976) where it is called "The Dutch National Flag Problem." Bentley (1986) gives some history and several solutions for the maximum subsequence sum problem (Exercise 4.59). The data in Table 1.2 and all but the exponential column of Table 1.1 come from solutions to this problem. Exercise 4.61 was contributed by Roger Whitney.

Adaptive sorting procedures are procedures that take advantage of favorable input permutations to sort more efficiently. Estivill-Castro and Wood (1996) study this subject in depth.

5

Selection and Adversary Arguments

5.1 Introduction

In this chapter we study several problems that can be grouped under the general name, *selection*. Finding the median element of a set is a well-known example. Besides finding algorithms to solve the problems efficiently, we also explore *lower bounds* for the problems. We introduce a widely applicable technique known as *adversary arguments* for establishing lower bounds.

5.1.1 The Selection Problem

Suppose E is an array containing n elements with keys from some linearly ordered set, and let k be an integer such that $1 \leq k \leq n$. The *selection* problem is the problem of finding an element with the kth smallest key in E. Such an element is said to *have rank k*. As with most of the sorting algorithms we studied, we will assume that the only operations that may be performed on the keys are comparisons of pairs of keys (and copying or moving elements). In this chapter keys and elements are considered identical, because our focus is on the number of key comparisons, and we are usually not concerned with element movement. Also, when storing keys in an array, we will use positions $1, \ldots, n$, to agree with common ranking terminology, rather than $0, \ldots, n-1$. Position 0 of the array is simply left unused.

In Chapter 1 we solved the selection problem for the case $k = n$, for that problem is simply to find the largest key. We considered a straightforward algorithm that did $n - 1$ key comparisons, and we proved that no algorithm could do fewer. The dual case for $k = 1$, that is, finding the smallest key, can be solved similarly.

Another very common instance of the selection problem is the case where $k = \lceil n/2 \rceil$, that is, where we want to find the middle, or *median*, element. The median is helpful for interpreting very large sets of data, such as the income of all people in a particular country, or in a particular profession, the price of houses, or scores on college entrance tests. Instead of including the whole set of data, news reports, for example, summarize by giving us the mean (average) or median. It is easy to compute the average of n numbers in $\Theta(n)$ time. How can we compute the median efficiently?

Of course, all instances of the selection problem can be solved by sorting E; then, for whatever rank k we are interested in, $E[k]$ would be the answer. Sorting requires $\Theta(n \log n)$ key comparisons, and we have just observed that for some values of k, the selection problem can be solved in linear time. Finding the median seems, intuitively, to be the hardest instance of the selection problem. Can we find the median in linear time? Or can we establish a lower bound for median finding that is more than linear, maybe $\Theta(n \log n)$? We answer these questions in this chapter, and we sketch an algorithm for the general selection problem.

5.1.2 Lower Bounds

So far we have used the decision tree as our main technique to establish lower bounds. Recall that the internal nodes of the decision tree for an algorithm represent the comparisons the algorithm performs, and the leaves represent the outputs. (For the search problem in Section 1.6, the internal nodes also represented outputs.) The number of comparisons done in the worst case is the height of the tree; the height is at least $\lceil \lg L \rceil$, where L is the number of leaves.

In Section 1.6 we used decision trees to get the worst-case lower bound of $\lceil \lg(n + 1) \rceil$ for the search problem. That is exactly the number of comparisons done by Binary Search, so a decision tree argument gave us the best possible lower bound. In Chapter 4 we used decision trees to get a lower bound of $\lceil \lg n! \rceil$, or roughly $\lceil n \lg n - 1.5n \rceil$, for sorting. There are algorithms whose performance is very close to this lower bound, so once again, a decision tree argument gave a very strong result. However, decision tree arguments do not work very well for the selection problem.

A decision tree for the selection problem must have at least n leaves because any one of the n keys in the set may be the output, that is, the kth smallest. Thus we can conclude that the height of the tree (and the number of comparisons done in the worst case) is at least $\lceil \lg n \rceil$. But this is not a good lower bound; we already know that even the easy case of finding the largest key requires at least $n - 1$ comparisons. What's wrong with the decision tree argument? In a decision tree for an algorithm that finds the largest key, some outputs appear at more than one leaf, and there will in fact be more than n leaves. To see this, Exercise 5.1 asks you to draw the decision tree for FindMax (Algorithm 1.3) with $n = 4$. The decision tree argument fails to give a good lower bound because we don't have an easy way of determining how many leaves will contain duplicates of a particular outcome.

Instead of a decision tree, we use a technique called an *adversary argument* for establishing better lower bounds for the selection problem. This technique is described next.

5.1.3   Adversary Arguments

Suppose you are playing a guessing game with a friend. You are to pick a date (a month and day), and the friend will try to guess the date by asking yes/no questions. You want to force your friend to ask as many questions as possible. If the first question is, "Is it in the winter?" and you are a good adversary, you will answer "No," because there are more dates in the three other seasons. To the question, "Is the first letter of the month's name in the first half of the alphabet?" you should answer "Yes." But is this cheating? You didn't really pick a date at all! In fact, you will not pick a specific month and day until the need for consistency in your answers pins you down. This may not be a friendly way to play a guessing game, but it is just right for finding lower bounds for the behavior of an algorithm.

Suppose we have an algorithm that we think is efficient. Imagine an adversary who wants to prove otherwise. At each point in the algorithm where a decision (a key comparison, for example) is made, the adversary tells us the result of the decision. The adversary chooses its answers to try to force the algorithm to work hard, that is, to make a lot of decisions. You may think of the adversary as gradually constructing a "bad" input for the algorithm while it answers the questions. The only constraint on the adversary's answers is that they must be internally consistent; there must be *some* input for the problem for which its answers would be correct. If the adversary can force the algorithm to perform $f(n)$ steps, then $f(n)$ is a lower bound for the number of steps done in the worst case. This approach is explored in Exercise 5.2 for sorting and merging by key comparisons.

In fact, "designing against an adversary" is often a good technique for solving a comparison-based problem efficiently. In thinking about what comparison to make in a given situation, imagine that the adversary will give the least favorable answer—then choose a comparison where both outcomes are about equally favorable. This technique is discussed in more detail in Section 5.6. However, here we are primarily interested in the role of adversary arguments in lower-bound arguments.

We want to find a lower bound on the complexity of a *problem*, not just a particular algorithm. When we use adversary arguments, we will assume that the algorithm is any algorithm whatsoever from the class being studied, just as we did with the decision tree arguments. To get a good lower bound we need to construct a clever adversary that can thwart any algorithm.

5.1.4 Tournaments

In the rest of this chapter we present algorithms for selection problems and adversary arguments for lower bounds for several cases, including the median. In most of the algorithms and arguments, we use the terminology of contests, or tournaments, to describe the results of comparisons. The comparand that is found to be larger will be called the *winner*; the other will be called the *loser*.

5.2 Finding max and min

Throughout this section we use the names max and min to refer to the largest and smallest keys, respectively, in a set of n keys.

We can find max and min by using Algorithm 1.3 to find max, eliminating max from the set, and then using the appropriate variant of Algorithm 1.3 to find min among the remaining $n - 1$ keys. Thus max and min can be found by doing $(n - 1) + (n - 2)$, or $2n - 3$, comparisons. This is not optimal. Although we know (from Chapter 1) that $n - 1$ key comparisons are needed to find max or min independently, when finding both, some of the work can be "shared." Exercise 1.25 asked for an algorithm to find max and min with only about $3n/2$ key comparisons. A solution (for even n) is to pair up the keys and do $n/2$ comparisons, then find the largest of the winners, and, separately, find the smallest of the losers. If n is odd, the last key may have to be considered among the winners and the losers. In either case, the total number of comparisons is $\lceil 3n/2 \rceil - 2$. In this section we give an adversary argument to show that this solution is optimal. Specifically, in the remainder of this section we prove:

Theorem 5.1   Any algorithm to find max and min of n keys by comparison of keys must do at least $3n/2 - 2$ key comparisons in the worst case.

Proof   To establish the lower bound we may assume that the keys are distinct. To know that a key x is max and a key y is min, an algorithm must know that every key other than x has lost some comparison and every key other than y has won some comparison. If we count each win and loss as one unit of information, then an algorithm must have

Status of keys x and y compared by an algorithm	Adversary response	New status	Units of new information
N, N	$x > y$	W, L	2
W, N or WL, N	$x > y$	W, L or WL, L	1
L, N	$x < y$	L, W	1
W, W	$x > y$	W, WL	1
L, L	$x > y$	WL, L	1
W, L or WL, L or W, WL	$x > y$	No change	0
WL, WL	Consistent with assigned values	No change	0

Table 5.1 The adversary strategy for the min and max problem

(at least) $2n - 2$ units of information to be sure of giving the correct answer. We give a strategy for an adversary to use in responding to the comparisons so that it gives away as few as possible units of new information with each comparison. Imagine the adversary constructing a specific input set as it responds to the algorithm's comparisons.

We denote the status of each key at any time during the course of the algorithm as follows:

Key status	Meaning
W	Has won at least one comparison and never lost
L	Has lost at least one comparison and never won
WL	Has won and lost at least one comparison
N	Has not yet participated in a comparison

Each W or L is one unit of information. A status of N conveys no information. The adversary strategy is described in Table 5.1. The main point is that, except in the case where both keys have not yet been in any comparison, the adversary can give a response that provides at most one unit of new information. We need to verify that if the adversary follows these rules, its replies are consistent with some input. Then we need to show that this strategy forces any algorithm to do as many comparisons as the theorem claims.

Observe that in all cases in Table 5.1 except the last, either the key chosen by the adversary as the winner has not yet lost any comparison, or the key chosen as the loser has not yet won any. Consider the first possibility; suppose that the algorithm compares x and y, the adversary chooses x as the winner, and x has not yet lost any comparison. Even if the value already assigned by the adversary to x is smaller than the value it has assigned to y, the adversary can change x's value to make it beat y without contradicting any of the responses it gave earlier. The other situation, where the key to be the loser has never won, can be handled similarly—by reducing the value of the key if necessary. So the

Compar-ison	x_1 Status	Value	x_2 Status	Value	x_3 Status	Value	x_4 Status	Value	x_5 Status	Value	x_6 Status	Value
x_1, x_2	W	20	L	10	N	*	N	*	N	*	N	*
x_1, x_5	W	20							L	5		
x_3, x_4					W	15	L	8				
x_3, x_6					W	15					L	12
x_3, x_1	WL	20			W	25						
x_2, x_4			WL	10			L	8				
x_5, x_6									WL	5	L	3
x_6, x_4							L	2			WL	3

Table 5.2   An example of the adversary strategy for max and min

adversary can construct an input consistent with the rules in the table for responding to the algorithm's comparisons. This is illustrated in the following example.

Example 5.1   Constructing an input using the adversary's rules

The first column in Table 5.2 shows a sequence of comparisons that might be carried out by some algorithm. The remaining columns show the status and value assigned to the keys by the adversary. (Keys that have not yet been assigned a value are denoted by asterisks.) Each row after the first contains only the entries relevant to the current comparison. Note that when x_3 and x_1 are compared (in the fifth comparison), the adversary increases the value of x_3 because x_3 is supposed to win. Later, the adversary changes the values of x_4 and x_6 consistent with its rules. After the first five comparisons, every key except x_3 has lost at least once, so x_3 is max. After the last comparison, x_4 is the only key that has never won, so it is min. In this example the algorithm did eight comparisons; the worst-case lower bound for six keys (still to be proved) is $3/2 \times 6 - 2 = 7$.   ■

To complete the proof of Theorem 5.1, we just have to show that the adversary rules will force any algorithm to do at least $3n/2 - 2$ comparisons to get the $2n - 2$ units of information it needs. The only case where an algorithm can get two units of information from one comparison is the case where the two keys have not been included in any previous comparisons. Suppose for the moment that n is even. An algorithm can do at most $n/2$ comparisons of previously unseen keys, so it can get at most n units of information this way. From each other comparison, it gets at most one unit of information. The algorithm needs $n - 2$ additional units of information, so it must do at least $n - 2$ more comparisons. Thus to get $2n - 2$ units of information, it must do at least $n/2 + n - 2 = 3n/2 - 2$ comparisons in total. The reader can easily check that for odd n, at least $3n/2 - 3/2$ comparisons are needed. This completes the proof of Theorem 5.1.   □

5.3 Finding the Second-Largest Key

We can find the second-largest element of a set by finding and eliminating the largest, then finding the largest remaining element. Is there a more efficient method? Can we prove a certain method is optimal? This section answers these questions.

5.3.1 Introduction

Throughout this section we use max and secondLargest to refer to the largest and second-largest keys, respectively. For simplicity in describing the problem and algorithms, we will assume that the keys are distinct.

The second-largest key can be found with $2n - 3$ comparisons by using FindMax (Algorithm 1.3) twice, but this is not likely to be optimal. We should expect that some of the information discovered by the algorithm while finding max can be used to decrease the number of comparisons performed in finding secondLargest. Specifically, any key that loses to a key other than max cannot possibly be secondLargest. All such keys discovered while finding max can be ignored during the second pass through the set. (The problem of keeping track of them will be considered later.)

Using Algorithm 1.3 on a set with five keys, the results might be as follows:

Comparands	Winner
x_1, x_2	x_1
x_1, x_3	x_1
x_1, x_4	x_4
x_4, x_5	x_4

Then max $= x_4$ and secondLargest is either x_5 or x_1 because both x_2 and x_3 lost to x_1. Thus only one more comparison is needed to find secondLargest in this example.

It may happen, however, that during the first pass through the set to find max we don't obtain any information useful for finding secondLargest. If max were x_1, then each other key would be compared only to max. Does this mean that in the worst case $2n - 3$ comparisons must be done to find secondLargest? Not necessarily. In the preceding discussion we used a specific algorithm, Algorithm 1.3. No algorithm can find max by doing fewer than $n - 1$ comparisons, but another algorithm may provide more information that can be used to eliminate some keys from the second pass through the set. The tournament method, described next, provides such information.

5.3.2 The Tournament Method

The tournament method is so named because it performs comparisons in the same way that tournaments are played. Keys are paired off and compared in "rounds." In each round after the first one, the winners from the preceding round are paired off and compared. (If at any round the number of keys is odd, one of them simply waits for the next round.) A tournament can be described by a binary-tree diagram as shown in Figure 5.1. Each leaf contains a key, and at each subsequent level the parent of each pair contains the winner.

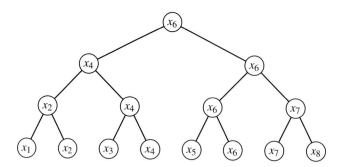

Figure 5.1 An example of a tournament; max $= x_6$; secondLargest may be x_4, x_5, or x_7.

The root contains the largest key. As in Algorithm 1.3, $n - 1$ comparisons are done to find max.

In the process of finding max, every key except max loses in one comparison. How many lose directly to max? If n is a power of 2, there are exactly $\lg n$ rounds; in general, the number of rounds is $\lceil \lg n \rceil$. Since max is involved in at most one comparison in each round, there are at most $\lceil \lg n \rceil$ keys that lost only to max. These are the only keys that could possibly be secondLargest. The method of Algorithm 1.3 can be used to find the largest of these $\lceil \lg n \rceil$ keys by doing at most $\lceil \lg n \rceil - 1$ comparisons. Thus the tournament finds max and secondLargest by doing a total of $n + \lceil \lg n \rceil - 2$ comparisons in the worst case. This is an improvement over our first result of $2n - 3$. Can we do better?

5.3.3 An Adversary Lower-Bound Argument

Both methods we considered for finding the second-largest key first found the largest key. This is not wasted effort. Any algorithm that finds secondLargest must also find max because, to know that a key is the second largest, one must know that it is not the largest; that is, it must have lost in one comparison. The winner of the comparison in which secondLargest loses must, of course, be max. This argument gives a lower bound on the number of comparisons needed to find secondLargest, namely $n - 1$, because we already know that $n - 1$ comparisons are needed to find max. But one would expect that this lower bound could be improved because an algorithm to find secondLargest should have to do more work than an algorithm to find max. We will prove the following theorem, which has as a corollary that the tournament method is optimal.

Theorem 5.2 Any algorithm (that works by comparing keys) to find the second largest in a set of n keys must do at least $n + \lceil \lg n \rceil - 2$ comparisons in the worst case.

Proof For the worst case, we may assume that the keys are distinct. We have already observed that there must be $n - 1$ comparisons with distinct losers. If max was a comparand in $\lceil \lg n \rceil$ of these comparisons, then all but one of the $\lceil \lg n \rceil$ keys that lost to max must lose again for secondLargest to be correctly determined. Then a total of at least $n + \lceil \lg n \rceil - 2$

comparisons would be done. Therefore we will show that there is an adversary strategy that can force any algorithm that finds secondLargest to compare max to $\lceil \lg n \rceil$ distinct keys.

The adversary assigns a "weight" $w(x)$ to each key x in the set. Initially $w(x) = 1$ for all x. When the algorithm compares two keys x and y, the adversary determines its reply and modifies the weights as follows.

Case	Adversary reply	Updating of weights
$w(x) > w(y)$	$x > y$	New $w(x) = $ prior $(w(x) + w(y))$; new $w(y) = 0$.
$w(x) = w(y) > 0$	Same as above.	Same as above.
$w(y) > w(x)$	$y > x$	New $w(y) = $ prior $(w(x) + w(y))$; new $w(x) = 0$.
$w(x) = w(y) = 0$	Consistent with previous replies.	No change.

To interpret the weights and adversary rules, imagine that the adversary builds trees to represent the ordering relations between the keys. If x is the parent of y, then x beat y in a comparison. Figure 5.2 shows an example. The adversary combines two trees only when their roots are compared. If the algorithm compares nonroots, no change is made in the trees. The weight of a key is simply the number of nodes in that key's tree, if it is a root, and zero otherwise.

We need to verify that if the adversary follows this strategy, its replies are consistent with some input, and max will be compared to at least $\lceil \lg n \rceil$ distinct keys. These conclusions follow from a sequence of easy observations:

1. A key has lost a comparison if and only if its weight is zero.
2. In the first three cases, the key chosen as the winner has nonzero weight, so it has not yet lost. The adversary can give it an arbitrarily high value to make sure it wins without contradicting any of its earlier replies.
3. The sum of the weights is always n. This is true initially, and the sum is preserved by the updating of the weights.
4. When the algorithm stops, only one key can have nonzero weight. Otherwise there would be at least two keys that never lost a comparison, and the adversary could choose values to make the algorithm's choice of secondLargest incorrect.

Let x be the key that has nonzero weight when the algorithm stops. By facts 1 and 4, $x = $ max. Using fact 3, $w(x) = n$ when the algorithm stops.

To complete the proof of the theorem, we need to show that x has directly won against at least $\lceil \lg n \rceil$ distinct keys. Let $w_k = w(x)$ just after the kth comparison won by x against a previously undefeated key. Then by the adversary's rules,

$$w_k \leq 2w_{k-1}.$$

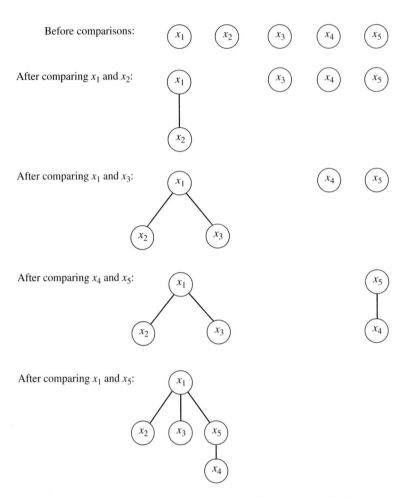

Figure 5.2   Trees for the adversary decisions in Example 5.2

Now let K be the number of comparisons x wins against previously undefeated keys. Then

$$n = w_K \leq 2^K w_0 = 2^K.$$

Thus $K \geq \lg n$, and since K is an integer, $K \geq \lceil \lg n \rceil$. The K keys counted here are of course distinct, since once beaten by x, a key is no longer "previously undefeated" and won't be counted again (even if an algorithm foolishly compares it to x again).   □

Example 5.2   The adversary strategy in action

To illustrate the adversary's action and show how its decisions correspond to the step-by-step construction of an input, we show an example for $n = 5$. Keys in the set that have not yet been specified are denoted by asterisks. Thus initially the keys are *, *, *, *, *. Note that

Comparands	Weights	Winner	New weights	Keys
x_1, x_2	$w(x_1) = w(x_2)$	x_1	2, 0, 1, 1, 1	20, 10, *, *, *
x_1, x_3	$w(x_1) > w(x_3)$	x_1	3, 0, 0, 1, 1	20, 10, 15, *, *
x_5, x_4	$w(x_5) = w(x_4)$	x_5	3, 0, 0, 0, 2	20, 10, 15, 30, 40
x_1, x_5	$w(x_1) > w(x_5)$	x_1	5, 0, 0, 0, 0	41, 10, 15, 30, 40

Table 5.3 Example of the adversary strategy for the Second-Largest Key problem

values assigned to some keys may be changed at a later time. See Table 5.3, which shows just the first few comparisons (those that find max, but not enough to find secondLargest). The weights and the values assigned to the keys will not be changed by any subsequent comparisons. ∎

5.3.4 Implementation of the Tournament Method for Finding max and secondLargest

To conduct the tournament to find max we need a way to keep track of the winners in each round. After max has been found by the tournament, only those keys that lost to it are to be compared to find secondLargest. How can we keep track of the elements that lose to max when we don't know in advance which key is max? Since the tournament is conceptually a binary tree that is as balanced as possible, the *heap structure* of Section 4.8.1 suggests itself. For a set of n elements, a heap structure of $2n - 1$ nodes is used; that is, an array E[1], ..., E[2*n−1]. Initially, place the elements in positions $n, \ldots, 2n - 1$. As the tournament progresses, positions $1, \ldots, n - 1$ will be filled (in reverse order) with winners. Exercise 5.4 covers the additional details. This algorithm uses linear extra space and runs in linear time.

5.4 The Selection Problem

Suppose we want to find the median of n elements in an array E in positions $1, \ldots, n$. (That is, we want the element of rank $\lceil n/2 \rceil$.) In earlier sections we found efficient methods for finding ranks near one extreme or the other, such as the maximum, the minimum, both maximum *and* minimum, and the second-largest key. The exercises explore more variations, but all of the techniques for these problems lose efficiency as we move away from the extremes, and are not useful for finding the median. If we are to find a solution that is more efficient than simply sorting the whole set, then a new idea is needed.

5.4.1 A Divide-and-Conquer Approach

Suppose we can partition the keys into two sets, S_1 and S_2, such that all keys in S_1 are smaller than all keys in S_2. Then the median is in the larger of the two sets (that is, the set with more keys, not necessarily the set with larger keys). We can ignore the other set and restrict our search to the larger set.

But what key do we look for in the larger set? Its median is not the median of the original set of keys.

Example 5.3   Partitioning in search of the median

Suppose $n = 255$. We are seeking the median element (whose rank is $k = 128$). Suppose, after partitioning, that S_1 has 96 elements and S_2 has 159 elements. Then the median of the whole set is in S_2, and it is the 32nd-smallest element in S_2. Thus the problem reduces to finding the element of rank 32 in S_2, which has 159 elements.   ∎

The example shows that this approach to solving the median problem naturally suggests that we solve the general selection problem.

Thus we are developing a divide-and-conquer solution for the general selection problem that, like Binary Search and FixHeap, divides the problem to be solved into *two* smaller problems, but needs to solve only *one* of the smaller problems. Quicksort uses Partition to divide the elements into subranges of elements "small" and "large" relative to a pivot element (see Algorithm 4.2). We can use a modified version of Quicksort for the selection problem, called findKth, in which only one recursive subproblem needs to be solved. The details are worked out in Exercise 5.8.

In the analysis parts of Exercise 5.8 we learn that the same pattern emerges that we found when we analyzed Quicksort. Although findKth works well on average, the worst case is plagued by the same problem that confronts Quicksort: The pivot element may give a very uneven division of the elements into S_1 and S_2. To develop a better solution, consider what we learned from Quicksort.

Seeing that the crux of the problem is to choose a "good" pivot element, we can review the suggestions of Section 4.4.4, but none of them guarantees that the pivot will divide the set of elements into subsets of equal, or almost equal, size. In the next section we will see that, by investing more effort, it is possible to choose a pivot that is guaranteed to be "good." It guarantees that each set will have at least $0.3\,n$ and at most $0.7\,n$ elements. With this "high-quality" pivot element, the divide-and-conquer method works efficiently in the worst case, as well as the average case.

⋆ 5.4.2   A Linear-Time Selection Algorithm

The algorithm we present in this section is a simplification of the first linear algorithm discovered for solving the selection problem. The simplification makes the general strategy easier to understand (though the details are complicated and tricky to implement), but it is less efficient than the original. The algorithm is important and interesting because it solves the selection problem in general, not just for the median, because it *is* linear, and because it opened the way for improvements.

As usual, to simplify the description of the algorithm, we assume the keys are distinct. It is not hard to modify if there are duplicate keys.

Algorithm 5.1   Selection

Input: S, a set of n keys; and k, an integer such that $1 \leq k \leq n$.

Output: The kth smallest key in S.

Remark: Recall that $|S|$ denotes the number of elements in S.

Element select(SetOfElements S, **int** k)
0. **if** $(|S| \leq 5)$
    return direct solution for kth element of S.

1. Divide the keys into sets of five each, and find the median of each set. (The last set may have fewer than five keys; however, later references to "set of five keys" include this set, too.) Call the set of medians M. Let $n_M = |M| = \lceil n/5 \rceil$. At this point we can imagine the keys arranged as shown in Figure 5.3(a). In each set of five keys, the two larger than the median appear above the median, and the smaller two appear below the median.

2. $m^* = \mathsf{select}(M, \lceil |M|/2 \rceil);$
    (m^* is now the median of M, i.e., the median of medians.)
    Now imagine the keys as in Figure 5.3(b), where the sets of five keys have been arranged so that the sets whose medians are larger than m^* appear to the right of the set containing m^*, and the sets with smaller medians appear to the left of the set containing m^*. Observe that, by transitivity, all keys in the section labeled B are larger than m^*, and all keys in the section labeled C are smaller than m^*.

3. Compare each key in the sections labeled A and D in Figure 5.3(b) to m^*.
    Let $S_1 = C \cup \{$keys from $A \cup D$ that are smaller than $m^*\}$.
    Let $S_2 = B \cup \{$keys from $A \cup D$ that are larger than $m^*\}$.
    This completes the partitioning process with m^* as pivot.

4. Divide and conquer:
    if $(k = |S_1| + 1)$
        m^* is the kth-smallest key, so:
        return m^*;
    else if $(k \leq |S_1|)$
        the kth-smallest key is in S_1, so:
        return select(S_1, k);
    else
        the kth-smallest key is in S_2, so:
        return select$(S_2, k - |S_1| - 1)$;

Algorithm 5.1 is expressed in terms of a set S and rank k. Here we briefly discuss implementation for an array E, using indexes 1 through n, rather than 0 through $n - 1$. Finding an element with rank k is equivalent to answering the question: If this array were sorted, which element would be in E[k]? If S_1 has n_1 elements, then we rearrange E so that

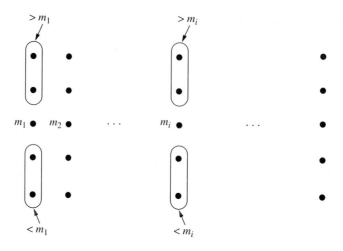

(a) m_i is the median of the ith group of five keys. There are $n_M = \lceil n/5 \rceil$ groups. This diagram assumes n is a multiple of 5 for simplicity.

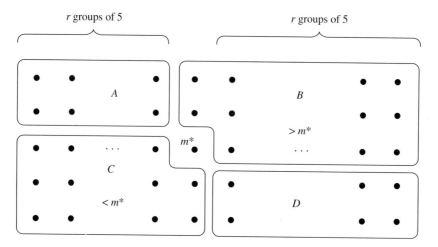

(b) Medians less than m^* are to its left; medians greater than m^* are to its right. This diagram assumes n is an odd multiple of 5 for simplicity. Therefore $n = 5(2r + 1)$ for some r.

Figure 5.3   Steps 1 and 2 for the linear-time selection algorithm

all elements of S_1 are in positions $1, \ldots, n_1$, m^* is in position $n_1 + 1$, and all elements of S_2 are in positions $n_1 + 2, \ldots, n$.

First we observe that if $k = n_1 + 1$, then m^* is the desired element. If $k \leq n_1$, then for the next call to select, the question is: If the segment $E[1], \ldots, E[n_1]$ were sorted, which element would be in $E[k]$? If $k \geq n_1 + 2$, then for the next call to select, the question is:

If the segment $E[n_1 + 2], \ldots, E[n]$ were sorted, which element would be in $E[k]$? (This is equivalent to the problem of finding an element of rank $k - n_1 - 1$ in set S_2 by itself.) The point here is that the variable k will be the same for all recursive calls. However, some changes are needed in the details of the tests to determine which subrange to search recursively. These are left as an exercise (Exercise 5.9).

⋆ 5.4.3 Analysis of the Selection Algorithm

We next show that select is a linear algorithm. We will not completely prove this claim, but we will give the structure of the argument assuming that n is an odd multiple of 5 to simplify the counting.

Let $W(n)$ be the number of key comparisons done by select in the worst case on inputs with n keys. Assuming $n = 5(2r + 1)$ for some nonnegative integer r (and ignoring the problem that this might not be true of the sizes of the inputs for the recursive calls), we count the comparisons done by each step of select. Brief explanations of the computation are included after some of the steps.

1. Find the medians of sets of five keys: $6(n/5)$ comparisons.
   The median of five keys can be found using six comparisons (Exercise 5.14). There are $n/5$ such sets.
2. Recursively find the median of the medians: $W(n/5)$ comparisons.
3. Compare all keys in sections A and D to m^* (see Figure 5.3b): $4r$ comparisons.
4. Call select recursively: $W(7r + 2)$ comparisons.
   In the worst case, all $4r$ keys in sections A and D will be on the same side of m^* (i.e., all smaller than m^* or all greater than m^*). B and C each have $3r + 2$ elements. So the size of the largest possible input for the recursive call to select is $7r + 2$.

Since $n = 5(2r + 1)$, r is approximately $n/10$. So

$$W(n) \leq 1.2n + W(0.2n) + 0.4n + W(0.7n) = 1.6n + W(0.2n) + W(0.7n). \quad (5.1)$$

Although this recurrence equation (actually inequality) is of the divide-and-conquer type, the two subproblems are not of equal size, so we cannot simply apply the Master Theorem (Theorem 3.17). However, we can develop a recursion tree (Section 3.7), as shown in Figure 5.4. Since the row-sums form a decreasing geometric series, whose ratio is 0.9, the total is Θ of the largest term, which is $\Theta(n)$. Equation (1.10) gives the exact expression for the geometric series, which is $16n$ minus some very small term. This result can also be verified by induction. Thus the selection algorithm is a linear algorithm.

The original presentation of the algorithm in the literature included improvements to cut the number of key comparisons down to approximately $5.4\,n$. The best currently known algorithm for finding the median does $2.95\,n$ comparisons in the worst case. (It, too, is complicated.)

Since select is recursive, it uses space on a stack; it is not an in-place algorithm. However, the depth of recursion is in $O(\log n)$, so it is unlikely to cause a problem.

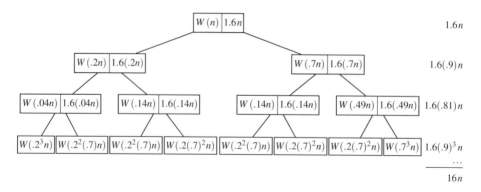

Figure 5.4   Recursion tree for select

5.5 A Lower Bound for Finding the Median

We are assuming that E is a set of n keys and that n is odd. We will establish a lower bound on the number of key comparisons that must be done by any key-comparison algorithm to find median, the $(n + 1)/2$-th key. Since we are establishing a lower bound, we may, without loss of generality, assume that the keys are distinct.

We claim first that to know median, an algorithm must know the relation of every other key to median. That is, for each other key, x, the algorithm must know that $x >$ median or $x <$ median. In other words, it must establish relations as illustrated by the tree in Figure 5.5. Each node represents a key, and each branch represents a comparison. The key at the higher end of the branch is the larger key. Suppose there were some key, say y, whose relation to median was not known. (See Figure 5.6(a) for an example.) An adversary could change the value of y, moving it to the opposite side of median, as in Figure 5.6(b), without contradicting the results of any of the comparisons done. Then median would not be the median; the algorithm's answer would be wrong.

Since there are n nodes in the tree in Figure 5.5, there are $n - 1$ branches, so at least $n - 1$ comparisons must be done. This is neither a surprising nor exciting lower bound. We will show that an adversary can force an algorithm to do other "useless" comparisons before it performs the $n - 1$ comparisons it needs to establish the tree of Figure 5.5.

Definition 5.1   Crucial comparison

A comparison involving a key x is a *crucial comparison for x* if it is the first comparison where $x > y$, for some $y \geq$ median, or $x < y$ for some $y \leq$ median. Comparisons of x and y where $x >$ median and $y <$ median are *noncrucial*.   ■

A crucial comparison establishes the relation of x to median. Note that the definition does not require that the relation of y to median be already known at the time the crucial comparison for x is done.

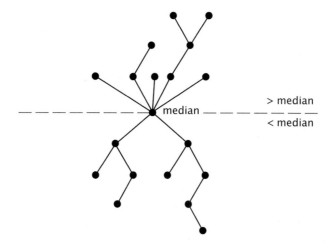

Figure 5.5 Comparisons relating each key to median

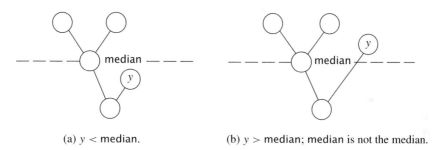

(a) $y <$ median. (b) $y >$ median; median is not the median.

Figure 5.6 An adversary conquers a bad algorithm

We will exhibit an adversary that forces an algorithm to perform *noncrucial* comparisons. The adversary chooses some value (but not a particular key) to be median. It will assign a value to a key when the algorithm first uses that key in a comparison. So long as it can do so, the adversary will assign values to new keys involved in a comparison so as to put the keys on opposite sides of median. The adversary may not assign values larger than median to more than $(n - 1)/2$ keys, nor values smaller than median to more than $(n - 1)/2$ keys. It keeps track of the assignments it has made to be sure not to violate these restrictions. We indicate the status of a key during the running of the algorithm as follows:

L   Has been assigned a value *Larger* than median.

S   Has been assigned a value *Smaller* than median.

N   Has not yet been in a comparison.

Comparands	Adversary's action
N, N	Make one key larger than median, the other smaller.
L, N or N, L	Assign a value smaller than median to the key with status N.
S, N or N, S	Assign a value larger than median to the key with status N.

Table 5.4   The adversary strategy for the median-finding problem

The adversary's strategy is summed up in Table 5.4. In all cases, if there are already $(n - 1)/2$ keys with status S (or L), the adversary ignores the rule in the table and assigns value(s) larger (or smaller) than median to the new key(s). When only one key without a value remains, the adversary assigns the value median to that key. Whenever the algorithm compares two keys with statuses L and L, S and S, or L and S, the adversary simply gives the correct response based on the values it has already assigned to the keys.

All of the comparisons described in Table 5.4 are noncrucial. How many can the adversary make any algorithm do? Each of these comparisons creates at most one L-key, and each creates at most one S-key. Since the adversary is free to make the indicated assignments until there are $(n - 1)/2$ L-keys or $(n - 1)/2$ S-keys, it can force any algorithm to do at least $(n - 1)/2$ noncrucial comparisons. (Since an algorithm could start out by doing $(n - 1)/2$ comparisons involving two N-keys, this adversary can't guarantee any more than $(n - 1)/2$ noncrucial comparisons.)

We can now conclude that the total number of comparisons must be at least $n - 1$ (the crucial comparisons) + $(n - 1)/2$ (noncrucial comparisons). We sum up the result in the following theorem.

Theorem 5.3   Any algorithm to find the median of n keys (for odd n) by comparison of keys must do at least $3n/2 - 3/2$ comparisons in the worst case.   □

Our adversary was not as clever as it could have been in its attempt to force an algorithm to do noncrucial comparisons. In the past several years the lower bound for the median problem has crept up to roughly $1.75n - \log n$, then roughly $1.8n$, then a little higher. The best lower bound currently known is slightly above $2n$ (for large n). There is still a small gap between the best known lower bound and the best known algorithm for finding the median.

5.6 Designing Against an Adversary

Designing against an adversary can be a powerful technique for developing an algorithm with operations like comparisons, which elicit information about the input elements. The main idea is to anticipate that any "question" (i.e., comparison or other test performed by the algorithm) is going to receive an answer chosen by an adversary to be as unfavorable as possible for the algorithm, usually by giving the least information. To counter this, the algorithm should choose comparisons (or whatever the operation is) for which both answers give the same amount of information, as far as possible.

The idea that a good algorithm uses some notion of balance has come up before, when we studied decision trees. The number of comparisons done in the worst case is the height of a decision tree for the algorithm. To keep the height small, for a fixed problem size, means keeping the tree as balanced as possible. A good algorithm chooses comparisons such that the number of possible outcomes (outputs) for one result of the comparison is roughly equal to the number of outcomes for the other result.

We have seen several examples of this technique already: Mergesort, finding both max and min, and finding the second-largest element. The first phase of the tournament method for finding the second-largest element, that is, the tournament that finds the maximum element, is the clearest example. In the first round each key comparison is between two elements about which nothing is known, so an adversary has no basis for favoring one answer over another. In subsequent rounds, to the extent possible, elements that have equal win–loss records are compared, so the adversary never can give one answer that is less informative than the other. In contrast, the straightforward algorithm to find the maximum first compares x_1 with x_2, then compares the winner (say x_2) with x_3. In this case, the adversary *can* give one answer that is less informative than the other. (Which?)

In general, for comparison-based problems, the complete status of an element includes more than the number of prior wins and losses. Rather, an element's status includes the number of elements known to be smaller and the number of elements known to be larger by transitivity. Tree structures like those in Figure 5.2 can be used to represent the status information graphically.

To further illustrate the technique of designing against an adversary, we consider two problems whose optimum solution is difficult: finding the median of five elements and sorting five elements (Exercises 5.14 and 5.15). The median can be found with six comparisons, and five elements can be sorted with seven comparisons. Many students (and instructors) have spent hours trying various strategies, looking unsuccessfully for the solutions. The optimal algorithms squeeze the most information possible out of each comparison. The technique we are describing in this section gives a big boost in getting started right. The first comparison is arbitrary; it is necessarily between two keys about which we have no information. Should the second comparison include either of these keys? No; comparing two new keys, which have equal status, gives more information. Now we have two keys that (we know) are each larger than one other, two keys that (we know) are each smaller than one other, and one unexamined key. Which two will you compare next?

Are you beginning to wonder which problem we are working on? The technique of designing against an adversary suggests the same first three comparisons for both the median problem and the sorting problem. Finishing the algorithms is still tricky and makes instructive exercises.

Exercises

Section 5.1   *Introduction*

5.1   Draw the decision tree for FindMax (Algorithm 1.3) with $n = 4$.

5.2   Consider the problem of sorting n elements. Essentially, there are only $n!$ distinct outcomes, one for each permutation. Adversaries are not limited in how much computation they are allowed to do in deciding the outcome, or answer, for a comparison that is "asked" by the algorithm. In principle, an adversary for the sorting problem could look at all permutations before arriving at a decision.

a.   Use the above idea to develop an adversary strategy for comparison-based sorting. Find a lower bound based on your strategy. How does your result compare with the lower bound of Theorem 4.10?

⋆ **b.**   Develop an adversary strategy for the problem of merging two sorted sequences, each containing $n/2$ keys. It should be a simple modification of your strategy for part (a). Find a lower bound for the worst case of comparison-based algorithms for this problem, based on your strategy. How does your result compare with the lower bound of Theorem 4.4? *Hint*: Look at Exercise 4.25.

Section 5.2   *Finding* max *and* min

5.3   We used an adversary argument to establish the lower bound for finding the minimum and maximum of n keys. What lower bound do we get from a decision tree argument?

Section 5.3   *Finding the Second-Largest Key*

5.4   In this exercise you will write an algorithm based on the heap structure (Section 4.8.1) for the tournament method to find max and secondLargest.

a.   Show that the following procedure places the max in E[1]. Array E is allocated for indexes $1, \ldots, 2n - 1$. (Recall that "last -= 2" subtracts 2 from last.)

```
heapFindMax(E, n)
    int last;
    Load n elements into E[n], . . ., E[2*n-1].
    for (last = 2*n - 2; last ≥ 2; last -= 2)
        E[last/2] = max(E[last], E[last+1]);
```

b.   Explain how to determine which elements lost to the winner.

c.   Complete the code to find secondLargest after heapFindMax finishes.

5.5   How many comparisons are done by the tournament method to find secondLargest on the average,

a.   if n is a power of 2?

b.   if n is not a power of 2?

   Hint: Consider Exercise 5.4.

5.6   The following algorithm finds the largest and second-largest keys in an array E of n keys by sequentially scanning the array and keeping track of the two largest keys seen so far. (It assumes $n \geq 2$.)

```
if (E[1] > E[2])
    max = E[1];
    second = E[2];
else
    max = E[2];
    second = E[1];
for (i = 3; i ≤ n; i ++)
    if (E[i] > second)
        if (E[i] > max)
            second = max;
            max = E[i];
        else
            second = E[i];
```

a.   How many key comparisons does this algorithm do in the worst case? Give a worst-case input for $n = 6$ using integers for keys.

★ **b.**   How many key comparisons does this algorithm do on the average for n keys assuming any permutation of the keys (from their proper ordering) is equally likely?

★ **5.7**   Write an efficient algorithm to find the third-largest key from among n keys. How many key comparisons does your algorithm do in the worst case? Is it necessary for such an algorithm to determine which key is max and which is secondLargest?

Section 5.4   The Selection Problem

5.8   Quicksort can be modified to find the kth-smallest key among n keys so that in most cases it does much less work than is needed to sort the set completely.

a.   Write a modified Quicksort algorithm called findKth for this purpose.

b.   Show that when this algorithm is used to find the median, the worst case is in $\Theta(n^2)$.

c.   Develop a recurrence equation for the average running time of this algorithm.

★ **d.**   Analyze your algorithm's average running time. What is the asymptotic order?

5.9   Following the pseudocode outline for the Selection algorithm (Algorithm 5.1), we briefly discussed implementation in an array. Finding an element with rank k in an array E with n elements is equivalent to answering the question: If this array were sorted, which element would be in $E[k]$? The point was that the parameter k will be the same for all recursive calls. Rewrite the test conditions in the two **if** statements in step 4 to work properly with this implementation.

5.10 Suppose we use the following algorithm to find the k largest keys in a set of n keys. (See Section 4.8 for heap algorithms.)

```
Build a heap H out of the n keys;
for (i = 1; i ≤ k; i ++)
    output(getMax(H));
    deleteMax(H);
```

How large can k be (as a function of n) for this algorithm to be linear in n?

★ **5.11** Generalize the tournament method to find the k largest of n keys (where $1 \le k \le n$). Work out any implementation details that affect the order of the running time. How fast is your algorithm as a function of n and k?

Section 5.5   A Lower Bound for Finding the Median

5.12 Suppose n is even and we define the median to be the $n/2$th-smallest key. Make the necessary modifications in the lower bound argument and in Theorem 5.3 (where we assumed n was odd).

Section 5.6   Designing Against an Adversary

5.13 How well do the sorting algorithms below meet the criterion of performing comparisons for which either outcome is about equally informative? How would an adversary respond to the comparisons using a "least new information" strategy? Does this push the algorithms into their worst cases?

a. Insertion Sort?
b. Quicksort?
c. Mergesort?
d. Heapsort?
e. Accelerated Heapsort?

★ **5.14** Give an algorithm to find the median of five keys with only six comparisons in the worst case. Describe the steps, but don't write code. Using tree diagrams like those in Figure 5.2 may be helpful in explaining what your algorithm does. *Hint*: A useful strategy and the first few steps were partly sketched in Section 5.6.

★ **5.15** Give an algorithm to sort five keys with only seven comparisons in the worst case. Describe the steps, but don't write code. Using tree diagrams like those in Figure 5.2 may be helpful in explaining what your algorithm does. *Hint*: A useful strategy and the first few steps were partly sketched in Section 5.6.

Additional Problems

5.16 Prove Theorem 1.16 (the lower bound for searching an ordered array) by means of an adversary argument. *Hint*: Define an *active range* consisting of the minimum and maximum indexes of the array that might contain K, the key being searched for.

5.17 Let E be an array with elements defined for indexes $0, \ldots, n$ (thus there are $n + 1$ elements). Suppose it is known that E is *unimodal*, which means that E[i] is strictly increasing up to some index M, and is strictly decreasing for indexes $i > M$. Thus E[M] is the maximum. (Note that M may be 0 or n.) The problem is to find M.

   a.   As a warm-up, show that for $n = 2$, two comparisons are necessary and sufficient.

   b.   Write an algorithm to find M, by comparing various keys in E.

   c.   How many comparisons does your algorithm do in the worst case? (You should be able to devise an algorithm that is in $o(n)$.)

★ **d.**   Suppose that $n = F_k$, the kth Fibonacci number, as defined in Equation (1.13), where $k \geq 2$. Describe an algorithm to find M with $k - 1$ comparisons. Describe the ideas, but don't write code.

★ **e.**   Devise an adversary strategy that forces any comparison-based algorithm to do at least $\lg n + 2$ comparisons to find M, for $n \geq 4$. This shows that the problem is at least a little harder than searching an ordered array. *Hint*: Try a more elaborate version of the adversary strategy suggested for Exercise 5.16.

★ **5.18** Suppose E1 and E2 are arrays, each with n keys sorted in ascending order.

   a.   Devise an $O(\log n)$ algorithm to find the nth smallest of the $2n$ keys. (This is the median of the combined set.) For simplicity, you may assume the keys are distinct.

   b.   Give a lower bound for this problem.

5.19

   a.   Give an algorithm to determine if the n keys in an array are all distinct. Assume three-way comparisons; that is, the result of a comparison of two keys is $<$, $=$, or $>$. How many key comparisons does your algorithm do?

★ **b.**   Give a lower bound on the number of (three-way) key comparisons needed. (Try for $\Omega(n \log n)$.)

5.20 Consider the problem of determining if a bit string of length n contains two consecutive zeroes. The basic operation is to examine a position in the string to see if it is a 0 or a 1. For each $n = 2, 3, 4, 5$ either give an adversary strategy to force any algorithm to examine every bit, or give an algorithm that solves the problem by examining fewer than n bits.

5.21 Suppose you have a computer with a small memory and you are given a sequence of keys in an external file (on a disk or tape). Keys can be read into memory for processing, but no key can be read more than once.

a. What is the minimum number of storage cells needed for keys in memory to find the largest key in the file? Justify your answer.

b. What is the minimum number of cells needed for keys in memory to find the median? Justify your answer.

5.22

a. You are given n keys and an integer k such that $1 \leq k \leq n$. Give an efficient algorithm to find *any one* of the k smallest keys. (For example, if $k = 3$, the algorithm may provide the first-, second-, or third-smallest key. It need not know the exact rank of the key it outputs.) How many key comparisons does your algorithm do? *Hint*: Don't look for something complicated. One insight gives a short, simple algorithm.

b. Give a lower bound, as a function of n and k, on the number of comparisons needed to solve this problem.

⋆ **5.23**   Let E be an n-element array of positive integers. A *majority element* in E is an element that occurs *more than $n/2$ times* in the array. The *majority element problem* is to find the majority element in an array if it has one, or return -1 if it does not have one. The only operations you may perform on the elements are to compare them to each other and move or copy them.

Write an algorithm for the majority element problem. Analyze the time and space used by your algorithm in the worst case. (There are easy $\Theta(n^2)$ algorithms, but there is a linear solution. *Hint*: Use a variation of the technique in Section 5.3.2.)

⋆ **5.24** M is an $n \times n$ integer matrix in which the keys in each row are in increasing order (reading left to right) and the keys in each column are in increasing order (reading top to bottom). Consider the problem of finding the position of an integer x in M, or determining that x is not there. Give an adversary argument to establish a lower bound on the number of comparisons of x with matrix entries needed to solve this problem. The algorithm is allowed to use three-way comparisons; that is, a comparison of x with M[i][j] tells if $x <$ M[i][j], $x =$ M[i][j], or $x >$ M[i][j].

Note: Finding an efficient algorithm for the problem was Exercise 4.58 in Chapter 4. If you did a good job on both your algorithm and your adversary argument, the number of comparisons done by the algorithm should be the same as your lower bound.

Notes and References

Knuth (1998) is an excellent reference for the material in this chapter. It contains some history of the selection problem, including the attempt by Charles Dodgson (Lewis Carroll), in 1883, to work out a correct algorithm so that second prize in lawn tennis tournaments could be awarded fairly. The tournament algorithm for finding the second-largest key appeared in a 1932 paper by J. Schreier (in Polish). It was proved optimal in 1964 by S. S. Kislitsin (in Russian). The lower bound argument given here is based on Knuth (1998).

The algorithm and lower bound for finding min and max and Exercise 5.21 are attributed to I. Pohl by Knuth.

The first linear selection algorithm is in Blum, Floyd, Pratt, Rivest, and Tarjan (1973). Other selection algorithms and lower bounds appear in Hyafil (1976), Schönhage, Paterson, and Pippenger (1976), and Dor and Zwick (1995, 1996a, 1996b).

6

Dynamic Sets and Searching

6.1 Introduction

Dynamic sets are sets whose membership varies during computation. In some applications the sets are initially empty and elements are inserted as the computation progresses. Often the maximum size to which a set might grow is not known very accurately in advance. Other applications begin with a large set and delete elements as the computation progresses (often terminating when the set becomes empty). Some applications both insert and delete elements. Various data structures have been developed to represent these dynamic sets. Depending on the needed operations and the access patterns, different data structures are efficient. First we describe the array-doubling technique, which is a basic tool. Then we introduce the basics of amortized time analysis, which is a technique that is often needed to demonstrate the efficiency of sophisticated implementations of dynamic sets. Finally, we survey several popular data structures that have been found useful for representing dynamic sets. They are presented as implementations of appropriate abstract data types (ADTs).

Red-black trees provide a form of balanced binary trees, which are useful to implement binary search trees efficiently. Binary search trees and hash tables are popular implementations of the Dictionary ADT.

Dynamic equivalence relations occur in numerous applications, and their operations are closely related to the Union-Find ADT, which has a very efficient implementation in certain cases, using the In-Tree ADT.

Priority queues are the workhorses of many algorithms, especially *greedy* algorithms. Two efficient implementations of the Priority Queue ADT are binary heaps (used also for Heapsort) and pairing forests, which are also called lazy pairing heaps.

This chapter introduces these topics. For further reading and more extensive treatments, consult Notes and References at the end of the chapter.

6.2 Array Doubling

A typical situation that arises in connection with dynamic sets is that we don't know how big an array we might need when the computation begins. Allocating the "largest possibly needed" array is usually not very satisfactory, although it is one common solution. A simple, more flexible solution is to allocate a small array initially with the intention of doubling its size whenever it becomes apparent that it is too small. For this to work we need to keep track of how full the current array is and how many entries are currently allocated. Java keeps track of the latter information automatically with the length field, but the first number is the programmer's responsibility and it depends on the application for which the array is used.

Let's assume we have an organizer class setArray with two fields, setSize and elements, the latter being an array of the element type, which we assume is simply **Object**. Initially, we might construct an object in this class as follows:

```
setArray  mySet = new setArray();
mySet.setSize = 0;
mySet.elements = new Object[100];
```

Now each time an element is added to mySet the program also increments setSize. Before inserting a new element, however, the program should be sure there is room, and if not, double the array size. This is accomplished by allocating a new array that is twice as large as the current array, and then transferring all the elements into the new array. The application code might be the following:

```
if (mySet.setSize == mySet.elements.length)
    arrayDouble(mySet);
Continue with insertion of new element.
```

The arrayDouble subroutine takes the following form:

```
arrayDouble(set)
    newLength = 2 * set.elements.length;
    newElements = new Object[newLength];
    Transfer all elements from the set.elements array to the newElements array.
    set.elements = newElements;
```

The expensive part is the transfer of elements. However, we will now show that total overhead for inserting n elements into a set that is stored this way is in $\Theta(n)$.

Suppose that inserting the $(n + 1)$-th element triggers an array-doubling operation. Let t be the cost of transferring one element from the old array to the new array (we assume t is some constant). Then n transfers occur as part of this array-doubling operation. But then $n/2$ transfers occurred in the previous array-doubling operation, and $n/4$ before that, and so on. The total cost of all transfers since the set was created cannot exceed $2tn$.

This is a simple example in which it is possible to *amortize*, or spread out, the cost of occasional expensive operations, so that the average overhead per operation is bounded by a constant. Amortized time analysis is explained in the next section.

6.3 Amortized Time Analysis

As we saw in the previous section, situations can arise in which the work done for individual operations of the same type varies widely, but the total time for a long sequence of operations is much less than the worst-case time for one operation multiplied by the length of the sequence. These situations arise fairly frequently in connection with dynamic sets and their associated operations. A technique called *amortized time analysis* has evolved to provide more accurate analysis in these situations. The name *amortized* comes (somewhat loosely interpreted) from the business accounting practice of spreading a large cost, which was actually incurred in a single time period, over multiple time periods that are related to the reason for incurring the cost. In the case of algorithm analysis, the large cost of one operation is spread out over many operations, where the others are less expensive. This section gives a brief introduction to amortized time analysis. The technique is simple in concept, although it requires creativity to come up with effective schemes for difficult problems.

Suppose we have an ADT and we want to analyze its operations using amortized time analysis. We use the term *individual operation* to mean a single execution of an operation. Amortized time analysis is based on the following equation, which applies to each individual operation of this ADT that occurs in the course of some computation:

$$amortized\ cost = actual\ cost + accounting\ cost. \tag{6.1}$$

The creative part is to design a system of *accounting costs* for individual operations that achieves these two goals:

1. In *any* legal sequence of operations, beginning from the creation of the ADT object being analyzed, the sum of the *accounting costs* is nonnegative.

2. Although the *actual cost* may fluctuate widely from one individual operation to the next, it is feasible to analyze the *amortized cost* of each operation (i.e., it is fairly regular).

If these two goals are achieved, then the total *amortized* cost of a sequence of operations (always starting from the creation of the ADT object) is an upper bound on the total *actual* cost, *and* the total amortized cost is amenable to analysis.

Intuitively, the sum of the accounting costs is like a savings account. When times are good, we make a deposit to save up for a rainy day. When the rainy day arrives, in the form of an unusually expensive individual operation, we make a withdrawal. However, to remain solvent, our account balance cannot go negative.

The main idea for designing a system of accounting costs is that "normal" individual operations should have a positive accounting cost, while the unusually expensive individual operations receive a negative accounting cost. The negative accounting cost should offset the unusual expense, that is, the high actual cost, so that the amortized cost comes out about the same for "normal" and "unusually expensive" individual operations. The amortized cost might depend on how many elements are in the data structure, but it should be relatively independent of details of the data structure. Working out how big to make the positive charges often requires creativity, and may involve a degree of trial and error to arrive at an amount that is reasonably small, yet large enough to prevent the "account balance" from going negative.

Example 6.1   Accounting scheme for Stack with array doubling

Consider the Stack ADT, which has two operations, push and pop, and is implemented with an array. (We will ignore the costs of access operations in this example, because they do not change the stack and they are in $O(1)$.) Array doubling, as described in Section 6.2, is used behind the scenes to enlarge the array as necessary. Say the actual cost of push or pop is 1 when no resizing of the array occurs, and the actual cost of push is $1 + nt$, for some constant t, if it involves doubling the array size from n to $2n$ and copying n elements over to the new array. (Exercise 6.2 considers schemes in which both push and pop might cause array resizing.)

The worst-case actual time for push is in $\Theta(n)$. Looking at the worst-case actual time might make it seem that this implementation is very inefficient, since $\Theta(1)$ implementations for these operations are possible. However, the technique of amortized analysis gives a more accurate picture. We can set up the following accounting scheme:

1. The *accounting cost* for a push that does not require array doubling is $2t$.
2. The *accounting cost* for a push that requires doubling the array from n to $2n$ is $-nt + 2t$.
3. The *accounting cost* for a pop is 0.

The coefficient of 2 in the accounting costs was chosen to be large enough that, from the time the stack is created, the sum of the accounting costs can never be negative. To see this informally, assume that doubling will occur at stack sizes of N, $2N$, $4N$, $8N$, and so on. Let's consider the worst case, in which only pushes occur. The "account balance"—net sum of accounting costs—will grow to $2Nt$, then the first negative charge will reduce it to $Nt + 2t$, then it will grow back to $3Nt$ before the second array doubling, at which time it drops back to $Nt + 2t$. From there is grows to $5Nt$, gets cuts to $Nt + 2t$, grows to $9Nt$, gets cut to $Nt + 2t$, and so on. Therefore, this is a valid accounting scheme for the Stack ADT. (With some experimentation we can convince ourselves that any coefficient less than 2 will lead to eventual bankruptcy in the worst case.)

With this accounting scheme, the *amortized cost* of each individual push operation is $1 + 2t$, whether it causes array doubling or not, and the *amortized cost* of each pop operation is 1. Thus we can say that both push and pop run in worst-case *amortized time* that is in $\Theta(1)$.   ∎

More complicated data structures often require more complicated accounting schemes, which require more creativity to think up. In later sections of this chapter (Sections 6.6.6 and 6.7.2) we will encounter ADTs and implementations that require amortized time analysis to demonstrate their efficiency.

6.4 Red-Black Trees

Red-black trees are binary trees that satisfy certain structural requirements. These structural requirements imply that the height of a red-black tree with n nodes cannot exceed $2\lg(n + 1)$. That is, its height is within a factor of two of the height of the most balanced binary tree with n nodes. The most popular use of red-black trees is for binary search trees, but this is not the only application. This section shows how to use red-black trees to maintain balanced binary search trees (with the degree of balance just mentioned) very efficiently. Some other schemes for maintaining balanced binary trees are mentioned in Notes and References at the end of the chapter. We have chosen to focus on red-black trees because the deletion procedure is simpler than most of the alternatives.

After introducing some notation here, we review binary search trees. Then we introduce the structural properties that are required for red-black trees, and show how to maintain them efficiently in insert and delete operations.

Red-black trees are objects in a class RBtree, whose implementation will probably have many similarities to an implementation of the BinTree ADT of Section 2.3.3; however, the specifications and the interface are quite different. This is because a red-black tree has a more specific purpose than a general binary tree in the BinTree ADT, and has operations that modify its structure, whereas the BinTree ADT has no such operations defined. An empty tree is represented by nil as in the BinTree ADT. The operations on red-black trees are rbtInsert, rbtDelete, and rbtSearch. They respectively insert, delete, or search for a given key in the tree. No direct access to subtrees of a red-black tree is provided, as it is with the BinTree ADT. However, such access functions can be added with the understanding that the subtrees are binary search trees, but are not necessarily red-black trees.

The RBtree class is suitable for use in an implementation of the Dictionary ADT, or other ADTs that need balanced binary trees. Nodes of a red-black tree are objects in some class Element; the details are not important for the red-black tree algorithms. This would be the type of the elements being stored in the dictionary. Many of the same conventions regarding elements, keys, and comparison of keys that were introduced for sorting (Chapter 4) are carried over here. We assume that one of the fields in the Element class is named key and is in the class Key. For notational convenience, we assume that keys can be compared with the usual operators such as "<".

Properly Drawn Trees

The idea of a *properly drawn* tree helps to visualize many of the concepts involving binary search trees and red-black trees. This book uses properly drawn trees for all illustrations.

Definition 6.1

A tree is *properly drawn* in a two-dimensional plane if:

1. Each node is a point and each edge is a line segment or a curve connecting a parent to a child. (In a drawing in which a node is a circle or similar figure, its "point" is considered to be at the center, and the edges are considered to go to these points.)
2. The left and right child of any node are to the left and right, respectively, of that node, in terms of horizontal locations.
3. For any edge uv, u being the parent node, no point on the edge uv has the same horizontal location as (i.e., is directly under or over) any proper ancestor of u. ∎

In a properly drawn tree, all nodes in the left subtree of a given tree are to the left of the root, and all nodes in the right subtree are to the right of the root, considering only their horizontal locations. If a binary tree is properly drawn, then sweeping a vertical line from left to right encounters the nodes in their inorder traversal order.

Empty Trees as External Nodes

For binary search trees and particularly for red-black trees, it is convenient to treat empty trees as a special kind of node, called an *external node*. External nodes were introduced in connection with 2-trees (Section 3.4.2) and used for analyzing decision trees (Section 4.7). In this scheme, an external node cannot have any children, and an internal node must have two children. Only internal nodes contain any data, including a key. In terms of the BinTree ADT, we may think of an empty subtree (nil, as returned by the functions leftSubtree and rightSubtree) as an edge to an external node. All other subtrees are rooted at internal nodes.

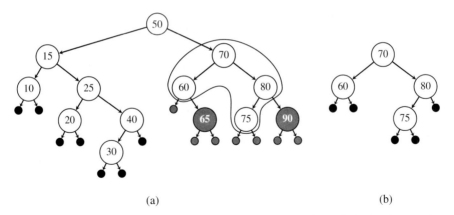

(a)   (b)

Figure 6.1   (a) A node group with four nodes, circled, and its five principal subtrees, shown in gray: Small nodes denote external nodes. (b) The new tree T: The principal subtrees are replaced by external nodes.

Definition 6.2   Node groups and their principal subtrees

A *node group* is any connected group of internal nodes of a binary tree. A subtree S is a *principal subtree* of a node group if the parent of the root of S is in the group, but no node of S is. A principal subtree of a node group can be an external node (empty tree).   ■

Figure 6.1(a) shows a node group and its principal subtrees. A node group can be thought of as the internal nodes of a new tree T, as suggested in Figure 6.1(b). The node group is extracted, and external nodes are attached where the principal subtrees were. The number of principal subtrees of a node group is always one more than the number of nodes in the group. (What property of 2-trees is related to this fact?)

6.4.1   Binary Search Trees

In a binary search tree the keys at the nodes satisfy the following constraints.

Definition 6.3   Binary search tree property

A binary tree in which the nodes have *keys* from an ordered set has the *binary search tree property* if the key at each node is greater than all the keys in its left subtree and less than or equal to all keys in its right subtree. In this case the binary tree is called a *binary search tree* (abbreviated to BST).   ■

An inorder traversal of a binary search tree produces a sorted list of the keys. Whether a properly drawn binary tree is a binary search tree is easily determined by inspection, by passing a vertical line from left to right, as mentioned in connection with Definition 6.1. See Figure 6.2 for examples. As this figure shows, binary search trees can vary greatly in their degree of balance.

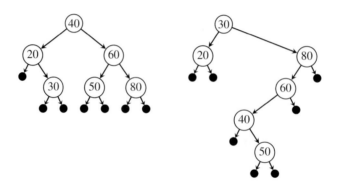

Figure 6.2   Two binary search trees on the same set of keys, with different degrees of balance: Black dots denote empty trees, also called external nodes in this section.

To search for a particular key, we begin at the root and follow the left or right branch depending on whether the key sought is less than or greater than the key at the current node. This procedure sets the pattern for all BST operations. The insertion and deletion operations for red-black trees developed in Sections 6.4.5 and 6.4.6 contain the same search logic embedded within them.

Algorithm 6.1   Binary Search Tree Retrieval

Input: bst, the binary search tree; and K, the key sought.

Output: An object in the tree whose key field is K, or **null** if K is not the key of any node in the tree.

```
Element  bstSearch(BinTree bst, Key K)
    Element  found;
    if (bst == nil)
        found = null;
    else
        Element  root = root(bst);
        if (K == root.key)
            found = root;
        else if (K < root.key)
            found = bstSearch(leftSubtree(bst), K);
        else
            found = bstSearch(rightSubtree(bst), K);
    return found;
```

We use as our measure of work the number of internal nodes of the tree that are examined while searching for a key. (Although, in the high-level language algorithm, K is compared to a key in the tree twice, it is reasonable to count it as one three-way comparison, as we argued in Section 1.6. Either way, the number of comparisons is proportional to the number of nodes examined.) In the worst case (including cases where K is not in the tree), the number of nodes examined is the height of the tree. (In this section the height of a tree with one internal node is 1, because empty trees are treated as external nodes; in Section 2.3.3 the height of such a tree was defined as 0; the difference is not important as long as one convention is used consistently.)

Suppose there are n internal nodes in the tree. If the tree structure is arbitrary (hence may consist of one long chain), the worst case is in $\Theta(n)$. If the tree is as balanced as possible, the number of nodes examined in the worst case is roughly $\lg n$. All operations on binary search trees follow the pattern of bstSearch and have worst cases proportional to the height of the tree. The goal of a balanced-tree system is to reduce the worst case to $\Theta(\log n)$.

6.4.2 Binary Tree Rotations

The structure of a binary tree can be modified locally by operations known as *rotations*, without upsetting the binary search tree property. Although the rebalancing operations for red-black trees can be described without using rotations, rotations are valuable operations in their own right, and they provide a good introduction for more complex restructuring operations. In fact, the more complex restructuring operations can be built up by a sequence of rotations.

A rotation involves a group of two connected nodes, say p and c, for parent and child, and the three principal subtrees of the group. Figure 6.3 illustrates the following description, with 15 in the role of p and 25 in the role of c. The edge between p and c changes direction and the *middle* principal subtree (shown in gray in the figure) changes parent, from c to p. Since c is now the root of the group, the former parent of p (50 in the figure) is now the parent of c, so it must now have an edge to c instead of p. Thus three edges are revised altogether during a rotation.

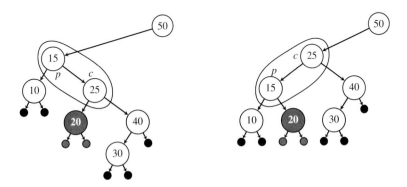

Figure 6.3 A left rotation on (15, 25) transforms the tree on the left into the tree on the right. (The right subtree of node 50 is not shown.) A right rotation on (25, 15) transforms the tree on the right into the tree on the left.

In a left rotation p is to the left of c, so p sinks, c rises, and the edge to the middle subtree moves to the left to hook up with p. The left principal subtree sinks along with p; the right principal subtree rises along with c; the middle principal subtree remains at the same level. A right rotation is the inverse of a left rotation; that is, doing a left rotation followed by a right rotation on the same group of two nodes leaves the tree unchanged. As Figure 6.3 suggests, properly chosen rotations may improve the balance of a binary tree.

6.4.3   Red-Black Tree Definitions

Red-black trees are objects in a class RBtree. We define this class to have four instance fields, root, leftSubtree, rightSubtree, and color. The color field specifies the color of the *root node* of the tree. Although individual nodes (of class Element) do not have a color field, every node is the root of *some* subtree, hence every node has a color associated with it. For implementation purposes, we define color as a field for the tree instead of the node, so that node types do not have to be specific to red-black trees. However, when we are discussing trees and nodes abstractly, we speak of nodes as having a color.

Node colors may be red or black (constants defined in the class). A node may be temporarily gray during deletion but the structure is not a red-black tree until this condition is changed. The color of an empty tree (represented by the constant nil, and also called an external node) is, by definition, black.

Definition 6.4   Red-black tree

Let T be a binary tree in which each node has a color, red or black, and all external nodes are black. An edge to a black node is called a *black edge*. The *black length* of a path is the number of black edges on that path. The *black depth* of a node is the black length of the path from the root of the tree to that node. A path from a specified node to an external node is called an *external path* for the specified node. A tree T is a *red-black tree* (*RB tree* for short) if and only if:

1. No red node has a red child.
2. The black length of all external paths from a given node u is the same; this value is called the *black height* of u.
3. The root is black.

A tree T is an *almost-red-black tree* (ARB tree) if the root is red, but the other conditions above hold.   ■

Figure 6.4 shows some possible red-black trees on the same keys as Figure 6.2. The light nodes are red. The root of each tree has black height two. The rightmost tree has the largest height possible for a red-black tree with six nodes. Notice that its height is less than the height of the right tree of Figure 6.2.

We can gain greater insight into the structure of red-black trees by drawing them so that *red nodes are on the same level as their parents*. With this convention, geometric depth corresponds to black depth and all external nodes (empty trees) appear at the same depth!

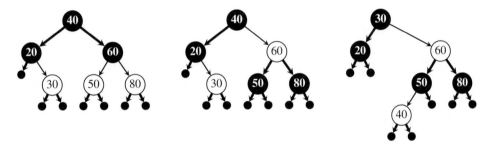

Figure 6.4   Several red-black trees on the same set of keys: Thicker edges are *black edges*.

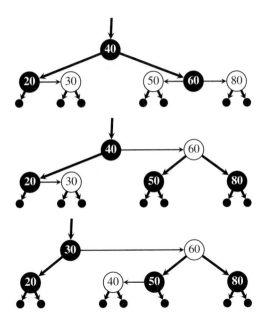

Figure 6.5   Red-black trees drawn with the black-depth convention. We draw an arrow to the root for clarity.

The trees of Figure 6.4 are redrawn in Figure 6.5 using this convention, which is called the *black-depth convention*.

Now let us look at some ARB trees. In Figure 6.5, the subtree rooted at 60 in the lowest figure is an example of an ARB tree. If this subtree were the whole tree, we could simply change the color of the root to black and we would have an RB tree. In fact, looking at the other subtrees of that figure that have red roots, we see that all of them are ARB trees. The following inductive definition is equivalent to Definition 6.4 in that both definitions define the same structures, but the new definition gives more details. Notice that an RB_h tree is a red-black tree of black height h.

Definition 6.5 RB_h trees and ARB_h trees

Binary trees whose nodes are colored red or black, with external nodes being black, are RB_h trees or ARB_h trees, as follows:

1. An external node is an RB_0 tree.
2. For $h \geq 1$, a binary tree is an ARB_h tree if its root is red and its left and right subtrees are each an RB_{h-1} tree.
3. For $h \geq 1$, a binary tree is an RB_h tree if its root is black and its left and right subtrees are each either an RB_{h-1} tree or an ARB_h tree. ■

Doing Exercise 6.4 (drawing some RB_h and ARB_h trees) will help make this definition clear.

Lemma 6.1 The black height of any RB_h tree or ARB_h tree is well defined and is h.
Proof Exercise 6.5. □

6.4.4 Size and Depth of Red-Black Trees

Just from the definitions, without looking at any algorithms, we can derive several useful facts about red-black trees. These facts are easy to prove by induction, using Definition 6.5, and are left as exercises.

Lemma 6.2 Let T be an RB_h tree. That is, let T be a red-black tree with black height h. Then:

1. T has at least $2^h - 1$ internal black nodes.
2. T has at most $4^h - 1$ internal nodes.
3. The depth of any black node is at most twice its black depth.

Let A be an ARB_h tree. That is, let A be an almost-red-black tree with black height h. Then:

1. A has at least $2^h - 2$ internal black nodes.
2. A has at most $\frac{1}{2}\left(4^h\right) - 1$ internal nodes.
3. The depth of any black node is at most twice its black depth. □

This lemma leads to bounds on the depth of any node in terms of n, the number of internal nodes. The following theorem shows that the longest path in a red-black tree is at most twice as long as the longest path in the most balanced binary tree with the same number of nodes.

Theorem 6.3 Let T be a red-black tree with n internal nodes. Then no node has depth greater than $2 \lg(n + 1)$. In other words, the height of T in the usual sense is at most $2 \lg(n + 1)$.

Proof   Let h be the black height of T. The number of internal nodes, n, is at least the number of internal black nodes, which is at least $2^h - 1$, by Lemma 6.2. So $h \leq \lg(n + 1)$. The node with greatest depth is some external node, and the black depth of all external nodes is h. By Lemma 6.2, the depth of any external node is therefore at most $2h$.   □

6.4.5   Insertion into a Red-Black Tree

The red-black tree definition specifies a constraint on colors and a constraint on black height. The idea of insertion into a red-black tree is to insert a red node, thereby guaranteeing that the black-height constraint remains intact. However, the new red node may violate the requirement that no red node has a red child. We can repair this violation while maintaining the black-height constraint, by changing some combination of colors and structure.

The first phase of the procedure to insert key K is essentially the same as searching for key K in a BST and arriving at an external node (empty tree) because the search fails to find the key (see Algorithm 6.1). The next step is to replace that empty tree with a tree containing one node: K. The final phase, which is carried out while returning from recursive calls, is to fix up any color violations. There are no violations of the black-height constraint at any time.

Example 6.2   Phase one of red-black insertion

Before looking at the full algorithm, let us consider what happens in phase one of insertion if we insert a new key 70 in the red-black trees shown in Figure 6.5. In all three trees 70 is compared to the root and is larger, so the search descends into the right subtree. Then 70 is compared to 60 and again the search descends right, where 70 is compared to 80. Now the search goes left and encounters the external node that is the left subtree of the node containing 80. This external node is replaced by a new red node that contains key 70 and has two external nodes as children. The present configuration for the upper tree is shown in Figure 6.6. In the lower and middle trees, the location of the new node is similar, but its parent is black, so there is no color violation, and the procedure is finished. In the upper tree, shown in Figure 6.6, a color violation has occurred, because the red node 80 has a red child 70. This violation must be repaired to complete the insertion operation. We will return to this example after describing the repair method.   ■

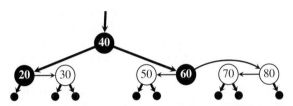

Figure 6.6   A violation of red-black tree color constraint after inserting key 70 in the upper tree of Figure 6.5.

Definition 6.6   Clusters and critical clusters

We define a *cluster* as the set of internal nodes consisting of a black node and all the red nodes that can be reached from that black node by following only nonblack edges. (Hence, each cluster has exactly one black node, called the *root of the cluster*.)

If any node in a cluster is reached by a path of length greater than one from the root of the cluster, the cluster is called a *critical cluster*. (Since all paths within a cluster consist of nonblack edges, a path of length two implies that some red node has an edge to another red node.)   ■

By Definition 6.2, the *principal subtrees* of a cluster are those subtrees whose roots are not in the cluster, but whose parents are in the cluster. By the definition of cluster, the roots of principal subtrees of a cluster are black. A principal subtree can be an external node (empty tree).

Example 6.3   Clusters in red-black trees

In Figure 6.6 node 40 is a cluster, nodes (20, 30) are a cluster, and nodes (60, 50, 80, 70) are a cluster. The latter cluster is a critical cluster because 70 is reached by a path of length two from 60, the root of that cluster. The principal subtrees of cluster 40 are rooted at 20 and 60. The principal subtrees of cluster (60, 50, 80, 70) are five external nodes, and the principal subtrees of cluster (20, 30) are three external nodes.   ■

If the black height is well defined for the root of a cluster, and has the value h, then it is well defined and equals h for all the other nodes in the cluster, because they are all red nodes. This black height is well defined and equals h if and only if every principal subtree has black height $h - 1$. We will see that this condition does hold at all times during the insertion procedure.

Using the terminology of clusters and critical clusters, we can describe in general terms the violations of the red-black tree definition that might occur during insertion of a new node. If there is no critical cluster in the tree, there is no violation, and the operation is complete. A critical cluster can have either three or four nodes; Figure 6.6 shows an example with four nodes. If node 50 were absent (replaced by an external node), then the cluster would still be a critical cluster and it would have three nodes.

Before an insertion operation begins, a red-black tree has no critical clusters (by definition). As we saw, phase one of the insertion may create one critical cluster. During rebalancing (phase two) the strategy is to repair the one critical cluster either leaving no critical clusters or creating one new critical cluster higher in the tree. At no time is there more than one critical cluster. Eventually, if the root of the critical cluster is the root of the entire tree, the repair will succeed, so the rebalancing eventually succeeds. The repair method depends on whether the critical cluster has three or four nodes.

First, consider a critical cluster of four nodes, as in Figure 6.6, for the cluster (60, 50, 80, 70). We perform a *color flip* with the root of the cluster, call it r (r is initially black), and its two children (which are both initially red). That is, we make the root, r, red and

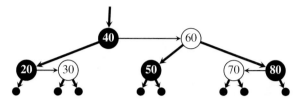

Figure 6.7   Color flip repairs the critical cluster of four nodes in Figure 6.6.

the two children black. This increases the black height of r by one, as seen in Figure 6.7 where r is node 60. However, the edge from the parent of r (node 40 in the figure) to r is no longer a black edge, so the black length of paths from the parent through r does not change, and the black height of the parent remains well defined. The color flip cures the color violation: The path that was black, red, red is now red, black, red.

If r happens to be the root of the whole tree, and it is turned red by a color flip, it will be turned back to black at the end of the insertion procedure. (The root of the whole tree also becomes red when the first node is inserted into an empty tree.) The only times that the black height of the whole tree changes is when the root becomes red during an insertion.

Since a color flip changes r, the root of the former cluster, to red and puts it in a different cluster, there is a possibility that the parent of r is a red node and the new cluster becomes a critical cluster. In this case the new critical cluster must be repaired.

Example 6.4   Red-black tree insertion and color flips

Suppose keys 85, then 90, are inserted into the tree shown in Figure 6.7. The first insertion creates no color violation. Phase one of the second insertion creates the situation shown at the top of Figure 6.8. The critical cluster consists of (80, 70, 85, 90). The situation after performing a color flip is shown at the bottom of Figure 6.8. Node 80 has joined the cluster (40, 60), making this cluster into a critical cluster of three nodes. Color flips are not useful on critical clusters of three nodes (see Exercise 6.7), so a new technique is needed to repair this critical cluster.   ∎

Now we turn to the technique for repairing a critical cluster of three nodes. Call the nodes L, M, and R, in left-to-right order (remember, the tree is assumed to be properly drawn). This cluster has four principal subtrees. Call them, again in left-to-right order, LL, LR, RL, RR. Recall that the root of each principal subtree must be black, or else it would be part of the cluster. The root of the critical cluster is either L or R, since otherwise it could not contain a path of length two. The four possible configurations are shown as trees (a) through (d) in Figure 6.9. Viewed as a tree of three nodes, the cluster is unbalanced. The solution is simply to rebalance the cluster itself, preserving its black height. That is, M becomes the new root of the cluster and becomes black; L becomes the new left child, and R becomes the new right child, and they both become red. Now the principal subtrees are reattached, preserving their order (hence preserving the binary

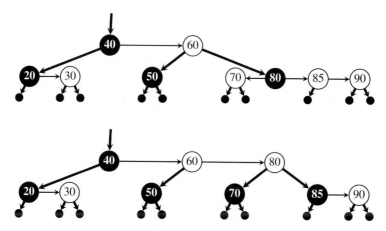

Figure 6.8 Color flip repairs the critical cluster of four nodes in the upper tree, giving the lower tree, but this tree has a new critical cluster, (40, 60, 80).

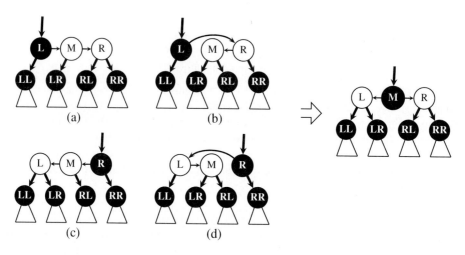

Figure 6.9 Rebalancing repairs any critical cluster of three nodes. Four possible initial arrangements, (a) through (d), become the same final arrangement, right.

search tree property). *LL* and *LR* become the left and right children of *L*, respectively; *RL* and *RR* become the left and right children of *R*, respectively. Notice that four different arrangements of the cluster are possible before rebalancing, but they are all the same after rebalancing.

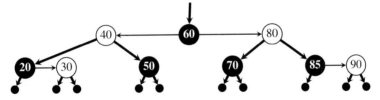

Figure 6.10 The result of rebalancing the critical cluster (40, 60, 80) in the lower tree of Figure 6.8: Node 60 is now the root of the tree.

Example 6.5   Red-black tree insertion and rebalancing

The critical cluster (40, 60, 80) in the lower tree of Figure 6.8 is repaired by rebalancing: $L = 40$, $M = 60$, $R = 80$, LL is rooted at 20, LR is rooted at 50, RL is rooted at 70, and RR is rooted at 85. After rebalancing, the root of the tree is 60, as shown in Figure 6.10.   ■

We are now ready to describe an implementation of the insertion procedure. See Figure 6.11 for the specifications and Figure 6.12 for the instance fields of the RBtree class.

The insertion procedure rbtInsert uses a recursive procedure rbtIns. The return type for rbtIns is an organizer class, InsReturn (see Figure 6.12), because it is desirable for recursive calls to return both the subtree that has the new node inserted and status information to permit detection and repair of any violations.

RBtree rbtInsert(RBtree oldRBtree, Element newNode)

Precondition: oldRBtree has the binary search tree property and satisfies the red-black tree properties of Definition 6.4.

Postconditions: The tree returned has newNode properly inserted. oldRBtree may be destroyed.

RBtree rbtDelete(RBtree oldRBtree, Key K)

Precondition: oldRBtree has the binary search tree property and satisfies the red-black tree properties of Definition 6.4.

Postconditions: If oldRBtree contained no node with key K, the tree returned is identical to oldRBtree; if oldRBtree contained exactly one node with key K, the tree returned does not contain that node; otherwise, *one* node with key K is deleted. oldRBtree may be destroyed.

Element rbtSearch(RBtree T, Key K)

Precondition: T has the binary search tree property.

Postconditions: The returned value is an element in T with the key K, or **null** if no such key is in T.

RBtree nil

Constant denoting the empty tree.

Figure 6.11   Specifications of the RBtree class

```
class RBtree
    Element root;
    RBtree leftSubtree;
    RBtree rightSubtree;
    int color;


    static class InsReturn
        public RBtree newTree;
        public int status;
```

Figure 6.12 Private instance fields of the RBtree class, and the inner InsReturn class. In addition, the constant nil and several methods are public.

We use the following symbolic constants. They should be defined as distinct integer values in the RBtree class. The three-letter status constants represent the colors of the top three nodes (left child, root, right child) in the tree returned by rbtIns.

color	red	root node is red
	black	root node is black
status	ok	operation completed, root is same as input root
	rbr	root is black, final repair was applied
	brb	root is red, both children black
	rrb	root and left child are red
	brr	root and right child are red

Algorithm 6.2   Red-Black Tree Insertion

Input: A red-black tree, oldRBtree, that is also a BST; newNode, the node (with key K) to be inserted. If K duplicates an existing key it will be inserted anyway.

Output: A red-black tree with the same nodes as oldRBtree and also newNode.

Remarks:

1. The recursive procedure rbtIns is called by the wrapper rbtInsert. The preconditions and postconditions of rbtIns are contained in Lemma 6.4.
2. If the newTree returned by rbtIns to rbtInsert has a red root, the wrapper sets it to black.
3. Additional subroutines appear in Figures 6.13 and 6.14.
4. A number of subroutines are left for the exercises: colorOf, colorFlip, repairRight, and rebalRight.

```
RBtree  rbtInsert(RBtree oldRBtree, Element newNode)
    InsReturn  ans = rbtIns(oldRBtree, newNode);
    if (ans.newTree.color ≠ black)
        ans.newTree.color = black;
    return ans.newTree;

InsReturn  rbtIns(RBtree oldRBtree, Element newNode)
    InsReturn  ans, ansLeft, ansRight;
    if (oldRBtree == nil)
        ans = new InsReturn();
        ans.newTree = single-node RBtree with red root = newNode.
        ans.status = brb;
    else
        if (newNode.key < oldRBtree.root.key)
            ansLeft = rbtIns(oldRBtree.leftSubtree, newNode);
            ans = repairLeft(oldRBtree, ansLeft);
        else
            ansRight = rbtIns(oldRBtree.rightSubtree, newNode);
            ans = repairRight(oldRBtree, ansRight);
    return ans;
```

Lemma 6.4   If the parameter oldRBtree of rbtIns is an RB_h tree or an ARB_{h+1} tree, then the newTree and status fields returned are one of the following combinations:

1. status = ok and newTree is an RB_h tree or an ARB_{h+1} tree.
2. status = rbr and newTree is an RB_h tree.
3. status = brb and newTree is an ARB_{h+1} tree.
4. status = rrb and newTree.color = red, newTree.leftSubtree is an ARB_{h+1} tree, and newTree.rightSubtree is an RB_h tree.
5. status = brr and newTree.color = red, newTree.rightSubtree is an ARB_{h+1} tree, and newTree.leftSubtree is an RB_h tree.

Proof   Exercise 6.12.   □

Theorem 6.5   Algorithm 6.2 correctly inserts a new node in a red-black tree with n nodes in $\Theta(\log n)$ time in the worst case.

Proof   The proof follows from Lemma 6.4 and Theorem 6.3. For example, if rbtIns returns status rrb or brr, then rbtInsert changes the color of the root to black, and the tree now satisfies all the red-black tree properties of Definition 6.4, as the color violation is removed. Similarly, if the returned status is brb or ok, changing the root to black ensures that the tree is a red-black tree.   □

```
/** Precondition for repairLeft:
 * oldTree has well-defined black height, but possibly has
 * two consecutive red nodes. */
/** Postcondition: Let ans be the value returned.
 * ans.newTree is the result of a color flip, or rebalance,
 * if needed, on oldTree. Otherwise ans.newTree = oldTree.
 * ans.status indicates which: If a color flip was done,
 * ans.status = brb and ans.newTree has a red root.
 * If a rebalance occurred, ans.status = rbr and ans.newTree
 * is a red-black tree.
 * If neither, ans.status = ok and ans.newTree is a
 * red-black tree.
 */
InsReturn  repairLeft(RBtree oldTree, InsReturn ansLeft)
    InsReturn  ans = new InsReturn();
    if (ansLeft.status == ok)
        // Nothing to change
        ans.newTree = oldTree;
        ans.status = ok;
    else
        oldTree.leftSubtree = ansLeft.newTree;
        if (ansLeft.status == rbr)
            // No more repair needed
            ans.newTree = oldTree;
            ans.status = ok;
        else if (ansLeft.status == brb)
            // Left subtree OK; check root color
            if (oldTree.color == black)
                ans.status = ok;
            else
                ans.status = rrb;
            ans.newTree = oldTree;
        else if (colorOf(oldTree.rightSubtree) == red)
            // Critical cluster is 4.
            colorFlip(oldTree);
            ans.newTree = oldTree;
            ans.status = brb;
        else
            // Critical cluster is 3.
            ans.newTree = rebalLeft(oldTree, ansLeft.status);
            ans.status = ok;
    return ans;
```

Figure 6.13   The repairLeft subroutine for Algorithm 6.2

```
/** Precondition for rebalLeft:
 * oldTree has black root and well-defined black height, but
 * has 2 consecutive red nodes, as specified by leftStatus.
 * oldTree.leftSubtree is red in all cases, and one of its
 * children (grandchild of oldTree) is red.
 * If leftStatus = rrb, it is the left-left grandchild.
 * If leftStatus = brr, it is the left-right grandchild.
 */
/** Postcondition: The tree returned is a
 * red-black tree that results from rebalancing oldTree.
 */
RBtree  rebalLeft(RBtree oldTree, int leftStatus)
    RBtree  L, M, R, LR, RL;
    if (leftStatus == rrb)  // case (c)
        R = oldTree;
        M = oldTree.leftSubtree;
        L = M.leftSubtree;
        RL = M.rightSubtree;
        R.leftSubtree = RL;
        M.rightSubtree = R;
    else
        // leftStatus == brr, case (d)
        R = oldTree;
        L = oldTree.leftSubtree;
        M = L.rightSubtree;
        LR = M.leftSubtree;
        RL = M.rightSubtree;
        R.leftSubtree = RL;
        L.rightSubtree = LR;
        M.rightSubtree = R;
        M.leftSubtree = L;
    // Now cluster is rooted at M.
    L.color = red;
    R.color = red;
    M.color = black;
    return M;
```

Figure 6.14 The rebalLeft subroutine for Algorithm 6.2: Variables L, M, R, LR, and RL correspond to Figure 6.9. This subroutine handles cases (c) and (d) in that figure, where R is the root of the critical cluster before rebalancing. In case (c), rrb was returned from the subtree rooted at M. In case (d), brr was returned from the subtree rooted at L. The tree is reconfigured as shown at the right of Figure 6.9.

6.4.6   Deletion from a Red-Black Tree

Deleting a node from a red-black tree is rather more complicated than insertion. First, deleting a node from any BST is more complicated than inserting into a BST. The reason for this, intuitively, is that we always are able to insert at a leaf, but we may be forced to delete anywhere in the tree.

In addition, for a red-black tree, it is necessary to restore the balance of black height in some cases. Whereas the insertion procedure was always able to maintain the correct black height, and just had to repair color violations, the deletion procedure never encounters a color violation, but must repair height errors. In particular, deleting a black node causes its parent to be out of balance. (That is, the parent will no longer have a well-defined black height as required in the second condition of Definition 6.4.) In several cases, simply recoloring a red node to black is sufficient to restore the balance. The difficult cases arise when this simple expedient is not available.

Deletion from a Binary Search Tree

First, we need to develop a procedure to delete from a BST, without worrying about it being a red-black tree. The thing to remember is that the node that is to be *logically* deleted, in the sense that its key disappears, is not usually the node that is *structurally* deleted. The *structurally* deleted node is normally the *tree successor* (defined below) of the *logically* deleted node, and the information (including the key) in the structurally deleted node replaces the information in the logically deleted node. This does not upset the key order for the BST property because the key of the tree successor immediately follows that of the logically deleted node; in other words, in a left-to-right sweep of a properly drawn tree, the tree successor appears immediately after the node to be logically deleted.

Definition 6.7   Tree successor

In a 2-tree the *tree successor* of any internal node u is the leftmost internal node in the right subtree of u, or simply the right subtree of u if it is an external node.   ■

If the tree successor of u is an external node, then u is the maximum key in its tree, and it can simply be structurally deleted, moving its left child up to its position. For the rest of the discussion, we assume this case does not apply.

Suppose node u is to be logically deleted. Let σ be the tree successor of u, let S be the subtree rooted at σ, and let π be the parent of σ. The left subtree of S is necessarily empty, because the tree successor is a leftmost node. Therefore structural deletion can be accomplished by attaching the right subtree of S as a subtree of π, replacing S. If $\pi = u$, then S was the right subtree of π; otherwise S was the left subtree of π. Note that the right subtree of S might be an external node.

Example 6.6   BST deletion

Figure 6.15 shows several examples of logical and structural deletion. Although node colors are included for later reference, they do not affect the basic BST deletion procedure. In the original tree, the tree successor of 80 is 85, the tree successor of 60 is 70, and so on.

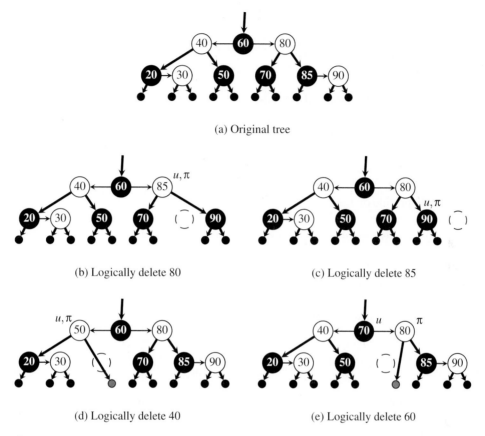

(a) Original tree

(b) Logically delete 80

(c) Logically delete 85

(d) Logically delete 40

(e) Logically delete 60

Figure 6.15 The result of logically deleting various nodes (marked as u) in a red-black tree (or any binary search with a similar node structure), as discussed in Examples 6.6 and 6.7: The structurally deleted node, σ, is indicated by a dashed circle and its prior parent is marked as π. The parent of the gray node does not have a well-defined black height.

For parts (b), (c), and (d), $\pi = u$. That is, the tree successor of u is its right child. (This would be unusual in a larger tree.) The successor's right subtree will become the right subtree of u after the successor's information is copied into u. Specifically, to logically delete 80, the information from its tree successor, 85, is copied into the node that contained 80; then the tree successor is structurally deleted. The subtree rooted at 90 was the right subtree of the former tree successor, so now it becomes the right subtree of π. In the case of logically deleting 85, the structure looks the same as after deleting 80, but a different node was structurally deleted in each case.

The more typical case is illustrated by deleting 60 in part (e) of Figure 6.15, because here u and π are different nodes. The tree successor is 70. Information is copied from 70 into u, the node that contained 60; then the tree successor is structurally deleted. The right subtree of the former tree successor (in this case an external node) becomes the left subtree of π.

We will return to these examples to consider the balancing implications for red-black trees.   ■

Overview of Red-Black Deletion

The procedure for red-black tree deletion can be summarized as follows:

1. Do a standard BST search to locate the node to be logically deleted; call it u.
2. If the right child of u is an external node, identify u as the node to be structurally deleted.
3. If the right child of u is an internal node, find the tree successor of u, copy the key and information from the tree successor to u. (The color of u is not changed at this point.) Identify the tree successor as the node to be structurally deleted.
4. Carry out the structural deletion and repair any imbalance of black height.

We now consider the last step in more detail.

Example 6.7   Red-black tree deletion

Let's take another look at Figure 6.15. In part (b), although a black node was structurally deleted, its right child was an internal node, so it was necessarily red (why?), and could be changed to black to restore the balance of black heights. In part (c), a red node was structurally deleted, so no imbalance of black height occurred.

Parts (d) and (e) show the result when the tree successor is black and its right subtree is black (and is necessarily an external node). The remaining subtree after deletion (just an external node) has insufficient black height, which is indicated by the color gray. For example, consider the case when 60 is to be deleted; 70 is its tree successor. Before the deletion, node 70 has black height 1, and is the left child of node 80. After 70 is copied and its former node structurally deleted (the lower right diagram), the external node in its place has black height 0. Now the tree rooted at node 80 is out of balance with respect to the black lengths of external paths. The situation is similar after logically deleting node 40. These are examples in which we need a repair that goes beyond a simple color change.   ■

Restoring Black Height

A gray node is the root of a subtree that is itself an RB_{h-1} tree, but is in a position where its parent requires an RB_h tree. (More precisely, the subtree is an RB_{h-1} tree if the gray node is interpreted as being black.) That is, the subtree rooted at a gray node has a black height that is well defined, but is one less than what is required for its parent to have a well defined black height. The gray node initially is an external node, but the gray color might propagate up the tree.

The theme of repairing this imbalance is to find some nearby red node that can be changed to black. Then by local restructuring, the black lengths of paths can be brought

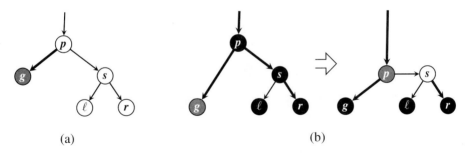

(a)   (b)

Figure 6.16 (a) Nodes in the vicinity of g, the gray node, whose tree's black height is too small, during deletion from a red-black tree. Colors of p, s, ℓ and r vary, creating different cases. (b) Propagation of the gray node when all nearby nodes are black. The operation is symmetric when g is a right child.

back into balance. If there is no such red node sufficiently nearby, then the imbalance must be propagated to a higher level of the tree, and repaired recursively.

Let's introduce some nomenclature. We call the gray node g, call its parent p, and call its sibling s (the other child of p). Two other important nodes are the left and right children of s, which we call ℓ and r, respectively (see Figure 6.16a).

The case that cannot be handled directly is that in which p, s, ℓ and r are all black. The method of propagation is to change the color of s to red and g to black, bringing p back into balance, as shown in Figure 6.16(b). However, this decreases the black height of p by one, compared to its value before the deletion began, so p is now the gray node. This is the only case in which the gray node propagates up the tree, and it involves color changes only, no structural changes to the tree.

Notice that, if p is the root of the whole tree and becomes gray, it has no parent to throw out of balance, and the red-black properties have been restored (after p is colored black). Therefore it is all right if the gray node propagates all the way to the root of the tree. We now concentrate on the cases when the gray node does *not* propagate.

If any of p, s, ℓ, or r are red, then the black height imbalance can be repaired without propagation. The cases get complicated and there are quite a few of them, but there is a common theme. Recall that g is the root of an RB_{h-1} tree. Form a node group with p as the root, such that all the principal subtrees of the group (Definition 6.2) are RB_{h-1} trees. Call this the *deletion rebalance group*. Now restructure the deletion rebalance group (isolated from the rest of the tree, with external nodes in place of the principal subtrees) as follows:

1. If p was red, the group should form an RB_1 or ARB_2 tree;
2. If p was black, the group should form an RB_2 tree.

Now attach the restructured group as a subtree of the parent of p, replacing the former edge to p with an edge to the (possibly) new root of the group; also, reattach all the principal subtrees, in correct order.

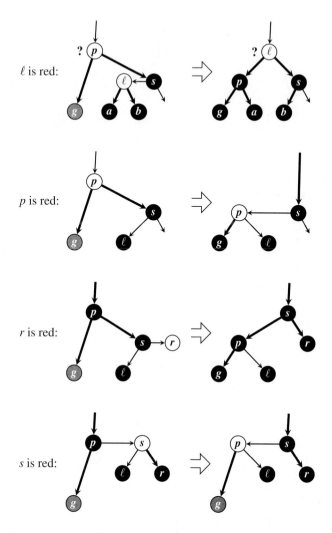

ℓ is red:

p is red:

r is red:

s is red:

Figure 6.17   Repairs of black height errors during deletion: Cases are considered in order from top to bottom. The last case does not remove the gray node, but transforms into one of the first two cases. Cases are symmetric when g is the right child of p, and then the order is r, p, ℓ, s.

The number of cases can be reduced by following a certain order in looking for red nodes: When g is a left child, check them in the order ℓ, p, r, and finally s. Figure 6.17 shows the appropriate transformations; note that it shows only the relevant part of each deletion rebalance group. For example, in the first case, where ℓ is red, the right child of s is *in* the deletion rebalance group if it is red, but is the root of a principal subtree of the group if it is black. However, the appropriate transformation is the same in both cases.

A question mark next to a node means that it might be either red or black, but both nodes that have question marks, one before and one after the transformation, must be the same color.

The last case, when only s is red, does not remove the gray node, but transforms into one of the first two cases, depending on the color of ℓ's left child. (Node ℓ will be called s, the sibling of g, for the final restructuring.)

When g is a right child, the order is symmetric: check r, p, ℓ, and finally s. (To help remember the order, s is always last, and the first three are in alphabetical order when g is a left child, and in reverse alphabetical order when g is a right child.)

Example 6.8   Black-height repair

Consider the tree in the upper part of Figure 6.18(a), which resulted from logical deletion of 60 in Figure 6.15(e). The deletion created a gray node. Now node 80 is in the role of p, 85 is s, 90 is r, and the external (left) child of 85 is ℓ. The case that applies in Figure 6.17 is the one in which p is red (and ℓ is black), that is, the second case. Therefore 80 descends to the level of 85, which is its new parent; 80 takes the former left child of 85 as its new right child. When the group is reattached to the tree, 70 will have 85 as its right child instead of 80. The final tree is shown in the lower part of Figure 6.18(a).

The tree in the upper part of Figure 6.18(b) resulted from logically deleting 40 in Figure 6.15(d). In this case the gray node is a right child, so the mirror images of Figure 6.17 are needed; note that ℓ and r interchange their roles. Node 50 is in the role of p, 20 is s, 30 is r and the external child of 20 is ℓ. Therefore the *first* case of Figure 6.17 applies (r is red): 30 moves up to the former level of 50 and adopts its color, while 50 drops one level and turns black. The former children of 30 are distributed to 20 and 50. When the group is reattached, 30 becomes the new left child of 60. The final tree is shown in the lower part of Figure 6.18(b).   ∎

As with repairs for insertion, repairs for deletion do $O(1)$ structural changes, but may do $O(\log n)$ color changes. The implementation is tedious because of all the cases, but is straightforward, and is left as an exercise.

6.5   Hashing

Hashing is a technique often used to implement a Dictionary ADT, although it has other uses too. Imagine that we could assign a unique array index to every possible key that could occur in an application. Then locating, inserting, and deleting elements could be done very easily and quickly.

Normally, of course, the key space (the set of all possible keys) is much too large. A typical example is the key space of strings of characters, perhaps names. Suppose a name is assumed to be at most 20 letters and spaces. The key space has more than 2^{100} elements. That is, if we are using an array, it would need 2^{100} cells to assign a different index to each string, which is completely infeasible. Even though the key space is extremely large, only a small fraction of the possible keys will occur in a particular application. The actual set of

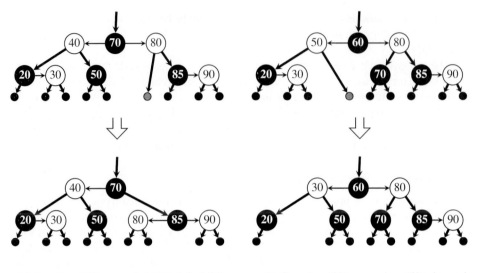

(a) Case 2: p (80) was red; ℓ (85's left child) was black.

(b) Case 1: r (30) was red; p (50) changed color.

Figure 6.18 The result of rebalancing after deletions, according to cases of Figure 6.17: Note that part (b),the example for case 1, has its gray node as the *right* child of p, so the operation is the mirror image of case 1 in Figure 6.17.

elements being used might number in the hundreds, or even up to a few million. An array with 4 million would be enough to give a different index to each element, and such array sizes are feasible.

The purpose of hashing is to translate an extremely large key space into a reasonably small range of integers. The translated value of the key is called the *hash code* for that key, and it is computed by some *hash function*. We can use an array to store each element according to its hash code.

The name "hash" originates from the early practice of "chopping up" the key and selecting certain bits to make up the hash code for that key.

The job of the hash function is to assign integers to keys in such a way that it is unlikely that two keys in a "typical" set of n elements are mapped to the same integer. When this happens, the event is called a *collision*. To reduce the chance of collisions, if we have n elements, we typically use a range of integers up to about $2n$ for hash codes.

The most common, but not the only, use of hashing is to maintain a *hash table*. The hash table is an array H on indexes $0, \ldots, h - 1$; that is, the table has h entries. The entries of H are called *hash cells*. The hash function maps each key into an integer in the range $0, \ldots, h - 1$.

Example 6.9 Hashing

For a small example, suppose the key space is four-digit integers, and it is desired to translate them into the integers $0, \ldots, 7$. We choose the hash function:

$$\text{hashCode}(x) = (5x \bmod 8).$$

Assume our actual set consists of six important historical dates: 1055, 1492, 1776, 1812, 1918, and 1945. They map into the range $0, \ldots, 7$ as follows:

hash code	0	1	2	3	4	5	6	7
key	1776			1055	1492 1812	1945	1918	

If we have a hash table consisting of an array with eight entries, elements can be stored according to their hash code and they will be spread out over the whole table. However, some elements do have the same hash code, so some provision must be made for this event. In this example, keys 1492 and 1812 *collided*, meaning that they mapped to the same hash code. ■

The two issues to be addressed in designing a hash table are: What is the hash function and what is the method of handling collisions? The two issues are fairly independent. The question of what function makes a good hash function may depend on the application. We will look at the collision issue.

6.5.1 Closed Address Hashing

Closed address hashing, also called *chained hashing*, is the simplest collision policy. Each entry in the hash table, say $H[i]$, is a linked list (see Section 2.3.2) whose elements have hash code i. Initially, all entries in H are empty lists. To insert an element, first compute its hash code, say i, then insert the element into the linked list $H[i]$. If the table H is currently storing n elements, the *load factor* is defined to be $\alpha = n/h$. Note that α is the average number of elements in one linked list.

To search for a given key K, first compute its hash code, say i, then search through the linked list at $H[i]$, comparing the keys of the elements in the list with the key K. Notice that we can't assume, just because an element's hash code is i that its key is K. The hash function is a many-to-one function.

Suppose any element in the table is equally likely to be searched for, and n elements are stored. What is the average cost of a successful search? Let's assume that the cost of computing the hash code is equal to the cost of doing a small number, say a, of key comparisons. If an element hashes into a cell i, whose linked list has L_i elements, then the average number of comparisons needed to locate the element is $(L_i + 1)/2$. Then the average cost of a successful search is given by

$$a + \frac{1}{n} \sum_{i=0}^{h-1} (L_i + 1)/2.$$

For the arrangement of Example 6.9, this is $a + 7/6$. A total of seven key comparisons would be done to locate each element once.

If some fixed fraction of the elements, say $n/10$, hash into the same cell, then the average successful search takes more than $n/200$ key comparisons. In the worst case, *all* elements hash into the same cell, and the average successful search takes about $n/2$, or $\Theta(n)$, key comparisons. These cases are no better (in growth rate) than searching an unordered array, as in Algorithm 1.1. They demonstrate the importance of spreading the hash codes fairly evenly over the entire range of h integers.

If we assume that the hash code for each key in our set is equally likely to be any integer in the range $0, \ldots, h-1$, then it can be shown that the average successful search takes $O(1 + \alpha)$ key comparisons, where $\alpha = n/h$ is the load factor. (See Notes and References at the end of the chapter for sources that have all analytical results not derived in the text.) If h is proportional to n (which can be accomplished with array doubling, as described in Section 6.2), this is $O(1)$ key comparisons, on average, for a successful search.

In practical situations it is unlikely that we can rigorously justify a claim that hash codes are uniformly distributed. Nevertheless, with well-chosen hash functions, experience supports this assumption in many cases.

Now consider the cost for an unsuccessful search for a key K that hashes to index i. It is clear that the worst case is proportional to the longest list in the hash table, and the average depends on the assumed distribution of unsuccessful search requests. Costs of unsuccessful searches are about a factor of two worse than costs for successful searches.

Besides searching for a key in response to a retrieval request, the other operations to consider are insertion and deletion. Clearly, insertion involves no key comparisons, and just depends on the cost of computing the hash code. Deletion cost is proportional to the cost for a successful search if the deletion is successful (only one key is deleted in case of duplicates), and is proportional to the cost of an unsuccessful search otherwise.

Instead of a linked list at each hash cell, why not use a balanced binary search tree? While this has theoretical advantages, it is rarely done because, in practice, load factors are kept small, and people rely on getting something resembling the favorable behavior of uniformly distributed hash codes. Therefore the space and time overheads for more sophisticated data structures are not usually considered worthwhile.

6.5.2   Open Address Hashing

Open addressing is a strategy for storing all elements right in the array of the hash table, rather than using linked lists to accommodate collisions. Thus $H[i]$ contains an actual key, rather than a list of keys. Open addressing is less flexible than closed addressing because load factors in excess of 1 are impossible. However, it is usually more space efficient because linked lists are not used (but see Exercise 6.19). Searching takes place right in the hash table instead of traversing through linked lists, so it is likely to be more efficient in time also.

The fundamental idea of open addressing is that, if the hash cell corresponding to the hash code is occupied by a different element, then a sequence of alternative locations for the current element is defined. The process of computing alternative locations is called *rehashing*.

The simplest rehashing policy is *linear probing*. Suppose a key K hashes to location i. Suppose some other key occupies $H[i]$. The following function is used to generate alternative locations:

$$\text{rehash}(j) = (j + 1) \bmod h$$

where j is the location most recently probed. Initially $j = i$, the hash code for K. Notice that this version of rehash does not depend on K.

Example 6.10   Linear probing

Consider the linear probing policy for storing the keys given in Example 6.9. Assume the keys are inserted in the order given: 1055, 1492, 1776, 1812, 1918, 1945.

1. 1055 hashes to 3 and is stored in $H[3]$.
2. 1492 hashes to 4 and is stored in $H[4]$.
3. 1776 hashes to 0 and is stored in $H[0]$.
4. 1812 hashes to 4, but $H[4]$ is occupied, so linear probing rehashes 4 to 5, which is empty, so 1812 is stored in $H[5]$.
5. 1918 hashes to 6 and is stored in $H[6]$.
6. 1945 hashes to 5, but $H[5]$ is occupied. Note that $H[5]$ is *not* occupied by a key that hashed to 5. This shows how collisions can occur among keys with different hash codes under open addressing. However, since $H[5]$ is occupied, linear probing rehashes 5 to 6 for the next location in which to try to store 1945. This cell is also occupied, so 6 is rehashed to 7, which finally becomes the home for 1945.

The final array layout for H is the following:

index	0	1	2	3	4	5	6	7
H	1776			1055	1492	1812	1918	1945

∎

The retrieval procedure imitates the insertion procedure, more or less. To search for key K, compute its hash code, say i. If $H[i]$ is empty, K is not in the table. Otherwise, if $H[i]$ contains some key other than K, rehash to $i_1 = ((i + 1) \bmod h)$. If $H[i_1]$ is empty, K is not in the table. Otherwise, if $H[i_1]$ contains some key other than K, rehash to $i_2 = ((i_1 + 1) \bmod h)$, and so on.

Example 6.11   High load factor for linear probing

Consider searching for each of the keys in the table created in Example 6.10. Keys 1055, 1492, 1776, and 1918 are found with one "probe"; that is, they are found in the first cell inspected, the cell of their hash codes. Key 1812 requires two probes and 1945 requires three probes. Thus the total probes, or key comparisons, for the set is 9, compared to 7 for the closed addressing policy.

Now suppose we search for the key 1543, which is not in the table. This key hashes to 3. So $H[3]$ is inspected, but does not contain 1543. Linear probing rehashes 3 to 4, 4 to 5,

5 to 6, and 6 to 7, but each time, the hash cell is occupied by a different key. Are we done finally? No! Rehashing "wraps around." The next probe is at $((7 + 1) \bmod 8) = 0$. And $H[0]$ is occupied by a different key! Finally, 0 rehashes to 1, where an empty cell is found. This confirms that 1543 is not in the table. (You should work out why it is unnecessary to check $H[2]$.)

This example shows the weakness of open addressing with linear probing when the load factor approaches 1. Long chains of keys with different hash codes build up, making it necessary to travel a long way to find an empty cell.   ∎

As you might suspect from the previous example, even with the favorable assumption that all hash codes are equally likely to occur among the elements of the set, the average cost of a successful search is not proportional to α, the load factor, under the policy of open addressing with linear probing. In fact, with high-powered mathematics, it can be shown to approach $\sqrt{n}$ for a load factor of 1. (See Notes and References at the end of the chapter.)

With all these problems lurking, why even consider open addressing? One reason is that performance is quite good at low load factors. With array doubling, the load factor can always be kept under 0.5, for example. Long chains at a load factor of 0.5 are unlikely.

Example 6.12   Expansion of hash table

Consider again the keys of Example 6.9: 1055, 1492, 1776, 1812, 1918, and 1945. Suppose the hash table has been doubled to 16 entries and the new hash function is $\mathsf{hashCode}(x) = (5x \bmod 16)$. Now the hash code mapping looks like this:

	0	1	2	3	4	5	6	7	8	9	10	11	12	13	14	15
H	1776				1492	1812	1918					1055		1945		

All keys are stored in the cells of their hash code except for 1812, which still collides with 1492. The previous chain of six contiguous filled cells has been broken up into four separate chains.   ∎

Another reason why open addressing is still an effective method is that a more sophisticated rehashing scheme alleviates the problem of long chains of occupied cells, for moderate load factors, say up to 0.7. One such scheme is *double hashing*. Instead of having rehash increment by 1, as in linear probing, it increments by an amount d, calculated from the key K. That is, we compute $d = \mathsf{hashIncr}(K)$ using a hash function different from hashCode, then compute

$$\mathsf{rehash}(j, d) = (j + d) \bmod h.$$

Thus if the hash code of K is i and the increment is d, the sequence of cells to be searched is i, $(i + d)$, $(i + 2d)$, and so on. Pseudocode for the search procedure would look something like this, assuming the constant emptyCell denotes an empty hash cell.

```
Element  hashFind(Key K)
    Element  ans;
    int  code = hashCode(K);
    int  incr = hashIncr(K);
    int  loc = code;
    ans = null;  // Default is failure
    while (H[loc] ≠ emptyCell)
        if (H[loc].key == K)
            ans = H[loc];
            break;
        loc = rehash(loc, incr);
        if (loc == code)
            break;
    return ans;
```

The second **break** prevents an infinite loop; it is unnecessary if d and h are chosen in a way that all cells in the array are eventually visited by the sequence that rehash generates, *and* it is known that the array has at least one empty cell.

Deletion under Open Addressing

Another complication arises if elements might be deleted from a hash table. The search procedure stops searching when it encounters an empty cell. Look at the table set up in Example 6.10, and recall that 1945 hashes to 5 in this example, but due to rehashing, 1945 was stored in cell 7. Suppose 1918 is subsequently deleted, and $H[6]$ is set back to emptyCell. Now a subsequent search for 1945 will start at 5, rehash to 6, and terminate in failure. Key 1945 has been "cut off" from the cell of its hash code.

The simplest way to avoid this problem is to define another constant, obsolete. When 1918 is deleted, the value of $H[6]$ is set to obsolete. Now the search procedure will continue over $H[6]$ as though it had an element in it, but will *not* attempt to match the search key K to this cell. However, the "obsolete" cell *may* be reused for a new element, if the occasion arises. In judging the load factor, "obsolete" cells count as elements. If the number of "obsolete" cells becomes excessive over time, it may be advisable to "clean up" by allocating a new (empty) hash table, then going through the old array sequentially and reinserting all genuine elements into the new hash table.

6.5.3 Hash Functions

As we have seen, the main criterion for a good hash function is that it spreads the keys around fairly uniformly. See the Notes and References at the end of the chapter for theoretical work on the subject. We offer some simple prescriptions in this section.

Intuitively, one way to judge if a function spreads the keys around is to ask whether its output is "predictable." The opposite of predictability is randomness, so a simple approach to choosing a hash function is to pattern it after a pseudorandom number generator. One class of pseudorandom number generators is called "multiplicative congruential." In words of fewer syllables, this means "multiply by a constant, then take the remainder after dividing by another constant." The second constant is called the *modulus*. For a hash function the modulus is h, the size of the hash table.

For strings, computing the hash code is likely to be the dominant cost in a search or insert operation, because all characters of the string are usually involved. (In most string comparisons, only one or two characters need to be checked before a difference is found.) Considering this fact, our prescription is the following:

1. Choose h as a power of 2, say 2^x, and $h \geq 8$.

2. Implement "mod" by extracting the x low-order bits. (The code in Java, C or C++ can be "(num & ($h-1$))" because h is a power of 2.)

3. Choose the multiplier $a = 8 \lfloor h/23 \rfloor + 5$.

4. If the key type is integer, the hash function is

$$\text{hashCode}(K) = (a\,K) \bmod h.$$

5. If the key type is a pair of integers, (K_1, K_2), the hash function can be

$$\text{hashCode}(K_1, K_2) = (a^2\,K_1 + a\,K_2) \bmod h.$$

6. If the key type is a string of characters, treat them as a sequence of integers, $k_1, k_2, \ldots$, and use as the hash function:

$$\text{hashCode}(K) = (a^\ell\,k_1 + a^{\ell-1}\,k_2 + \cdots + a\,k_\ell) \bmod h \qquad \text{where } \ell \text{ is length of } K.$$

Use the identity

$$(a^\ell\,k_1 + a^{\ell-1}\,k_2 + \cdots + a\,k_\ell) = ((\cdots (((k_1\,a) + k_2)\,a) + \cdots + k_\ell)\,a)$$

to make the computation efficient. It might be a good idea to take the mod after each multiplication to avoid overflow.

7. Use array doubling whenever the load factor gets high, say above 0.5. After allocating a new array for the hash table of size 2^{x+1}, set up the constants h and a for the new hash function. Now go through the old array sequentially and, for each cell that contains a genuine key, insert that key into the new hash table using the new hash function.

8. If double hashing is desired, the second hash function (called hashIncr in the search procedure in Section 6.5.2) can be simpler, to save time. For example, if the key type is strings of characters, use $(2\,k_1 + 1) \bmod h$. Computing an odd increment ensures that the whole hash table is accessed in the search for an empty cell (provided h is a power of two).

As we said, this is a prescription to get a hash table up and running, with a minimum of work. It is handy for the implementation of a dictionary ADT.

6.6 Dynamic Equivalence Relations and Union-Find Programs

Dynamic equivalence relations arise in a variety of problems on sets or graphs. The Union-Find abstract data type provides a tool for maintaining dynamic equivalence relations. Although it has a very efficient (and simple!) implementation, the analysis is challenging.

The applications include a minimum spanning tree algorithm, discussed in Section 8.4, and some problems mentioned at the end of this section.

6.6.1 Dynamic Equivalence Relations

An *equivalence relation R* on a set S is a binary relation on S that is reflexive, symmetric, and transitive (Section 1.3.1). That is, for all s, t, and u in S, it satisfies these properties: $s\,Rs$; if $s\,Rt$, then $t\,Rs$; and, if $s\,Rt$ and $t\,Ru$, then $s\,Ru$. The equivalence class of an element s in S is the subset of S that contains all elements equivalent to s. The equivalence classes form a partition of S, that is, they are disjoint and their union is S. The symbol "$\equiv$" will be used from now on to denote an equivalence relation.

The problem studied in this section is to represent, modify, and answer certain questions about an equivalence relation that changes during a computation. The equivalence relation is initially the equality relation, that is, each element is in a set by itself. The problem is to process a sequence of instructions of the following two types, where s_i and s_j are elements of S:

1. IS $s_i \equiv s_j$?
2. MAKE $s_i \equiv s_j$ (where $s_i \equiv s_j$ is not already true).

Question 1 is answered "yes" or "no." The correct answer depends on the instructions of the second type that have been received already; the answer is yes if and only if the instruction "MAKE $s_i \equiv s_j$" has already appeared or $s_i \equiv s_j$ can be derived by applying the reflexive, symmetric, and transitive properties to pairs that were explicitly made equivalent by the second type of instruction. The response to the latter, that is, the MAKE instructions, is to modify the data structure that represents the equivalence relation so that later instructions of the first type will be answered correctly.

Consider the following example where $S = \{1, 2, 3, 4, 5\}$. The sequence of instructions is in the left-hand column. The right-hand column shows the response—either a yes or no answer, or the set of equivalence classes for the relation as defined at the time.

Equivalence classes to start: $\{1\}$, $\{2\}$, $\{3\}$, $\{4\}$, $\{5\}$

1.	IS $2 \equiv 4$?	No
2.	IS $3 \equiv 5$?	No
3.	MAKE $3 \equiv 5$.	$\{1\}, \{2\}, \{3, 5\}, \{4\}$
4.	MAKE $2 \equiv 5$.	$\{1\}, \{2, 3, 5\}, \{4\}$
5.	IS $2 \equiv 3$?	Yes
6.	MAKE $4 \equiv 1$.	$\{1, 4\}, \{2, 3, 5\}$
7.	IS $2 \equiv 4$?	No

6.6.2 Some Obvious Implementations

To compare various implementation strategies we will count operations of various kinds done by each strategy to process a sequence of m MAKE and/or IS instructions on a set S with n elements. We start by examining two fairly obvious data structures for representing the relation: matrices and arrays.

A matrix representation of an equivalence relation requires n^2 cells (or roughly $n^2/2$ if the symmetry is used). For an IS instruction only one entry need be examined; however, a MAKE instruction would require copying several rows. A sequence of m MAKE instructions (hence, a worst-case sequence of m MAKES and ISS) would require at least mn operations.

The amount of space used can be reduced to n by using an array, say, eqClass, where eqClass[i] is a label or name for the equivalence class containing s_i. An instruction IS $s_i \equiv s_j$? requires looking up and comparing eqClass[i] and eqClass[j]. For MAKE $s_i \equiv s_j$, each entry is examined to see if it equals eqClass[i] and, if so, is assigned eqClass[j]. Again, for a sequence of m MAKES (hence, for a worst-case sequence) at least mn operations are done.

Both methods have inefficient aspects—the copying in the first and the search (for elements in eqClass[i]) in the latter. Better solutions use links to avoid the extra work.

6.6.3 Union-Find Programs

The effect of a MAKE instruction is to form the union of two subsets of S. An IS can be answered easily if we have a way of finding out which set a given element is in. The Union-Find abstract data type (Section 2.5.2) provides just these operations. Initially, makeSet is run on each element of S to make n singleton sets. The find and union operations would be used as follows to implement the equivalence instructions:

IS $s_i \equiv s_j$	MAKE $s_i \equiv s_j$
$t = \text{find}(s_i)$;	$t = \text{find}(s_i)$;
$u = \text{find}(s_j)$;	$u = \text{find}(s_j)$;
$(t == u)$?	$\text{union}(t, u)$

We regard create(n) as a shorthand for

create(0), makeSet(1), makeSet(2), . . ., makeSet(n).

This assumes that $S = \{1, \ldots, n\}$. The result is a collection of sets, each containing a single element i, $1 \leq i \leq n$. If elements need to be added one by one during the program, instead of all at the beginning, we assume makeSet is run on them is numerical sequence, with no gaps: makeSet(1), makeSet(2), . . ., makeSet(k). If this is not the natural numbering for the elements, a Dictionary ADT (Section 2.5.3) can be used for the translation.

Thus we turn our attention to the makeSet, union, and find operators and a particular data structure in which they can be implemented easily. We will represent each equivalence class, or subset, by an in-tree. Recall that the In-Tree abstract data type (Section 2.3.5) provides the following operations:

makeNode	construct a tree of one node
setParent	change the parent of a node
setNodeData	set an integer data value for the node
isRoot	return **true** if the node has no parent
parent	return the parent of the node
nodeData	return the data value

Each root will be used as a label or identifier for its tree. The instruction r = find(v) finds and assigns to r the root of the tree containing v. The parameters of union must be roots; union(t, u) attaches together the trees with roots t and u ($t \neq u$).

The In-Tree ADT makes it easy to implement union, and find. To combine roots t and u with u being the root of the resulting in-tree, as required by union, simply execute the in-tree operation setParent(t, u). To find the root of a node, use the parent function repeatedly to find the ancestor for which isRoot is **true**. Implementing create and makeSet are also easy, using the in-tree operation makeNode.

If the nodes of an in-tree are numbered $1, \ldots, n$, where $n = |S|$, we can implement the in-tree with a few arrays of $n + 1$ entries each. Since this is usually the case in practice, and to focus on the essential points, we will adopt this assumption for the rest of this section. We can "un-abstract" the in-tree and simply access the array entry parent[i] instead of calling parent(i) as an access function or setParent(i) as a manipulation procedure. We adopt the convention that -1 as a parent value denotes that this in-tree node is a root, so no array is needed for isRoot. Another array can hold nodeData, but this name is overly general for this application, so we will give it the more specific name weight, anticipating the weighted union method that will be described next. Array doubling (Section 6.2) can be used if the number of elements is not known in advance.

Using arrays simplifies the code; however, for understanding the logic of the algorithms, it is best to keep in mind the underlying in-tree structure and to interpret the array accesses in terms of the tree operations. This implementation of in-trees using arrays comes up in several other algorithms, so it is worth remembering.

A create(n) operation (considered as n makeSets) followed by a sequence of m union and/or find operations interspersed in any order will be considered an input, or *Union-Find* program, of length m. That is, the initial makeSets are not counted in the length of the program. To simplify the discussion, we assume that makeSet is not used after the initial create. The analysis reaches the same general conclusions if makeSet is used later (see Exercise 6.31).

We take the number of accesses to the parent array as the measure of work done; each access is either a *lookup* or an *assignment*, and we assume they each take time $O(1)$. (It will be clear that the total number of operations is proportional to the number of parent accesses.) Each makeSet or union does one parent assignment, and each find(i) does $d + 1$ parent lookups, where d is the depth of node i in its tree. The parent assignments and lookups collectively will be called *link* operations.

The program in Figure 6.19 builds the tree shown in Figure 6.20(a) and does $n + n - 1 + (m - n + 1)n$ link operations, in total. This demonstrates that, using these methods,

1.   *Union* (1, 2)

2.   *Union* (2, 3)

$\vdots$

$n-1$.   *Union* $(n-1, n)$

n.   *Find* (1)

$\vdots$

m.   *Find* (1)

Figure 6.19 A *Union-Find* program P with $S = \{1, \ldots, n\}$, consisting of $n - 1$ unions, followed by $m - n + 1$ finds

the worst-case time for a *Union-Find* program is in $\Omega(mn)$. (We are assuming $m > 0$; otherwise we should write $\Omega(mn + n)$.) It is not hard to show that no such program does more than $mn + n$ link operations so the worst case is in $\Theta(mn)$. This is not generally better than the methods described earlier. We will improve the implementation of the union and find instructions.

6.6.4 Weighted Union

The cost of the program in Figure 6.19 is high because the tree constructed by the union instructions, Figure 6.20(a), has large height. It could be reduced by a more careful implementation of union aimed at keeping the trees short. Let wUnion (for "weighted union") be the strategy that makes the tree with fewer nodes a subtree of the root of the other tree (and, say, makes the first tree a subtree of the second if the trees have the same number of nodes). (Exercise 6.22 examines the possibility of using the height rather than the number of nodes as the "weight" of each tree.) To distinguish between the two implementations of the union operation, we will call the first one unwUnion, for unweighted union. For wU-nion the number of nodes in each tree is stored in the weight array (which corresponds to nodeData in ADT terms). Actually, the value is needed only in the root. wUnion must compare the numbers of nodes, compute the size of the new tree, and do assignments to parent and weight. The cost of a wUnion is still a small constant, including one link operation. Now if we go back to the program in Figure 6.19 (call it P) to see how much work it requires using wUnion, we find that P is no longer a valid program because the parameters of union in instructions 3 through $n - 1$ will not all be roots. We may expand P to the program P' by replacing each instruction of the form union(i, j) by the three instructions

```
t = find(i);
u = find(j);
union(t, u);
```

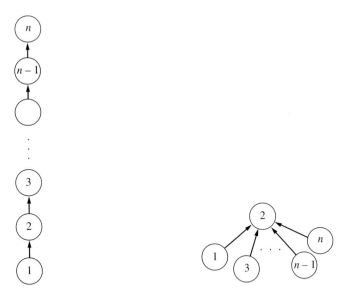

(a) Tree for P, using unweighted union   (b) Tree for P', using weighted union

Figure 6.20   Trees obtained using unweighted union and weighted union

Then, using wUnion, P' requires only $2m + 2n - 1$ link operations! Figure 6.20 shows the trees constructed for P and P' using unwUnion and wUnion, respectively. We can't conclude that wUnion allows linear time implementations in all cases; P' is not a worst-case program for wUnion. The following lemma helps us obtain an upper bound on the worst case.

Lemma 6.6   If union(t, u) is implemented by wUnion—that is, so that the tree with root u is attached as a subtree of t if and only if the number of nodes in the tree with root u is smaller, and the tree with root t is attached as a subtree of u otherwise—then, after any sequence of union instructions, any tree that has k nodes will have height at most $\lfloor \lg k \rfloor$.

Proof   The proof is by induction on k. The base case is $k = 1$; a tree with one node has height 0, which is $\lfloor \lg 1 \rfloor$. Now suppose $k > 1$ and any tree constructed by a sequence of union instructions and containing m nodes, for $m < k$, has height at most $\lfloor \lg m \rfloor$. Consider the tree T in Figure 6.21 which has k nodes, height h, and was constructed from the trees T_1 and T_2 by a union instruction. Suppose, as indicated in the figure, that u, the root of T_2, was attached to t, the root of T_1. Let k_1 and h_1 be the number of nodes in and the height of T_1, and similarly let k_2 and h_2 be the number of nodes in and the height of T_2. By the inductive hypothesis, $h_1 \le \lfloor \lg k_1 \rfloor$ and $h_2 \le \lfloor \lg k_2 \rfloor$. The height of the new tree is $h = \max(h_1, h_2 + 1)$. Clearly, $h_1 \le \lfloor \lg k \rfloor$. Since $k_2 \le k/2$, $h_2 \le \lfloor \lg k \rfloor - 1$, and $h_2 + 1 \le \lfloor \lg k \rfloor$. So in both cases $h \le \lfloor \lg k \rfloor$. $\square$

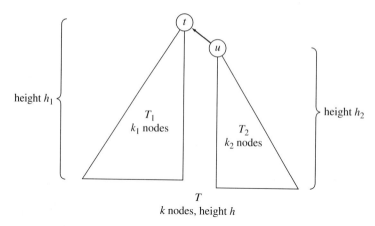

Figure 6.21   An example for the proof of Lemma 6.6

Theorem 6.7   A *Union-Find* program of size m, on a set of n elements, performs $\Theta(n + m \log n)$ link operations in the worst case if wUnion and the straightforward find are used.

Proof   With n elements, at most $n - 1$ wUnion instructions can be done, building a tree with at most n nodes. Hence by the lemma, each tree has height at most $\lfloor \lg n \rfloor$, so the cost of each find is at most $\lfloor \lg n \rfloor + 1$. Each wUnion does one link operation, so the cost of m find operations is an upper bound on the cost of any combination of m wUnion or find operations. The total number of link operations is therefore less than $m(\lfloor \lg n \rfloor + 1)$, which is in $O(n + m \log n)$.   □

Showing, by example, that programs requiring $\Omega(n + m \log n)$ steps can be constructed is left for Exercise 6.23.

The algorithms for wUnion (as well as create and makeSet) are very easy to write; we leave them as exercises.

6.6.5   Path Compression

The implementation of the find operation can also be modified to improve the speed of a *Union-Find* program by performing a process called *path compression*. Given parameter v, cFind (for "compressing-find") follows parents from the node for v to the root, and then resets the parents in all the nodes on the path just traversed so that they all point to the root. See Figure 6.22.

The effect of cFind is illustrated in Figure 6.23. Omitting lines 6 and 7 gives the procedure for the straightforward find.

There is one link operation in line 1 (done by find and cFind) and one link operation done in line 7 (by cFind only). Thus, the function cFind does twice as many link operations as the straightforward find for a given node in a given tree, but the use of cFind keeps

```
int cFind(int v)
     int root;
1.   int oldParent = parent[v];
2.   if (oldParent == -1)  // v is a root
3.       root = v;
4.   else
5.       root = cFind(oldParent);
6.       if (oldParent ≠ root)  // This if statement
7.           parent[v] = root);  // does path compression.
8.   return root;
```

Figure 6.22   Procedure for cFind

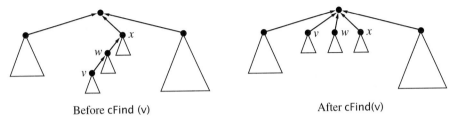

Before cFind (v)   After cFind(v)

Figure 6.23   Find with path compression (cFind)

the trees very short so that, overall, the work will be reduced. It can be shown (see Notes and References at the end of the chapter) that, using cFind and unwUnion (the *unweighted* union), the worst-case running time for programs of length m is in $O(n + m \log n)$. Exercises 6.25 through 6.29 show that there is in fact a program that requires $\Theta(n + m \log n)$ steps. Thus using either the improved implementation of union or the improved implementation of find lowers the worst-case complexity of a program from $\Theta(n + mn)$ to $\Theta(n + m \log n)$. The next step is to combine the two improvements, hoping for a further reduction.

Compatibility of wUnion and cFind

Are cFind and wUnion compatible? cFind changes the structure of the tree it acts on but it does not alter the number of nodes in that tree. It may, however, change the height. Recall that it might have seemed more natural for wUnion to compare the heights of the trees it was joining rather than the number of nodes in each since the point was to keep the trees short. It would be difficult to update the height of a tree correctly after cFind modified it. The number of nodes was used as the weight specifically to make wUnion and cFind compatible.

⋆ 6.6.6   Analysis of wUnion and cFind

We will now derive an upper bound on the number of link operations done by a *Union-Find* program using wUnion and cFind, using the amortized analysis technique introduced in Section 6.3. In this discussion P is a *Union-Find* program of length m on the set of elements $S = \{1, \ldots, n\}$. Several definitions and lemmas are needed to get the desired result, Theorem 6.13.

Definition 6.8   Forest F, node height, rank

For a specified *Union-Find* program P, let F be the forest constructed by the sequence of union instructions in P, assuming wUnion is used and the finds are ignored. The *height* of a node v in any tree is the height of the subtree rooted at v. The height of a node v in F is defined as the *rank of v*.   ■

We derive a few properties of F.

Lemma 6.8   In the set S there are at most $n/2^r$ nodes with rank r, for $r \geq 0$.

Proof   It follows from Lemma 6.6 that any tree with height r constructed by a sequence of wUnions has at least 2^r nodes. Each subtree in F (i.e., a node and all its descendants) was at one time a separate tree, so any subtree in F rooted at a node of rank r has at least 2^r nodes. Since the subtrees with root at rank r are disjoint, there can be at most $n/2^r$ of them.   □

Lemma 6.9   No node of S has rank greater than $\lfloor \lg n \rfloor$.

Proof   Use Lemma 6.6 and the fact that S has only n nodes.   □

Lemmas 6.8 and 6.9 describe properties of the forest F constructed by the union instructions of a *Union-Find* program, ignoring the finds. If the find instructions are executed as they occur in P, using cFind, a different forest results and the heights of the various nodes will be different from their ranks, which are based on F.

Lemma 6.10   At any time during execution of a *Union-Find* program P, the ranks of the nodes on a path from a leaf to a root of a tree form a strictly increasing sequence. When a cFind operation changes the parent of a node, the new parent has higher rank than the old parent of that node.

Proof   Certainly in F the ranks form an increasing sequence on a path from leaf to root. If, during execution of P, a node v becomes a child of a node w, v must be a descendant of w in F, hence the rank of v is lower than the rank of w. If v is made a child of w by a cFind, then w was an ancestor of the previous parent of v; hence the second statement of the lemma follows.   □

i	0	1	2	3	4	5	6	. . .	16	17	. . .	65536	65537
$H(i)$	1	2	4	16	65536	2^{65536}	??						
$\lg^*(i)$		0	1	2	2	3	3	. . .	3	4	. . .	4	5

Table 6.1 The functions H and $\lg^*$

In Theorem 6.13 we will establish an upper bound of $O(n \lg^*(n))$ on the running time of a *Union-Find* program using wUnion and cFind, where $\lg^*$ is a function that grows extremely slowly.

Definition 6.9 Log-star

To define $\lg^*$ we first define the function H as follows:

$$H(0) = 1,$$
$$H(i) = 2^{H(i-1)} \qquad \text{for } i > 0.$$

For example,

$$H(5) = 2^{2^{2^{2^2}}}.$$

$\lg^*(j)$ is defined for $j \geq 1$ as the least i such that $H(i) \geq j$; that is, informally, $\lg^*(j)$ is the number of 2's that must be "piled up" to reach or exceed j. ∎

It can be seen from the definition that $\lg^*(n)$ is in $o(\log^{(p)} n)$ for any constant $p \geq 0$. (We use the convention that $\lg^{(0)} n = n$.) Some values of H and $\lg^*$ are shown in Table 6.1. For any conceivable input that might ever be used, $\lg^* n \leq 5$.

We now partition the nodes of S into groups, according to their ranks. The accounting scheme for amortized cost will be based on these node groups.

Definition 6.10 Node groups

Define s_i for $i \geq 0$ to be the set of nodes $v \in S$ such that $\lg^*(1 + \text{rank of } v) = i$. The relationship of ranks to groups for "small" values is given by this table.

r (rank)	0	1	2–3	4–15	16–65535	65536–$(2^{65536} - 1)$
i (group)	0	1	2	3	4	5

∎

Lemma 6.11 The number of distinct node groups for S is at most $\lg^*(n + 1)$.

Proof The rank of any node is at most $\lfloor \lg n \rfloor$. The maximum group index is

$$\lg^*(1 + \lfloor \lg n \rfloor) = \lg^*(\lceil \lg(n + 1) \rceil) = \lg^*(n + 1) - 1,$$

and the minimum group index is 0. □

We are now ready to define accounting costs, from which we will derive amortized costs, using Equation (6.1), repeated here for convenience:

$$amortized\ cost = actual\ cost\ +\ accounting\ cost.$$

Recall that the program consists of n makeSets, followed by an arbitrary mixture of m union and find operations, except that there are at most $n - 1$ unions. Exercise 6.31 considers the case in which makeSets might be spread throughout the program and n is not known in advance.

Definition 6.11   Costs for wUnion and cFind

Costs for the Union-Find ADT operations are as follows. The unit of cost is "link operations" (parent assignments and lookups).

1. The accounting cost for makeSet is $4 \lg^*(n + 1)$. Let's think of these positive accounting costs as deposits into a savings account. The actual cost is 1 (for assigning -1 to the parent). The amortized cost is $1 + 4 \lg^*(n + 1)$.

2. The accounting cost for a wUnion is 0. The actual cost is 1. The amortized cost is 1.

3. The accounting cost for cFind is the most involved. Suppose, at the time that cFind(v) is called (but not recursively from another cFind invocation), the path from v to the root of its in-tree is given by the sequence $v = w_0, w_1, \ldots, w_k$, where w_k is the root. We use the convention that $k = 0$ if v is a root. If k is 0 or 1, the accounting cost is 0 (and no parents change).

   For $k \geq 2$, the accounting cost is -2 for each pair (w_{i-1}, w_i) such that $1 \leq i \leq k - 1$ and the node groups of w_{i-1} and w_i, as defined in Definition 6.10, are the same. Each such charge of -2 is called a *withdrawal for* w_{i-1}. Notice that the ranks of w_i increase with i, so the node groups form a nondecreasing sequence.

   The actual cost of the cFind is $2k$, because the root and the child of the root do a lookup, but no parent assignment. Therefore the *amortized cost* is 2 plus 2 times the number of cases that w_{i-1} is in a *different* node group from w_i, for $1 \leq i \leq k - 1$. By Lemma 6.11, the amortized cost of any cFind is at most $2 \lg^*(n + 1)$. ∎

Although the worst-case cost of a cFind might be $2 \lg n$, the amortization scheme has spread some of the cost onto the initial create operation. Is this robbing Peter to pay Paul? Not exactly. Observe that the accounting charges incurred by makeSets depend only on n, the number of elements in the set. But the number of cFind operations is at least $m - n + 1$, which may be arbitrarily larger than n. Nevertheless, the amortized cost per cFind is only $2 \lg^*(n + 1)$, a significant savings over $2 \lg n$. This is all very nice, but it remains to prove that we can "afford" it—that the "savings account" established by create will never be overdrawn.

Lemma 6.12   The system of accounting costs in Definition 6.11 produces a valid amortized cost scheme in the sense that the sum of the accounting costs is never negative.

Proof The initial makeSet operations set the sum of accounting costs to $4n \lg^*(n + 1)$. It suffices to show that the sum of the negative charges, incurred by cFind operations, does not exceed this total.

Each negative charge is identified as a withdrawal for some node, say w. This occurs if w is on the path traversed by a cFind and it is in the same node group as its parent, and the parent is not a root. Let i be that node group. So w will be assigned a new parent by this cFind, and by Lemma 6.10 the new parent will have a higher rank than the old parent. Once w is assigned a new parent in a higher *node group* it will not be associated with any more withdrawals. Therefore, w cannot be associated with more withdrawals than there are ranks in its node group. The number of ranks in group i is less than $H(i)$, as defined by Definition 6.9, and this is an upper bound for the number of withdrawals for w.

The number of withdrawals for all $w \in S$ is at most

$$\sum_{i=0}^{\lg^*(n+1)-1} H(i)(\text{number of nodes in group } i). \tag{6.2}$$

By Lemma 6.8, there are at most $n/2^r$ nodes of rank r so the number of nodes in group i is

$$\sum_{r=H(i-1)}^{H(i)-1} \frac{n}{2^r} \leq \frac{n}{2^{H(i-1)}} \sum_{j=0}^{\infty} \frac{1}{2^j} = \frac{2n}{2^{H(i-1)}} = \frac{2n}{H(i)}.$$

Thus the summation in Equation (6.2) is bounded above by

$$\sum_{i=0}^{\lg^*(n+1)-1} H(i) \left(\frac{2n}{H(i)} \right) = 2n \lg^*(n + 1).$$

Each withdrawal is -2, so the sum of withdrawals cannot exceed $4n \lg^*(n + 1)$. □

Theorem 6.13 The number of link operations done by a *Union-Find* program implemented with wUnion and cFind, of length m on a set of n elements is in $O((n + m) \lg^*(n))$ in the worst case.

Proof The amortization scheme defined in Definition 6.11 gives amortized costs of at most $1 + 4 \lg^*(n + 1)$ for each Union-Find operation. There are $n + m$ operations, including the makeSets. An upper bound for the total amortized cost is $(n + m)(1 + 4 \lg^*(n + 1))$. By Lemma 6.12, the sum of the actual costs never exceeds the sum of the amortized costs, so the upper bound applies to the actual costs, as well. □

Since $\lg^* n$ grows so slowly and the estimates made in the proof of the theorem are fairly loose, it is natural to wonder if we can in fact prove a stronger theorem, that is, that the running time of *Union-Find* programs of length m on a set of n elements, implemented with wUnion and cFind, is in $\Theta(n + m)$. It has been shown that this is not true (see Notes and References at the end of the chapter). For any constant c, there are programs of length m on sets of size m that require more than cm operations using these (and a variety of other) techniques. However, see Exercise 6.30.

It is an open question whether there exist different techniques that implement *Union-Find* programs in linear time. Nevertheless, as Theorem 6.13 shows, the use of cFind and wUnion results in a very efficient implementation of *Union-Find* programs. We will assume this implementation when discussing later applications.

Equivalence Programs

We began by attempting to find a good way of representing a dynamic equivalence relation so that instructions of the forms MAKE $s_i \equiv s_j$ and IS $s_i \equiv s_j$? could be handled efficiently. We define an equivalence program of length m to be a sequence of m such instructions interspersed in any order. Since, as we observed earlier, each MAKE or IS instruction can be implemented by three instructions from the set wUnion, cFind, equality test, an equivalence program of length m on a set of n elements can be implemented in $O((m + n) \lg^* n)$ time.

6.6.7   Applications

One of the best known applications of an equivalence program is Kruskal's minimum spanning tree algorithm. This algorithm is discussed in Section 8.4, after we introduce needed material on graphs. Additional applications are briefly described here. References on these applications can be found in Notes and References at the end of the chapter. In general, an equivalence program is indicated when information needs to be processed as it is received, discovered, or computed. This is called *on-line* operation.

The union and find operators can be used to implement a sequence of two other types of instructions that act on the same kind of tree structures: link(r ,v), which makes the tree rooted at r a subtree of v, and depth(v), which determines the current depth of v. A sequence of n such instructions can be implemented in $O(n \lg^*(n))$ time.

The study of equivalence programs was motivated by the problem of processing **equivalence** declarations in Fortran and other programming languages. An **equivalence** declaration indicates that two or more variables or array entries are to share the same storage locations. The problem is to correctly assign storage addresses to all variables and arrays. The declaration

equivalence (A,B(3)), (B(4),C(2)), (X,Y,Z), (J(1),K), (B(1),X), (J(4),L,M)

indicates that A and B(3) share the same location, B(4) and C(2) share the same location, and so forth. (Fortran uses parentheses, not square brackets, for array indexes.) The complete storage layout indicated by this **equivalence** statement is shown in Figure 6.24, which assumes for simplicity that each array has five entries.

If there were no arrays, the problem of processing **equivalence** declarations (as soon as they appear in the source program) would be essentially the same as the problem of processing an equivalence program. The inclusion of arrays requires some extra bookkeeping and introduces the possibility of an unacceptable declaration. For example,

equivalence (A(1),B(1)), (A(2),C(3)), (B(5),C(5))

could not be allowed because the elements of each array must occupy consecutive memory locations.

		A					J(1)	J(2)	J(3)	J(4)	J(5)
B(1)	B(2)	B(3)	B(4)	B(5)			K			L	
X		C(1)	C(2)	C(3)	C(4)	C(5)				M	
Y											
Z											

Figure 6.24 Storage arrangement (with Fortran array syntax) for an **equivalence** (A,B(3)), (B(4),C(2)), (X,Y,Z), (J(1),K), (B(1),X), (J(4),L,M)

The union and find operations are only two of many possible operations on collections of subsets. Some others include insert, which inserts a new member in a set; delete, which removes an item from a set; min, which finds the smallest item in a set; intersect, which produces a new set consisting of the elements that occur in *both* of the two given sets; and member, which indicates whether or not a specified element is in a particular set. Techniques and data structures for efficiently processing "programs" consisting of sequences of two or three types of such instructions have been studied. In some cases, the union and find techniques can be used to implement such programs of size n in $O(n \lg^*(n))$ time.

6.7 Priority Queues with a Decrease Key Operation

Recall that the main access function for the priority queue ADT (Section 2.5.1) is getBest, where "best" is min or max. The operations in a full *minimizing* priority queue ADT are:

Constructor:	create
Access functions:	isEmpty, getMin, getPriority
Manipulation procedures:	insert, deleteMin, decreaseKey

The names are revised suitably for a *maximizing* priority queue. A delete operation, which deletes an arbitrary key, might also be added.

Partial order trees (Definition 4.2) are a family of data structures often used for the implementation of priority queues. The "best" element is at the root of the partial order tree, so it can be retrieved in constant time. A number of implementations of partial order trees have been developed over the years. The word "heap" is often seen in their names because the earliest structure for partial order trees was named "heap" by its inventor.

The binary heap, introduced for Heapsort in Section 4.8.1, permits all manipulation procedures to be implemented in $O(\log n)$ time when the priority queue contains n elements. The driving force for further research was that some applications use the de-creaseKey operation far more often than any other, so it was desirable to make that operation more efficient without blowing up the other costs too much. Pairing forests were chosen for inclusion in this section because they are the simplest of many systems designed to make the decreaseKey operation very efficient. See Notes and References at the end of the chapter for sources that offer more sophisticated alternatives.

In this section we first describe how to implement the decreaseKey operation in a binary heap. An auxiliary data structure is needed; this auxiliary structure can also make a delete operation on an arbitrary element efficient. Then we describe the pairing forest strategy, which also uses a similar auxiliary structure, but its main data structure is a general partial order forest, rather than a binary partial order tree.

Recall that a binary heap is a left-complete binary tree; that is, each level of the tree is full except possibly the deepest level, and all nodes on that level are packed to the left with no gaps. Consequently nodes can be stored in an array with the root in position 1, and the binary tree can be traversed by using the rule that the children of the node in position k are in positions $2k$ and $2k + 1$. The number of elements, n, is stored in a separate variable.

6.7.1   The Decrease Key Operation

The decreaseKey and getPriority operations are not needed by all priority-queue applications. When they are needed, the implementation becomes more complicated. The name decreaseKey implicitly assumes a minimizing heap, as is typical of optimization problems, and in this section we work with minimizing heaps.

The difficulty is that the decreaseKey operation specifies an element that is already *somewhere* in the priority queue. The getPriority operation is only needed in conjunction with decreaseKey; once the problems for decreaseKey are solved, getPriority will be easy, so it is not discussed further. Using a heap for the priority queue, the signature of decreaseKey would be something like:

void decreaseKey(Key[] H, **int** id, Key K)

where id is the identifier of the element to be modified, and K is the new key (priority) value. The task of the operation is to find that element, decrease its "key," which can be thought of as a cost, and adjust its position in the priority queue according to the new key. Once the element is located, and its key modified, it is clear that bubbleUpHeap (Algorithm 4.10) can be used to perform the adjustment of position (with "$\leq$" changed to "$\geq$" in the code in Section 4.8.6 where we were using a maximizing heap), because the element moves toward the root, if it moves at all.

It would be very inefficient to search through the whole heap to find the element with the required identifier, id. The technique is to maintain a supplementary data structure, organized by identifiers, that tells the current heap location of every element in the heap. If the identifiers are integers in a reasonably compact range, which is the most common case, the supplementary data structure can be an array. In general, the supplementary data structure could be in a Dictionary ADT. We will assume the simpler case, that the identifier is an integer, and call the supplementary array xref.

Example 6.13   Heap and xref array

Figure 6.25 shows a small example of a heap with a supplementary xref array to speed the location of arbitrary elements in the heap. If xref[id] = 0, then element id is not in the heap. To execute decreaseKey(H, 5, 2.8), the xref array is consulted to find that element 5

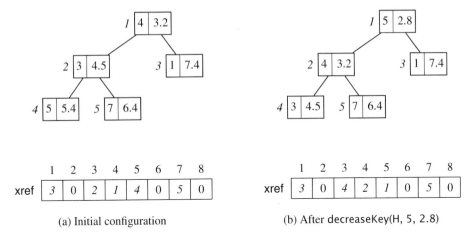

(a) Initial configuration   (b) After decreaseKey(H, 5, 2.8)

Figure 6.25 Heap H and supplementary xref array. The element identifier and key are shown inside the nodes; the key is floating point. Heap indexes are shown in italics outside the nodes.

is currently at heap index 4. (The decreaseKey operation can be executed on any node in the heap, not just on leaves.)

The key of element 5 is revised to 2.8. The whole element (5,2.8) is moved to a temporary location K. Heap index 4 is now vacant. Then bubbleUpHeap(H, 1, K, 4) is called. Element K is bubbled up to restore the partial order tree property. During the operation, element 3 moves to heap index 4, element 4 moves to heap index 2, and element 5 moves to heap index 1. The xref array is updated as each element movement occurs. Code needs to be added to bubbleUpHeap (and to all heap operations that move elements) to keep xref up to date. ∎

Since elements never move within the xref array (they are always accessed using their identifier as the array index), it might be more efficient or convenient in some cases to store the priorities there, instead of in the heap array.

6.7.2 Pairing Forests

The main goal of the Pairing Forest implementation of the Priority Queue ADT is to make the decreaseKey operation very efficient, without pushing up the costs of other operations too much. In later chapters we will encounter algorithms for which decreaseKey is done many more times than any of the other priority queue operations. In this section we concentrate on *minimizing* priority queues to simplify the discussion. Applications needing the decreaseKey operation are normally minimizing a cost of some kind, rather than maximizing something.

The Pairing Forest strategy uses a variant of a data structure called a *pairing heap*. The Pairing Forest is relatively simple to implement, and has performed well in practice.

However, it is known not to be asymptotically optimal. See Notes and References at the end of the chapter.

A Pairing Forest is a collection of general out-trees that have the partial order tree property (Definition 4.2); that is, on every path from the root of a tree to a leaf, nodes are encountered in increasing order of cost, or priority field value. The roots of the trees have the minimum priority of all nodes in their respective trees. However, no order relationship among roots of various trees in the forest is known.

The pairing forest itself can be represented as a linked list of the type TreeList; let's let the instance field forest in the class PairingForest be this list. Trees and subtrees in this forest are of type Tree. The Tree and TreeList ADTs were described in Section 2.3.4. We will use their operations, which include buildTree, root, children, as well as cons, first, and rest.

The essence of Pairing Forests is the method for finding the minimum. As long as there are two or more trees in the forest, trees are paired up, as if for a tournament. The basic operation, called pairTree, takes two trees, t1 and t2, compares their roots, and combines the two trees into a single tree with the "winning" root becoming the root of the combined tree. Since we are minimizing, the "winner" is the node with smaller priority. The combined tree is returned.

```
Tree  pairTree(Tree t1, Tree t2)  // OUTLINE
    Tree  newTree;
    if (root(t1).priority < root(t2).priority)
        newTree = buildTree(root(t1), cons(t2, children(t1)));
    else
        newTree = buildTree(root(t2), cons(t1, children(t2)));
    return newTree;
```

Notice the similarity with the weighted union operation in Section 6.6.4.

The forest is maintained as a list of trees. The operation pairForest performs pairTree on each pair of trees in the forest. If the forest started with k trees, pairForest cuts this number to $\lceil k/2 \rceil$, and returns the resulting list of trees.

```
pairForest(oldForest)  // OUTLINE
    Assume oldForest = t₁, t₂, . . ., tₖ.
    Apply pairTree to (t₁, t₂), (t₃, t₄), . . ., and put the resulting trees in the list
    newForest with the result of pairing (t₁, t₂) at the end of the list. If k is odd,
    tₖ is at the beginning of newForest, otherwise it is the result of pairing tₖ₋₁
    and tₖ.
    return newForest;
```

The getMin function carries out tournament rounds by calling pairForest repeatedly until a unique winner (minimum element) is established.

```
getMin(pq)  // OUTLINE
    while (pq.forest has more than one tree)
        pq.forest = pairForest(pq.forest);
    min = id field of root of only remaining tree.
    return min;
```

This tournament is essentially the same as that used in the algorithm to find the maximum and second largest elements of a set, in Section 5.3.2, except here we are finding the minimum and we are combining trees as we go, with the pairTree operation. Figure 6.26 shows an example.

As always, for finding the minimum of k elements (k roots of trees in the initial forest), $k - 1$ key comparisons are needed. Since k can be large, this operation can be expensive. However, it is not clear if it can be expensive time after time. For the example in Figure 6.26, the first getMin requires 7 comparisons. But if that element is deleted, there are only three candidates for the next minimum. The exact complexity of operations with this data structure is still not known.

Let's see what is involved in implementing the other priority queue operations. Nodes will be in an organizer class, PairingNode, that contains at least the id and priority fields. Insertion of a new node is very simple: create a tree of one node and add it as an additional tree in the forest:

```
insert(pq, v, w)  // OUTLINE
    Create newNode with id = v and priority = w.
    Tree  newTree = buildTree(newNode, TreeList.nil);
    xref[v] = newTree;
    pq.forest = cons(newTree, pq.forest);
```

Deleting the minimum, after it is found, simply makes all of its principal subtrees into trees in the forest.

```
deleteMin(pq)  // OUTLINE
    getMin(pq);  // Ensure forest has only 1 tree.
    Tree  t = first(pq.forest);
    pq.forest = children(t);
```

This may result in an empty forest.

For decreaseKey, we need to be able to locate the node, say oldNode, based on its id. An xref array, as was used for binary heaps in Section 6.7.1, can make this efficient. That is, oldNode = root(xref[id]). Now we need to evaluate the impact of decreasing a particular node's priority. The node oldNode is still less than all the children in its own subtree. Therefore if we detach the entire subtree rooted at oldNode, this subtree is a valid partial order tree in its own right, even after the priority of its root is decreased. We can add this subtree as a new tree of the Pairing Forest. Although the TreeList ADT does not give us an operation for actually detaching a subtree of a tree in the list, we can set a special

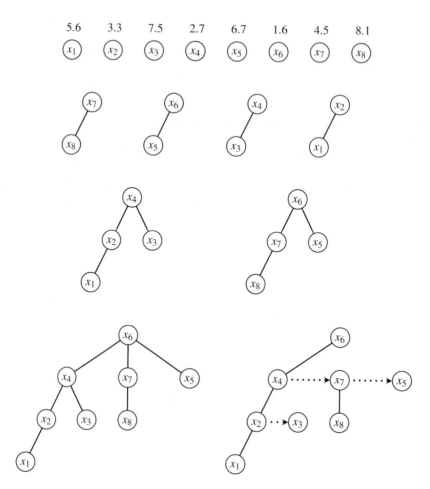

Figure 6.26 An example of a tournament with pairTree operations on 8 roots of trees. For this example, the eight original trees have one node each, with priorities shown over the nodes. The steps would be the same if these were the roots of larger trees. Each loser is attached as the new leftmost child of the winner, and the list order of the winners is reversed. For example, in round 2, x_7 lost to x_6 and x_2 lost to x_4. Winners of earlier rounds are paired up in later rounds. After three rounds, the minimum root is identified as x_6. The last row shows both the logical, or conceptual, view of the tree and the representation in which principal subtrees are in a list, as was introduced in Section 2.3.4. In the latter representation, downward sloping edges go to leftmost subtrees, while sideways arrows go to right sibling subtrees. In the last diagram an order relationship is implied only by paths that *begin* with a downward edge; thus x_4 must be less than or equal to x_3, but has no necessary relationship with x_7 or x_8.

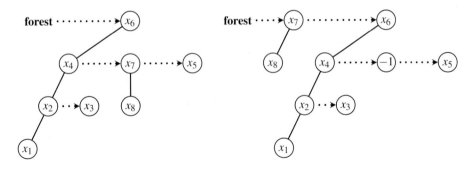

Figure 6.27   An example of decreaseKey on node x_7. The representation with principal sub-trees in a list is used. The tree that formerly contained x_7 at its root still exists, but its root now identifies it as obsolete. Before the operation x_6 was known to be less than or equal to x_7 in priority value, but now no relationship is known.

value in the id field of oldNode, to indicate that this tree is obsolete. We use -1 to denote this special id. Suppose that newNode has been created with the required id and priority.

```
decreaseKey(pq, v, w)  // OUTLINE
      Create newNode with id = v and priority = w.
      Tree  oldTree = xref[v];
      PairingNode  oldNode = root(oldTree);
      Tree  newTree = buildTree(newNode, children(oldTree));
      xref[v] = newTree;
      oldNode.id = -1;  // This tree is obsolete.
      pq.forest = cons(newTree, pq.forest);
```

Figure 6.27 shows an example.

Whenever a list of trees is traversed, any tree whose root has an id of -1 is simply bypassed. This does not entail a significant loss of efficiency in the context of pairing forests, because the only such list to be traversed is forest itself, and the only time it is traversed, it is rebuilt as part of the getMin operation. (Also, isEmpty(pq) might have to traverse over, and discard, obsolete nodes until it reaches a genuine node.) Therefore, an obsolete node is encountered only once, and is discarded at that time. Although there are some implementation details to work out, they are straightforward, and are left for the exercises.

Analysis

All operations run in constant time, except for the combination of getMin, deleteMin. Most applications call these one right after the other, so it is common to package them into one operation named extractMin. For purposes of analysis, we assume that this is done. The extractMin operation on a forest of k trees runs in time proportional to k, assuming that list ADT operations take constant time. Since k can be n, the number of nodes in the priority queue (and this can happen by simply inserting n nodes into an empty priority queue), the worst-case time for extractMin is in $\Theta(n)$. However, as with Union-Find operations, discussed in Section 6.6.6, the worst case cannot happen every time in a series of operations. Closer analysis requires advanced techniques that are beyond the scope of this book, and some questions are still unanswered. Empirical studies indicate that pairing forests perform efficiently in practice. We refer interested readers to Notes and References at the end of the chapter.

Most applications that would use a pairing forest know which elements will be in the priority queue, and so know n when the pairing forest is created. The space requirements are proportional to n, no matter how many operations are performed, provided the element ids remain in the range $1, \ldots, n$.

Exercises

Section 6.2   Array Doubling

6.1   Evaluate the time and space trade-offs for the policy of multiplying the current array size by four, instead of by two, whenever the array needs to be enlarged. (Assume elements are never deleted.)

Section 6.3   Amortized Time Analysis

6.2   To conserve space for a stack, it is proposed to shrink it when its size is some fraction of the number of allocated cells. This supplements the array-doubling strategy for growing it. Assume that the cost is tn if there are n stack elements, similar to the cost of array doubling.

Assume we stay with the policy that the array size is doubled whenever the stack size grows beyond the current array size. Evaluate each of these proposed shrinking policies, using amortized costs if possible. Do they offer constant amortized time per operation? Which scheme offers the lowest constant factor? The current array size is denoted as N.

a.   If a pop results in fewer than $N/2$ stack elements, reduce the array to $N/2$ cells.

b.   If a pop results in fewer than $N/4$ stack elements, reduce the array to $N/4$ cells.

c.   If a pop results in fewer than $N/4$ stack elements, reduce the array to $N/2$ cells.

★ **d.**   Can you devise a scheme with different parameters from those given above that does even better?

Section 6.4   Red-Black Trees

6.3   Show that the third part of Definition 6.1 is necessary. That is, draw a tree that does *not* have the binary search tree property (Definition 6.3), yet it satisfies parts 1 and 2 of Definition 6.1, and sweeping a vertical line from left to right encounters keys in ascending order.

6.4   Draw all RB_1 and RB_2 trees and all ARB_1 and ARB_2 trees.

6.5   Prove Lemma 6.1.

6.6   Prove Lemma 6.2.

6.7   Why does a color flip not work to repair a critical cluster of three nodes?

6.8   Beginning with an empty red-black tree, insert in succession the keys 10, 20, 30, 40, 50, 60, 70, 80, 90, 100.

6.9   Find a sequence in which to insert 15 nodes into an initially empty red-black tree so that the final result has black height two.

6.10   Write these color-related subroutines for Algorithm 6.2:

a.   The function colorOf that returns black if its parameter is an empty tree and returns the color of the root, otherwise.
b.   colorFlip, as described in Section 6.4.5.

6.11   Write the subroutines repairRight and rebalRight for Algorithm 6.2.

6.12   Prove Lemma 6.4.

6.13   Express the structural changes for rebalancing after an insertion (see Figure 6.9) in terms of rotations. *Hint*: The eventual root of the revised subtree participates in each rotation.

6.14   Delete nodes from the tree created by Exercise 6.8 according to each of the following rules.

a.   Logically delete each node independently of the others, from the original tree.
b.   Cumulatively, always logically delete the root of the tree that remains after the previous deletion.
c.   Cumulatively, always logically delete the least key remaining in the tree.

6.15   Delete nodes from the tree created by Exercise 6.9, cumulatively, always logically deleting the largest key remaining in the tree.

6.16   Express the structural changes for rebalancing after a deletion (see Figure 6.17) in terms of rotations.

6.17

a.   Does inserting a node into a red-black tree, then deleting it always result in the original tree? Prove it does, or give a counterexample where it does not.
b.   Does deleting a leaf node from a red-black tree, then reinserting the same key always result in the original tree? Prove it does, or give a counterexample where it does not.

Section 6.5   Hashing

6.18   Write out the open addressing procedures in more detail for searching, inserting, and deleting keys in a hash table. How do the conditions under which loops terminate differ among these procedures? Take into account the possibility of "obsolete" cells.

6.19   The type of a hash table H under closed addressing is an array of list references, and under open addressing is an array of keys. Assume a key requires one "word" of memory and a linked list node requires two words, one for the key and one for a list reference. Consider each of these load factors for *closed* addressing: 0.25, 0.5, 1.0, 2.0. Let h_C be the number of hash cells in the hash table for closed addressing.

a.   Estimate the total space requirement, including space for lists, under closed addressing, and then, assuming that the *same amount* of space is used for an open addressing hash table, what are the corresponding load factors under open addressing?

b.   Now assume that a key takes *four* words and a list node is five words (four for the key and one for the reference to the rest of the list), and repeat part (a).

Section 6.6   Dynamic Equivalence Relations and Union-Find Programs

6.20   Write algorithms for processing a sequence of MAKE and IS instructions using a matrix to represent the equivalence relation. The underlying set has n elements. Use the fact that the relation is symmetric to avoid extra work. How many matrix entries are examined or changed in the worst case when processing a list of m instructions?

6.21   Prove that a *Union-Find* program of length m on a set of n elements does at most $(n + m)n$ link operations if implemented with the unweighted union and straightforward find.

6.22   The weighted union, wUnion, uses the number of nodes in a tree as its weight. Let hUnion be an implementation which uses the height of a tree as its weight and makes the tree with the smaller height a subtree of the other.

a.   Write out an algorithm for hUnion.

b.   Either prove that the trees constructed for all *Union-Find* programs are the same regardless of whether wUnion or hUnion is used, or exhibit a program for which they differ. (For both implementations, if the trees are of equal sizes, attach the first tree as a subtree of the second.)

c.   What is the worst-case complexity of *Union-Find* programs using the straightforward find (without path compression) and hUnion?

6.23   Exhibit a *Union-Find* program of size n which requires $\Theta(n \log n)$ time using the straightforward find (without path compression) and the weighted union (wUnion).

6.24   Let $S = \{1, 2, \ldots, 9\}$ and assume wUnion and cFind are used. (If the sizes of the trees rooted at t and u are equal, union(t,u) makes u the root of the new tree.) Draw the

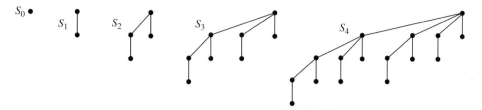

Figure 6.28   Binomial trees, also called S_k trees

trees after the last union and after each find in the following program. For each find, tell how many parent accesses (link operations) are used.

```
union(1,2)
union(3,4)
union(2,4)
union(6,7)
union(8,9)
union(7,9)
union(4,9)
find(1)
find(4)
find(6)
find(2)
find(1)
```

6.25   Binomial trees, also called S_k trees, are defined as follows: S_0 is a tree with one node. For $k > 0$, an S_k tree is obtained from two disjoint S_{k-1} trees by attaching the root of one to the root of the other. See Figure 6.28 for examples.

   Prove that, if T is an S_k tree, T has 2^k vertices, height k, and a unique vertex at depth k. The node at depth k is called the *handle* of the S_k tree.

6.26   Using the definitions and results of Exercise 6.25, prove the following characterization of an S_k tree: Let T be an S_k tree with handle v. There are disjoint trees $T_0, T_1, \ldots, T_{k-1}$, not containing v, with roots $r_0, r_1, \ldots, r_{k-1}$, respectively, such that

1. T_i is an S_i tree, $0 \le i \le k - 1$, and
2. T results from attaching v to r_0, and r_i to r_{i+1}, for $0 \le i < k - 1$.

This decomposition of an S_4 tree is illustrated in Figure 6.29.

6.27   Using the definitions and results of Exercise 6.25, prove the following characterization of an S_k tree: Let T be an S_k tree with root r and handle v. There are disjoint trees $T'_0, T'_1, \ldots, T'_{k-1}$ not containing r, with roots $r'_0, r'_1, \ldots, r'_{k-1}$, respectively, such that

1. T'_i is an S_i tree, $0 \le i \le k - 1$,

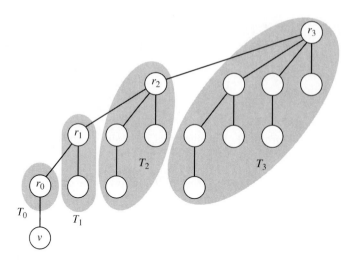

Figure 6.29   Decomposition of S_4 for Exercise 6.26

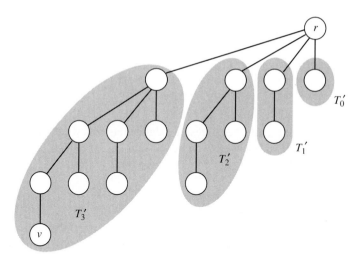

Figure 6.30   Decomposition of S_4 for Exercise 6.27

2. T is obtained by attaching each r_i' to r for $0 \leq i \leq k-1$, and
3. v is the handle of T_{k-1}'.

This decomposition of an S_4 tree is illustrated in Figure 6.30.

★ **6.28**   An *embedding* of a tree T in a tree U is a one-to-one function $f:T \to U$ (i.e., from the vertices of T to the vertices of U) such that for all w and x in T, x is the parent of

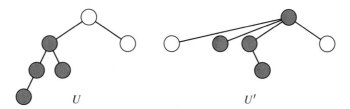

Figure 6.31   Binomial tree embeddings for Exercise 6.28: The shaded nodes are *properly embedded* in U (left) and are *initially embedded* in U' (right).

w if and only if $f(x)$ is the parent of $f(w)$. An embedding f is an *initial embedding* if it maps the root of T to the root of U; it is a *proper embedding* otherwise. See Figure 6.31 for examples.

Using the results of Exercises 6.25 through 6.27, show that, if T is an S_k tree with handle v, and f is a proper embedding of T in a tree U (which need not be a binomial tree), and U' is the tree that results from doing a cFind on $f(v)$ in U, then there is an S_k tree T' initially embedded in U'. Figure 6.31 illustrates the theorem with the shaded nodes in the roles of T (left) and T' (right).

★ **6.29**   Show that a *Union-Find* program of length $m = n$ on a set with n elements can be constructed so that, if cFind and unwUnion are used to implement it, $\Omega(n \log n)$ operations are done. (*Hint*: Read Exercises 6.25 through 6.28.)

★ **6.30**   We stated that there are examples of *Union-Find* programs that take more than linear time even when weighted union and find with path compression are used. Show that in a program of length m on a set of n elements, if all the unions occur before the finds, then the total number of operations is in $O(n + m)$. *Hint*: Modify the accounting costs in Definition 6.11.

★ **6.31**   Suppose we relax the assumption that all singleton sets are created before the *Union-Find* program begins. To be sure our "savings account" never goes negative, we need the sum of positive accounting costs to be at least $4 \lg^*(n + 1)$ if the set currently has n elements. The kth makeSet can occur anywhere in the program. Since we do not know n, the final number of elements, at the time of the kth makeSet, we cannot very well assign this operation an accounting cost based on n. However, we do know k at the time of the kth makeSet.

Show that an accounting cost of $4(2 + \lg^*(k + 1))$ for the kth makeSet is sufficient to ensure that the sum of positive accounting costs for n makeSets is at least $4 \lg^*(n + 1)$.

6.32   Design an algorithm to process **equivalence** declarations and assign memory addresses to all arrays and variables in the declarations. Assume that a **dimension** statement gives the dimensions of all the arrays. Does your algorithm detect invalid **equivalence**s?

Section 6.7   Priority Queues with a Decrease Key Operation

6.33   Show the intermediate stages of the decreaseKey operation of Example 6.13.

6.34   Show how the heap and the xref array evolve during a deleteMin operation on the heap shown on the left side of Figure 6.25.

6.35   Suppose the following elements are inserted into an empty pairing forest in the order given: (1, 4.5), (2, 1.4), (3, 6.2), (4, 5.1), (5, 7.5), (6, 9.6), (7, 3.3), (8, 8.4), (9, 2.0). Each element is written in the form (id, priority). Each part below assumes the operations in the previous parts have been carried out, so the results are cumulative. Be careful about order in all cases.

a.   Show the pairing forest after the above 9 inserts.
b.   Show the pairing forest after a getMin, also showing the intermediate results after each pairForest.
c.   Show the pairing forest after a deletemin.
d.   Show the pairing forest after the priority of 7 is decreased to 2.2. Be sure to include the obsolete node.
e.   Show the pairing forest after a second getMin.
f.   Show the pairing forest after a second deletemin.
g.   Show the pairing forest after a third getMin.

6.36   Consider the following algorithm for finding the second largest element. Insert all elements into a *maximizing* pairing forest. Perform getMax, then deleteMax, then getMax again. Does this algorithm always perform an optimal number of comparisons when n, the number of elements, is a power of 2? That is, does it always equal the lower bound given in Theorem 5.2? Either prove it does or give an example input where it fails.

6.37   Recall that decreaseKey leaves obsolete nodes in the pairing forest. Complete the implementation of these operations so that they detect and discard obsolete nodes.

a.   isEmpty(pq). Does your function run in time $O(1)$ in the worst case? If not, give a sequence of operations that causes isEmpty to require more than constant time.
b.   pairForest(pq). Does your function run in time $O(k)$ in the worst case, when there are k genuine trees in the forest (i.e., trees whose roots are not obsolete)?
c.   Devise an accounting scheme for the work of dealing with obsolete nodes. Assume that discarding a tree whose root is obsolete is one unit of work, that making the root of a tree obsolete is one unit of work, and that checking the root of a tree to see if it is obsolete is also one unit of work. Ignore all other work, because it is not related to obsolete nodes. Ensure that the amortized times for isEmpty and decreaseKey are in $O(1)$ by this work measure, and that pairForest has amortized time in $O(k)$ if there are k genuine trees in the forest.

6.38 Which functions and procedures for pairing forests need to update the xref array? Complete their implementations. *Hint*: Entries in xref are of type Tree, so look for places where the constructor for Tree is used.

6.39 The strategy for getMin that we described in the text is similar to the strategy called *multipass* in other reports. An alternative strategy, called *twopass*, works as follows: Call pairForest once on the initial forest, yielding an intermediate forest, say $t_1, t_2, \ldots t_j$. Note that pairForest reverses list order. Call pairTree on t_1 and t_2, getting the result w_2; then call pairTree on w_2 and t_3, getting the result w_3, and so on. The result w_j has the minimum element at its root. This is the usual "running minimum" method of finding the minimum, with calls to pairTree along the way. Work out the details of getMin2 using this strategy. Don't forget about the xref array.

Additional Problems

6.40 Evaluate the suitability of red-black trees for implementing both an *elementary* priority queue and a *full* priority queue, by treating the key of each element as its priority. (Recall that an elementary priority queue excludes the decreaseKey and getPriority operations.) Consider the worst-case asymptotic order of each operation. For a full priority queue, you can assume the elements have ids in the range 1, ..., n. What auxiliary data structures, such as the xref array mentioned in Section 6.7, are needed for decreaseKey to be efficient? Are they straightforward to implement? If not, explain some complications that arise.

Programs

1. Write a program to implement red-black trees, and test the operations. Include an option to count the number of key comparisons, the number of color flips, and the number of rebalances.

2. Write a program to implement the Union-Find ADT using the weighted union and find with path compression. It should test the operations by executing some *Union-Find* programs. Include an option to count the number of "link" operations.

3. Write a program to implement a pairing forest, and test the operations. Include an option to count the number of key comparisons. Note that each pairTree performs a key comparison, and no other operations do.

Notes and References

Red-black trees have a long history, having been invented with other names and rediscovered a few times. The original version was called "symmetric binary B-trees" in Bayer (1972). The name *red-black* was given by Guibas and Sedgewick (1978), who gave top-down insertion and deletion algorithms that required $O(\log n)$ structural changes (rotations). Another name is 2-3-4 trees. Algorithms to perform repairs after insertions and deletions with $O(1)$ structural changes are due to Tarjan (1983a, 1983b). The methods for repair after deletion given in this chapter are somewhat different. We adopted the term *black height* from Cormen, Leiserson and Rivest (1990); Tarjan used the term *rank*. Aho, Hopcroft, and Ullman (1974) surveys several other schemes for maintaining balanced binary trees, including AVL trees and 2-3 trees. Sleator and Tarjan (1985) introduced splay trees for the same purpose. Splay trees are the simplest to implement, but the most difficult to analyze, of all the balanced-tree methods mentioned. They do not have an efficient worst case per operation; however, their amortized cost is $O(\log n)$ per operation.

Hashing is analyzed in depth by Knuth (1998). A thorough treatment may also be found in Cormen, Leiserson and Rivest (1990) and in Gonnet and Baeza-Yates (1991). The latter book discusses practical hash functions.

Van Leeuwen and Tarjan (1983) describes and analyzes a large number of techniques for implementing *Union-Find*, or equivalence, programs. Galler and Fischer (1964) introduced the use of tree structures for the problem of processing **equivalence** declarations. Knuth (1968) describes the equivalence problem and some suggestions for a solution (see his Section 2.3.3, Exercise 11, also in Knuth (1997)). Fischer (1972) proves that, using the unweighted union and find with path compression, there are programs that do $\Omega(n \log n)$ link operations. Exercises 6.25 through 6.29 develop Fischer's proof. The upper bound of $O((m + n) \log n)$ was proved by M. Paterson (unpublished). Hopcroft and Ullman (1973) put wUnion and cFind together and proved Theorem 6.13—that is, that a program of length m on a set of n elements does $O((m + n) \lg^*(n))$ operations. Tarjan (1975) establishes a slightly above linear lower bound for the worst-case behavior of cFind and wUnion as measured by link operations; this is generalized by Fredman and Saks (1989) to the cell probe model of computation.

There has been extensive research on data structure for priority queues that make the decreaseKey operation very efficient. Pairing heaps were introduced by Fredman, Sedgewick, Sleator, and Tarjan (1986), and several variations were described. The version that we call "pairing forests" is similar to their "lazy multipass" method. Exercise 6.39 is similar to their "twopass." They were able to prove somewhat stronger bounds for "twopass" than for "multipass." Jones (1986) reported empirical studies of several priority queue data structures, and found pairing heaps to be competitive. Stasko and Vitter (1987) performed empirical studies in which they found that "multipass" did better than "twopass." They introduced new variations, called "auxiliary multipass" and "auxiliary twopass." Auxiliary twopass performed best of the four variants in their experiments, and they also proved a stronger amortized time bound for this variant than has been proven for any of the other variants in the literature, but only for the case that decreaseKey is not used.

Meanwhile Fredman and Tarjan (1987) introduced Fibonacci heaps as a priority queue data structure, and proved that they are of optimal asymptotic order in terms of amortized time. That is, decreaseKey and insert run in $O(1)$, while deleteMin runs in $O(\log n)$, in the amortized sense. Fredman (1999) closed the long-standing open question of whether pairing heaps might be optimal in the amortized sense, by demonstrating that they are not of optimal asymptotic order. He also presented additional empirical results and described an important class of applications in which "twopass" pairing heaps *are* of optimal asymptotic order. However, the exact asymptotic orders of all variations of pairing heaps are still unknown. Despite their theoretical advantages, Fibonacci heaps have been described as complicated to implement and as having significant overhead, compared to pairing heaps (Stasko and Vitter (1987), Fredman (1999)). Surveys of priority queue data structures may be found in Cormen, Leiserson, and Rivest (1990) and Gonnet and Baeza-Yates (1991).

7

Graphs and Graph Traversals

7.1   Introduction

A very rich group of problems can be cast as problems on some kind of graph. These problems originate not just in connection with computers, but throughout the sciences, industry, and business. The development of efficient algorithms to solve many graph problems has had a major impact on people's ability to solve real problems in all these fields. Yet, for many important graph problems no efficient solutions are known. For others, it is not known whether the currently known solutions are as efficient as possible or are amenable to further substantial improvements.

In this chapter we introduce the definitions and basic properties of graphs. Then we cover the primary methods for traversing graphs efficiently. It turns out that many natural problems can be solved very efficiently—in linear time, in fact—by using a graph traversal as a foundation. Loosely speaking, we may call these "easy" graph problems, not in the sense that the solution was easy to find or easy to program, but in the sense that, once programmed, instances of the problem can be solved very efficiently, and it is practical to solve very large problem instances (graphs with millions of nodes, in some cases).

Continuing our loose classification, the class of "medium" graph problems consists of those that can be solved in polynomial time, but require more work than one elementary graph traversal. That is, for each "medium" problem, an algorithm is known that solves instances of "size" n in time bounded above by some fixed polynomial, such as n^2, n^3, or n^d for some other fixed d. Several important problems in this class are covered in later chapters; see Chapters 8, 9 and 14. It is practical to solve fairly large problem instances (graphs with thousands or tens of thousands of nodes, say) on today's powerful computers.

Moving up the scale, we have "hard" graph problems, for which no polynomial-time algorithm is known. In some cases problems on graphs with 50 to 100 nodes cannot be solved by any known algorithm, even after running for a year. Yet, our current knowledge does not allow us to rule out the possibility that some efficient algorithm will be found. These problems truly represent the frontier of our knowledge, and a selection of them are discussed in Chapter 13.

One of the fascinating aspects of graph problems is that very slight changes in the way a problem is formulated can often place it in any of the three categories, easy, medium, or hard. Therefore a familiarity with what is known about existing problems, and what characteristics cause them to be easy, medium, or hard, can be very helpful when tackling a new problem.

7.2   Definitions and Representations

Informally, a graph is a finite set of points (vertices, or nodes), some of which are connected by lines or arrows (edges). If the edges are undirected or "two-way," the graph is said to be an *undirected graph*. If the edges are directed or "one-way," it is said to be a *directed graph*. "Directed graph" is often abbreviated to *digraph*. "Undirected graph" is sometimes abbreviated to "graph," but this can be ambiguous because people often refer to both undirected and directed graphs simply as "graphs." We will use the specific term

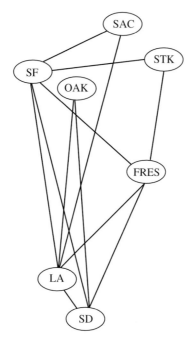

Figure 7.1   A (hypothetical) graph of nonstop airline flights between California cities

in any context where confusion might arise. In general discussions "graph" refers to both undirected and directed graphs.

7.2.1 Some Examples

Graphs are useful abstractions for numerous problems and structures in operations research, computer science, electrical engineering, economics, mathematics, physics, chemistry, communications, game theory, and many other areas. Consider the following examples:

Example 7.1   Airline route map

A map of airline routes can be represented by an undirected graph. The points are the cities; a line connects two cities if and only if there is a nonstop flight between them in both directions. See Figure 7.1 for a (hypothetical) map of airline routes between several California cities.   ■

Example 7.2   Flowcharts

A flowchart represents the flow of control in a procedure, or the flow of data or materials in a process. The points are the flowchart boxes; the connecting arrows are the flowchart arrows. Figure 7.2 shows an example in Pascal syntax.   ■

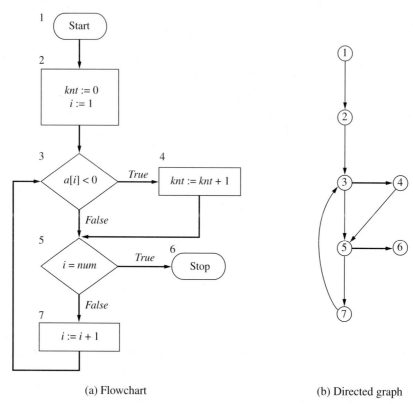

(a) Flowchart   (b) Directed graph

Figure 7.2   A flowchart and the corresponding directed graph: Arrows indicate the direction of flow.

Example 7.3   A binary relation

Binary relations are defined in Section 1.3.1. Define R to be the binary relation on the set $S = \{1, \ldots, 10\}$ consisting of ordered pairs (x, y) for which x is a proper factor of y; that is, $x \neq y$ and y/x has remainder 0. Recall that $x R y$ is an alternative notation for $(x, y) \in R$. In the digraph in Figure 7.3, the points are the elements of S and there is an arrow from x to y if and only if $x R y$. Notice that R is transitive: If $x R y$ and $y R z$ both hold, then $x R z$ also holds.   ∎

Example 7.4   Computer networks

The points are the computers. The lines (for an undirected graph) or arrows (for a directed graph) are the communication links. Figure 7.4 shows an example of each.   ∎

Example 7.5   An electrical circuit

The points could be diodes, transistors, capacitors, switches, and so on. Two points are connected by a line if there is a wire connecting them.   ∎

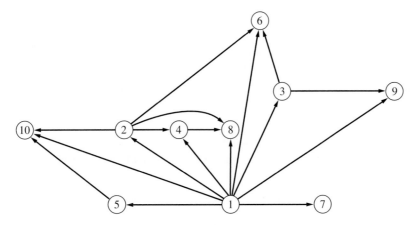

Figure 7.3 The relation R in Example 7.3, representing "x is a proper factor of y"

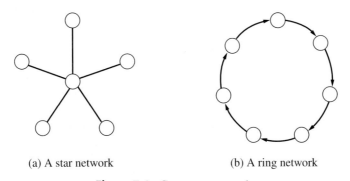

(a) A star network   (b) A ring network

Figure 7.4 Computer networks

The preceding five examples should be sufficient to illustrate that undirected and directed graphs provide a natural abstraction of relationships of diverse objects, including both physical objects and their arrangement, such as cities connected by airline routes, highways, or railway lines, and abstract objects, such as binary relations and the control structure of a program.

These examples should also suggest some of the questions we may wish to ask about the objects represented and their relationships, questions that will be rephrased in terms of the graph. Such questions can be answered by algorithms that work on the graphs. For example, the question "Is there a nonstop flight between San Diego and Sacramento?" translates into "Is there an edge between the vertices SD and SAC in Figure 7.1?" Consider the following questions:

1. What is the cheapest way to fly from San Diego to Sacramento?
2. Which route involves the least flying time?

3. If one city's airport is closed by bad weather, can you still fly between every other pair of cities?

4. If one computer in a network goes down, can messages be sent between every other pair of computers in the network?

5. How much traffic can flow from one specified point to another using certain specified roads?

6. Is a given binary relation transitive?

7. Does a given flowchart have any loops?

8. How should wires be attached to various electrical outlets so that all are connected together using the least amount of wire?

In this chapter and the next we will study algorithms to answer most of these questions.

7.2.2   Elementary Graph Definitions

This section is devoted to definitions and general remarks about graphs. Many statements and definitions are applicable to both undirected and directed graphs, and we will use a common notation for both to minimize repetition. However, certain definitions are different between undirected and directed graphs, and these differences will be emphasized.

Definition 7.1   Directed graph

A *directed graph*, or *digraph*, is a pair $G = (V, E)$ where V is a set whose elements are called *vertices*, and E is a set of *ordered* pairs of elements of V. Vertices are often also called *nodes*. Elements of E are called *edges*, or *directed edges*, or *arcs*. For directed edge (v, w) in E, v is its *tail* and w its *head*; (v, w) is represented in the diagrams as the arrow, $v \rightarrow w$. In text we simply write vw.   ∎

In the binary relation example (Example 7.3, Figure 7.3),

$$V = \{1, 2, \ldots, 10\},$$

$$E = \{(1,2), \ldots, (1,10), (2,4), (2,6), (2,8), (2,10), (3,6), (3,9), (4,8), (5,10)\}.$$

Definition 7.2   Undirected graph

An *undirected graph* is a pair $G = (V, E)$, where V is a set whose elements are called *vertices*, and E is a set of *unordered* pairs of distinct elements of V. Vertices are often also called *nodes*. Elements of E are called *edges*, or *undirected edges*, for emphasis. Each edge may be considered as a subset of V containing two elements; consequently, $\{v, w\}$ denotes an undirected edge. In diagrams this edge is the line v—w. In text we simply write vw. Of course, $vw = wv$ for undirected graphs.   ∎

For the graph of Example 7.1 and Figure 7.1, for example, we have

$$V = \{\text{SF, OAK, SAC, STK, FRES, LA, SD}\},$$

$$E = \left\{ \begin{array}{llllll} \{\text{SF, STK}\}, & \{\text{SF, SAC}\}, & \{\text{SF, LA}\}, & \{\text{SF, SD}\}, & \{\text{SF, FRES}\}, & \{\text{SD, OAK}\}, \\ \{\text{SAC, LA}\}, & \{\text{LA, OAK}\}, & \{\text{LA, FRES}\}, & \{\text{LA, SD}\}, & \{\text{FRES, STK}\}, & \{\text{SD, FRES}\} \end{array} \right\}.$$

The definition of undirected graph implies that there cannot be an edge that connects a vertex to itself: An edge is defined as a set containing two elements, and a set cannot have duplicate elements, by definition (Section 1.3.1).

Definition 7.3 Subgraph, symmetric digraph, complete graph

A *subgraph* of a graph $G = (V, E)$ is a graph $G' = (V', E')$ such that $V' \subseteq V$ and $E' \subseteq E$. By the definition of "graph" it is also required that $E' \subseteq V' \times V'$.

A *symmetric digraph* is a directed graph such that for every edge vw there is also the reverse edge wv. Every undirected graph has a corresponding symmetric digraph by interpreting each undirected edge as a pair of directed edges in opposite directions.

A *complete graph* is a (normally undirected) graph with an edge between each pair of vertices.

The edge vw is said to be *incident* upon the vertices v and w, and vice versa. ∎

Definition 7.4 Adjacency relation

The edges of a graph or digraph $G = (V, E)$ induce a relation called the *adjacency relation*, A, on the set of vertices. Let v and w be elements of V. Then vAw (read "w is *adjacent* to v") if and only if vw is in E. In other words, vAw means w can be reached from v by moving along one edge of G. If G is undirected, the relation A is symmetric. (That is, wAv if and only if vAw.) ∎

The concept of a path is very useful in many applications, including some that involve routing of people, telephone (or electronic) messages, automobile traffic, liquids or gases in pipes, and so on, and others where paths represent abstract properties (see Exercise 7.3). Consider Figure 7.1 again and suppose we wish to travel by airplane from Los Angeles (LA) to Fresno (FRES). There is an edge {LA, FRES} that is one possible route, but there are others. We could go from LA to SAC to SF to FRES, or we could go from LA to SD to FRES. These are all "paths" from LA to FRES in the graph.

Definition 7.5 Path in a graph

A *path from v to w* in a graph $G = (V, E)$ is a sequence of edges $v_0v_1, v_1v_2, \ldots, v_{k-1}v_k$, such that $v = v_0$ and $v_k = w$. The length of the path is k. A vertex v alone is considered to be a path of length zero from v to itself. A *simple path* is a path such that $v_0, v_1, \ldots, v_k$ are all distinct.

A vertex w is said to be *reachable* from v if there is a path from v to w. ∎

The path {SD, FRES}, {FRES, SF}, {SF, SAC} is shown in Figure 7.5. We denote a path by listing the sequence of vertices through which it passes (but remember that the length of a path is the number of edges traversed). Thus the path in Figure 7.5 is SD, FRES, SF, SAC, and has length three.

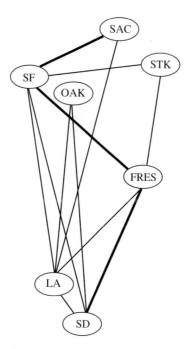

Figure 7.5   A path from SD to SAC

Definition 7.6   Connected, strongly connected

Definitions for *connectivity* require care because they differ between directed and undirected graphs.

An undirected graph is *connected* if and only if, for each pair of vertices v and w, there is a path from v to w.

A directed graph is *strongly connected* if and only if, for each pair of vertices v and w, there is a path from v to w.   ■

The reason for separate definitions that apparently read the same is that, in an undirected graph, if there is a path from v to w, then there is automatically a path from w to v. In a directed graph, this may not be true, hence the qualifier "strongly" is used to indicate that the condition is stronger. If we think of an undirected graph as a system of two-way streets and a directed graph as a system of one-way streets, then the condition of strong connectivity means that we can get from anywhere to anywhere, by traveling the one-way streets in their correct direction. This is clearly a more stringent condition than if they were all two-way streets.

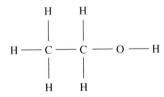

Figure 7.6   A free tree representing an alcohol molecule

Definition 7.7   Cycle in a graph

Definitions for *cycles* require care because they differ between directed and undirected graphs.

For a directed graph, a *cycle* is just a nonempty path such that the first and last vertices are identical, and a *simple cycle* is a cycle in which no vertex is repeated, except that the first and last are identical.

For undirected graphs the definitions are similar, but there is the added requirement that if any edge appears more than once, it always appears with the same orientation. That is, using the notation of Definition 7.5, if $v_i = x$ and $v_{i+1} = y$ for $0 \le i < k$, then there cannot be a j such that $v_j = y$ and $v_{j+1} = x$.

A graph is *acyclic* if it has no cycles.

An *undirected* acyclic graph is called an *undirected forest*. If the graph is also connected, it is a *free tree*, or *undirected tree*.

A *directed* acyclic graph is often abbreviated as *DAG*. (A DAG is not assumed to satisfy any connectivity condition.)   ∎

Figure 7.6 is an example of a free, or undirected, tree. Note that with this definition of a tree, no vertex is singled out as the root. A *rooted tree* is a tree with one vertex designated as the root. The parent and child relations often used with trees can be derived once a root is specified.

The reason for defining a *symmetric digraph* separately from an *undirected graph* involves cycles. If the notion of cycles is not important, then a procedure intended for directed graphs can often be used on the symmetric digraph that corresponds to an undirected graph. However, if cycles are important in the problem at hand, this substitution is not likely to work. For example, the simple undirected graph with the edge *ab* has no cycle, but its symmetric counterpart has two directed edges, *ab* and *ba*, and has a cycle.

Definition 7.8   Connected component

A *connected component* of an undirected graph G is a *maximal* connected subgraph of G. For directed graphs, the corresponding concept is more involved, and its definition is deferred until Definition 7.18.   ∎

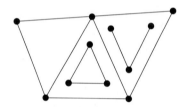

Figure 7.7   A graph with three connected components

We should clarify the meaning of "maximal" in the definition of "connected component." A graph is said to be *maximal* within some collection of graphs if it is not a proper subgraph of any graph in that collection. It need not have the most vertices nor the most edges of any graph in that collection. In Definition 7.8 the "collection" is all connected subgraphs of G.

When the term *component* is used in connection with graphs and other abstract structures, it usually carries the implication of maximality within some group. We will encounter the terms "strongly connected component" and "biconnected component" later in the chapter. In both cases there is a notion of maximality.

If an undirected graph is not connected, it may be partitioned into separate connected components, and this partitioning is unique. The graph in Figure 7.7 has three connected components.

In many applications of graphs it is natural to associate a number, usually called a *weight*, with each edge. The numbers represent costs or benefits derived from using the particular edge in some way. Consider Figure 7.1 once again and suppose that we want to fly from SD to SAC. There is no nonstop flight, but there are several routes or paths that could be used. Which one is best? To answer this question we need a standard by which to judge the various paths. Some possible standards are

1. the number of stops,
2. the total ticket cost, and
3. the total flying time.

After choosing a standard, we could assign to each edge in the graph the cost (in stops, money, or time) of traveling along that edge. The total cost of a particular path is the sum of the costs of the edges traversed by that route. Figure 7.8 shows the airline graph with the (hypothetical) cost of a plane ticket written beside each edge. You may verify that the cheapest way to get from SD to SAC is to make one stop in LA. The general problem of finding "best" paths is studied in Sections 8.3 and 9.4.

Figure 7.9, which shows some of the streets in a city, might be used to study the flow of automobile traffic. The number assigned to an edge indicates the amount of traffic that can flow along that section of the street in a certain time interval. The number is determined by the type and size of road, the speed limit, the number of traffic lights between the intersections shown in the graph as vertices (assuming not every street is shown in the graph), and various other factors.

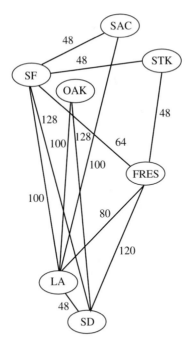

Figure 7.8   A weighted graph showing airline fares

The assignment of numbers to edges occurs often enough in applications to merit a definition.

Definition 7.9   Weighted graph

A *weighted graph* is a triple (V, E, W) where (V, E) is a graph (directed or undirected) and W is a function from E into $\mathbf{R}$, the reals. (Other types for weights, such as rationals or integers, may be appropriate for some problems.) For an edge e, $W(e)$ is called the *weight* of e.   ∎

The functional terminology may seem very technical, but it is easily understood, once we recall from Section 1.3.1 that, conceptually, a function is just a table of two columns: the argument to the function and the corresponding function value. In this case each edge appears on some row in column one and its weight is on the same row in column two. The representation in a data structure may be different, but it will carry the same information. In diagrams of graphs, we simply write the weight next to each edge, as we did in Figures 7.8 and 7.9. The weights in some applications will correspond to costs or undesirable aspects of an edge, whereas in other problems the weights are capacities or other beneficial properties of the edges. (The terminology varies with the application; thus the terms *cost, length*, or *capacity* may be used instead of *weight*.) In many applications weights cannot naturally be negative, as when they represent distances. The correctness of some algorithms depends

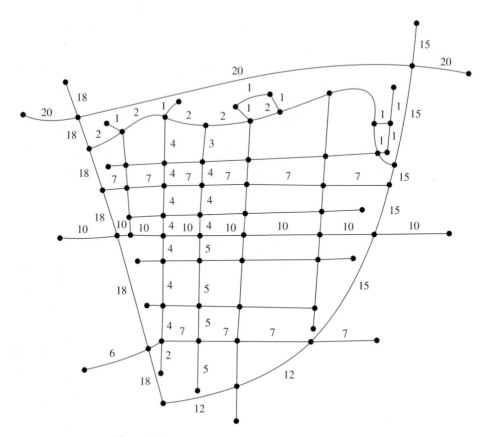

Figure 7.9 A street map showing traffic capacities

on restricting the weights to nonnegative values, while other algorithms are able to handle negative values.

7.2.3 Graph Representations and Data Structures

We have seen two ways of representing a graph on paper: by drawing a picture in which vertices are represented by points and edges as lines or arrows, and by listing the vertices and edges. This section discusses data structures that are useful for representing graphs in a computer program. Let $G = (V, E)$ be a graph with $n = |V|$, $m = |E|$, and $V = \{v_1, v_2, \ldots, v_n\}$.

Adjacency Matrix Representation

G can be represented by an $n \times n$ matrix $A = (a_{ij})$, called the *adjacency matrix* for G. A is defined by

$$a_{ij} = \begin{cases} 1 & \text{if } v_i v_j \in E \\ 0 & \text{otherwise} \end{cases} \qquad \text{for } 1 \leq i, j \leq n.$$

The adjacency matrix for an undirected graph is symmetric (and only half of it need be stored). If $G = (V, E, W)$ is a weighted graph, the weights can be stored in the adjacency matrix by modifying its definition as follows:

$$a_{ij} = \begin{cases} W(v_i v_j) & \text{if } v_i v_j \in E \\ c & \text{otherwise} \end{cases} \qquad \text{for } 1 \leq i, j \leq n,$$

where c is a constant whose value depends on the interpretation of the weights and the problem to be solved. If the weights are thought of as costs, ∞ (or some very high number) may be chosen for c because the cost of traversing a nonexistent edge is prohibitively high. If the weights are capacities, a choice of $c = 0$ is usually appropriate since nothing can move along an edge that is not there. See Figures 7.10(a, b) and 7.11(a, b) for examples.

Algorithms for solving some problems on graphs require that every edge be examined and processed in some way at least once. If an adjacency matrix representation is used, we may as well think of a graph as having edges between all pairs of distinct vertices, because many algorithms would examine each entry in the matrix to determine which edges really exist. Since the number of possible edges is n^2 in a directed graph, or $n(n - 1)/2$ in an undirected graph, the complexity of such algorithms will be in $\Omega(n^2)$.

Array of Adjacency Lists Representation

An alternative to the adjacency matrix representation is an array indexed by vertex number containing linked lists, called *adjacency lists*. For each vertex v_i the ith array entry contains a list with information on all edges of G that "leave" v_i. In a directed graph this means v_i is the tail of the edge; in an undirected graph, the edge is incident upon v_i. The list for v_i contains one element per edge. For definiteness, let's call this array adjInfo. It might be defined by

        List[] adjInfo = **new** List[n+1];

We will use indexes $1, \ldots, n$, so we allocate $n + 1$ positions and don't use the 0th position. Now adjInfo[i] will be a list with information about the edges leaving v_i.

The merit of an adjacency-list structure is that edges that don't exist in G don't exist in the representation either. If G is sparse (has many fewer than n^2 edges), it can be processed quickly. Note that if the elements within an adjacency list appear in a different order, the structure still represents the same graph, but an algorithm using the list will encounter the elements in a different order and may behave somewhat differently. An algorithm should not assume any particular ordering (unless, of course, the algorithm itself constructs the list in a special way).

The data in the adjacency lists will vary with the problem, but there are fairly standard basic structures that are useful for many algorithms. Suppose we define EdgeInfo to be an organizer class (see Section 1.2.2) with fields for each piece of information that we want to maintain about the edge. Then each element of an adjacency list will be an object in the EdgeInfo class. Three common fields are from, to, and weight, to record that the edge is from v_{from} to v_{to} and "weight" is its weight. We will write this information in the form

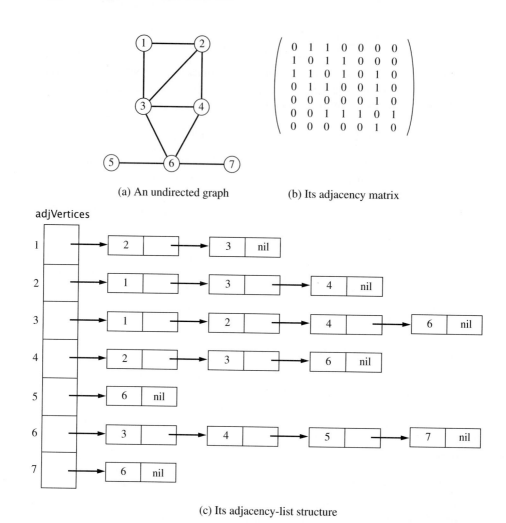

(a) An undirected graph   (b) Its adjacency matrix

(c) Its adjacency-list structure

Figure 7.10 Two representations for an undirected graph without edge weights are the adjacency matrix and the array of adjacency lists. It could also be a symmetric digraph.

(from, to, weight). However, in any single list, the from field will be the same for all edges. In particular, the list adjInfo[i] will have from = i for all elements. Therefore the from field is redundant and is normally omitted from the adjacency lists.

For unweighted graphs, there is no weight field either. Since EdgeInfo is reduced to a single field, to, in this case we don't need an organizer class. We simply use lists of integers, as provided by the IntList abstract data type (Section 2.3.2). Since there is no "info" except vertices now, we rename the array to adjVertices. Each element, say j, in the list adjVertices[i] indicates the presence of the edge $v_i v_j$ in G. For example, if 6 is in

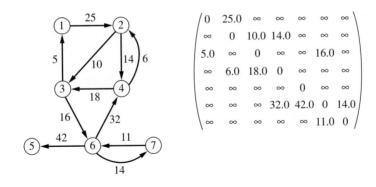

(a) A weighted digraph   (b) Its adjacency matrix

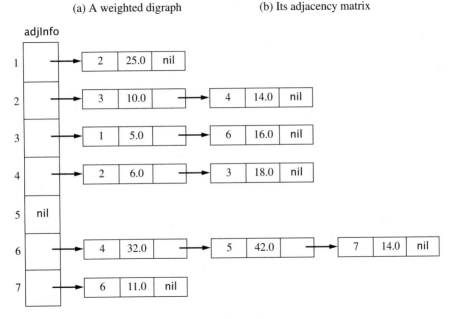

(c) Its adjacency-list structure

Figure 7.11   Two representations for a weighted directed graph

the list adjVertices[7], it represents the edge $(7, 6)$. This data structure is illustrated for an undirected graph (it could also be a symmetric digraph) by the example in Figure 7.10.

For weighted graphs, we might wish to define a class of lists in which the elements are in EdgeInfo, and call this class EdgeList. Let's denote an object in EdgeInfo as (to, weight). In this case an element (j, w_{ij}) in the adjacency list adjInfo[i] represents the edge (v_i, v_j) with weight w_{ij}. Figure 7.11 illustrates the conceptual structure for a weighted directed graph. Additional fields may be added to the array entries or the linked list elements as required by the algorithms to be used.

In an undirected graph, each edge is represented twice; that is, if vw is an edge, there is an element for w on the adjacency list for v and an element for v on the adjacency list for w. Thus there are $2m$ adjacency-list elements and n adjacency lists. For a directed graph each edge, being directed, is represented once. Notice that the adjacency-list representations of an undirected graph and the corresponding *symmetric digraph* are identical.

7.3   Traversing Graphs

Most algorithms for solving problems on a graph examine or process each vertex and each edge. Breadth-first search and depth-first search are two traversal strategies that provide an efficient way to "visit" each vertex and edge exactly once. (The terms *depth-first search* and *depth-first traversal* are interchangeable; similarly for *breadth-first search* and *breadth-first traversal*.) Consequently, many algorithms based on these foundations run in time that grows linearly with the size of the input graph.

7.3.1   Overview of Depth-First Search

The value of depth-first search was demonstrated by John Hopcroft and Robert Tarjan, who developed many important algorithms that use it. Several of these are presented in the rest of this chapter.

Depth-first search is a generalization of general tree traversal (Section 2.3.4). The starting vertex may be determined by the problem or chosen arbitrarily. As with tree traversal, depth-first search is usefully visualized as a journey around the graph. The analogy with tree traversal is easier to see with directed graphs because the edges are directed, as are tree edges. We begin by describing depth-first search for directed graphs, then see how to adapt it for undirected graphs in Section 7.6.

Imagine a directed graph as a cluster of islands connected by bridges. We'll assume that traffic is one-way on each bridge, but we are taking a walking tour, so we are allowed to walk in either direction. However, we decide on a policy that we will always walk across a bridge for the *first* time in the same direction as traffic; we call this *exploring* an edge (bridge). If we walk across a bridge in the reverse direction from traffic, then we must be returning to some place we have been before, so we call this *backtracking*. The theme of depth-first search is to explore if possible, otherwise backtrack. We have to add some restrictions on exploring, but we'll do that as we "walk" through an example in the persona of Terry the tourist.

Example 7.6   Depth-first search

Let's begin a depth-first search from vertex A in the graph below. For simplicity, when we have a choice of edges to explore, we will select them in alphabetical order.

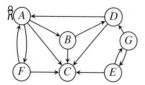 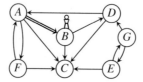 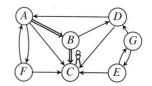

Terry the tourist begins at A in the left diagram, explores to B in the middle, and then to C in the right diagram. Double solid lines denote edges that have been explored and led to undiscovered vertices, or islands. We say that A, B, and C are *discovered* when Terry first arrives.

Remembering that exploration must be in the direction of traffic, there is nowhere to explore from C. We call this a *dead end*. So Terry *backtracks*. Backtracking is always done over the bridge that was used to arrive on the island for the first time. Once island C is backtracked from it will not be revisited, and is said to be *finished*. A heavy line indicates that an edge has both been explored and backtracked over.

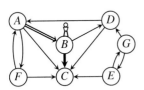 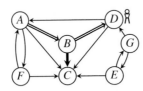 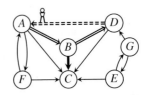

In the left diagram above, Terry has backtracked to B, and now applies the rule to explore if possible. The bridge to D has not been explored yet, so that is the next step, leading to the middle diagram. Now we have a situation that can't arise in tree traversal. The right diagram shows Terry en route over the bridge from D to A. This would complete a cycle, but of course, trees don't have cycles. For this reason, when searching a graph, it is necessary to remember where we have been—we must be able to distinguish undiscovered vertices from discovered vertices. We could walk around in circles forever if we don't remember that we have already discovered A.

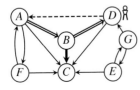 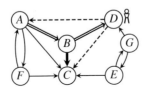 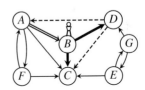

Let's assume Terry does recognize island A just before getting there, and backtracks to D, as shown in the left diagram above. We use dotted lines to indicate that an edge was explored, but it went to an already discovered vertex.

For the journey metaphor, we say that such an edge is explored and backtracked over, even though it goes to a vertex that was previously discovered. However, when we are thinking of the search algorithmically, we will say that such an edge is *checked*, and use the term *backtrack* only when the edge was explored and it led to an undiscovered vertex.

Similarly, the bridge from D to C is explored, but C has previously been discovered and even finished, so backtracking occurs without a visit, leading to the middle diagram. We also call D a *dead end*, even though it has edges leaving it, because they only go to discovered vertices.

Notice that edges DA and DC both led to discovered vertices, but there is a difference: The edge to A led to a vertex that was discovered, but not finished, whereas the edge to C

led to a finished vertex. This distinction is important in many applications of depth-first search.

There is nowhere else to explore from D, so Terry backtracks over the bridge by which D was discovered, returning to B in the right diagram. There are no further bridges to explore here either, so the next step is to backtrack to A.

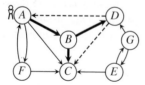 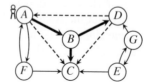 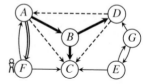

In the left diagram Terry has backtracked to A and is ready to explore in a new direction. The bridge AC is a third example of a bridge to an already discovered vertex, but again there is a slight difference from the other two. In this case, previous explorations carried Terry from A to C, and now this bridge is a shortcut. In the case of DC there was no previous path that was traveled from D to C. The middle diagram shows the situation after AC has been explored and backtracked over. In the right diagram Terry has explored AF, reaching an undiscovered vertex.

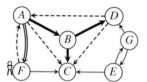 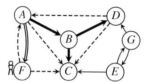 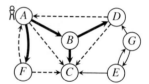

From island F, first FA is explored and backtracked over (left diagram above), then FC is explored and backtracked over (middle diagram). Like D, F is a dead end. Terry finally backtracks to A, completing the day's perambulations in the right diagram. Notice that Terry was never able to reach E or G.

Looking at the final diagram, we see that the edges drawn as heavy solid lines, which went to undiscovered vertices during the search, form a tree. This makes sense when we think about it, because a vertex can only be discovered once, so it can only have one such edge coming into it (or none, if the search starts there). Having only one edge coming into each vertex is a property of trees. The tree defined by the edges that led to undiscovered vertices during the search is called a *depth-first search tree*, or DFS tree for short. DFS trees are studied in more detail in Section 7.4.3. ■

Although we introduced depth-first search as a journey, our example shows that the journey has a certain structure: We always return the way we came. In other words, if the first step is from A to B, then eventually we return from B to A. What happened in the interim? Actually, we performed a depth-first search from B with the added condition that we could not revisit A.

More generally, whenever the journey returns (backtracks) to A, the added condition on further exploration is that *no* vertex that has been visited will be revisited. For example, the edge AC led to a discovered vertex, but AF did not, so a depth-first search from F

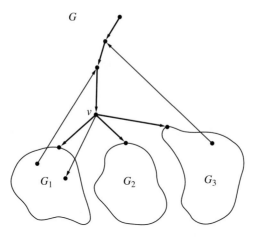

Figure 7.12   The structure of depth-first search: G_1 is completely traversed before exploring G_2, then G_3. Since G might not be a tree, there might be edges from the subgraphs to previously visited vertices.

was performed. Due to the rule against revisiting a vertex that has been discovered, the exploration from F did not visit A or C before backtracking to A. Instead the edges FA and FC are *checked*. These observations suggest a recursive decomposition of the search process:

```
dfs(G, v)  // OUTLINE
      Mark v as "discovered."
      For each vertex w such that edge vw is in G:
            If w is undiscovered:
                  dfs(G, w); that is, explore vw, visit w, explore from there
                  as much as possible, and backtrack from w to v.
            Otherwise:
                  "Check" vw without visiting w.
      Mark v as "finished."
```

To gain some further insight into the structure of depth-first search, let's look at Figure 7.12. Suppose the vertices that will be reached from v during a depth-first search can be partitioned into several subgraphs, G_1, G_2, G_3, such that there is no connection (via undiscovered vertices) among G_1, G_2, and G_3. We also assume for this example that the adjacency list of v happens to be arranged such that some vertex in G_1 is discovered before any vertex in G_2, and some vertex in G_2 is discovered before any vertex in G_3.

The depth-first strategy of always exploring a path as far as possible before backtracking (and exploring alternative paths as far as possible before backtracking further) has the effect of visiting all vertices in G_1 before going on to a new subgraph adjacent to v, in this case, G_2 or G_3. Then all vertices in G_2 will be visited before visiting anything in G_3.

This is analogous to tree traversal, which visits all vertices in one subtree before going to the next subtree. We will return to this analogy when we study the properties of depth-first search in more detail, in Section 7.4.1.

So far we have concentrated on directed graphs. Depth-first search is equally applicable to undirected graphs. However, we have some ambiguity to resolve concerning "forward direction" and "backward direction" of edges, because now the edges are undirected. We will return to this issue in Section 7.6.

Finally, we need to address the fact that not all vertices in a graph are necessarily reachable from the vertex at which a depth-first search commenced. We saw this for vertices *E* and *G* in Example 7.6. The following brief pseudocode describes how this is handled.

```
dfsSweep(G)  // OUTLINE
    Initialize all vertices of G to "undiscovered."
    For each vertex v ∈ G, in some order:
        If v is undiscovered:
            dfs(G, v); that is, perform a depth-first search beginning
            (and ending) at v; any vertices discovered during an earlier
            depth-first search visit are not revisited; all vertices visited
            during this dfs are now classified as "discovered."
```

Given the informal description of depth-first search, we see that dfsSweep (through calls to dfs) visits every vertex in *G* exactly once, and traverses every edge in *G* once in the forward direction (exploring) and once in the backward direction (backtracking). However, when the edge goes to a vertex that has already been discovered, rather than say that the edge is explored and immediately backtracked over, we say the edge is *checked*.

7.3.2 Overview of Breadth-First Search

Breadth-first search is quite different from depth-first search in terms of the order in which vertices are discovered. Rather than a journey by one individual, breadth-first search is best visualized as many simultaneous (or nearly simultaneous) explorations starting from a common point and spreading out independently. After giving an informal introduction, we develop a breadth-first search algorithm for a typical application, finding a breadth-first spanning tree.

Example 7.7 Breadth-first search

Let's see how breadth-first search works, starting from vertex *A* in the same graph as we used in Example 7.6. Instead of Terry the tourist, a *busload* of tourists start walking at *A* in the left diagram. They spread out and explore in all directions permitted by edges leaving *A*, looking for bargains. (We still think of edges as one-way bridges, but now they are one-way for walking, as well as traffic.)

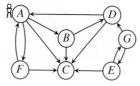 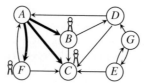 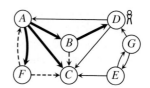

Various groups have arrived at B, C, and F in the middle diagram. We'll assume that only the *first* group to arrive at any island is able to find the best bargains—then they're all gone. Although they keep spreading out, only a contingent from B reaches an undiscovered location, D, as shown in the right diagram.

The dashed lines show edges that were explored but went to vertices that were previously discovered. (Again, in an algorithmic setting we will say these edges are *checked*, rather than *explored*.) The tourists that took these routes arrived at C (or back at A) too late to get any bargains. Not only that, but once they fall behind like this, they will be too late at any *future* islands that might be reached from A or C, so they might as well give up on bargain hunting.

In the last phase of the search (not shown) the edges DA and DC will similarly be explored. There is no backtracking in breadth-first search and E and G are unreachable, so the search will be over after these last two edges are explored.

Looking at the final diagram, we see that the edges drawn as heavy solid lines, which went to undiscovered vertices during the search, again form a tree, although it is different from the tree formed in Example 7.6. If there are two or more shortest paths to a particular vertex, the tie is broken somehow and only one edge is considered to "discover" the vertex. The winner depends on implementation details and details of the data structure, when a computer program is run.   ■

As we saw in the example, in a breadth-first search, vertices are visited in order of increasing distance from the starting point, say, s. The "distance" for this discussion is simply the number of edges in a shortest path. We now outline the procedure in a little more detail. Initially all vertices are undiscovered.

The central step of the breadth-first search, beginning with $d = 0$ and repeated until no new vertices are found, is to consider in turn each vertex, v, at distance d from s and examine all edges leading from v to adjacent vertices. For each edge vw, if w is undiscovered, then add w to the set of vertices at distance $d + 1$ from the starting point s; otherwise w is closer than that, and its distance is already known.

After all vertices at distance d are processed in this way, process vertices at distance $d + 1$, and so on. The search terminates when a distance d occurs such that there are no vertices at all at distance d.

Example 7.8   Breadth-first distances

For the breadth-first search in Example 7.7, the distances are 0 for A, 1 for B, C, and F, and 2 for D. In Exercise 7.5 you are asked to calculate the breadth-first distances for the graph in Example 7.7, with G as the starting vertex.   ■

Because breadth-first search has fewer applications than depth-first search, we will conclude our presentation of it here with a representative application. The following algorithm puts the preceding description of breadth-first search into action, and finds a *breadth-first spanning tree* rooted at a specified start vertex, s. The tree is stored as an in-tree in the array parent. The In-Tree ADT was described in Section 2.3.5, and we have encountered the array implementation of an in-tree earlier in Section 6.6.3.

A *breadth-first spanning tree* contains a tree vertex for every graph vertex that is reachable from s, hence the name "spanning." Moreover, the path in the tree from s to any vertex v contains the minimum possible number of edges; thus the depth of v in this tree is its minimum edge-distance from s. In the last part of the figure in Example 7.7 the solid-lined edges make up a breadth-first spanning tree.

As always with in-trees, the path from the starting vertex s to any vertex v can be discovered in reverse order by following parent entries from v back to s. The parent of s is set to -1 to denote that s is the root.

Algorithm 7.1   Breadth-First Search

Input: $G = (V, E)$, a graph represented by an adjacency list structure, adjVertices, as described in Section 7.2.3, where $V = \{1, \ldots, n\}$; $s \in V$, the vertex from which the search begins.

Output: A breadth-first spanning tree, stored in the parent array. The parent array is passed in and the algorithm fills it.

Remarks: For a queue Q, we assume operations of the Queue abstract data type (Section 2.4.2) are used. The array color[1], . . ., color[n] denotes the current search status of all vertices. Undiscovered vertices are white; those that are discovered but not yet processed (in the queue) are gray; those that are processed are black.

```
void  breadthFirstSearch(IntList[] adjVertices, int n, int s, int[] parent)
    int[]  color = new int[n+1];
    Queue pending = create(n);
    Initialize color[1], . . ., color[n] to white.

    parent[s] = -1;
    color[s] = gray;
    enqueue(pending, s);
    while (pending is nonempty)
        v = front(pending);
        dequeue(pending);
        For each vertex w in the list adjVertices[v]:
            if (color[w] == white)
                color[w] = gray;
                enqueue(pending, w);
                parent[w] = v;  // Process tree edge vw.
            // Continue through list.
        // Process vertex v here.
        color[v] = black;
    return;
```

Algorithm 7.1 serves as a skeleton for all breadth-first search applications. Comments indicate where code would be inserted for processing vertices and tree edges (edges to undiscovered vertices, which make up the breadth-first spanning tree). If it is desired to process nontree edges, an else for the if is needed; however, such a requirement is unusual in breadth-first search.

For the queue needed in Breadth-First Search (pending), the last part of Exercise 2.16 provides a simple and efficient implementation, because only n enqueues will be done during the course of the algorithm.

As we saw in Example 7.7, not all vertices are necessarily reachable from a selected starting vertex. If it is necessary to explore the entire graph, a "wrapper" procedure similar to dfsSweep in Section 7.3.1 can be used.

Analysis of Breadth-First Search

We assume G has n vertices and m edges, and assume the search reaches of all G. Also, we assume that each queue operation takes constant time. Finally, we assume that the application's processing for individual vertices and edges takes constant time for each; otherwise, the appropriate costs need to be multiplied by the time per processing operation.

Each edge is processed once in the **while** loop for a cost of $\Theta(m)$. Each vertex is put into the queue once and is removed from the queue and processed once, for a cost of $\Theta(n)$. Extra space is used for the color array and the queue, and these are in $\Theta(n)$.

7.3.3   Comparison of Depth-First and Breadth-First Searches

Before getting further into specific problems and algorithms, let's take a high-level look at some similarities and differences of the two traversal methods just outlined.

The descriptions of the two traversal methods are somewhat ambiguous. For example, if there are two vertices adjacent to v, which will be visited first? The answer depends on implementation details, for example, the way in which the vertices are numbered or arranged in the representation of G. An efficient implementation for either method must keep track of vertices that have been discovered but whose adjacent vertices have not yet all been discovered.

Note that when a depth-first search backs up from a dead end, it is supposed to branch out from the *most recently* discovered vertex before exploring new paths from vertices that were discovered earlier. Thus vertices from which exploration is incomplete are processed in a last-in first-out (LIFO) order that is characteristic of a stack. On the other hand, in a breadth-first search, to ensure that vertices close to v are visited before those farther away, the vertices to be explored are organized as a FIFO queue.

We presented high-level algorithms for both search methods in the preceding subsections. Many variations and extensions can be made to these algorithms, depending on what they are used for. It is often necessary, for example, to do some sort of processing on each edge. The descriptions of the algorithms do not mention all edges explicitly, but of course the implementation of the lines that require finding an undiscovered vertex adjacent to a given vertex, say v, would involve examining edges incident upon v, and the necessary processing of edges would be done there. In Section 7.4.4 we will consider how to fit other kinds of processing into a general depth-first search skeleton.

To conclude this comparison we observe that depth-first search contains two processing opportunities for v (when it is discovered and when it is marked "finished"), while breadth-first search contains only one (when it is dequeued). Upon closer inspection, we observe that in both searches, the *first* processing opportunity occurs while there are (possibly many) undiscovered vertices that are reachable from v and have not yet been discovered. Therefore the kind of computations that can be done at this point must be done in a state of relative ignorance about the rest of the graph. However, in depth-first search, there is a *postorder* processing opportunity, as well, just before the search finally backtracks from v. At this time, in general, many more vertices have been discovered and much more information may have accumulated during the search. The postorder processing step is often able to exploit this additional information to perform much more sophisticated computations than were possible at preorder time. The presence of this postorder processing opportunity in depth-first search explains, in a very profound way, why we see so many applications for depth-first search, and relatively few for breadth-first search.

7.4   Depth-First Search on Directed Graphs

We begin our detailed study of depth-first search with directed graphs. We will develop a general depth-first search skeleton that can be used to solve many problems, and we will apply it to solve several standard problems.

The general depth-first search procedure is somewhat more complicated for undirected graphs than it is for directed graphs, and so it is taken up in Section 7.6. This might seem surprising because undirected graphs seem to be simpler than directed graphs. However, a technically correct depth-first search explores each edge only once, and in undirected graphs each edge is represented *twice* in the data structure. In essence, depth-first search on an undirected graph transforms it into a directed graph on the fly, with each edge being oriented in the direction of exploration. We prefer to separate this issue from the main issues of depth-first search. We also note that several problems on undirected graphs can be recast as problems on symmetric digraphs, and the simpler directed depth-first search can then be used. As a rule of thumb, if the depth-first search on the undirected graphs ignores nontree edges, then the symmetric digraph can be substituted.

In many problems where we model something using a directed graph, it may be natural to assign edges in either direction. For example, consider a "call graph" in which the vertices are procedures. We might reasonably define edges by the rule that vw means "v calls w," or by the rule that vw means "v is called by w." For another example, consider a "genealogy chart" in which vertices are people. We might reasonably define edges in the direction from parent to child or from child to parent. Which choice is most useful is likely to depend on the specific problem at hand. Therefore it is convenient to be able to go back and forth between the two orientations. This motivates the next definition.

Definition 7.10   Transpose graph

The *transpose graph* of digraph G, denoted as G^T, is the graph that results from reversing the direction of each edge in G.   ■

Depth-first search explores in the forward direction, but there are some cases when we want to search "backwards" over a graph. It is possible to construct the adjacency-list structure of the transpose graph G^T from the adjacency-list structure of G in linear time, and do a standard search on G^T. Alternatively, if the need is anticipated when the adjacency-list structure is being built, both G and G^T can be built simultaneously.

7.4.1 Depth-First Search and Recursion

We have seen that depth-first search can be simply described by a recursive algorithm. In fact, there is a fundamental connection between recursion and depth-first search. In a recursive procedure, the call structure can be diagrammed as a rooted tree where each vertex represents a recursive call to the procedure, as we have seen in Sections 3.2.1 and 3.7. The order in which the calls are executed corresponds to a depth-first traversal of the tree.

Example 7.9   Fibonacci numbers

Consider the recursive definition of the Fibonacci numbers, $F_n = F_{n-1} + F_{n-2}$, from Equation (1.13). The call structure for a recursive computation of F_6 is shown in Figure 7.13. Each vertex is labeled with the current value of n, that is, the actual parameter of the activation frame that the vertex represents. Essentially, the subtree rooted at that vertex computes F_n for the current value of n.

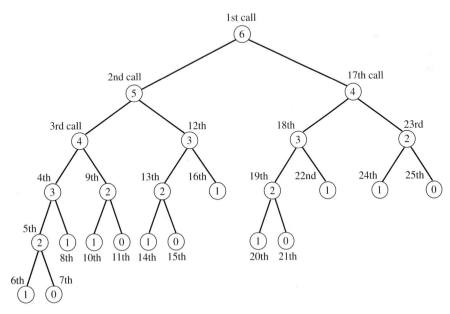

Figure 7.13   Call structure for recursive computation of Fibonacci numbers

The order of the execution of the recursive calls is indicated in the figure; it is the familiar preorder sequence. However, the order in which results are accumulated (by the "+" operation) is the postorder sequence. We saw a smaller example with more details on the activation frames in Example 3.1.

For the diagram in Figure 7.13 we assumed that each of the 25 vertices is distinct, even though many have duplicated labels, because each vertex corresponds not just to its label, but also to a specific function invocation. You might suspect that this is an extremely inefficient way to compute the Fibonacci numbers. You would be correct. It would be much more efficient to do a depth-first search on a graph with seven vertices, each with a unique label from 0 through 6. We will return to this topic in Chapter 10, Section 10.2. For now, this example is used only to illustrate the connection between depth-first search and recursion. ∎

Thus the logical structure of the solutions to a number of interesting problems solved by recursive algorithms is a depth-first traversal of a tree. The tree is not always explicitly part of the problem, nor is it explicitly represented as a data structure. As another example, let's look at the famous eight-queens problem.

Example 7.10   Eight queens on a chessboard

Consider the problem of placing eight queens on a chessboard so that none is under attack by any other; in other words, so that none can reach another by moving along one row, column, or diagonal. It is not obvious that this can be done.

We try as follows: Place a queen in the first (leftmost) square of the first (topmost) row. Then continue to place queens in each successive vacant row in the first column that is not under attack by any queen already on the board. Do this until all eight queens are on the board or all of the squares in the next vacant row are under attack. If the latter case occurs (which it does in the sixth row; see Figure 7.14), go back to the previous row, move the queen there as few places as possible farther to the right so that it is still not under attack, and then proceed as before.

What tree is involved in this problem, and in what sense are we doing a depth-first search of it? The tree is shown in Figure 7.14. Each vertex (other than the root) is labeled by a position on the chessboard. For $1 \leq i \leq 8$, the vertices at level i are labeled with board positions in row i. The children of a vertex, v, at level i are all board positions in row $i + 1$ that would not be under attack if there were queens in all board positions along the path from the root to v; in other words, the children are all the safe squares in the next row. In terms of the tree, the problem is to find a path from the root to a leaf of length eight. As an exercise, you might write a recursive program for the queens problem such that the order in which the recursive calls are executed corresponds to a depth-first search. If there actually is a solution, only part of the tree in Figure 7.14 is traversed. (Depth-first search, when used in a problem like this one, is also called backtrack search.) ∎

7.4.2   Finding Connected Components with Depth-First Search

This section develops in detail an algorithm for identifying connected components of a graph—or strongly connected components of a symmetric (directed) graph. Along the

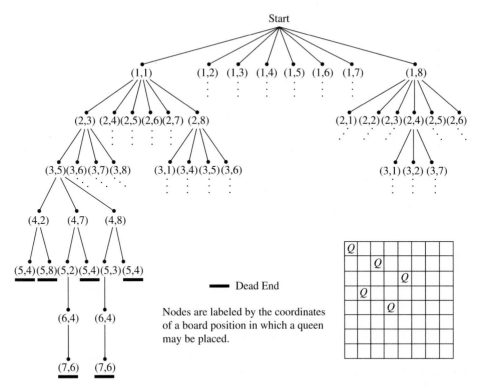

Figure 7.14 The eight-queens problem

way, we work out a number of implementation details that carry over to all applications of depth-first search. Connected components are associated with undirected graphs, but the representation for an undirected graph is the same as the representation for a symmetric digraph, and the components are the same in both cases. However, the depth-first search algorithm is somewhat simpler on directed graphs.

Let $G = (V, E)$ be an undirected graph with $n = |V|$ and $m = |E|$. The corresponding symmetric digraph has $2m$ directed edges. We will use G for this graph, too, since their representations are identical. Recall that a *connected component* of G is a maximal connected subgraph, that is, a connected subgraph that is not contained in any larger connected subgraph (Definition 7.8). The graph in Figure 7.7, for example, has three connected components. The problem of finding the connected components of a graph can be solved by using depth-first search with very little embellishment. We may start with an arbitrary vertex, do a depth-first search to find all other vertices (and edges) in the same component, and then, if there are some vertices remaining, choose one and repeat.

We use the outline of depth-first search (dfs) given in Section 7.3.1. Various parts of the algorithm could require a lot of work if we choose a poor implementation. The loop needs to find all ws that are adjacent to v (in the edges' forward directions). Certainly, we should use adjacency lists to represent the graph so that we can traverse the list for v and only look at ws for which there actually are edges from v; if we used the adjacency matrix we would have to scan through every w in the graph in this loop. Throughout the algorithm, each adjacency list is traversed only once. A local variable is used to keep track of our place in an adjacency list. (This means there is a variable saved on the frame stack to keep track of our place in each adjacency list that has been partly, but not completely, traversed at any time, as explained in Section 3.2.1.)

As an algorithm, depth-first search operates at two levels. The top level, or wrapper (dfsSweep), finds undiscovered vertices and initiates a depth-first search at each undiscovered vertex that is found. The lower level, called dfs, recursively carries out the actions of a depth-first search.

The problem of finding an undiscovered vertex in dfsSweep from which to start a new depth-first search can be handled analogously to the way dfs finds a new undiscovered vertex. Instead of checking through the array of vertices from the beginning each time a depth-first search is completed, we start wherever we left off the previous time.

It is crucial to record when a vertex changes its status from "undiscovered" to "discovered," to prevent repeated work, and even a nonterminating search. In some applications it is important also to record when a vertex has been completely processed, that is, "finished." This is also very useful for analysis. Thus we adopt a three-color system for recording vertex status.

Definition 7.11   Three-color code for search status of vertices

The color *white* denotes that a vertex is undiscovered. The color *gray* denotes that a vertex is discovered, but its processing is incomplete. The color *black* denotes that a vertex is discovered, and its processing is complete.   ■

Now let's turn our attention to the particular needs of the connected components problem. If the partition of the graph into connected components is to be recorded in the data structure for later use, it can be done by marking each vertex and/or edge with the number of the component to which it belongs. A more complex alternative is to make a separate linked list of the vertices and/or edges in each component. The particular method chosen would depend on how the information is to be used later.

The connected component algorithm is presented next, using a depth-first search procedure that makes the implementation explicit. The procedure connectedComponents in this algorithm corresponds to the generic dfsSweep mentioned above, and outlined in Section 7.3.1. We will treat the graph as a symmetric digraph, rather than an undirected graph, in the sense that we do a directed depth-first search. Depth-first search on an undirected graph entails some additional complications that are unnecessary for finding connected components; these details are addressed in Section 7.6.

Algorithm 7.2   Connected Components

Input: Array adjVertices of adjacency lists that represent a symmetric digraph $G = (V, E)$, as described in Section 7.2.3, and n, the number of vertices. The array is defined for indexes $1, \ldots, n$. G can also be interpreted as an undirected graph.

Output: Array cc in which each vertex is numbered to indicate which component it is in. The identifier for each connected component is the number of some vertex within that component (other identification systems are possible). (The caller allocates and passes in cc and this procedure fills it.)

Remarks: Color meanings are white = undiscovered, gray = active, black = finished. Note that the third and fourth parameters of ccDFS are both v in the top-level call, but have different meanings. The third parameter designates the current vertex to visit, and changes in every recursive call. The fourth parameter designates the identifier of the connected component and remains unchanged through recursive calls.

```
void  connectedComponents(IntList[] adjVertices, int n, int[] cc)
    int[]  color = new int[n+1];
    int  v;
    Initialize color array to white for all vertices.
    for (v = 1; v ≤ n; v ++)
        if (color[v] == white)
            ccDFS(adjVertices, color, v, v, cc);
    return;


void  ccDFS(IntList[] adjVertices, int[] color, int v, int ccNum, int[] cc)
    int  w;
    IntList  remAdj;

    color[v] = gray;
    cc[v] = ccNum;
    remAdj = adjVertices[v];
    while (remAdj ≠ nil)
        w = first(remAdj);
        if (color[w] == white)
            ccDFS(adjVertices, color, w, ccNum, cc);
        remAdj = rest(remAdj);
    color[v] = black;
    return;
```

Analysis of Connected Components

The number of operations done by connectedComponents, excluding the calls to ccDFS is clearly linear in n. In ccDFS($\ldots, v, \ldots$), the number of instructions executed is proportional to the number of elements in adjVertices[v], the adjacency list that was traversed, since the instruction "remAdj = rest(remAdj)" is executed once each time through the **while** loop. Since the adjacency lists are traversed only once, the complexity of the depth-first search, and hence the connected component algorithm, is in $\Theta(n + m)$. (Usually $m \geq n$.)

The space used by the adjacency-list structure is in $\Theta(n + m)$, but this is part of the input to the algorithm. Extra space is used for the *color* array ($n + 1$ entries) and recursion might cause the activation frame stack to grow to size n, so the amount of extra space used is in $\Theta(n)$.

Remarks on Connected Components

The output of the algorithm is simply an array cc containing an identifier (the term *leader* is often used) of the connected component for each vertex. One pass through the cc array is sufficient to assemble a set of linked lists in which each linked list contains just the vertices of one connected component. Similarly one pass through adjVertices, with references to cc is sufficient to assemble a set of linked lists in which each linked list contains just the edges of one connected component. These possible postprocessing steps do not increase the overall complexity, so there is little point in complicating the basic algorithm to tailor it to specific output formats.

The ccDFS procedure did not do any postorder vertex processing (which would consist of code placed just before the statement "color[v] = black"). This is a strong hint that breadth-first search will also solve this problem easily.

7.4.3   Depth-First Search Trees

Depth-first search trees and the depth-first search forest, defined below, provide important insights into the structure of depth-first search, which has many subtleties. Algorithm 7.4 will show how to construct depth-first search trees. Most problems do not require that they be constructed, but they are still useful for analysis. The definitions given here apply to directed graphs. Although many of them apply in a similar form to undirected graphs, there are often differences in the details, so the definitions for undirected graphs are deferred until Section 7.6.

Definition 7.12   Depth-first search tree, depth-first search forest

The edges that lead to undiscovered, that is, white, vertices during a depth-first search of a digraph G form a rooted tree called a *depth-first search tree* (sometimes called *depth-first spanning tree*, abbreviated to *DFS tree* in both cases). If not all of the vertices can be reached from the starting vertex (the root), then a complete traversal of G partitions the vertices into several trees, the entire collection being called the *depth-first search forest* (sometimes called *depth-first spanning forest*, abbreviated to *DFS forest* in both cases). ∎

Definition 7.13

We say that a vertex v is an *ancestor* of a vertex w in a tree if v is on the path from the root to w; v is a *proper* ancestor of w if v is an ancestor of w and $v \neq w$. The closest proper ancestor to v is the *parent* of v. If v is a (proper) ancestor of w, then w is a (proper) descendant of v. ∎

Definition 7.14

The edges of a directed graph G are classified according to how they are *explored* (traversed in their forward direction).

1. If w is undiscovered at the time vw is explored, then vw is called a *tree edge*, and v becomes the parent of w.

2. If w is an ancestor of v, then vw is called a *back edge*. (This includes vv.)

3. If w is a descendant of v, but w has been discovered earlier than the time vw is explored, then vw is called a *descendant edge* (other names are *forward edge* and *frond*).

4. If w has no ancestor/descendant relationship to v, then vw is called a *cross edge*.   ∎

Example 7.11   Depth-first search trees

Let's see how edges are classified by the depth-first search conducted by Terry the tourist in Example 7.6. Terry started at A (so A is the root of the first depth-first search tree), and explored to B, then C, then backtracked to B, and explored to D. So edges AB, BC, and BD are tree edges. Now Terry is at D and encounters the first nontree edges.

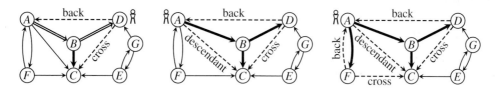

Double lines denote tree edges that have not yet been backtracked over, heavy solid lines denote tree edges that have been backtracked over, thin lines are unexplored edges, and dashed lines are nontree edges. In the left diagram above, A is a tree-ancestor of D, so DA is a *back edge*. However, C is neither an ancestor nor a descendant of D in the tree, so DC is a *cross edge*.

The middle diagram shows the situation after Terry has backtracked from D to B and from B to A. Vertex C is already a descendant of A in the tree at the time that edge AC is explored; C has been discovered by another route. Therefore AC is a *descendant* edge (also called *forward edge* or *frond*). A descendant edge is always a shortcut for a longer tree path.

The rightmost diagram shows the situation after the first depth-first tree has been completed. Although Terry has nowhere to go, the depth-first search of the graph is incomplete.

To complete the depth-first search of the graph a new search is started at E. The edge EC goes to a vertex that is finished (black) and is in a DFS tree that is already completed. It is very important that C is not revisited as part of the new DFS tree. The edge EC is classified as a cross edge; vertices in different trees obviously do not have an ancestor/descendant relationship. The edge EG is considered next, and it does go to an undiscovered (white) vertex, so it is a tree edge. Again the edge GD goes to a finished (black) vertex in a different DFS tree, so it is a cross edge. Edge GE is a back edge because it goes to an ancestor of G in the current DFS tree. Thus the second DFS tree, which completes the DFS forest, has two vertices and one edge. (It is also possible to have a tree with one vertex and no edge: suppose the first depth-first search of the graph

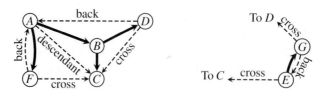

Figure 7.15 Heavy edges show the depth-first search forest for the graph of Examples 7.6 and 7.11. Dashed lines are nontree edges, as labeled.

happened to start at vertex C.) The final DFS forest is shown in Figure 7.15, along with the classifications of all nontree edges. ∎

Edge classifications can vary depending on the order of vertices within an adjacency list (see Exercise 7.4). Note that the head and tail of a cross edge may be in two different trees. The distinctions among the various types of edges are important in some applications of depth-first search—in particular, in the algorithms studied in Sections 7.5 and 7.7.

7.4.4 A Generalized Depth-First Search Skeleton

Depth-first search provides the structure for many elegant and efficient algorithms. As we have seen in several examples, a depth-first search encounters each vertex several times: when the vertex is first discovered and becomes part of the depth-first search tree, then several more times when the search backtracks *to* it and attempts to branch out in a different direction, and finally, after the last of these encounters, when the search backtracks *from* the vertex and does not pass through it again. Depending on the problem to be solved, an algorithm will process the vertices differently when they are encountered at various stages of the traversal. Many algorithms will also do some computation for the edges—perhaps for each edge, or perhaps only for edges in the depth-first search tree, or perhaps different kinds of computation for the different kinds of edges. The following skeleton algorithm shows exactly where the processing would be done for each kind of edge and for each kind of encounter with the vertices.

Algorithm 7.3 Directed Depth-First Search Skeleton (DFS Skeleton)

Input: Array adjVertices of adjacency lists that represent a directed graph $G = (V, E)$, as described in Section 7.2.3, and n, the number of vertices. The array is defined for indexes $1, \ldots, n$. Other parameters are as needed by the application.

Output: Return value depends on the application. Return type can vary; **int** is just an example.

Remarks: This skeleton is also adequate for some undirected graph problems that ignore nontree edges, but see Algorithm 7.8. Color meanings are white = undiscovered, gray = active, black = finished.

```
int  dfsSweep(IntList[] adjVertices, int n, . . .)
    int  ans;
    Allocate color array and initialize to white.
    For each vertex v of G, in some order:
        if(color[v] == white)
            int  vAns = dfs(adjVertices, color, v, . . .);
            (Process vAns)
        // Continue loop.
    return ans;
```

```
int  dfs(IntList[] adjVertices, int[] color, int v, . . .)
    int  w;
    IntList  remAdj;
    int  ans;
1.   color[v] = gray;
2.   Preorder processing of vertex v
3.   remAdj = adjVertices[v];
4.   while (remAdj ≠ nil)
5.       w = first(remAdj);
6.       if (color[w] == white)
7.           Exploratory processing for tree edge vw
8.           int  wAns = dfs(adjVertices, color, w, . . .);
9.           Backtrack processing for tree edge vw, using wAns (like inorder)
10.      else
11.          Checking (i.e., processing) for nontree edge vw
12.      remAdj = rest(remAdj)
13.  Postorder processing of vertex v, including final computation of ans
14.  color[v] = black;
15.  return ans;
```

For some applications, the problem may be solved by a partial search. This condition would be detected at line 9 of the skeleton, or possibly line 11. A **break** statement is recommended for making an early exit of the **while** loop, so postorder processing, including setting the color to black, will still be done.

Example 7.12   Use of DFS skeleton for connected components

To illustrate the versatility of the skeleton, let's use it to re-solve the connected components problem.

1. Pass an array cc as an additional parameter to dfsSweep. This array is to be filled with connected component numbers by the algorithm.

2. Add a fourth parameter, ccNum, and a fifth, cc, to dfs. In dfsSweep, when calling dfs, set the fourth parameter to v, which is also the third parameter, and set the fifth parameter to cc.

3. In the recursive call of dfs, use the same ccNum and cc that were passed in.

4. For preorder processing (line 2 of the skeleton), insert the statement "cc[v] = ccNum."

With these few changes, one new line of code and a few extra parameters passed, we have specialized the general-purpose skeleton to solve the connected components problem. We will see more examples of using the skeleton in the rest of this chapter, and in the exercises. ∎

7.4.5   Structure of Depth-First Search

In some applications of depth-first search, we may need to know which vertices are on the path from the root of the DFS tree to the current vertex, say v, which is being visited. They are exactly the gray vertices and are the v-parameters of calls further down in the frame stack (i.e., closer to the root of the activation frame tree). For some algorithms we need to know the order in which vertices are encountered for the first time or last time, or relationships between the two. A simple and useful way to keep track of these relationships is to maintain two arrays, discoverTime and finishTime. One global integer time variable is initialized to zero and is incremented whenever a vertex color changes.

Definition 7.15   Depth-first search terminology

While the color of v is white, we say it is *undiscovered*. When color[v] becomes gray, the current time is recorded in discoverTime[v] (at line 2 of the skeleton); now v is *active*. When color[v] becomes black, the current time is recorded in finishTime[v] (at line 13 of the skeleton), and now v is *finished*. The *active interval* for vertex v, denoted as $active(v)$, is defined as the integer interval

$$active(v) = \text{discoverTime[v]}, \ldots, \text{finishTime[v]}$$

including both endpoints, so v is gray precisely during its active interval. The final value of time will be $2n$ if the whole graph is searched. ∎

We can insert code into the DFS skeleton to compute discovery and finishing times and "construct" the depth-first search forest. We call this algorithm *Depth-First Search Trace*. Even if an algorithm that uses the DFS skeleton does not include this code, for analysis purposes we can use the values that would have been computed if the code had been inserted.

Algorithm 7.4   Depth-First Search Trace (DFS Trace)

Input: The same input as for the DFS skeleton (Algorithm 7.3) plus global arrays discoverTime, finishTime, and parent; also a global counter, time.

Output: The global arrays mentioned above are filled by the algorithm. Return types for this algorithm can be changed to **void**. The parent array stores the depth-first search forest as an in-tree. The other arrays have the meanings of Definition 7.15.

Strategy: Modify the DFS skeleton of Algorithm 7.3 as follows:

1. In dfsSweep initialize time to 0.

2. In dfsSweep before calling dfs (after the "if") insert "parent[v] = –1."
3. In dfs before the recursive call to dfs (after the "if") insert "parent[w] = v."
4. At preorder processing (line 2) of the skeleton, insert

>   time ++; discoverTime[v] = time

(This is the time at which v becomes active.)
5. At postorder processing (line 13) of the skeleton, insert

>   time ++; finishTime[v] = time

(This is the time at which v becomes inactive.) ∎

Figure 7.16 shows an example of Algorithm 7.4. The intervals during which vertices are *active*, according to Definition 7.15, are shown as d/f pairs, where d is the discovery time and f is the finishing time for the vertex. These intervals have an interesting and important relationship to each other, and to the relative positions of the vertices in the depth-first search forest (Definition 7.12).

Example 7.13   Nesting of *active* intervals

For the depth-first search forest shown in Figure 7.16, the *active* intervals are shown in Figure 7.17. Vertex A is the root of one depth-first search tree, and E is the root of the other. Their *active* intervals are disjoint. Notice that all cross edges proceed from late intervals to nonoverlapping earlier intervals. Also, where there is a descendant edge AC, there is a vertex B whose interval contains the interval of C and is contained in the interval of A. ∎

We summarize the relationships illustrated by the prior example.

Theorem 7.1   Let $active(v)$ be as defined in Definition 7.15, let edge classifications be as defined in Definition 7.14, and suppose a DFS Trace has been carried out on a directed graph $G = (V, E)$. Then for any $v \in V$ and $w \in V$,

1. w is a descendant of v in the DFS forest if and only if $active(w) \subseteq active(v)$. If $w \neq v$ the inclusion is proper.
2. If v and w have no ancestor/descendant relationship in the DFS forest, then their *active* intervals are disjoint.
3. If edge $vw \in E$, then:

    a. vw is a cross edge if and only if $active(w)$ entirely precedes $active(v)$.
    b. vw is a descendant edge if and only if there is some third vertex x such that $active(w) \subset active(x) \subset active(v)$.
    c. vw is a tree edge if and only if $active(w) \subset active(v)$, and there is *no* third vertex x such that $active(w) \subset active(x) \subset active(v)$.
    d. vw is a back edge if and only if $active(v) \subset active(w)$.

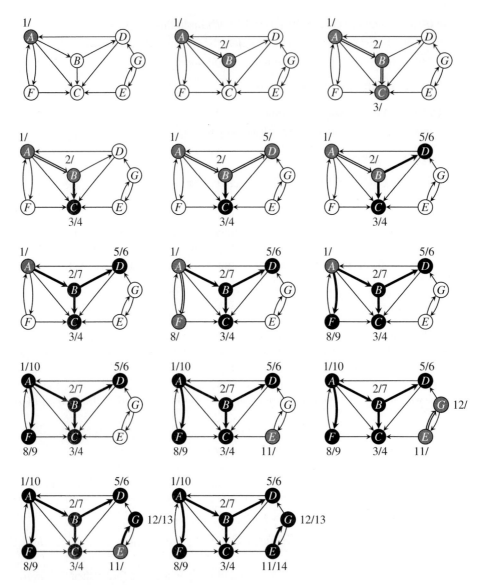

Figure 7.16 Progress of DFS Trace on the graph of Example 7.6. Double lines are tree edges that have not yet been backtracked over, so they go to gray vertices. Heavy lines are tree edges that have been backtracked over, so they go to black vertices. The d/f pairs designate discovery and finishing times for the vertices. Two depth-first search trees are constructed. A different vertex order can produce a different trace.

time

1	2	3	4	5	6	7	8	9	10	11	12	13	14

←——————— A ———————→   ← E ——→

←——— B ———→   ←F→   ←G→

←C→ ←D→

Figure 7.17   The *active* intervals for the depth-first search forest of Figure 7.16

Proof   Break up item 1 into item 1(if) and item 1(only-if), where item 1(if) is the statement, "if w is a descendant of v in the DFS forest, then $active(w) \subseteq active(v)$," and item 1(only-if) is the converse. Define a partial order on V by the rule that $w < v$ if and only if w is a proper descendant of v in its DFS tree. First we prove item 1(if) by induction on this partial order. The base cases are vertices v that are minimal in the partial order, that is, vertices with no proper descendants. Since v is a descendant of itself, item 1(if) is true.

For v not a minimal vertex, assume item 1(if) holds for all $x < v$. If w is any proper descendant of v in the DFS tree, there is some x such that $vx \in E$ is a tree edge on the tree path to w, so w is a descendant of x. By inspection of dfsTrace we see that $active(x) \subset active(v)$. By the inductive hypothesis, $active(w) \subset active(x)$. So $active(w) \subset active(v)$. This proves item 1(if).

Next we consider item 2. This is clearly true if v and w are in different DFS trees, because all the vertices in one tree are processed before any of the vertices in the later tree. Suppose v and w are in the same DFS tree (but have no ancestor/descendant relationship). Then there is some third vertex c, called their least common ancestor, such that there are tree paths from c to v and from c to w, and these paths have no edges in common (see Exercise 7.14). Suppose the first edge on the path from c to v is cy and the first edge on the path from c to w is cz. By inspection of dfsTrace we see that $active(y)$ and $active(z)$ are disjoint intervals. But by item 1(if), $active(v)$ is contained in $active(y)$ and $active(w)$ is contained in $active(z)$, so $active(v)$ and $active(w)$ are also disjoint intervals, completing the proof of item 2.

Now let us return to item 1(only-if). If w is *not* a descendant of v, then either w is a proper ancestor of v or there is no ancestor/descendant relationship. If w is a proper ancestor, then 1(if) showed that $active(w) \supset active(v)$, so $active(w) \not\subset active(v)$, so item 1(only-if) holds for this case. If there is no ancestor/descendant relationship, then item 2 implies item 1(only-if).

The proof of item 3 is left as an exercise.   □

Corollary 7.2   The vertices that are discovered while v is active are exactly the descendants of v in its depth-first search tree.   □

We have seen by example that a depth-first search discovers all vertices that are reachable by a path of *undiscovered* vertices. Exercise 7.13 asks for an example in which some vertices are reachable from v and are undiscovered when the depth-first search of v

begins, yet they will not be discovered or visited while v is active. The following theorem characterizes exactly which vertices *will* be discovered while v is active.

Theorem 7.3 (White Path Theorem)   In any depth-first search of a graph G, a vertex w is a descendant of a vertex v in a depth-first search tree if and only if, at the time vertex v is discovered (just before coloring it gray), there is a path in G from v to w consisting entirely of white vertices.

Proof   (Only if) If w is a descendant of v, by Theorem 7.1, the path of tree edges from v to w is a white path.

(If) The proof is by induction on k, the length of a white path from v to w. The base case is $k = 0$; then $v = w$ and the theorem holds.

For $k \geq 1$, let $P = (v, x_1, \ldots, x_k)$, where $x_k = w$, be a white path of length k from v to w. Now let x_i be the vertex other than v on this path that is discovered *earliest* during the *active* interval of v. In the diagram below, wavy lines are paths, possibly empty paths.

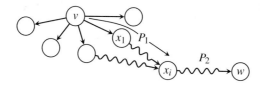

We claim that x_i must exist, because x_1 is white and has a direct edge from v, so at least x_1 is discovered during the *active* interval of v. Divide path P into P_1 from v to x_i, and P_2 from x_i to w (possibly $x_i = w$). But P_2 has fewer than k edges, and at the time x_i is discovered, P_2 is a white path. Therefore, by the inductive hypothesis, w is a descendant of x_i. But

$$\text{discoverTime}[v] < \text{discoverTime}[x_i] < \text{finishTime}[v]$$

so by Theorem 7.1, x_i is a descendant of v. By transitivity, w is a descendant of v. □

7.4.6   Directed Acyclic Graphs

Directed acyclic graphs (*DAGs* for short) are an important special case of general directed graphs. As the name implies, a DAG is any directed graph that has no cycles. Directed acyclic graphs are important for two primary reasons:

1. Many problems are naturally phrased in terms of a DAG, such as scheduling problems. In scheduling problems it is often required that certain tasks be completed before other tasks may begin. A cycle in task dependencies would mean a *deadlock*: no task in the cycle can ever be ready to begin.

2. Many problems on general directed graphs are easier—that is, more efficient—to solve on DAGs. The difference can be as great as exponential time vs. linear time. We will mention these problems as they come up in their general versions.

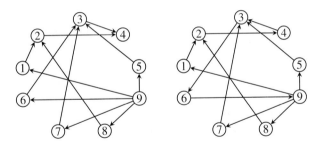

Figure 7.18 Two directed graphs. Which one is acyclic?

Also, we will see in Section 7.5 that every general directed graph is associated with a certain directed acyclic graph, called its *condensation graph*.

A directed acyclic graph corresponds mathematically to a partial order on its vertices. Wherever there is an edge vw, we can interpret it as the relationship $v < w$ between the vertices. If there is any directed path from v to w, we also interpret this as $v < w$ by transitivity. (All edges in a graph might be interpreted as $v > w$, instead. We just have to be consistent within the graph.) An order (or partial order) relation is not allowed to contain cycles. We will see that the order interpretation is useful in scheduling problems.

In this section we will study two applications of DAGs: topological order and critical paths.

Topological Order

When thinking about some problem on directed graphs, you might ask yourself, "If I could draw this graph so that all the edges were pointing generally left to right, would this help me to solve the problem?" Of course, if the graph has a cycle, this is clearly impossible. But if the directed graph has no cycles—is a DAG—then we will see that such an arrangement of vertices *is* possible. Finding such an arrangement is the problem of *topological ordering*.

Definition 7.16   Topological order

Let $G = (V, E)$ be a directed graph with n vertices. A *topological order* for G is an assignment of distinct integers $1, \ldots, n$ to the vertices of V, called their *topological numbers*, such that, for every edge $vw \in E$, the topological number of v is less than the topological number of w. A *reverse topological order* is similar except that for every edge $vw \in E$ the topological number of v is greater than the topological number of w.   ■

Figure 7.18 shows two graphs, only one of which is acyclic. Readers are invited to try to determine by trial and error which graph is acyclic, and for that graph to try to find a topological order. A little experimentation should convince you that trying to do this haphazardly on a graph of 50 to 100 vertices would be out of the question. We will see that this problem is solvable very efficiently, using the depth-first search skeleton as a basis. (Another efficient solution is mentioned in the exercises.)

Note that a topological order is equivalent to a permutation of the vertices. The definition does not specify that G needs to be acyclic. But the following lemma is easy to prove.

Lemma 7.4   If a directed graph G has a cycle, then G has no topological order.   □

In a sense, topological ordering is the fundamental problem on DAGs. We will see that every DAG has at least one topological order, providing the converse of Lemma 7.4. After a topological order for the vertices has been found, many other problems become straightforward. The concept of topological order alone may be enough to suggest an efficient solution without explicitly assigning the topological numbers.

Example 7.14   Scheduling with task dependencies

Consider the problem of scheduling a project consisting of a set of interdependent tasks to be done by one person. Certain tasks *depend on* others; that is, they cannot begin until all the tasks they depend on are completed. The most natural way to organize the information for such a problem is an array of tasks, each with a list of tasks that it depends on directly. Here is an example for the "project" of getting out of the house in the morning. Tasks are numbered in alphabetical order.

Task and Number		Depends on
choose clothes	1	9
dress	2	1, 8
eat breakfast	3	5, 6, 7
leave	4	2, 3
make coffee	5	9
make toast	6	9
pour juice	7	9
shower	8	9
wake up	9	—

If we choose the convention that vw means w depends directly on v, that is, edges go "forward in time," then we see that the above table gives us lists of *incoming* edges for each vertex. One of the graphs in Figure 7.18 corresponds to this set of tasks and dependencies with edges pointing "forward in time." On the other hand, if we interpret the lists of dependencies in the table as adjacency lists for the graph, we get the transpose of the "forward in time" graph. It is quite typical for scheduling problems to use this transpose graph, also called the *dependency graph* or *precedence graph*, in which edges point "backward in time."

There are numerous topological orders for the set of tasks in this table. We will find one after we give the algorithm for topological order.   ■

The algorithms for topological order and reverse topological order are simple modifications of the DFS skeleton. We give the version for reverse topological order because it comes up more often.

Algorithm 7.5   Reverse Topological Ordering

Input: The same input as for the DFS skeleton (Algorithm 7.3) plus global array topo and a global counter, topoNum.

Output: The global array topo is filled by the algorithm with a set of reverse topological numbers. Return types for this algorithm can be changed to **void**.

Remark: To compute "forward" topological order, initialize topoNum at $n + 1$ and count backwards.

Strategy: Modify the DFS skeleton of Algorithm 7.3 as follows:

1. In dfsSweep initialize topoNum to 0.
2. At postorder processing (line 13) of the skeleton, insert

    topoNum ++; topo[v] = topoNum   ∎

Comparing Algorithm 7.4 and Algorithm 7.5 it is clear that ordering vertices by their finishing times in the depth-first search gives the same ordering as Algorithm 7.5; the last vertex to finish has the largest number.

By its connection with the DFS skeleton it is clear that Algorithm 7.5 runs in time $\Theta(n + m)$ on a graph of n vertices and m edges. The correctness is proved in the following theorem.

Theorem 7.5   If G is a DAG with n vertices, then Algorithm 7.5 computes a reverse topological order for G in the array topo. Therefore every DAG has a reverse topological order and a topological order.

Proof   Since depth-first search visits each vertex exactly once, the code inserted at line 13 gets executed exactly n times, so the numbers in the array topo are distinct integers in the range $1, \ldots, n$. It remains only to verify that for any edge vw, topo[v] > topo[w]. Consider the possible classifications of vw, according to Definition 7.14. If vw were a back edge, then it would complete a cycle and G would not be a DAG. For the other edge types, at the time topo[v] is assigned a value vertex w is finished (colored black), so topo[w] has been assigned a value earlier. Since topoNum only increases, topo[v] > topo[w].   □

Example 7.15   Reverse topological order for dependency graph

There are many reverse topological orders for the dependency graph of Example 7.14. The one found by Algorithm 7.5 using the vertex numbers and edge lists in that example is the following:

9	1	8	2	5	6	7	3	4
wake up	choose clothes	shower	dress	make coffee	make toast	pour juice	eat breakfast	leave

The results of dfsTrace on this graph are shown in Figure 7.19. Notice that this graph is the transpose graph of one of the graphs in Figure 7.18. ∎

Critical Path Analysis

Critical path analysis is related to finding a topological order, but it is an optimization problem, in the sense that the longest path in the DAG is to be discovered. As with the scheduling example in Example 7.14, a project consists of a set of tasks, and the tasks have dependencies. But now, we assume that we are also given the time required to complete each task, once it is started. Furthermore, we assume that all tasks that are ready to be worked on *can be* worked on simultaneously; that is, there are enough workers to assign a different worker to each task. Certainly, the last assumption is questionable in many practical situations, but to get started we make this simplifying assumption.

We can define the *earliest finish time* for a task, assuming the project starts at time 0, as follows.

Definition 7.17   Earliest start and finish times, critical path

Let a *project* consist of a set of *tasks*, numbered 1, . . ., *n*, for each task a list of its *dependencies*, which are tasks upon which it depends directly, and for each task a nonnegative real number denoting its *duration*. The *earliest start time* (est) for a task *v* is:

1. If *v* has no dependencies, then est is 0.
2. If *v* has dependencies, then est is the maximum of the earliest finish time (see below) of its dependencies.

The *earliest finish time* (eft) for any task is its earliest start time plus its duration.

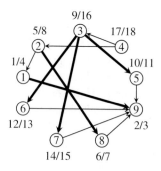

Figure 7.19   Results of dfsTrace on the dependency graph in Example 7.14. Heavy lines are tree edges, and *d/f* pairs designate discovery and finishing times for the vertices. Notice that there are four depth-first search trees. (Where is the fourth?)

A *critical path* in a project is a sequence of tasks $v_0, v_1, \ldots, v_k$ such that

1. v_0 has no dependencies;
2. for each subsequent task, v_i $(1 \leq i \leq k)$, v_{i-1} is a dependency of v_i such that est of v_i equals eft of v_{i-1}; and
3. eft of v_k is maximum for all tasks in the project.   ■

A critical path has no "slack." That is, there is no pause between the completion of one task on the path and the start of the next. In other words, if v_i follows v_{i-1} on a critical path, the eft of v_{i-1} must have been maximum among all the dependencies of v_i. Therefore v_{i-1} is a *critical dependency* of v_i, in the sense that any delay in v_{i-1} will force a delay in v_i. Taking a different point of view, suppose we are seeking a way to speed up completion of the entire set of tasks by finding a faster way to perform one of them. It is clear that reducing the time for one task doesn't help to reduce the total time required if the task is not on a critical path. The practical interest in critical paths is based on these properties.

To keep our problem simple, we have assumed that each task has a fixed duration. In many real situations, the duration can be shortened by allocating more resources to the task, perhaps withdrawing some resources from a task that is not on a critical path.

Example 7.16   Critical path

Let's keep the tasks and dependencies from Example 7.14 and add durations (in minutes):

9	1	8	2	5	6	7	3	4
wake up	choose clothes	shower	dress	make coffee	make toast	pour juice	eat breakfast	leave
0.0	3.0	8.5	6.5	4.5	2.0	0.5	6.0	1.0

Thus doing the tasks in sequence takes 32.0 minutes. Suppose we can do them all simultaneously, restricted only by the requirement to complete the dependencies before starting a task. The critical path goes from waking up to showering to getting dressed to leaving: only 16 minutes! To accomplish this, we need to overlap pouring juice and eating breakfast with getting dressed (not too far fetched), but we also need to choose clothes and make toast and coffee while showering (a bit trickier).   ■

We have given the natural definitions in terms of tasks and durations. It takes a little manipulation to relate these terms to longest paths, because we haven't defined how long edges are. Furthermore, the number of edges in a path is one less than the number of tasks, so how would the duration of *all* tasks on the path be taken into account by a path length? We can solidify the connection with a few technical revisions:

1. Add a special task to the project, called *done*, with duration 0; it can be task number $n + 1$.
2. Every regular task that is not a dependency of any task (i.e., is a potential final task) is made a dependency of *done*.

3. The *project DAG* has a weighted edge vw whenever v depends on w, and the weight of this edge is the duration of w.

Notice that we have chosen to make edges point from the task to its dependent task, to agree with the way dependency information is usually organized; this is "backwards in time." If it is more convenient to make the edges point "forward in time," this can be done instead.

Now we can see that a longest path in the project DAG corresponds to a critical path as originally defined; it just has the *done* vertex as an extra vertex at the beginning. The distance from the *done* task to any task v on this path is the difference between the earliest start times of *done* and v. This distance is maximized when the earliest start time of v is 0. Thus an algorithm to compute longest paths in a DAG can be used to find critical paths.

Example 7.17   Critical path as longest path

The weighted graph with the *done* vertex for the critical path problem of Example 7.16 is shown, with heavy lines identifying the critical path and critical subpaths.

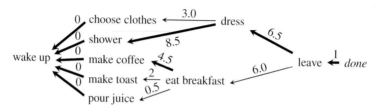

A critical subpath is a longest path leaving a vertex, not necessarily the *done* vertex. For example, we can't starting eating breakfast until the coffee is made; other preparations will finish earlier.   ■

Like the algorithm for reverse topological order, an algorithm for critical paths is strongly based on the DFS skeleton.

Algorithm 7.6   Critical Path

Input: The same input as for the DFS skeleton (Algorithm 7.3) plus global arrays dura-tion, critDep, and eft. A precondition is that G is a DAG. Edges of G point from tasks to their dependencies (backwards in time).

Output: The global arrays critDep and eft are filled by the algorithm; eft[v] is the earliest finishing time for v and critDep[v] is a critical dependency of v. A critical path can be found by tracing back from a vertex with a maximum value of eft and following critDep values as links. Return types for this algorithm can be changed to **void**.

Remark: The algorithm works with minor adjustments if the edges point "forward in time."

Strategy: In the recursive dfs procedure, a local variable est will store the earliest start time, which is the maximum of the eft values of the current task's dependencies. Modify the DFS skeleton of Algorithm 7.3 as follows:

1. At preorder processing (line 2) of the skeleton, insert

    est = 0; critDep[v] = −1;

2. At backtrack time for both tree edges (line 9) and nontree edges (line 11) of the skeleton, insert

    if (eft[w] ≥ est)
        est = eft[w];
        critDep[v] = w;

    It is important here that the nontree edge cannot be a back edge, because then eft[w] would be uninitialized.

3. At postorder processing (line 13) of the skeleton, insert

    eft[v] = est + duration[v];   ∎

Again it is immediate that the algorithm runs in time $\Theta(n + m)$ for n vertices and m edges. By the nature of depth-first search, each entry in the eft array is assigned a value exactly once, for indexes 1 through n. Therefore the inserted code simply implements the definitions of eft and est, provided that the accessed values eft[w] are defined at the time they are accessed. But this follows by the same argument as in the proof of Theorem 7.5 that w is finished (colored black) at these times.

Summary of Directed Acyclic Graphs

We have seen that directed acyclic graphs arise in connection with scheduling problems and that the topological order problem and critical path problem can be solved with a few insertions of code into the DFS skeleton. DAGS have many other applications, and we have just scratched the surface of this topic. Some additional problems appear in the exercises. In the next section we will learn that *every* directed graph has a certain DAG associated with it, called its *condensation graph*. Thus applications on DAGs may extend into applications on graphs with cycles in some cases.

7.5 Strongly Connected Components of a Directed Graph

An undirected graph is connected if and only if there is a path between each pair of vertices. Connectivity for directed graphs can be defined in either of two ways, depending on whether or not we require that edges be traversed only from tail to head. Recall from Definition 7.6 that a directed graph (digraph) $G = (V, E)$ is *strongly connected* if, for each pair of vertices v and w, there is a path from v to w (and hence by interchanging the roles of v and w in the definition, there is a path from w to v as well). That is, edges must be followed in the direction of their "arrows." G is *weakly connected* if, after making all edges undirected and consolidating any duplicate edges, the resulting undirected graph is connected. We will focus on strong connectivity.

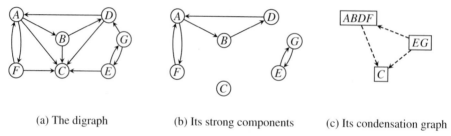

| (a) The digraph | (b) Its strong components | (c) Its condensation graph |

Figure 7.20   The strong components and condensation graph of the digraph used in Figure 7.16 and several examples

Definition 7.18   Strongly connected component

A *strongly connected component* (hereinafter called a *strong component*) of a digraph G is a maximal strongly connected subgraph of G. (The meaning of "maximal" was discussed following Definition 7.8.)   ■

We may give an alternative definition in terms of an equivalence relation, S, on the vertices. For v and w in V, let vSw if and only if there is a path from v to w and a path from w to v. (Recall that vSw is an alternative notation for $(v, w) \in S$, where $S \subseteq V \times V$. Here, (v, w) is any ordered pair of vertices, not necessarily an edge of G. Equivalence relations were defined in Section 1.3.1.) Then a strong component consists of one equivalence class, C, along with all edges vw such that v and w are in C. See the example in Figure 7.20. We sometimes use the term *strong component* to refer only to the vertex set C; the meaning should be clear from the context.

The strong components of a digraph can each be collapsed to a single vertex yielding a new digraph that has no cycles.

Definition 7.19   Condensation graph

Let $S_1, S_2, \ldots, S_p$ be the strong components of G. The *condensation graph of G (condensation of G* for short), denoted as $G{\downarrow}$, is the digraph $G{\downarrow} = (V', E')$, where V' has p elements, $s_1, s_2, \ldots, s_p$, and $s_i s_j$ is in E' if and only if $i \neq j$ and there is an edge in E from some vertex in S_i to some vertex in S_j. In other words, all vertices in S_i are condensed into a single vertex s_i.   ■

See Figure 7.20 for an example. In small examples we use the convention that the name of a condensed vertex is simply the concatenation of the names of all vertices in the strong component. Notice that the original edges AC, BC, DC, and FC have collapsed into one edge.

Solutions to some problems on digraphs can be simplified by treating the strong components and the condensation separately, taking advantage of the special properties of each—the former are strongly connected and the latter acyclic. (For example, consider the relationship of the strong components and the condensation of a program flowchart to the loop structure of the program.)

7.5.1 Properties of Strongly Connected Components

Strong components have several interesting properties, which we discuss next. The algorithm for finding strong components is presented in Section 7.5.2, and its mechanics can be understood without reading this subsection. However, this material is important for understanding *why* it works.

We recall from Definition 7.10 that G^T, the transpose graph of G, results from reversing the direction of each edge in G. It is immediate from the definition that the strong components of G^T are identical, in terms of vertices, to the strong components of G. The edges are also identical, except for direction. Also, $(G\!\downarrow)^T = (G^T)\!\downarrow$; that is, the condensation of G is the same as the condensation of G^T, except that the direction of each edge is reversed.

Now let's consider the relationship between depth-first search trees and strong components. We will see that *leaders*, defined next, essentially represent their entire strong components for structural purposes.

Definition 7.20   Leader of a strong component

Given a digraph G with strong components $S_i, i = 1, \ldots, p$, and a depth-first search of G, the first vertex in S_i to be discovered in the search is called the *leader* of S_i and is denoted by v_i.   ■

Suppose G is entirely undiscovered. If a depth-first search begins at v_1 (i.e., v_1 is the root of a depth-first search tree and v_1 is the leader of the strong component S_1), then by the White Path Theorem (Theorem 7.3) all vertices in S_1 will be descendants of v_1 in the depth-first search tree. Moreover, if any vertex of another strong component, say S_j, is reachable, then the first such vertex to be discovered is v_j, and applying the White Path Theorem at the time that v_j is discovered, we see that all of S_j is discovered in this tree. The same applies for subsequent depth-first search trees. This proves the following lemma.

Lemma 7.6   Each depth-first search tree in a depth-first search forest of a digraph G contains one or more complete strong components of G. There are no "partial" strong components in any depth-first search tree.   □

Corollary 7.7   The leader v_i is the last vertex to finish (i.e., reach postorder processing and be colored black) among all vertices of S_i.   □

Is there some way to arrange the search order so that a tree contains *exactly one* strong component? For a clue, let's look again at Figure 7.20(c). From the condensation graph, it is clear that if we start our first depth-first search anywhere in a strong component that has no arrows *coming out* of it, then this search must discover exactly one strong component. The C subgraph qualifies. But how can this help in practice? We don't *know* the condensation graph until we find the strong components! The secret is revealed in the next subsection, but its correctness depends on some further properties of leaders.

Although we don't know the strong components or the leaders, we can still draw some conclusions. Suppose an edge emerges from a strong component S_i and enters another, S_j. This means there is a path from v_i to v_j in G. Of course, it is possible that v_j is a descendant of v_i in the depth-first search tree that contains v_i. In this case $active(v_j) \subset active(v_i)$. What are the other possibilities? Clearly v_j cannot be an ancestor of v_i or they would be in the same strong component. For general vertices, the *active* interval of v_j might be entirely before that of v_i or entirely after (as well as contained in). We will show that, for leaders with a path from one to the other, one of these possibilities can be ruled out. You are invited to try to work out which before continuing.

■   ■   ■

Lemma 7.8   At the time a leader v_i is discovered in a depth-first search (just before it is colored gray), there is no path from v_i to any gray vertex, say x.

Proof   At this time, every gray vertex is a proper ancestor of v_i and has been discovered before v_i, so must be in a different strong component. Since there is a path from x to v_i there must not be a path from v_i to x.   □

Lemma 7.9   If v is the leader of its strong component S, and x is in a different strong component, and there is a path from v to x in G, then at the time v is discovered, either x is black, or there is a white path from v to x (and x is white). In either case, v finishes later than x.

Proof   Consider any path from v to x, and consider the last vertex, say z, on that path that is *not* white. If z does not exist, the path is all white and we are done. Suppose z exists. By Lemma 7.8, z must be black. If $z = x$ the proof is done. Assume $z \neq x$. But now consider the (earlier) time at which z was discovered. The path from z to x was white at that time, so by the White Path Theorem x is a descendant of z and is now also black.   □

So, if there is an edge from S_i to S_j, we have ruled out the possibility that the *active* interval of v_j, the leader of S_j, is entirely after that of v_i, the leader of S_i. You should construct examples to prove that the lemma would not hold (and $active(v_j)$ might be entirely after $active(v_i)$) if we did not require v_i to be the leader of its strong component. Exercise 7.13 is related.

7.5.2   A Strong Component Algorithm

We will study an algorithm for finding strong components that exploits most of the properties discussed in the previous section. The first linear-time strong components algorithm is due to R. E. Tarjan, and is based on depth-first search. The algorithm we present is due to M. Sharir, is also based on depth-first search. It is elegant for its simplicity and subtlety.

The algorithm has two main phases:

1. A standard depth-first search on G is performed, and the vertices are put in a stack at their finishing times.
2. A depth-first search is performed on G^T, the transpose graph. However, an unusual method is used to find white vertices from which to start a search (i.e., a new tree): Vertices are popped off the stack that was built during Phase 1, rather than being accessed in numerical order by a **for** loop (as in dfsSweep in Algorithm 7.3, which was used in Phase 1). During this search, the algorithm stores the leader of each vertex v's strong component in scc[v].

Each depth-first search tree generated in Phase 2 will be exactly one strong component. Because the strong components are found in Phase 2, we are really finding strong components of G^T. However, as we have noted, the strong components of G^T and G are identical in terms their vertices, and their edges agree except for a reversal of direction.

Algorithm 7.7   Strongly Connected Components

Input: Array adjVertices of adjacency lists that represent a directed graph $G = (V, E)$, as described in Section 7.2.3, and n, the number of vertices. The array is defined for indexes $1, \ldots, n$; the 0th entry is unused.

Output: Array scc in which each vertex is numbered to indicate which strong component it is in. The identifier for each strong component is the number of some vertex within that strong component (other identification systems are possible). (The caller allocates and passes in scc and this procedure fills it.)

Remark: The transpose graph G^T may be an input, rather than being computed in the procedure. Note that the third and fourth parameters of dfsT are both v in the top-level call, but have different meanings. The third parameter designates the current vertex to visit, and changes in every recursive call. The fourth parameter designates the identifier of the strong component and remains unchanged through recursive calls. The Stack ADT operations described in Section 2.4.1 are used; the class-name qualifiers are omitted for readability.

```
void strongComponents(IntList[] adjVertices, int n, int[] scc)
// Phase 1
  1. IntStack finishStack = create(n);
  2. Perform a depth-first search on G, using the DFS skeleton of Algorithm 7.3.
       At postorder processing for vertex v (line 13 in the skeleton), insert the
       statement: push(finishStack, v);
// Phase 2
  3. Compute G^T, the transpose graph, represented as the array adjTrans of
       adjacency lists.
  4. dfsTsweep(adjTrans, n, finishStack, scc);
     return;
```

```
void dfsTsweep(IntList[] adjTrans, int n, IntStack finishStack, int[] scc)
// dfsSweep on transpose graph
    Allocate color array and initialize to white.
    while (finishStack is not empty)
        int  v = top(finishStack);
        pop(finishStack);
        if(color[v] == white)
            dfsT(adjTrans, color, v, v, scc);
        // Continue loop.
    return;
```

```
void  dfsT(IntList[] adjTrans, int[] color, int v, int leader, int[] scc)
    Use the standard depth-first search skeleton of Algorithm 7.3. At preorder
    processing for vertex v (line 2 of the skeleton) insert the statement:
        scc[v] = leader;
    Pass leader and scc into recursive calls.
```

The stack finishStack can be implemented very simply as an array of n entries, since only n pushes will occur in the course of the algorithm.

Example 7.18   Strong components

To see the algorithm in action, let's look at the graph in Figure 7.20(a). The Phase 1 DFS was worked out in detail in Figure 7.16.

With the push operation that is inserted at postorder time, finishStack develops as shown Figure 7.21(a). Before continuing, let's check the relative positions of the leaders of the strong components. (Even though the algorithm does not know them, we do by peeking at Figure 7.20 and checking discovery times in Figure 7.16.) The leaders are A, C, and E. There is a path from E to the rest and E finished last. There is a path from A to C, and A is higher in the stack than C, hence finished later. Therefore Lemma 7.9 is confirmed.

Now strongComponents continues to lines 3 and 4, calling dfsTsweep. The transpose graph is shown in Figure 7.21(b). In the first pass through dfsTsweep's **while** loop, a dfsT begins at E, the current top of finishStack. Notice that E is passed in the fourth parameter as the leader and in the third parameter as the vertex to visit.

In the transpose graph, edges DG and CE are oriented *toward* G and E, respectively. This dfsT is "trapped" in the single strong component, $S_E = \{E, G\}$, and those vertices comprise the first depth-first spanning tree of Phase 2, in G^T. (The algorithm does not actually build the tree; this is done only in our analysis.) According to the description of dfsT, E is passed in to recursive calls as the leader, and is stored in the scc array whenever a vertex is discovered and visited. This brings us to Figure 7.21(c).

Control backtracks into dfsTsweep, where the search for another white vertex resumes by popping finishStack. Vertex G is popped and bypassed because it is black at this point. Then A is popped, and it becomes the root of a new tree. We will prove later that every white vertex that is popped is a leader, as A is. Again, we note that the edges are from C to A, B, D, and F, so this search cannot "leak" off into C's strong component. But there

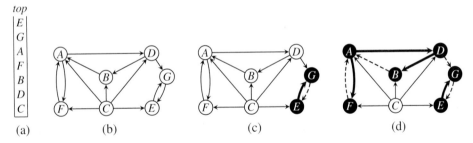

Figure 7.21 Phase 2 of the Strong Components Algorithm: (a) finishStack at the beginning of Phase 2. (b) The transpose graph. (c) The first DFS tree identifies one strong component. Heavy-lined edges are tree edges; dashed edges are processed nontree edges; thin-lined edges have not been processed yet. (d) The second DFS tree identifies another strong component. Note that DG is a cross edge to a different DFS tree. Also note that C will be the last DFS tree and will have no edges.

is an edge now from D to G, which *does* lead out of the strong component of A. However, it is not a coincidence that G has already been discovered before this second search began, and is currently a black vertex. Therefore this last attempt to "escape" from the strong component of A is also thwarted. This brings us to Figure 7.21(d).

Finally the tree with C at the root, and no edges, is finished. This completes the work of dfsTsweep and the overall algorithm. Again, we remind readers that the algorithm does not actually build the trees; this is done only in our analysis. ∎

At first it seems like an amazing coincidence that whenever a depth-first search in the transpose graph might stray out of the strong component of its root, the "stray" vertex has been discovered in an earlier tree. However, after trying various vertex orders (for Phase 1) in Figure 7.20, and trying other graphs, you will discover that it always seems to work out. The next lemmas prove why.

Lemma 7.10 In Phase 2, each time a white vertex is popped from finishStack, that vertex is the Phase 1 leader of a strong component.

Proof Popping is in reverse order of finishing time in Phase 1. By Corollary 7.7, the leader is the first vertex of a strong component to get popped. Suppose vertex x is popped and is not a leader. That would imply that some other vertex in the strong component of x is the first to have been visited within that strong component. By Lemma 7.6 and the White Path Theorem, x is already in a completed tree, so x is not white. ☐

Theorem 7.11 In Phase 2, each depth-first search tree contains exactly one strong component of vertices.

Proof Lemma 7.6 shows that each depth-first search tree contains one or more complete strong components. So we must show there is only one. Let v_i be the Phase 1 leader of

S_i. Assume v_i is popped from finishStack and is white. Then v_i is the root of a depth-first search tree in Phase 2. If no other strong component is reachable from v_i, by a path in G^T, then there is no problem.

Suppose some other strong component, say S_j, with leader v_j, *is* reachable from v_i, by a path in G^T. Then there is a path in G from v_j to v_i. By Lemma 7.9, v_j finished later than v_i in Phase 1, and so has been popped from finishStack, and all vertices in S_j are black at the time v_i is popped. Therefore the current depth-first search tree cannot "escape" from S_i.
□

Theorem 7.12   The algorithm strongComponents correctly identifies the strong components of G^T, which are the same, in terms of vertices, as the strong components of G.

Proof   By Theorem 7.11, each depth-first search tree contains exactly one strong component (of G^T), and by properties of depth-first search, every vertex of G^T is in some depth-first search tree.   □

7.5.3 Analysis

Much of the analysis of Algorithm 7.2, Connected Components, carries over to the strong component algorithm with small changes. It performs two depth-first searches, each of which is in time $\Theta(n + m)$. The computation of G^T, if necessary, is also in $\Theta(n + m)$ (see Exercise 7.8). The extra space used for various arrays is in $\Theta(n)$. The recursion stack also uses $\Theta(n)$ space in the worst case. So, including the adjacency lists for G^T, the space used is in $\Theta(n + m)$.

7.6 Depth-First Search on Undirected Graphs

Depth-first search on an undirected graph has the same theme as on a directed graph: explore further whenever possible, and backtrack when necessary. Many of the aspects of the DFS skeleton carry over without change. We can use the same system for vertex colors, discovery times, finishing times, and DFS trees. However, depth-first search on an undirected graph is complicated by the fact that edges should be *explored* in one direction only, but they are represented twice in the data structure.

For some problems it doesn't matter if an edge is processed twice, as we saw in the connected components problem, so the graph can be treated as a symmetric digraph. This section deals with the situations where this simplification would not work. As a rule of thumb, problems involving *cycles* in undirected graphs must process each edge only once. We will study one such problem in detail in Section 7.7.

For an undirected graph, the depth-first search provides an orientation for each of its edges; they are oriented in the direction in which they are first encountered, (*explored*, in the sense introduced at the beginning of Section 7.3.1). Even if the edge does not go to an undiscovered vertex, it is oriented *away from* the vertex that first encounters it during the search; this vertex is said to *check* the edge, as with directed depth-first search. Processing of nontree edges occurs when they are checked. Tree edges are also oriented away from the vertex that first encounters them; they are explored and later backtracked over, just as with directed depth-first search.

When a vertex encounters an edge in the data structure (adjacency list or adjacency matrix) that has been oriented *toward* it, it bypasses that edge as though it did not exist. The DFS skeleton for undirected graphs is modified to recognize these situations. We can find out how these situations arise by studying nontree edges in symmetric digraphs (Definition 7.3). With a little study we realize the following:

1. A *cross edge* simply cannot occur in a symmetric digraph.

2. A *back edge* from a vertex v to p, its parent in the DFS tree, would be the second encounter of the undirected edge between these two vertices, the first being as the tree edge pv, so vp needs to be bypassed. Other back edges are first encounters.

3. A *forward edge* in a symmetric digraph is always the second encounter of the undirected edge. Say a forward edge from v to w is found. Then w was discovered earlier and wv was processed in this orientation as a *back edge*. Since cross edges can't occur, any edge to a black vertex must be a forward edge in the symmetric digraph and needs to be bypassed in the undirected graph.

This analysis suggests the following modifications to the DFS skeleton of Algorithm 7.3. First, pass the DFS parent p as an additional parameter to dfs. This allows item 2 above to be implemented. Second, in processing edge vw, if w is not white, then test whether w is gray and is different from p, the parent of v (as passed in). If so, it is a "real" back edge; if not, bypass it for the reasons described in items 2 and 3 above. This test is incorporated in line 10 of the undirected depth-first search skeleton, given next. Exercise 7.28 asks you to prove that undirected depth-first search classifies every edge as a tree edge or a back edge.

The dfsSweep routine for undirected graphs is modified from Algorithm 7.3 only in that the call to dfs has the value -1 for the parent parameter. This indicates that the current vertex is the root of its depth-first search tree. Compare also with Algorithm 7.4.

Algorithm 7.8   Undirected Depth-First Search Skeleton

Input: Array adjVertices of adjacency lists that represent an undirected graph $G = (V, E)$, as described in Section 7.2.3, and n, the number of vertices. The array is defined for indexes $1, \ldots, n$. Also the array color recording search status, vertex v for next visit, and vertex p, the parent of v. Other parameters are as needed by the application.

Output: (Does a depth-first search beginning at the vertex v.) Parameters and return value ans are as needed by the application. Return type **int** is just an example. Array color is also updated so that all vertices discovered during this dfs are black; all others are unchanged.

Remarks: The wrapper dfsSweep is like Algorithm 7.3, except that it calls dfs with the fourth parameter (p) set to -1. Color meanings are white = undiscovered, gray = active, black = finished.

```
int dfs(IntList[] adjVertices, int[] color, int v, int p, . . .)
    int w;
    IntList remAdj;
    int ans;
```

1. color[v] = gray;
2. Preorder processing of vertex v
3. remAdj = adjVertices[v];
4. **while** (remAdj ≠ nil)
5.   w = first(remAdj);
6.   **if** (color[w] == white)
7.   Exploratory processing for tree edge vw
8.   **int** wAns = dfs(adjVertices, color, w, v, . . .);
9.   Backtrack processing for tree edge vw, using wAns (like inorder)
10.   **else if** (color[w] == gray && w ≠ p)
11.   Checking (i.e., processing) back edge vw
        // else wv was traversed, so ignore vw.
12.   remAdj = rest(remAdj)
13. Postorder processing of vertex v, including final computation of ans
14. color[v] = black;
15. **return** ans;

Analysis

The running time and space requirements are the same as for Algorithm 7.3: time is in $\Theta(n + m)$ and extra space for the color array is in $\Theta(n)$. The application might add code that increases the asymptotic order, but if each inserted statement runs in constant time, the time remains linear.

Undirected Breadth-First Search

As with depth-first search, the question of reprocessing an undirected edge arises for breadth-first search on an undirected graph. One simple solution is to treat the undirected graph as a symmetric digraph. We do not know of any applications of breadth-first search where this treatment would be wrong. Each edge is processed once in the "forward" direction, so for an undirected edge, whichever direction is encountered first is considered "forward" for the duration of the search. When the edge is encountered in the other direction, it goes to an already discovered vertex, and is normally ignored. However, see Exercise 7.7.

7.7 Biconnected Components of an Undirected Graph

In Section 7.2 we raised these questions:

1. If one city's airport is closed by bad weather, can you still fly between every other pair of cities?

2. If one computer in a network goes down, can messages be sent between every other pair of computers in the network?

In this section we consider undirected graphs only. As a graph problem, the question is:

Problem 7.1

If any one vertex (and the edges incident upon it) are removed from a connected graph, is the remaining subgraph still connected?   ∎

This question is important in graphs that represent all kinds of communication or transportation networks. It is also important to find those vertices, if any, whose removal can disconnect the graph. The purpose of this section is to present an efficient algorithm for answering these questions. This algorithm was discovered by R. E. Tarjan, and was one of the early algorithms that demonstrated the tremendous power of depth-first search.

7.7.1 Articulation Points and Biconnected Components

We begin by establishing some terminology and basic properties.

Definition 7.21   Biconnected component

A connected undirected graph G is said to be *biconnected* if it remains connected after removal of any one vertex and the edges that are incident upon that vertex.

A *biconnected component* (*bicomponent* for short) of an undirected graph is a maximal biconnected subgraph, that is, a biconnected subgraph not contained in any larger biconnected subgraph.   ∎

Definition 7.22   Articulation point

A vertex v is an *articulation point* (also called a *cut point*) for an undirected graph G if there are distinct vertices w and x (distinct from v also) such that v is in every path from w to x.   ∎

Clearly, the removal of an articulation point would leave an unconnected graph, so a connected graph is *biconnected* if and only if it has no articulation points. Figure 7.22 gives an illustration of biconnected components. Observe that, although the biconnected components partition the edges into disjoint sets, they do not partition the vertices; some vertices are in more than one component. (Which vertices are these?)

There is an alternative characterization of biconnected components, in terms of an equivalence relation on the edges, that is sometimes useful. Two edges e_1 and e_2 are equivalent if $e_1 = e_2$ or if there is a simple cycle containing both e_1 and e_2. Then each subgraph consisting of the edges in one equivalence class and the incident vertices is a biconnected component. (Verifying that the relation described is indeed an equivalence relation and verifying that it characterizes the biconnected components are left as an exercise; see Exercise 7.34.)

The applications that motivate the study of biconnectivity should suggest a dual problem: how to determine if there is an *edge* whose removal would disconnect a graph, and

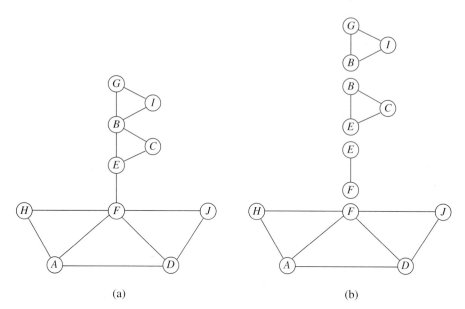

(a)   (b)

Figure 7.22   (a) An undirected graph. (b) Its biconnected components.

how to find such an edge if there is one. For example, if a railroad track is damaged, can trains still travel between any pair of stations? Relationships between the two problems are examined in Exercise 7.41.

The algorithm we will study for finding biconnected components uses the depth-first search skeleton of Algorithm 7.8 and the idea of a depth-first search tree from Section 7.4.3. During the search, information will be computed and saved so that the edges (and, implicitly, the incident vertices) can be divided into biconnected components as the search progresses. What information must be saved? How is it used to determine the biconnected components? Several *wrong* answers to these questions seem reasonable until they are examined carefully. Two edges are in the same biconnected component if they are in a simple cycle, and every cycle must include at least one back edge. You should work on Exercise 7.35 before proceeding; it requires looking at a number of examples to determine relationships between back edges and biconnected components.

From now on we will use the shorter term *bicomponent* in place of *biconnected component*.

7.7.2   The Bicomponent Algorithm

Processing of vertices in depth-first search may be done when a vertex is *discovered* (preorder time, line 2 in the skeleton of Algorithm 7.8), when the search backtracks *to* it (inorder time, line 9 in the skeleton), and just before it is finished (postorder time, line 13 in the skeleton). The bicomponent algorithm tests to see if a vertex in the depth-first search tree is an articulation point each time the search backtracks *to* it. All references to trees in

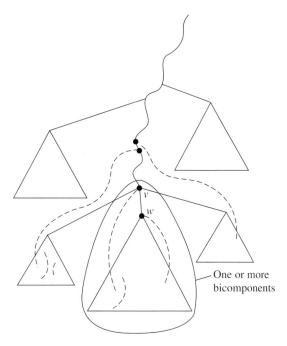

Figure 7.23   An articulation point in a depth-first search tree

this discussion mean the depth-first search tree. Recall that, in a depth-first search of an undirected graph, every edge is either a tree edge or a back edge.

Suppose the search is backing up to v from w. If there is no back edge from any vertex in the subtree rooted at w to a proper ancestor of v, then v must be on every path in G from the root of the DFS tree to w and is therefore an articulation point. See Figure 7.23 for illustration. (Note that this argument is not valid if v is the root.) The subtree rooted at w, along with all back edges leading from it and along with the edge vw, can be separated from the rest of the graph at v, but it is not necessarily one bicomponent; it may be a union of several. We ensure that bicomponents are properly separated by removing each one as soon as it is detected. Vertices at the outer extremities of the tree are tested for articulation points before vertices closer to the root, ensuring that when an articulation point is found, the subtree in question (along with the additional edges mentioned above) forms one bicomponent.

This discussion suggests that the algorithm must keep track of how far back in the tree one can get from each vertex by following tree edges (implicitly directed away from the root) and certain back edges. This information will be stored in a local variable, back. (There is a separate copy of back for each active vertex.) When a vertex finishes its search, it returns its final value of back to the caller. The depth-first search procedure will compute discoverTime and finishTime as described in Definition 7.15. Values of back will be these discoverTimes. For a vertex v, back may be assigned (or modified) when:

1. v is first discovered and visited (preorder time), to initialize back;
2. the search is trying to explore, but a back edge from v is encountered (as in Figure 7.24(b) with $v = F$, in Figure 7.24(c) with $v = C$, and in Figure 7.24(e) with $v = I$);
3. the search backtracks to v (as in Figure 7.24(d) with $v = B$ and in Figure 7.24(f) with $v = G$), since any vertex that can be reached from a child of v can also be reached from v.

Determining which of two vertices is farther back in the tree is easy: If v is a proper ancestor of w, then discoverTime[v] < discoverTime[w]. Thus we can formulate the following rules for setting back:

1. At preorder time, back = discoverTime[v] (but see Exercise 7.38).
2. When trying to explore from v and a back edge vw is detected, back = min(back, discoverTime[w]).
3. When backtracking from w to v, say that the value returned from the visit of w is wBack. Then for v, back = min(back, wBack).

The condition tested to detect a bicomponent when backing up from w to v is
    wBack $\geq$ discoverTime[v].

(This condition is tested but not satisfied in Figures 7.24(d) and 7.24(f); it is satisfied in Figures 7.24(g) and 7.24(h).) When the test is satisfied, v is an articulation point (except perhaps if v is the root of the tree); a complete bicomponent has been found and may be removed from further consideration.

The problem of exactly when and how to test for bicomponents is subtle but critical to the correctness of an algorithm. (See Exercise 7.40.) The essence of the correctness argument is contained in the following theorem.

Theorem 7.13   In a depth-first search tree, a vertex v, other than the root, is an articulation point if and only if v is not a leaf and some subtree of v has no back edge incident with a proper ancestor of v.

Proof   (Only if) Suppose that v, a vertex other than the root, is an articulation point. Then there are vertices x and y such that v, x, and y are distinct and v is on every path from x to y. At least one of x and y must be a proper descendant of v, since otherwise there would be a path between them using (undirected) edges in the tree without going through v. Thus v is not a leaf. Now suppose every subtree of v has a back edge to a proper ancestor of v; we claim that this contradicts the assumption that v is an articulation point. There are two cases: when only one of x and y is a descendant of v, and when both are descendants of v. For the first case, paths between x and y that do not use v are illustrated in Figure 7.25. We leave the latter case as an exercise. The "if" part of the proof is also left as an exercise. $\Box$

Theorem 7.13 does not tell us under what conditions the root is an articulation point. See Exercise 7.37.

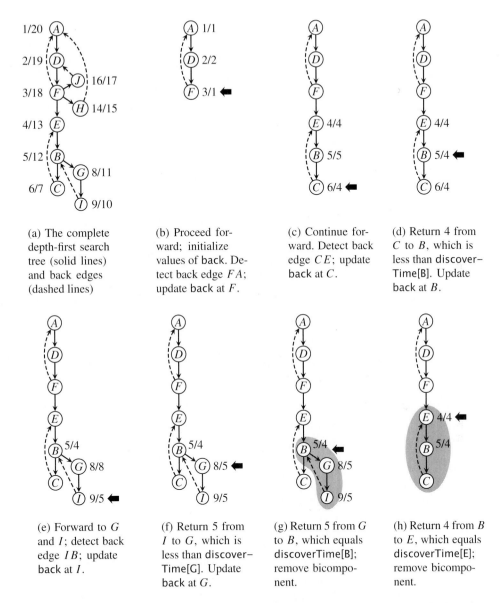

(a) The complete depth-first search tree (solid lines) and back edges (dashed lines)

(b) Proceed forward; initialize values of back. Detect back edge FA; update back at F.

(c) Continue forward. Detect back edge CE; update back at C.

(d) Return 4 from C to B, which is less than discover-Time[B]. Update back at B.

(e) Forward to G and I; detect back edge IB; update back at I.

(f) Return 5 from I to G, which is less than discover-Time[G]. Update back at G.

(g) Return 5 from G to B, which equals discoverTime[B]; remove bicomponent.

(h) Return 4 from B to E, which equals discoverTime[E]; remove bicomponent.

Figure 7.24 The action of the bicomponent algorithm on the graph in Figure 7.22 (detecting the first two bicomponents): Part (a) shows discovery and finishing times. Vertex labels for parts (b) through (h) are discoverTime/back.

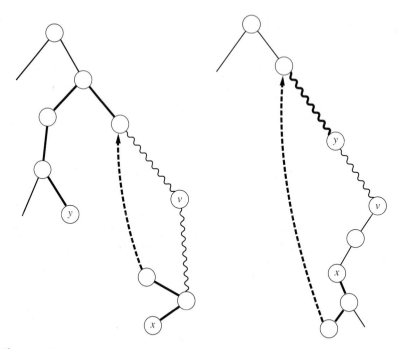

Figure 7.25   Examples for the proof of Theorem 7.13. Wavy lines denote paths.

We can now outline the work to be done in the depth-first search. Note that code will be inserted into the undirected depth-first search skeleton of Algorithm 7.8. However, before developing the complete algorithm, we want to outline it at a high level.

```
int  bicompDFS(v)  // OUTLINE
    color[v] = gray;
    time ++; discoverTime[v] = time;
    back = discoverTime[v];
    while (there is an untraversed edge vw)
        If vw is a tree edge:
            wBack = bicompDFS(w);
            // Now backtracking to v
            if (wBack ≥ discoverTime[v])
                Output a new bicomponent consisting of the subtree rooted at w
                and incident edges, but excluding edges in bicomponents that were
                output earlier.
            back = min(back, wBack);
        else if vw is a back edge:
            back = min(discoverTime[w], back);
        // Continue while loop.
    return back;
```

The algorithm must keep track of the edges traversed during the search so that those in one bicomponent can easily be identified and removed from further consideration at the appropriate time. As the example in Figure 7.24 illustrates, when a bicomponent is detected, its edges are the edges most recently processed. Thus edges are stacked on edgeStack as they are encountered. When a bicomponent is detected when backtracking from, say, w to v, the edges in that bicomponent are the edges from the top of edgeStack down to (and including) vw. These edges may then be popped.

Incorporating the outline into the skeleton of Algorithm 7.8, with some top-level control code, gives the final algorithm. (Computing finishTime is done for consistency with DFS Trace, Algorithm 7.4, but may be omitted.)

Algorithm 7.9   Biconnected Components

Input: Array adjVertices of adjacency lists for an undirected graph $G = (V, E)$; n, the number of vertices. Global arrays discoverTime and finishTime, and global variable time are also used. All arrays should be defined for indexes $1, \ldots, n$; the 0th entry is unused.

Output: Sets (e.g., lists) of the edges in each biconnected component of G.

Remarks: The Stack ADT operations described in Section 2.4.1 are used. Color meanings are white = undiscovered, gray = active, black = finished.

Procedure: See Figure 7.26. ■

Since edgeStack might grow to the number of edges in G, a flexible implementation is suggested, perhaps built upon the List ADT.

7.7.3 Analysis

As usual, $n = |V|$ and $m = |E|$. The initialization in bicomponents includes $\Theta(n)$ operations. bicompDFS is the undirected depth-first search skeleton with appropriate processing of vertices and edges added. The undirected depth-first search skeleton takes time in $\Theta(n + m)$. The amount of space used is $\Theta(n + m)$.

Thus if the amount of processing for each vertex and edge is bounded by a constant, the complexity of bicomponents is in $\Theta(n + m)$. It is easy to see that this is the case. The only place where the needed observation is nontrivial is when the search backs up from w to v. Sometimes the *output* loop popping edges from edgeStack is executed, sometimes not, and the number of edges popped each time varies. But each edge is stacked and popped exactly once. So, overall, the amount of work done is in $\Theta(m)$.

7.7.4 Generalizations

The prefix *bi* means "two." Informally speaking, a biconnected graph has two vertex-disjoint paths between any pair of vertices (see Exercise 7.33). We can define triconnectivity (and, in general, k-connectivity) to denote the property of having three (in general, k) vertex-disjoint paths between any pair of vertices. An efficient algorithm that uses depth-first search to find the triconnected components of a graph has been developed (see Notes and References at the end of the chapter), but it is much more complicated than the algorithm for bicomponents.

```
void  bicomponents(IntList[] adjVertices, n)
    int  v;
    IntStack  edgeStack;
    int[]  color = new int[n+1];

    Initialize color array to white for all vertices.
    time = 0;
    edgeStack = create();
    for (v = 1; v ≤ n; v ++)
        if (color[v] == white)
            bicompDFS(adjVertices, color, v, −1);
    return;

int  bicompDFS(IntList[] adjVertices, int[] color, int v, p)
    int  w;
    IntList  remAdj;
    int  back;
```

```
  1.  color[v] = gray;
 2a.  time ++; discoverTime[v] = time;
 2b.  back = discoverTime[v];
  3.  remAdj = adjVertices[v];
  4.  while (remAdj ≠ nil)
  5.      w = first(remAdj);
  6.      if (color[w] == white)
  7.          push(edgeStack, vw);
  8.          int  wBack = bicompDFS(adjVertices, color, w, v);
 9a.          // Backtrack processing of tree edge vw
 9b.          if (wBack ≥ discoverTime[v])
 9c.              Initialize for new bicomponent.
 9d.              Pop and output edgeStack down through vw.
 9e.          back = min(back, wBack);
 10.      else if (color[w] == gray && w ≠ p)
11a.          // Process back edge vw.
11b.          push(edgeStack, vw);
11c.          back = min(discoverTime[w], back);
             // else wv was traversed, so ignore vw.
 12.      remAdj = rest(remAdj);
 13.  time ++; finishTime[v] = time;
 14.  color[v] = black;
 15.  return back;
```

Figure 7.26   Procedure for Algorithm 7.9

Exercises

Section 7.2   Definitions and Representations

7.1   Make a connected undirected graph (whose edges may represent two-way streets) such that every vertex is in some undirected cycle, yet no matter how the edges are oriented (i.e., made into directed edges, or one-way streets), the graph is not strongly connected.

7.2   This exercise is about Euler paths.

a.   A popular game among grade-school children is to draw the following figure without picking up your pencil and without retracing a line. Try it.

b.   Figure 7.27 provides a similar but slightly harder problem. It shows a river with two islands in it connected to each other and to the banks by seven bridges. The problem is to determine if there is a way to take a walk starting on either bank of the river or on either island and crossing each bridge exactly once. (No swimming allowed.) Try it.

★ **c.**   The problems in parts (a) and (b) may be studied abstractly by examining the following graphs. G_2 is obtained by representing each bank and island as a vertex and each bridge as an edge. (Some pairs of vertices are connected by two edges, but this departure from the definition of a graph will not cause trouble here.) The general problem is: Given a graph (with multiple edges between pairs of vertices permitted), find a path through the graph that traverses each edge exactly once. Such a path is called an Euler path. This problem is solvable for G_1 but not for G_2. That is, there is no way to walk across

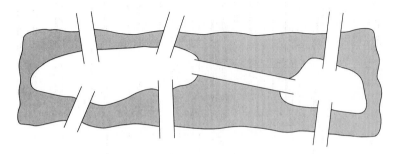

Figure 7.27   The Königsberg bridges

each bridge exactly once. Find a necessary and sufficient condition for a graph to have an Euler path.

G_1 G_2

7.3   Suppose that a digraph G represents a binary relation R. Describe a condition on G that holds if and only if R is transitive.

Section 7.3   Traversing Graphs

7.4   Find the depth-first search tree for the graph used in Example 7.6 (see Figure 7.28) with G as the starting vertex under two assumptions about the adjacency-list order:

a.   Each adjacency list is in alphabetical order.

b.   Each adjacency list is in reverse alphabetical order.

7.5   Find the breadth-first search tree and breadth-first distances for the graph used in Example 7.7 (see Figure 7.28) with G as the starting vertex under two assumptions about the adjacency list order.

a.   Each adjacency list is in alphabetical order.

b.   Each adjacency list is in reverse alphabetical order.

7.6   Let G be a connected graph, and let s be a vertex in G. Let T_D be a depth-first search tree formed by doing a depth-first search of G starting at s. Let T_B be a breadth-first spanning tree formed by doing a breadth-first search of G starting at s. Is it always true that height(T_D) $\geq$ height(T_B)? Does it matter whether the graph is directed or undirected? Give a clear argument or a counterexample.

7.7   Prove that when a breadth-first search is done on an undirected graph every edge in the graph is either a tree edge or a cross edge. (A cross edge for breadth-first search is an

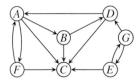

Figure 7.28   Digraph from Examples 7.6 and 7.7, used for various exercises

edge between two vertices such that neither is a descendant of the other in the breadth-first spanning tree.)

Section 7.4 *Depth-First Search on Directed Graphs*

7.8 Outline an algorithm to compute the transpose graph, given the original graph in the form of an array of adjacency lists. Your algorithm should run in linear time.

a. Give pseudocode for the procedure and any subroutines.

b. Show how your algorithm works on Figure 7.28, assuming the adjacency lists of the original graph are in alphabetical order. Be specific about the order of vertices in the adjacency lists of the transpose graph. (Remember, you are not going to sort them; that might be expensive.)

7.9 Classify the edges of the graph used in Example 7.6 (see Figure 7.28) according to Definition 7.14, assuming that the depth-first search begins at vertex G, and adjacent vertices are processed in alphabetical order.

7.10 In case 2 of Definition 7.14 (back edge), what color(s) can w have when edge vw is checked?

7.11 Carry out DFS Trace (Algorithm 7.4) on the digraph in Figure 7.29, and classify all the edges.

a. Assume the vertices are indexed in alphabetical order in the adjVertices array and that each adjacency list is in alphabetical order.

b. Assume the vertices are indexed in reverse alphabetical order in the adjVertices array and that each adjacency list is in alphabetical order.

c. Assume the vertices are indexed in alphabetical order in the adjVertices array and that each adjacency list is in reverse alphabetical order.

d. Assume the vertices are indexed in reverse alphabetical order in the adjVertices array and that each adjacency list is in reverse alphabetical order.

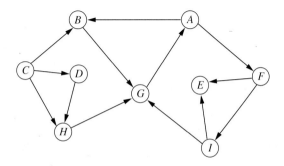

Figure 7.29 Digraph for Exercises 7.11 and 7.23

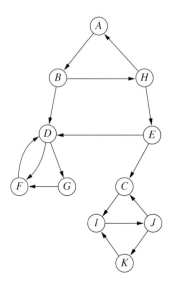

Figure 7.30   Digraph for Exercises 7.12 and 7.24

7.12   Carry out DFS Trace (Algorithm 7.4) on the digraph in Figure 7.30, and classify all the edges.

a.   Assume the vertices are indexed in alphabetical order in the adjVertices array and that each adjacency list is in alphabetical order.

b.   Assume the vertices are indexed in reverse alphabetical order in the adjVertices array and that each adjacency list is in alphabetical order.

c.   Assume the vertices are indexed in alphabetical order in the adjVertices array and that each adjacency list is in reverse alphabetical order.

d.   Assume the vertices are indexed in reverse alphabetical order in the adjVertices array and that each adjacency list is in reverse alphabetical order.

7.13   Give an example of a graph in which a depth-first search backs up from a vertex before all the vertices that can be reached from it via one or more edges are discovered.

7.14   Suppose v and w are distinct vertices in the same directed tree, but have no an-cestor/descendant relationship. Show that there is some third vertex c, called their least common ancestor, such that there are tree paths from c to v and from c to w, and these paths have no edges in common. *Hint*: Use the fact that every vertex in a tree has exactly one path from the root to it.

7.15   Prove item 3 of Theorem 7.1.

7.16   Describe how to modify the DFS skeleton to produce an algorithm for a digraph whose output is a list of the edges in the depth-first search tree.

7.17

a. Write an algorithm to determine if a digraph has a cycle.

b. If you used depth-first search for the preceding algorithm, try to write an algorithm for the same problem using breadth-first search, and vice versa. Do you see any strong reasons to prefer either of the search strategies for this problem?

7.18   Show the result of Algorithm 7.4 and indicate what topological numbers are assigned by Algorithm 7.5 if the dependency graph defined in Example 7.14 is processed in reverse order. That is, assume the **for** loop in dfsSweep goes from 9 to 1, and adjacency lists are in reverse order also.

7.19   For each graph in Figure 7.18 manually run Algorithm 7.5 with the modification that causes it to compute a topological order instead of a reverse topological order. Assume that vertices in adjacency lists are in numerical order. Also check as you are running it whether the graph has a cycle (what condition should you look for during dfs?). Stop as soon as a cycle is detected, and explain how it was detected, or find the complete topological order if there is no cycle. Compare your topological order with the reverse topological order of Example 7.15 (which used the transpose graph). Are they the same?

7.20   A DAG is called a *lattice* if there is one vertex that can reach every vertex and one vertex that can be reached by every vertex.

a. Outline an algorithm to determine if a DAG is a lattice.

b. What is the asymptotic order of its running time?

c. Show the operation of your algorithm on the graph in Example 7.15. Is it a lattice?

⋆ **7.21**   Another strategy for topological sorting is to keep track of "source" vertices. Initially, each vertex has an *indegree* that is the number of directed edges *entering* the vertex. A *source* is a vertex with indegree 0. The idea is to give topological numbers in ascending sequence to source vertices. Each time a vertex v is numbered, each vertex with an incoming edge from v should have its indegree reduced. This is as though v were taken out of the graph after being numbered. As other indegrees reduce to 0, other vertices become sources. Write an algorithm to implement this strategy. Specify what data structures you need for bookkeeping. What is the asymptotic order of your algorithm on a DAG with n vertices and m edges?

Section 7.5   *Strongly Connected Components of a Digraph*

7.22   Prove that the condensation of a digraph is acyclic.

7.23   Find the strong components of the digraph in Figure 7.29 by carefully following the steps of the algorithm. (It is helpful to calculate the discoverTime and finishTime of the vertices, although the algorithm does not require it.)

a. Assume the vertices are indexed in alphabetical order in the adjVertices array and that each adjacency list is in alphabetical order.

b.   Assume the vertices are indexed in reverse alphabetical order in the adjVertices array and that each adjacency list is in alphabetical order.

c.   Assume the vertices are indexed in alphabetical order in the adjVertices array and that each adjacency list is in reverse alphabetical order.

d.   Assume the vertices are indexed in reverse alphabetical order in the adjVertices array and that each adjacency list is in reverse alphabetical order.

7.24   Find the strong components of the digraph in Figure 7.30 by carefully following the steps of the algorithm. (It is helpful to calculate the discoverTime and finishTime of the vertices, although the algorithm does not require it.)

a.   Assume the vertices are indexed in alphabetical order in the adjVertices array and that each adjacency list is in alphabetical order.

b.   Assume the vertices are indexed in reverse alphabetical order in the adjVertices array and that each adjacency list is in alphabetical order.

c.   Assume the vertices are indexed in alphabetical order in the adjVertices array and that each adjacency list is in reverse alphabetical order.

d.   Assume the vertices are indexed in reverse alphabetical order in the adjVertices array and that each adjacency list is in reverse alphabetical order.

7.25   Extend or modify the strong component algorithm so that it outputs a list of all the edges, as well as the vertices, in each strong component. Try to minimize the amount of extra time used to do so.

7.26   Can either depth-first search in the strong components algorithm be (easily) replaced by a breadth-first search? Explain why or why not.

Section 7.6   Depth-First Search on Undirected Graphs

7.27   Write a depth-first search algorithm for an undirected graph such that the output is a list of the edges encountered, with each edge appearing once.

7.28   Prove that if G is a connected undirected graph, each of its edges either is in the depth-first search tree or is a back edge.

7.29

a.   Write an algorithm to determine if an undirected graph has a cycle.

b.   If you used depth-first search for the preceding algorithm, try to write an algorithm for the same problem using breadth-first search, and vice versa. Do you see any strong reasons to prefer either of the search strategies for this problem?

c.   How, if at all, do these algorithms differ from the ones for Exercise 7.17?

7.30 Describe an algorithm to determine if an undirected graph $G = (V, E)$, with $n = |V|$ and $m = |E|$, is a tree. Would you use the same algorithm if you could assume that the graph is connected? If not, describe one that uses that assumption as well.

⋆ **7.31** Consider the problem of finding the length of a shortest cycle in an undirected graph. Here is a proposed solution that is not correct. Show why it does not always work.

> When a back edge, say vw, is encountered during a depth-first search, it forms a cycle with the tree edges from w to v. The length of the cycle is depth[v] − depth[w] + 1, where depth is the depth in the DFS tree. So, do a depth-first search, keeping track of the depth of each vertex. Each time a back edge is encountered, compute the cycle length and save it if it is smaller than the shortest one previously seen.

Look for a fundamental flaw in the strategy, not a detail.

Section 7.7 Biconnected Components of an Undirected Graph

7.32 List the articulation points in the graph with the depth-first search tree shown in Figure 7.31.

7.33 Is the following property on a graph $G = (V, E)$ necessary and sufficient for G to be biconnected? Prove your answer.

> For each pair of distinct vertices v and w in V, there are two distinct paths from v to w that have no vertices in common except v and w.

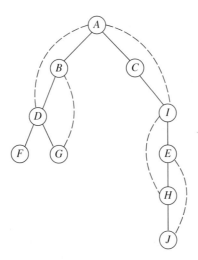

Figure 7.31 Depth-first search tree for Exercise 7.32

7.34 For an undirected graph $G = (V, E)$, consider the following relation, R, on the edges E: $e_1 R e_2$ if and only if $e_1 = e_2$ or there is a simple cycle in G containing e_1 and e_2.

a. Show that R is an equivalence relation.

b. How many equivalence classes are there in the following graph?

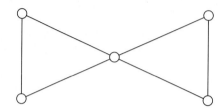

c. Show that a subgraph consisting of the edges in one equivalence class of the relation R and the incident vertices is a maximal biconnected subgraph of G.

⋆ **7.35** The following two definitions of functions on the vertices in a depth-first search tree of an undirected graph are attempts to provide necessary and/or sufficient conditions for two vertices to be in the same biconnected component of the graph. Show by exhibiting counterexamples that these attempts fail.

a. Define $old_1(x) =$ the "oldest"—that is, closest to the root—ancestor of x that can be reached by following tree edges (away from the root) and back edges; or $old_1(x) = x$ itself if no such path leads to an ancestor of x. Show that $old_1(v) = old_1(w)$ is neither necessary nor sufficient for v and w to be in the same bicomponent.

b. Define $old_2(x) =$ the oldest ancestor of x that can be reached by following directed tree edges (away from the root) and *one* back edge; or $old_2(x) = x$ itself if no such path leads to an ancestor of x. Show that $old_2(v) = old_2(w)$ is neither necessary nor sufficient for v and w to be in the same bicomponent.

7.36 Complete the proof of Theorem 7.13.

7.37 Find a necessary and sufficient condition for the root of a depth-first search tree for a connected graph to be an articulation point. Prove it.

7.38 Would the bicomponent algorithm work properly if back were initialized to ∞ (or $2(n + 1)$) instead of discoverTime[v]? Explain your answer.

7.39 Give an example of a graph that shows that the bicomponent algorithm may produce incorrect answers if no attempt is made to avoid stacking an edge the second time it is encountered in the adjacency-list structure. This amounts to treating G as a symmetric digraph instead of an undirected graph. The test in line 10 of Algorithm 7.9 would be omitted and that line would be a simple **else**.

7.40 Would the bicomponent algorithm work properly if the test for a bicomponent were changed to back $\geq$ discoverTime[v]? If so, explain why; if not, give an example in which it does not work.

7.41 A connected graph is *edge biconnected* if there is no edge whose removal disconnects the graph. Which, if either, of the following statements is true? Give a proof or counterexample for each.

a. A biconnected graph with three or more vertices is edge biconnected.

b. An edge biconnected graph with three or more vertices is biconnected.

7.42 Suppose G is a connected graph. An edge e whose removal disconnects the graph is called a *bridge*. For example, the edge EF in Figure 7.22 is a bridge. Give an algorithm for finding the bridges in a graph. What is the worst-case complexity of your algorithm?

Additional Problems

7.43 We mentioned in Section 7.2 that, if a graph is represented by an adjacency matrix, then almost any algorithm that operates on the graph will have worst-case complexity in $\Omega(n^2)$, where n is the number of vertices. There are, however, some problems that can be solved quickly, even when the adjacency matrix is used. Here is one.

a. Let $G = (V, E)$ be a digraph with n vertices. Let's call a vertex s a *hypersink* if, for every v in V such that $s \neq v$, there is an edge vs and there is no edge of the form sv. Give an algorithm to determine whether or not G has a hypersink, assuming that G is given by its $n \times n$ adjacency matrix.

b. How many matrix entries are examined by your algorithm in the worst case? It is easy to give an algorithm that looks at $\Theta(n^2)$ entries, but there is a linear solution.

$\star$ **7.44** Find the best lower bound you can for the number of adjacency matrix entries that must be examined to solve the problem described in Exercise 7.43. Prove that it is a lower bound. *Hint*: You should easily be able to give a clear argument for $2n - 2$. An adversary argument similar to the one in Section 5.3.3 can be used to get a stronger lower bound.

7.45 Design an efficient algorithm to find a path in a connected undirected graph that goes through each edge exactly once in each direction.

$\star$ **7.46** An *Euler circuit* in an undirected graph is a circuit (i.e., a cycle that may go through some vertices more than once) that includes every edge exactly once. Give an algorithm that finds an Euler circuit in a graph, or tells that the graph doesn't have one.

7.47 Consider the following question:

Problem 7.2

Is there a vertex v in G such that every other vertex in G can be reached by a path from v?

■

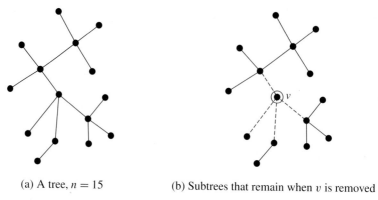

(a) A tree, $n = 15$ (b) Subtrees that remain when v is removed

Figure 7.32   Example for Exercise 7.49

If G is an undirected graph, the question can be answered easily by a simple depth-first (or breadth-first) search and a check to see if every vertex was visited. Write an algorithm to solve the problem for a directed graph. What is the complexity of your algorithm?

7.48   A *bipartite* graph is a graph whose vertices may be partitioned into two subsets such that there is no edge between any two vertices in the same subset. Write an algorithm to determine if an undirected graph is bipartite. What is the worst-case complexity of your algorithm?

★ **7.49**   When a vertex and its incident edges are removed from a tree, a collection of subtrees remains. Write an algorithm that, given a graph that is a tree with n vertices, finds a vertex v whose removal leaves no subtree with more than $n/2$ vertices. See Figure 7.32 for an example. What is the worst-case complexity of your algorithm? (You should be able to get a linear solution.)

Programs

Each of the following program assignments requires a *graph-loading* procedure that reads in a description of a graph from a file and sets up the adjacency lists. Appendix A contains sample Java code to serve as a starter. Assume the input contains the number of vertices on the first line, followed by a sequence of lines, with each line containing a pair of vertices representing one edge. Write this procedure so that, with small changes, it could be used for any of the problems.

For a fancier user interface, arrange for the graph to be loaded from a named file so that "queries" that direct the main program (*not* the graph-loading procedure above) to solve a particular problem or produce a particular output can be entered at the terminal by the user after the loading is completed. In this case, don't forget to have a "query" that exits the program.

Test data should be chosen so that all aspects of a program are tested. Include some of the examples in the text.

1. A depth-first search algorithm to determine if an undirected graph has a cycle.
2. A breadth-first search algorithm to determine if a directed graph has a cycle.
3. The strong component algorithm described in Algorithm 7.7.
4. The bicomponent algorithm, Algorithm 7.9.

Notes and References

The adjacency-list structure used in this chapter was suggested by Tarjan and is described, along with the algorithms for biconnected components, topological sorting, and many more, in Tarjan (1972) and Hopcroft and Tarjan (1973b). Hopcroft and Tarjan (1973a) presents an algorithm for finding the triconnected components of a graph. See Hopcroft and Tarjan (1974) for a very efficient algorithm to test graphs for planarity—another important problem for graphs. The strong component algorithm in Algorithm 7.7 is due to Sharir (1981). Using three vertex colors for "housekeeping" in depth-first search, as well as using a single time counter for discoverTime and finishTime, is due to Cormen, Leiserson, and Rivest (1990).

See King and Smith-Thomas (1982) for optimal solutions to Exercises 7.43 and 7.44. Knuth (1998) has Exercise 7.21.

Gibbons (1985) is a book on graph theory and algorithms; it covers topics in this chapter and many others. See also Even (1973) and Even (1979); Aho, Hopcroft, and Ullman (1974); Deo (1974); Reingold, Nievergelt, and Deo (1977); and Sedgewick (1988).

8

Graph Optimization Problems and Greedy Algorithms

8.1   Introduction

In this chapter we will study several graph optimization problems that can be solved exactly by greedy algorithms. Typically, in optimization problems the algorithm needs to make a series of choices whose overall effect is to minimize the total cost, or maximize the total benefit, of some system. The greedy method consists of making the choices in sequence such that each individual choice is best according to some limited "short-term" criterion that is not too expensive to evaluate. Once a choice is made, it can't be undone, even if it becomes evident later that it was a poor choice. For this reason, greedy methods don't necessarily find the exact optimum solution to many problems. However, for the problems studied in this chapter we are able to prove that the *appropriate* greedy strategy produces optimum solutions. In Chapter 13 we will see problems for which very similar greedy strategies fail. In Chapter 10 we will see other problems for which greedy strategies fail.

This chapter presents an algorithm for finding a minimum spanning tree in an undirected graph, due to R. C. Prim, a closely related algorithm for finding shortest paths in directed and undirected graphs, due to E. W. Dijkstra, and a second algorithm for finding a minimum spanning tree, due to J. B. Kruskal. All three algorithms use a priority queue to select the best current choice from a set of candidate choices.

8.2   Prim's Minimum Spanning Tree Algorithm

The first problem we will study is the problem of finding a minimum spanning tree for a connected, weighted, undirected graph. For unconnected graphs the natural extension of the problem is to find a minimum spanning tree for each connected component We saw that connected components can be found in linear time (Section 7.4.2).

Minimum spanning trees are meaningful only for undirected graphs, with edge weights, so all references to "graph" in this section mean "undirected graph," and weights are always edge weights. Recall that the notation $G = (V, E, W)$ means that W is a function that assigns a weight to each edge in E. This is just the mathematical description. In the implementation, there normally is no "function"; the weight of each edge is simply stored in the data structure for that edge.

8.2.1   Definition and Examples of Minimum Spanning Trees

Definition 8.1   Minimum spanning tree

A *spanning tree* for a connected, undirected graph, $G = (V, E)$, is a subgraph of G that is an undirected tree and contains all the vertices of G. In a weighted graph $G = (V, E, W)$, the weight of a subgraph is the sum of the weights of the edges in the subgraph. A *minimum spanning tree* (*MST* for short) for a weighted graph is a spanning tree with minimum weight.   ∎

There are many situations in which minimum spanning trees must be found. Whenever one wants to find the cheapest way to connect a set of terminals, be they cities, electrical terminals, computers, or factories, by using, say, roads, wires, or telephone lines, a solution

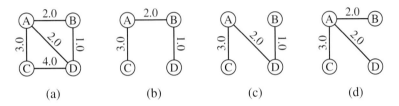

Figure 8.1   A graph and some spanning trees: Two of these are *minimum* spanning trees.

is a minimum spanning tree for the graph with an edge for each possible connection weighted by the cost of that connection. Finding minimum spanning trees is also an important subproblem in various routing algorithms, that is, algorithms for finding efficient paths through a graph that visit every vertex (or every edge).

As the simple example in Figure 8.1 shows, a weighted graph may have more than one minimum spanning tree. In fact, the method of transforming one minimum spanning tree into another in this example is an illustration of a general property of minimum spanning trees, which is discussed in Section 8.2.3.

8.2.2   An Overview of the Algorithm

Since an undirected tree is connected, and any vertex can be thought of as the root, a natural approach to finding a minimum spanning tree is to "grow" it one edge at a time from some starting vertex. We should first try using our standard traversal methods, depth-first search and breadth-first search. If we can annotate one of these skeletons to solve the problem, then we have a linear-time solution, which is surely optimal. You should take some time out to try some ideas using these search methods, and construct example graphs where they fail to find the minimum (see Exercise 8.1).

Having convinced ourselves that a simple traversal seems to be inadequate, and considering that this is an optimization problem, the next natural idea to try is the *greedy method*. The theme of the greedy method is to make progress by choosing an action that incurs the minimum short-term cost, in the hope that a lot of small short-term costs add up to a small overall cost. (The possible drawback is that actions with a small short-term cost may lead to a situation where further large costs are unavoidable.) We have a very natural way to minimize the short-term cost of adding an edge to the tree we are growing: Simply add an edge that is attached to the tree at exactly one end and has minimum weight among all such edges. Prim's algorithm takes this greedy approach.

Having come up with an idea to solve the problem, we should ask ourselves the usual two questions. Does it work correctly? How fast does it run? As we have mentioned, a series of small short-term costs might lead into an unfavorable situation, so even though we are sure that we get a spanning tree, we still need to consider whether its weight is minimum among all spanning trees. Also, since we need to choose among many edges at each step, and the set of candidates changes after each choice, we will want to consider what data structures can make these operations efficient. We will return to these questions after fleshing out the general idea.

Prim's algorithm begins by selecting an arbitrary starting vertex, and then "branches out" from the part of the tree constructed so far by choosing a new vertex and edge at each iteration. The new edge connects the new vertex to the previous tree. During the course of the algorithm, the vertices may be thought of as divided into three (disjoint) categories as follows:

1. *tree* vertices: in the tree constructed so far,
2. *fringe* vertices: not in the tree, but adjacent to some vertex in the tree,
3. *unseen* vertices: all others.

The key step in the algorithm is the selection of a vertex from the fringe and an incident edge. Actually, since the weights are on the edges, the focus of the choice is on the edge, not on the vertex. Prim's algorithm always chooses an edge of minimum weight from a tree vertex to a fringe vertex. The general structure of the algorithm may be described as follows:

```
primMST(G, n)  // OUTLINE
    Initialize all vertices as unseen.
    Select an arbitrary vertex s to start the tree; reclassify it as tree.
    Reclassify all vertices adjacent to s as fringe.
    While there are fringe vertices:
        Select an edge of minimum weight between a tree vertex t and a
            fringe vertex v;
        Reclassify v as tree; add edge t v to the tree;
        Reclassify all unseen vertices adjacent to v as fringe.
```

Example 8.1   Prim's algorithm, one iteration

Figure 8.2(a) shows a weighted graph. Assume A is the starting vertex. The steps before the loop lead to Figure 8.2(b). In the first iteration of the loop, the minimum-weight edge to a fringe vertex is found to be AB. Thus B is added to the tree, and the unseen vertices adjacent to B enter the fringe, leading to Figure 8.2(c).   ■

Can we be sure that this strategy will yield a minimum spanning tree? Is being greedy in the short term a good long-term strategy? In this case, yes. The next two subsections discuss a general property shared by all minimum spanning trees, and use the property to show that the tree built at each stage of Prim's algorithm is a minimum spanning tree on the subgraph spanned by this tree. We return to implementation considerations in Section 8.2.5.

8.2.3   Properties of Minimum Spanning Trees

Figure 8.1 demonstrated that a weighted graph may have more than one minimum spanning tree. In fact, minimum spanning trees have a general property that gives us a way to transform any minimum spanning tree into any other in a step-by-step manner. Examining this property also helps us to become more familiar with undirected trees, generally.

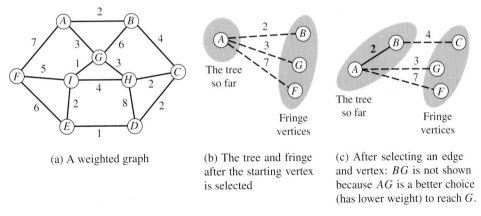

(a) A weighted graph

(b) The tree and fringe
after the starting vertex
is selected

(c) After selecting an edge
and vertex: BG is not shown
because AG is a better choice
(has lower weight) to reach G.

Figure 8.2   One iteration of the loop for Prim's algorithm: Solid lines are tree edges and dashed
lines are edges to fringe vertices.

Definition 8.2   Minimum spanning tree property

Let a connected, weighted graph $G = (V, E, W)$ be given, and let T be any spanning tree
of G. Suppose that for every edge uv of G that is *not* in T, if uv is added to T it creates
a cycle such that uv is a maximum-weight edge on that cycle. Then the tree T has the
minimum spanning tree property (*MST property* for short).   ■

First, let us see what the definition means. Then we will prove that the name is well
chosen; just calling it "minimum spanning tree property" does not mean that it has anything
to do with minimum spanning trees!

Example 8.2   Minimum spanning tree property

By definition an undirected tree connects any two vertices in the tree, and has no cycles.
Let's look at Figure 8.1, which shows a simple graph, which we'll call G, and three
spanning trees. First let T be the tree in part (b). Suppose we add an edge of G that isn't in T
to T, making a new subgraph G_1 (we'll add the one of weight 2). This creates a cycle (and
only one cycle) in the subgraph G_1. (Why?) All the other edges in the cycle have weight at
most 2, which is the new edge's weight. Alternatively, if we add the edge of weight 4, all
the other edges in the cycle that *it* forms have weight at most 4 (at most 3, in fact). There
are no other missing edges to try, so T has the minimum spanning tree property. The tree
in part (c) is similar.

However, now consider letting T be the tree in part (d), and add the missing edge
of weight 1. This time some other edge in the cycle it formed has weight greater than 1.
Therefore this T does *not* have the minimum spanning tree property. Notice that we can
pluck any edge out of this cycle making a new subgraph G_2, and G_2 must again be a tree, in
fact, a spanning tree. These facts are proved in Exercise 8.2, and are used to prove the next
lemma and theorem. Since there is an edge of weight greater than 1, we choose to pluck

one such edge. That means G_2 has lower weight than T, so T could not be a minimum spanning tree.   ∎

Lemma 8.1   In a connected, weighted graph $G = (V, E, W)$, if T_1 and T_2 are two spanning trees that have the MST property, then they have the same total weight.

Proof   The proof is by induction on k, the number of edges that are in T_1 and not in T_2. (There are likewise exactly k edges in T_2 that are not in T_1.) The base case is $k = 0$; in this case, T_1 and T_2 are identical, so they have the same weight.

For $k > 0$ assume the lemma holds for trees that differ by j edges, where $0 \le j < k$. Let uv be a *minimum-weight* edge that is in one of the trees T_1 or T_2 but not in both. Assume $uv \in T_2$; the case when $uv \in T_1$ is symmetrical. Consider the (unique) path from u to v in T_1: $w_0, w_1, \ldots, w_p$, where $w_0 = u$, $w_p = v$, and $p \ge 2$. This path must contain some edge that is not in T_2. (Why?) Let $w_i w_{i+1}$ be such an edge. By the MST property of T_1, $w_i w_{i+1}$ cannot have a weight *greater* than the weight of uv. By the fact that uv was chosen to be of minimum weight among all differing edges, $w_i w_{i+1}$ cannot have a weight *less* than the weight of uv. Therefore $W(w_i w_{i+1}) = W(uv)$. Add uv to T_1, creating a cycle, then remove $w_i w_{i+1}$, breaking that cycle, and leaving a new spanning tree T_1', with the same total weight as T_1. But T_1' and T_2 differ on only $k - 1$ edges, so by the inductive hypothesis, they have the same total weight. Therefore T_1 and T_2 have the same total weight.   □

The proof of this lemma also shows us the step-by-step method to transform any minimum spanning tree, T_1, into any other, T_2. Choose a lightest edge in T_2 that is not in T_1; call it uv. Look at the path from u to v in T_1. Somewhere on that path is an edge with the same weight as uv that is not in T_2; say this edge is xy (see Exercise 8.3). Remove xy and add uv. This brings us one step closer to T_2. Repeat this step until the trees agree.

Theorem 8.2   In a connected, weighted graph $G = (V, E, W)$, a tree T is a minimum spanning tree if and only if T has the MST property.

Proof   (Only if) Assume T is a minimum spanning tree for G. Suppose there is some edge uv that is not in T such that adding uv creates a cycle in which some *other* edge xy has weight $W(xy) > W(uv)$. Then removing xy creates a new spanning tree with total weight less than T, contradicting the assumption that T was of minimum weight.

(If) Assume T has the MST property. Let T_{min} be *any* minimum spanning tree of G. By the first half of the theorem, T_{min} has the MST property. By Lemma 8.1, T has the same total weight as T_{min}.   □

8.2.4   Correctness of Prim's MST Algorithm

We now use the MST property to show that Prim's algorithm constructs a minimum spanning tree. This proof takes a form that occurs frequently when using induction: The statement to be proved by induction is somewhat more detailed than the theorem we are interested in. So first we prove this more detailed statement as a *lemma*. Then the theorem simply extracts the interesting part of the lemma. In this sense, the theorem is very much like the "wrapper" for a recursive procedure, as discussed in Section 3.2.2.

Lemma 8.3   Let $G = (V, E, W)$ be a connected, weighted graph with $n = |V|$; let T_k be the tree with k vertices constructed by Prim's algorithm, for $k = 1, \ldots, n$; and let G_k be the subgraph of G induced by the vertices of T_k (i.e., uv is an edge in G_k if it is an edge in G and both u and v are in T_k). Then T_k has the MST property in G_k.

Proof   The proof is by induction on k. The base case is $k = 1$. In this case, G_1 and T_1 contain the start vertex s and no edges, so T_1 has the MST property in G_1.

For $k > 1$ assume that T_j has the MST property in G_j for $1 \leq j < k$. Assume that the kth vertex to be added to the tree by Prim's algorithm is v and that the edges between v and vertices in T_{k-1} are $u_1v, \ldots, u_dv$. For definiteness, assume u_1v is the edge of minimum weight among these that is chosen by the algorithm. We need to verify that T_k has the MST property. That is, if xy is any edge in G_k that is not in T_k, we need to show that xy has maximum weight in the cycle that would be created by adding xy to T_k. If $x \neq v$ and $y \neq v$, then xy was also in G_{k-1}, but not in T_{k-1}, so by the inductive hypothesis, it is maximum in the cycle created by adding it to T_{k-1}. But this is the same cycle in T_k, so T_k has the MST property in this case. It remains to show that the property holds when xy is one of the edges $u_2v, \ldots, u_dv$ (since u_1v is in T_k). If $d < 2$ we are done, so assume not.

It may be helpful to refer to Figure 8.3 throughout the rest of the proof. Consider the path from v to u_i in T_k for any i, $2 \leq i \leq d$. Suppose some edge on this path has a weight *greater* than the weight of u_iv, which in turn is at least the weight of u_1v. (If not, the MST property is satisfied.) Specifically, let the path be $v, w_1, \ldots, w_p$, where $w_1 = u_1$ and $w_p = u_i$. Then $w_1, \ldots, w_p$ is a path in T_{k-1}. Let w_aw_{a+1} be the *first* edge on this path with weight greater than $W(u_iv)$ and let $w_{b-1}w_b$ be the *last* edge on this path with weight greater than $W(u_iv)$ (possibly $a + 1 = b$; see Figure 8.3). We claim that w_a and w_b cannot exist in T_{k-1} if it was constructed by Prim's algorithm. Suppose w_a was added to the tree before w_b. Then all edges on the path from w_1 (which is u_1) to w_a would be added before either w_aw_{a+1} or $w_{b-1}w_b$ because they all have lower weights, and u_1v would also have been added before either of them. Similarly, if w_b was added to the tree before w_a, then u_iv would have been added before either w_aw_{a+1} or $w_{b-1}w_b$. But neither u_1v nor u_iv is in T_{k-1}, so no edge on the path $w_1, \ldots, w_p$ has weight greater than $W(u_iv)$, and the MST property is established for T_k.   □

Theorem 8.4   Prim's algorithm outputs a minimum spanning tree.

Proof   In the terminology of Lemma 8.3, $G_n = G$ and T_n is the output of the algorithm, so it follows that T_n has the MST property in G. By Theorem 8.2, T_n is a minimum spanning tree of G.   □

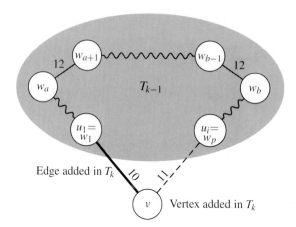

Figure 8.3 Illustration for Lemma 8.3. Weights shown are examples. Wiggly lines are paths in T_{k-1}. The dashed edge would create a cycle, as shown. Edges on the path between $u_1 (= w_1)$ and w_a, and edges on the path between w_b and $u_i (= w_p)$ all have weights not exceeding $W(u_i v)$, which is 11 in this example. Possibly $w_b = w_{a+1}$ and $w_{b-1} = w_a$.

8.2.5 Managing the Fringe Efficiently with a Priority Queue

After each iteration of the algorithm's loop, there may be new fringe vertices, and the set of edges from which the next selection is made will change. Figure 8.2(c) suggests that we need not consider all edges between tree vertices and fringe vertices. After AB was chosen, BG became a potential edge choice, but it is discarded because AG has lower weight and would be a better choice for reaching G. If BG had lower weight than AG, then AG could be discarded. For each fringe vertex, we need keep track of only one edge to it from the tree: the one with lowest weight. We call such edges *candidate edges*.

The priority queue ADT (Section 2.5.1) has just the operations we need for implementing the outline of the algorithm given in Section 8.2.2. The insert operation enters a vertex into the priority queue. The getMin operation can be used to choose the fringe vertex that can be attached to the current tree while incurring minimal cost. The deleteMin operation transfers that vertex out of the fringe. The decreaseKey operation records a more favorable cost for attaching a fringe vertex when a better candidate edge is discovered. The minimum known cost of attaching any fringe vertex is called the fringeWgt of that vertex. This value serves as the priority of the vertex, and is returned by the getPriority access function.

Using the priority queue ADT operations, the high-level algorithm is as follows. A subroutine updateFringe has been introduced to process the vertices adjacent to the selected vertex v. Figure 8.4 contains an example of the action of the algorithm.

```
primMST(G, n)  // OUTLINE
    Initialize the priority queue pq as empty.
    Select an arbitrary vertex s to start the tree;
    Set its candidate edge to (−1, s, 0) and call insert(pq, s, 0).
    While pq is not empty:
        v = getMin(pq); deleteMin(pq);
        Add the candidate edge of v to the tree.
        updateFringe(pq, G, v);

updateFringe(pq, G, v)  // OUTLINE
    For all vertices w adjacent to v, letting newWgt = W(v, w):
        If w is unseen:
            Set its candidate edge to (v, w, newWgt).
            insert(pq, w, newWgt);
        Else if newWgt < fringeWgt of w:
            Revise its candidate edge to (v, w, newWgt).
            decreaseKey(pq, w, newWgt);
```

Preliminary Analysis

What can we say about the running time of this algorithm without knowing how the priority queue ADT is implemented? The first step is to estimate how many times each ADT operation is performed. Then we can write an expression in which the costs of the ADT operations are parameters. Let us assume, as usual, that the graph has n vertices and m edges. Then we easily see that the algorithm does insert, getMin, and deleteMin about n times, while it does decreaseKey at most m times. (There are $2m$ iterations of the **for** loop that does decreaseKey because each edge is processed from both directions, but we will see later that the condition in the second **if** statement is satisfied at most once for each edge.) With a little work we can construct examples where virtually every edge triggers a decreaseKey. We can reasonably assume that insert is less expensive than deleteMin. Thus we have the expression, where the T's on the right denote the average time for the indicated operation over the course of one run of the algorithm:

$$T(n, m) = O(n\, T(\text{getMin}) + n\, T(\text{deleteMin}) + m\, T(\text{decreaseKey})). \qquad (8.1)$$

For general graphs m may be much larger than n, so clearly we want an implementation that concentrates on the efficiency of decreaseKey.

Here we realize the advantage of designing with abstract data types. We have already reasoned that our algorithm is correct, no matter how the priority queue ADT is implemented, provided the implementation meets the logical specifications of the ADT. We are now free to customize the implementation to minimize, or at least reduce, the right side of Equation (8.1).

We have already seen that a heap provides an efficient implementation of a priority queue (Section 4.8.1). How does it fare in Equation (8.1)? This question is the subject of

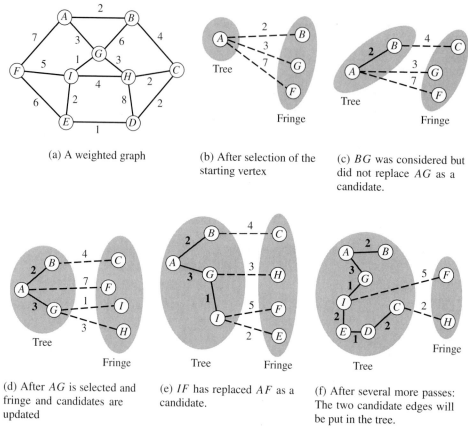

(a) A weighted graph

(b) After selection of the starting vertex

(c) *BG* was considered but did not replace *AG* as a candidate.

(d) After *AG* is selected and fringe and candidates are updated

(e) *IF* has replaced *AF* as a candidate.

(f) After several more passes: The two candidate edges will be put in the tree.

Figure 8.4   An example for Prim's minimum spanning tree algorithm.

Exercise 8.9, where we discover that the worst case is worse than $\Theta(n^2)$. Can we do any better?

If we are to improve upon the heap time in general, clearly we need to consider implementations for which decreaseKey runs faster than $\Theta(\log n)$. However, we can afford to make getMin and deleteMin *slower* than $\Theta(\log n)$ in the trade-off. Can we think of an implementation for which decreaseKey is $O(1)$ and the others are no worse than $O(n)$? Then Equation (8.1) would evaluate to $\Theta(n^2 + m) = \Theta(n^2)$. Readers are invited to consider alternatives before continuing.

■   ■   ■

The answer is so simple, we are likely to overlook it. Simply store the information in one or more arrays, indexed by vertex number. That is, we can use a separate array for each field, or we can collect fields in an organizer class and have one array whose entries are objects in this class. We will proceed with separate arrays because it simplifies the syntax slightly. The decreaseKey operation is $O(1)$ because we simply index to the vertex and update two or three fields. The getMin operation is accomplished by scanning all n entries in the arrays; deleteMin can either use the result of the preceding getMin or do its own scan if the previous result is obsolete. One of the arrays should be the *status* flag to indicate whether each vertex is in the fringe; only these vertices are eligible for selection as the minimum. Another array contains the vertex priority. For our algorithm, the vertex priority should always correspond to fringeWgt, the weight of the candidate edge for that vertex. Similarly, the candidate edges can be maintained as an array named parent, as was done in breadth-first and depth-first searches. That is, (v, parent[v]) is the candidate edge for v. With this implementation we have arrived essentially at the classic Prim algorithm.

Although the encapsulation theme of ADT design suggests that the priority queue data structures should be hidden, we will "un-abstract" them so all parts of the algorithm have simple access. However, we still use the ADT operations to *update* these data structures.

Prim's algorithm was published before priority queues were invented, and before programming languages supported modern data structures, so its implementation was based simply on arrays. Since that time, there has been substantial research on the efficiency of priority queues. After presenting the most straightforward implementation of Prim's algorithm, we will show in Section 8.2.8 how to adapt the *pairing forest* data structure (Section 6.7.2) for this algorithm. This can serve as a guide for using other advanced implementations of the priority queue, such as the *Fibonacci heap*, which is beyond the scope of this book. (See Notes and References at the end of the chapter.)

8.2.6 Implementation

The main data structures for the algorithm (besides those for the graph itself) are three arrays, status, fringeWgt, and parent, indexed by vertex number. The classification of vertices is given by the status array and we assume that we have constants defined with the names unseen, fringe, and tree. These are strongly correlated to the colors white, gray, and black used by breadth-first search (Algorithm 7.1). Sometimes, search based on the priority queue instead of the FIFO queue is called *best-first search*.

The three main arrays status, parent, and fringeWgt are collected in the pq object for convenience in passing them to subroutines. Also, we customize the insert and decreaseKey operations slightly to record the parent, as well as the priority, of the vertex that is being inserted or updated. When pq is first constructed, all elements have the unseen status.

When insert is called for a vertex, its parent and fringeWgt acquire values, and its status changes to fringe. Note that insert is called on the start vertex to create the first fringe vertex; its parent is not a real vertex.

When deleteMin is called, the status of the currently minimum vertex is switched to tree, thereby removing it from the priority queue, in effect. This also has the effect of freezing its fringeWgt and parent fields.

In the main loop of the primMST algorithm, as each currently minimum vertex (v) is retrieved, its adjacency list is processed (by the subroutine updateFringe), to see if any of these edges (v, w), provide a lower-cost connection to the adjacent vertex w. The adjacency

	A	B	C	D	E	F	G	H	I
fringeWgt	0	2	4			7	3	3	1
parent	−1	A	B			A	A	G	G
status	tree	tree	fringe	unseen	unseen	fringe	tree	fringe	fringe

Figure 8.5 Minimum spanning tree data structure for the situation in Figure 8.4(d): Adjacency lists are not shown. Vertices are assumed to be in alphabetical order within each list.

lists are assumed to contain elements in the organizer class EdgeInfo, with two fields, to and weight as described in Section 7.2.3 and illustrated in Figure 7.11.

Figure 8.5 shows the data structure at an intermediate point in the execution of the algorithm on the example in Figure 8.4 (specifically at the point illustrated in Figure 8.4d). To make it a little easier to read, we show the vertex names as letters, as in Figure 8.4.

When the algorithm terminates, the tree edges are implied by the parent array. That is, for each vertex v other than the start vertex (root), (v, parent[v]) is an edge in the MST and fringeWgt[v] is its weight.

The counter numPQ keeps track of how many vertices have status = fringe, so that isEmpty(pq) can execute in constant time. If the input graph is not connected, then parent[v] and fringeWgt[v] will be undefined for v that are not connected to the start vertex when the algorithm terminates. This condition should never occur because a precondition of the algorithm is that the graph is connected.

Algorithm 8.1 (Prim) Minimum Spanning Tree

Input: Array adjInfo of adjacency lists that represent a weighted, connected, undirected graph $G = (V, E, W)$, as described in Section 7.2.3; n, the number of vertices; and s, the desired start vertex. All arrays should be defined for indexes 1, ..., n; the 0th entry is unused. The entries of adjInfo are lists in the EdgeList ADT, described below.

Output: A minimum spanning tree, stored in the parent array as an in-tree, and the array fringeWgt containing, for each vertex v, the weight of the edge between parent[v] and v. (The root's parent is −1.) The caller allocates and passes in the arrays, and the algorithm fills them.

Remarks: The array status[1], ..., status[n] denotes the current search status of all vertices. Undiscovered vertices are unseen; those that are discovered but not yet processed (in the priority queue) are fringe; those that are processed are tree. The adjacency lists are type EdgeList and have the standard List ADT operations (Section 2.3.2). The elements are in the organizer class EdgeInfo, with two fields, to and weight.

```
void  primMST(EdgeList[] adjInfo, int n, int s, int[] parent, float[] fringeWgt)
    int[]  status = new int[n+1];
    MinPQ  pq = create(n, status, parent, fringeWgt);

    insert(pq, s, -1, 0);
    while (isEmpty(pq) == false)
        int  v = getMin(pq);
        deleteMin(pq);
        updateFringe(pq, adjInfo[v], v);
    return;

/** See if a better connection is found to any vertex in
 * the list adjInfoOfV, and decreaseKey if so.
 * For a new connection, insert the vertex. */
void  updateFringe(MinPQ pq, EdgeList adjInfoOfV, int v)
    EdgeList  remAdj;
    remAdj = adjInfoOfV;
    while (remAdj ≠ nil)
        EdgeInfo  wInfo = first(remAdj);
        int  w = wInfo.to;
        float  newWgt = wInfo.weight;
        if (pq.status[w] == unseen)
            insert(pq, w, v, newWgt);
        else if (pq.status[w] == fringe)
            if (newWgt < getPriority(pq, w))
                decreaseKey(pq, w, v, newWgt);
        remAdj = rest(remAdj);
    return;
```

The priority queue implementation is shown in Figures 8.6 through 8.8.

8.2.7 Analysis (Time and Space)

We now complete the analysis of Algorithm 8.1 running on $G = (V, E, W)$. We pick up from Equation (8.1). The main procedure is primMST, which calls the subroutine update-Fringe, and both call the MinPQ ADT operations. Let $n = |V|$ and $m = |E|$. The number of initialization operations (create) is linear in n. The body of the **while** loop is executed n times, because each pass does a deleteMin. We need to estimate the time required for the procedure calls in this loop: isEmpty, getMin, deleteMin, and updateFringe.

A parameter of updateFringe is the list adjVerts, and the body of its **while** loop is executed once for each element of this list (the call could be omitted for the last vertex to be deleted from the priority queue). Over the course of the algorithm the adjacency list of each vertex is processed by updateFringe once, so the total number of passes through

```
class MinPQ
    // Instance fields
    int numVertices, numPQ;
    int minVertex;
    float oo;
    int[] status;
    int[] parent;
    float[] fringeWgt;

    /** Construct pq on n vertices, all "unseen". */
    MinPQ create(int n, int[] status, int[] parent, float[] fringeWgt)
        MinPQ pq = new MinPQ();
        pq.parent = parent;
        pq.fringeWgt = fringeWgt;
        pq.status = status;
        Initialize status[1], . . ., status[n] to unseen.
        pq.numVertices = n; pq.numPQ = 0;
        pq.minVertex = –1;
        pq.oo = Float.POSITIVE_INFINITY;
        return pq;
```

Figure 8.6 A priority queue implementation for Prim's minimum spanning tree algorithm, part 1: data structures and ADT constructor. Arrays have one element per graph vertex; the element with index 0 is unused.

the body of the **while** loop is about $2m$. One pass through that loop calls first, rest, and getPriority, which we assume are in $\Theta(1)$, and it also calls insert or decreaseKey. For the implementation given in Figure 8.7, insert and decreaseKey are also in $\Theta(1)$, but we should keep in mind that other implementations might not achieve this—it is a critical choice: decreaseKey might be called for almost all edges of G, a total of about $m - n$ calls. For our chosen implementation, the total time for all invocations of updateFringe is in $\Theta(m)$.

So far it looks as though the running time of the algorithm may be linear in m (G is connected, so m can't be much smaller than n, but could be much larger). However, getMin is called about n times from primMST and it must call the subroutine findMin for each of these calls. The subroutine findMin does a weight comparison for each vertex "in" the priority queue, to find the minimum candidate edge. In the worst case there are no "unseen" vertices after the first updateFringe call. Then the average number of vertices requiring a weight comparison is about $n/2$, since one is deleted after each getMin call. (We focus on weight comparisons because they are unavoidable; some other implementation might avoid checking status.) This is a total of (roughly) $n^2/2$ comparisons, even if the number of edges is smaller. Again, we emphasize that the time for findMin is implementation-dependent,

```
/** Record newPar, newW as parent, priority of v
 * and make status[v] = fringe. */
void  insert(MinPQ pq, int v, int newPar, float newW)
    pq.parent[v] = newPar;
    pq.fringeWgt[v] = newW;
    pq.status[v] = fringe;
    pq.minVertex = -1;
    pq.numPQ ++;
    return

/** Record newPar, newW as parent, priority of v. */
void  decreaseKey(MinPQ pq, int v, int newPar, float newW)
    pq.parent[v] = newPar;
    pq.fringeWgt[v] = newW;
    pq.minVertex = -1;
    return

/** Delete fringe vertex with min wgt from pq. */
void  deleteMin(MinPQ pq)
    int  oldMin = getMin(pq);

    pq.status[oldMin] = tree;
    pq.minVertex = -1;
    pq.numPQ --;
    return
```

Figure 8.7 A priority queue implementation for Prim's minimum spanning tree algorithm, part 2: manipulation procedures.

and is a critical choice for the overall efficiency of primMST. Observe that deleteMin is also called about n times, but requires only $O(1)$ per call; a different implementation might shift the work from getMin to deleteMin. The pair of calls usually must be analyzed together.

Thus the worst-case running time, as well as the worst-case number of comparisons done, is in $\Theta(m + n^2) = \Theta(n^2)$. (We encourage you to investigate ways to reduce the work performed to find the minimum candidates, but see Exercises 8.7 through 8.9.)

The data structure in Figure 8.5 uses $3n$ cells in addition to those in the adjacency-list representation of the graph. This is more extra space than is used by any of the algorithms we have studied so far, and it may seem like quite a lot. However, it allows a time-efficient implementation of the algorithm. (It would be worse if the extra space requirement were in $\Theta(m)$ since for many graphs $\Theta(m) = \Theta(n^2)$).

```
boolean isEmpty(MinPQ pq)
    return (numPQ == 0);

float getPriority(MinPQ pq, int v)
    return pq.fringeWgt[v];

/** Return fringe vertex with min wgt.
 ** Return −1 if no fringe vertex remains.
 */
int getMin(MinPQ pq)
    if (pq.minVertex == −1)
        findMin(pq);
    return pq.minVertex;

// This subroutine does most of the work!
void findMin(MinPQ pq)
    int v;
    float minWgt;

    minWgt = pq.oo;
    for (v = 1; v ≤ pq.numVertices; v++)
        if (pq.status[v] == fringe)
            if (pq.fringeWgt[v] < minWgt)
                pq.minVertex = v;
                minWgt = pq.fringeWgt[v];
        // Continue loop
    return;
```

Figure 8.8   A priority queue implementation for Prim's minimum spanning tree algorithm, part 3: access functions and the findMin subroutine of getMin.

8.2.8   The Pairing Forest Interface

The general pairing forest data structure and the implementations of the priority queue operations were described in Section 6.7.2. Minor adaptations allow it to be used in Prim's algorithm.

First, the general pairing forest structure assumes that a tree node contains fields for both the element id and the priority. But the id (vertex number) is sufficient in this case because the priority of v can be accessed as fringeWgt[v]. So the steps in Section 6.7.2 that say "create newNode . . ." should be modified to say "store the priority in fringeWgt[v] and create newNode with id = v." The xref array is an additional array like status that is maintained by the priority queue ADT operations. (With some special artificial values of type Tree to represent the unseen and tree statuses, the xref array can replace the status array, as a space optimization.) What is gained by using the pairing forest? The insert and decreaseKey operations continue to run in constant time. The possible savings are in the getMin operation. In the straightforward implementation, getMin must scan the whole status array and possibly a large part of the fringeWgt array for each operation. The pairing forest has the property that only the roots of the trees in the forest are candidates for the minimum. Although it is difficult to analyze how many trees there might be at various times during the algorithm, it is clear that there will normally be multiple nodes per tree, so not all vertices need to be checked.

The precise worst-case asymptotic order is not known, in general. However, a partial optimality result has been found for a variant of the pairing forest ADT, called *two-pass pairing heaps*. For the class of graphs in which m grows as $\Theta(n^{1+c})$ for some constant $c > 0$, the amortized cost of getMin is in $\Theta(\log n)$, and the amortized cost of insert and decreaseKey are in $\Theta(1)$. These bounds imply that Prim's algorithm with two-pass pairing heaps runs in $\Theta(m + n \log n) = \Theta(m)$ on this class of graphs.

It is also known that Prim's algorithm with Fibonacci heaps runs in $\Theta(m + n \log n)$ on all graphs, which is asymptotically optimal. However, the constant factors for Fibonacci heaps have been reported to be rather large, and the operations themselves are quite complicated and difficult to implement. For these reasons the pairing heap or pairing forest is seen as a practical alternative. The subject is discussed in Notes and References at the end of the chapter.

8.2.9 Lower Bound

How much work is essential for finding a minimum spanning tree? We claim that any minimum spanning tree algorithm requires time that is in $\Omega(m)$ in the worst case because it must examine, or process in some way, every edge in the graph. To see this, let G be a connected, weighted graph where each edge has weight at least 2, and suppose there were an algorithm that did nothing at all to an edge, xy, in G. Then xy is not in the output tree, T, of the algorithm. Change the weight of xy to 1. This could not change the action of the algorithm because it never examined xy. But now T fails the MST property and so, by Theorem 8.2, it is not a minimum spanning tree. In fact, to produce a lighter tree, simply add xy to T creating a cycle, and remove any other edge in that cycle. Therefore an algorithm that does not examine xy is not correct.

8.3 Single-Source Shortest Paths

In Section 7.2 we briefly considered the problem of finding the best route between two cities on a map of airline routes, such as Figure 7.8. Using as our criterion the price of the plane tickets, we observed that the best—that is, cheapest—way to get from San Diego to Sacramento was to make one stop in Los Angeles. This is one instance, or application, of a very common problem on a weighted graph: finding a minimum-weight path between two specified vertices.

It turns out that, in the worst case, it is no easier to find a minimum-weight path between a specified pair of nodes s and t than it is to find minimum-weight paths between

s and every vertex reachable from s. The latter problem is called the *single-source shortest path problem*. The same algorithm is used for both problems.

This section considers the problem of finding the minimum-weight path from a specified source vertex to every other vertex in a weighted directed or undirected graph. The weight (length, or cost) of a path is the sum of the weights on the edges in that path. When weight is interpreted as distance, a minimum-weight path is called a *shortest path*, and this is the name most often used. (It is, alas, conventional to mix the terminology of weight, cost, and length.)

How did we determine the shortest path from SD to SAC in Figure 7.8? In fact, for this small example we used a very unalgorithmic method, full of assumptions, such as that the fares are proportional to the distance between the cities and that the map is drawn approximately to scale. Then, we picked a route that "looked" short, and totaled up its cost. Finally, we checked some other paths (somewhat haphazardly) and did not notice any improvements, so we declared the problem solved. This is hardly an algorithm we would expect to program for a computer. We mention it to answer the above question honestly; people generally use very unrigorous ways to solve problems, especially on very small sets of data.

In practice, the problem of finding shortest paths in a graph arises in applications in which V may contain hundreds, thousands, or even millions of vertices. An algorithm theoretically could consider all possible paths and compare their weights, but in practice that could take a very long time, possibly centuries. To try to find a better approach, it is helpful to look at some general properties of shortest paths, and see if they suggest a more efficient approach. The algorithm we present is due to E. W. Dijkstra. This algorithm requires that edge weights be nonnegative. Other algorithms that don't impose this requirement are mentioned in Notes and References at the end of the chapter.

8.3.1   Properties of Shortest Paths

In general, when trying to solve a large problem, we want to break it down into smaller problems. What can we say about shortest paths between distant nodes, in terms of shortest paths between less distant nodes? Can we use some sort of divide-and-conquer approach? Suppose path P is a shortest path from x to y and Q is a shortest path from y to z. Does this mean that P followed by Q is a shortest path from x to z? It does not take long to work out an example where this is not true. However, there is a subtle variation on this theme that *does* hold true. The proof of this lemma is left as an exercise.

Lemma 8.5 (Shortest path property)   In a weighted graph G, suppose that a shortest path from x to z consists of path P from x to y followed by path Q from y to z. Then P is a shortest path from x to y, and Q is a shortest path from y to z.   □

Suppose we are trying to find a shortest path from x to z. Possibly a direct edge xz exists and provides the shortest route. However, if the shortest path involves two or more edges, then the lemma tells us that it can be broken down into two paths, each with fewer edges than the whole path, and each being a shortest path in its own right. To develop an algorithm, we need to establish some organized scheme for breaking down paths.

Example 8.3   A busload of tourists

Another useful insight can be gained by thinking of a physical process in connection with shortest paths from a source vertex s. Think of the graph as a collection of islands connected by one-way bridges, as in Example 7.7, but now the bridges are of various lengths. The length of the bridge for edge uv is $W(uv)$.

Imagine a busload of tourists all departing from a source vertex s at time zero, as in that example. They spread out from s and walk at a uniform rate, say one meter per second (about 2.5 miles per hour, but using 2.5 requires more arithmetic). When they arrive at any new island (vertex) there are a lot of them, and they divide up, with some taking each bridge (edge) leaving that island. Clearly, the first tourists to arrive at any island have followed a shortest path. In this example "shortest" can refer to time or distance.

Consider the situation when tourists are first arriving at vertex z. Suppose they are traversing an edge yz. Then a shortest path from s to z goes through y, and by Lemma 8.5, consists of a shortest path from s to y, followed by the edge yz.   ■

Simulating the Busload of Tourists

Now suppose we want to *predict* when tourists will first arrive at z, and assume we have an array, arrive, to store when tourists first arrive at each vertex. Let the vertices with an edge to z be y_1, y_2, ..., y_k. The shortest path must use one of these vertices, so we consider them all. As soon as tourists arrive at y_i, say at time arrive[y_i], we can predict that the first tourists to arrive at z will arrive *no later than* arrive[y_i] + $W(y_iz)$. Thus arrive[z] will be the minimum of these predictions. Because we have disallowed negative weights (no backwards time travel for these tourists), we don't need to worry about any y_i's where the tourists arrive later than arrive[z].

Can we use depth-first search to organize this computation? Since we need to look at vertices with edges *to* z, instead of edges leaving z, we want to search in G^T, the transpose graph (see Definition 7.10). The general idea is that the search from z would traverse to each y_i, and when backtracking from y_i to z, we would compute arrive[y_i] + $W(y_iz)$, and compare it with the value previously stored in arrive[z]. Whenever a smaller value is found, it is saved as arrive[z]. This idea is pursued in Exercise 8.21, where it is shown that it works on an important class of graphs, but not all graphs.

Another natural idea for organizing the computation is the greedy approach, since we have observed that arrive[z] can be calculated when we know the values of arrive[y_i] that are smaller than arrive[z]. The greedy heuristic in this case is to find the vertex where the tourists will arrive *soonest*, given that they have already arrived at certain vertices.

8.3.2   Dijkstra's Shortest-Path Algorithm

In this section we study Dijkstra's shortest-path algorithm; it is very similar in approach and timing to Prim's minimum spanning tree algorithm in the previous section.

Definition 8.3

Let P be a nonempty path in a weighted graph $G = (V, E, W)$ consisting of k edges xv_1, v_1v_2, ..., $v_{k-1}y$ (possibly $v_1 = y$). The *weight* of P, denoted as $W(P)$ is the sum of the weights, $W(xv_1)$, $W(v_1v_2)$, ..., $W(v_{k-1}y)$. If $x = y$, the empty path is considered to be a path from x to y. The weight of the empty path is zero.

If no path between x and y has weight less than $W(P)$, then P is called a *shortest path*, or *minimum-weight path*.   ∎

The preceding definition was carefully phrased to permit the possibility of negative weights. However, in this section we assume that weights are nonnegative. Under these circumstances, shortest paths can be restricted to simple paths.

Problem 8.1   Single-source shortest paths

We are given a weighted graph $G = (V, E, W)$ and a source vertex s. The problem is to find a shortest path from s to each vertex v.   ∎

Before proceeding, we should consider whether we need a new algorithm at all. Suppose we use the minimum spanning tree algorithm, starting at s. Will the path to v in the tree constructed by the algorithm always be a shortest path from s to v? Consider the path from A to C in the minimum spanning tree in Figure 8.4. It is *not* a shortest path; the path A, B, C is shorter.

Dijkstra's shortest-path algorithm will find shortest paths from s to the other vertices in order of increasing distance from s. The algorithm, like Prim's MST algorithm in Section 8.2, starts at one vertex (s) and "branches out" by selecting certain edges that lead to new vertices. The tree built by this algorithm is called a *shortest-path tree*. (Naming it that does not make it true; it must be proved that the paths in the tree really are shortest paths.)

Also like Prim's MST algorithm, Dijkstra's algorithm is greedy; it always chooses an edge to a vertex that appears to be "closest"; but in this case the sense of "closest" is "closest to s," not "closest to the tree." The vertices are again divided into three (disjoint) categories as follows:

1. *tree* vertices: in the tree constructed so far,
2. *fringe* vertices: not in the tree, but adjacent to some vertex in the tree,
3. *unseen* vertices: all others.

Also, as in Prim's algorithm, we keep track of only one candidate edge (the best found so far) for each fringe vertex. For each fringe vertex z, there is at least one tree vertex v such that vz is an edge of G. For each such v there is a (unique) path in the tree from s to v (possibly $s = v$); $d(s, v)$ denotes the weight of that path. Adding the edge vz to this path gives a path from s to z, and its weight is $d(s, v) + W(vz)$. The candidate edge for z is the edge vz such that $d(s, v) + W(vz)$ is minimized over all choices of vertex v in the tree built so far.

Example 8.4   Growing a shortest-path tree

Look at the graph in Figure 8.9(a). Each undirected edge is treated as a pair of directed edges in opposite directions. Assume the source vertex is A. Let us trace the steps of

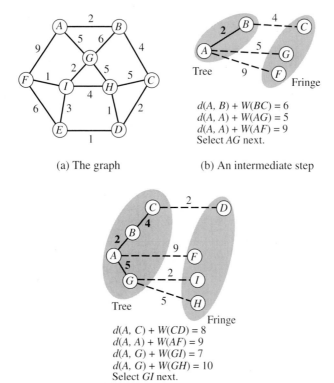

(a) The graph

(b) An intermediate step

$d(A, B) + W(BC) = 6$
$d(A, A) + W(AG) = 5$
$d(A, A) + W(AF) = 9$
Select AG next.

$d(A, C) + W(CD) = 8$
$d(A, A) + W(AF) = 9$
$d(A, G) + W(GI) = 7$
$d(A, G) + W(GH) = 10$
Select GI next.

(c) An intermediate step: CH was considered,
but not chosen, to replace GH as a candidate.

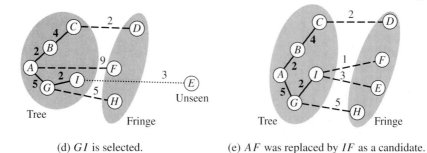

(d) GI is selected.

(e) AF was replaced by IF as a candidate.

Figure 8.9 An example for Dijkstra's shortest-path algorithm: The problem is to find a shortest
path from A to H.

growing the tree. Initially, it has only the vertex A, and $d(A, A) = 0$. The tourists get off the tour bus at A at time 0, and start walking over the bridges AB, AG, and AF. As in Example 7.7, the first tourists to reach an island snap up the bargains. Once any group of tourists arrives late, they will not be the first to arrive at any future island because the earlier group split up and explored all bridges leaving the island. The algorithm will not keep track of these groups.

In part (b) of the figure, edge AB has been added because B is closest to the source A, and $d(A, B) = 2$. A group of tourists has arrived at B at time 2, and they split up into subgroups that start walking across the bridges BA, BC, and BG. The other groups continue across AG and AF.

All vertices that can be reached by an edge from either A or B are now in the fringe, unless they are already in the tree, of course. For each fringe vertex, the candidate edge is shown as a dashed line; observe that BG is not a candidate edge. We know tourists will arrive at G no later than time 5 (from A), so those on the BG bridge will not be the earliest, and we can stop tracking them.

Based on tree edges and candidate edges, G is the fringe vertex that is closest to A, so AG is the next edge to be added to the tree, and $d(A, G) = 5$. That is, tourists arrive at G at time 5, and split up into groups exploring GA, GB, GH, and GI. The algorithm only tracks those heading for H (predicted arrival at 10) and I (predicted arrival at 7). However, the tourists on bridge BC arrive at C at time 6, so edge BC will be added next, and $d(A, C) = 6$. Tourists depart from C at time 6 on the bridges CB, CD, and CH. We can ignore those on CB because B has been visited, and we can ignore those on CH because they will arrive at H at time 11, which is later than the "competing" tourists on GH. This leads to part (c) of the figure.

Given the situation in Figure 8.9(c), the next step is to select a candidate edge and fringe vertex. We choose a candidate edge yz for which $d(s, y) + W(yz)$ is minimum. This is the weight of the path obtained by adjoining yz to the known (hopefully shortest) path from s to y. Vertex z is selected from D, F, I, and H, the current fringe vertices. In this case, GI is the selected edge, and $d(A, I) = 7$. ∎

The general structure of Dijkstra's algorithm may be described as follows:

dijkstraSSSP(G, n) *// OUTLINE*
    Initialize all vertices as *unseen*.
    Start the tree with the specified source vertex s; reclassify it as *tree*;
    define $d(s, s) = 0$.
    Reclassify all vertices adjacent to s as *fringe*.
    While there are fringe vertices:
        Select an edge between a tree vertex t and a fringe vertex v such that
        $(d(s, t) + W(tv))$ is minimum;
        Reclassify v as *tree*; add edge tv to the tree;
        define $d(s, v) = (d(s, t) + W(tv))$.
        Reclassify all *unseen* vertices adjacent to v as *fringe*.

Since the quantity $d(s, y) + W(yz)$ for a candidate edge yz may be used repeatedly, it can be computed once and saved. To compute it efficiently when yz first becomes a candidate, we also save $d(s, y)$ for each y in the tree. Thus we could use an array dist as follows:

dist[y] $= d(s, y)$ for y in the tree;

dist[z] $= d(s, y) + W(yz)$ for z on the fringe, where yz is the candidate edge to z.

As in Prim's algorithm, after a vertex and the corresponding candidate edge are selected, the information in the data structure must be updated for some fringe and previously unseen vertices.

Example 8.5   Updating distance information

In Figure 8.9(d) the vertex I and edge GI have just been selected. The candidate edge for F was AF (with dist[F] $= 9$), but now AF must be replaced by IF because IF yields a shorter path to F. We must also recompute dist[F]. On the other hand, IH does not yield a shorter path to H because dist[H] $= 10$, currently, so this edge is discarded from further consideration. The vertex E, which was unseen, is now on the fringe because it is adjacent to I, now in the tree. The edge IE becomes a candidate. These changes lead to Figure 8.9(e). Values of dist for new fringe vertices must be computed.   ■

Does this method work? The crucial step is the selection of the next fringe vertex and candidate edge. For an arbitrary candidate yz, $d(s, y) + W(yz)$ is not necessarily the shortest distance from s to z because shortest paths to z might not pass through y. (In Figure 8.9, for example, the shortest path to H does not go through G, although GH is a candidate in parts c, d, and e.) We claim that, if $d(s, y)$ is the shortest distance for each tree vertex y, and yz is chosen by minimizing $d(s, y) + W(yz)$ over all candidates, then yz does give a shortest path. This claim is proved in the following theorem.

Theorem 8.6   Let $G = (V, E, W)$ be a weighted graph with nonnegative weights. Let V' be a subset of V and let s be a member of V'. Assume that $d(s, y)$ is the shortest distance in G from s to y, for each $y \in V'$. If edge yz is chosen to minimize $d(s, y) + W(yz)$ over all edges with one vertex y in V' and one vertex z in $V - V'$, then the path consisting of a shortest path from s to y followed by the edge yz is a shortest path from s to z.

Proof   Look at Figure 8.10. Suppose $e = yz$ is chosen as indicated, and let $s, x_1, \ldots, x_r, y$ be a shortest path from s to y (possibly $y = s$). Let $P = s, x_1, \ldots, x_r, y, z$. $W(P) = d(s, y) + W(yz)$. Let $s, z_1, \ldots, z_a, \ldots, z$ be any shortest path from s to z; call it P'. Vertex z_a is chosen to be the first vertex in P' that is not in V' (possibly $z_a = z$). We must show that $W(P) \leq W(P')$. (In the algorithm, $z_{a-1}z_a$ would be a candidate edge; if $a = 1, z_0 = s$.) By the choice of e,

$$W(P) = d(s, y) + W(e) \leq d(s, z_{a-1}) + W(z_{a-1}z_a). \tag{8.2}$$

By Lemma 8.5, $s, z_1, \ldots, z_{a-1}$ is a shortest path from s to z_{a-1}, so the weight of this path

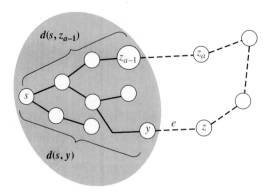

Figure 8.10 For the proof of Theorem 8.6

is $d(s, z_{a-1})$. Since $s, z_1, \ldots, z_{a-1}, z_a$ is part of the path P' and any remaining edges must have nonnegative weights,

$$d(s, z_{a-1}) + W(z_{a-1}z_a) \leq W(P'). \tag{8.3}$$

Combining Equations (8.2) and (8.3), $W(P) \leq W(P')$. ☐

Theorem 8.7 Given a directed weighted graph G with nonnegative weights and a source vertex s, Dijkstra's algorithm computes the shortest distance (weight of a minimum-weight path) from s to each vertex of G that is reachable from s.

Proof The proof is by induction on the sequence in which vertices are added to the shortest-path tree. The details are left for Exercise 8.16. ☐

8.3.3 Implementation

The shortest-path algorithm can use exactly the same Priority Queue ADT as Prim's algorithm; see Figures 8.6 through 8.8. When the algorithm terminates, the shortest-path tree edges are implied by the parent array. That is, for each vertex v other than the source vertex, (v, parent[v]) is an edge in the shortest-path tree and fringeWgt[v] is the distance from s to v. If not all vertices are reachable from the given source s, then parent[v] and fringeWgt[v] will be undefined for v that are unreachable from s. It is easy to adjust the algorithm to give these entries some special values, such as $n + 1$ and ∞.

Algorithm 8.2 (Dijkstra) Single-Source Shortest Paths

Input: Array adjInfo of adjacency lists that represent a weighted directed or undirected graph $G = (V, E, W)$, as described in Section 7.2.3; n, the number of vertices; and s, the desired start vertex. All arrays should be defined for indexes 1, ..., n; the 0th entry is unused. The entries of adjInfo are lists in the EdgeList ADT, described below.

Output: A shortest-path tree, stored in the parent array as an in-tree, and the array fringeWgt containing, for each vertex v, the shortest distance from s to v. (The root's parent is -1.) The caller allocates and passes in the arrays, and the algorithm fills them.

Remarks: The array status[1], ..., status[n] denotes the current search status of all vertices. Undiscovered vertices are unseen; those that are discovered but not yet processed (in the priority queue) are fringe; those that are processed are tree. The adjacency lists are type EdgeList and have the standard List ADT operations (Section 2.3.2). The elements are in the organizer class EdgeInfo, with two fields, to and weight.

```
void shortestPaths(EdgeList[] adjInfo, int n, int s, int[] parent, float[] fringeWgt)
    int[] status = new int[n+1];
    MinPQ  pq = create(n, status, parent, fringeWgt);

    insert(pq, s, -1, 0);
    while (isEmpty(pq) == false)
        int v = getMin(pq);
        deleteMin(pq);
        updateFringe(pq, adjInfo[v], v);
    return;


/** See if a better connection is found to any vertex in
 * the list adjInfoOfV, and decreaseKey if so.
 * For a new connection, insert the vertex. */
void updateFringe(MinPQ pq, EdgeList adjInfoOfV, int v)
    float  myDist = pq.fringeWgt[v];
    EdgeList  remAdj;
    remAdj = adjInfoOfV;
    while (remAdj ≠ nil)
        EdgeInfo  wInfo = first(remAdj);
        int  w = wInfo.to;
        float  newDist = myDist + wInfo.weight;
        if (pq.status[w] == unseen)
            insert(pq, w, v, newDist);
        else if (pq.status[w] == fringe)
            if (newDist < getPriority(pq, w))
                decreaseKey(pq, w, v, newDist);
        remAdj = rest(remAdj);
    return;
```

Analysis

The analysis in Section 8.2.7 of Prim's minimum spanning tree algorithm, Algorithm 8.1, carries over to Dijkstra's shortest path algorithm, Algorithm 8.2, without change. Dijkstra's algorithm also runs in $\Theta(n^2)$ time in the worst case. The same lower bound of $\Omega(m)$ and space requirements of $\Theta(n)$ carry over, as well.

If a significant number of vertices are expected to be unreachable, it might be more efficient to test for reachability as a preprocessing step, eliminate unreachable vertices, and renumber the remaining vertices as $1, \ldots, n_r$. The total cost would be in $\Theta(m + n_r^2)$, rather than $\Theta(n^2)$.

The pairing forest (Section 6.7.2), pairing heap, or Fibonacci heap may be used to implement the priority queue in Dijkstra's algorithm in the same manner as described in Section 8.2.8 for Prim's algorithm. The asymptotic bounds are the same: Using a Fibonacci heap gives the optimum asymptotic order of $\Theta(m + n \log n)$, but poses practical difficulties.

8.4   Kruskal's Minimum Spanning Tree Algorithm

Let $G = (V, E, W)$ be a weighted undirected graph. In Section 8.2 we studied Prim's algorithm to find a minimum spanning tree for G (with the condition that G be connected). The algorithm started at an arbitrary vertex and then branched out from it by "greedily" choosing edges with low weight. At any time, the edges chosen formed a tree. Here we examine an algorithm that uses a greedier strategy. Throughout this section all graphs are undirected graphs.

8.4.1   The Algorithm

The general outline of Kruskal's algorithm is as follows. At each step it chooses the lowest-weighted remaining edge from anywhere in the graph, but discards any edge that would form a cycle with those already chosen. At any time the edges chosen so far will form a forest but not necessarily one tree. It terminates when all edges have been processed.

```
kruskalMST(G, n)  // OUTLINE
    R = E;  // R is remaining edges.
    F = ∅;  // F is forest edges.
    while (R is not empty)
        Remove the lightest (shortest) edge, vw, from R;
        if (vw does not make a cycle in F)
            Add vw to F;
    return F;
```

Before even thinking about how to implement this idea, we should ask whether it works. Since the graph may not be connected, we first need a definition.

Definition 8.4   Spanning tree collection

Let $G = (V, E, W)$ be a weighted undirected graph. A *spanning tree collection* for G is a set of trees, one for each connected component of G, such that each tree is a spanning tree for its connected component. A *minimum spanning tree collection* is a spanning tree collection whose edges have minimum total weight, that is, a collection of minimum spanning trees.   ∎

First, is every vertex of G represented in some tree (there may be multiple trees if the graph is not connected)? Let v be an arbitrary vertex of G. If at least one edge is incident upon v, then the first edge withdrawn from S that is incident upon v will be taken into F. But if v is an isolated vertex (no incident edges), then it will *not* be represented in F, and it needs to be considered separately if it is not to be overlooked.

The next question is whether a spanning tree collection is created by the algorithm, assuming that G has no isolated vertices. That is, is there exactly one tree in F for each connected component of G? The following lemma provides some insight into this question. The proof is easy and is left as an exercise.

Lemma 8.8   Let F be a forest; that is, any undirected acyclic graph. Let $e = vw$ be an edge that is not in F. There is a cycle consisting of e and edges in F if and only if v and w are in the same connected component of F. $\square$

Now suppose some connected component of G corresponds to two or more trees in the forest F that is computed by Kruskal's algorithm. There must be some edge in G that goes between two of these trees, call it vw; that is, v and w are in different connected components of F. Therefore, when the algorithm processed vw, it must have formed a cycle in the forest at that time, say F', because vw was not added to F'. By Lemma 8.8, v and w were in the same connected component of F at that time. But then it is impossible that v and w are in different connected components of F when the algorithm terminates. Therefore F can contain only one tree for each connected component of G.

Having determined that the algorithm computes *some* spanning tree collection, the last question of correctness is whether the trees are of minimum weight. This question is answered by the following theorem, the proof of which is left as an exercise.

Theorem 8.9   Let $G = (V, E, W)$ be a weighted undirected graph. Let $F \subseteq E$. If F is contained in a minimum spanning tree collection for G and if e is an edge of minimum weight in $E - F$ such that $F \cup \{e\}$ has no cycles, then $F \cup \{e\}$ is contained in a minimum spanning tree collection for G. $\square$

The algorithm starts with $F = \emptyset$ and continues adding edges to F until all edges have been processed. The theorem guarantees that F is always contained within some minimum spanning tree collection, and we have already realized that the final value of F *is* a spanning tree collection for G, except for trivial trees, each consisting of an isolated node and no edges.

We are now ready to consider implementation methods. To access the edges in order of increasing weight, a minimizing priority queue is used (Section 2.5.1), such as a heap (Section 4.8.1). The edges of F can be stored in a list, stack, or other convenient data structure.

One problem to be resolved is how to determine whether an edge will form a cycle with others already in F. Lemma 8.8 provides the criterion: If v and w are in the same connected component of F, then (and only in this case) adding edge vw to F will create a cycle. Therefore we would like to keep track of the connected components of F as it is

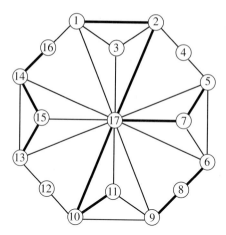

Figure 8.11   The darkened edges are in the subgraph F. The equivalence classes are $\{1, 2, 5, 7, 10, 11, 17\}$, $\{6, 8, 9\}$, $\{13, 14, 15, 16\}$, $\{3\}$, $\{4\}$, and $\{12\}$.

built. In particular, given two vertices v and w, we want to be able to determine efficiently whether they are in the same connected component of F. The methodology of dynamic equivalence relations that was developed in Section 6.6 can be applied.

We define a relation, "$\equiv$", on the vertices in a subgraph F by $v \equiv w$ if and only if v and w are in the same connected component of F. It is easy to check that $\equiv$ is an equivalence relation. (See Figure 8.11 for an example.) Thus, by Lemma 8.8, an edge vw is chosen by Kruskal's algorithm if and only if $v \not\equiv w$. Initially, each vertex of G is in the $\equiv$ relation as a separate equivalence class, and F is a graph consisting of all vertices in G, but no edges (this also takes care of isolated vertices). Each time an edge is chosen, the subgraph F and the equivalence relation $\equiv$ change; each new edge causes two connected components, or two equivalence classes, to be merged into one.

Maintaining and querying the $\equiv$ relation are accomplished through the Union-Find ADT. Recall that $\mathrm{find}(v)$ returns the unique identifier of the equivalence class of vertex v and if s and t are identifiers for distinct equivalence classes, then $\mathrm{union}(s, t)$ merges them.

Algorithm 8.3   (Kruskal) Minimum Spanning Tree

Input: $G = (V, E, W)$, a weighted graph, with $|V| = n$, $|E| = m$.

Output: F, a subset of E which forms a minimum spanning tree for G, or a minimum spanning tree collection if G is not connected.

Remarks: The structure sets defined in the algorithm corresponds to the equivalence relation $\equiv$ in the discussion. The class-name qualifiers are omitted from the operations of the Union-Find ADT and the priority-queue ADT for easier readability.

```
kruskalMST(G, n, F)  // OUTLINE
    int count;
    Build a minimizing priority queue, pq, of edges of G, prioritized by weight.
    Initialize a Union-Find structure, sets, in which each vertex of G is in its
    own set.
    F = Ø;
    while (isEmpty(pq) == false)
        vwEdge = getMin(pq);
        deleteMin(pq);
        int  vSet = find(sets, vwEdge.from);
        int  wSet = find(sets, vwEdge.to);
        if (vSet ≠ wSet)
            Add vwEdge to F;
            union(sets, vSet, wSet);
    return;
```

8.4.2 Analysis

The priority queue of edges can be implemented efficiently as a heap, since the de-creaseKey operation is not used in this algorithm. It can be built in time $\Theta(m)$. Deleting all the edges requires $\Theta(m \log m)$ time in the worst case, but might be $\Theta(n \log m)$, which is the same as $\Theta(n \log n)$, if only $O(n)$ lightest edges need to be processed to construct the spanning tree collection.

As an additional optimization, if the number of connected components in G is known to be ncc, then the number of edges in the spanning tree collection is known to be $n - \text{ncc}$, and the algorithm can terminate as soon as this many edges have been added to F, which is now the minimum spanning tree collection, without processing the remaining edges. Finding the number of connected components can be done in linear time. This would make it possible to take advantage of the favorable case mentioned in the previous paragraph.

For the Union-Find operations, find might be called about $2m$ times, while union is called at most $n - 1$ times. Thus the total number of Union-Find operations done is bounded by $(2m + n)$. Assume $m \geq n$, as it normally is, to simplify the expressions. With the weighted-union, path-compression implementation of Section 6.6, the total time for these operations is in $O(m \lg^*(m))$, where $\lg^*$ is the very slowly growing function of Definition 6.9.

Thus the worst-case running time of Kruskal's MST algorithm is in $\Theta(m \log m)$. Prim's algorithm, Algorithm 8.1, is in $\Theta(n^2)$ in the worst case. Which is better depends on the relative sizes of n and m. For dense graphs, the Prim algorithm is better. For sparse graphs, Kruskal's is faster than Algorithm 8.1. However, consider the alternative of Exercise 8.9 and the fact that Prim's algorithm can use the data structures discussed in Section 8.2.8.

If the edges of G were already sorted, then a trivial priority queue could be used, and each edge could be deleted in $O(1)$ time, in which case Kruskal's algorithm would run in $O(m \lg^*(m))$ time, which is quite good.

Exercises

Section 8.2   *Prim's Minimum Spanning Tree Algorithm*

8.1   Give a connected, weighted, undirected graph and a start vertex such that neither the depth-first search tree nor the breadth-first search tree is an MST, regardless of how the adjacency lists are ordered.

8.2   Let T be any spanning tree of an undirected graph G. Suppose that uv is any edge in G that is not in T. The following proofs are easy by using the definitions of undirected tree, spanning tree, and cycle.

a.   Let G_1 be the subgraph that results from adding uv to T. Show that G_1 has a cycle involving uv, say $(w_1, w_2, \ldots, w_p, w_1)$, where $p \geq 3$, $u = w_1$ and $v = w_p$.

b.   Suppose any one edge, $w_i w_{i+1}$, is removed from the cycle created in part (a), creating a subgraph G_2 (which depends on i). Show that G_2 is a spanning tree for G.

8.3   Suppose T_1 and T_2 are distinct minimum spanning trees for graph G. Let uv be the lightest edge that is in T_2 and is not in T_1. Let xy be *any* edge that is in T_1 and is not in T_2. Show that $W(xy) \geq W(uv)$.

8.4   Prove that if the weights on the edges of a connected, undirected graph are distinct, then there is a unique minimum spanning tree.

8.5

a.   Describe a family of connected, weighted, undirected graphs G_n, for $n \geq 1$, such that G_n has n vertices and the number of weight comparisons done by Prim's MST algorithm (Algorithm 8.1) for G_n is linear in n.

b.   Describe a family of connected, weighted, undirected graphs G_n such that G_n has n vertices and Prim's MST algorithm does no comparisons among weights when G_n is the input. A comparison of a weight with ∞ (pq.oo) does not count for this purpose (because the findMin procedure can check whether minVertex is -1 to avoid it). (The algorithm will require time at least proportional to n because it must succeed in finding a minimum spanning tree.)

8.6   Execute Prim's minimum spanning tree algorithm by hand on the graph in Figure 8.4(a), showing how the data structures evolve. Clearly indicate which edges become part of the minimum spanning tree and in what order.

a.   Start at vertex G.

b.   Start at vertex H.

c.   Start at vertex I.

8.7   Let $G = (V, E, W)$ where $V = \{v_1, v_2, \ldots, v_n\}$, $E = \{v_1 v_i \mid i = 2, \ldots, n\}$, and for $i = 2, \ldots, n$, $W(v_1 v_i) = 1$. With this G as input and v_1 as the start vertex, how many comparisons of edge weights will be done by Prim's MST algorithm, in total, to find minimum candidate edges? (Working through this problem may suggest to you that saving information about the ordering of the weights of candidate edges could decrease the number of comparisons. The next two exercises suggest that it may not be easy.)

8.8

a.   How many comparisons of edge weights will be done by the MST algorithm, in total, if the input is a complete undirected graph with n vertices and v_1 is the start vertex?

b.   Suppose the vertices are $v_1, \ldots, v_n$, and $W(v_i v_j) = n + 1 - i$ for $1 \leq i < j \leq n$. How many of the edges are candidate edges at some time during the execution of the algorithm?

⋆ **8.9**   Consider storing candidate edges in a min-heap (a heap where each node is smaller than its children, see Section 4.8.1). In this exercise we evaluate Prim's MST algorithm under this assumption, for graphs in general, and for certain restricted classes of graphs. Use $|V| = n$ and $|E| = m$.

a.   Find the asymptotic order of the number of comparisons of edge weights that will be done by Prim's MST algorithm, based on Equation (8.1) in the worst case. Remember to consider the work that is necessary for the decreaseKey operation, when a candidate edge is replaced by another.

b.   A *bounded-degree family of graphs* is any family for which there is a constant k such that all vertices of any graph in the family have degree at most k. Find the asymptotic order, as a function of n, of the number of comparisons of edge weights that would be done by Prim's MST algorithm on a bounded-degree family.

⋆ c.   A *planar graph* is a connected graph that can somehow be drawn in a plane without any crisscrossing edges. For this class, Euler's theorem states that $|V| - |E| + |F| = 2$, where $|F|$ is the number of faces (regions surrounded by edges, plus one region from the outer edges to infinity) formed when the graph is drawn. For example, if the graph is a simple triangle, it has two faces—one inside the triangle and one outside. The outer face extends to infinity in all directions. Find the asymptotic order, as a function of n, of the number of comparisons of edge weights that would be done by Prim's MST algorithm on a planar graph. *Hint*: Note that all edges are in two faces.

8.10   The use of the priority queue can be simplified by initially entering all vertices with a fringeWgt of "∞" and a status of fringe. The value "∞" merely needs to be bigger than the cost of any edge that is actually in the graph; it doesn't have to really represent "infinity." Then decreaseKey will lower the cost of a vertex below "∞" when the first connection for a vertex is found, and insert will not be needed. Show the modifications of Algorithm 8.1 and the priority queue operations that implement this strategy. Does it improve the asymptotic order?

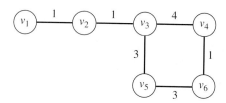

Figure 8.12   Graph for Exercise 8.13

8.11   Suppose we want to use Prim's algorithm on a weighted, undirected graph that is not known to be connected. Show how to modify Prim's algorithm to find a minimum spanning tree collection (Definition 8.4) without first finding the connected components. Try not to increase the asymptotic order of the algorithm.

Section 8.3   Single-Source Shortest Paths

8.12   Give a weighted directed graph and a source vertex such that neither the depth-first search tree nor the breadth-first search tree is a shortest-path tree, regardless of how the adjacency lists are ordered.

8.13   For the graph in Figure 8.12, indicate which edges would be in the minimum spanning tree constructed by Prim's MST algorithm (Algorithm 8.1), and which would be in the tree constructed by Dijkstra's shortest-path algorithm (Algorithm 8.2) using v_1 as the source.

8.14   Will Dijkstra's shortest-path algorithm (Algorithm 8.2) work correctly if weights may be negative? Justify your answer by an argument or a counterexample.

8.15   Here are the adjacency lists (with edge weights in parentheses) for a digraph. For convenience, the digraph is also shown in Figure 8.13.

$$A: B(4.0), F(2.0)$$
$$B: A(1.0), C(3.0), D(4.0)$$
$$C: A(6.0), B(3.0), D(7.0)$$
$$D: A(6.0), E(2.0)$$
$$E: D(5.0)$$
$$F: D(2.0), E(3.0)$$

a.   This digraph has *three* shortest paths from C to E (i.e., all with the *same* total weight). Find them. (List the sequence of vertices in each path.)

b.   Which of these paths is the one that would be found by Dijkstra's shortest-path algorithm, with $s = C$? (Give a convincing explanation or show the main steps of the algorithm.)

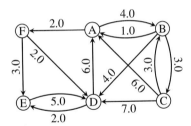

Figure 8.13   Digraph for Exercise 8.15

c.   Execute Dijkstra's shortest-path algorithm by hand on this graph, showing how the data structures evolve, with $s = A$. Clearly indicate which edges become part of the shortest-path tree and in what order.

d.   Repeat part (c) with $s = B$.

e.   Repeat part (c) with $s = F$.

8.16   Complete the proof of Theorem 8.7.

8.17   Explain how to find an actual shortest path from s to a specified vertex z using the parent array that is filled by Dijkstra's shortest-path algorithm.

⋆ **8.18**   Let $G = (V, E, W)$ be a weighted graph, and let s and z be distinct vertices. As Exercise 8.15 suggests, there can be more than one shortest path from s to z. Explain how to modify Dijkstra's shortest-path algorithm to determine the number of distinct shortest paths from s to z. Assume all edge weights are positive.

8.19   Consider the problem of finding just the distance, but not a shortest path, from s to a specified vertex z in a weighted graph. Outline a modified version of Dijkstra's shortest-path algorithm to do this with the aim of eliminating as much work and extra space usage as possible. Indicate what changes, if any, you would make in the data structure used by the algorithm, and indicate what work or space you would eliminate.

8.20   Some graph algorithms are written with the assumption that the input is always a complete graph (where an edge has weight ∞ or 0 to indicate its absence from the graph for which the user really wants to solve the problem). Such algorithms are usually shorter and "cleaner" because there are fewer cases to consider. In the algorithms in Sections 8.2 and 8.3, for example, there would be no unseen vertices since all vertices would be adjacent to vertices in the tree constructed so far.

a.   With the aim of simplifying as much as possible, rewrite Dijkstra's shortest-path algorithm with the assumption that $G = (V, E, W)$ is a complete graph and $W(uv)$ may be ∞. Describe any changes you would make in the data structures used.

b. Compare your algorithm and data structures with those in the text, using the criteria of simplicity, time (worst case and other cases), and space usage (for graphs with many edges that have weight ∞ and for graphs with few).

⋆ **8.21** Consider this general approach to computing shortest paths from vertex s in a weighted graph $G = (V, E, W)$. Form G^T, the transpose graph (see Definition 7.10). Define an array named arrive with indexes $1, \ldots, n$, and all entries initialized to ∞. Perform a complete depth-first search of G^T, and compute values for arrive[v] according to this scheme:

1. arrive[s] = 0;
2. When backtracking from w to v, compute arrive[w] + $W(wv)$ and compare it with the value previously stored in arrive[v]. Whenever a smaller value is found, it is saved as arrive[v].

The intention is that arrive[v] will be the shortest-path distance from s to v when the DFS is finished.

a. Complete the above sketch by inserting statements into the depth-first search skeleton for directed graphs, Algorithm 7.3.

b. Does the algorithm find shortest paths in all cases? Prove it does or find a counter-example.

c. On what (well-known) class of graphs does the algorithm find shortest paths in all cases? Prove your answer. *Hint*: What constraint on the graph would permit the proof in part (b) to be completed successfully?

Section 8.4   Kruskal's Minimum Spanning Tree Algorithm

8.22 Prove Lemma 8.8.

8.23 Prove Theorem 8.9. *Hint*: Use the MST property (Definition 8.2).

8.24 Find the minimum spanning tree for the graph in Figure 8.14 that would be output by Kruskal's algorithm (Algorithm 8.3), assuming the edges are sorted as shown.

Additional Problems

8.25 In this exercise you will develop a *best-first search* skeleton, analogous to the breadth-first search skeleton in Chapter 7.

a. Consider whether to use the strategy of Exercise 8.20 (no inserts, create the priority queue with all elements present and infinite weights where needed) or the MinPQ ADT given in Figures 8.6 through 8.8 as the basis for your skeleton. Which offers the most generality? Which is likely to be more efficient? Are both about equal?

b. Write the skeleton with whichever strategy you chose.

c. Show how to annotate your skeleton (insert a few statements at specified points) to produce Prim's algorithm, and how to produce Dijkstra's algorithm.

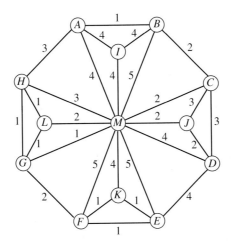

Figure 8.14   Sorted edges: *AB, EF, EK, FK, GH, GL, GM, HL, BC, CM, DJ, FG, JM, LM, AH, CD, CJ, HM, AI, AM, BI, DE, DM, IM, KM, BM, EM, FM.*

d. Discuss the interface of pairing forests with your skeleton. Is the interface independent of the applications your skeleton might be used for, or does it need to be modified depending on each application?

8.26   Suppose we want to find a shortest path from *s* to *w* in a graph *G* where the length of a path is simply the number of edges in the path (e.g., to plan an airline trip with the fewest stops). Which of the algorithms or traversal strategies from this chapter or Chapter 7 *could* you use? Which one *would* you use, and why?

8.27   Suppose you need to determine if a large graph is connected. It has *n* vertices, $V = \{1, \ldots, n\}$, and *m* edges, where *m* is quite a bit larger than *n*. The input will consist of the integers *n* and *m* and a sequence of edges (pairs of vertices). You don't have enough space to store the whole graph; you can use *cn* units of space, where *c* is a small constant, but you can't use space proportional to *m*. Thus you can process each edge when you read it, but you can't save edges or reread them. Describe an algorithm to solve the problem. How much time does your algorithm take in the worst case?

Programs

Each of the following program assignments requires a procedure that reads in a description of an edge-weighted graph and sets up the adjacency lists. A minor modification of the graph-loading procedure in Chapter 7 is sufficient. Assume the input contains the number of vertices followed by a sequence of lines, with each line containing a pair of nodes representing one edge and a third number representing its weight. Write this procedure so that, with small changes, it could be used for any of the problems.

Test data should be chosen so that all aspects of a program are tested. Include some of the examples in the text.

1. Prim's minimum spanning tree algorithm, Algorithm 8.1. The program should complete the algorithm, building a data structure to record the minimum spanning tree found. Output should be from a separate procedure and should include the graph, the set of edges in the tree, along with their weights, and the total weight of the tree.

2. Kruskal's minimum spanning tree algorithm, Algorithm 8.3. The program should complete the algorithm, building a data structure to record the minimum spanning tree found. Output should be from a separate procedure and should include the graph, the set of edges in the tree, along with their weights, and the total weight of the tree.

3. Dijkstra's shortest-path algorithm, Algorithm 8.2. The program should complete the algorithm, building a data structure to record the shortest paths found. Output should be from a separate procedure and should include the graph (or digraph), the source vertex, each vertex reachable from the source, along with the edges in the shortest path found to that vertex, their weights, and the total weight of the path.

4. After writing Program 1 or Program 3, modify it to use pairing forests for the priority queue. Run timing tests on some large graphs and compare the timings before and after the modifications.

Notes and References

The first minimum spanning tree algorithm is from Prim (1957). The single-source shortest-path algorithm is from Dijkstra (1959), but that paper does not discuss implementation. Dijkstra (1959) also describes a minimum spanning tree algorithm like Prim's. The terminology for categorizing vertices in Sections 8.2 and 8.3 (e.g., *fringe vertex*) is from Sedgewick (1988). Alternatives for implementing priority queues, such as pairing forests, pairing heaps, and Fibonacci heaps are discussed in Notes and References for Chapter 6. The upper bound for Prim's and Dijkstra's algorithms, using pairing heaps, on graphs for which $m = \Theta(n^{1+c})$ is from Fredman (1999).

In some applications it is necessary to find a spanning tree with minimum weight among those that satisfy other criteria required by the problem, so it is useful to have an algorithm that generates spanning trees in order by weight so that each can be tested for the other criteria. Gabow (1977) presents algorithms that do this.

Kruskal's strategy for finding minimum spanning trees is from Kruskal (1956). The implementation using equivalence programs was apparently folklore; it is mentioned in Hopcroft and Ullman (1973), who report that M. D. McIlroy and R. Morris carried out such an implementation. Much of the material in this section, plus additional applications and extensions, appear in Aho, Hopcroft, and Ullman (1974). Additional shortest-path algorithms, including some that do not require nonnegative edge weights, can be found in Cormen, Leiserson, and Rivest (1990).

In Section 7.2 we listed several questions that might be asked about graphs and digraphs. One of the questions that we did not answer in this book is: How much of a commodity can flow from one vertex to another given capacities of the edges? This is the network flow problem; it has a rich variety of solutions and applications. Interested readers may consult Even (1979), Ford and Fulkerson (1962), Tarjan (1983), Wilf (1986), and Cormen, Leiserson, and Rivest (1990).

9

Transitive Closure, All-Pairs Shortest Paths

9.1 Introduction

This chapter studies two related problems that can be informally described as answering the following questions about *all* pairs of vertices in a graph:

1. Is there a path from u to v?
2. What is the *shortest* path from u to v?

In Chapters 7 and 8 we saw algorithms for these problems for the cases where the first vertex is special, and only the second vertex ranges over the whole graph. In this chapter, we investigate the more global problem.

The main algorithmic idea presented in this chapter has very broad application. It was discovered independently, and for different applications, by Kleene (for synthesis of a regular language, not covered in this book), by Warshall (for transitive closure), and by Floyd (for all-pairs shortest paths). Consequently, it is sometimes called the Kleene-Floyd-Warshall algorithm. It is applicable to a whole class of problems called *semi-ring closure* problems, which are beyond the scope of this book. See Notes and References at the end of the chapter for further reading.

9.2 The Transitive Closure of a Binary Relation

In this section we define *transitive closure* in terms of binary relations, and look at its relationship to paths in directed graphs. We also introduce some notation that is used throughout the chapter. We then examine a few straightforward approaches to computing the transitive closure. Later sections will present more sophisticated algorithms.

9.2.1 Definitions and Background

Let S be a set with elements $s_1, s_2, \ldots$. Recall from Section 1.3.1 that a *binary relation* on S is a subset, say A, of $S \times S$. If $(s_i, s_j) \in A$, we say that s_i is A-related to s_j and use the notation $s_i A s_j$.

Suppose S has n elements. The relation A can be represented by an $n \times n$ Boolean matrix with entries

$$a_{ij} = \begin{cases} true & \text{if } s_i A s_j \\ false & \text{otherwise.} \end{cases}$$

We will start with this representation, but later we will also consider representations using bits 1 and 0 for *true* and *false*; also, diagrams show 1 and 0. For Boolean matrices, the term *zero matrix*, denoted as 0, means the matrix in which all entries are *false*, and the *identity matrix*, denoted as I, means the matrix in which all entries are *false* except for those on the main diagonal (a_{ii}), which are *true*.

The adjacency relation on the set of vertices of a graph, used extensively in Chapter 7, is an important example of a relation. Other common examples of relations are equivalence relations and partial orders. Conversely, any binary relation A on set S can be interpreted as the directed graph

$$G = (S, A); \tag{9.1}$$

that is, interpret elements of S as the vertices, and ordered pairs in A as the edges.

We will use the same (capital) letter to denote a relation and its matrix representation (which assumes a particular ordering on the elements of the underlying set), and the corresponding lowercase letters for the matrix entries. Unless otherwise stated, we assume the set in question is $S = \{s_1, \ldots, s_n\}$.

Boolean Operator Notation

In the pseudocode we will use the mathematical symbols "$\wedge$", "$\vee$", and "$\neg$" for the logical operators *and, or,* and *not,* respectively. Sometimes, "$\vee$" is called the *Boolean sum,* following the custom in electrical engineering of using the symbols "$+$" for binary *or* and Σ for multi-way *or;* we will use this notation in certain cases. This notation should not be confused with the *exclusive or* operator (also denoted as "$+$" sometimes); this chapter does not use *exclusive or.* For Boolean matrices, $A \vee B$ means that each entry is computed as $(a_{ij} \vee b_{ij})$. (The definitions for the other logical operators are similar, but we will not have occasion to use them.)

Transitive Closure

Recall from Definition 1.2 that a relation A on S is *transitive* if and only if for all s_i, s_j, and s_k in S: $s_i A s_j$ and $s_j A s_k$ implies $s_i A s_k$. Equivalence relations and partial orders are transitive relations. Usually, the adjacency relation for a graph is not transitive.

Definition 9.1   Transitive closure

Let S be a set and let A be a binary relation on S. Let $G = (S, A)$, as in Equation (9.1). The *reflexive transitive closure* of A (called the *transitive closure* of A for short) is the binary relation R defined by: $s_i R s_j$ if and only if there is a path from s_i to s_j in G. The transitive closure of the adjacency relation for a graph is also called the *reachability relation.*

Note that the (reflexive) transitive closure of A is reflexive because there is a path from each vertex to itself of length zero. The *irreflexive transitive closure* of A is defined similarly except that the path from s_i to s_j must be nonempty.   ∎

The transitive closure of a transitive and reflexive relation A is the relation A itself. More generally, it can be shown that the transitive closure of any relation A is the *minimum* relation R such that $A \subseteq R$ and R is transitive and reflexive.

Example 9.1   Transitive closure of a relation

For the relation A below, the transitive closure is R.

$$A = \begin{bmatrix} 0 & 1 & 0 & 0 & 1 \\ 0 & 0 & 0 & 1 & 0 \\ 0 & 1 & 0 & 0 & 0 \\ 0 & 0 & 1 & 0 & 0 \\ 0 & 0 & 0 & 1 & 0 \end{bmatrix}, \quad R = \begin{bmatrix} 1 & 1 & 1 & 1 & 1 \\ 0 & 1 & 1 & 1 & 0 \\ 0 & 1 & 1 & 1 & 0 \\ 0 & 1 & 1 & 1 & 0 \\ 0 & 1 & 1 & 1 & 1 \end{bmatrix}.$$

We can verify that R is transitive by inspection. For example, $s_1 R s_5$ and $s_5 R s_3$, so it should be the case that $s_1 R s_3$, and it is. ∎

In Sections 9.2, 9.3, 9.5, and 9.6 we study a variety of methods for finding the transitive closure of a relation. The application to graphs is a useful one. The form in which the input is given will depend on how the problem arises in a particular application. We assume throughout that $|S| = n$ and $|A| = m$.

9.2.2   Finding the Reachability Matrix by Depth-First Search

A fairly obvious way to construct R, the reachability matrix for a digraph $G = (S, A)$, is to do a depth-first search (see Section 7.3) from each vertex to find all other vertices that can be reached from it. Initially R would be the zero matrix. Visiting, or processing, a vertex s_j encountered in the depth-first search from s_i would consist of assigning *true* to r_{ij}. Thus each depth-first search fills one row of R. This may seem overly simpleminded and inefficient since during a depth-first search from, say, s_i, entries may be made in rows other than the ith row; specifically, when a vertex s_j is encountered, r_{kj} may be assigned *true* for all k such that s_k is on the path from s_i to s_j. These vertices s_k are gray and may be found on the stack. How significant is this modification? Does it eliminate the need to do a depth-first search from s_k? How does it affect the amount of work done in the worst case?

Since depth-first search was illustrated by many examples in Chapter 7, we will not work out the details of an algorithm here, but just make a few comments about the amount of work done. If the adjacency list structure described in Chapter 7 is used for G and a depth-first search is done for each vertex, the worst-case running time will be in $\Theta(nm)$. Inserting *true*'s in more than one row of R during each depth-first search, as just suggested, can improve the algorithm's behavior for many graphs, but the worst case will still be in $\Theta(nm)$. (See Exercise 9.2.)

In Chapter 7 we defined the condensation of a digraph. Informally, the condensation is the digraph obtained by collapsing each strongly connected component to a single point; it is acyclic. We mentioned that some problems may be simplified by working with the condensation instead of the original digraph. The reachability relation for a digraph $G = (S, A)$ can be computed as follows:

1. Find the strong components of G (in $\Theta(n + m)$ time). Let $G{\downarrow}$ be the condensation of G.

2. Find the reachability relation for $G{\downarrow}$. (Any of the methods presented in this chapter can be used.)

3. Expand the reachability relation for $G{\downarrow}$ by replacing each vertex of $G{\downarrow}$ by all the vertices in G that were collapsed to it ($O(n^2)$ time).

The amount of work done at step 2 and hence by this method as a whole depends on the particular digraph G. If G has several large strong components, reduction to $G{\downarrow}$ may save a lot of time.

Efficient depth-first search uses adjacency lists. In the next section we present a fairly simple $\Theta(n^3)$ algorithm for finding the reachability matrix using the adjacency matrix as the digraph representation.

9.2.3 Transitive Closure by Shortcuts

If we interpret a binary relation A on a finite set S as a digraph, then finding elements of R, the transitive closure of the relation, corresponds to inserting edges in the digraph. In particular, for any pair of edges $s_i s_k$ and $s_k s_j$ inserted so far, we add the edge $s_i s_j$. That is, we can conclude that $s_i R s_j$ if we already know that, for some k, $s_i R s_k$ and $s_k R s_j$. We can think of $s_i R s_j$ as a "shortcut" in the corresponding digraph that allows us to get from s_i to s_j in one step instead of two. Relation R is transitive if there are no more shortcuts that can be added. Thus we can easily convince ourselves that the following algorithm computes R.

Algorithm 9.1   Transitive Closure by Shortcuts

Input: A and n, where A is an $n \times n$ **boolean** matrix that represents a binary relation.

Output: R, the **boolean** matrix for the transitive closure of A.

```
void simpleTransitiveClosure(boolean[][] A, int n, boolean[][] R)
    int i, j, k;
    Copy A into R.
    Set all main diagonal entries, r_ii, to true.
    while (any entry of R changed during one complete pass)
        for (i = 1; i ≤ n; i ++)
            for (j = 1; j ≤ n; j ++)
                for (k = 1; k ≤ n; k ++)
                    r_ij = r_ij ∨ (r_ik ∧ r_kj);
```

Example 9.2   Transitive closure by shortcuts

Consider the relation A from Example 9.1. The corresponding digraph is shown in Figure 9.1(a). Self-edges are added by Algorithm 9.1 before its **while** loop begins, but are not shown in the figure. After one pass through the **while** loop of Algorithm 9.1, the edges shown as dashed lines in Figure 9.1(b) have been added. Notice that $(5, 2)$ was able to be added even though the path from 5 to 2 is length 3, because $(4, 2)$ was added earlier. However, $(1, 3)$ cannot be added during this pass. During the second pass $(1, 3)$ has been added, as shown in Figure 9.1(c). No edges are added on the third pass.   ■

Figure 9.1 illustrates that the **while** loop cannot be omitted. When a particular s_i and s_j are first considered, there may be no s_k that joins them. Later in the processing, because of the insertion of other edges, we may be able to insert $s_i s_j$; hence we must reconsider it. The complexity of Algorithm 9.1 is proportional to n^3 times the number of repetitions of the triple **for** loop. Investigating this number is left to Exercise 9.4, since we will revise the algorithm to reduce the amount of work done in Section 9.3. Later, in Section 9.5,

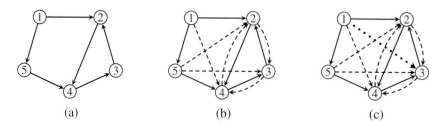

(a) (b) (c)

Figure 9.1   (a) A digraph representing a relation A. (b) Dashed lines show shortcuts added after one pass. (c) Dotted line shows another shortcut added in the second pass. Self-edges are omitted from the pictures.

we will return to the idea of Algorithm 9.1 and reinterpret it in terms of Boolean matrix multiplication.

We refer to the work done in the statement "$r_{ij} = r_{ij} \vee (r_{ik} \wedge r_{kj})$" as *processing the triple* (i, k, j). In Figure 9.1, if the triples were processed in reverse order, so that $(5, 4, 3)$ is processed early, then no triples would have to be considered twice. Is there some order that always eliminates the need for processing any triple more than once? Or, no matter what order we try, can we find an example in which repetition is required? We suggest that you try to answer these questions before proceeding.

9.3   Warshall's Algorithm for Transitive Closure

Warshall's algorithm is simply an algorithm that processes the triples mentioned in Section 9.2.3 in the correct order, specifically, with k varying in the outermost loop. First, we describe the basic algorithm, using Boolean matrices. A proof of correctness follows the algorithm. Then we describe an optimization using bit strings.

9.3.1   The Basic Algorithm

Algorithm 9.2   (Warshall) Transitive Closure

Input: A and n, where A is an $n \times n$ matrix that represents a binary relation.

Output: R, the $n \times n$ matrix for the transitive closure of A.

```
void transitiveClosure(boolean[][] A, int n, boolean[][] R)
    int i, j, k;
    Copy A into R.
    Set all main diagonal entries, rii, to true.
    for (k = 1; k ≤ n; k ++)
        for (i = 1; i ≤ n; i ++)
            for (j = 1; j ≤ n; j ++)
                rij = rij ∨ (rik ∧ rkj);
```

Clearly the total number of triples processed is n^3. Initializing R takes $\Theta(n^2)$ time so the number of matrix entries examined and/or changed for any input is in $\Theta(n^3)$.

The correctness of the algorithm hinges on the following definition, and the lemma that follows.

Definition 9.2   Highest-numbered intermediate vertex

Let G be a digraph whose vertices are indexed by the integers $1, 2, \ldots, n$, and denoted as $(s_1, s_2, \ldots, s_n)$; that is, they are considered to be an ordered sequence, not just a set. For any nonempty path in G the *highest-numbered intermediate vertex* of that path is a vertex that is neither the initial nor final vertex of the path, and has the highest index among all such vertices in the path. If the path consists of a single edge, the highest-numbered intermediate vertex is considered to be 0.   ∎

Lemma 9.1   In Algorithm 9.2, let $r_{ij}^{(0)}$ be the value of r_{ij} after the initializations, and for each k in $1, \ldots, n$, let $r_{ij}^{(k)}$ be the value of r_{ij} after the body of the "**for** $(k \ldots)$" loop is executed for the kth time. If there is any simple path from s_i to s_j $(i \neq j)$ for which the highest-numbered intermediate vertex is s_k, then $r_{ij}^{(k)} = true$.

Proof   The proof is by induction on k, the number of times the "**for** $(k \ldots)$" loop has been executed. The base case is $k = 0$, that is, when the **for** loop has not yet been executed but the initializations are completed. Then $r_{ij}^{(0)} = a_{ij}$, so $r_{ij}^{(0)} = true$ if and only if there is an edge $s_i s_j$. In this case the highest-numbered intermediate vertex is 0.

For $k > 0$, assume the lemma holds for $0 \leq h < k$. The simple path, call it P_{ij}, from s_i to s_j with highest-numbered intermediate vertex s_k can be split into two nonempty paths, P_{ik} from s_i to s_k, and P_{kj} from s_k to s_j, as shown in Figure 9.2.

The highest-numbered intermediate vertices on P_{ik} and P_{kj} have indexes strictly less than k, because P_{ij} is a simple path. By the inductive hypothesis $r_{ik}^{(h)} = true$ for some $h < k$. But once r_{ik} becomes *true*, due to the "∨" operator, it remains *true*, so

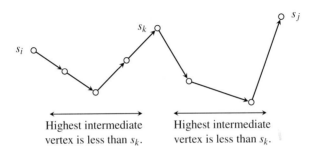

Highest intermediate vertex is less than s_k.   Highest intermediate vertex is less than s_k.

Figure 9.2   A path from s_i to s_j with highest-numbered intermediate vertex s_k. (Vertical positions of vertices reflect their vertex numbers.)

$r_{ik}^{(k-1)} = true$. A similar argument holds for $r_{kj}^{(k-1)}$. Therefore the execution of the statement "$r_{ij} = r_{ij} \vee (r_{ik} \wedge r_{kj})$" makes $r_{ij}^{(k)}$ *true*. $\square$

The key to the proof of Warshall's algorithm is the shape of the path in Figure 9.2, which is easy to remember, because it looks like a W in this example. The important part of this shape is the middle peak; other aspects may vary considerably.

Theorem 9.2   When Algorithm 9.2 terminates, R is the matrix representing the transitive closure of A.

Proof   Note that a path exists from s_i to s_j if and only if a *simple* path exists from s_i to s_j. By initialization, each r_{ii} is *true*. By Lemma 9.1, r_{ij} is *true* for all pairs such that there is a nonempty simple path from s_j to s_j (since the final value of r_{ij} is $r_{ij}^{(n)}$, and once $r_{ij}^{(k)}$ is *true* it ensures that $r_{ij}^{(n)}$ will be true). For any $s_i \neq s_j$, since r_{ij} is initialized to *false* unless there is an edge (s_i, s_j), and r_{ij} can only be set to *true* inside the loop when a simple path is found, it follows that r_{ij} is *false* if there is *no* path from s_i to s_j. $\square$

9.3.2 Warshall's Algorithm for Bit Matrices

If the matrices A and R are stored with one entry per bit, then Warshall's algorithm has the following fast implementation using the bitwise *or* (or Boolean *sum*, or union) instruction available on most large general-purpose computers. In Java, C, and C++ bitwise *or* on integers is implemented as the "|" operator. In our pseudocode we continue to use "$\vee$".

Definition 9.3   Bit string, bit matrix, bitwiseOR

A *bit string* of length n is a sequence of n bits occupying contiguous storage, beginning on a computer-word boundary, and being padded out to a computer-word boundary at the end, if needed. That is, if a computer word holds c bits, then a bit string of n bits is stored in an array of $\lceil n/c \rceil$ computer words.

A *bit matrix* is an array of bit strings, with each bit string representing one row of the matrix. If A is a bit matrix, then $A[i]$ denotes the ith row of A and is a bit string. Also, a_{ij} denotes the jth bit of $A[i]$.

The procedure bitwiseOR(a, b, n), where a and b are bit strings and n is an integer, is defined to compute $a \vee b$ bitwise for n bits and leave the result in a.   ∎

Algorithm 9.3   (Warshall) Transitive Closure for Bit Matrices

Input: A and n as in Algorithm 9.2 but A is a bit matrix. (We assume for the pseudocode that the class BitMatrix has been defined.)

Output: R, the transitive closure of A, also as a bit matrix.

```
void warshallBitMatrices(BitMatrix A, int n, BitMatrix R)
    int i, k;
    Copy A into R.
    Set all r_ii to 1.
    for (k = 1; k ≤ n; k ++)
        for (i = 1; i ≤ n; i ++)
            if (r_ik == 1)
                bitwiseOR(R[i], R[k], n);
```

At most n^2 bitwise *or*'s are done on rows of R. However, a row may not fit in one memory word and more than one *or* instruction may be needed to implement bitwiseOR. (On some computers one machine instruction will compute the Boolean *or* of two long bit strings, say, up to 256 bytes—that is, 2048 bits—though the time required to execute the instruction depends on the length of the operands.) The number of *or*'s required for each row is $\lceil n/c \rceil$, where c is the word size (or the size of the operand of the Boolean *or* instruction), so Algorithm 9.3 does $\lceil n^3/c \rceil$ Boolean *or* instructions in the worst case. The complexity is in $\Theta(n^3)$, but the constant multiple of n^3 is small.

9.4 All-Pairs Shortest Paths in Graphs

In Chapter 8 we studied Dijkstra's algorithm (Algorithm 8.2), which finds a shortest path and the distance between a specified *source vertex* and all other vertices in a weighted graph. The algorithm uses the adjacency list structure and runs in $\Theta(n^2)$ time in the worst case. (It requires that there be no negative weights.) Now we consider the following problem:

Problem 9.1   All-pairs shortest paths

Given a weighted graph $G = (V, E, W)$ with $V = \{v_1, \ldots, v_n\}$, represented by the weight matrix with entries

$$w_{ij} = \begin{cases} W(v_i v_j) & \text{if } v_i v_j \in E, \\ \infty & \text{if } v_i v_j \notin E \text{ and } i \neq j, \\ \min(0, W(v_i v_i)) & \text{if } v_i v_i \in E, \\ 0 & \text{if } v_i v_i \notin E, \end{cases} \qquad (9.2)$$

compute the $n \times n$ matrix D defined by d_{ij} = the shortest-path distance from v_i to v_j. (The *distance* is the weight of a minimum-weight path.)   ∎

See Figure 9.3 for an example. The problem may be extended to require a *routing table* from which shortest paths can be extracted. If negative-weight cycles exist, some pairs of vertices will not have a shortest path defined—paths can be made shorter by running around this cycle arbitrarily many times.

One approach to computing D (if G has no negative weights) would be to use Algorithm 8.2 repeatedly, starting over at each vertex. However, we can use an extension of

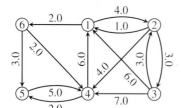

$$W = \begin{bmatrix} 0 & 4 & \infty & \infty & \infty & 2 \\ 1 & 0 & 3 & 4 & \infty & \infty \\ 6 & 3 & 0 & 7 & \infty & \infty \\ 6 & \infty & \infty & 0 & 2 & \infty \\ \infty & \infty & \infty & 5 & 0 & \infty \\ \infty & \infty & \infty & 2 & 3 & 0 \end{bmatrix} \qquad D = \begin{bmatrix} 0 & 4 & 7 & 4 & 5 & 2 \\ 1 & 0 & 3 & 4 & 6 & 3 \\ 4 & 3 & 0 & 7 & 9 & 6 \\ 6 & 10 & 13 & 0 & 2 & 8 \\ 11 & 15 & 18 & 5 & 0 & 13 \\ 8 & 12 & 15 & 2 & 3 & 0 \end{bmatrix}$$

Figure 9.3   The weight matrix and distance matrix for a digraph

Warshall's algorithm, due to R. W. Floyd, to get a more streamlined algorithm (eliminating the data structures used in Algorithm 8.2).

How do we compute $D[i][j]$? A shortest path may go through any of the other vertices in any order. As in Warshall's algorithm, we classify paths according to their highest-numbered intermediate vertex (see Definition 9.2).

Recall the shortest path property from Lemma 8.5: If a shortest path from v_i to v_j goes through intermediate vertex v_k, then the segments of that path from v_i to v_k and from v_k to v_j are themselves shortest paths. If we choose k to have the highest index of any intermediate vertex on the path from v_i to v_j (assuming the path has more than one edge), then each of the segments mentioned has a highest-numbered intermediate vertex whose index is strictly less than k. (See Figure 9.2, which shows the same idea for Warshall's algorithm.) This suggests computing a distance matrix D in rounds, according to the following recurrence equation.

$$D^{(0)}[i][j] = w_{ij}$$
$$D^{(k)}[i][j] = \min\left(D^{(k-1)}[i][j], D^{(k-1)}[i][k] + D^{(k-1)}[k][j]\right) \qquad (9.3)$$

where w_{ij} was defined in Equation (9.2). By the above observations about the shortest path property and the same argument as was used in Lemma 9.1, the following lemma can be proved (the proof is left as an exercise).

Lemma 9.3   For each k in $0, \ldots, n$, let $d_{ij}^{(k)}$ be the weight of a shortest simple path from v_i to v_j with highest-numbered intermediate vertex v_k, and let $D^{(k)}[i][j]$ be defined by Equation (9.3). Then, $D^{(k)}[i][j] \leq d_{ij}^{(k)}$.   □

Example 9.3   Computation of distance matrix

The computation of $D^{(6)}[4][3]$ for the digraph in Figure 9.3 illustrates the case in which $D^{(6)}[4][3] < d_{43}^{(6)}$. $D^{(5)}[4][3] = 13$ (because the best path from 4 to 3 using only $\{1, \ldots, 5\}$ is the path 4,1,2,3, which has weight 13). Now allowing the use of vertex 6 does not give a better path. We have $D^{(5)}[4][6] = 8$ (by the path 4,1,6), and $D^{(5)}[6][3] = 15$ (by the path 6,4,1,2,3), so $d_{43}^{(6)} = 23$.

Computing $D^{(6)}[1][5]$ illustrates a case for which vertex 6 does help. $D^{(5)}[1][5] = 10$ (because the best path from 1 to 5 using only $\{1, \ldots, 5\}$ is the path 1, 2, 4, 5, which has weight 10). Allowing the use of vertex 6 gives a shorter path: 1, 6, 5, with weight 5. We get this by adding $D^{(5)}[1][6] = 2$ and $D^{(5)}[6][5] = 3$. ∎

Equation (9.3) computes a sequence of matrices: $D^{(0)}, D^{(1)}, \ldots, D^{(n)}$. Since the computation of $D^{(k)}$ uses only $D^{(k-1)}$, we don't have to save the earlier matrices. It appears we need only two $n \times n$ matrices. In fact, we need only one; the computation can all be done in the matrix D. Since matrix entries can only decrease, if $D^{(k-1)}[i][k]$ is supposed to be used, but $D^{(k)}[i][k]$ is accessed instead, we have $D^{(k)}[i][k] \leq D^{(k-1)}[i][k] \leq d_{ik}^{(k-1)}$, and the computation may find an even better path.

Algorithm 9.4   (Floyd) All-Pairs Shortest Paths

Input: W, the weight matrix for a graph with vertices $v_1, \ldots, v_n$; and n.

Output: D, an $n \times n$ matrix such that D[i][j] is the shortest-path distance from v_i to v_j, provided that the graph has no negative-weight cycles. (If negative-weight cycles exist, some pairs of vertices will not have a shortest path defined—paths can be made shorter by running around this cycle arbitrarily many times.) Matrix D is passed in; the algorithm fills it.

```
void allPairsShortestPaths(float[][] W, int n, float[][] D)
    int i, j, k;
    Copy W into D.
    for (k = 1; k ≤ n; k ++)
        for (i = 1; i ≤ n; i ++)
            for (j = 1; j ≤ n; j ++)
                D[i][j] = min(D[i][j], D[i][k]+ D[k][j]);
```

Clearly Algorithm 9.4 does $\Theta(n^3)$ operations.

The algorithm can be modified to construct a *routing table* from which shortest paths can be extracted, as well as computing the shortest-path distance. A matrix go is a routing table if, whenever go[i][j] $= k$, then there is a shortest path from v_i to v_j whose first edge is (v_i, v_k). After arriving at k, one consults go[k][j] to find the next step. (See Exercise 9.10.)

The all-pairs shortest paths problem is more general than the problem of finding R, the reachability matrix, and Algorithm 9.4 is a generalization of Warshall's algorithm, Algorithm 9.2. R can be obtained from D simply by changing all entries less than ∞ to *true*'s and all ∞'s to *false*'s. For D, processing the triple (i, k, j) means computing

D[i][j] = min(D[i][j], D[i][k] + D[k][j]).

Here too, the order in which triples are processed is critical to getting the correct result without repeated processing.

9.5   Computing Transitive Closure by Matrix Operations

Suppose A is the matrix for a binary relation on $S = \{s_1, \ldots, s_n\}$ and we interpret A as the adjacency relation on the digraph $G = (S, A)$. Then $a_{ij} = true$ if and only if there is a path of length one from s_i to s_j since a path of length one is an edge. Suppose we define matrices $A^{(p)}$ by

$$a_{ij}^{(p)} = \begin{cases} true & \text{if there is a path of length } p \text{ from } s_i \text{ to } s_j \\ false & \text{otherwise.} \end{cases}$$

Then $A^{(0)} = I$, the identity matrix, and $A^{(1)} = A$. How can we compute $A^{(2)}$? By definition, $a_{ij}^{(2)} = true$ if and only if there is a path of length two from s_i to s_j, hence if and only if there is a vertex s_k such that $a_{ik} = true$ and $a_{kj} = true$. Thus

$$a_{ij}^{(2)} = \bigvee_{k=1}^{n} (a_{ik} \wedge a_{kj}),$$

The formula for $a_{ij}^{(2)}$ is the formula for an entry in the *Boolean matrix product*, AA, or A^2.

Definition 9.4   Boolean matrix operations

The *Boolean matrix product* $C = AB$ of $n \times n$ Boolean matrices A and B is the Boolean matrix with entries

$$c_{ij} = \bigvee_{k=1}^{n} (a_{ik} \wedge b_{kj}) \qquad \text{for } 1 \leq i, j \leq n.$$

Powers of a boolean matrix are defined as usual: for integer $p \geq 0$, A^p is the product $AA \cdots A$ (p factors).

The *Boolean matrix sum* $D = A + B$ is defined by

$$d_{ij} = a_{ij} \vee b_{ij} \qquad \text{for } 1 \leq i, j \leq n.$$

Notice that the definitions are just like arithmetic matrix product and sum, with addition replaced by "$\vee$" (*or*) and multiplication replaced by "$\wedge$" (*and*).   ■

With this notation we see that $A^{(2)} = A^2$. That is, A^2 indicates which vertices are connected by paths of length 2. It is easy to generalize and prove the following lemma by induction on p. The proof is left as an exercise (see Exercise 9.13).

Lemma 9.4   Let A be the Boolean adjacency matrix for a digraph with vertices $\{s_1, \ldots, s_n\}$. Denote elements of A^p, for $p \geq 0$, by $A^p[i][j]$. Then $A^p[i][j] = true$ if and only if there is a path of length p from s_i to s_j. That is, $A^p[i][j] = a_{ij}^{(p)}$, as defined at the beginning of the section.   □

The entries of R, the transitive closure of A, are defined by $r_{ij} = true$ if and only if there is a path of *any* length from s_i to s_j. However, the next lemma allows us to restrict our attention to certain paths; its proof is also left as an exercise.

Lemma 9.5   In a digraph with n vertices, if there is a path from vertex v to vertex w, then there is a simple path from v to w, which necessarily is of length at most $n - 1$.   □

Therefore we only need to identify paths of lengths through $n - 1$ to obtain the transitive closure. Observe that for any p and q, the (i, j)-th entry of the matrix $A^p + A^q$ is *true* if and only if there is a path of length p *or* a path of length q from s_i to s_j. Thus

$$R = \sum_{p=0}^{n-1} A^p. \tag{9.4}$$

The straightforward computation of this formula would do $n - 2$ Boolean matrix multiplications, to obtain A^2, A^3, ..., A^{n-1}. Each multiplication takes time in $\Theta(n^3)$ (by the straightforward method), so the total time is in $\Theta(n^4)$. However, we can do much better than this straightforward method.

First, we observe that it is harmless to replace the upper limit of $(n - 1)$ in Equation (9.4) by some value $s \geq n - 1$. The additional terms denote paths of length n or longer, so they are not simple paths, and they do not connect any pairs of nodes that are not already identified in R. But how can raising the upper limit help? Doesn't that just mean more work to do?

One key idea is that exponents that are powers of 2 can be computed by repeated squaring, rather than going up one power at a time. Thus we could compute A^{32} with five multiplications, by computing A^2, then A^4, then A^8, and so on. But A^{31} would require quite a few more than five. So we can obtain *certain* high powers quickly, but we need *all* powers through $n - 1$.

The second key idea involves some algebraic manipulations on the formula in Equation (9.4) to put it in a form that suggests a more efficient computation. Some of the following properties of Boolean matrix operations will be useful. Assume that A, B, and C are $n \times n$ Boolean matrices.

Absorption of $+$: $A + A = A$.

Commutativity of $+$: $A + B = B + A$.

Associativity of $+$ and $\times$: $A + (B + C) = (A + B) + C$, $A(BC) = (AB)C$.

Distributivity of $+$ over $\times$: $A(B + C) = (AB) + (AC)$, $(B + C)A = (BA) + (CA)$.

Multiplicative identity: $IA = AI = A$.

Now, let s be the least power of 2 such that $s \geq n - 1$. Then the following equation for R also holds.

$$R = \sum_{p=0}^{s} A^p = I + A + A^2 + \cdots + A^s.$$

The second key idea is to replace the sum of many powers by a power of a single matrix.

Intuitively, suppose we have a Boolean matrix that tells us about all paths of lengths 0–k. Then multiplying it by itself tells us about any path that can be made by combining one path of any length 0–k with another path of any length 0–k. This gives us all paths of lengths 0–$2k$. To get started, $(I + A)$ tells us about all paths of lengths 0–1. Then we keeping squaring the matrix until we have covered paths of lengths through $n - 1$, at least. (We can look back and see that this is almost what Algorithm 9.1 is doing inside its **while** loop.) Adding I to A is what keeps us from losing the shorter paths as the powers increase. The following lemma and theorem formalize this intuition.

Lemma 9.6 $I + A + A^2 + \cdots + A^s = (I + A)^s$, where A is a Boolean matrix and $s \geq 0$.

Proof The proof is by induction on s. The base case is $s = 0$, in which case both sides are equal to I. For $s > 0$, assume that $I + A + \cdots + A^{s-1} = (I + A)^{s-1}$, that is, the lemma equality holds for $s - 1$. Then

$$(I + A)^s = (I + A)^{s-1}(I + A) = (I + A)^{s-1}I + (I + A)^{s-1}A.$$

Using the inductive hypothesis,

$$(I + A)^{s-1}I = I + A + \cdots + A^{s-1},$$

$$(I + A)^{s-1}A = A + A^2 \cdots + A^s.$$

But $A^i + A^i = A^i$ by the absorption property, so the conclusion of the lemma follows. □

Theorem 9.7 Let A be an $n \times n$ Boolean matrix representing a binary relation. Then R, the matrix for the transitive closure of A, is $(I + A)^s$ for any $s \geq n - 1$. □

Although the theorem holds for many s, as we mentioned, we choose s to be the least power of 2 such that $s \geq n - 1$. How much work is needed to compute R using the formula of Theorem 9.7? Computing $I + A$ requires copying A and inserting *true*'s in the diagonal of A, for $\Theta(n^2)$ operations. Then $(I + A)^s$ can be computed by doing $\lg s = \lceil \lg(n - 1) \rceil$ Boolean matrix multiplications.

A Boolean matrix product can be computed as indicated by the definition in $\Theta(n^3)$ time. However, in Section 12.3.4 we will see that it is possible to perform an *integer* matrix multiplication in $o(n^3)$ time (for example, using Strassen's algorithm); the asymptotic order is about $\Theta(n^{2.81})$. (The actual exponent is $\lg 7$ and 2.81 is its approximate value.) Another alternative for Boolean matrix multiplication is to convert to an integer matrix by substituting 1 for *true* and 0 for *false*. Then use an $o(n^3)$ integer matrix multiplication algorithm, and finally convert back to a Boolean matrix by substituting *true* for all positive entries and *false* for 0. Thus R can be computed in about $\Theta(n^{2.81} \log n)$ time. Therefore R can be computed (asymptotically) faster than $\Theta(n^3)$.

None of the algorithms we have examined for transitive closure are of the same asymptotic order as the (asymptotically) fastest matrix multiplication algorithms. However, a transitive closure algorithm is known, due to I. Munro, that is about 32 times as expensive as a Boolean matrix multiplication of the same size, but is of the same asymptotic order. It is an involved use of the divide-and-conquer method. (See Notes and References at the end of the chapter.)

Multiplying Boolean matrices is a more specialized problem than multiplying matrices with real entries, and it is worth seeking specialized algorithms. In the next section, we develop a fast Boolean matrix multiplication algorithm for bit matrices.

9.6 Multiplying Bit Matrices—Kronrod's Algorithm

We use the terminology of Definition 9.3 throughout this section. Let A and B be $n \times n$ Boolean matrices stored with one entry per bit. Recall that A[i] denotes the ith row of A and is a bit string. Using the bitwise *or* instruction, the product $C = AB$ can be computed as follows, where C[i] and B[k] are the ith row of C and kth row of B, respectively.

> Initialize C to the zero matrix (all entries *false*).
> **for** (i = 1; i $\leq$ n; i ++)
>   **for** (k = 1; k $\leq$ n; k ++)
>   **if** (a_{ik} == *true*)
>   bitwiseOR(C[i], B[k], n);

(Compare this to Algorithm 9.3, where bitwiseOR was defined; notice how similar the procedures are, although they compute different things.) We may think of the bitwise *or* operation as performing a union of sets. That is, if we view A[i] as the set $\{k \mid a_{ik} = true\}$ (a subset of $\{1, 2, \ldots, n\}$), and similarly for rows of B and C, then

$$C[i] = \cup_{k \in A[i]} B[k].$$

The algorithm above does at most n^2 row unions (each of which may require several bitwise *or* machine instructions). We will derive an algorithm that does fewer row unions. The algorithm presented below is sometimes referred to as the Four Russians' Algorithm, though it is apparently the work of M. A. Kronrod, one of the four.

9.6.1 Kronrod's Algorithm

Certain groups of rows of B may appear in the unions for several different rows of C. For example, suppose A is as shown in Figure 9.4. Then $B[1] \cup B[3] \cup B[4]$ is contained in rows 1, 3, and 7 of the product, and nine unions are done where three would suffice. How can some or all of the duplicated work be reduced? The approach that suggests itself is to first compute a lot of unions of small numbers of rows of B (like $B[1] \cup B[3] \cup B[4]$), and then to combine these unions appropriately to get the rows of the product. Several questions come to mind immediately:

1. How many and which rows of B should be combined in the first step?
2. How can these unions be stored so that they can be accessed efficiently during the second step?
3. How much additional storage is needed?
4. Will any time really be saved in the worst case? If so, how much?

The answers to most of the questions depend on the answer to the first.

$$
\begin{array}{l}
A_1 \\
A_2 \\
A_3 \\
A_4 \\
A_5 \\
A_6 \\
A_7 \\
A_8 \\
A_9 \\
A_{10} \\
A_{11} \\
A_{12}
\end{array}
\left[
\begin{array}{cccccccccccc}
1 & 0 & 1 & 1 & 0 & 1 & 0 & 1 & 0 & 0 & 0 & 1 \\
 & & & & & & & & & & & \\
1 & 0 & 1 & 1 & 1 & 0 & 0 & 1 & 1 & 0 & 1 & 1 \\
 & & & & & & & & & & & \\
 & & & & & & & & & & & \\
 & & & & 0 & 1 & 0 & 1 & & & & \\
1 & 0 & 1 & 1 & 1 & 0 & 0 & 1 & 1 & 1 & 1 & 0 \\
 & & & & & & & & & & & \\
 & & & & & & & & & & & \\
 & & & & & & & & & & & \\
 & & & & & & & & & & & \\
 & & & & & & & & & & &
\end{array}
\right]
$$

Figure 9.4   A bit matrix

We adopt a straightforward strategy: Divide up the rows of B into several groups of t rows each and compute all possible unions within each group. We will ignore all implementation details until we see if, with an appropriate choice for t, this strategy can produce an algorithm that does fewer than n^2 row unions.

Let $g = \lceil n/t \rceil$, the number of groups we will use. The rows of B are grouped as follows:

$$
\begin{array}{ll}
\text{Group 1:} & B[1], \ldots, B[t] \\
\text{Group 2:} & B[t+1], \ldots, B[2t] \\
& \vdots \\
\text{Group } g: & B[(g-1)t+1], \ldots, B[n].
\end{array}
$$

Example 9.4   Groups of bits

Suppose that the matrix A in Figure 9.4 is to multiply a 12×12 matrix B and let $t = 4$. Unions of all combinations of rows $B[1]$, $B[2]$, $B[3]$, and $B[4]$ would be computed once. If done in the right order (first all combinations of two rows, then three, and finally all four), all the unions can be obtained by doing 11 row union operations. The same would be done for the groups $B[5], \ldots, B[8]$ and $B[9], \ldots, B[12]$. Then, to get the first row of AB, only two more row union operations would be needed: They would compute

$$(B[1] \cup B[3] \cup B[4]) \cup (B[6] \cup B[8]) \cup (B[12]).$$

The value of $B[1] \cup B[3] \cup B[4]$ is used again in the third and seventh rows and $B[6] \cup B[8]$ is used again in the sixth row of the product.   ■

We make a rough estimate of the total number of unions done as a function of t, and then see if we can choose a value for t that gives a total lower than n^2. For each group of rows (except perhaps the last), there are 2^t sets of rows to be combined. No unions are needed to compute the empty set or the sets consisting of just one row (eliminating

$t + 1$ unions). Since each union of rows within a group can be computed by combining sets already computed with one more row, a total of $2^t - (t + 1)$ union operations are done for each group. There are g groups, so roughly $g(2^t - (t + 1))$ unions are done in the first phase of the proposed algorithm. Now any desired union of rows from B can be obtained by computing the union of at most one combination from each of the groups. Therefore computing each row of the product matrix requires at most $g - 1$ additional unions, or at most $n(g - 1)$ additional unions for all n rows. The total number of unions done by this method is at most $g(2^t - (t + 1)) + n(g - 1)$. To simplify our work, we approximate, and consider only the high-order terms:

$$g(2^t - (t + 1)) + n(g - 1) \approx \frac{n\,2^t}{t} + \frac{n^2}{t}. \tag{9.5}$$

If $t = 1$ or $t = n$, this expression is in $\Theta(n^2)$ or $\Theta(2^n)$, respectively. Suppose that we try to minimize the right-hand side of Equation (9.5) under the assumption that the first term is of higher order than the second. We would want to make t as small as possible but if $t < \lg n$, the first term would no longer dominate. Similarly, if we assume that the second term is of higher order, we would want t to be as large as possible, but it can't be larger than $\lg n$. This by no means rigorous argument suggests that we try $t \approx \lg n$. The number of unions done for $t \approx \lg n$ is roughly $2n^2/\lg n$, which is of lower order than n^2. Thus this approach is worth pursuing with $t \approx \lg n$. Since 2^t is the fastest growing term, we use $t = \lfloor \lg n \rfloor$. We will now work out some of the implementation details and determine how much extra space is needed.

For each group of rows of B there are 2^t, or $2^{\lfloor \lg n \rfloor}$, sets to be stored. First we will store the sets for all groups in a two-dimensional array of bit strings for simplicity. Later, we will see how to store only the sets for the current group, thereby saving some space. Sets for all groups are stored in the array allUnions according to the following scheme, where allUnions[j][i] stores set i for group j. The rows of B in group j have indexes $(j - 1)t + 1$ through jt. Interpret the second index for allUnions as a t-bit binary number $b_1 b_2 \cdots b_t$. The bits of an index i indicate which rows of B within group j are included in the union stored in allUnions[j][i]; in particular, B[(j–1)t+k] is included if and only if bit b_k in i is one. Thus group 1 of unions is stored as follows:

i	Contents of allUnions[1][i]
$00\ldots00$	$\emptyset$
$00\ldots01$	$B[t]$
$00\ldots10$	$B[t - 1]$
$00\ldots11$	$B[t - 1] \cup B[t]$
$\vdots$	$\vdots$
$11\ldots11$	$B[1] \cup B[2] \cup \cdots \cup B[t]$

Exactly 2^t cells (each the size of one row of B) are used to store the unions for each group of rows. We may suppose for now that the unions for the other groups are stored in

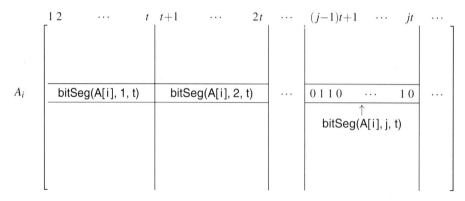

Figure 9.5   The jth segment of t bits in row i of bit matrix A

blocks of cells whose first index is their group number. Later we will show how to make do with only 2^t (roughly n) cells, instead of using $2^t g$, or roughly $n^2/\lg n$.

This storage setup was devised to make it easy to find the unions needed for a given row of the product. Recall that the ith row of the product is $\cup_{k \in A[i]} B[k]$. Suppose we break up each row of A into segments of t entries each, with the following notation:

Definition 9.5   Segments of t bits within a bit string

Let b be a bit string. The subroutine bitSeg(b, j, t) returns the jth segment of t bits, starting with index 1. That is, bits $(j-1)t + 1$ through jt are returned as a t-bit integer, with bit jt of b becoming the least significant bit of the integer (see Figure 9.5).   ∎

Interpreted as a binary number, bitSeg(A[i], j, t) is the correct second index in the array allUnions for the union of rows of B from the jth group. For example, with the matrix of Figure 9.4, bitSeg(A[7], 1, 4) is 11 in decimal, or 1011 in binary.

So far, the algorithm we have developed looks like this:

```
t = ⌊lg n⌋; g = ⌈n/t⌉;
Compute and store in allUnions unions of all combinations of rows of B
within each group of t successive rows.
// i indexes rows of A and C.
// j indexes groups of rows of B.
for (i = 1; i ≤ n; i ++)
    Initialize C[i] to 0.
    for (j = 1; j ≤ g; j ++)
        C[i] = C[i] ∪ allUnions[j][bitSeg(A[i], j, t)];
```

The amount of space used to store the unions can be cut down merely by changing the order in which the work is done. In its present form the algorithm computes one complete *row* of C before going on to the next, so all groups of unions must be available. If instead it works with one *group* at a time, selecting the union needed from that group for each row of C, succeeding groups of unions could use the same memory locations.

The last two details to work out are an efficient scheme for computing the unions within each group and a way of handling the case when the last group has fewer than t rows. We leave the latter problem as an exercise. The former is easily taken care of in the final form of the algorithm, now using a one-dimensional array unions with 2^t entries.

Algorithm 9.5   (Kronrod) Bit Matrix Multiplication

Input: A, B, and n, where A and B are $n \times n$ bit matrices. (We assume for the pseudocode that the class BitMatrix has been defined. Its entries begin with index 0, although some bit matrices may leave that row unused.)

Output: C, the Boolean matrix product. The matrix is passed in and the algorithm fills it.

Remarks: A[i] and C[i] are the ith rows of A and C. As written, the algorithm assumes n is an exact multiple of t. The subroutine bitwiseOR was defined in Definition 9.3, and implements "row union". The subroutine bitSeg was defined in Definition 9.5.

```
void  kronrod(BitMatrix A, BitMatrix B, int n, BitMatrix C)
    int  t, g, i, j, k;
    t = ⌊lg n⌋; g = ⌈n/t⌉;
    BitMatrix  unions = new BitMatrix();
    Initialize C to the zero matrix.
    for (j = 1; j ≤ g ; j ++)

        // Compute all unions within j-th group of rows of B.
        unions[0] = 0;
        for (k = 0; k ≤ t − 1; k ++)
            for (i = 0; i ≤ 2ᵏ − 1; i ++)
                Copy unions[i] into unions[i + 2ᵏ].
                bitwiseOR(unions[i + 2ᵏ], B[j∗t−k], n);

        // Select the appropriate union for each row of C.
        for (i = 1; i ≤ n; i ++)
            bitwiseOR(C[i], unions[bitSeg(A[i], j, t)], n);
        // Continue loop on j.
```

Analysis

Note that $2^t - 1$ union operations are done to get all unions within a group (in the **for** k, **for** i loop). Algorithm 9.5 does a total of $(n/t)(2^t - 1 + n)$ row unions, which is less than $2n^2/\lg(n)$ for $n > 8$. (See Exercise 9.17 for a possible improvement in the choice of t, lowering the leading coefficient to 1.) The number of row unions is in $\Theta(n^2/\log n)$ in any case. In Section 9.6.2 we will derive a lower bound of the same asymptotic order for a class of algorithms that do bit-matrix multiplication by row unions.

Row unions are implemented with the bitwiseOR subroutine. This subroutine requires $\lceil n/w \rceil$ bitwise *or* instructions (where w is the word size, or the size of the operand of the bitwise *or* instruction), so the running time is in $\Theta(n^3/\log n)$, but is a fairly small multiple of $n^3/\lg n$. The running time does not depend on the particular input; the same operations are done for all inputs of size n. The extra space required for the unions array is in $\Theta(n^2)$ bits.

The formula derived in Section 9.5 for the matrix of the transitive closure of a relation (Theorem 9.7) uses approximately $\lg n$ Boolean matrix multiplications. Thus using Kronrod's algorithm, the transitive closure can be computed with only $\Theta(n^2)$ row unions.

Note that both Warshall's algorithm for transitive closure (Section 9.3) and Kronrod's Boolean matrix algorithm save time or space by doing their computations in a particular order. In both cases the natural, or more usual, order in which one would think of doing the work is less efficient.

★ 9.6.2   A Lower Bound for Bit Matrix Multiplication

Is Kronrod's algorithm optimal? If we consider the time it takes to do the row unions, then it is not; it takes $\Theta(n^3/\log n)$ time, and $n^{2.81}$ (the order of Strassen's algorithm) is of a lower asymptotic order. The various algorithms for Boolean matrix multiplication assume different representations for the matrices (bit matrices versus one entry per word) and do different kinds of operations (for example, Boolean operations on words, arithmetic operations if Strassen's method is used, or row unions as in Kronrod's algorithm). If we restrict our attention to the class of algorithms that compute rows of the bit matrix product by forming unions of rows of the second factor matrix, then we can show that, within this class, Kronrod's algorithm is of optimal asymptotic order: number of unions done by an optimal algorithm would also be in $\Theta(n^2/\log n)$.

One of the reasons for including the proof of the theorem is that it illustrates a "counting argument," a useful approach for establishing lower bounds that involves counting all possible algorithms (ignoring differences not relevant to the sequence of basic operations—in this case, row unions done by the algorithms).

To derive the lower bound we use an abstracted model of algorithms (as we did with decision trees for sorting). Let $\mathbf{A}$ be an algorithm that computes $C = AB$ by forming unions of rows of B (and possibly copying rows) and can do no other operations on B. For a particular input, A and B, we can make an indexed list of the union operations done by $\mathbf{A}$, denoting such an operation by union(r, s), where r and s may be a row of B or the result of a previous union specified by its index in the list.

The sequence of unions done is not sufficient to describe the result produced by the algorithm; we must know which unions computed in the sequence are to be rows of the product, and which rows in the product they are. Suppose that A and B are $n \times n$, and let steps be the number of steps in the list of union operations. Then the additional information needed can be provided by an n-vector $V = (j_1, \ldots, j_n)$, where $-n \le j_i \le$ steps and j_i describes the ith row of the product matrix C, as follows: If $j_i > 0$, the ith row is the result of the j_i-th union operation; if $j_i = 0$, the ith row is all zeros (the empty set); and if $j_i < 0$, the ith row is the $|j_i|$-th row of B.

Example 9.5 Row unions and the vector V

If

$$A = \begin{bmatrix} 1 & 1 & 0 & 1 \\ 1 & 0 & 1 & 1 \\ 1 & 1 & 1 & 1 \\ 0 & 0 & 0 & 1 \end{bmatrix}$$

an algorithm might carry out the following sequence of union and copy operations:

1. tmp1 = union(B[1], B[4]);
2. C[1] = union(tmp1, B[2]);
3. C[2] = union(tmp1, B[3]);
4. C[3] = union(C[1], C[2]);
5. C[4] = B[4];

The vector V for this example is $(2, 3, 4, -4)$. ∎

Theorem 9.8 For sufficiently large n, in particular, $n > 1024$, any algorithm that does Boolean matrix multiplication using row unions must do at least $n^2/5 \lg(n)$ union operations to multiply $n \times n$ matrices in the worst case.

Proof Let **A** be an algorithm that computes $C = AB$, and suppose **A** does at most $2n^2/\lg n$ row unions for $n > 1024$. Let $F(n)$ be the number of unions done by **A** to multiply an arbitrary $n \times n$ matrix A and the identity matrix I_n in the worst case. The number of unions done by **A** in the worst case for all inputs is at least $F(n)$, and any lower bound derived for $F(n)$ is a lower bound for any algorithm in the class under consideration. We will show that $F(n) \geq n^2/5 \lg n$, for sufficiently large n. (The details of showing that 1024 is large enough are omitted, but are easily filled in by direct calculations.)

Let S_n be the set of all valid sequences of $F(n)$ union operations. (A sequence is valid if, for each i, the ith operation refers to rows of B between 1 and n and/or to the results of operations with indexes between 1 and $i - 1$.) Let V_n be the set of all n vectors with integer entries between $-n$ and $F(n)$. The operations done by **A** and **A**'s output for a given input A are described by an element of $S_n \times V_n$. If **A** does fewer than $F(n)$ unions for a particular A, S_n contains a sequence that does the work of **A** and is then padded out to length $F(n)$ with repetitions of, say, union(1, 1). We will derive an upper bound and a lower bound on $|S_n \times V_n|$ and use the resulting inequality to get a lower bound for $F(n)$.

Since each union has two operands, each of which is a row of B or an index between 1 and $F(n)$, there are $(n + F(n))^2$ choices for each union operation. Therefore $|S_n| \leq (n + F(n))^{2F(n)}$. $|V| = (n + 1 + F(n))^n$, so $|S_n \times V_n| \leq (n + 1 + F(n))^{2F(n)+n}$.

To get a lower bound on $|S_n \times V_n|$, observe that $S_n \times V_n$ contains a distinct element for each $n \times n$ matrix A since $A_1 I_n \neq A_2 I_n$ if $A_1 \neq A_2$. Thus $|S_n \times V_n| \geq 2^{n^2}$, since there are 2^{n^2} $n \times n$ Boolean matrices. So

$$2^{n^2} \leq |S_n \times V_n| \leq (n+1+F(n))^{2F(n)+n}$$

or

$$n^2 \leq (2F(n)+n) \lg(n+1+F(n)) \qquad \text{for all } n > 0. \tag{9.6}$$

We observe that $F(n) > n^{3/2}$ for sufficiently large n, because if not, Equation (9.6) would imply that n^2 is in $O(n^{3/2} \log n)$, and this is not true. Since $F(n) > n^{3/2}$, $2F(n) + n < 2.1\ F(n)$ for sufficiently large n.

Also, $F(n) \leq 2n^2 / \lg n$ (by choice of **A**), so $n+1+F(n) < 2n^2$ for sufficiently large n. Substituting these inequalities in Equation (9.6) gives

$$n^2 \leq 2.1\ F(n)\ \lg(2n^2) = 2.1\ F(n)(1 + 2\ \lg n) \qquad \text{for sufficiently large } n.$$

We also have $1 + 2 \lg n \leq 2.1\ \lg n$ for sufficiently large n, so

$$n^2 \leq 2.1^2 F(n) \lg n \qquad \text{for sufficiently large } n.$$

But $2.1^2 < 5$, so $n^2 < 5\ F(n) \lg n$, or $F(n) > n^2/5 \lg(n)$, for sufficiently large n. $\quad\square$

Exercises

Section 9.2   The Transitive Closure of a Binary Relation

9.1   Let $G = (V, E)$ be an undirected graph and let R be a relation on V defined by vRw if and only if there exists a path from v to w. (Recall there is a path of length zero from any vertex to itself.)

a.   Show that R is an equivalence relation.

b.   What are the equivalence classes of this relation?

c.   Show that the reachability matrix R for an undirected graph with n vertices can be constructed in $O(n^2)$ time.

9.2

a.   Try to write an algorithm using depth-first search to construct R, the reachability matrix for a directed graph, given A, the adjacency matrix. The algorithm should use the suggestion in Section 9.2.2 that entries of R in several rows be computed during one depth-first search. Use whatever other tricks you can think of to design an efficient algorithm.

b.   What is the asymptotic order of the worst-case running time of your algorithm?

c.   Test your algorithm on the digraph in Figure 9.6. If it does not work correctly, modify it so that it does and redo part (b).

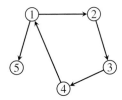

Figure 9.6   Digraph for Exercise 9.2

Section 9.3   *Warshall's Algorithm for Transitive Closure*

9.3   Use Algorithm 9.2 to compute the transitive closure of the relation A given in Example 9.1. Show the matrix after each pass of the outermost **for** loop.

9.4   Construct the worst example you can for Algorithm 9.1, that is, an example for which the triple **for** loop is repeated many times. How many times will the loop be repeated on your example?

9.5   Use Algorithm 9.3 to compute the transitive closure of the relation A given in Example 9.1. Specify which bitwiseOR operations are performed, and show their results. Also show the matrix after each pass of the outermost **for** loop.

Section 9.4   *All-Pairs Shortest Paths in Graphs*

9.6   Construct an example of a weighted digraph on which Algorithm 9.4 would not work correctly if k were varied in the innermost loop instead of the outermost.

9.7   Use Algorithm 9.4 to compute the distance matrix for the digraph whose adjacency matrix is

$$\begin{bmatrix} 0 & 2 & 4 & 3 \\ 3 & 0 & \infty & 3 \\ 5 & \infty & 0 & 3 \\ \infty & 1 & 4 & 0 \end{bmatrix}$$

9.8

a.   Use Algorithm 9.4 to compute the distance matrix for the digraph whose adjacency matrix is

$$\begin{bmatrix} 0 & 2 & 4 & 3 \\ 3 & 0 & \infty & 3 \\ 5 & \infty & 0 & -3 \\ \infty & -1 & 4 & 0 \end{bmatrix}$$

b. Explain why this algorithm will work correctly even if some of the weights are negative, so long as there are no negative cycles. (A negative cycle is a cycle for which the sum of the weights of its edges is negative.)

9.9 Prove Lemma 9.3.

9.10 Show how to modify Algorithm 9.4 to construct a *routing table*, as described in the text after the algorithm. Call the matrix for the routing table go. *Hint*: If D[i][j] is being updated because a shorter path was found, and that path goes through intermediate vertex k, what would be the first step of that path?

9.11 Compute the routing table go for the weighted graph in Exercise 9.7. Note that this is easiest to do simultaneously with computing the distance matrix.

9.12 Give an algorithm to find the length of a shortest cycle in a directed graph. Does your algorithm also work for undirected graphs? Explain why or why not.

Section 9.5 Computing Transitive Closure by Matrix Operations

9.13 Prove Lemma 9.4.

9.14 Prove Lemma 9.5.

9.15 Show that A^+, the irreflexive transitive closure of the Boolean matrix A, can be computed with one matrix multiplication if the (reflexive) transitive closure, A^*, is known.

Section 9.6 Multiplying Bit Matrices—Kronrod's Algorithm

9.16 Prove that if A and B are $n \times n$ Boolean matrices with rows interpreted as subsets of $\{1, 2, \ldots, n\}$ as described at the beginning of Section 9.6, and if $C = AB$, then the ith row of C is $\cup_{k \in A[i]} B[k]$.

9.17 Analyze a variation of Algorithm 9.5 in which the group size is $t = \lfloor \lg(n/\lg(n)) \rfloor = \lfloor \lg(n) - \lg \lg(n) \rfloor$. How many row unions are done in this variation, as opposed to the value of t used in the algorithm?

Additional Problems

9.18 A *triangle* in a graph is a cycle of length 3. Outline an algorithm that uses the adjacency matrix of an undirected graph to determine if it has a triangle. How many operations on matrix entries are done by your algorithm?

Programs

1. Write a program to multiply two bit matrices using Kronrod's algorithm (Algorithm 9.5). Allow for n to be larger than the number of bits per word. How much space is used?

Notes and References

Algorithms 9.2 and 9.3 are from Warshall (1962). Proofs of the correctness of Algorithm 9.2 (Theorem 9.2) and Algorithm 9.3 can be found there and in Wegner (1974). Algorithm 9.4, for finding distances in graphs, is from Floyd (1962). Semi-ring closure is a generalization of both problems, and is discussed in Aho, Hopcroft, and Ullman (1974) and in Cormen, Leiserson, and Rivest (1990). The earliest algorithm in this genre may be found in Kleene (1956), and applies to finite automata. The proof that computing the reflexive transitive closure can be done in the same order as Boolean matrix multiplication is from Munro (1971) and also appears in Aho, Hopcroft, and Ullman (1974).

Kronrod's algorithm (Algorithm 9.5) is from Arlazarov, Dinic, Kronrod, and Faradzev (1970) (where it appears without any discussion of implementation). The proof of Theorem 9.8, the lower bound on Boolean matrix multiplication by row unions, is based on Angluin (1976). This result and generalizations of Kronrod's algorithm appear in Savage (1974).

10

Dynamic Programming

10.1   Introduction

Those who cannot remember the past are condemned to repeat it.

> —George Santayana, *The Life of Reason; or,*
> *The Phases of Human Progress* (1905)

Dynamic programming has evolved into a major paradigm of algorithm design in computer science. However, its name is something of a mystery to many people. The name was coined in 1957 by Richard Bellman to describe a type of optimum control problem. Actually, the name originally described the problem more than the technique of solution. The sense in which *programming* is meant is "a series of choices," like the programming of a radio station. The word *dynamic* conveys the idea that choices may depend on the current state, rather than being decided ahead of time. So in this original sense, a radio show in which listeners call in requests might be said to be "dynamically programmed" to contrast it with the more usual format where the selections are decided before the show begins. Bellman described a method of solution for "dynamic programming" problems, which has become the inspiration for many computer algorithms. The main feature of his method was that it replaced an exponential-time computation by a polynomial-time computation. That continues to be a common feature of dynamic programming algorithms.

This chapter differs from most of the others in that we usually focus on one problem or application area and consider a variety of algorithms for it; in this chapter, however, we focus on a technique, developing dynamic programming solutions for problems from different application areas.

Top-down algorithm design is natural and powerful. We think and plan in a general way first, then add more detail. We solve a high-level, complex problem by breaking it down to subproblems. Using recursion, we solve a large problem by breaking it down to smaller instances of the same problem. Divide and Conquer, a recursive algorithm design technique, proved especially useful for getting fast sorting algorithms. But, as good as recursion is, if not controlled properly, it can become very inefficient. The Fibonacci numbers provide a simple and dramatic example.

Example 10.1   Recursive Fibonacci function

Recall from Equation (1.13) that the Fibonacci numbers are defined by the recurrence $F_n = F_{n-1} + F_{n-2}$ for $n \geq 2$, with boundary values $F_0 = 0$ and $F_1 = 1$. They are defined recursively, and it is natural to compute them with a recursive function, fib(n), as given in Example 3.1. However, as Figure 7.13 illustrates, the natural recursive computation is terribly inefficient because a lot of work is repeated. That figure essentially shows the activation tree for fib(6). In general, the activation tree for fib(n) is a full binary tree down to depth $n/2$ (the rightmost path being the shortest), and has more nodes at lower depths, so the running time is *at least* in $\Omega(2^{n/2})$. The exact asymptotic order is the subject of Exercise 10.1. But F_n can be computed with $\Theta(n)$ simple statements by computing *and remembering* n smaller values, each of which can be computed with a constant number of operations if the smaller values are accessible. (Recall from Section 3.2.1 that a *simple statement* is one that involves no function calls, and is assumed to require constant time.) Assuming a large enough array f has been allocated, the following procedure does the job:

```
f[0]=0; f[1]=1;
for (i=2; i ≤ n; i++)
    f[i]=f[i−1]+f[i−2];
```

Exercise 10.2 dispenses with the array.   ∎

A dynamic programming algorithm stores the results, or solutions, for small subproblems, and later looks them up, rather than recomputing them, when it needs them to solve larger subproblems. Thus dynamic programming is especially well suited to problems where a recursive algorithm would solve many of the subproblems repeatedly.

We will introduce a characterization of dynamic programming algorithms that provides a unified framework for a wide variety of published algorithms that might seem quite different on the surface. This framework permits a recursive solution to be converted into a dynamic programming algorithm, and provides a way to analyze the complexity of the dynamic programming algorithm.

10.2 Subproblem Graphs and Their Traversal

As stated earlier, problems are often solved by decomposing the main problem into smaller problems of the same kind, solving the smaller problems recursively, then combining the solutions. Suppose we have such a solution method in mind. We can define a directed graph based on the relationships between problems and their relevant subproblems.

Definition 10.1   Subproblem graph

Suppose a recursive algorithm **A** is known for a problem. The *subproblem graph for* **A** is the directed graph whose vertices are the instances, or inputs, for this problem and whose directed edges are $I \to J$ for all pairs such that when algorithm **A** is invoked on problem instance I it makes a recursive call (directly) on instance J. (Here we use the notation "$I \to J$" rather than "IJ" to emphasize that edges are directed.) Unlike most of the graphs we have considered so far, which were explicitly represented by a data structure, this graph is abstract and is not explicitly represented.

Let P be a problem instance for algorithm **A**; that is, we assume $\mathbf{A}(P)$ is not a recursive call. Then the *subproblem graph for* $\mathbf{A}(P)$ is the portion of the subproblem graph for **A** that is reachable from vertex P.   ∎

Example 10.2   Subproblem graph for Fibonacci function

For the recursive Fibonacci function, fib(n), the problem instances are just the nonnegative integers, so these are the vertices of the subproblem graph for F. The directed edges are $\{i \to i - 1 \mid i \geq 2\} \cup \{i \to i - 2 \mid i \geq 2\}$. Although the graph is infinite, for any particular

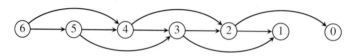

Figure 10.1   The subproblem graph for fib(6)

n the portion that is relevant to the computation of fib(n) (i.e., reachable from vertex n) has only $n + 1$ vertices and about $2n$ edges. Figure 10.1 shows an example. ∎

If algorithm **A** always terminates, then its subproblem graph must be acyclic. Directed acyclic graphs (DAGs) were studied in Section 7.4.6, and we will soon get a chance to use some of those results. By looking at the tree of activation frames (Section 3.2.1) generated by a particular top-level call, say **A**(P), it is apparent that each path in the tree corresponds to a path in the subproblem graph for **A**(P) beginning at vertex P and terminating at a base-case vertex, which has no outgoing edges. Keep in mind that vertices are problem instances in this abstract graph. Directed edges correspond to recursive calls that would be invoked during the execution of **A**(P).

Consider a graph traversal procedure that is like the depth-first search skeleton (Algorithm 7.3), but does not color the vertices to record which ones have been discovered or finished. We call this a *memoryless* graph traversal. A memoryless graph traversal traverses every path in an acyclic graph (and may not terminate in a graph with cycles). A natural recursive computation, which simply makes recursive calls as needed, is like a memoryless traversal of the subproblem graph for **A**(P). As long as the subproblem graph is acyclic the procedure eventually terminates. However, an acyclic graph can have an exponential number of paths.

To summarize where we stand, if we have a recursive strategy to solve a problem, and P is the problem instance we wish to solve, then we need to solve it for all vertices in the subproblem graph that are reachable from P. If there are multiple paths to a subproblem, the natural recursive procedure will solve it multiple times.

If I is any subproblem that must be solved, and I has edges to $J_1, J_2, \ldots, J_k$, then it is necessary to solve those subproblems before solving I. In other words, the subproblem graph can also be viewed as a *dependency graph*, as in Example 7.14. If we find an order to schedule the solutions of the subproblems, and remember the solutions for later use, each subproblem needs to be solved only once.

As we learned in Section 7.4.6, any reverse topological order produces an acceptable schedule for a dependency graph. The essence of dynamic programming is to find a reverse topological order for the subproblem graph, to schedule the subproblems according to the reverse topological order, and to record the subproblem solutions for later use by other subproblems.

In many cases, a reverse topological order can be determined by knowledge of the problem. For the Fibonacci numbers, it is simply ascending order. For some of the problems we will study in later sections, it is more subtle, but one can still be worked out by knowledge of the problem. However, in Section 7.4.6 we developed a general tool for finding a reverse topological numbering of *any* DAG, Algorithm 7.5. This algorithm simply executes the DFS skeleton and assigns the reverse topological number at postorder time. So if we don't see an easy way to define a reverse topological order for a certain problem, we could turn the job over to this algorithm. Next, we will see that we don't need to do this as a separate step. Readers might wish to review the depth-first search skeleton of Algorithm 7.3 before proceeding.

The DFS skeleton is just a recursive procedure itself. When applied to the subproblem graph, it just mimics the recursive algorithm, say **A**, for the problem we wish to solve; remember that the subproblem graph is based on the pattern of recursive calls that are made by **A**. That is, exploring each edge in the DFS skeleton corresponds to a recursive call in **A**, and at postorder time all the information that **A** needs to complete the solution has been accumulated. However, **A** explores *every* edge in the sense of making the recursive call, while the DFS skeleton only explores edges to undiscovered vertices, and it *checks* the other edges. In a nutshell, the DFS skeleton remembers where it has been by coloring the vertices it has visited. This observation leads us to the characterization of dynamic programming algorithms.

Definition 10.2   Dynamic programming version of a recursive algorithm

A *dynamic programming version* of a given recursive algorithm **A**, denoted as $\mathcal{DP}(\mathbf{A})$, is a procedure that, given a top-level problem to solve, say P, performs a depth-first search on the subproblem graph for $\mathbf{A}(P)$. As solutions are found for subproblems, they are recorded in a *dictionary*, say soln. That is, soln is an object of a Dict abstract data type. The process of recording solutions of subproblems is often called *memo-ization*. Recall that the operations of the Dict ADT are create, member, retrieve, and store (Section 2.5.3).

In general, the procedure of **A** is converted into $\mathcal{DP}(\mathbf{A})$ by inserting a few statements, according to this scheme. Assume P is the current problem.

1. Before any recursive call, say on subproblem Q, check the dictionary soln to see if a solution for Q has been stored.

   a. If no solution has been stored, go ahead with the recursive call, thereby treating Q as a white vertex and treating $P \rightarrow Q$ as a tree edge.

   b. If a solution has been stored for Q, retrieve the stored solution, and do *not* make the recursive call, thereby treating Q as a black vertex.

2. Just before returning the solution for P, store it in the dictionary soln; this has the effect of coloring vertex P black.

In this scheme, it is essential that the subproblem graph be acyclic, because vertices are not colored gray, which is normally done to prevent traversing around cycles.

As with depth-first search, $\mathcal{DP}(\mathbf{A})$ requires a "wrapper" to prepare for execution of the recursive procedure. At a minimum, this wrapper creates soln as an empty dictionary, which has the effect of making all reachable vertices of the subproblem graph white. This dictionary depends on the top-level problem, say P, because it must be able to store a solution for each subproblem reachable from P in the subproblem graph.

In many cases the original recursive algorithm **A** required a wrapper, usually to initialize certain global structures that depend on the top-level problem. In these cases the dynamic programming wrapper must include the processing done by the original wrapper, as well as creating the empty dictionary.   ∎

We will see that the number of reachable subproblems, hence the size of the dictionary, is a critical factor in the design and analysis of efficient dynamic programming algorithms.

Example 10.3 $\mathcal{DP}$(fib)

The dynamic programming version of the Fibonacci function fib would be something like this.

```
fibDPwrap(n)
    Dict  soln = create(n);
    return fibDP(soln, n);

fibDP(soln, k)
    int  fib, f1, f2;
    if (k < 2)
        fib = k;
    else
        if (member(soln, k−1) == false)
            f1 = fibDP(soln, k−1);
        else
            f1 = retrieve(soln, k−1);

        if (member(soln, k−2) == false)
            f2 = fibDP(soln, k−2);
        else
            f2 = retrieve(soln, k−2);

    fib = f1 + f2;
    store(soln, k, fib);
    return fib;
```

Of course, for this simple example, many simplifications are easy to find, resulting in an algorithm like the one in Exercise 10.1. Its purpose is to illustrate the general nature of the transformation from **A** to $\mathcal{DP}(\mathbf{A})$. Notice that, just as depth-first search requires a wrapper around its recursive procedure, so does $\mathcal{DP}(\mathbf{A})$. Thus fibDPwrap initializes a dictionary suitable for the top-level problem (n in this case), then calls fibDP(soln, n).   ∎

Even when we can find a reverse topological order by inspection, the DFS point of view can be valuable for analyzing the complexity. We know that DFS processes each vertex once and each *edge* once; usually there are more edges than vertices. If we can allocate all the work of the algorithm to various vertices and edges, that may help to get a good estimate of the running time.

10.3 Multiplying a Sequence of Matrices

In this section we present the matrix multiplication order problem, which is one of the classical examples of dynamic programming. In the next section we will study a problem that originates from a quite different application, but has a very similar solution. Together they should serve as a good introduction to dynamic programming.

The purpose of this section is not to demonstrate how to solve the matrix multiplication order problem, but rather how to apply the principles of developing a dynamic programming algorithm, step by step. We hope these principles help readers to solve new problems, and to develop a sense of when dynamic programming is a likely strategy. However, the treatment of the matrix multiplication order problem is more involved than would be necessary if the only purpose were to exhibit and explain the solution of this one problem.

10.3.1 The Matrix Multiplication Order Problem

Suppose we want to determine the best order in which to carry out matrix multiplications when a string of more than two matrices are to be multiplied together. We use the ordinary matrix multiplication algorithm (Algorithm 1.2) each time we multiply two matrices. Thus to multiply a $p \times q$ matrix and a $q \times r$ matrix, we do pqr element-wise multiplications. There are two important observations to be made. One, we get the same result no matter in which order the multiplications are done. That is, matrix multiplication is *associative*: $A(BC) = (AB)C$. Second, the order can make a big difference in the amount of work done. Consider the following example.

Example 10.4   Various multiplication orders

We want to multiply arrays with the sizes shown:

$$A_1 \quad \times \quad A_2 \quad \times \quad A_3 \quad \times \quad A_4$$
$$30 \times 1 \quad\quad 1 \times 40 \quad\quad 40 \times 10 \quad\quad 10 \times 25$$

The following computations show how many multiplications are done for several orderings.

$$
\begin{array}{lllll}
((A_1 A_2)A_3)A_4 & 30 \cdot 1 \cdot 40 & + \quad 30 \cdot 40 \cdot 10 & + \quad 30 \cdot 10 \cdot 25 & = \quad 20{,}700 \\
A_1(A_2(A_3 A_4)) & 40 \cdot 10 \cdot 25 & + \quad 1 \cdot 40 \cdot 25 & + \quad 30 \cdot 1 \cdot 25 & = \quad 11{,}750 \\
(A_1 A_2)(A_3 A_4) & 30 \cdot 1 \cdot 40 & + \quad 40 \cdot 10 \cdot 25 & + \quad 30 \cdot 40 \cdot 25 & = \quad 41{,}200 \\
A_1((A_2 A_3)A_4) & 1 \cdot 40 \cdot 10 & + \quad 1 \cdot 10 \cdot 25 & + \quad 30 \cdot 1 \cdot 25 & = \quad 1{,}400 \quad \blacksquare
\end{array}
$$

For the general problem, suppose we are given matrices $A_1, A_2, \ldots, A_n$, where the dimensions of A_i are $d_{i-1} \times d_i$ (for $1 \le i \le n$). How should we compute

$$A_1 \quad \times \quad A_2 \quad \times \quad \cdots \quad \times \quad A_n$$
$$d_0 \times d_1 \quad\quad d_1 \times d_2 \quad\quad\quad\quad d_{n-1} \times d_n$$

and what is the minimum cost of doing so? Our cost is the number of element-wise multiplications. (Some other cost function might be used, also.) For now we will focus on the problem of finding the minimum cost; later, we make the algorithm "remember" how the minimum is achieved. We denote the multiplication operator between A_k and A_{k+1} as the kth multiplication.

10.3.2   A Greedy Attempt

Any sequence of the $n - 1$ multiplications is legal, and the algorithm needs to determine which sequence has the minimum total cost. The greedy approach is a plausible one. First choose the multiplication with minimum cost. Determine the dimensions of the matrices in the modified matrix chain after this multiplication. Again choose the multiplication with minimum cost, and continue in this vein. This strategy works on Example 10.4. However, it fails to be optimal for some sequences of three matrices (only two matrix multiplications). Another greedy strategy is explored in Exercise 10.6. Typically, dynamic programming algorithms are more expensive than greedy algorithms, so they are used only when no greedy strategy can be found that delivers the optimal solution.

10.3.3   Toward a Dynamic Programming Solution

We next attempt to develop a recursive algorithm. Suppose, after choosing a first multiplication, say at position i in the sequence, we recursively solve the remaining problem optimally. We do this for each i that represents a valid first choice, and finally select the i that gives the lowest combined cost. This is called a *backtracking* algorithm because after trying one complete choice sequence, the algorithm backtracks to the point before the most recent choice and tries an alternative; when alternatives are exhausted at this point, it backtracks to an earlier point and tries alternatives there, and continues until all alternatives are exhausted. We saw an example of this idea in the eight-queens problem (see Figure 7.14).

Suppose the dimensions $d_0, \ldots, d_n$ are in an array dim. We can leave the array intact and just identify a subproblem by a sequence of integers, giving the indexes of the dimensions of the remaining matrices. The initial index sequence is $0, \ldots, n$. Notice that all indexes of the sequence, except the first and last, specify multiplication operators, as well.

After making a first choice of multiplication i, the index sequence for the remaining problem is $0, \ldots, i - 1, i + 1, \ldots, n$. That is, the chosen first multiplication multiplies $A_i \times A_{i+1}$, for which the dimensions are d_{i-1}, d_i, and d_{i+1}. Let $B = A_i \times A_{i+1}$; then the dimensions of B are d_{i-1} by d_{i+1}. The remaining subproblem is to multiply

$$A_1 \quad \times \cdots \times \quad A_{i-1} \quad \times \quad B \quad \times \quad A_{i+2} \quad \times \cdots \times \quad A_n$$
$$d_0 \times d_1 \qquad\qquad d_{i-2} \times d_{i-1} \quad d_{i-1} \times d_{i+1} \quad d_{i+1} \times d_{i+2} \qquad\qquad d_{n-1} \times d_n$$

Assume the index sequence itself is stored in a zero-based array seq, and len is the length of seq. The outline of the method is

```
mmTry1(dim, len, seq)  // OUTLINE
    if (len < 3)
        bestCost = 0;  // base case, one array or none.
    else
        bestCost = ∞;
        for (i = 1; i ≤ len−1; i ++)
            c = cost of multiplication at position seq[i].
            newSeq = seq with ith element deleted.
            b = mmTry1(dim, len−1, newSeq);
            bestCost = min(bestCost, b + c);
    return bestCost;
```

The recurrence equation for this algorithm is

$$T(n) = (n - 1)T(n - 1) + n.$$

The solution is in $\Theta((n - 1)!)$, but our ambition is to improve the performance of the recursive algorithm by converting it into a dynamic programming algorithm.

To design a dynamic programming version, we first need to analyze the subproblem graph. How many subproblems are reachable from the initial problem, which is described by the index sequence $0, \ldots, n$? Here we encounter a serious difficulty. Although subsequences start out as a few continuous subranges, they get more and more fragmented as the subproblem depth increases. For example, with $n = 10$ after choosing multiplication operators 1, 4, 6, 9, the subsequence of remaining indexes becomes 0, 2, 3, 5, 7, 8, 10. There is no concise way to specify these subsequences. Essentially, every subsequence (with at least three elements) of the initial sequence $(0, \ldots, n)$ is a reachable subproblem. There are about 2^n such subsequences (see Exercise 10.3), hence exponentially many subproblems. This graph is simply too large to be searched efficiently.

This illustrates one of the most important principles of designing a dynamic programming algorithm. The subproblems should have a *concise identifier*. This limits the maximum size of the subproblem graph (in terms of vertices—there may be more edges) and the dictionary to the number of possible identifiers (within the ranges that need to be solved). Recall that the *identifier*, or *id*, of an element uniquely identifies it in the dictionary (Section 2.5.3). There cannot be more elements in the dictionary than there are distinct *identifiers*. Therefore, if we focus on making the maximum dictionary size a polynomial function of the input size, and as small as possible, we will ensure that the depth-first search of the subproblem graph can be carried out in polynomial time.

Based on these considerations, we realize that we need a different idea for how to decompose the problem into subproblems. Looking at the subproblem created after the first matrix multiplication did not work. How about the subproblem created by choosing the *last* matrix multiplication? Suppose the *last* matrix multiplication is at position i? This actually creates *two* subproblems:

1. Multiply $A_1, \ldots, A_i$ with dimension indexes $0, \ldots, i$; that is,

$$
\underset{d_0 \times d_1}{A_1} \quad \times \quad \underset{d_1 \times d_2}{A_2} \quad \times \cdots \times \quad \underset{d_{i-1} \times d_i}{A_i} \quad = \quad \underset{d_0 \times d_i}{B_1}
$$

2. Multiply $A_{i+1}, \ldots, A_n$ with dimension indexes $i, \ldots, n$.

$$
\underset{d_i \times d_{i+1}}{A_{i+1}} \quad \times \quad \underset{d_{i+1} \times d_{i+2}}{A_{i+2}} \quad \times \cdots \times \quad \underset{d_{n-1} \times d_n}{A_n} \quad = \quad \underset{d_i \times d_n}{B_2}
$$

The last step is to multiply $B_1 B_2$ and the cost for that is based on (d_0, d_i, d_n).

It is not immediately obvious that this is any better than our first approach. However, we note that each subproblem can be identified (so far) by a pair of integers, $(0, i)$ and (i, n). That is, the sequence of indexes for the first subproblem is $(0, 1, \ldots, i)$, but since the elements are contiguous, it is only necessary to list the endpoints. (A pair $(j - 1, j)$ represents A_j alone and has cost 0.) As before, the array of dimensions, $d_0, \ldots, d_n$, is not modified and might be a global array.

Upon checking further we see that whenever a choice for index of the last multiplication is made on a subproblem, each new subproblem that it creates is also describable by a single pair of integers. For example, if the choice in subproblem (i, n) is k, the new subproblems are (i, k) and (k, n). Thus we see that this method of problem decomposition creates only $\Theta(n^2)$ distinct subproblems in the subproblem graph.

As before, we don't know which choice for the last multiplication will produce the least overall cost, so we need to evaluate all choices. The objective of mmTry2(dim, low, high) is to find the optimum cost for the subproblem specified by (low, high), where low < high. The outline is similar to mmTry1:

```
mmTry2(dim, low, high)  // OUTLINE
 1.  if (high – low == 1)
 2.      bestCost = 0;  // Base case: only one matrix.
 3.  else
 4.      bestCost = ∞;
 5.  for (k = low+1; k ≤ high–1; k ++)
 6.      a = mmTry2(dim, low, k);
 7.      b = mmTry2(dim, k, high);
 8.      c = cost of matrix multiplication at position k, with
            dimensions dim[low], dim[k], dim[high].
 9.      bestCost = min(bestCost, a + b + c);
10.  return bestCost;
```

Like mmTry1, this is a backtracking algorithm. The exact recurrence equation for this algorithm is complicated but we can get a simplified version that shows that the time is greater than 2^n (see Exercise 10.4). We expected this, because backtracking algorithms are typically exponential, but we hope that we can improve the performance of the natural recursive algorithm by converting it into a dynamic programming algorithm.

Again, let's consider the subproblem graph, where the initial problem is described by the pair $(0, n)$. The vertices (subproblems) are identified by a pair of integers, say (i, j), in the range $0, \ldots, n$, with $i < j$, so there are about $n^2/2$ of them. For the subproblem identified by the pair (i, j) there are two subproblems to be solved by recursive calls for each k between $i + 1$ and $j - 1$, so this is less than $2n$ edges leaving the vertex (i, j). In all, the whole subproblem graph has fewer than n^3 edges, so depth-first search can traverse it in time $O(n^3)$. This looks tractable so we can carry out the conversion of mmTry2 to a dynamic programming algorithm mmTry2DP by inserting tests to look up solutions, rather than recompute them, and to store solutions as they are found.

In the next procedure outline, the dictionary is named cost, and the identifier for an element is a pair of integers. To use a generic ADT, we would have to package the identifier into an organizer class, but instead we will assume that we have customized this dictionary interface to take the two integers, low and high, as separate parameters. We continue to use the dictionary operations create, member, retrieve, and store. The line numbers correspond to mmTry2.

```
mmTry2DP(dim, low, high, cost)  // OUTLINE
 1.  if (high − low == 1)
 2.       bestCost = 0;  // Base case: only one matrix.
 3.  else
 4.       bestCost = ∞;
 5.  for (k = low+1; k ≤ high−1; k ++)
6a.       if (member(low, k) == false)
6b.            a = mmTry2DP(dim, low, k, cost);
6c.       else
6d.            a = retrieve(cost, low, k);

7a.       if (member(k, high) == false)
7b.            b = mmTry2DP(dim, k, high, cost);
7c.       else
7d.            b = retrieve(cost, k, high);

 8.       c = cost of matrix multiplication at position k, with
              dimensions dim[low], dim[k], dim[high].
 9.       bestCost = min(bestCost, a + b + c);
10a. store(cost, low, high, bestCost);
10b. return bestCost;
```

Since subproblems are identified by a pair of integers in the range $0, \ldots, n$, the dictionary can be implemented with an $(n + 1) \times (n + 1)$ array. In mmTry2DP we stored and retrieved the optimum cost for the subproblems. In the complete algorithm below, the cost array is supplemented by the last array, which will contain the optimum *choice* of multiplication index for the subproblem. An entry with a cost of ∞ denotes an unsolved subproblem. We "un-abstract" the dictionary and access the arrays directly.

We have already seen that mmTry2 can be converted into mmTry2DP with a few mechanical changes, which implement *memo-ization*. The result looks very much like the DFS skeleton: lines 6 and 7 test for unsolved subproblems (undiscovered, or white vertices) in a loop that goes through all needed subproblems (all edges to adjacent vertices). The solved subproblems (black vertices) are just looked up. At line 10 (postorder time) the current subproblem becomes solved (the current vertex is colored black). Since mmTry2DP corresponds to the recursive part of the skeleton (that is, dfs), to complete the implementation we need a "wrapper," analogous to dfsSweep, to initialize the cost array to ∞ and to make the top-level call of mmTry2DP.

An alternative, starting from mmTry2, is to determine a convenient reverse topological order by inspection. If we can do this, then we simply solve problems in this order, and as each subproblem comes up for solution, all the subproblems that are its dependencies will have been solved (see Section 7.4.6 and Example 7.14). We see that the subproblem (low, high) depends on (has dependency edges to) (low, k) and (k, high) for low $< k <$ high. Can we arrive at a simple order that causes all the edges to point from a higher topological number to a lower one? Readers are invited to try to come up with such an order before reading on.

■   ■   ■

From the edges mentioned in the previous paragraph we see that decreasing the second index and keeping the first index the same should lead to a lower topological number. Turning this around, increasing the second index and keeping the first index the same should lead to a higher topological number. Similarly, decreasing the first index and keeping the second index the same should lead to a higher topological number. There are several schemes that work. Let's decide to make a double **for** loop that ranges over the needed subproblems and to vary the first index in the outer loop. Then it needs to decrease as the loop proceeds. Similarly the second index, varying in the inner loop, needs to increase as the loop proceeds. Here is an outline of that strategy:

```
matrixOrder(n, cost, last)  // OUTLINE
    for (low = n−1; low ≥ 1; low −−)
        for (high = low+1; high ≤ n; high ++)
            Compute solution of subproblem (low, high) and store it in
            cost[low][high] and last[low][high].
    return cost[0][n];
```

The procedure to compute the solution of subproblem (low, high) is similar to mmTry2DP, except that we know the tests on lines 6a and 7a will always be false, so only lines 6d and 7d are needed from those compound statements.

The final algorithm computes the optimum choices and costs and stores them in last and cost, then calls another subroutine, extractOrderWrap (Algorithm 10.2), to extract the actual optimum multiplication sequence from last.

Algorithm 10.1   Optimal Matrix Multiplication Order

Input: An array dim containing $d_0, \ldots, d_n$, the dimensions of the matrices; n, the number of matrices to be multiplied.

Output: An array multOrder in which the ith entry, for $1 \le i \le n - 1$, contains the index of the ith multiplication in an optimum sequence. The array is passed in and the algorithm fills it. The algorithm also returns the total cost of the best multiplication order.

Remarks: The subproblem identified by the pair (low, high) is the problem of optimizing the computation of $A_{low+1} \times \cdots \times A_{high}$. Thus the top-level problem is specified as $(0, n)$. This algorithm uses two-dimensional arrays cost and last, where last represents the index of the last multiplication to be done for the subproblem. The cost is computed by the subroutine multCost, which is implemented to return the number of multiplications needed, but could be coded to compute any desired cost function.

```
float  matrixOrder(int[] dim, int n, int[] multOrder)
    int[][]  last = new int[n+1][n+1];
    float[][]  cost = new float[n+1][n+1];
    int  low, high, k, bestLast;
    float  bestCost;

    for (low = n-1; low ≥ 0; low --)
        for (high = low+1; high ≤ n; high ++)
            // Compute solution of subproblem (low, high) and
            // store it in cost[low][high] and last[low][high].
            if (high - low == 1)
                bestCost = 0;
                bestLast = -1;
            else
                bestCost = ∞;
            for (k = low+1; k ≤ high-1; k ++)
                float  a = cost[low][k];
                float  b = cost[k][high];
                float  c = multCost(dim[low], dim[k], dim[high]);
                if (a + b + c < bestCost)
                    bestCost = a + b + c;
                    bestLast = k;
                // Continue for (k)
            cost[low][high] = bestCost;
            last[low][high] = bestLast;

    extractOrderWrap(n, last, multOrder);
    return cost[0][n];

float  multCost(float leftD, float midD, float rightD)
    return leftD * midD * rightD;
```

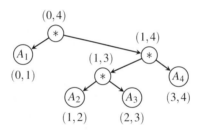

Figure 10.2 The arithmetic-expression tree corresponding to the solution in Example 10.5. Each node is identified with a subproblem and represents either a matrix or a multiplication to be performed.

Example 10.5 Matrices for cost and last

For the sequence of matrices in Example 10.4, $d_0 = 30$, $d_1 = 1$, $d_2 = 40$, $d_3 = 10$, and $d_4 = 25$. Algorithm matrixOrder would produce the following cost and last tables. Entries of "." were not computed. Entries in which last is -1 and cost is zero are subproblems consisting of a single matrix.

$$\mathsf{cost} = \begin{bmatrix} . & 0 & 1200 & 700 & 1400 \\ . & . & 0 & 400 & 650 \\ . & . & . & 0 & 10000 \\ . & . & . & . & 0 \\ . & . & . & . & . \end{bmatrix} \qquad \mathsf{last} = \begin{bmatrix} . & -1 & 1 & 1 & 1 \\ . & . & -1 & 2 & 3 \\ . & . & . & -1 & 3 \\ . & . & . & . & -1 \\ . & . & . & . & . \end{bmatrix}$$

The cost of the best way of multiplying the matrices is cost[0][4], which is 1400. Later, we will see how to extract the best multiplication order from the table. ∎

Observe that choosing the *last* multiplication to perform is equivalent to choosing the root of an arithmetic-expression tree for the multiplications; each internal node denotes a matrix multiplication and the leaves are the matrices. Figure 10.2 shows an example for the solution in Example 10.5. In mmTry2DP the first subproblem recursively decides upon the best left subtree and the second subproblem recursively decides upon the best right subtree; the order of matrixOrder doesn't make this so clear. A postorder tree traversal lists the multiplications in the order that standard expression evaluation performs them. This is done in Algorithm 10.2.

Analysis of mmTry2DP and matrixOrder

We have not looked at the extractOrder subroutine yet, but its cost will be minor, compared to the main algorithm. We have two versions, mmTry2DP and matrixOrder, that do about the same work, but in different orders. For mmTry2DP, we simply observe that it is essentially a depth-first search on a graph of $\Theta(n^2)$ vertices and $\Theta(n^3)$ edges, with a constant amount of processing per edge and vertex. For matrixOrder, the body of the innermost **for** loop requires constant time and it is executed $\Theta(n^3)$ times. So either implementation runs in $\Theta(n^3)$ time. This is far better than doing an exponential number of steps.

The extra space required for the two-dimensional arrays cost and last is in $\Theta(n^2)$. This is quadratic in the size of the input and output, both of which are in $\Theta(n)$. A recursive solution would use only $\Theta(n)$ space (for the activation frame stack). The investment of the extra space to produce the much faster algorithm is worthwhile.

There is a $\Theta(n^2)$ algorithm for determining the best multiplication order for a sequence of matrices. However, it is specialized to the cost function given by multCost in Algorithm 10.1, whereas Algorithm 10.1 does not depend on any particular cost function. See Notes and References at the end of the chapter.

10.3.4   Extracting the Optimal Order

The following recursive procedure, extractOrder, extracts an optimal order for multiplying the matrices from the last table that was computed by matrixOrder. It is called from its wrapper, extractOrderWrap, which is called from matrixOrder as the last step of its computation.

First, extractOrderWrap initializes a global variable, multOrderNext, which is the index for filling the output array multOrder. Then it calls extractOrder to do the work. The objective of extractOrder(low, high, last, multOrder) is to fill in the multOrder array with the optimal multiplication order for the subproblem specified by (low, high).

The algorithm may be recognized as a postorder traversal of a binary tree that is implicitly defined in last as follows. Let k = last[low][high] (when high − low > 1). Tree node (low, high) has as its left and right children the nodes (low, k) and (k, high), respectively. When high − low = 1, the node is a leaf. Note that extractOrder is recursive. Why is recursion, rather than dynamic programming, appropriate here?

Algorithm 10.2   Extracting Optimal Multiplication Order

Input: The number of matrices, n; the matrix last, which was computed by matrixOrder in Algorithm 10.1.

Output: Array multOrder as described in Algorithm 10.1. The array is passed in and this procedure fills positions 1 through $n - 1$.

```
int  multOrderNext;

extractOrderWrap(n, last, multOrder);
    multOrderNext = 0;
    extractOrder(0, n, last, multOrder);

extractOrder(low, high, last, multOrder)
    int  k;
    if (high – low > 1)
        k = last[low][high];
        extractOrder(low, k, last, multOrder);
        extractOrder(k, high, last, multOrder);
        multOrder[multOrderNext] = k;
        multOrderNext ++;
```

Example 10.6   Extracting multiplication order

For the last table in Example 10.5, the implicit tree traversed by extractOrder is shown in Figure 10.2. The postorder of the nodes is $(0, 1)$, $(1, 2)$, $(2, 3)$, $(1, 3)$, $(3, 4)$, $(1, 4)$, $(0, 4)$. Only the internal nodes cause an entry to be written in the multOrder array; these are $(1, 3)$, $(1, 4)$, and $(0, 4)$. Thus

$$\text{multOrder}[1] = \text{last}[1][3] = 2$$
$$\text{multOrder}[2] = \text{last}[1][4] = 3$$
$$\text{multOrder}[3] = \text{last}[0][4] = 1$$

That is, the optimal order found by the algorithm is 2, 3, 1. It corresponds to the optimal factoring $A_1((A_2A_3)A_4)$ shown in Exercise 10.4.   ∎

Analysis of extractOrder

Each invocation of extractOrder (Algorithm 10.2) visits a new node in the expression tree, which has $2n - 1$ nodes, so there are $2n - 1$ invocations, and extractOrder takes $\Theta(n)$ time. The tree might have depth that is in $\Theta(n)$, so the activation frame stack would require $\Theta(n)$ space. However, since the data structure being processed uses $\Theta(n^2)$ space, this algorithm's space requirement is probably negligible.

10.4 Constructing Optimal Binary Search Trees

In this section we consider the problem of how best to arrange a set of keys (from some linearly ordered set) in a binary search tree to minimize the average search time if we know that some keys are looked up more often than others. In a binary search tree the keys at the nodes satisfy the binary search tree property given in Definition 6.3. Recall that an in-order traversal of a binary search tree visits the nodes in increasing order of their keys. See Figure 10.3 for an example. Readers may wish to review Algorithm 6.1 for Binary Search Tree retrieval before proceeding.

We use as our measure of work the number of key comparisons done, or the number of nodes of the tree that are examined, while searching for a key. We assume, as in Section 6.4,

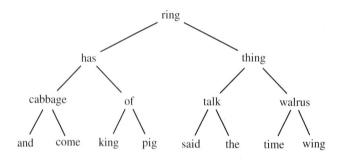

Figure 10.3   A binary search tree

that three-way comparisons are available, so the number of comparisons done to find a key in the tree is one plus the depth of the node containing the key.

Now, let's assume the keys are $K_1, K_2, \ldots, K_n$ and the probability of each key being sought is $p_1, p_2, \ldots, p_n$, respectively. The probabilities would usually come from past experience or other knowledge about the application. Frequencies (which need not sum to 1) may be used instead of probabilities.

Suppose we have arranged the keys in a binary search tree T. Let c_i be the number of comparisons done by Algorithm 6.1 to locate K_i (that is, the depth of K_i plus one). The average number of nodes examined for T is

$$A(T) = \sum_{i=1}^{n} p_i c_i. \tag{10.1}$$

If all keys are equally likely to be sought ($p_i = 1/n$ for all i), it is best to keep the tree as balanced as possible; the average number of comparisons is roughly $\lg n$ (Exercise 10.8), which is about the same as the worst case, for a balanced tree. However, if some keys are much more likely to be retrieved than others, an unbalanced structure may have a lower average number of comparisons.

Example 10.7   Computing average search time

Table 10.1 shows a list of keys and data on the number of times each key was looked up in a (hypothetical) test. The probability for each key is computed from the data. (The data were chosen to make the computation easy; they are not particularly realistic.) Now, suppose a

Key	Number of searches	Probability (p_i)
and	30	.150
cabbage	5	.025
come	10	.050
has	5	.025
king	10	.050
of	25	.125
pig	5	.025
ring	15	.075
said	15	.075
talk	10	.050
the	30	.150
thing	15	.075
time	10	.050
walrus	5	.025
wing	10	.050
	Total = 200	Total = 1.000

Table 10.1   Data on the keys

Key	Probability (p_i)	Comparisons (c_i)	$p_i c_i$
and	.150	4	.600
cabbage	.025	3	.075
come	.050	4	.200
has	.025	2	.050
king	.050	4	.200
of	.125	3	.375
pig	.025	4	.100
ring	.075	1	.075
said	.075	4	.300
talk	.050	3	.150
the	.150	4	.600
thing	.075	2	.150
time	.050	2	.100
walrus	.025	3	.075
wing	.050	4	.200
		Total =	3.250

Table 10.2   Computation of average search time

binary search tree has been constructed as in Figure 10.3. Table 10.2 shows the computation of the average search time.

The average search time is 3.25. It should seem pretty clear that this tree is not optimal. The two keys sought most often, *and* and *the*, are at the bottom level, hence require the maximum search time. Putting *and* at the root might not improve the average because, to maintain the binary search tree property, all the other keys would be in the right subtree. The prospects look better for putting *the* at the root. But let's tackle the problem systematically.   ■

We want to find a binary search tree for the keys $K_1, K_2, \ldots, K_n$ with search probabilities $p_1, p_2, \ldots, p_n$ that has minimum average search time. Assume that the keys are in sorted order. If we choose K_k as the root for the tree, then $K_1, \ldots, K_{k-1}$ must go in the left subtree, and $K_{k+1}, \ldots, K_n$ must go in the right subtree, and we now need optimal arrangements for the two subtrees. See Figure 10.4. Since we don't know which is the best choice for the root, we minimize over all choices.

The above plan looks very much like the way the matrix multiplication order problem was decomposed. This suggests that we identify each subproblem by the pair, (low, high), the low and high indexes of the subrange of keys represented by that subproblem. Thus subproblem (low, high) is to find the binary search tree with minimum *weighted* retrieval cost for keys $K_{low}, \ldots, K_{high}$ and weights $p_{low}, \ldots p_{high}$. We are switching our terminology from probabilities to weights because, in the subproblems, the p's do not sum to 1.

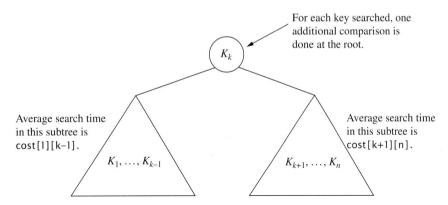

Figure 10.4   Choosing K_k as the root

Definition 10.3

We adopt the following notation:

1. Define $A(\text{low}, \text{high}, r)$ to be the minimum weighted cost for subproblem (low, high) when K_r is chosen as the root of its binary search tree.

2. Define $A(\text{low}, \text{high})$ to be the minimum weighted cost for subproblem (low, high) over all choices of root key.

3. Define $p(\text{low}, \text{high}) = p_{low} + \cdots + p_{high}$; that is, the probability that the key being searched for is *some* key in the range K_{low} through K_{high}. We will call this the *weight of the subproblem* (low, high).   ∎

If the weighted retrieval cost for a particular tree containing $K_{low}, \ldots, K_{high}$ is W (assuming it is the whole tree, so its root is at depth zero), then if the root of the subtree is at depth 1, the weighted retrieval cost is $(W + p(\text{low}, \text{high}))$. That is, every search that goes into this subtree involves one more comparison than if it is the whole tree, and the probability that the search that goes into this subtree is just $p(\text{low}, \text{high})$. (See Figure 10.4.) This relationship allows us to combine recursive solutions of subproblems to obtain the solution of the larger problem.

$$A(\text{low}, \text{high}, r) = p_r + p(\text{low}, r - 1) + A(\text{low}, r - 1)$$
$$+ p(r + 1, \text{high}) + A(r + 1, \text{high})$$
$$= p(\text{low}, \text{high}) + A(\text{low}, r - 1) + A(r + 1, \text{high}), \qquad (10.2)$$
$$A(\text{low}, \text{high}) = \min \{A(\text{low}, \text{high}, r) \mid \text{low} \le r \le \text{high}\} . \qquad (10.3)$$

We can write a recursive procedure to compute $A(\text{low}, \text{high})$, based on Equations (10.2) and (10.3). However, as with the matrix multiplication order problem studied in Section 10.3, we would observe that a lot of repeated work is done by a recursive solution. The running time of the algorithm would be exponential. Again, to avoid the repeated work, we

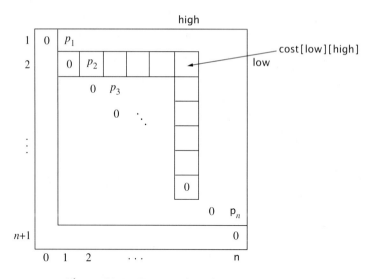

Figure 10.5   Computation of cost[low][high]

define a dictionary, implemented as two two-dimensional arrays of size $(n + 2) \times (n + 1)$, named cost and root.

As in the matrix multiplication order problem, the subproblems that cost[low][high] depends upon are in a higher numbered row (first index) or a lower numbered column (second index). See Figure 10.5. Rather than follow the order that would be taken by the recursive procedure, we can compute them in a double loop that works backwards on the first index and forwards on the second, as we did in Algorithm 10.1.

Algorithm 10.3   Optimal Binary Search Tree

Input: An array prob containing the probabilities $p_1, \ldots, p_n$ for each key; n, the number of keys.

Output: Two-dimensional arrays cost and root, allocated for size $(n + 2) \times (n + 1)$, 0-based. The arrays are passed in; the algorithm fills them. First index 0 is not used. For the subrange of keys $K_{low}, \ldots, K_{high}$, where $1 \leq low \leq high \leq n$, cost[low][high] gives the minimum weighted search cost and root[low][high] gives the best choice of root for the binary search tree on this subrange of keys. The optimal cost for whole tree is in cost[1][n].

Remarks: A pair $(i, i - 1)$ represents an empty tree, which has cost zero. Array cost has an extra row (index $n + 1$) to simplify the boundary conditions. The extra row is only used to store the empty tree $(n + 1, n)$. Note that $p(i, j) = p_i + \cdots + p_j$, as in the text, and $p(i, i - 1) = 0$.

```
optimalBST(prob, n, cost, root)  // OUTLINE
    for (low = n + 1; low ≥ 1; low --)
        for (high = low-1; high ≤ n; high ++)
            bestChoice(prob, cost, root, low, high);
    return cost;


/** Compute solution of subproblem (low, high) */
bestChoice(prob, cost, root, low, high)  // OUTLINE
    if (high < low)
        bestCost = 0;  // empty tree
        bestRoot = -1;
    else
        bestCost = ∞;
    for (r = low; r ≤ high; r ++)
        rCost = p(low, high) + cost[low][r-1] + cost[r+1][high];
        if (rCost < bestCost)
            bestCost = rCost;
            bestRoot = r;
        // Continue loop
    cost[low][high] = bestCost;
    root[low][high] = bestRoot;
    return;
```

A recursive function to construct (and return) the optimal binary search tree, using the BinTree ADT of Section 2.3.3, is similar to Algorithm 10.2 (see Exercise 10.10).

Analysis

Much of the analysis is similar to that of Algorithm 10.1. The function $p(i, j) = p_i + \cdots + p_j$ need not be computed "from scratch" each time. We leave it as an exercise to devise an efficient way of computing these sums (Exercise 10.11). Also, if integer computation is faster or more convenient for any reason, data on past searches for the keys (as in the second column in Table 10.1) could be used directly, instead of probabilities, as weights for the keys. In any case, the amount of work done by Algorithm 10.3 is clearly in $\Theta(n^3)$.

10.5 Separating Sequences of Words into Lines

This section addresses the problem of separating a sequence of words into a series of lines that comprise a paragraph. The objective is to avoid a lot of extra spaces on any line. This is an important problem in computerized typesetting. Because extra spaces on the last line of the paragraph are not objectionable, the paragraph is a natural unit to optimize. Of course, the order of the words must be maintained as they are placed in lines. Optimization of line-breaking, as this problem is often called, was introduced in the $T_{E}X$ (pronounced "tech") typesetting system developed by Don Knuth and his students at Stanford University. The version we will study is greatly simplified: We assume all letters and spaces are the same width.

The input to the line-breaking problem is a sequence of n word lengths, $w_1, \ldots, w_n$, representing the lengths of words that make up a paragraph, and a line width W. To simplify the arithmetic, we will assume that each w_i includes one space at the end of the word in its count (i.e., for "the," w would be 4), and that W includes one extra space at the end of the line (that is, for an actual line width of 80, specify $W = 81$).

The basic constraint on word placement is that, if words i through j are placed on a single line, then $w_i + \cdots + w_j \le W$. In this case the number of extra spaces is

$$X = W - (w_i + \cdots + w_j).$$

The penalty for extra spaces is assumed to be some function of X. For our discussion, the line penalty is specified as X^3, but the method of solution should work on a variety of penalty functions. (A more realistic penalty might also depend on the number of words on the line, because extra space can be distributed among the words.) There is no penalty for extra spaces on the last line of the paragraph. The penalty for the paragraph is the sum of the penalties for individual lines, and is to be minimized.

There is a simple greedy algorithm for this problem: Simply pack as many words as possible into the first line, then into the second line, and so on, until the paragraph is completed. Even though this does not guarantee an optimal line-breaking (you should make up a counterexample), in practice it works "pretty well" most of the time, and is the method used in many software packages.

Example 10.8   Line-breaking

Consider the quotation at the beginning of the chapter, which we take to be the whole paragraph:

i	1	2	3	4	5	6	7	8	9	10	11
	Those	who	cannot	remember	the	past	are	condemned	to	repeat	it.
w_i	6	4	7	9	4	5	4	10	3	7	4

Suppose $W = 17$. The greedy strategy groups words into lines as follows:

words	(1, 2, 3)	(4, 5)	(6, 7)	(8, 9)	(10, 11)
X	0	4	8	4	0
penalty	0	64	512	64	0

Is this optimal?   ∎

Let's approach the problem by decomposing it into subproblems, as we did for the problems of earlier sections of this chapter. Suppose we break words $1, \ldots, k$ into lines and then break words $k + 1, \ldots, n$ into lines, independently. If we solve each subproblem optimally, is their combination optimal? Not necessarily, because k might be a bad place for a line break. However, if we backtrack over all choices of k, then one of them will be optimal. This looks similar to the approaches of the matrix multiplication order and optimal binary search tree problems. A subproblem is identified as a pair of indexes (i, j). The objective of the subproblem is to break words i through j into lines with minimum penalty.

Does the above plan give a correct recursive solution? We have to be careful, because the penalty on the last line of the paragraph is zero, but the penalty on the last line of all subproblems that do *not* end the paragraph is computed as usual. So we really have two kinds of subproblem. With this proviso we may try to prove that, for some choice of k, the combination of the optimal solutions for the subranges $(1, k)$ and $(k + 1, n)$ gives an optimal solution for $(1, n)$.

Before going into a proof, let's consider the size of the dictionary and the subproblem graph. There are about $n^2/2$ subproblems (vertices), and each subproblem (i, j) has an edge to about $j - i$ other subproblems. There will be $\Theta(n^3)$ edges altogether. Certainly, a simple backtracking recursive procedure will run in exponential time, and the dynamic programming version will be in polynomial time, just as we saw in the earlier problems of this chapter. But is this the best bound we can achieve? If we can come up with a *more concise* way to identify subproblems than a pair of integers, then the dictionary will be smaller, and the subproblem graph will be smaller. Readers are encouraged to try to find a different strategy for problem decomposition that leads to more concise identifiers and a smaller dictionary, before reading on.

·   ■   ■

There is a clue to the solution in the observation we made that there were two kinds of subproblem in the proposed strategy: One kind includes the last line of the paragraph; the other kind does not. But the first kind is really identified by a *single* integer, the beginning of its subrange. If it concludes the paragraph, the end of its subrange must be n. That is, the identifier must be of the form (k, n), where $1 \le k \le n$, but n is part of the input and is fixed throughout the problem. Therefore n is not a necessary part of the dictionary identifier for these subproblems. In fact, we only have about n subproblems of the form (k, n).

Do we really need the subproblems of the form (i, j) where $j \ne n$? Let's apply Method 99 (Section 3.2.2). Assume we *already have* a subroutine that can find optimal line-breaking solutions for problems of 99 words or less—call it lineBreak99—and it assumes the end of the problem is the end of the paragraph. How can we exploit this to solve the line-breaking problem for $n = 100$ words or less, that is, to write lineBreak100? After a little thought we see that we can iterate over the choices of how many words to place on the *first* line. Letting this number be k, the remaining problem is how to optimally place words $k + 1, \ldots, n$ on the remaining lines. But we can use lineBreak99 for this! We choose the k that minimizes the combined penalty for the first line and the remaining lines. Now we drop the suffixes "100" and "99" to get a recursive procedure.

This is still a backtracking algorithm, because we don't know the best choice of k, so we must backtrack over all the choices. But we only need choices that fit all the chosen words on one line, so there are at most $W/2$ choices for k. (Recall W is the line width, and there is at least one space after each word.) The outline of the backtracking procedure follows. Its correctness is easy to prove by induction.

lineBreak(w, W, i, n, L) *// OUTLINE*
    if $(w_i + \cdots + w_n \leq W)$
        Put all words on line L and set penalty to 0.
    else
        Set penalty to the minimum of kPenalty over all $k > 0$ such that
        $w_i + \cdots + w_{i+k-1} \leq W$, where $X = W - (w_i + \cdots + w_{i+k-1})$, and
        kPenalty = lineCost(X) + lineBreak(w, W, i+k, n, L+1);
        Let k_{min} be the k that produced the minimum penalty.
        Put words i through $i + k_{min} - 1$ on line L.
    return penalty;

The identifier for the dictionary to go with lineBreak is a single integer in the range $1, \ldots, n$. Therefore the dictionary can be a simple array. The conversion of lineBreak into lineBreakDP follows the method described in Definition 10.2:

1. Before making a recursive call, see if the solution is already in the dictionary;

2. Before returning from the procedure, *store* the solution just computed.

Analysis

The subproblem graph has about n vertices (subproblems) and has at most $W/2$ edges at any vertex, so the running time is in $\Theta(Wn)$. The extra storage space used for the dictionary is $\Theta(n)$. Normally, W is regarded as a constant, so the running time is in $\Theta(n)$. By reducing the size of the dictionary from n^2 to n we saved *two* degrees in the polynomial for the running time: from $\Theta(n^3)$ to $\Theta(n)$.

10.6 Developing a Dynamic Programming Algorithm

The essence of dynamic programming algorithms is that they trade space for speed by storing solutions to subproblems rather than recomputing them. From the examples we have seen, we can make some general comments about how to develop a dynamic programming solution to a problem.

1. It is usually useful to tackle the problem "top-down" as if we were going to develop a recursive algorithm; we figure out how to solve a large problem assuming we know solutions for smaller problems.

2. If it appears that saving results from smaller problems can avoid repeated computation, define an appropriate dictionary for saving results, and make a clear statement to characterize the entries in the dictionary. Try to make the identifier for dictionary entries as concise as possible; this keeps the dictionary and the number of subproblems small. For example, in Section 10.5 we saw that one problem-decomposition strategy required two integers to specify a subproblem and led to a $\Theta(n^3)$ algorithm, while a different strategy required only one integer to specify a subproblem and led to a $\Theta(n)$

algorithm. Carry out the conversion described in Definition 10.2. The appropriate initialization can be determined at this point.

3. Based on the number of subproblems (maximum size of the dictionary is an upper bound) and the number of edges in the subproblem graph, the complexity of the dynamic programming procedure can be analyzed by its relationship to depth-first search on the subproblem graph.

4. Decide on an appropriate data structure for the dictionary. Often it is a one- or two-dimensional array. In these simple cases, the "abstraction" can be simplified out. If a more involved dictionary is needed (e.g., because the identifiers are too sparse for a simple array to be practical), it is probably best to stay with the division of tasks that the ADT methodology imposes.

5. If possible, analyze the structure of the subproblem graph, and figure out a simpler order in which the dictionary entries can be computed. The requirement is that they be computed in *some* reverse topological order. Then all the subproblems that the current subproblem depends on have been computed earlier.

6. Determine how to get the solution to the problem from the data in the dictionary. For problems such as those in Sections 10.3, 10.4, and 10.5, the optimum cost is in a particular place in the dictionary. The dictionary may serve as input for another algorithm to extract the choices that produced the optimum cost. We saw examples to extract the optimal matrix multiplication order or construct the optimal binary search tree. Since the dictionary has data for all subproblems in the subproblem graph, usually only a small subset of the data is related to the final optimum solution.

Experience with dynamic programming (and recursion) helps provide good intuition about what will work best for various problems. Some problems that have appeared earlier in the text can also be solved within the dynamic programming framework, such as maximum independent set in a tree (Exercise 3.13) and maximum subsequence sum (Exercise 4.59). Others will appear in Chapters 11 and 13.

Exercises

Section 10.1   Introduction

⋆ **10.1**   Define A_n to be the number of activation frames created in the computation of F_n, the nth Fibonacci number, using the natural recursive function fib(n), given in Example 3.1. Note that $A_0 = 1$, $A_1 = 1$, and $A_2 = 3$. By counting nodes in Figure 7.13, we find that $A_6 = 25$.

⋆ **a.**   Let $\phi = \frac{1}{2}(\sqrt{5} + 1) \approx 1.618$. This is called the Golden Ratio. Show that F_n is in $\Theta(\phi^n)$.

   b.   Show that $A_n = 2 F_{n+1} - 1$ for $n \geq 1$. Combined with part (a), this establishes the asymptotic order of the procedure fib(n). Interestingly, the time complexity of fib(n) is $\Theta(F_n)$, and F_n is the value it computes.

10.2   Modify the procedure of Example 10.1, which computes Fibonacci numbers, to use only a constant number of integers for work space and still compute F_n in $\Theta(n)$ time.

Section 10.3   Multiplying a Sequence of Matrices

10.3   This exercise counts subsequences of the sequence $(0, 1, \ldots, n)$. (A subsequence is any subset of the sequence elements in the same order; they need not be contiguous in the original sequence.)

a.   Show that there are 2^{n+1} distinct subsequences, including the empty subsequence.

b.   Show that there are fewer than $n^3/4$ subsequences of length three or less.

c.   Conclude that there are at least 2^n distinct subsequences of length four of more, for $n \geq 5$.

10.4   The recursive backtracking procedure mmTry2 in Section 10.3 computes the optimal cost for multiplying a sequence of matrices. Show that the number of recursive calls made during the execution of mmTry2 is bounded from below by an exponential function of n. (A similar argument would show that the corresponding recursive solution for the optimal binary search tree problem in Section 10.4 is also exponential.)

Hint: The exact recurrence equation for mmTry2 is complicated but we can get a simplified version by ignoring all but the two largest subproblems, which are of size $n - 1$ when the overall problem is of size n. Derive the *inequality*:

$$T(n) \geq 2T(n - 1) + n$$

and find a lower bound on its solution.

10.5   Suppose the dimensions of the matrices A, B, C, and D are $20 \times 2, 2 \times 15, 15 \times 40$, and 40×4, respectively, and we want to know how best to compute $A \times B \times C \times D$. Show the arrays cost, last, and multOrder computed by Algorithms 10.1 and 10.2.

10.6   Let $A_1, \ldots, A_n$ be matrices where the dimensions of A_i are $d_{i-1} \times d_i$, for $i = 1, \ldots, n$. Here is a proposal for a greedy algorithm to determine the best order in which to perform the matrix multiplications to compute $A_1 \times A_2 \times \ldots \times A_n$.

> greedyOrder(dim, n) // OUTLINE
> > At each step, choose the largest remaining dimension (among dim[1], . . . ,
> > dim[n−1]), and multiply two adjacent matrices that share that dimension.

Observe that this strategy produces the optimal order of multiplications for the matrices in Example 10.4.

a.   What is the order of the running time of this algorithm (only to determine the order in which to multiply the matrices, not including the actual multiplications)?

b.   Either give a convincing argument that this strategy will always minimize the number of multiplications, or give an example where it does not do so.

10.7 Construct an example with only three or four matrices where the worst multiplication order does at least 100 times as many element-wise multiplications as the best order.

Section 10.4 Constructing Optimal Binary Search Trees

10.8 Suppose all keys are equally likely to be searched for in a binary search tree that is completely balanced, with $n = 2^k - 1$ nodes. Find an expression for the average number of comparisons for a retrieval, assuming three-way comparisons are available. (Note that the worst case is $k = \lg(n + 1)$.)

10.9

a. Compute the values in the matrices cost and root in the dynamic programming algorithm for finding the optimal binary search tree (Algorithm 10.3) for the following keys. (The probabilities are given in parentheses for each key.)

$$A\ (.20),\quad B\ (.24),\quad C\ (.16),\quad D\ (.28),\quad E\ (.04),\quad F\ (.08)$$

b. Draw the optimal tree.

10.10 Suppose Algorithm 10.3 has been run for the keys $K_1, \ldots, K_n$ with probabilities $p_1, \ldots, p_n$. Write an algorithm that uses the root array computed by Algorithm 10.3 to construct the optimal binary search tree. Use the BinTree ADT of Section 2.3.3 to construct the result. What is the asymptotic order of the running time of your algorithm? (It should be in $O(n)$.) *Hint*: Look at Algorithm 10.2.

⋆ **10.11** Show how $p(i, j)$, as used in Algorithm 10.3, can be calculated in $\Theta(1)$ per call, after $\Theta(n)$ preprocessing.

10.12 Describe a straightforward greedy algorithm for the problem of constructing optimal binary search trees. Does it always produce the optimal tree? Justify your answer with an argument or a counterexample.

Section 10.5 Separating Sequences of Words into Lines

10.13 Show that the greedy algorithm for line breaking that was mentioned in Section 10.5 does not produce the minimum penalty in all cases.

10.14

a. Find an optimal line breaking for Example 10.8 by using $\mathcal{DP}$(lineBreak).
b. How many subproblems need to be evaluated?
⋆ c. How many subproblems would be evaluated using lineBreak in its natural recursive form? *Hint*: Use dynamic programming to count how many calls the natural recursive form makes.

10.15 Complete the sketch of the line-breaking algorithm in Section 10.5. The output of the overall algorithm should be an array lastWord with the meaning (after the algorithm terminates) that lastWord[L] is the index of the last word to be placed on line L. (When lastWord[L] is n, the paragraph is completed on line L.)

Additional Problems

10.16   The binomial coefficients can be defined by the recurrence equation:

$$C(n, k) = C(n - 1, k - 1) + C(n - 1, k) \qquad \text{for } n > 0 \text{ and } k > 0$$
$$C(n, 0) = 1 \qquad \text{for } n \geq 0$$
$$C(0, k) = 0 \qquad \text{for } k > 0.$$

$C(n, k)$ is also called "n choose k" and denoted $\binom{n}{k}$. It is the number of ways to choose k distinct objects from a set of n objects. (See Equation (1.1) and Exercise 1.2.) Consider the following four ways to compute $C(n, k)$ for $n \geq k$.

1. A recursive function as suggested by the recurrence relation given for $C(n, k)$.
2. A dynamic programming algorithm.
3. The formula $C(n, k) = \dfrac{n(n - 1) \cdots (n - k + 1)}{k!}$.
4. The formula $C(n, k) = \dfrac{n!}{k!(n - k)!}$.

Evaluate these methods as follows.

a.   Write out an outline of each method to make it clear you understand what work is to be done for each.

b.   Compare the amount of work done by each method. Indicate what operations you are counting. Compare the amount of space used by each method.

c.   Are there any other strong advantages or disadvantages of any of the four methods? (For example, is one of them more likely to cause an arithmetic overflow error? What about truncations caused by integer division?)

10.17   Let E be an array of n distinct integers. Give an algorithm to find the length of a longest increasing subsequence of entries in E. The subsequence is not required to be contiguous in the original sequence. For example, if the entries are 11, 17, 5, 8, 6, 4, 7, 12, 3, a longest increasing subsequence is 5, 6, 7, 12. Analyze the worst-case running time and space requirements of your algorithm.

10.18   Two character strings may have many common substrings. Substrings are required to be contiguous in the original string. For example, *photograph* and *tomography* have several common substrings of length one (i.e., single letters), and common substrings *ph*, *to*, and *ograph* (as well as all the substrings of *ograph*). The maximum common substring length is 6.

Let $X = x_1 x_2 \cdots x_n$ and $Y = y_1 y_2 \cdots y_m$ be two character strings. Give an algorithm to find the maximum common substring length for X and Y. Analyze the worst-case running time and space requirements of your algorithm as functions of n and m. *Note:* There is a $\Theta(nm)$ dynamic programming solution, and there are other $\Theta(nm)$ non–dynamic-programming solutions. Try to find two solutions.

10.19 Let A and B be arrays of n integers each. A *common subsequence* of A and B is a sequence that is a subsequence of A and is a subsequence of B. The subsequence is not required to be contiguous in A or B. For example, if the entries of A are 5, 8, 6, 4, 7, 1, 3, and the entries of B are 4, 5, 6, 9, 7, 3, 2, a longest common subsequence is 5, 6, 7, 3. Give an algorithm to find a longest common subsequence of A and B. Analyze the worst-case running time and space requirements of your algorithm.

10.20 Suppose we are given three strings of characters: $X = x_1x_2\cdots x_m$, $Y = y_1y_2\cdots y_n$, and $Z = z_1z_2\cdots z_{m+n}$. Z is said to be a *shuffle* of X and Y if Z can be formed by interspersing the characters from X and Y in a way that maintains the left-to-right ordering of the characters from each string. For example, *cchocohilaptes* is a shuffle of *chocolate* and *chips*, but *chocochilatspe* is not. Devise a dynamic programming algorithm that takes as input X, Y, Z, m, and n, and determines whether or not Z is a shuffle of X and Y. Analyze the worst-case running time and space requirements of your algorithm. *Hint*: The values in your dictionary should be Boolean, not numeric.

⋆ **10.21** The *partition problem* is, given a sequence of n nonnegative integers as input, to find a way to partition this sequence into two disjoint subsequences so that the sums of the integers in each of the two subsequences are equal. More formally, given nonnegative integers $s_1, \ldots, s_n$ that sum to S, find a subset I of $\{1, 2, \ldots, n\}$ such that

$$\sum_{i \in I} s_i = \sum_{j \notin I} s_j = S/2,$$

or determine that there is no such subset. Give a dynamic programming algorithm for the partition problem. Analyze the worst-case running time and space requirements of your algorithm as functions of n and S.

⋆ **10.22** Suppose you have n dollars to invest in any of m enterprises. Assume that n is an integer, and all investments must be in integer amounts. The input table invReturn describes the expected returns for individual investments. Specifically, invReturn[d][j] is the expected return for an investment of d dollars in enterprise j.

    a. Write an algorithm to determine the maximum possible expected return for investing n dollars. (You may assume that the columns of invReturn are nondecreasing; that is, investing more money in one enterprise won't decrease your return from that enterprise.)

    b. Analyze the worst-case running time and space requirements of your algorithm as functions of n and m.

    c. Expand your algorithm to determine the optimal investment plan. (Do whatever is needed to tell how much to invest in each enterprise.) Analyze the worst-case running time and space requirements.

d. Suppose you can't make the assumption made in part (a)? In other words, suppose investing additional dollars in one enterprise can reduce your overall return from that enterprise. Either prove that your algorithm already works correctly in such cases, or give an example where it does not compute the maximum possible return, and then show how to modify it so that it works correctly in general.

10.23 Suppose the denominations of the coins in a country are $c_1 > c_2 > \ldots > c_n$ (e.g., 50, 25, 10, 5, 1 for the United States). The *coin changing problem* is, given a sequence of coin denominations and an amount, a cents, as input, to determine the minimum number of coins needed to make a cents in change. (You may assume that $c_n = 1$, so that it is always possible to make change for any amount a.)

a. Describe a greedy algorithm for this problem. Explain how it would work to make change for $1.43 (U.S.).

b. Prove that your greedy algorithm works for U.S. coins; that is, it will make the change using the minimum possible number of coins.

c. Make up an example of denominations for a fictitious country's coin system where your greedy algorithm won't give the minimum number of coins.

d. Give a dynamic programming algorithm to solve the problem. Analyze the worst-case running time and space requirements of your algorithm as functions of n and a.

10.24 Give an algorithm to determine how many distinct ways there are to give a cents in change using any coins from among pennies, nickels, dimes, quarters, and half-dollars. For example, there are six ways to give 17 cents change: a dime, a nickel, and two pennies; a dime and seven pennies; three nickels and two pennies; two nickels and seven pennies; one nickel and 12 pennies; and 17 pennies.

★ **10.25** An n-sided *polygon* is an undirected graph with n vertices and n edges that form a simple cycle, $v_0, v_1, \ldots, v_{n-1}, v_0$. (It is conventional to index polygon vertices from 0.) A *chord* of a polygon is an edge (undirected) between any two nonadjacent vertices of the polygon. Two distinct chords, say wx and yz, are *nonintersecting* if there is a path of polygon edges from w to x that does not contain either y or z as an intermediate vertex. If two chords share exactly one vertex, they are nonintersecting. A *triangulation* of a polygon is a maximal set of mutually nonintersecting chords. A *triangulated polygon* is the graph consisting of the original polygon and a set of chords that comprise a triangulation of it.

The definitions are motivated by thinking of the vertices of the polygon as being positioned in counterclockwise sequence around a circle; however, this positioning is not required by the definitions. The figure below shows a polygon with its vertices on a circle, an example of intersecting chords, then two possible triangulations.

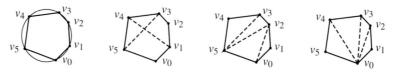

Suppose real weights are associated with all the possible chords. For example, if the polygon vertices are points in space, the weight of a chord might be the distance between its two vertices, but other weighting schemes are possible, also. The problem for this exercise is, given a polygon and a set of weights for its chords as input, to find a *minimum-weight triangulation*, that is, one whose sum of chord weights is minimized.

a. Show that each polygon edge is in exactly one triangle of a triangulated polygon.

★ **b.** Design a dynamic programming algorithm to solve the minimum-weight polygon triangulation problem in general. Analyze its worst-case running time and the space requirements as functions of n.

★ **c.** Now suppose the polygon vertices are at given positions on the rim of a circle and the weight of a chord $v_i v_j$ is the amount of circular arc between v_i and v_j, in degrees. For example, if a chord cuts off a quarter of the circle, its weight is 90. Thus each weight is positive and is at most 180. Can you design an algorithm for this special case that runs faster than the one in part (b)? Analyze its worst-case running time and the space requirements as functions of n.

★ **10.26** Suppose you have inherited the rights to 500 previously unreleased songs recorded by the popular group Raucous Rockers. You plan to release a set of five compact disks (numbered 1 through 5) with a selection of these songs. Each disk can hold a maximum of 60 minutes of music, and a song can't overlap from one disk to the next. Since you are a classical music fan and have no way of judging the artistic merits of these songs, you decide on the following criteria for making the selection:

1. The songs will be recorded on the set of disks in order by the date they were written.

2. The number of songs included will be maximized.

Suppose you have a list of the lengths of the songs, $l_1, l_2, \ldots, l_{500}$, in order by the date they were written. (Each song is less than 60 minutes long.)

Give an algorithm to determine the maximum number of songs that can be included in the set satisfying the given criteria. *Hint*: Let T[i][j] be the minimum amount of time needed for any i songs selected from among the first j songs. T should be interpreted to include the blank time, if any, at the end of a completed disk. In other words, if a selection of songs uses one disk plus the first 15 minutes of a second disk, count the time for that selection as 75 minutes even if there are a few blank minutes at the end of the first disk.

Programs

1. Write a program to construct an optimal binary search tree using Algorithm 10.3 and your solution to Exercise 10.10.

2. Write a program to perform line breaking on a sequence of words that makes up a paragraph. Implement several strategies, including the simple greedy strategy and the minimum-penalty dynamic programming solution. Try some variants for the lineCost function, such as X^3 as in the text, and $(X/k)^3$, where X is the number of extra spaces

and k is the number of words on the line. For the total penalty, try taking the minimum of lineCost over all lines in the paragraph, instead of the sum.

Notes and References

Bellman (1957) and Bellman and Dreyfus (1962) are standard references for dynamic programming from the control theoretical point of view.

For a much more extensive discussion of optimal binary search trees, see Knuth (1998). Yao (1982) describes techniques for speeding up dynamic programming solutions, and contains $O(n^2)$ algorithms for the matrix multiplication order and binary search tree problems covered in Sections 10.3 and 10.4.

Exercise 10.26 was contributed by J. Frankle.

Thompson (1986) describes the use of dynamic programming to solve chess endgames with a specific set of pieces on the board by working backwards from all possible checkmate positions. The work is also summarized in Bentley (1986). Later results appear in Thompson (1990, 1991, and 1996).

11

String Matching

11.1 Introduction

In this chapter we study the problem of detecting the occurrence of a particular substring, called a *pattern*, in another string, called the *text*. The problem is usually presented in the context of character strings and arises often in text processing, and we will assume this context in our discussion and examples. However, the solutions presented are applicable to other contexts, such as matching a string of bytes containing graphical data, machine code, or other data, and matching a sublist of a linked list. The first three algorithms described in this chapter look for an exact match of the pattern. The problem of approximate matching is addressed in Section 11.5. We use the following nomenclature throughout the chapter.

Definition 11.1   Notation for patterns and text

This chapter uses the following notational conventions.

P	The pattern being searched for
T	The text in which P is sought
m	The length of P
n	The length of T, not known to the algorithm, used for analysis only
p_i, t_i	The ith characters in P and T are denoted with lowercase letters and subscripts. The initial index of both P and T is assumed to be 1.
j	Current position within T
k	Current position within P

We assume a **boolean** function is given that tells us when we are beyond the last character of the text: endText(T, j) returns **true** if j is greater than the index of the last character of T, and returns **false** otherwise.   ■

For the pseudocode in this chapter we assume that both P and T are arrays of characters. This is a reasonable assumption for P because it is assumed to be of relatively short length, and available for preprocessing by the string-matching algorithms. However, T may well be a different type, may be extremely long, and may not be available all at once in memory. However, we will see that the algorithms perform only limited operations on T, and do not use the full flexibility of array access, so they can be adapted easily for applications in which T is not an array. Some of these issues are addressed in the exercises. We will assume that n is fairly large relative to m. Through the use of endText, algorithms do not need to know n. However, n appears in the analysis.

Java sidelight: Java provides a built-in class named **String**, which is not the same as an array of characters. In the interest of language independence we do not use this built-in class.

You should think about the string-matching problem and write out, or at least outline, an algorithm to solve it before proceeding. Your algorithm will probably be very similar to the first one we present here, which is fairly straightforward.

$$
\begin{array}{c}
p_1 \quad \cdots \quad p_{k-1} \quad \boxed{p_k \quad \cdots \quad p_m} \\
\downarrow \qquad \cdots \qquad \downarrow \\
t_1 \quad \cdots \quad t_i \quad \cdots \quad t_{j-1} \quad t_j \qquad \cdots \qquad t_n
\end{array}
$$

Matched   Next comparison

Figure 11.1 The general picture for Algorithm 11.1

11.2 A Straightforward Solution

Let us first examine a very straightforward procedure for string matching. Starting at the beginning of each string, we compare characters, one after the other, until either the pattern is exhausted or a mismatch is found. In the former case we are done; a copy of the pattern has been found in the text. In the latter case we start over again, comparing the first pattern character with the second text character. In general, when a mismatch is found, we (figuratively) slide the pattern one more place forward over the text and start again comparing the first pattern character with the next text character.

Example 11.1 Straightforward string matching

Comparisons are done (in left-to-right order) on the pairs of characters indicated by arrows. When a mismatch occurs, the pattern is moved one position forward with respect to the text, and the comparisons start again at the left end of the pattern.

Observe that moving the pattern all the way past the point where the first mismatch occurred could fail to detect an occurrence of the pattern. ■

Algorithm 11.1 Simple String Matching

Input: P and T, the pattern and text strings; m, the length of P. The pattern is assumed to be nonempty.

Output: The return value is the index in T where a copy of P begins, or -1 if no match for P is found.

Remarks: The general picture is shown in Figure 11.1. The index variable i is not really needed in the algorithm since it can be computed from j and k (that is, $i = j - k + 1$). The function endText is as defined in Definition 11.1.

```
int simpleScan(char[] P, char[] T, int m)
    int match;  // value to return
    int i, j, k;
    // i is the current guess at where P begins in T;
    // j is the index of the current character in T;
    // k is the index of the current character in P.
    match = −1;
    j = 1; k = 1;
    i = j;
    while (endText(T, j) == false)
        if (k > m)
            match = i;  // Match found
            break;

        if (t_j == p_k)
            j ++; k ++;
        else
            // Back up over matched characters.
            int backup = k − 1;
            j = j − backup; k = k − backup;
            // Slide pattern forward, start over.
            j ++;
            i = j;
        // Continue loop.
    return match;
```

Analysis

We will count the character comparisons done by our string-matching algorithms. This is certainly reasonable for Algorithm 11.1, given its simple loop structure. There are a few easy cases. If the pattern appears at the beginning of the text, m comparisons are done. If p_1 is not in T at all, n comparisons are done. What is the worst case? The number of comparisons would be maximized if for each value of i—that is, each possible starting place for P in T—all but the last character of P matched the corresponding text characters. Thus the number of character comparisons in the worst case is at most mn, and the complexity of the algorithm is in $O(mn)$.

For some algorithms, inputs that require a lot of work at one step may require very little work at another step. Thus adding up the maximum possible work at each step gives an upper bound but not necessarily an exact value for the work done in the worst case.

To show that the worst case *requires* (roughly) mn comparisons (i.e., to show that the worst-case complexity is in $\Theta(mn)$), we must show that the situation described can really occur, that is, that P and T can be constructed so that all characters in P but the last one match corresponding characters beginning anywhere in T. Let $P = `AA \cdots AB$' ($m − 1$ $A$'s followed by a $B$) and $T = `A \cdots A$' (n A's).

This worst-case example is not one that occurs often in natural language text. In fact, Algorithm 11.1 works quite well on the average for natural language. In some empirical studies the algorithm did only about 1.1 character comparisons for each character in T (up to the point where a match was found or to the end of T if no match was found). Thus few characters in the text had to be examined more than once.

Algorithm 11.1 has a property that in some applications is undesirable: It may often be necessary to back up in the text string (by the amount backup $- 1$, since backup is subtracted from j, and 1 is added to initiate a new match attempt in the **while** loop). If the text is being read from an input source that does not permit backing up, this makes the algorithm difficult to use (see Exercise 11.4 for a space-efficient solution). The algorithm we present in the next section was devised specifically to eliminate the need to back up in the text. It turned out to be faster (in the worst case) as well.

11.3 The Knuth-Morris-Pratt Algorithm

We first describe briefly, without formal algorithms, an approach to the pattern-matching problem that has some important good points but also some drawbacks. The construction used by the main algorithm of this section was suggested by the method we describe now and salvages some of its advantages while eliminating the disadvantages.

11.3.1 Pattern Matching with Finite Automata

Given a pattern P, it is possible to construct a *finite automaton* that can be used to scan the text for a copy of P very quickly. A finite automaton can easily be interpreted as a special kind of machine or flowchart, and a knowledge of automata theory is not necessary to understand this method.

Definition 11.2

Let Σ be the alphabet, or set of characters, from which the characters in P and T may be chosen, and let $\alpha = |\Sigma|$. The flowchart, or finite automaton, has two types of nodes:

1. Some *read* nodes, which mean "Read the next text character. If there are no further characters in the text string, halt; there is no match." One *read* node is designated the *start* node.
2. A *stop* node, which means "Stop; a match was found." It is marked with a $*$. ∎

The flowchart has α arrows leading out from each *read* node. Each arrow is labeled with a character from Σ. The arrow that matches the text character just read is the arrow to be followed; that is, it indicates which node to go to next. You should study the example in Figure 11.2 to understand why the arrows point where they do. The *read* nodes serve as a sort of memory. For instance, if execution reaches the third *read* node, the last two characters read from the text were A's. What preceded them is irrelevant. For a successful match, they must be followed immediately by a B and a C. If the next character is a B we can move on to node 4, which remembers that AAB has appeared. On the other hand, if

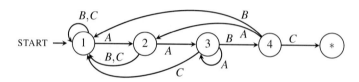

Figure 11.2   The finite automaton for P = '$AABC$'

the next character read at node 3 were a C, we would have to return to node 1 and wait for another A to begin the pattern.

Once the flowchart for the pattern is constructed, the text can be tested for an occurrence of the pattern by examining each text character only once, hence in $O(n)$ time. This is a big improvement over Algorithm 11.1, both in timing and in the fact that, once a text character has been examined, it never has to be reconsidered; there is no backing up in the text. The difficulty is constructing the finite automaton—that is, deciding where all the arrows go. There are well-known algorithms to construct the finite automaton to recognize a particular pattern, but in the worst case these algorithms require a lot of time. The difficulty arises from the fact that there is an arrow for each character in Σ leading out from each *read* node. It takes time to determine where each arrow should point, and space to represent $m\alpha$ arrows. Thus a better algorithm will have to eliminate some of the arrows.

11.3.2   The Knuth-Morris-Pratt Flowchart

When constructing the finite automaton for a pattern P, it is easy to put in the arrows that correspond to a successful match. For example, when drawing Figure 11.2 for the pattern '$AABC$', the first step is to draw

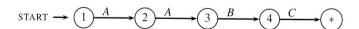

The difficult part is the insertion of the rest of the arrows. The Knuth-Morris-Pratt algorithm (which, for brevity, will be called the KMP algorithm) also constructs a sort of flowchart to be used to scan the text. The KMP flowchart contains the easy arrows— that is, the ones to follow if the desired character is read from the text—but it contains only one other arrow from each node, an arrow to be followed if the desired character was *not* read from the text. The arrows are called the success links and the failure links, respectively. The KMP flowchart differs from the finite automaton in several details: The character labels of the KMP flowchart are on the nodes rather than on the arrows; the next character from the text is read only after a success link has been followed; the same text character is reconsidered if a failure link is followed; there is an extra node that causes a new text character to be read. The scan starts at this node. As in the finite automaton, if the node labeled with the $*$ is reached, a copy of the pattern has been found; if the end of the text is reached elsewhere in the flowchart, the scan terminates unsuccessfully. This

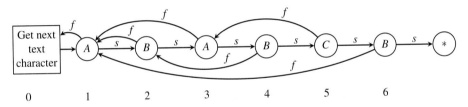

Figure 11.3   The KMP flowchart for $P =$ '$ABABCB$'

KMP cell number	Text being scanned		Success (s) or Failure (f)
	Index	Character	
1	1	A	s
2	2	C	f
1	2	C	f
0	2	C	get next char.
1	3	A	s
2	4	B	s
3	5	A	s
4	6	A	f
2	6	A	f
1	6	A	s
2	7	B	s
3	8	A	s
4	9	B	s
5	10	A	f
3	10	A	s
4	11	none	failure

Table 11.1   Action of the KMP flowchart in Figure 11.3 for the pattern '$ABABCB$' on the text '$ACABAABABA$'

informal description of the scanning procedure should enable you to use the KMP flowchart in Figure 11.3 to scan a text string. Try '$ACABAABABA$' and refer to Table 11.1 if you have difficulty.

We now need a computer representation of the KMP flowchart, an algorithm to construct it (to determine how to set the failure links), a formal algorithm for the scan procedure, and an analysis of the two algorithms.

11.3.3   Construction of the KMP Flowchart

The flowchart representation is quite simple; it uses two arrays, one containing the characters of the pattern and one containing the failure links. The success links are implicit in the ordering of the array entries.

Let fail be the array of failure links; fail[k] will be the index of the node pointed to by the failure link at the kth node, for $1 \leq k \leq m$. The special node that merely forces the next text character to be read is considered to be the zero-th node; fail[1] = 0. To see how to set the other failure links, we consider an example.

Example 11.2   Setting fail links for the KMP algorithm

Let $P = $ '$ABABABCB$' and suppose that the first six characters have matched six consecutive text characters as indicated:

$$
\begin{array}{lll}
P: & \text{A B A B A B} & \text{C B} \\
   & \downarrow \downarrow \downarrow \downarrow \downarrow \downarrow & \\
T: & \dots \quad \text{A B A B A B} & x \quad \dots
\end{array}
$$

Suppose that the next text character, x, is not a 'C'. The next possible place where the pattern could begin in the text is at the third position shown, that is, as follows:

$$
\begin{array}{lll}
P: & \text{A B A B} & \text{A B C B} \\
T: & \dots \quad \text{A B} \quad \text{A B A B} & x \quad \dots
\end{array}
$$

The pattern is moved forward so that the longest initial segment that matches part of the text preceding x is lined up with that part of the text. Now x should be tested to see if it is an A to match the third A of the pattern. Thus the failure link for the node containing the C should point to the node containing the third A.   ∎

The general picture is shown in Figure 11.4. When a mismatch occurs, we want to slide P forward, but maintain the longest overlap of a prefix of P with a suffix of the part of the text that has matched the pattern so far. Thus the current text character should be compared to p_r next; that is, fail[k] should be r. But we want to construct the flowchart before we ever see T. How do we determine r without knowing T? The key observation is that when we do scan T, the part of T just scanned will have matched the part of P just scanned, so we just need to find the longest overlap of a prefix of P with a suffix of the part of P just scanned.

Definition 11.3   Fail links

We define fail[k] as the largest r (with $r < k$) such that $p_1 \cdots p_{r-1}$ matches $p_{k-r+1} \cdots p_{k-1}$. That is, the $(r-1)$-character *prefix* of P is identical to the $(r-1)$-character substring *ending* at index $k-1$. Thus the fail links are determined by repetition within P itself.   ∎

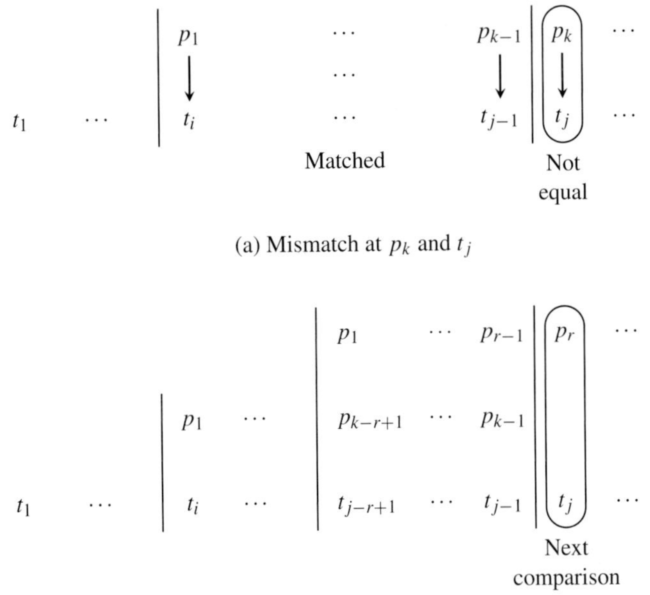

(a) Mismatch at p_k and t_j

(b) Slide p to line up the longest prefix that matches a suffix of the scanned characters.

Figure 11.4   Sliding the pattern for the KMP algorithm

An occurrence of the pattern could be missed if r were chosen too small. (Consider what would happen if in Example 11.2 the failure link for C was set to point to the second A, and if $x = A$ and is followed by BCB in the text.)

Although we have described the correct values for the failure links, we still don't have an algorithm for efficiently computing them. We can define fail recursively. Suppose that the first $k - 1$ failure links have been computed. Then we have the picture in Figure 11.5(a). To assign fail[k] we need to match a substring of P ending at $k - 1$. To simplify the notation, we will let $s = $ fail[k − 1]. The easy case is when $p_{k-1} = p_s$, because we already know that $p_1 \cdots p_{s-1}$ matches the $(s - 1)$-character substring ending at $k - 2$. Then the two matching sequences in Figure 11.5(a) can be extended by one more character, so in this case fail[k] is assigned $s + 1$.

Example 11.3   Computing KMP fail links—a simple case

In Figure 11.6, fail[6] = 4 because $p_1 p_2 p_3$ matches $p_3 p_4 p_5$. Since $p_6 = p_4$, fail[7] is assigned 5. This tells us that $p_1 \cdots p_4$ matches the four-character substring ending at index 6.   ■

What if $p_{k-1} \neq p_s$? We must find a prefix of P that matches a substring ending at $k - 1$. In this case the match in Figure 11.5(a) cannot be extended, so we look farther back. Let $s_2 = $ fail[s]. By the properties of the failure links we have the matches shown in

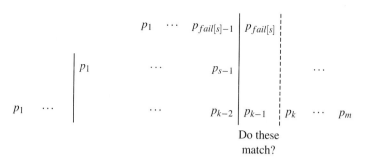

(a) By definition of fail[k−1] (which is s)

(b) Looking back for a match for p_{k-1}

Figure 11.5 Computing fail links: Index s is equal to fail[k−1].

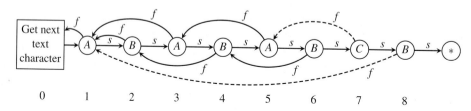

Figure 11.6 Computing fail links: Dashed edges are discussed in Examples 11.3 and 11.4.

Figure 11.5(b). If $p_{k-1} = p_{s_2}$, we have a prefix (of length s_2) to match the substring ending at $k − 1$ and so fail[k] should be $s_2 + 1$. If $p_{k-1} \neq p_{s_2}$, we must follow the failure link from node s_2 and try again. This process continues until we find a failure link s such that $s = 0$ or $p_{k-1} = p_s$. In either case, fail[k] should be $s + 1$.

Example 11.4 Computing KMP fail links—the recursive case

Again look at Figure 11.6. To compute fail[8], $s =$ fail[7] = 5. But $p_7 \neq p_5$, so recompute $s =$ fail[5] = 3. But $p_7 \neq p_3$ either, so recompute $s =$ fail[3] = 1. Still $p_7 \neq p_1$. Finally, $s =$ fail[1] = 0 ends the search, and fail[8] is assigned $s + 1 = 1$. ∎

Algorithm 11.2   KMP Flowchart Construction

Input: P, a string of characters; m, the length of P.

Output: fail, the array of failure links, defined for indexes $1, \ldots, m$. The array is passed in and the algorithm fills it.

```
void kmpSetup(char[] P, int m, int[] fail)
    int k, s;
1.  fail[1] = 0;
2.  for (k = 2; k ≤ m; k ++)
3.      s = fail[k−1];
4.      while (s ≥ 1)
5.          if (pₛ == pₖ₋₁)
6.              break;
7.          s = fail[s];
8.      fail[k] = s + 1;
```

11.3.4 Analysis of KMP Flowchart Construction

Let m be the length of the pattern, P. For this discussion we assume $m \geq 2$. It is easy to see that the complexity of Algorithm 11.2 is in $O(m^2)$. The body of the **for** loop is executed $m - 1$ times, and each time, the body of the **while** loop is executed at most m times because s starts somewhere in P and "jumps" backward, at worst to zero. But this analysis is not careful enough.

We will count character comparisons, as we did for Algorithm 11.1. Since the character comparison is executed in each pass through the **while** loop, the running time of the algorithm is bounded by a multiple of the number of character comparisons. (Actually, since the character comparison is not executed when $s = 0$, we should also note that the condition $s = 0$ cannot occur more than $m - 1$ times.)

We call a comparison *successful* if $p_s = p_{k-1}$ and *unsuccessful* otherwise. A successful comparison breaks out of the **while** loop so at most $m - 1$ successful comparisons are done (one for each k from 2 through m). After every unsuccessful comparison s is decreased (since fail[s] < s), so we can bound the number of unsuccessful comparisons by determining how many times s can decrease. Observe the following:

1. s is initially assigned 0, when $k = 2$.
2. s is increased only by executing line 8 on one pass of the **for** loop, followed by line 3 on the subsequent pass; these two statements increase s by 1. This occurs $m - 2$ times.
3. s is never negative.

Therefore s cannot be decreased more than $m - 2$ times. Thus the number of unsuccessful comparisons is at most $m - 2$ and the total number of character comparisons is at most $2m - 3$. Observe that, to count character comparisons, we actually counted the number of times the index s changed. The latter is another good measure of the work done by the algorithm. The important conclusion is that the complexity of the construction of the flowchart is linear in the length of the pattern.

11.3.5 The Knuth-Morris-Pratt Scan Algorithm

We have already informally described the procedure for using the KMP flowchart to scan the text. The algorithm follows.

Algorithm 11.3 KMP Scan

Input: P and T, the pattern and text strings; m, the length of P; fail, the array of failure links set up in Algorithm 11.2. The length of P would have been found when setting up the fail array. The pattern is assumed to be nonempty.

Output: The return value is the index in T where a copy of P begins, or -1 if no match for P is found.

Remark: The function endText is as defined in Definition 11.1.

```
int  kmpScan(char[] P, char[] T, int m, int[] fail)
    int  match;
    int  j, k;
    // j indexes text characters;
    // k indexes the pattern and fail array.
    match = –1;
    j = 1; k = 1;
    while (endText(T, j) == false)
        if (k > m)
            match = j – m;  // Match found
            break;

        if (k == 0)
            j ++;
            k = 1;  // Start pattern over
        else if (tⱼ == pₖ)
            j ++;
            k ++;
        else
            // Follow fail arrow.
            k = fail[k];
        // Continue loop.
    return match;
```

The analysis of the scan algorithm uses an argument very similar to that used to analyze the algorithm to set up the failure links, and it is left as Exercise 11.8. The number of character comparisons done by Algorithm 11.3 is at most $2n$, where n is the length of the text, T. Thus the Knuth-Morris-Pratt pattern-matching algorithm, which is comprised of Algorithms 11.2 and 11.3, does $\Theta(n + m)$ operations in the worst case, a significant improvement over the $\Theta(mn)$ worst-case complexity of Algorithm 11.1. Some empirical studies have shown that the two algorithms do roughly the same number of character comparisons on the average (for natural language text), but the KMP algorithm never has to back up in the text.

11.4 The Boyer-Moore Algorithm

The chief defect of Henry King
Was chewing little bits of string.
    —Hillaire Belloc, *Cautionary Tales* (1907)

For both simpleScan (Algorithm 11.1) and kmpScan (Algorithm 11.3), if the pattern P is found beginning at the ith position in the text, then each of the text characters preceding the ith position has also been examined (that is, has participated in at least one comparison). The key insight of the Boyer-Moore algorithm is that some text characters may be skipped over entirely. In fact, our intuition suggests that the longer the pattern, the more information the algorithm has about what it has to find, so a good algorithm should be able to jump faster past places in the text where the pattern can't appear.

11.4.1 The New Idea

The Boyer-Moore (from now on, BM) algorithm always scans the pattern from right to left. It uses two heuristics for deciding how far the pattern may be slid over the text string after a mismatch. As usual, let P be a pattern of length m and T a text string of length n. The first heuristic for sliding P is illustrated in the following example.

Example 11.5   Boyer-Moore's first heuristic

We are searching for the pattern *must* in a quotation from Oscar Wilde: "If you wish to understand others you must intensify your own individualism." The pattern is positioned over the string at each place where a potential match will be checked. The comparisons are indicated by arrows. The first four comparisons are as follows:

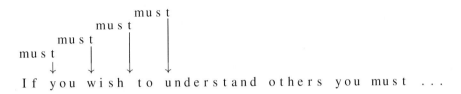

When the last character in *must*, the '*t*', is compared to the *y* in *you* we observe not only that there is no match at this position, but also, since there is no *y* at all in *must*, there can be no match that overlaps the *y*. We may slide the pattern four places to the right. Similarly, after each of the next two comparisons we slide the pattern four places because there is no *w* or blank in *must*. At the fourth comparison we have a mismatch, but there is a *u* in the pattern, so we slide the pattern to line up the *u*'s, as shown for the first comparison in the next diagram, and check for a match. (As always in BM, we start checking at the right end of the pattern.) The next several comparisons are as follows:

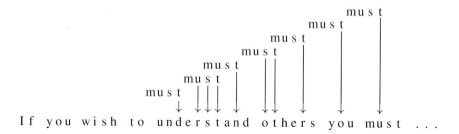

After the mismatch of the *u* in *must* and the *r* in *understand*, the pattern slides just far enough to pass the *r*. Similarly with the *s* in *must* and the *o* in *others*. The last comparison shown is a mismatch, but the text character *u* does appear in the pattern, so the pattern is slid over to line up the *u*'s. Four more comparisons (right to left) will confirm that a match has been found. ■

In this example only 18 character comparisons are done, but since the match occurs at position 38 in T, the other algorithms would do at least 41 comparisons. However, unlike KMP, this algorithm must be able to back up in the text by the length of the pattern.

The number of positions we can "jump" forward when there is a mismatch depends on the text character being read, say t_j. We will store these numbers in an array charJump indexed by the character set Σ.

Java sidelight: Characters (type **char**) in Java are 16 bits, so an array with an entry for each character would have 65,536 cells. Type **byte** is only 8 bits, requiring an array of 256 cells. If it is known (or assumed) that the text and pattern contain only 8-bit characters (which includes all the characters on most keyboards), the smaller array can be used.

For controlling the scanning algorithm, it is more convenient to know the amount by which the text index j should be incremented to begin the next right-to-left scan of the pattern, rather than the amount by which P slides forward. As can be seen in Example 11.5 and Figure 11.7, this jump in j may be larger than the distance P slides. If t_j does not appear in P at all, we can jump forward m places. Figure 11.7 illustrates how to calculate the jump for the case when t_j does occur in P. In fact, t_j may occur more than once in P. We need to make the smallest possible jump, lining up the rightmost instance of t_j in P; otherwise we might go past a copy of P. (We never want to slide the pattern backwards; when our current position in P is already left of the rightmost instance of t_j in P, charJump[t_j] will not be useful.)

Algorithm 11.4   Computing Jumps for the Boyer-Moore Algorithm

Input: Pattern string P; m, the length of P; alphabet size alpha = $|\Sigma|$.

Output: Array charJump, defined on indexes 0, . . ., alpha−1. The array is passed in and the algorithm fills it.

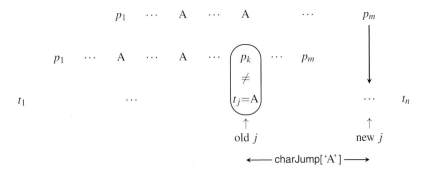

Figure 11.7 Sliding the pattern to line up a matching character

```
void computeJumps(char[] P, int m, int alpha, int[] charJump)
    char ch;
    int k;
    for (ch = 0; ch < alpha; ch++)
        charJump[ch] = m;
    for (k = 1; k ≤ m; k ++)
        charJump[pₖ] = m − k;
```

Clearly the amount of time used to compute the jumps is in $\Theta(|\Sigma| + m)$ where m is the length of the pattern, P.

11.4.2 And the "Old" Idea

Simply using charJump to skip through the text makes the Boyer-Moore algorithm run much faster than the Knuth-Morris-Pratt algorithm for many cases. Combining charJump with an idea similar to that of the fail arrows in the KMP algorithm can improve the algorithm further.

Example 11.6 Boyer-Moore's second heuristic

Suppose some (rightmost) segment of P has matched part of T before a mismatch occurs.

```
P :             b a t s a n d c a t s
                            ↓ ↓ ↓
T :    . . .               d a t s   . . .
                          ↑
                          j
```

The current text character is a 'd'. Using charJump['d'], we would slide the pattern only one place right to line up its 'd' over the 'd' in T. However, we know that the letters in T to the right of the current position are 'ats', the same letters that form the suffix of P that was just scanned. If we know that P does not have another instance of '*ats*', then we can slide P all the way past the '*ats*' in T. If P does have an earlier instance of '*ats*', we could slide P so that earlier '*ats*' lines up with the matched letters in T. For the previous example, the next position for a potential match is as follows:

$$
\begin{array}{lcc}
P : & & \text{b}|\text{a t s}|\text{a n d c a t s} \\[4pt]
T : & \cdots & \text{d}|\text{a t s}| \cdots \\
& & \qquad\quad \uparrow \\
& & \qquad\ \text{new } j
\end{array}
$$

In order not to miss a potential match, if P has more than one substring that matches the matched suffix, we line up the rightmost one (of course excluding the suffix itself). ∎

The general picture is shown in Figure 11.8(a); the mismatch occurs at p_k and t_j. Figure 11.8(b) shows the pattern slid to the right to line up a substring with the matched suffix. Figure 11.8(c) shows another possibility, where the entire matched suffix does not occur elsewhere in the pattern. In this case a prefix that matches *some* suffix is found, and the pattern is slid to the right to line them up. We want matchJump[k] to be the amount to increment j, the text position index, to begin the next right-to-left scan of the pattern after a mismatch has occurred at p_k.

Definition 11.4   matchJump and slide

For $1 \le k \le m$, we define

$$\text{matchJump}[k] = \text{slide}[k] + m - k \tag{11.1}$$

and define slide[k] as described below. Intuitively, slide[k] is how far we can slide the pattern forward after a mismatch on p_k, and $m - k$ is how many characters were matched before the mismatch. Their sum is how far the text index, j, can jump.

Let r be the largest index such that $p_{k+1} \cdots p_m$ matches $p_{r+1} \cdots p_{r+m-k}$, and $p_k \ne p_r$. (Notice that $r < k$.) That is, the $(m-k)$-character *suffix* of P is identical to the $(m-k)$-character substring beginning at index $r + 1$, the match cannot be extended to the left, and r is the largest index for which this is true. Then slide[k] = k − r. Shifting the pattern forward by this amount causes the substring beginning at $r + 1$ to line up with the text at the place where the substring beginning at $k + 1$ used to line up.

The condition $p_r \ne p_k$ is included because, if we are going to use matchJump[k] at this point, we already know that p_k does not match t_j. If $p_r = p_k$, then p_r will not match t_j either, so there is no point in lining them up. If $k = m$, the suffix $p_{k+1} \cdots p_m$ is empty, so the matching requirement is satisfied for every choice of r. In this case r is the largest index such that $p_r \ne p_k$.

Sometimes there is no substring of P that matches the matched suffix, $p_{k+1} \cdots p_m$. Then we line up the longest *prefix* of P that matches some suffix of P. If this prefix has q characters, then slide[k] = m − q. ∎

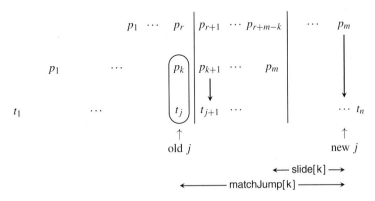

(a) A mismatch occurs at p_k and t_j.

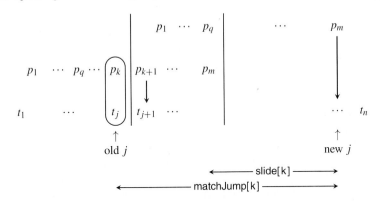

(b) Line up the rightmost substring of p that matches the matched suffix (and satisfies $p_r \neq p_k$).

(c) If no substring of P matches $p_{k+1} \cdots p_m$, line up a prefix that gives a partial match.

Figure 11.8   Sliding the pattern to line up a matched substring

Example 11.7   Computing slide and matchJump

Let P be '*wowwow*', for which $m = 6$. We compute the slide and matchJump values beginning at the right end of the pattern. Values for matchJump that are already computed are shown below the pattern. The question mark indicates the position we are currently working on. At each step we slide the pattern to the right to line up a substring that

$$
\begin{array}{c}
\text{w o w}|\text{w}|\text{o w} \\
\text{w o w w o}|\text{w}| \\
\text{? 1}
\end{array}
$$

$\longleftrightarrow$

(a) Matched = 1, slide = 2, jump = 3.

$$
\begin{array}{c}
|\text{w}|\text{o w w o w} \\
\text{w o w w}|\text{o w}| \\
\text{? 3 1}
\end{array}
$$

$\longleftrightarrow$

(b) Matched = 2, slide = 5, jump = 7. Note that the match of the first '*ow*' and the second '*ow*' was not used because both are preceded by a '*w*'; if a mismatch occurs at position 4 in the pattern, there is no point in lining up another '*w*' at that position when scanning the text.

$$
\begin{array}{c}
|\text{w o w}|\text{w o w} \\
\text{w o w}|\text{w o w}| \\
\text{? 7 3 1}
\end{array}
$$

$\longleftrightarrow$

(c) Matched = 3, slide = 3, jump = 6.

$$
\begin{array}{c}
\text{w o w}|\text{w o w} \\
\text{w o}|\text{w w o w}| \\
\text{? 6 7 3 1}
\end{array}
$$

$\longleftrightarrow$

(d) Matched = 4, slide = 3, jump = 7.

$$
\begin{array}{c}
\text{w o w}|\text{w o w} \\
|\text{w}|\text{o w w o w}| \\
\text{? 7 6 7 3 1}
\end{array}
$$

$\longleftrightarrow$

(e) Matched = 5, slide = 3, jump = 8.

P:	w	o	w	w	o	w
matchJump:	8	7	6	7	3	1

(f) Final values

Figure 11.9 Computing matchJump—an example: *Matched* is the number of characters matched before the mismatch, as in Definition 11.4.

matches a suffix. The character preceding the substring must be different from the character preceding the suffix. For the rightmost pattern position, matchJump is assigned 1 because $p_5 \neq p_6$.

See Figure 11.9. Note that this example illustrates the values for matchJump, but not the actual steps carried out by the algorithm below to compute them. We will return to this example after presenting the algorithm. ■

Algorithm 11.5   Computing Jumps Based on Partial Matches

Input: *P*, the pattern string; *m*, the length of *P*.

Output: Array matchJump, defined on indexes 1, . . ., *m*. The array is passed in and the algorithm fills it.

Remark: The initialization and first two phases actually compute slide[k], as described in Definition 11.4, but store it in matchJump[k]. The last phase converts the entries from slide to matchJump per Equation (11.1). The array sufx is a right-to-left analog of KMP fail. When sufx[k] = x, this means that the substring $p_{k+1} \cdots p_{k+m-x}$ matches the suffix $p_{x+1} \cdots p_m$. Note that sufx[0] tells what suffix matches a *prefix* of P.

```
void computeMatchJumps(char[] P, int m, int[] matchJump)
    int  k, r, s, low, shift;
    int[] sufx = new int[m+1];

    for (k = 1; k ≤ m; k ++)
        matchJump[k] = m + 1;  // Impossibly large slide

    // Compute sufx links (like KMP fail links, but right-to-left).
    // Detect if substring equals matched suffix and is
    // preceded by mismatch at s; compute its slide.
    sufx[m] = m + 1;
    for (k = m − 1; k ≥ 0; k −−)
        s = sufx[k+1];
        while (s ≤ m)
            if (pk+1 == ps)
                break;  // Exit while loop.
            // Mismatch between k+1 and s.
            matchJump[s] = min(matchJump[s], s − (k+1));
            s = sufx[s];
        sufx[k] = s − 1;
        // Continue for loop.

    // If no suffix match at k+1, compute slide based on prefix
    // that matches suffix. Prefix length = (m − shift).
    low = 1; shift = sufx[0];
    while (shift ≤ m)
        for (k = low; k ≤ shift; k ++)
            matchJump[k] = min(matchJump[k], shift);
        low = shift + 1; shift = sufx[shift];

    // Add number of matched characters to slide amount.
    for (k = 1; k ≤ m; k ++)
        matchJump[k] += (m − k);
    return;
```

Example 11.8 Computing slide and matchJump by the algorithm

Consider the pattern '*wowwow*' that was discussed in Example 11.7. In the first phase, sufx and matchJump (logically slide, see Definition 11.4) are given the following values (blanks indicate that no value has been computed, so the impossibly large initial value remains).

P		w	o	w	w	o	w
sufx	3	4	5	5	6	6	7
matchJump						2	1

In the second phase, since sufx[0] = 3, the value 3 is assigned to positions 1 through 3 of matchJump. Then sufx[3] is retrieved and found to be 5. The value 5 is assigned to matchJump[4]. However, matchJump[5] already has a value (and this value is necessarily less than 5), so it remains unchanged. Similarly, matchJump[6] retains its previous value. At this point we have the final slide values (stored in matchJump to save space).

P	w	o	w	w	o	w
matchJump	3	3	3	5	2	1

Finally, the number of matched characters prior to the mismatch at k is added to convert slide to matchJump, in accordance with Equation (11.1).

P	w	o	w	w	o	w
matchJump	8	7	6	7	3	1

These agree with the values computed by inspection in Example 11.7.   ∎

The central point for understanding correctness of Algorithm 11.5 is that the sufx array is a right-to-left analog of the fail array. Thus sufx[k] > k holds in place of fail[k] < k, sufx[m] = m + 1 holds in place of fail[1] = 0, and so on. The important property is that sufx[k] = x if and only if the substring $p_{k+1} \cdots p_{k+m-x}$ matches the suffix $p_{x+1} \cdots p_m$. The proof that the computation makes this property true follows the lines of that for KMP fail links, which was given informally in Section 11.3.3.

Now consider the sequence of indexes defined by $r_0 = \text{sufx}[0]$, $r_{i+1} = \text{sufx}[r_i]$, for $i \geq 0$ until $r_{i+1} = m + 1$. These are the values taken on by the shift variable. From the above property of the sufx array it follows that each suffix of the pattern beginning at $r_i + 1$ (and ending at m, of course) is also a prefix of P.

There are still quite a few details involved in showing that the algorithm is correct, but the above points cover the main ideas. For additional details, please refer to the sources in Notes and References at the end of the chapter.

Analysis of Computing Match Jumps

The time for the first phase of computeMatchJumps, in which the sufx array is computed, can be analyzed with arguments similar to those used for analyzing the computation of KMP fail links, in Section 11.3.4. This is in $\Theta(m)$. It is easy to see that the rest of the algorithm is also in $\Theta(m)$. It also uses $\Theta(m)$ extra space for the sufx array.

11.4.3 The Boyer-Moore Scan Algorithm

Algorithm 11.6   Boyer-Moore Scan

Input: P and T, the pattern and text strings; m, the length of P; charJump and match-Jump, the arrays described in Sections 11.4.1 and 11.4.2. The pattern is assumed to be nonempty.

Output: The return value is the index in T where a copy of P begins, or -1 if no match for P is found.

Remark: The function endText is as defined in Definition 11.1.

```
int boyerMooreScan(char[] P, char[] T, int m, int[] charJump, int[] matchJump)
    int match;
    int j, k;
    // j indexes text characters;
    // k indexes the pattern.
    match = -1;
    j = m; k = m;
    while (endText(T, j) == false)
        if (k < 1)
            match = j + 1;  // Match found
            break;

        if (t_j == p_k)
            j --; k --;
        else
            // slide P forward
            j += max(charJump[t_j], matchJump[k]);
            k = m;
        // Continue loop.
    return match;
```

11.4.4 Remarks

The behavior of the Boyer-Moore algorithm depends on the size of the alphabet and the repetition within the strings. In empirical studies using natural language text and $m \geq 5$, the algorithm did only roughly 0.24 to 0.3 character comparisons per character in the text, up to the point of the match or the end of the text. In other words, it examined only roughly one-quarter to one-third of the characters. See Figure 11.10 for the results of one such study comparing the three algorithms. The experiments used 20 patterns of length m from 1 to 14. The text length was 5000.

For binary strings, BM does not do quite as well (charJump does not help much); in another study, roughly 0.7 comparisons were done for each text character.

In all cases with $m \geq 5$, the average number of comparisons is bounded by cn for a constant $c < 1$. If the pattern is quite small ($m \leq 3$), then the overhead of preprocessing the pattern is not worthwhile; BM does more comparisons than the straightforward approach, simpleScan (Algorithm 11.1).

There are several improvements and modifications to the BM algorithm that make it run faster. (See Notes and References at the end of this chapter.) Like Algorithm 11.1, BM does some backing up in the text string (because it scans the pattern right-to-left).

Two extensions to the pattern-matching problem are often useful: Find *all* occurrences of the pattern in the text, and find any one of a finite set of patterns in the text.

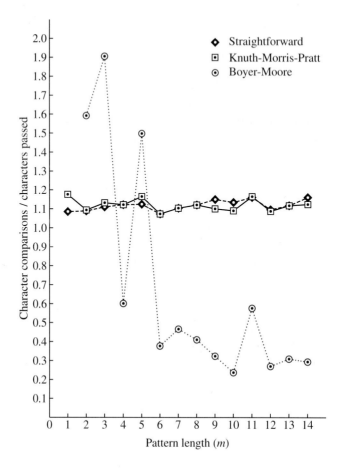

Figure 11.10 Comparison of string-matching algorithms. (From G. de V. Smit, "A Comparison of Three String Matching Algorithms," *Software: Practice and Experience*, vol. 12, Copyright 1982, John Wiley and Sons, Ltd. Reprinted by permission of John Wiley and Sons, Ltd.)

11.5 Approximate String Matching

In Sections 11.2 through 11.4 we studied several algorithms to find a copy of a character string called the *pattern* in another string called the *text*. Those algorithms searched for an exact copy of the pattern. However, in many applications we can't expect an exact copy. A spelling correcter, for example, may search a dictionary for an entry that is similar to a given (misspelled) word. In speech recognition, samples may vary. Other applications in which close, but not exact, matches are sought range from identifying sequences of amino acids to recognizing bird songs. As in the earlier sections, we use character strings here, but the method is clearly applicable to strings in "alphabets" of other kinds of data, as would be appropriate, for example, for speech recognition.

In this section we show a dynamic programming solution to the problem of finding an approximate match for a pattern in a string. The dynamic programming paradigm was introduced in Chapter 10. Familiarity with dynamic programming will give you a better perspective on this problem.

Let $P = p_1 p_2 \cdots p_m$ be the pattern and $T = t_1 t_2 \cdots t_n$ be the text. We assume that n is large relative to m. The terminology introduced next adopts the point of view that P is a "correct" pattern, while T may be only approximate. In many applications T may have "noise." However, the algorithm does not depend on this viewpoint.

Definition 11.5 k-approximate match

Let k be a nonnegative integer. A *k-approximate match* is a match of P in T that has at most k differences. The differences can be any of the following three types. The name of the difference is the operation needed on T to bring it closer to P.

> *revise*: The corresponding characters in P and T are different.
>
> *delete*: T contains a character that is missing from P.
>
> *insert*: T is missing a character that appears in P. ∎

Example 11.9

The match shown below is a 3-approximate match. It has one of each of the permissible differences. There are no blanks in P and T; the spaces are used to show the match more clearly.

```
P :                     u n n e   c e s s a r i l y
                          ↓ ↓               ↓
T :            . . .     u n   e s c e s s a r a l y   . . .
```
∎

The inputs for the problem are P, T, m (the length of P), and k (the acceptable number of differences). The problem is to find a substring of T that provides a k-approximate match for P, or determine that no k-approximate match exists.

In the exact matching problem, when the current text character does not match the pattern, there is one action: Shift the pattern. In this problem, there are four choices (unless k is exceeded): Either shift the pattern or perform one of the three operations in Definition 11.5. There is no obvious way to know which will turn out the best, so the straightforward approach is to develop a recursive procedure to evaluate the alternatives. In Chapter 10 we encountered several optimization problems that could be solved in the following framework:

1. For each current choice:

    a. Determine what subproblem(s) would remain if this choice were made.
    b. Recursively find the optimal costs of those subproblems.
    c. Combine those costs with the cost of the current choice itself to obtain an overall cost for this choice.

2. Select a current choice that produced the minimum overall cost.

With a little experimentation we can see that this procedure will encounter many repeated subproblems.

Example 11.10

Suppose two pattern letters are transposed in the text:

$$P: \qquad\qquad A\,B\,C\,D\,E$$
$$T: \qquad ...\quad A\,C\,B\,D\,E \quad ...$$

Assuming the pattern is scanned left-to-right, these differences can be explained as two *revisions*, or as *delete*(C) followed by a later *insert*(C), or as *insert*(B) followed by a later *delete*(B). In all three cases, the subproblem of matching 'DE' remains to be solved. A backtracking search would solve it anew in each branch of the search. This is exactly the kind of behavior that indicates that the dynamic programming paradigm may be applicable.
∎

To prepare for a dynamic programming solution, we need to formalize the recursive backtracking solution and decide on identifiers for the subproblems. We might want to scan the pattern left-to-right, as in KMP, or right-to-left, as in BM. (We assume the text is processed generally from left to right in either case, although there might be some backing up.)

For the left-to-right pattern scan, a natural way to identify a subproblem is by a pair of integers (i, j) where i denotes the beginning of a suffix of the pattern and j denotes the position in the text at which the match should begin. The subproblem (i, j), then, is specified as finding the minimum-difference match of $p_i \cdots p_m$ to a segment of T beginning at t_j. This might introduce some complications if looking far ahead in the text is inconvenient. Notice that on the branches of the backtrack search where *delete* is the chosen operation, (i, j) depends on $(i, j + 1)$, which depends on $(i, j + 2)$, and so on. We are forced to look ahead in the text without making any progress in the pattern. Let us see if the alternative, a right-to-left pattern scan, looks any simpler.

For the right-to-left pattern scan, a natural way to identify a subproblem is by a pair of integers (i, j) where i denotes the *end* of a *prefix* of the pattern, and j denotes the position in the text at which the match should *terminate*. The subproblem (i, j) now is specified as finding the minimum-difference match of $p_1 \cdots p_i$ to a segment of T *ending* at t_j. Now, on the branches of the backtrack search where *delete* is the chosen operation, (i, j) depends on $(i, j - 1)$, which depends on $(i, j - 2)$, and so on. But if our strategy for the dynamic programming algorithm is generally to solve the problem in increasing order of j, these subproblems will have been encountered and solved earlier. Thus the right-to-left pattern scan appears to be the superior foundation upon which to build a dynamic programming solution.

To solve subproblem (i, j) recursively, we need to solve these subproblems: $(i, j - 1)$, due to *delete*; $(i - 1, j)$, due to *insert*; and $(i - 1, j - 1)$, due to *revise* or due to matching characters. However, if we solve subproblems "bottom-up" in an order such that the latter three subproblems are solved before the solution for (i, j) is started, then we can solve (i, j) by looking up the earlier solutions. For the dynamic programming solution, we define:

Definition 11.6   Differences table

$D[i][j]$ = the minimum number of differences between $p_1 \cdots p_i$ and a segment of T ending at t_j.   ∎

There will be a k-approximate match ending at t_j for any j such that $D[m][j] \le k$. Thus if we want to find the first k-approximate match, we can stop as soon as we find an entry less than or equal to k in the last row of D. The rules for computing entries of D consider each of the possible differences that could occur at p_i and t_j, and, of course, the possibility that those two characters might match. $D[i][j]$ is the minimum of the following four values:

$$\text{matchCost} = D[i - 1][j - 1] \qquad \text{if } p_i = t_j$$
$$\text{reviseCost} = D[i - 1][j - 1] + 1 \qquad \text{if } p_i \ne t_j$$
$$\text{insertCost} = D[i - 1][j] + 1$$
$$\text{deleteCost} = D[i][j - 1] + 1$$

Each entry requires only entries above it and to its left in the table (see Figure 11.11), so the computation can be done in a forward row-by-row or column-by-column order. Since n may be much larger than m, it is more efficient to compute the entries of D column by column. To start the computation, we use a row 0, with $D[0][j] = 0$ for all j (intuitively, because a null section of the pattern differs in zero places from the null suffix of $t_1 \cdots t_j$),

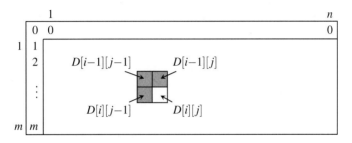

Figure 11.11   Computation of $D[i][j]$: The three shaded entries are used.

		H	a	v	e		a		h	s	p	p	y	d	a	y	.
	0	0	0	0	0	0	0	0	0	0	0	0	0				
h	1	1	1	1	1	1	1	1	0	1	1	1	1				
a	2	2	2	1	2	2	2	1	2	1	1	2	2	2			
p	3	3	3	2	2	3	3	2	2	2	2	1	2	3			
p	4	4	4	3	3	3	4	3	3	3	3	2	1	2			
y	5	5	5	4	4	4	4	4	4	4	4	3	2	1			

Table 11.2   The table D for Example 11.11

and a column 0, with $D[i][0] = i$ (because $p_1 \cdots p_i$ differs in i places from a null prefix of T).

Example 11.11   Computing the table D

Suppose $P =$ 'happy', $k = 1$, and T is the mistyped sentence 'Have a hsppy day.' Table 11.2 shows the values of D. The entries are computed column by column, and as soon as an entry in the fifth row is found to have the value 1, the computation terminates.   ∎

The work done to compute each entry of D is a small constant, so the total work done is in $O(nm)$. This is about as fast (within a constant factor) as the first, straightforward, algorithm for exact pattern matching (Algorithm 11.1).

What about space? The space used by a dynamic programming algorithm for its table is often a reasonable price to pay for saving time. The table D in this algorithm, though, is m by n, and n is very large. Clearly, the whole table does not have to be stored. Only entries from the current column and the previous one are needed, so the algorithm can be written using roughly $2m$ cells.

Writing out the algorithm should be an easy exercise (see Exercise 11.22). For an algorithm for k-approximate matching that runs in $O(kn)$ time, see sources in Notes and References at the end of the chapter.

Exercises

Section 11.2   A Straightforward Solution

11.1   Rewrite Algorithm 11.1 eliminating the variable i.

11.2   Rewrite Algorithm 11.1 to work on inputs that are linked lists. For simplicity, assume the element type is **int**. Use the IntList abstract data type operations of Section 2.3.2, and assume that T and P are objects in this class.

11.3   In this exercise you will design operations for a Text abstract data type that will do what simpleScan needs to do with T, without having to assume that T is an array. Try to make them general enough that other string-matching algorithms can probably use them. We have already assumed endText was available. Some other suggested names are advanceText, backupText, and getTextChar.

a.   Write the specifications, but do not implement the operations.

b.   Show how to modify simpleScan to use your operations on T.

11.4   Suppose the text T is too long to store all at once in memory, so it is read in as needed. Algorithm 11.1 may need about m previous characters of T, to the left of t_j. That is, it may need to back up about m positions.

In this exercise you will design a modification of the Queue ADT, called OpenQueue, which keeps elements (characters in this case) in FIFO order, as does a regular queue, but permits access to any element in the queue, not just the front element.

a.   Write the specifications for your new operations.

b.   Show how to implement the needed operations efficiently using an array, using suggestions from Exercise 2.16.

c.   Outline how to implement the Text ADT of Exercise 11.3 using the OpenQueue ADT. The idea is to keep enough characters in the queue to accommodate any backing up the algorithm may need to do. Assume the algorithm knows the maximum amount it might ever need to back up at the time the OpenQueue object is created.

Section 11.3   The Knuth-Morris-Pratt Algorithm

11.5   Draw the finite automaton (flowchart) for the pattern '$ABAABA$', where $\Sigma = \{A, B, C\}$.

11.6   Give the fail indexes used by the KMP algorithm for the following patterns:

a.   *AAAB*

b.   *AABAACAABABA*

c.   *ABRACADABRA*

d.   *ASTRACASTRA*

11.7   Give a pattern beginning with an A and using only letters from $\{A, B, C\}$ that would have the following fail indexes (for the KMP algorithm):

$$0 \ 1 \ 1 \ 2 \ 3 \ 4 \ 2 \ 2$$

11.8   Show that kmpScan (Algorithm 11.3) does at most $2n$ character comparisons.

11.9   How will the KMP algorithms behave if the pattern and/or the text are null (have length zero)? Will they "crash"? If not, will their output be meaningful and correct?

11.10   Recall that the pattern $P =$ '$A \cdots AB$' ($m - 1$ A's followed by one B) and the text string $T =$ '$A \cdots A$' (n A's) are a worst-case input for Algorithm 11.1.

a.   Give the values of the fail indexes for P. Exactly how many character comparisons are done by Algorithm 11.2 to compute them?

b. Exactly how many character comparisons are done by kmpScan to scan T for an occurrence of P?

c. Given an arbitrarily large m, find a pattern Q with m letters such that kmpSetup does more character comparisons for Q than it does for the pattern P with m letters described above.

11.11   Prove that Algorithm 11.2 sets the KMP failure links so that fail[k] is the largest r (with $r < k$) such that $p_1 \cdots p_{r-1}$ matches $p_{k-r+1} \cdots p_{k-1}$.

⋆ **11.12**   The strategy for setting the fail links for the KMP algorithm has a flaw that is illustrated by Figure 11.3. If a mismatch occurs at the fourth character, a B, fail[4] points us back to another B, which of course will not match the current text character either. Modify Algorithm 11.2 so that fail values satisfy the condition stated in Section 11.3.3 (and repeated in the previous exercise) *and also* the condition that $p_r \neq p_k$. (Be careful; a common first guess does not work.)

11.13   Rewrite the KMP algorithms to work on inputs that are linked lists. For simplicity, assume the element type is **int**. Use the IntList abstract data type operations of Section 2.3.2, and assume that T and P are objects in this class.

11.14   How would you modify kmpScan (Algorithm 11.3) to read the text from input, one character at a time, instead of accessing string T? Assume the function read() returns an **int**, which equals the next input character, unless end of file has been reached, in which case it returns -1. Do you need the full capabilities of the Text ADT proposed in Exercise 11.3? Explain why or why not.

Section 11.4   The Boyer-Moore Algorithm

11.15   List the values in the charJump array for the Boyer-Moore algorithm for the following patterns assuming that the alphabet is $\{A, B, \ldots, Z\}$.

a.   *ABRACADABRA*

b.   *ASTRACASTRA*

11.16   List the values in the sufx and matchJump arrays for the Boyer-Moore algorithm for the following patterns.

a.   *AAAB*

b.   *AABAACAABABA*

c.   *ABRACADABRA*

d.   *ASTRACASTRA*

11.17   As Example 11.5 showed, just using the charJump values, without using match-Jump, can give a very fast scan. However, the statement

$$j \mathrel{+}= \max(\text{charJump}[t_j], \text{matchJump}[k])$$

in Algorithm 11.6 cannot simply be replaced by

$$j \mathrel{+}= \mathsf{charJump}[t_j].$$

Why not? What other (small) change is needed to make the scan algorithm work?

11.18 Recall that the pattern $P = \text{`} A \cdots A B\text{'}$ ($m - 1$ $A$'s followed by one $B$) and the text string $T = \text{`} A \cdots A\text{'}$ (n A's) are a worst-case input for Algorithm 11.1.

a. Give the values of the charJump, sufx, and matchJump arrays for P assuming that the alphabet is $\{A, B, \ldots, Z\}$.

b. Exactly how many character comparisons are done by boyerMooreScan to scan T for an occurrence of P?

11.19 Suppose the text is being read as needed, one character at a time. Give a formula relating k, m, and matchJump[k] to the number of new text characters needed when there is a mismatch at p_k.

11.20 Suppose P and T are bitstrings.

a. Show the values in the charJump, sufx, and matchJump arrays for the pattern 1101101011.

b. For bitstrings in general, which array, charJump or matchJump, will yield the longer "jumps"?

Section 11.5 *Approximate String Matching*

11.21 An algorithm for finding an exact string match need tell us only where the pattern begins in the text or where it ends in the text. We can determine the unspecified end of the match in the text because we know the length of the pattern. This is not the case with approximate matching because we don't know how many characters are missing from the pattern or the text. Show how to modify or extend the algorithm for detecting k-approximate matches so that it tells where the approximate match of the pattern begins in T.

11.22

a. Write out the algorithm for k-approximate matching. How much space does it require?

b. Show how to use a version of the OpenQueue ADT, introduced in Exercise 11.4, to avoid using an amount of space that depends on n. *Hint*: Let the elements stored in the open queue be arrays of $m + 1$ integers, corresponding to the columns of the table D. What is the maximum number of columns that needs to be available at any one time?

Additional Problems

11.23 Rewrite each of the three scan algorithms (Algorithms 11.1, 11.3, and 11.6) so that they find all occurrences of the pattern in the text.

11.24 P is a character string (of length m) consisting of letters and at most one asterisk ('*'). The asterisk is a "wild-card" character; it can match any sequence of zero or more characters. For example, if P = '$sun*day$' and T = '$happysundaemonday$', there is a match beginning at the 's' and ending at the last 'y'; the asterisk "matches" $daemon$. Give an algorithm to find a match of P in a text string T (consisting of n characters), if there is one, and give an upper bound on the order of its worst-case time.

11.25   Let $X = x_1x_2 \cdots x_n$ and $Y = y_1y_2 \cdots y_n$ be two character strings. We say that X is a *cyclic shift* of Y if there is some r such that $X = y_{r+1} \cdots y_ny_1 \cdots y_r$. Give an $O(n)$ algorithm to determine if X is a cyclic shift of Y.

11.26

    a.   Write an efficient algorithm to determine if a (long) string of text contains 25 consecutive blanks. (Do not just give an exact copy of an algorithm in the text; customize it.)

 ★ **b.**   Construct a worst-case (or near worst-case) example for your algorithm. How many character comparisons are done in this case?

    c.   Suppose the text string contains ordinary English text where blanks separate words and sentences, but there is very rarely more than one blank together. If the text length is n, approximately how many character comparisons will your algorithm do?

★ **11.27**   Investigate the problem of finding any one of a finite set of patterns in a text string. Can you extend any of the algorithms in this chapter to produce an algorithm that does better than scan for each of the patterns separately?

Programs

1. Implement all three exact string searching algorithms, including a counter for the number of character comparisons done; run a large set of test cases; and compare the results. Use the techniques of Exercises 11.3 and 11.4 to manage backing up and jumping forward in text, so that you don't need to store the entire text in memory.

2. Write a program for the k-approximate matching algorithm, storing at most two columns at a time. Include the enhancements for Exercise 11.21.

Notes and References

Crochemore and Rytter (1994) is a book on text algorithms in general. It includes the Knuth-Morris-Pratt and Boyer-Moore algorithms and k-approximate matching. The main references for the algorithms presented here are Knuth, Morris, and Pratt (1977) and Boyer and Moore (1977). The first phase of Algorithm 11.5 is based on Knuth, Morris, and Pratt (1977) and the second phase is based on an idea attributed to K. Mehlhorn by Smit (1982). Guibas and Odlyzko (1977), Galil (1979), and Apostolico and Giancarlo (1986) present various worst-case linear versions of the Boyer-Moore algorithm. See also Aho and Corasick (1975). Boyer and Moore and Smit give empirical comparisons of the algorithms described in this chapter. The graph in Figure 11.10 is from Smit (1982).

Section 11.5 is based on Wagner and Fischer (1974). Hall and Dowling (1980) is a survey of approximate string-matching techniques. An $O(kn)$ algorithm for k-approximate string matching is in Landau and Vishkin (1986).

12

Polynomials and Matrices

12.1 Introduction

The problems examined in this chapter are polynomial evaluation (with and without pre-processing of the coefficients), polynomial multiplication (as an illustration of the discrete Fourier transform), and multiplication of matrices and vectors. The operations usually used for such tasks are multiplication and addition. On older computers, multiplication took a lot more time than addition, and some of the algorithms presented "improve" upon the straightforward or most widely known methods by reducing the number of multiplications at the expense of some extra additions. Hence their value depends on the relative costs of the two operations. Other algorithms presented reduce the number of both operations (for large input sizes).

Several algorithms in this chapter use the divide-and-conquer method: evaluating a polynomial with preprocessing of coefficients (Section 12.2.3), Strassen's matrix multiplication algorithm (Section 12.3.4), and the Fast Fourier Transform (Section 12.4).

Many lower-bound results are stated without proof in this chapter. See Notes and References at the end of the chapter for further comment and references on these results.

12.2 Evaluating Polynomial Functions

Consider the polynomial $p(x) = a_n x^n + a_{n-1} x^{n-1} + \cdots + a_1 x + a_0$ with real coefficients and $n \geq 1$. Suppose the coefficients $a_0, a_1, \ldots, a_n$ and x are given and that the problem is to evaluate $p(x)$. In this section we look at some algorithms and some lower bounds for this problem.

The number of multiplications and additions done may seem a reasonable measure of work, but some algorithms may use division and subtraction and do fewer multiplications and additions. Thus, particularly when discussing lower bounds, we will consider the total number of multiplications and divisions and the total number of additions and subtractions.

12.2.1 Algorithms

The two types of operations will be denoted $*/$ and $\pm$, respectively.

The obvious way to solve the problem is to compute each term and add it to the sum of the others already computed. The following algorithm does this.

Algorithm 12.1 Polynomial Evaluation—Term by Term

Input: The coefficients of polynomial $p(x)$ in the array a; $n \geq 0$, the degree of p; and x, the point at which to evaluate p.

Output: The value of $p(x)$.

```
float poly(float[] a, int n, float x)
    float p, xpower;
    int i;
    p = a[0]; xpower = 1;
    for (i = 1; i ≤ n; i ++)
        xpower = xpower * x;
        p += a[i] * xpower;
    return p;
```

Algorithm 12.1 does $2n$ multiplications and n additions.

Horner's method

Is there a better way? Is there a way to compute $ab + ac$, given a, b, and c, with fewer than two multiplications? Yes, of course, by factoring it as $a(b + c)$. Similarly, the key to Horner's method for evaluating $p(x)$ is simply a particular factorization of p:

$$p(x) = (\cdots((a_n x + a_{n-1})x + a_{n-2})x + \cdots + a_1)x + a_0.$$

The computation is done in a short loop with only n multiplications and n additions.

Algorithm 12.2   Polynomial Evaluation—Horner's Method

Input: a, n, and x as in Algorithm 12.1.

Output: The value of $p(x)$.

```
float hornerPoly(float[] a, int n, float x)
    float p;
    int i;
    p = a[n];
    for (i = n − 1; i ≥ 0; i −−)
        p = p * x + a[i];
    return p;
```

Thus simply by factoring p we have cut the number of multiplications in half without increasing the number of additions. Can the number of multiplications be reduced further? Can the number of additions be reduced?

12.2.2 Lower Bounds for Polynomial Evaluation

Just as we used decision trees as an abstract model for establishing lower bounds for sorting (and other problems), we need a model for polynomial evaluation algorithms (and other related computation problems). Recall that the algorithms represented by decision trees worked for a fixed input size and had no loops. Here we use a model called *straight-line programs*. The programs perform a sequence of arithmetic operations; they do no looping and no branching. The operands may be elements from the set of inputs to the problem, I, elements from some set of constants, C, and intermediate results already computed. The constants may seem unnecessary—we did not use any in the two polynomial evaluation algorithms we examined—but allowing constants simplifies the lower-bound arguments, and any lower bound derived in a model that allows constants will be valid for a more restricted model that does not.

Formally, a straight-line program is a finite sequence of steps of the form

$$s_i = q \text{ op } r$$

where q and r are inputs, constants, or the results of earlier steps, that is, q and r are in $I \cup C \cup \{s_j \mid j < i\}$ and op is an arithmetic operator. The last step should compute $p(x)$. For the problem of evaluating a polynomial $p(x) = a_n x^n + a_{n-1}x^{n-1} + \cdots + a_1 x + a_0$, the input set is $I = \{x, a_0, a_1, \ldots, a_n\}$. The inputs should be thought of as indeterminates, that is, abstract symbols with no assumptions about their values.

Example 12.1   A straight-line program for Horner's method with $n = 2$

$$s_1 = a_2 * x$$
$$s_2 = s_1 + a_1$$
$$s_3 = s_2 * x$$
$$s_4 = s_3 + a_0 \quad \blacksquare$$

The number of steps in a straight-line program is clearly a reasonable measure of the work it does. Most of the theorems count $*/$ and $\pm$ steps separately. We will illustrate the proof techniques by showing that, if divisions are not permitted, a straight-line program to evaluate a polynomial of degree n must do at least n $\pm$'s. It can be shown by a similar but more complicated argument that, if divisions are not permitted, at least n multiplications are needed. It is also known that, if divisions are permitted, at least n $*/$'s are required. Thus Horner's method uses the optimal number of $*/$'s, and, since division takes at least as much time as multiplication, it uses the best mix of these two operators.

We say that a step $s_i = q \text{ op } r$ *uses* an input α if and only if $q = \alpha$ or $r = \alpha$, or $q = s_j$ for some $j < i$ and s_j uses α, or $r = s_j$ for some $j < i$ and s_j uses α. In other words, if we "expanded" s_i by replacing the results from earlier steps until only inputs and constants remained, then α would appear in the expression. In Example 12.1, for example, s_3 uses a_2, a_1, and x.

Lemma 12.1   A straight-line program (using only $*, +$, and $-$) to compute $a_0 + \cdots + a_n$ must have at least n $\pm$ steps.

Proof   The proof is by induction on n. For $n = 0$, we observe that any program has at least zero $\pm$ steps. For $n > 0$, suppose P is a program for $a_0 + \cdots + a_n$. The idea of the proof is to substitute 0 for a_n to produce a program that computes $a_0 + \cdots + a_{n-1}$, then use the induction hypothesis. Let

$$s_i = q \text{ op } r$$

be the first $\pm$ step that uses a_n. (There must be such a step; otherwise the result of the computation would be a multiple of a_n.) Since no previous $\pm$ step used a_n, q or r must be a_n itself or a multiple of a_n. If we substitute 0 for a_n we would have one of the following cases:

1. $s_i = q \pm 0$
2. $s_i = 0 + r$
3. $s_i = 0 - r$

For cases 1 and 2, eliminate this step from the program and substitute q or r, respectively for s_i in all other steps where s_i appears. For case 3, replace this step with

$$s_i = -1 * r.$$

In all cases, we have eliminated one $\pm$ step. Replace a_n by 0 in all steps where it appears. We now have a program that computes $a_0 + \cdots + a_{n-1}$. By the induction hypothesis, it has at least $n - 1 \pm$ steps. Therefore the original program P had at least $n \pm$ steps.   □

Theorem 12.2   A straight-line program using only $*$, $+$, and $-$ to evaluate

$$p(x) = a_n x^n + a_{n-1} x^{n-1} + \cdots + a_1 x + a_0,$$

where $a_0, \ldots, a_n$ and x are arbitrary inputs, must have at least $n \pm$ steps.

Proof   Let P be a program to compute $a_n x^n + a_{n-1} x^{n-1} + \cdots + a_1 x + a_0$. Replace every reference to x with "1." This does not change the number of $\pm$ steps. The resulting program now computes $a_n + \cdots + a_0$, so it must have at least $n \pm$ steps.   □

12.2.3   Preprocessing of Coefficients

Preprocessing (also called preconditioning) some of the data in a problem means, informally, that some of the input is known in advance and a specialized program can be written. Suppose that a problem has inputs I and I' and that we denote an algorithm for the problem by A. When we speak of preprocessing I, we mean finding an algorithm A_I with input I' which produces the same output as A with inputs I and I'. Thus the preprocessing problem has two parts: the algorithm A_I which depends on I, and an algorithm that, with I as input, produces the algorithm A_I. Rigorously speaking, A and A_I solve different problems and, as we will see, their complexities may differ.

In some situations one polynomial has to be evaluated for a large number of different arguments. One example is a power series approximation of a function. In such cases, preprocessing of the coefficients may reduce the number of $*/$'s required for each evaluation. Let $p(x) = a_n x^n + a_{n-1} x^{n-1} + \cdots + a_1 x + a_0$, where $n = 2^k - 1$ for some $k \geq 1$. Thus p has 2^k terms, some of which may be zero. The procedure for evaluating $p(x)$ described here uses a divide-and-conquer method to factor p. We assume that p is monic (i.e., that $a_n = 1$). Extending the algorithm to the general case is left as an exercise.

$$
\begin{array}{r|l}
 & \overbrace{x^{2^{k-1}-1} + a_{2^k-2}x^{2^{k-1}-2} + \cdots + a_{2^{k-1}}}^{q(x)} \\
\hline
x^{2^{k-1}}+b \,\big)\; x^{2^k-1} + a_{2^k-2}x^{2^k-2} + \cdots + a_{2^{k-1}}x^{2^{k-1}} & + a_{2^{k-1}-1}x^{2^{k-1}-1} \quad + \cdots + a_1x + a_0 \\
x^{2^k-1} + a_{2^k-2}x^{2^k-2} + \cdots + a_{2^{k-1}}x^{2^{k-1}} & + bx^{2^{k-1}-1} \quad + \cdots + ba_{2^{k-1}} \\
\hline
0 & \underbrace{(a_{2^{k-1}-1} - b)x^{2^{k-1}-1} + \cdots + (a_0 - ba_{2^{k-1}})}_{r(x)}
\end{array}
$$

Figure 12.1 $p(x)$ divided by $x^j + b$

If $n = 1$, then $p(x) = x + a_0$ and is evaluated by doing one addition. Suppose $n > 1$ and p is written as follows for some j and b:

$$p(x) = (x^j + b)q(x) + r(x),$$

where q and r are monic polynomials of degree $2^{k-1} - 1$ (i.e., with half as many terms as p, counting zero terms, if any). Then $p(x)$ can be evaluated by carrying out the following steps:

1. Evaluate $q(x)$ and $r(x)$.
2. Compute x^j.
3. Multiply $(x^j + b)$ by $q(x)$ and add $r(x)$.

Since q and r satisfy the same conditions as p—that is, they are monic and their degree is $2^m - 1$ for some m—we could use the same scheme recursively to evaluate them. How must j and b be chosen to ensure that q and r have the desired properties? Clearly $j = \text{degree}(p) - \text{degree}(q) = 2^k - 1 - (2^{k-1} - 1) = 2^{k-1}$. Note that, since j is a power of 2, x^j can be computed fairly quickly. The correct value for b becomes clear when we divide $p(x)$ by $x^j + b$ to obtain $q(x)$, the quotient, and $r(x)$, the remainder. See Figure 12.1. For r to be monic, $a_{2^{k-1}-1} - b$ must be 1, so $b = a_{2^{k-1}-1} - 1$. Thus the preprocessing algorithm factors p as follows:

$$p(x) = \left(x^{2^{k-1}} + (a_{2^{k-1}-1} - 1)\right) q(x) + r(x)$$

and factors q and r recursively by the same procedure. The factorization is complete when q and r have degree 1. The following example illustrates the entire procedure.

Example 12.2

Let $p(x) = x^7 + 6x^6 + 5x^5 + 4x^4 + 3x^3 + 2x^2 + x + 1$. Then $k = 3$, $j = 2^{k-1} = 4$, $b = a_{2^{k-1}-1} - 1 = a_3 - 1 = 2$, and $x^j + b = x^4 + 2$. Figure 12.2(a) shows the computation of $q(x)$ and $r(x)$. Thus

$$p(x) = (x^4 + 2)(x^3 + 6x^2 + 5x + 4) + (x^3 - 10x^2 - 9x - 7).$$

$$
\begin{array}{rll}
 & \overbrace{x^3+6x^2+5x+4}^{q(x)} & \\
\cline{2-3}
x^4+2 \big) & x^7+6x^6+5x^5+4x^4 & +3x^3+\ \ 2x^2+\ \ \ x+1 \\
 & x^7+6x^6+5x^5+4x^4 & +2x^3+12x^2+10x+8 \\
\cline{3-3}
 & & \underbrace{x^3-10x^2-\ \ 9x-7}_{r(x)}
\end{array}
$$

(a) Computing $q(x)$ and $r(x)$

$q(x) = x^3+6x^2+5x+4$

$k=2;\quad j=2^{k-1}=2$

$b = a_{2^{k-1}-1}-1 = a_1-1 = 4$

$$
\begin{array}{rll}
 & x\ +6 & \\
\cline{2-3}
x^2+4 \big) & x^3+6x^2 & +5x+\ 4 \\
 & x^3+6x^2 & +4x+24 \\
\cline{3-3}
 & & \ \ x-20
\end{array}
$$

(b) Recursively factoring $q(x)$: Thus $q(x) = (x^2+4)(x+6) + (x-20)$.

$r(x) = x^3-10x^2-9x-7$

$k=2;\quad j=2^{k-1}=2$

$b = a_{2^{k-1}-1}-1 = a_1-1 = -10$

$$
\begin{array}{rll}
 & x\ -10 & \\
\cline{2-3}
x^2-10 \big) & x^3-10x^2 & -\ \ 9x-\ \ \ 7 \\
 & x^3-10x^2 & -10x+100 \\
\cline{3-3}
 & & \ \ x-107
\end{array}
$$

(c) Recursively factoring $r(x)$: Thus $r(x) = (x^2-10)(x-10) + (x-107)$.

Figure 12.2 Computational details for Example 12.2

Now factor $q(x)$ and $r(x)$ in the same way, as shown in Figures 12.2(b) and 12.2(c). Thus

$$p(x) = (x^4+2)\left((x^2+4)(x+6)+(x-20)\right) + \left((x^2-10)(x-10)+(x-107)\right).$$

Using this formula, evaluating $p(x)$ requires five multiplications: three that appear explicitly in the factorization and two to compute x^2 and x^4. Horner's method would have required seven. Observe, however, that 10 additions (and subtractions) are done instead of seven. ■

Analysis of Polynomial Evaluation with Preprocessing of Coefficients

We can easily count the number of operations done to evaluate $p(x)$ (after the preprocessing work has been done) by considering the three steps used to describe the procedure:

1. Evaluate $q(x)$ and $r(x)$ recursively.

   This suggests the use of a recurrence equation.

2. Compute x^j.

      The largest j used is 2^{k-1} and x^2, x^4, x^8, ..., $x^{2^{k-1}}$ can be computed by doing $k-1$ multiplications.

3. Multiply $(x^j + b)$ by $q(x)$ and add $r(x)$.

      One multiplication and two additions.

Let $M(k)$ be the number of multiplications done to evaluate a monic polynomial of degree $2^k - 1$, *not* counting the powers of x (since they can be computed once and used as needed). Let $A(k)$ be the number of additions (and subtractions). Then:

$$M(1) = 0$$
$$M(k) = 2M(k-1) + 1 \qquad \text{for } k > 1$$

and

$$A(1) = 1$$
$$A(k) = 2A(k-1) + 2 \qquad \text{for } k > 1.$$

By expanding $M(k)$ a few times we see that

$$M(k) = 4M(k-2) + 2 + 1 = 8M(k-3) + 4 + 2 + 1 = \sum_{i=0}^{k-2} 2^i = 2^{k-1} - 1.$$

The total number of multiplications, then, is $2^{k-1} - 1 + k - 1$. (The $k-1$ term is for computing powers of x.) Since $n = 2^k - 1$, the number of multiplications is $n/2 + \lg(n+1) - 3/2$, or roughly $n/2 + \lg n$. It is easy to show that $A(k) = (3n-1)/2$. (You should check that these formulas describe the number of operations done in the example.)

    Whether or not eliminating $n/2 - \lg n$ multiplications by doing $n/2$ extra additions is a time-saver, we have illustrated an important point: Lower bounds that have been obtained for a problem without preprocessing, in this case n $*/$'s for evaluating a polynomial of degree n, may no longer be valid. The particular operations permitted in the preprocessing (for example, division of polynomials, as in this case, or finding roots of polynomials) can also affect the number of operations required. A lower bound of $\lceil n/2 \rceil$ $*/$'s has been established for polynomial evaluation, allowing a variety of preprocessing operations.

12.3   Vector and Matrix Multiplication

We begin by reviewing the well-known methods for multiplying matrices and vectors, noting the number of operations done by these methods, and giving the known lower bounds for the number of multiplications and divisions ($*/$'s). Then we will look at some more sophisticated strategies. One of these, using a divide-and-conquer approach, is able to improve on the asymptotic order of the straightforward matrix multiplication procedure.

    Throughout this section we use capital letters for the names of vectors and matrices and the corresponding small letters for their components. The components are real numbers.

12.3.1 Review of Standard Algorithms

Let $V = (v_1, v_2, \ldots, v_n)$ and $W = (w_1, w_2, \ldots, w_n)$ be two n-vectors, that is, vectors with n components in each. The dot product of V and W, denoted $V \cdot W$, is defined as $V \cdot W = \sum_{i=1}^{n} v_i w_i$. The computation of $V \cdot W$ implied by the definition requires n multiplications and $n - 1$ additions. It has been shown that, even if one of the vectors is known in advance and some preprocessing of its components is permitted, at least n $*/$'s are required in the worst case. Thus the straightforward computation of dot products is optimal.

Let A be an $m \times n$ matrix and let V be an n-vector. Let W be the product AV. By definition, the ith component of W is the dot product of the ith row of A with V. That is, for $1 \le i \le m$, $w_i = \sum_{j=1}^{n} a_{ij} v_j$. The computation of AV implied by the definition requires mn multiplications. This is known to be optimal. The number of additions done is $m(n - 1)$.

Let A be an $m \times n$ matrix, let B be an $n \times q$ matrix, and let C be the product of A and B. By definition, c_{ij} is the dot product of the ith row of A and the jth column of B. That is, for $1 \le i \le m$ and $1 \le j \le q$, $c_{ij} = \sum_{k=1}^{n} a_{ik} b_{kj}$. If the entries of C are computed by the usual matrix multiplication algorithm, that is, as indicated by this formula, mnq multiplications and $m(n - 1)q$ additions are done. Much to the surprise of people studying the problem, attempts to prove that mnq $*/$'s are required for matrix multiplication were unsuccessful, and eventually algorithms that do fewer $*/$'s were sought and found. Two of these are presented here.

12.3.2 Winograd's Matrix Multiplication

Suppose that the dot product of $V = (v_1, v_2, v_3, v_4)$ and $W = (w_1, w_2, w_3, w_4)$ is computed by the following formula:

$$V \cdot W = (v_1 + w_2)(v_2 + w_1) + (v_3 + w_4)(v_4 + w_3) - v_1 v_2 - v_3 v_4 - w_1 w_2 - w_3 w_4.$$

Observe that the last four multiplications involve only components of V or only components of W. There are only two multiplications that involve components of both vectors. Also observe that the formula relies on the commutativity of multiplication; for example, it uses the fact that $w_2 v_2 = v_2 w_2$. Hence it would not hold if multiplication of the components were not commutative; in particular, it would not hold if the components were matrices.

Generalizing from the example, when n is even (say, $n = 2p$),

$$V \cdot W = \sum_{i=1}^{p} (v_{2i-1} + w_{2i})(v_{2i} + w_{2i-1}) - \sum_{i=1}^{p} v_{2i-1} v_{2i} - \sum_{i=1}^{p} w_{2i-1} w_{2i}. \quad (12.1)$$

If n is odd, we let $p = \lfloor n/2 \rfloor$ and add the final term $v_n w_n$ to Equation (12.1). In each summation, p, or $\lfloor n/2 \rfloor$, multiplications are done, so in all $3\lfloor n/2 \rfloor$ multiplications are done. This is worse than the straightforward way of computing the dot product. Even if one of the vectors is known in advance and the second or third summation can be considered preprocessing, n multiplications would still be done. If *both* vectors are known in advance, then the whole computation could be thought of as preprocessing, thus eliminating the whole problem! So what has been gained by looking at a more complicated formula for the dot product?

Suppose we are to multiply the $m \times n$ matrix A with the $n \times q$ matrix B. Each row of A is involved in q dot products, one with each column of B, and each column of B is involved in m dot products, one with each row of A. Thus terms like the last two summations in Equation (12.1) can be computed once for each row of A and each column of B and used many times.

Algorithm 12.3   Winograd's Matrix Multiplication

Input: A, B, m, n, and q, where A and B are $m \times n$ and $n \times q$ matrices, respectively.

Output: Matrix $C = AB$. The $m \times q$ matrix C is passed in and the algorithm fills it.

```
void winograd(float[][] A, float[][] B, int n, int m, int q, float[][] C)
    int i, j, k;
    int p = n / 2;
    float[] rowTerm = new float[m+1];
    float[] colmTerm = new float[q+1];
    // These arrays are for the results of the "preprocessing"
    // of the rows of A and the columns of B.

    // "Preprocess" rows of A.
    for (i = 1; i ≤ m; i ++)
        rowTerm[i] = ∑ᵖⱼ₌₁ a_{i,2j−1} * a_{i,2j};

    // "Preprocess" columns of B.
    for (i = 1; i ≤ q; i ++)
        colmTerm[i] = ∑ᵖⱼ₌₁ b_{2j−1,i} * b_{2j,i};

    // Compute entries of C.
    for (i = 1; i ≤ m; i ++)
        for (j = 1; j ≤ q; j ++)
            c_{ij} = ∑ᵖₖ₌₁ (a_{i,2k−1} + b_{2k,j}) * (a_{i,2k} + b_{2k−1,j})
                − rowTerm[i] − colmTerm[j];

    // If n is odd, add a final term to each entry of C.
    if (odd(n))
        for (i = 1; i ≤ m; i ++)
            for (j = 1; j ≤ q; j ++)
                c_{ij} = c_{ij} + a_{in} * b_{nj};
```

Analysis

Assume that n is even. (The case of odd n is left as an exercise.) We count multiplications first. Processing rows of A does mp, processing columns of B does qp, and computing the entries of C does mqp multiplications. The total, since $p = n/2$, is $(mnq/2) + (n/2)(q + m)$. If A and B are square matrices, both $n \times n$, then Winograd's algorithm does $(n^3/2) +$

n^2 multiplications instead of the usual n^3. (See Algorithm 1.2.) The difference is significant even for small n. Unfortunately, Winograd's algorithm does extra $\pm$'s. We count the $\pm$'s as follows:

Processing rows of A:	$m(p-1)$
Processing columns of B:	$q(p-1)$
Computing elements of C:	For each of the mq entries of C, we do:

two pluses in each term of the summation:	$2p$
add the terms in the summation:	$p-1$
subtract rowTerm[i] and colmTerm[j]:	2

Thus to compute the elements of C the algorithm does $mq(3p+1)$ $\pm$'s, and the total, again assuming n is even, is $(3/2)(mnq) + (n/2)(m+q) + mq - m - q$. For square $n \times n$ matrices, where the comparison between algorithms is a little easier to see, Winograd's algorithm does $(3/2)n^3 + 2n^2 - 2n$ $\pm$'s instead of the usual $n^3 - n^2$.

Observe that Winograd's algorithm contains fewer instructions that require incrementing and testing loop counters than does the usual method. On the other hand, Winograd's algorithm uses more complex subscripting and requires fetching matrix entries more often. These differences are explored in the exercises.

12.3.3   Lower Bounds for Matrix Multiplication

Winograd's algorithm shows that $m \times n$ and $n \times q$ matrices can be multiplied using fewer than mnq multiplications. How many $*/$'s are necessary? Is it in $\Theta(mnq)$ or can the cubic term be eliminated? The best known lower bound is surprisingly low: mn, or n^2 for square matrices. We stated earlier that mn $*/$'s are necessary to multiply an $m \times n$ matrix by an n-vector. We would expect matrix multiplication to be at least as hard, hence to require at least as many $*/$'s, and Figure 12.3 illustrates that this is true by showing that an algorithm to multiply matrices can be used to obtain a matrix-vector product. (The two problems are the same, of course, if $q = 1$.) No known matrix multiplication algorithm does only

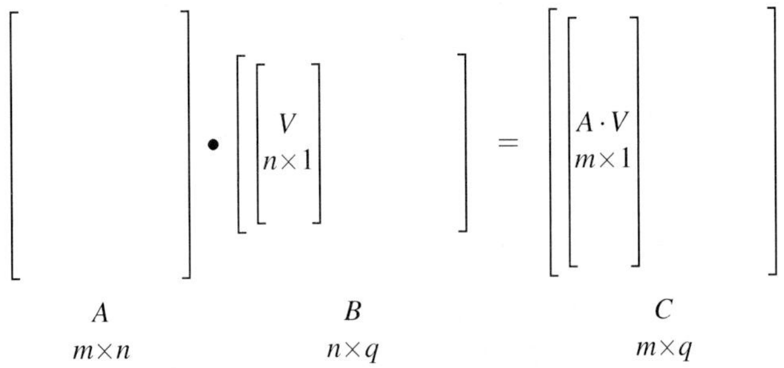

Figure 12.3   Lower bound for matrix multiplication

mn $*/$'s. However, there are algorithms that, for large matrices, do significantly fewer multiplications *and* $\pm$'s than Winograd's.

12.3.4 Strassen's Matrix Multiplication

For the remainder of this section we assume the matrices to be multiplied are $n \times n$ square matrices, A and B. Strassen's algorithm is a divide-and-conquer algorithm. The key to the algorithm is a method for multiplying 2×2 matrices using seven multiplications instead of the usual eight. (Winograd's algorithm also uses eight.) For $n = 2$, first compute the following seven quantities, each of which requires exactly one multiplication:

$$
\begin{aligned}
x_1 &= (a_{11} + a_{22}) * (b_{11} + b_{22}) & x_5 &= (a_{11} + a_{12}) * b_{22} \\
x_2 &= (a_{21} + a_{22}) * b_{11} & x_6 &= (a_{21} - a_{11}) * (b_{11} + b_{12}) \\
x_3 &= a_{11} * (b_{12} - b_{22}) & x_7 &= (a_{12} - a_{22}) * (b_{21} + b_{22}) \\
x_4 &= a_{22} * (b_{21} - b_{11})
\end{aligned}
\tag{12.2}
$$

Let $C = AB$. The entries of C are

$$
\begin{aligned}
c_{11} &= a_{11}b_{11} + a_{12}b_{21} & c_{12} &= a_{11}b_{12} + a_{12}b_{22} \\
c_{21} &= a_{21}b_{11} + a_{22}b_{21} & c_{22} &= a_{21}b_{12} + a_{22}b_{22}
\end{aligned}
$$

They are computed as follows:

$$
\begin{aligned}
c_{11} &= x_1 + x_4 - x_5 + x_7 & c_{12} &= x_3 + x_5 \\
c_{21} &= x_2 + x_4 & c_{22} &= x_1 + x_3 - x_2 + x_6
\end{aligned}
\tag{12.3}
$$

Thus 2×2 matrices can be multiplied using seven multiplications and 18 additions. It is critical to Strassen's algorithm that commutativity of multiplication is not used in the formulas in Equations 12.2, so they can be applied to matrices whose components are also matrices. Let n be a power of 2. Strassen's method consists of partitioning A and B each into four $n/2 \times n/2$ matrices as shown in Figure 12.4 and multiplying them using the formulas in Equations 12.2 and 12.3; the formulas are used recursively to multiply the component matrices. Before considering extensions for the case when n is not a power of 2, we compute the number of multiplications and $\pm$'s done.

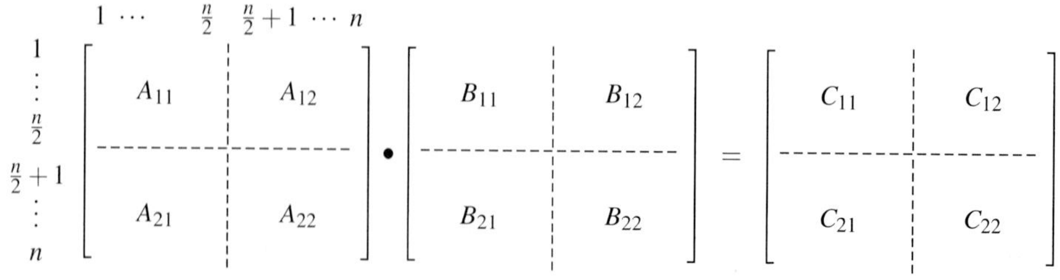

Figure 12.4 Partitioning for Strassen's matrix multiplication

Suppose $n = 2^k$ for some $k \geq 0$. Let $M(k)$ be the number of multiplications (of the underlying matrix components, i.e., real numbers) done by Strassen's method for $n \times n$ matrices. Then, since the formulas of Equation (12.2) do seven multiplications of $2^{k-1} \times 2^{k-1}$ matrices,

$$M(0) = 1$$
$$M(k) = 7M(k-1) \qquad \text{for } k > 0.$$

This recurrence equation is very easy to solve. $M(k) = 7^k$, and $7^k = 7^{\lg n} = n^{\lg 7} \approx n^{2.81}$. Thus the number of multiplications is in $o(n^3)$.

Let $P(k)$ be the number of $\pm$'s done. Clearly $P(0) = 0$. There are 18 $\pm$'s in the formulas of Equations 12.2 and 12.3, so $P(1) = 18$. For $k \geq 1$, multiplying $2^k \times 2^k$ matrices involves 18 additions of $2^{k-1} \times 2^{k-1}$ matrices, plus all the $\pm$'s done by the seven matrix multiplications in Equations 12.2. So

$$P(0) = 0$$
$$P(k) = 18\left(2^{k-1}\right)^2 + 7P(k-1) \qquad \text{for } k > 0.$$

We can expand the recursion tree (see Section 3.7.2) to see what the row-sums look like, or expand the recurrence equation to see what the terms look like.

$$
\begin{aligned}
P(k) &= 18(2^{k-1})^2 + 7P(k-1) \\
&= 18(2^{k-1})^2 + 7 \cdot 18(2^{k-2})^2 + 7^2 P(k-2) \\
&= 18(2^{k-1})^2 + 7 \cdot 18(2^{k-2})^2 + 7^2 \cdot 18(2^{k-3})^2 + 7^3 P(k-3) \\
&\;\;\vdots \\
&= 18 \cdot 2^{2(k-1)} + 7 \cdot 18 \cdot 2^{2(k-2)} + 7^2 \cdot 18 \cdot 2^{2(k-3)} + \cdots + 7^{k-1} \cdot 18
\end{aligned}
$$

A geometric series has developed, with ratio $r = 7/4$, so the sum is in Θ of its largest term (see Theorem 1.13). The largest term is $18 \cdot 7^{k-1}$, which is in $\Theta(7^k)$. As we just saw for $M(k)$, this is in $\Theta\left(n^{\lg 7}\right)$.

For a more accurate value, we can use Equation (1.9).

$$P(k) = \sum_{i=0}^{k-1} 7^i 18(2^{k-i-1})^2 = 18\left(2^k\right)^2 \sum_{i=0}^{k-1} \frac{7^i}{\left(2^{i+1}\right)^2}$$

$$= \frac{9}{2}2^{2k} \sum_{i=0}^{k-1} \left(\frac{7}{4}\right)^i = \frac{9}{2}2^{2k}\left(\frac{\left(\frac{7}{4}\right)^k - 1}{\frac{7}{4} - 1}\right) = 6 \cdot 7^k - 6 \cdot 4^k$$

$$\approx 6n^{2.81} - 6n^2.$$

Thus for large n this algorithm does about $7\,n^{2.81}$ arithmetic operations.

If n is not a power of 2, some extension of Strassen's algorithm must be used and more work will be done. There are two simple approaches, both of which can be very

	The usual algorithm	Winograd's algorithm	Strassen's algorithm (without enhancements)
Multiplications	n^3	$\frac{1}{2}n^3 + n^2$	$7^k \approx n^{2.81}$, where $n = 2^k$
Additions/subtractions	$n^3 - n^2$	$\frac{3}{2}n^3 + 2n^2 - 2n$	$6 \cdot 7^k - 6 \cdot 4^k \approx 6n^{2.81} - 6n^2$, where $n = 2^k$
Total	$2n^3 - n^2$	$2n^3 + 3n^2 - 2n$	$7n^{\lg 7} - 6n^2 \approx 7n^{2.81} - 6n^2$

Table 12.1   Comparison of matrix multiplication methods for $n \times n$ matrices

slow. The first possibility is to add extra rows and columns of zeros to make the dimension a power of 2. The second is to use Strassen's formulas as long as the dimension of the matrices is even and then use the usual algorithm when the dimension is odd. Another more complicated possibility is to modify the algorithm so that at each level of the recursion, if the matrices to be multiplied have odd dimensions, one extra row and column are added. Strassen described a fourth strategy, one that combines the advantages of the first two, and also improves performance when n is a power of 2. The matrices are embedded in (possibly) larger ones with dimension $2^k m$, where $k = \lfloor \lg n - 4 \rfloor$ and $m = \lceil n/2^k \rceil$. Strassen's formulas are used recursively until the matrices to be multiplied are $m \times m$; then the usual method is applied. With this enhancement, the total number of arithmetic operations done on the matrix entries will be less than $4.7n^{\lg 7}$ (see Exercise 12.11).

Table 12.1 compares the numbers of arithmetic operations done by the three matrix multiplication methods for $n \times n$ matrices. For large n, Strassen's algorithm does fewer multiplications *and* fewer $\pm$'s than either of the other methods. In practice, however, because of its recursive nature, implementing this algorithm requires a lot of bookkeeping that might be slow and is complicated. The other, much simpler algorithms are more efficient for moderate-size n.

The primary importance of Strassen's algorithm is that it broke the $\Theta(n^3)$ barrier for matrix multiplication *and* the $\Theta(n^3)$ barrier for a number of other matrix problems. These problems, which include matrix inversion, computing determinants, and solving systems of simultaneous linear equations, have well-known $\Theta(n^3)$ solutions, but they can be reduced to matrix multiplication, so they too can be solved in $O(n^{\lg 7})$ time. Strassen's result has been improved upon theoretically several times. There is a matrix multiplication algorithm with running time in $O(n^{2.376})$. The lower bound of n^2 multiplications has not been increased; whether matrix multiplication can be done in $\Theta(n^2)$ steps is still an open question.

⋆ 12.4   The Fast Fourier Transform and Convolution

The Fourier transform has widespread applications in engineering, physical sciences, and mathematics. Its discrete version is used in interpolation problems, in finding solutions of partial differential equations, in circuit design, in crystallography, and, very extensively, in signal processing. This was one of the earliest problems for which the divide-and-conquer strategy was used to develop an algorithm of lower asymptotic order than the straightforward computation. The improved algorithm is called the fast Fourier transform.

This algorithm had a widespread impact because many other mathematical computations can be expressed in terms of Fourier transforms. In some cases it turns out to be faster to convert the natural problem into a Fourier transform problem, and do two Fourier transforms, than to compute a solution of the original problem in the straightforward way. Convolution is one such example.

Definition 12.1   Convolution

Let U and V be n-vectors with components indexed from 0 to $n - 1$. The *convolution* of U and V, denoted $U \star V$, is, by definition, an n-vector W with components $w_i = \sum_{j=0}^{n-1} u_j v_{i-j}$, where $0 \leq i \leq n - 1$ and the indexes on the right-hand side are taken modulo n. ∎

For example, for $n = 5$,

$$w_0 = u_0 v_0 + u_1 v_4 + u_2 v_3 + u_3 v_2 + u_4 v_1$$
$$w_1 = u_0 v_1 + u_1 v_0 + u_2 v_4 + u_3 v_3 + u_4 v_2$$

$$\vdots$$

$$w_4 = u_0 v_4 + u_1 v_3 + u_2 v_2 + u_3 v_1 + u_4 v_0.$$

The problem of computing the convolution of two vectors arises naturally and frequently in probability problems, engineering, and other areas. Symbolic polynomial multiplication, which is examined in this section, is a convolution computation.

The discrete Fourier transform of an n-vector and the convolution of two n-vectors can each be computed in a straightforward way using n^2 multiplications and fewer than n^2 additions. We present a divide-and-conquer algorithm to compute the discrete Fourier transform using $\Theta(n \log n)$ arithmetic operations. This algorithm (which appears in the literature in many variations) is known as the fast Fourier transform, or FFT. We then use the FFT to compute convolutions in $\Theta(n \log n)$ time. This time-saving is very valuable in the applications.

Throughout this section all matrix, array, and vector indexes begin at 0. The complex *roots of unity* (also called *roots of* 1) and some of their elementary properties are used in the FFT. The basic definitions and required properties are reviewed in the appendix for this section (Section 12.4.3). Readers who are unfamiliar with complex numbers or nth roots of unity should read the appendix before proceeding.

12.4.1   The Fast Fourier Transform

The discrete Fourier transform transforms a complex n-vector (i.e., an n-vector with complex components) into another complex n-vector. To transform a real n-vector, simply treat it as a complex n-vector in which all imaginary parts are zero.

Definition 12.2   Discrete Fourier transform and the matrix F_n

For $n \geq 1$, let ω be a primitive nth root of 1, and let F_n be the $n \times n$ matrix with entries $f_{ij} = \omega^{ij}$, where $0 \leq i, j \leq n-1$. The *discrete Fourier transform* of the n-vector $P = (p_0, p_1, \ldots, p_{n-1})$ is the product $F_n P$.   ∎

The components of $F_n P$ are

$$\omega^0 p_0 + \omega^0 p_1 + \cdots + \omega^0 p_{n-2} + \omega^0 p_{n-1}$$

$$\omega^0 p_0 + \omega p_1 + \cdots + \omega^{n-2} p_{n-2} + \omega^{n-1} p_{n-1}$$

$$\vdots$$

$$\omega^0 p_0 + \omega^i p_1 + \cdots + \omega^{i(n-2)} p_{n-2} + \omega^{i(n-1)} p_{n-1}$$

$$\vdots$$

$$\omega^0 p_0 + \omega^{n-1} p_1 + \cdots + \omega^{(n-1)(n-2)} p_{n-2} + \omega^{(n-1)(n-1)} p_{n-1}.$$

Rewritten in a slightly different form, the ith component is

$$p_{n-1}(\omega^i)^{n-1} + p_{n-2}(\omega^i)^{n-2} + \cdots + p_1 \omega^i + p_0.$$

Thus if we interpret the components of P as coefficients of the polynomial $p(x) = p_{n-1}x^{n-1} + p_{n-2}x^{n-2} + \cdots + p_1 x + p_0$, then the ith component is $p(\omega^i)$ and computing the discrete Fourier transform of P means evaluating the polynomial $p(x)$ at $\omega^0, \omega, \omega^2, \ldots, \omega^{n-1}$, that is, at each of the nth roots of 1. We will approach the problem from this point of view. We will develop a recursive divide-and-conquer algorithm first and then examine it closely to remove the recursion. We assume that $n = 2^k$ for some $k \geq 0$. (Adjustments to the algorithm can be made if it is to be used for n not a power of 2.)

The divide-and-conquer strategy is to divide the problem into smaller instances, solve those, and use the solutions to get the solution for the current instance. Here, to evaluate p at n points, we evaluate two smaller polynomials at a subset of the points and then combine the results appropriately. Recall that $\omega^{n/2} = -1$ and thus for $0 \leq j \leq (n/2) - 1$, $\omega^{(n/2)+j} = -\omega^j$. Group the terms of $p(x)$ with even powers and the terms with odd powers as follows:

$$p(x) = \sum_{i=0}^{n-1} p_i x^i = \sum_{i=0}^{n/2-1} p_{2i} x^{2i} + x \sum_{i=0}^{n/2-1} p_{2i+1} x^{2i}.$$

Define

$$p_{even}(x) = \sum_{i=0}^{n/2-1} p_{2i} x^i \quad \text{and} \quad p_{odd}(x) = \sum_{i=0}^{n/2-1} p_{2i+1} x^i.$$

Then

$$p(x) = p_{even}(x^2) + x p_{odd}(x^2) \quad \text{and} \quad p(-x) = p_{even}(x^2) - x p_{odd}(x^2). \qquad (12.4)$$

Equation (12.4) shows that, to evaluate p at $1, \omega, \ldots, \omega^{(n/2)-1}, -1, -\omega, \ldots, -\omega^{(n/2)-1}$, it suffices to evaluate p_{even} and p_{odd} at $1, \omega^2, \ldots, (\omega^{(n/2)-1})^2$ and then do $n/2$ multiplications (for $x \, p_{odd}(x^2)$) and n additions and subtractions. The polynomials p_{even} and p_{odd} can be evaluated recursively by the same scheme. That is, they are polynomials of degree $n/2 - 1$ and will be evaluated at the $n/2$-th roots of unity: $1, \omega^2, \ldots, (\omega^{(n/2)-1})^2$. Clearly, when the polynomial to be evaluated is a constant, there is no work to be done.

The recursive algorithm follows.

Algorithm 12.4   Fast Fourier Transform (Recursive Version)

Input: The vector $P = (p_0, p_1, \ldots, p_{n-1})$, as a **Complex** array with n entries, where $n = 2^k$; integer $k > 0$; and integer $m > 0$. (To process a vector of **float**, copy it into the real part of the **Complex** array P, and set all the imaginary parts to 0.)

Output: The discrete Fourier transform of P stored in the **Complex** array transform. This array (with indexes $0, \ldots, 2^k - 1$) is passed in and the algorithm fills it.

Remark: We assume the class **Complex** provides complex arithmetic to simplify the pseudocode. This class does not currently exist in Java.

We assume the 2^k-th roots of 1: $\omega^0, \omega, \ldots, \omega^{2^k-1}$, are stored in the global array omega in the order listed here. We use m to select roots from this array. Procedure recursiveFFT would be called initially with $m = 1$. In general, the set consisting of every mth entry, that is, $\omega^0, \omega^m, \omega^{2m}, \ldots$, is the set of $(2^k/m)$-th roots of 1.

```
void recursiveFFT(Complex[] P, int k, int m, Complex[] transform)
    if (k==0)
        transform[0] = p₀;
    else
        int n = 2ᵏ;
        Complex[] evens = new Complex[n/2];
        Complex[] odds = new Complex[n/2];
        Complex xPOdd;
        int j;
        // Evaluate p_even at the 2ᵏ⁻¹th roots of 1.
        recursiveFFT((p₀, p₂, . . . , p₂ᵏ₋₂), k−1, 2m, evens);
        // Evaluate p_odd at the 2ᵏ⁻¹th roots of 1.
        recursiveFFT((p₁, p₃, . . . , p₂ᵏ₋₁), k−1, 2m, odds);
        for (j = 0; j ≤ 2ᵏ⁻¹ − 1; j ++)
            // Evaluate p(ωʲ) and p(ω²ᵏ⁻¹⁺ʲ).
            xPOdd = omega[m∗j] ∗ odds[j];
            // Compute p(ωʲ).
            transform[j] = evens[j] + xPOdd;
            // Compute p(ω²ᵏ⁻¹⁺ʲ).
            transform[2ᵏ⁻¹ + j] = evens[j] − xPOdd;
```

The recursive nature of the algorithm makes it easy to find a recurrence equation for the number of operations done. We count the arithmetic operations done on components of P and roots of 1. Let $M(k)$, $A(k)$, and $S(k)$ be the number of multiplications, additions, and subtractions, respectively, done by recursiveFFT to compute the discrete Fourier transform of a 2^k-vector. The three operations are done, one each, in the body of the **for** loop, so $M(k) = A(k) = S(k)$. We solve for $M(k)$.

$$M(0) = 0$$

$$M(k) = 2^{k-1} + 2M(k-1),$$

where the first term on the right-hand side, that is, 2^{k-1}, counts the multiplications in the **for** loop, and the second term, $2M(k-1)$, counts multiplications done by the recursive calls to recursiveFFT to compute the values in the arrays evens and odds. It is easy to see that $M(k) = 2^{k-1}k$. Thus $M(k) = A(k) = S(k) = 2^{k-1}k$, or $(n/2) \lg n$. Since the operations are done on complex numbers, this result should be multiplied by a small constant to reflect the fact that each complex operation requires several ordinary ones.

Algorithm 12.4 would require a lot of extra time and space for the bookkeeping necessitated by the recursion. Yet the breakdown of the polynomial seems systematic enough that we should be able to obtain a scheme for carrying out the same computation "from the bottom up" without using a recursive program. The example in the tree diagram of Figure 12.5 should help suggest the pattern of the computation. The depths of the tree correspond to the depth of recursion, but we could eliminate the recursion if we start the computation at the leaves. The leaves are the components of the vector P permuted in a particular way. Determining the correct permutation, π_k, is the key to constructing an efficient implementation of the evaluation scheme. We will give π_k (and prove its correctness) after the presentation of the nonrecursive algorithm. Readers are invited to try to determine how to define π_k before proceeding.

■   ■   ■

Observe that, at each level of the tree, the same number of values is to be computed: 2^k, since at depth d there are 2^d nodes, or polynomials, to be evaluated at 2^{k-d} roots of unity. Since the values computed at one level are needed only for the computation of two values in the next level, one array, transform, with 2^k entries suffices to store the results of the computations. Figure 12.6 illustrates how two values at a node at depth d are computed using one value from each of its children. The diagram may help clarify the algorithm's indexing.

Algorithm 12.5   The Fast Fourier Transform

Input: The vector $P = (p_0, p_1, \ldots, p_{n-1})$, as a **Complex** array with n entries, where $n = 2^k$; and integer $k > 0$. (To process a vector of **float**, copy it into the real part of the **Complex** array P, and set all the imaginary parts to 0.)

Output: **Complex** array transform, the discrete Fourier transform of P, with n entries. The array is passed in and the algorithm fills it.

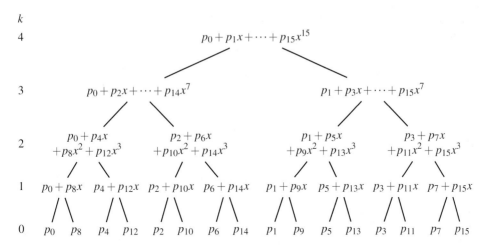

Figure 12.5 Polynomial evaluation at roots of unity: For a polynomial p at any internal node, the left child is p_{even} and the right child is p_{odd}.

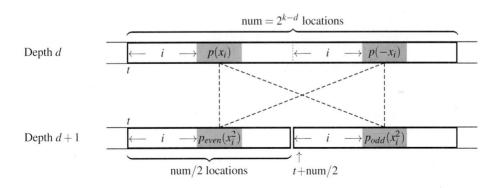

Figure 12.6 Illustration for FFT: At the node shown in depth d, the polynomial p is to be evaluated at $x_0, x_1, \ldots, x_{2^{k-(d+1)}-1}, -x_0, -x_1, \ldots, -x_{2^{k-(d+1)}-1}$, where $p(x_i) = p_{even}(x_i^2) + x_i p_{odd}(x_i^2)$ and $p(-x_i) = p_{even}(x_i^2) - x_i p_{odd}(x_i^2)$. The diagram shows which values from the previous depths are used to compute $p(x_i)$ and $p(-x_i)$.

Remarks: We assume the class **Complex** provides complex arithmetic to simplify the pseudocode. This class does not currently exist in Java.

We assume omega is a **Complex** array containing the nth roots of 1: $\omega^0, \omega, \ldots, \omega^{n-1}$. The **Complex** array transform is initialized to contain the values for depth $k - 1$, not the leaves, in the tree of Figure 12.5. π_k is a certain permutation on $\{0, 1, \ldots, n - 1\}$.

```
void  fft(Complex[] P, int k, Complex[] transform)
    int  n = 2^k;
    int  d;  // the current depth in the tree
    int  num;
    // num is the number of values to be computed at
    // each node at depth d.
    int  t;
    // t is the index in transform for the first of
    // these values for a particular node
    int  j;
    // j counts the pairs of values to be computed
    // for that node.
    int  m;
    // m is used as in recursiveFFT to pick out
    // the correct entry from omega
    Complex  prevTrans;  // temporary variable

    // To initialize transform, evaluate polynomials of
    // degree 1 = 2^1 − 1 at square roots of 1.
    for (t = 0; t ≤ n − 2; t += 2)
        transform[t] = P[π_k(t)] + P[π_k(t + 1)];
        transform[t+1] = P[π_k(t)] − P[π_k(t + 1)];

    // The main computation
    m = n/2; num = 2;
    for (d = k − 2; d ≥ 0; d −−)
        m = m/2; num = 2 * num;
        for (t = 0; t ≤ (2^d − 1) * num; t += num)
            for (j = 0; j ≤ (num/2) − 1; j ++)
                xPOdd = omega[m*j] * transform[t + num/2 + j];
                prevTrans = transform[t + j];
                transform[t+j] = prevTrans + xPOdd;
                transform[t + num/2 + j] = prevTrans − xPOdd;
```

An analysis of the number of operations done by fft gives a result only slightly different from that obtained for recursiveFFT. The statements that do the bulk of the computation (one complex multiplication, one complex addition, and one complex subtraction) are in a triply nested **for** loop. It is easy to verify that $num = 2^{k-d}$ so the ranges of the loop indexes indicate that the number of each operation done in these statements is

$$\sum_{d=0}^{k-2} 2^d \frac{num}{2} = \sum_{d=0}^{k-2} 2^d 2^{k-d-1} = \sum_{d=0}^{k-2} 2^{k-1} = (k-1)2^{k-1} = \tfrac{1}{2}n(\lg(n) - 1).$$

The first **for** loop, initializing transform, does $n/2$ additions and $n/2$ subtractions, so the total is $\frac{3}{2}n \lg(n) - \frac{1}{2}n$ complex arithmetic operations. We claim that the permutation π_k can be computed easily enough so that the running time of fft is in $\Theta(n \log n)$.

Note that the fast Fourier transform allows us to evaluate a polynomial of degree $n - 1$ at n distinct points at a cost of only $\frac{1}{2}n(\lg(n) - 1)$ complex multiplications. The lower bound on polynomial evaluation given in Section 12.2 suggests that this is not possible for n arbitrary points. The speed of the FFT derives from its use of some of the properties of roots of unity.

Now, what is π_k? Let t be an integer between 0 and $n - 1$, where $n = 2^k$. Then t can be represented in binary by $[b_0 b_1 \cdots b_{k-1}]$, where each b_j is 0 or 1. Let $rev_k(t)$ be the number represented by these bits in reverse order, that is, by $[b_{k-1} \cdots b_1 b_0]$. We claim that $\pi_k(t) = rev_k(t)$. Lemma 12.3 describes the values computed by the FFT using $\pi_k = rev_k$. It is used in Theorem 12.4 to establish the correctness of the algorithm, thus also establishing the correctness of this choice of π_k. The proof of the lemma follows the theorem. First, we need some notation.

Definition 12.3

Let P be the complex n-vector P[0], P[1], . . ., P[n−1], where $n = 2^k$. Thinking of n (and k) as fixed, for each t such that $0 \le t \le n-1$ and for each d such that $0 \le d \le k-1$, we define the vector of coefficients $c_{t,d}[j]$ as

$$c_{t,d}[j] = P[2^d j + rev_k(t)] \qquad \text{for } 0 \le j \le 2^{k-d} - 1.$$

Now we define $P_{t,d}$ to be the polynomial of degree $2^{k-d} - 1$ with coefficients $c_{t,d}[j]$. ∎

Lemma 12.3   Let π_k in Algorithm 12.5 be rev_k. The following statements hold for $d = k - 1$ before the triply nested **for** loop is first entered and for each d such that $k - 2 \ge d \ge 0$ at the end of each execution of the body of the outer **for** loop.

1. $m = 2^d$ and num $= 2^{k-d}$.
2. For $t = r2^{k-d}$ where $0 \le r \le 2^d - 1$, transform[t], . . ., transform[t+num−1] contain the values of $P_{t,d}$ evaluated at the (2^{k-d})-th roots of 1, where $P_{t,d}$ was defined in Definition 12.3.

Theorem 12.4   Algorithm 12.5 computes the values of

$$p(x) = P[0] + P[1]x + \cdots + P[n - 2]x^{n-2} + P[n - 1]x^{n-1}$$

at the nth roots of 1. That is, it computes the discrete Fourier transform of P.

Proof   Let $d = 0$ in Lemma 12.3. Then the only value for t is 0 and the lemma says that transform[0], . . ., transform[$2^k - 1$] contain the values of $P_{0,0}$ at the 2^k-th roots of 1. The coefficients of $P_{0,0}$ are $c_{0,0}[j] = P[2^0 j + rev_k(0)] = P[j]$ for $0 \le j \le 2^k - 1$, so $P_{0,0}$ is the polynomial p.   □

Proof of Lemma 12.3   We prove the lemma by induction on d, where d ranges from $k - 1$ down to 0. Let $d = k - 1$ for the basis. Statement 1 is clearly true. Statement 2 states that t ranges from 0 to $2^k - 2$ (i.e., $n - 2$) in steps of 2, and that, for each t, transform[t] and transform[$t+1$] contain $P_{t,k-1}(1)$ and $P_{t,k-1}(-1)$. But (using Lemma 12.5) the coefficients of $P_{t,k-1}$ are

$$c_{t,k-1}[0] = P[2^{k-1}0 + rev_k(t)] = P[rev_k(t)],$$

$$c_{t,k-1}[1] = P[2^{k-1}1 + rev_k(t)] = P[rev_k(t + 1)].$$

That is, $P_{t,k-1}(x) = P[rev_k(t)] + P[rev_k(t + 1)]x$. This corresponds exactly to the initial values assigned to transform in the first **for** loop.

Now suppose that $0 \leq d < k - 1$ and statements 1 and 2 hold for $d + 1$. It follows easily that statement 1 holds for d. Note that ω^{2^d} and $\omega^{2^{d+1}}$ are primitive (2^{k-d})-th and $(2^{k-(d+1)})$-th roots of 1, respectively. Using the induction hypothesis, we see that for $0 \leq i \leq \text{num}/2 - 1$, the body of the triply nested **for** loop computes

$$\text{xPOdd} = \left(\omega^{2^d}\right)^i P_{t+\text{num}/2,\,d+1}\left(\left(\omega^{2^{d+1}}\right)^i\right),$$

$$\text{transform}[t + i] = P_{t,\,d+1}\left(\left(\omega^{2^{d+1}}\right)^i\right) + \left(\omega^{2^d}\right)^i P_{t+\text{num}/2,\,d+1}\left(\left(\omega^{2^{d+1}}\right)^i\right),$$

$$\text{transform}[t + \text{num}/2 + i] = P_{t,\,d+1}\left(\left(\omega^{2^{d+1}}\right)^i\right) - \left(\omega^{2^d}\right)^i P_{t+\text{num}/2,\,d+1}\left(\left(\omega^{2^{d+1}}\right)^i\right).$$

Thus $P_{t,\,d}(x) = P_{t,\,d+1}\left(x^2\right) + x\,P_{t+\text{num}/2,\,d+1}\left(x^2\right)$ and the array entries transform[0], . . ., transform[t+num-1] contain $P_{t,d}$ evaluated at

$$\left(\omega^{2^d}\right)^0, \omega^{2^d}, \ldots, \left(\omega^{2^d}\right)^{2^{k-d-1}}, -\left(\omega^{2^d}\right)^0, -\omega^{2^d}, \ldots, -\left(\omega^{2^d}\right)^{2^{k-d-1}},$$

that is, at the (2^{k-d})-th roots of 1. The coefficients of $P_{t,d}$ are derived as follows for $0 \leq j \leq 2^{k-d}-1$:

$$c_{t,d}[j] = \begin{cases} c_{t,\,d+1}[j/2] & \text{for even } j, \\ c_{t+\text{num}/2,\,d+1}[(j - 1)/2] & \text{for odd } j. \end{cases}$$

Therefore, using the induction hypothesis, for even j,

$$c_{t,d}[j] = c_{t,d+1}[j/2] = P[2^{d+1}(j/2) + rev_k(t)] = P[2^d j + rev_k(t)]$$

as required. For odd j,

$$c_{t,d}[j] = c_{t+\text{num}/2,\,d+1}[(j - 1)/2] = P[2^{d+1}(j - 1)/2 + rev_k(t + 2^{k-(d+1)})]$$

$$= \text{(by Lemma 12.5) } P[2^d(j - 1) + rev_k(t) + 2^d] = P[2^d j + rev_k(t)],$$

also as required. $\square$

The proof used the following lemma, whose proof is left as an exercise.

Lemma 12.5 For $k, a, b > 0$, $b \le k$, and $a + 2^{k-b} < 2^k$, if a is a multiple of 2^{k-b+1}, then $rev_k(a + 2^{k-b}) = rev_k(a) + 2^{b-1}$. □

12.4.2 Convolution

To motivate the convolution computation we will examine the problem of symbolic polynomial multiplication. Suppose we are given the coefficient vectors

$$P = (p_0, p_1, \ldots, p_{m-1}),$$
$$Q = (q_0, q_1, \ldots, q_{m-1}),$$

for the polynomials $p(x) = p_{m-1}x^{m-1} + p_{m-2}x^{m-2} + \cdots + p_1x + p_0$ and $q(x) = q_{m-1}x^{m-1} + q_{m-2}x^{m-2} + \cdots + q_1x + q_0$. The problem is to find the vector $R = (r_0, r_1, \ldots, r_{2m-1})$ of coefficients of the product polynomial $r(x) = p(x)q(x)$. The coefficients of r are given by the formula

$$r_i = \sum_{j=0}^{i} p_j q_{i-j} \qquad \text{for } 0 \le i \le 2m - 1$$

with p_k and q_k taken as 0 for $k > m - 1$. (Note that $r_{2m-1} = 0$ since r has degree $2m - 2$; it is included as a convenience.) R is very much like the convolution of P and Q. Let $\vec{P}$ and $\vec{Q}$ be the $2m$-vectors obtained by adding m zeros to P and Q, respectively. Then $R = \vec{P} \star \vec{Q}$. So our investigation of polynomial multiplication should lead to a convolution algorithm.

Consider the following outline for polynomial multiplication:

1. Evaluate $p(x)$ and $q(x)$ at $2m$ points: $x_0, x_1, \ldots, x_{2m-1}$.
2. Multiply pointwise to find the values of $r(x)$ at these $2m$ points; that is, compute $r(x_i) = p(x_i)q(x_i)$ for $0 \le i \le 2m - 1$.
3. Find the coefficients of the unique polynomial of degree $2m - 2$ that passes through the points $\{(x_i, r(x_i)) \mid 0 \le i \le 2m - 1\}$. (It is a well-known theorem that the coefficients of a polynomial of degree d can be determined if the values of the polynomial are known at $d + 1$ points.)

If the points $x_0, \ldots, x_{2m-1}$ were chosen arbitrarily, the method outlined would require much more work than a straightforward computation of $\vec{P} \star \vec{Q}$, but the FFT can evaluate p and q at the $(2m)$-th roots of 1 very efficiently (assume that m is a power of 2). So step 1 can be done in $\Theta(m \log m)$ time. Step 2 requires only $2m$ multiplications. How do we carry out step 3?

Let ω be a primitive $(2m)$-th root of 1, and for $0 \le j \le 2m-1$, let $w_j = r(\omega^j) = p(\omega^j)q(\omega^j)$. We can find the coefficients of r by solving the following set of simultaneous linear equations for $r_0, r_1, \ldots, r_{2m-1}$.

$$r_0 + r_1\omega^0 + \cdots + r_{2m-2}\left(\omega^0\right)^{2m-2} + r_{2m-1}\left(\omega^0\right)^{2m-1} = w_0,$$

$$r_0 + r_1\omega + \cdots + r_{2m-2}\left(\omega\right)^{2m-2} + r_{2m-1}(\omega)^{2m-1} = w_1,$$

$$\vdots \qquad\qquad (12.5)$$

$$r_0 + r_1\omega^{2m-1} + \cdots + r_{2m-2}\left(\omega^{2m-1}\right)^{2m-2} + r_{2m-1}\left(\omega^{2m-1}\right)^{2m-1} = w_{2m-1}.$$

If r had been evaluated at $2m$ arbitrary points, a $\Theta(m^3)$ algorithm such as Gaussian elimination might be used to solve the equations. Again, we take advantage of the fact that the points are roots of unity to obtain a $\Theta(m \log m)$ algorithm. The formulas of Equation (12.5) can be written as a matrix equation $F_{2m}R = W$, where F_{2m} is as in Definition 12.2 and W is the vector $(w_0, w_1, \ldots, w_{2m-1})$. Thus

$$\vec{P} \star \vec{Q} = R = F_{2m}^{-1} W = F_{2m}^{-1}(F_{2m}\vec{P} * F_{2m}\vec{Q}),$$

where $\star$ denotes convolution and $*$ denotes component-wise multiplication. Three problems remain: to show that F_n is in fact invertible for all $n > 0$, to show that the formula $U \star V = F_n^{-1}(F_n U * F_n V)$ holds for arbitrary n-vectors U and V, and to find an efficient way to compute the inverse transform. The formula for $U \star V$ does not follow immediately from the formula for R because $\vec{P}$ and $\vec{Q}$ have the property that half of their components are zero.

Lemma 12.6 For $n > 0$, F_n is invertible and the (i, j)-th entry of its inverse is $(1/n)\omega^{-ij}$ for $0 \le i, j \le n-1$.

Proof Let $\widetilde{F}_n$ be the matrix which the lemma claims is F_n^{-1}. We show that $F_n \widetilde{F}_n = I$; $\widetilde{F}_n F_n = I$ similarly.

$$(F_n \widetilde{F}_n)_{ij} = \sum_{k=0}^{n-1} \omega^{ik} \frac{1}{n}\omega^{-kj} = \frac{1}{n}\sum_{k=0}^{n-1} \left(\omega^{i-j}\right)^k.$$

For nondiagonal entries (i.e., $i \neq j$), $(F_n \widetilde{F}_n)_{ij} = 0$ by Proposition 12.8 for roots of unity since $0 < |i - j| < n$ (see Section 12.4.3). For diagonal entries (i.e., for $i = j$),

$$(F_n \widetilde{F}_n)_{ij} = \frac{1}{n}\sum_{k=0}^{n-1} \left(\omega^0\right)^k = \frac{1}{n}\sum_{k=0}^{n-1} 1 = 1. \quad \square$$

Theorem 12.7 Let U and V be n-vectors. Then $U \star V = F_n^{-1}(F_n U * F_n V)$, where $\star$ denotes convolution and $*$ denotes component-wise multiplication.

Proof We show that $F_n(U \star V) = F_n U * F_n V$. For $0 \le i \le n - 1$, the ith component of $F_n U * F_n V$ is

$$\left(\sum_{j=0}^{n-1} \omega^{ij} u_j\right)\left(\sum_{k=0}^{n-1} \omega^{ik} v_k\right) = \sum_{j=0}^{n-1}\sum_{k=0}^{n-1} u_j v_k \omega^{i(j+k)}.$$

The tth component of $U \star V$ is $\sum_{j=0}^{n-1} u_j v_{t-j}$ where subscripts are taken modulo n. Thus the ith component of $F_n(U \star V)$ is

$$\sum_{t=0}^{n-1} \left(\omega^{it} \sum_{j=0}^{n-1} u_j v_{t-j} \right) = \sum_{j=0}^{n-1} \sum_{t=0}^{n-1} u_j v_{t-j} \omega^{it}.$$

Let $k = t - j \pmod{n}$ in the inner summation. For each j, since t ranges from 0 to $n - 1$, k will also range from 0 to $n - 1$, although in a different order. Also, for any p, $\omega^p = \omega^{p \bmod n}$, so the ith component of $F_n(U \star V)$ is

$$\sum_{j=0}^{n-1} \sum_{k=0}^{n-1} u_j v_k \omega^{i(j+k)}$$

which is exactly the ith component of $F_n U * F_n V$. $\square$

Lemma 12.6 indicates that the matrix F_n^{-1} is not very different from F_n. The entries of $n F_n^{-1}$ are ω^{-ij}. Its rows are the rows of F_n arranged in a different order. Specifically, since $\omega^{n-i} = \omega^{-i}$, for $1 \le i \le n - 1$ the ith row of F_n is the $(n - i)$-th row of $n F_n^{-1}$. Row 0 is the same for both matrices. Thus the inverse discrete Fourier transform of an n-vector A may be computed as follows.

Algorithm 12.6 Inverse Discrete Fourier Transform

Input: The vector $A = (a_0, a_1, \ldots, a_{n-1})$, as a **Complex** array with n entries, where $n = 2^k$; and integer $k > 0$.

Output: The **Complex** vector $B = (b_0, b_1, \ldots, b_{n-1})$, the inverse discrete Fourier transform of A; that is, $B = F_n^{-1} A$. The array is passed in and the algorithm fills it.

Remark: The remarks for Algorithm 12.5 apply to this algorithm also.

```
void inverseFFT(Complex[] A, int k, Complex[] B)
    int n = 2^k;
    int i;
    Complex[] transform = new Complex[n];
    fft(A, k, transform);
    b_0 = transform[0] / n;
    for (i = 1; i ≤ n - 1; i ++)
        b_i = transform[n - i] / n;
```

Analysis

The FFT does $\frac{1}{2} n (\lg(n) - 1)$ complex multiplications (and the same number of complex additions and subtractions), so Algorithm 12.6 does $\frac{1}{2} n (\lg(n) + 1)$ complex $*/$'s, and both run in $\Theta(n \log n)$ time. Computing the convolution of two n-vectors using the FFT takes $\Theta(n \log n)$ time.

12.4.3   Appendix: Complex Numbers and Roots of Unity

The field $\mathbf{C}$ of complex numbers is obtained by joining i, the square root of -1, to the field of real numbers $\mathbf{R}$. Thus $\mathbf{C} = \mathbf{R}(i) = \{a + bi \mid a, b \in \mathbf{R}\}$. If $z = a + bi$, a is called the real part of z and b the imaginary part. Let $z_1 = a_1 + b_1 i$ and $z_2 = a_2 + b_2 i$. Then by definition,

$$z_1 + z_2 = (a_1 + a_2) + (b_1 + b_2)i,$$
$$z_1 z_2 = (a_1 a_2 - b_1 b_2) + (a_1 b_2 + b_1 a_2)i,$$
$$\frac{1}{z_1} = \frac{a_1}{a_1^2 + b_1^2} - \frac{b_1 i}{a_1^2 + b_1^2} \qquad \text{for } z_1 \neq (0 + 0i).$$

Division and subtraction can be defined easily using the above equations.

Java sidelight: To simplify the representation of complex numbers and operations in the pseudocode of the algorithms, we assume that a class **Complex** exists and permits the arithmetic operations $*$, $/$, $+$, and $-$; such a class does not currently exist in Java, but C++ and Fortran support this notation. It is easy to define a class with two instance fields, re and im, each of type **float** or **double**. (The abbreviations re and im are commonly used in mathematics texts for the real and imaginary parts of a complex number.) However, the programmer would have to define the arithmetic operations as functions (static methods), and use functional notation in the actual code, rather than operator notation.

A complex number can be represented as a vector in a plane using the real and imaginary parts for the Cartesian coordinates. The geometric interpretation of multiplication of complex numbers is more easily seen by using polar coordinates, r and θ, where r is the length of the vector and θ is the angle (measured in radians) that it subtends with the horizontal, or real, axis. (See Figure 12.7.) The product of two complex numbers (r_1, θ_1) and (r_2, θ_2) is $(r_1 r_2, \theta_1 + \theta_2)$. An example is given in Figure 12.8.

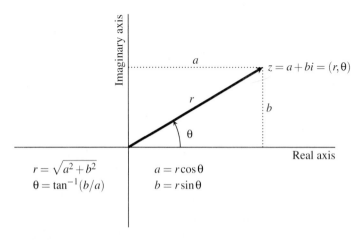

Figure 12.7   Cartesian and polar coordinates for complex numbers

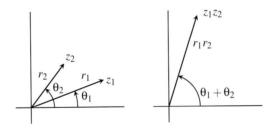

Figure 12.8 Multiplication of complex numbers: Magnitudes r_1 and r_2 multiply; angles θ_1 and θ_2 add.

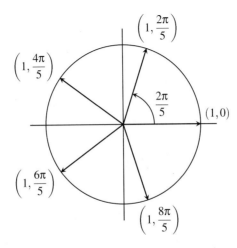

Figure 12.9 Fifth roots of unity (polar coordinates)

The complex field **C** is *algebraically closed*. This means that every polynomial of degree n with coefficients in **C** has n roots (not necessarily distinct). Therefore $x^n - 1$ has n roots, which are called the *nth roots of unity*, or the *nth roots of 1*. The polar coordinates of 1 are (1,0). To find a root (r, θ) of $x^n - 1$ we solve the equation $(r^n, n\theta) = (1, 0)$. Since r is real and nonnegative, r must be 1, so all roots of unity are represented by vectors of unit length. Since $n\theta = 0$, $\theta = 0$ so we have found that (1,0)—that is, 1—is a solution, hardly a surprise. To find the other roots of unity, we use the fact that an angle of 0 radians is equivalent to an angle of $2\pi j$ radians for any integer j. The n distinct roots are $\{(1, 2\pi j/n) \mid 0 \le j \le n - 1\}$. The vectors representing these numbers slice the unit circle into n equal pie slices as shown in Figure 12.9.

If ω is an nth root of 1, then ω^k is also an nth root of 1, since $(\omega^k)^n = \omega^{nk} = (\omega^n)^k = 1^k = 1$. If ω is an nth root of 1 and $1, \omega, \omega^2, \ldots, \omega^{n-1}$ are all distinct, then ω

is called a *primitive nth root of unity*. One primitive nth root of unity is $(1, 2\pi/n)$, or $\cos(2\pi/n) + i\sin(2\pi/n)$. The following properties are used in Section 12.4.

Proposition 12.8   For $n \geq 2$, the sum of all the nth roots of 1 is zero. Also, if ω is a primitive nth root of 1 and c is an integer not divisible by n, then $\sum_{j=0}^{n-1}(\omega^c)^j = 0$.

Proof   Let ω be a primitive nth root of 1. Then $\omega^0, \omega, \omega^2, \ldots, \omega^{n-1}$ are all of the nth roots of 1. Their sum is

$$\sum_{j=0}^{n-1} \omega^j = \frac{\omega^n - 1}{\omega - 1} = \frac{1 - 1}{\omega - 1} = 0.$$

The second statement is proved similarly.   □

Proposition 12.9   If n is even and ω is a primitive nth root of 1, then

1. ω^2 is a primitive $(n/2)$-th root of 1, and
2. $\omega^{n/2} = -1$.

Proof   The proof is left as an exercise.   □

Exercises

Section 12.2   *Evaluating Polynomial Functions*

12.1   Any polynomial $p(x) = a_n x^n + a_{n-1} x^{n-1} + \cdots + a_1 x + a_0$ can be factored into

$$p(x) = a_n(x - r_1)(x - r_2) \cdots (x - r_n),$$

where $r_1, \ldots, r_n$ are the roots of p. Could this factorization be used as the basis of an algorithm to evaluate $p(x)$? How, or why not?

12.2   We claimed that an algorithm to evaluate a polynomial of degree n must do at least n multiplications and/or divisions in the worst case. For special cases, we may get algorithms that do better. Devise a fast algorithm for evaluating each of the following polynomials. The inputs are n and x.

a. $p(x) = x^n + x^{n-1} + \cdots + x + 1$.
   How many arithmetic operations does your algorithm do?

b. $p(x) = \sum_{k=0}^{n} \binom{n}{k} x^k$, where $\binom{n}{k}$ are the binomial coefficients (Equation 1.1).
   How many arithmetic operations does your algorithm do?

12.3   Write out the factorization that would be used to evaluate $p(x) = x^7 + 6x^6 - 7x^5 + 12x^4 + 2x^2 - 3x - 8$ by

a. Horner's method.

b. preprocessing coefficients.

12.4 What part(s) of the proofs of Theorem 12.2 and/or Lemma 12.1 would not work if division were permitted?

12.5 What modifications or additions must be made to the procedure for evaluating polynomials with preprocessing of coefficients so that it will work for nonmonic polynomials? How many multiplications and/or divisions are done by the extended algorithm?

12.6 Suppose that $A(1) = 1$ and for $k > 1$, $A(k) = 2A(k - 1) + 2$. Show that the solution of this recurrence equation is $A(k) = (3n - 1)/2$, where $n = 2^k - 1$.

12.7 Using the terminology of the first paragraph of Section 12.2.3, what are I, I', A_I, and the algorithm that gives A_I from I for the problem of evaluating a polynomial with preprocessing of coefficients by the method described in Section 12.2.3?

Section 12.3 Vector and Matrix Multiplication

12.8 In Section 12.3.1, we stated that computing the dot product $U \cdot V$ of two n-vectors with real components requires at least n $*/$'s. How many $*/$'s are required if U always has integer components? Why?

12.9 Compute exactly the number of multiplications and additions done by Algorithm 12.3 when n is odd.

12.10 Let A and B be $n \times n$ matrices that are to be multiplied and suppose that a matrix entry must be fetched from storage each time it is used in the computation. How many times is each entry of A and B fetched to compute AB

a. by the usual algorithm?

b. by Winograd's algorithm (for n even)?

⋆⋆ 12.11

a. Prove that Strassen's algorithm, using the fourth modification described toward the end of Section 12.3.4, does fewer than $4.7 \, n^{\lg 7}$ arithmetic operations on the matrix entries, whether or not n is a power of 2.

b. Show how to reduce the 18 additions given for one invocation of Strassen's algorithm to 15.

Section 12.4 The Fast Fourier Transform and Convolution

12.12

a. Why are the restrictions "$n \geq 2$" and "c is not divisible by n" needed in Proposition 12.8?

$$
\begin{array}{c}
\text{column}\\
\begin{array}{ccccccccc}
\text{row} & 0 & 1 & & \tfrac{n}{2}-1 & \tfrac{n}{2} & \tfrac{n}{2}+1 & & n-1
\end{array}\\
\begin{array}{c}
0\\ 1\\ \vdots\\ \tfrac{n}{2}-1\\[2pt] \tfrac{n}{2}\\ \tfrac{n}{2}+1\\ \vdots\\ n-1
\end{array}
\left[
\begin{array}{ccc:ccc}
1 & 1 & \cdots\ 1 & 1 & 1 & \cdots\ 1\\
1 & \omega^2 & \cdots\ \omega^{n-2} & \omega & \omega^3 & \cdots\ \omega^{n-1}\\
 & (G_1) & & & (G_2) & \\
1 & \left(\omega^{\frac{n}{2}-1}\right)^2 & \cdots\ \left(\omega^{\frac{n}{2}-1}\right)^{n-2} & \omega^{\frac{n}{2}-1} & \left(\omega^{\frac{n}{2}-1}\right)^3 & \cdots\ \left(\omega^{\frac{n}{2}-1}\right)^{n-1}\\
\hdashline
1 & \left(\omega^{\frac{n}{2}}\right)^2 & \cdots\ \left(\omega^{\frac{n}{2}}\right)^{n-2} & \omega^{\frac{n}{2}} & \left(\omega^{\frac{n}{2}}\right)^3 & \cdots\ \left(\omega^{\frac{n}{2}}\right)^{n-1}\\
1 & \left(\omega^{\frac{n}{2}+1}\right)^2 & \cdots\ \left(\omega^{\frac{n}{2}+1}\right)^{n-2} & \omega^{\frac{n}{2}+1} & \left(\omega^{\frac{n}{2}+1}\right)^3 & \cdots\ \left(\omega^{\frac{n}{2}+1}\right)^{n-1}\\
 & (G_3) & & & (G_4) & \\
1 & \left(\omega^{n-1}\right)^2 & \cdots\ \left(\omega^{n-1}\right)^{n-2} & \omega^{n-1} & \left(\omega^{n-1}\right)^3 & \cdots\ \left(\omega^{n-1}\right)^{n-1}
\end{array}
\right]
\left[
\begin{array}{c}
v_0\\ v_2\\ \vdots\\ (V_1)\\ v_{n-2}\\ v_1\\ v_3\\ \vdots\\ (V_2)\\ v_{n-1}
\end{array}
\right]
\end{array}
$$

$$\widetilde{F}_n \qquad\qquad\qquad \widetilde{V}$$

Figure 12.10   Matrix and vector for Exercise 12.16

b.   Prove Proposition 12.9 for roots of unity.

12.13   Let $p(x) = p_7 x^7 + p_6 x^6 + \cdots + p_1 x + p_0$. Carry out the steps of the FFT on p to show how it evaluates p at the 8th roots of 1: $1, \omega, i, i\omega, -1, -\omega, -i, -i\omega$.

12.14   Suppose you are given the real and imaginary parts of two complex numbers. Show that the real and imaginary parts of their product can be computed using only three multiplications.

12.15   Prove Lemma 12.5.

★ **12.16**   Let $n = 2^k$ for some $k > 0$, let ω be a primitive nth root of 1, and let F_n be as in Definition 12.2. Let V be a complex n-vector. This problem describes the FFT (recursively) from the point of view of the matrix-vector product $F_n V$ rather than as polynomial evaluation. Note the correspondence of various steps of this algorithm with steps of recursiveFFT.

Let $\widetilde{F}_n$ be the $n \times n$ matrix obtained from F_n by putting all the even-indexed columns before the odd-indexed columns. (Note that this is not the same as the $\widetilde{F}_n$ in the proof of Lemma 12.6.) Let $\widetilde{V}$ have all the even-indexed components of V before all the odd-indexed components of V. That is, for $0 \le j \le n/2 - 1$, $\widetilde{f}_{ij} = \omega^{i(2j)}$, $\widetilde{f}_{i,j+n/2} = \omega^{i(2j+1)}$, $\widetilde{v}_j = v_{2j}$, and $\widetilde{v}_{j+n/2} = v_{2j+1}$. Partition $\widetilde{F}_n$ into four $(n/2) \times (n/2)$ matrices $G_1, G_2, G_3,$ and G_4, and partition $\widetilde{V}$ into two $(n/2)$-vectors V_1 and V_2 as shown in Figure 12.10. Now

$$\tilde{F}_n \tilde{V} = \begin{bmatrix} G_1 V_1 + G_2 V_2 \\ G_3 V_1 + G_4 V_2 \end{bmatrix}.$$

Prove the following statements.

a. $F_n V = \tilde{F}_n \tilde{V}$.

b. $G_1 = G_3$.

c. $G_4 = -G_2$.

d. $G_2 = D G_1$, where D is an $(n/2) \times (n/2)$ diagonal matrix (i.e., all off-diagonal elements are zero) with $d_{ii} = \omega^i$ for $0 \le i \le (n/2) - 1$.

e. G_1 has entries $g_{ij} = \gamma^{ij}$, where γ is a primitive $(n/2)$-th root of 1. Thus $G_1 = F_{n/2}$, a discrete Fourier transform matrix for $(n/2)$-vectors, and

$$F_n V = \begin{bmatrix} F_{n/2} V_1 + D F_{n/2} V_2 \\ F_{n/2} V_1 - D F_{n/2} V_2 \end{bmatrix}.$$

That is, the computation can be carried out by recursively computing the discrete Fourier transform of V_1 and V_2, both $(n/2)$-vectors.

f. Derive recurrence equations for the number of multiplications, additions, and subtractions done by the algorithm described here. Let $\vec{D} = (1, \omega, \dots, \omega^{(n/2)-1})$. (Note that the product $D(F_{n/2} V_2)$ can be computed as a component-wise product of $\vec{D}$ with $F_{n/2} V_2$, requiring $n/2$ multiplications.) Compare your recurrence equations with those obtained for recursiveFFT.

Additional Problems

12.17 Observe that the Fibonacci numbers (Equation 1.13) satisfy the following matrix equation for $n \ge 2$:

$$\begin{bmatrix} F_n \\ F_{n-1} \end{bmatrix} = A \begin{bmatrix} F_{n-1} \\ F_{n-2} \end{bmatrix} \qquad \text{where } A = \begin{bmatrix} 1 & 1 \\ 1 & 0 \end{bmatrix}.$$

Then

$$\begin{bmatrix} F_n \\ F_{n-1} \end{bmatrix} = A \begin{bmatrix} F_{n-1} \\ F_{n-2} \end{bmatrix} = A^2 \begin{bmatrix} F_{n-2} \\ F_{n-3} \end{bmatrix} = \dots = A^{n-1} \begin{bmatrix} F_1 \\ F_0 \end{bmatrix} = A^{n-1} \begin{bmatrix} 1 \\ 0 \end{bmatrix}.$$

How many arithmetic operations are done if F_n is computed using the following formula:

$$\begin{bmatrix} F_n \\ F_{n-1} \end{bmatrix} = A^{n-1} \begin{bmatrix} 1 \\ 0 \end{bmatrix}?$$

How does this method compare with the recursive and iterative algorithms for computing Fibonacci numbers?

Programs

1. Write and debug efficient subroutines for Winograd's matrix multiplication algorithm and for the usual algorithm. How many instructions are executed by each program to multiply two $n \times n$ matrices?

2. Implement the FFT (Algorithm 12.5). Make the computation of rev_k and the other bookkeeping as efficient as you can.

Notes and References

The lower bounds given in Sections 12.2 and 12.3 for polynomial evaluation, with or without preprocessing of coefficients, and for vector-matrix products are established in Pan (1966), Reingold and Stocks (1972), and Winograd (1970). Winograd's matrix multiplication algorithm also appears in the latter. Winograd's proofs use field theory. Reingold and Stocks use simpler arguments such as that in the proof of Theorem 12.2.

Strassen's matrix multiplication algorithm is presented in Strassen (1969), a short paper that gives no indication of how he discovered his formulas. An improvement to use 15 additions instead of 18, the subject of Exercise 12.11(b), is given in Aho, Hopcroft, and Ullman (1974), where it is attributed to S. Winograd. Some additional details are given in Gonnet and Baeza-Yates (1991). The $O(n^{2.376})$ method is in Coppersmith and Winograd (1987). Several matrix problems that can be reduced to multiplication and therefore have $O(n^{2.376})$ solutions are described in Aho, Hopcroft, and Ullman (1974).

Versions of the fast Fourier transform are presented in Cooley and Tukey (1965) and in Aho, Hopcroft, and Ullman (1974). Brigham (1974) is a book on the FFT. Press, Flannery, Teukolsky, and Vettering (1988) give a thorough discussion of the theory and implementation issues for the FFT. Aho, Hopcroft, and Ullman (1974) present an application of the FFT to integer multiplication. (The string of digits $d_n d_{n-1} \ldots d_1 d_0$ representing an integer in base b is a polynomial $\sum_{i=0}^{n} d_i b^i$.) There are many other references on the FFT since it is widely used.

13

$\mathcal{NP}$-Complete Problems

13.1 Introduction

In the previous chapters we have studied quite a variety of problems and algorithms. Some of the algorithms are straightforward, while others are complicated and tricky, but virtually all of them have complexity in $O(n^3)$, where n is the appropriately defined input size. From the point of view taken in this chapter, we will accept all the algorithms studied so far as having fairly low time requirements. Take another look at Table 1.1. We saw there that algorithms whose complexity is described by simple polynomial functions can be run for fairly large inputs in a reasonable amount of time. The last column in the table shows that if the complexity is 2^n, the algorithm is useless except for very small inputs. In this chapter we are concerned with problems whose complexity may be described by exponential functions, problems for which the best known algorithms would require many years or centuries of computer time for moderately large inputs. We will present definitions aimed at distinguishing between the *tractable* (i.e., "not-so-hard") problems we have encountered already and *intractable* (i.e., "hard," or very time-consuming) ones. We will study a class of important problems that have an irksome property—we do not even know whether they can be solved efficiently. No reasonably fast algorithms for these problems have been found, but no one has been able to prove that the problems require a lot of time. Because many of these problems are optimization problems that arise frequently in applications, the lack of efficient algorithms is of real importance.

13.2 $\mathcal{P}$ and $\mathcal{NP}$

For this chapter, "$\mathcal{P}$" is a class of problems that can be solved in "polynomial time." "$\mathcal{NP}$" is more complicated to describe. Before getting into the formal definitions and theorems, we describe several problems that we use as examples throughout this chapter. Then we give the definitions of $\mathcal{P}$ and $\mathcal{NP}$.

13.2.1 Decision Problems

Many of the problems described in this chapter occur naturally as optimization problems (they are called *combinatorial optimization problems*), but they can also be formulated as *decision problems*. The classes $\mathcal{P}$ and $\mathcal{NP}$, which will be defined in the following subsections, are classes of decision problems. Basically, a *decision problem* is a question that has two possible answers, *yes* and *no*. The question is about some *input*. A *problem instance* is the combination of the problem and a specific input. Usually the statement of a decision problem has two parts:

1. The *instance description* part defines the information expected in the input.
2. The *question* part states the actual yes-or-no question; the question contains variables defined in the instance description.

A decision problem's output is either *yes* or *no* according to the correct answer to the question, as applied to a given input. Thus a decision problem can be thought of abstractly as a mapping from all inputs into the set $\{yes, no\}$.

To see why a precise statement of the input is important, consider these two problems:

1. *Instance*: an undirected graph $G = (V, E)$.
   Question: Does G contain a clique of k vertices? (A clique is a complete subgraph: every pair of vertices in the subgraph has an edge between them.)
2. *Instance*: an undirected graph $G = (V, E)$ and an integer k.
   Question: Does G contain a clique of k vertices?

The question is the same in both problems, but in the first problem k is not part of the input, so it does not vary from one instance to the other; in other words, k is some *constant*. It happens that this question can be answered by an algorithm that runs in $O(k^2 n^k)$. If k is regarded as a constant, the algorithm runs in polynomial time. In the second question, k is part of the input, so it is a variable. The algorithm still runs in $O(k^2 n^k)$, but this expression is not a polynomial because the exponent of n is variable.

13.2.2   Some Sample Problems

Here are some problems we will study in this chapter. In some cases the problem is a simplification or abstraction of a problem that occurs in realistic applications. Frequently, difficult problems are simplified to try to make some progress and gain insights, in the hope that the insights can then be used to make progress on the original problem.

Definition 13.1   Graph coloring and chromatic number

A *coloring* of a graph $G = (V, E)$ is a mapping $C : V \rightarrow S$, where S is a finite set (of "colors"), such that if $vw \in E$ then $C(v) \neq C(w)$; in other words, adjacent vertices are not assigned the same color.

The *chromatic number* of G, denoted $\chi(G)$, is the smallest number of colors needed to color G (that is, the smallest k such that there exists a coloring C for G and $|C(V)| = k$).
∎

Problem 13.1   Graph coloring

We are given an undirected graph $G = (V, E)$ to be colored.

Optimization Problem: Given G, determine $\chi(G)$ (and produce an optimal coloring, that is, one that uses only $\chi(G)$ colors).

Decision Problem: Given G and a positive integer k, is there a coloring of G using at most k colors? (If so, G is said to be *k-colorable*.)

The graph coloring problem is an abstraction of certain types of scheduling problems. For example, suppose the final exams at your university are to be scheduled during one week with three exam times each day, for a total of 15 time slots. Some courses, say, Calculus 1 and Physics 1, must have their exams at different times because many students are in both classes. Let V be the set of courses, and let E be the pairs of courses whose exams must not be at the same time. Then the exams can be scheduled in the 15 time slots without conflicts if and only if the graph $G = (V, E)$ can be colored with 15 colors.   ∎

Problem 13.2   Job scheduling with penalties

Suppose there are n jobs $J_1, \ldots, J_n$ to be executed one at a time. We are given execution times $t_1, \ldots, t_n$, deadlines $d_1, \ldots, d_n$ (measured from the starting time of the first job executed), and penalties for missing the deadlines $p_1, \ldots, p_n$. Assume the execution times, deadlines, and penalties are all positive integers. A *schedule* for the jobs is a permutation π of $\{1, 2, \ldots, n\}$, where $J_{\pi(1)}$ is the job done first, $J_{\pi(2)}$ is the job done next, and so on.

For a particular schedule, the penalty for the jth job is denoted as P_j, and is defined as $P_j = p_{\pi(j)}$ if job $J_{\pi(j)}$ completes *after* the deadline $d_{\pi(j)}$, otherwise $P_j = 0$. The total penalty for a particular schedule is

$$ P_\pi = \sum_{j=1}^{n} P_j. $$

Optimization Problem: Determine the minimum possible penalty (and find an optimal schedule—one that minimizes the total penalty).

Decision Problem: Given, in addition to the inputs described, a nonnegative integer k, is there is a schedule with $P_\pi \le k$?   ■

Problem 13.3   Bin packing

Suppose we have an unlimited number of bins each of capacity one, and n objects with sizes $s_1, \ldots, s_n$ where $0 < s_i \le 1$ (s_i are rational numbers).

Optimization Problem: Determine the smallest number of bins into which the objects can be packed (and find an optimal packing).

Decision Problem: Given, in addition to the inputs described, an integer k, do the objects fit in k bins?

Applications of bin packing include packing data in computer memories (e.g., files on disk tracks, program segments into memory pages, and fields of a few bits each into memory words) and filling orders for a product (e.g., fabric or lumber) to be cut from large, standard-sized pieces.   ■

Problem 13.4   Knapsack

Suppose we have a knapsack of capacity C (a positive integer) and n objects with sizes $s_1, \ldots, s_n$ and "profits" $p_1, \ldots, p_n$ (where $s_1, \ldots, s_n$ and $p_1, \ldots, p_n$ are positive integers).

Optimization Problem: Find the largest total profit of any subset of the objects that fits in the knapsack (and find a subset that achieves the maximum profit).

Decision Problem: Given k, is there a subset of the objects that fits in the knapsack and has total profit at least k?

The knapsack problem has a variety of applications in economic planning and loading, or packing, problems. For example, it could describe a problem of making investment decisions where the "size" of an investment is the amount of money required, C is the total amount one has to invest, and the "profit" of an investment is the expected return. In an application of a more complicated version of the problem, the objects are tasks or experiments various organizations want to have performed on a space flight. In addition to its size (the volume of the equipment needed), each task may have a power requirement and a requirement for a certain amount of crew time. The space, power, and time available on the flight are all limited. Each task has some value, or profit. Which feasible subset of the tasks has the largest total value? ∎

Notice that the first three problems we described are minimization problems, but the knapsack problem is a maximization problem.

The next problem is a simpler version of the knapsack problem.

Problem 13.5   Subset sum

The input is a positive integer C and n objects whose sizes are positive integers $s_1, \ldots, s_n$.

Optimization Problem: Among subsets of the objects with sum at most C, what is the largest subset sum?

Decision Problem: Is there a subset of the objects whose sizes add up to exactly C? ∎

Problem 13.6   Satisfiability

A propositional (or Boolean) variable is a variable that may be assigned the value *true* or *false*. If v is a propositional variable, then $\bar{v}$, the negation of v, has the value *true* if and only if v has the value *false*. A *literal* is a propositional variable or the negation of a propositional variable. A propositional formula is defined inductively as an expression that is either a propositional variable or a propositional constant (i.e., *true* or *false*) or an expression consisting of a Boolean operator and its operand(s), which are propositional formula(s). A propositional formula may be represented in several forms, including functional notation (e.g., $and(x, y)$), operator notation (e.g., $(x \wedge y)$), or as an expression tree in which each internal node is a Boolean operator and each leaf is a propositional variable or one of the constants *true* or *false*. If truth values are assigned to the variables, the formula has a truth value that is obtained by applying the rules for the operators.

A certain regular form for propositional formulas, called *conjunctive normal form*, turns out to be very useful. A *clause* is a sequence of literals separated by the Boolean *or* operator ($\vee$). A propositional formula is in *conjunctive normal form* (*CNF*) if it consists of a sequence of clauses separated by the Boolean *and* operator ($\wedge$). An example of a propositional formula in CNF is

$$(p \vee q \vee s) \wedge (\bar{q} \vee r) \wedge (\bar{p} \vee r) \wedge (\bar{r} \vee s) \wedge (\bar{p} \vee \bar{s} \vee \bar{q})$$

where p, q, r, and s are propositional variables. Throughout this chapter "CNF formula" always refers to a propositional CNF formula.

A *truth assignment* for a set of propositional variables is an assignment of one of the values *true* or *false* to each propositional variable in the set, in other words, a Boolean-valued function on the set. A truth assignment is said to *satisfy* a formula if it makes the value of the entire formula *true*. Notice that a CNF formula is satisfied if and only if each clause evaluates to true, and a clause evaluates to true if and only if at least one literal in the clause is true.

Decision Problem: Given a CNF formula, is there a truth assignment that satisfies it?

This decision problem is called *CNF-satisfiability*, or simply *satisfiability*, and is often abbreviated as *CNF-SAT* or *SAT*. The satisfiability problem has applications in automated theorem proving. It played a central role in the development of the ideas in this chapter.

The following simplification of the satisfiability problem, called *3-satisfiability*, *3-CNF-satisfiability*, *3-SAT*, and *3-CNF-SAT*, is also important. (We list the multiple names and abbreviations because nomenclature is not standard, and the problem is mentioned often.)

Decision Problem: Given a CNF formula, in which each clause is permitted to contain at most three literals, is there a truth assignment that satisfies it?   ■

Problem 13.7   Hamiltonian cycles and Hamiltonian paths

A *Hamiltonian cycle* in an undirected graph is a simple cycle that passes through every vertex exactly once. The word *circuit* in place of *cycle* is sometimes seen.

Decision Problem: Does a given undirected graph have a Hamiltonian cycle?

A related optimization problem is the traveling salesperson, or minimum tour, problem, described below.

A *Hamiltonian path* in an undirected graph is a simple path that passes through every vertex exactly once.

Decision Problem: Does a given undirected graph have a Hamiltonian path?

Both problems may also be posed for *directed* graphs, in which case they are called the "directed Hamiltonian cycle (or path) problem." A variant of the Hamiltonian path problem includes a specified starting and ending vertex for the path.   ■

Problem 13.8   Traveling salesperson

This problem is widely known as the *traveling salesperson problem* (abbreviated *TSP*), but is also known as the *minimum tour problem*. The salesperson wants to minimize the total traveling cost (time, or distance) required to visit all the cities in a territory, and return to the starting point. Other applications include routing trucks for garbage pickup and package delivery.

Optimization Problem: Given a complete, weighted graph, find a minimum-weight Hamiltonian cycle.

Decision Problem: Given a complete, weighted graph and an integer k, is there a Hamiltonian cycle with total weight at most k?

The traditional version treats the graph as undirected; that is, the weights are the same in each direction. As with the Hamiltonian cycle problem, there is also a directed version. For this chapter, all edge weights are integers or rational numbers.   ∎

The usefulness and apparent simplicity of these problems may intrigue you; you are invited to try to devise algorithms for some of them before proceeding.

13.2.3   The Class $\mathcal{P}$

None of the algorithms known for the problems just described are guaranteed to run in a reasonable amount of time. We will not rigorously define "reasonable," but we will define a class $\mathcal{P}$ of problems that *includes* those with reasonably efficient algorithms.

Definition 13.2   Polynomially bounded

An algorithm is said to be *polynomially bounded* if its worst-case complexity is bounded by a polynomial function of the input size (i.e., if there is a polynomial p such that for each input of size n the algorithm terminates after at most $p(n)$ steps).

A problem is said to be polynomially bounded if there is a polynomially bounded algorithm for it.   ∎

All of the problems and algorithms studied in Chapters 1 through 12 are polynomially bounded, except for occasional exercises.

Definition 13.3   The class $\mathcal{P}$

$\mathcal{P}$ is the class of decision problems that are polynomially bounded.   ∎

$\mathcal{P}$ is defined only for decision problems, but you usually will not go wrong by thinking of the kinds of problems studied earlier in this book as being in $\mathcal{P}$.

It may seem rather extravagant to use the existence of a polynomial time bound as the criterion for defining the class of more or less reasonable problems—polynomials can be quite large. There are, however, a number of good reasons for this choice.

First, while it is not true that every problem in $\mathcal{P}$ has an acceptably efficient algorithm, we can certainly say that if a problem is *not* in $\mathcal{P}$, it will be extremely expensive and probably impossible to solve in practice. All of the problems described at the beginning of this section are probably not in $\mathcal{P}$; there are no algorithms for them that are known to be polynomially bounded and it is believed by most researchers in the field that no such algorithms exist. Thus while the definition of $\mathcal{P}$ may be too broad to provide a criterion for problems with truly reasonable time requirements, it provides a useful criterion—not being in $\mathcal{P}$—for problems that are intractable.

A second reason for using a polynomial bound to define $\mathcal{P}$ is that polynomials have nice "closure" properties. An algorithm for a complex problem may be obtained by combining several algorithms for simpler problems. Some of the simpler algorithms may work on the output or intermediate results of others. The complexity of the composite algorithm may be bounded by addition, multiplication, and composition of the complexities of its component algorithms. Since polynomials are closed under these operations, any algorithm built from several polynomially bounded algorithms in various natural ways will also be polynomially bounded. No smaller class of functions that are useful complexity bounds has these closure properties.

A third reason for using a polynomial bound is that it makes $\mathcal{P}$ independent of the particular formal model of computation used. A number of formal models (formal definitions of algorithms) are used to prove rigorous theorems about the complexity of algorithms and problems. The models differ in the kinds of operations permitted, the memory resources available, and the costs assigned to different operations. A problem that requires $\Theta(f(n))$ steps on one model may require more than $\Theta(f(n))$ steps on another, but for virtually all of the realistic models, if a problem is polynomially bounded for one, then it is polynomially bounded for the others.

13.2.4 The Class $\mathcal{NP}$

Many decision problems (including all our sample problems) are phrased as existence questions: Does there exist a k-coloring of the graph G? Does there exist a truth assignment that makes a given CNF formula true? For a given input, a "solution" is an object (e.g., a graph coloring or a truth assignment) that satisfies the criteria in the problem and hence justifies a *yes* answer (e.g., the graph coloring uses at most k colors; the truth assignment makes the CNF formula true). A "proposed solution" is simply an object of the appropriate kind—it may or may not satisfy the criteria. We sometimes use the term *certificate* for a proposed solution. Loosely speaking, $\mathcal{NP}$ is the class of decision problems for which a given proposed solution for a given input can be checked quickly (in polynomial time) to see if it really is a solution (i.e., if it satisfies all the requirements of the problem). More formally, inputs for a problem and proposed solutions must be described by strings of symbols from some finite set, for example, the set of characters on the keyboard of a computer terminal. We need some conventions for describing graphs, sets, functions, and so on, using these symbols. The set of conventions that is adopted for a particular problem is called the *encoding* of that problem. The size of a string is the number of symbols in it. Some strings of symbols from the chosen set are not valid encodings of objects relevant to the problem at hand; they are just gibberish. Formally, an input for a problem and a proposed solution for that instance of the problem can be any string from the character set. Checking a proposed solution includes checking that the string makes sense (that is, has the correct syntax) as a description of the required kind of object, as well as checking that it satisfies the criteria of the problem. Thus any string of characters can be thought of as a certificate for a problem instance.

There may be decision problems where there is no natural interpretation for "solutions" and "proposed solutions." A decision problem is, abstractly, just some function from a set of input strings to the set $\{yes, no\}$. A formal definition of $\mathcal{NP}$ considers all decision problems. The definition uses nondeterministic algorithms, which we define next.

Although such algorithms are not realistic or useful in practice, they are useful for classifying problems.

Definition 13.4   Nondeterministic algorithm

A *nondeterministic algorithm* has two phases and an output step:

1. The nondeterministic "guessing" phase. Some completely arbitrary string of characters, s, is written beginning at some designated place in memory. Each time the algorithm is run, the string written may differ. (This string is the certificate; it may be thought of as a guess at a solution for the problem, so this phase may be called the guessing phase, but s could just as well be gibberish.)
2. The deterministic "verifying" phase. A deterministic (i.e., ordinary) subroutine begins execution. In addition to the decision problem's input, the subroutine may use s, or it may ignore s. Eventually it returns a value *true* or *false*—or it may get in an infinite loop and never halt. (Think of the verifying phase as checking s to see if it is a solution for the decision problem's input, i.e., if it justifies a *yes* answer for the decision problem's input.)
3. The output step. If the verifying phase returned *true*, the algorithm outputs *yes*. Otherwise, there is no output.   ■

The number of steps carried out during one execution of a nondeterministic algorithm is defined as the sum of the steps in the two phases; that is, the number of steps taken to write s (simply the number of characters in s) plus the number of steps executed by the deterministic second phase.

We can also describe a nondeterministic algorithm with an explicit subroutine structure. Assume genCertif generates an arbitrary certificate.

```
void nondetA(String input)
    String s = genCertif();
    boolean checkOK = verifyA(input, s);
    if (checkOK)
        Output "yes".
    return;
```

Normally, an algorithm terminates for every input, and each time we run an algorithm with the same input, we get the same output. This does not happen with nondeterministic algorithms; for a particular input x, the output (or lack of output) from one run may differ from that of another run because it may depend on s. So what is the "answer" computed by a nondeterministic algorithm, say, **A**, for a particular decision problem with input x? **A**'s answer for x is defined to be *yes* if and only if there is *some* execution of **A** that gives a *yes* output. The answer is *no* if for all s, there is no output. Using our informal notion of s as a proposed solution, **A**'s answer for x is *yes* if and only if there is some proposed solution that "works."

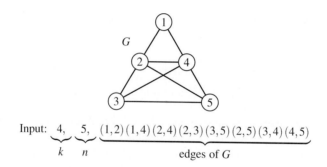

Input: $\underbrace{4,}_{k}$ $\underbrace{5,}_{n}$ $\underbrace{(1,2)\,(1,4)\,(2,4)\,(2,3)\,(3,5)\,(2,5)\,(3,4)\,(4,5)}_{\text{edges of } G}$

Figure 13.1   Input for nondeterministic graph coloring (Example 13.1)

Example 13.1   Nondeterministic graph coloring

Suppose the problem is to determine if an undirected graph G is k-colorable. The first phase of a nondeterministic algorithm will write some string s, which the second phase can interpret as a proposed coloring. The string s can be interpreted as a list of integers c_1, $c_2, \ldots, c_q$ for some q that depends on the length of s. The second phase of the algorithm can interpret these integers as colors to be assigned to the vertices: Assign c_i to v_i. To verify that the coloring is valid, the second phase does these steps:

1. Check that there are n colors listed (i.e., that $q = n$).
2. Check that each c_i is in the range $1, \ldots, k$.
3. Scan the list of edges in the graph (or scan an adjacency matrix) and for each edge $v_i v_j$ check that $c_i \neq c_j$; that is, the two vertices incident upon one edge have different colors.

If all of these tests are passed, the verifier returns *true* and the algorithm outputs *yes*. If s does not satisfy all the requirements, the verifier may return *false* or go into an infinite loop, and the algorithm produces no output for this particular execution.

As an example, let the input instance be the graph G in Figure 13.1 and $k = 4$, so the question in this case is, "Can G be 4-colored?" For readability, we denote colors by letters B (blue), R (red), G (green), Y (yellow), and O (orange), rather than integers $1, \ldots, 5$. Here is a list of a few possible certificate strings s and the values returned by the verifier.

s	Output	Reason
RGRBG	*false*	v_2 and v_5, both green, are adjacent
RGRB	*false*	Not all vertices are colored
RBYGO	*false*	Too many colors used
RGRBY	*true*	A valid 4-coloring
R%*,G@	*false*	Bad syntax

Since there is (at least) one possible computation of the verifier that returns a *true*, the answer of the nondeterministic algorithm for the input $(G, 4)$ is *yes*.   ∎

A nondeterministic algorithm is said to be polynomially bounded if there is a (fixed) polynomial p such that for each input of size n for which the answer is *yes*, there is some execution of the algorithm that produces a *yes* output in at most $p(n)$ steps.

Definition 13.5   The class $\mathcal{NP}$

$\mathcal{NP}$ is the class of decision problems for which there is a polynomially bounded nondeterministic algorithm. (The name $\mathcal{NP}$ comes from "*N*ondeterministic *P*olynomially bounded.")   ∎

Theorem 13.1   Graph coloring, Hamiltonian cycle, Hamiltonian path, job scheduling with penalties, bin packing, the subset sum problem, the knapsack problem, satisfiability, and the traveling salesperson problem (Problems 13.1 through 13.8) are all in $\mathcal{NP}$.

Proof   The proofs are straightforward and are left for the exercises. The work described earlier to check a possible graph coloring, for example, can easily be done in polynomial time.   □

Theorem 13.2 $\mathcal{P} \subseteq \mathcal{NP}$.

Proof   An ordinary (deterministic) algorithm for a decision problem is, with a minor modification, a special case of a nondeterministic algorithm. If **A** is a deterministic algorithm for a decision problem, just let **A** be the second phase of a nondeterministic algorithm, but modify **A** so that whenever it would have output *yes*, it returns *true* and whenever it would have output *no*, it returns *false*. **A** just ignores whatever was written by the first phase and proceeds with its usual computation. A nondeterministic algorithm can do zero steps in the first phase (writing the null string), so if **A** runs in polynomial time, the nondeterministic algorithm with the modified **A** as its second phase also runs in polynomial time. It will output *yes* if **A** would have, and will output nothing otherwise.   □

The big question is, does $\mathcal{P} = \mathcal{NP}$ or is $\mathcal{P}$ a proper subset of $\mathcal{NP}$? In other words, is nondeterminism more powerful than determinism in the sense that some problems can be solved in polynomial time with a nondeterministic "guesser" that cannot be solved in polynomial time by an ordinary algorithm? If a problem is in $\mathcal{NP}$, with polynomial time bound, say, p, we can (deterministically) give the proper answer (*yes* or *no*) if we check all strings of length at most $p(n)$ (i.e., run the second phase of the nondeterministic algorithm on each possible string, one at a time). The number of steps needed to check each string is at most $p(n)$. The trouble is that there are too many strings to check. If our character set contains c characters, then there are $c^{p(n)}$ strings of length $p(n)$. The number of strings is exponential, not polynomial in n. Of course there is another way to solve problems: Use some properties of the objects involved and some cleverness to devise an algorithm that does not have to examine all possible solutions. When sorting, for example, we do not check each of the $n!$ permutations of the given n keys to see which one puts the keys in order. The difficulty with the problems discussed in this chapter is that this approach has not yielded efficient algorithms; all the known algorithms either examine all possibilities or, if they use tricks to reduce the work, the tricks are not good enough to give polynomially bounded algorithms.

It is believed that $\mathcal{NP}$ is a much larger set than $\mathcal{P}$, but there is not one single problem in $\mathcal{NP}$ for which it has been proved that the problem is not in $\mathcal{P}$. There are no polynomially bounded algorithms known for many problems in $\mathcal{NP}$ (including all the sample problems in Section 13.2.2), but no larger-than-polynomial lower bounds have been proved for these problems. Thus the question we asked above, does $\mathcal{P} = \mathcal{NP}$?, is still open.

13.2.5 The Size of the Input

Consider the following problem.

Problem 13.9

Given a positive integer n, are there integers $j, k > 1$ such that $n = jk$? (that is, is n nonprime?)   ∎

Is this problem in $\mathcal{P}$? Consider the following algorithm, which looks for a factor of n.

```
factor = 0;
for (j = 2; j < n; j ++)
    if ((n mod j) == 0)
        factor = j;
        break;
return factor;
```

The loop body is executed fewer than n times, and certainly $(n \bmod j)$ can be evaluated in $O(\log^2(n))$, so the running time of the algorithm is in $O(n^2)$ with room to spare. Yet the problem of determining whether an integer is prime or is factorable is *not* known to be in $\mathcal{P}$, and, in fact, the difficulty of finding factors of large integers is the basis for various encryption algorithms exactly because it is considered a hard problem. What is the resolution of the apparent paradox?

The input for the prime testing algorithm is the integer n, but what is the *size* of n? Until now, we have used any convenient and reasonable measure of input size; it wasn't important to count individual characters or bits. When our measure of the size of an input may make the difference of whether an algorithm is polynomial or exponential, we have to be more careful. The size of an input is the number of characters it takes to write the input. If $n = 150$, for example, we write three digits, not 150 digits. Thus an integer n written in decimal notation has size roughly $\log_{10} n$. If we choose to think of the internal representation inside a computer where an integer is represented in binary, then the size of n is roughly $\lg n$. These representations differ by a constant factor; that is, $\log_2 n = \log_2 10 \log_{10} n$, so which we use is not critical. The point, however, is that if the input size s is $\log_{10} n$ and the running time of an algorithm is n, then the running time of the algorithm is an exponential function of the input size ($n = 10^s$). Thus the algorithm above for determining if n is prime is not in $\mathcal{P}$. There is no algorithm presently known for prime testing in polynomial time. However, the question, "Is integer n prime?" is in $\mathcal{NP}$ (see Exercise 13.4).

In the problems we considered earlier in this book, the variable we used to describe the input size corresponded (more or less) to the amount of data in the input. For example, we used n as the input size when sorting a list of n keys. Each of the keys would be represented in, say, binary, but since there are n keys, there are at least n symbols in the input. So, if the complexity of an algorithm is bounded by a polynomial in n, it is bounded by a polynomial in the exact size of the input.

Similarly, we used $(m + n)$ as the input size of graphs, but all edges needed to be listed explicitly, so that requires at least m symbols in the input. Although it is not necessary to list all n vertices in the input, in all problems of interest every vertex will be incident upon some edge so $(n + m)$ is at most three times the number of symbols in the input. Again, if the complexity of an algorithm is bounded by a polynomial in $(n + m)$, it is bounded by a polynomial in the exact size of the input.

If each of two measures of input size is bounded by a polynomial function of the other, then determining if the problem is in $\mathcal{P}$ will not depend on the specific measure used. For the sorting example, if one measure is the number of keys, n, and the second measure is $n \lg(\text{maximum key})$, which counts individual bits, we have $n \in O(n \log(\text{maximum key}))$ and $n \lg(\text{maximum key}) \in O(n^2)$. Therefore each measure is within a polynomial function of the other.

So, usually, we do not have to be entirely precise about the input size. We must be careful, however, when the running time of an algorithm is expressed as a polynomial function of one of the input *values*, as is the case with the prime testing problem.

A few of the sample problems described earlier have dynamic programming solutions that appear to be polynomially bounded at first glance, but, like the prime testing program, are not. For example, recall the subset sum problem: Is there a subset of the n objects with sizes $s_1, s_2, \ldots, s_n$ that adds up to exactly C? Using the techniques of Chapter 10, this can be solved with an $n \times C$ table with only a few operations needed to compute each table entry (see Exercise 13.5a). Similar dynamic programming solutions exist for various versions of the knapsack problem.

The dynamic programming solution for the subset sum problem runs in $\Theta(nC)$ time. Since there are n objects in the input, the term n is no problem, but the value of the number C is exponentially bigger (in general) than the input, because the datum C in the input would be represented in $\lg C$ bits. Thus the dynamic programming solution is not a polynomially bounded algorithm. Of course, if C is not too large, the algorithm may be useful in practice.

13.3 $\mathcal{NP}$-Complete Problems

$\mathcal{NP}$-*complete* is the term used to describe decision problems that are the hardest ones in $\mathcal{NP}$ in the sense that, if there were a polynomially bounded algorithm for an $\mathcal{NP}$-complete problem, then there would be a polynomially bounded algorithm for each problem in $\mathcal{NP}$.

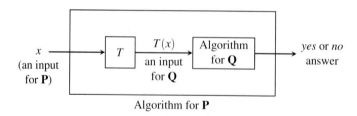

Figure 13.2 Reduction of a problem **P** to a problem **Q**: Problem **Q**'s answer for $T(x)$ must be the same as **P**'s answer for x.

Some of the sample problems described in Section 13.2.2 may seem easier than others and, in fact, the worst-case complexities of the algorithms that have been devised and analyzed for them do differ (they are fast-growing functions like $2^{\sqrt{n}}$, 2^n, $(n/2)^{n/2}$, $n!$, etc.), but, surprisingly, they are all equivalent in the sense that if any one is in $\mathcal{P}$, they all are. They are all $\mathcal{NP}$-complete.

13.3.1 Polynomial Reductions

The formal definition of "$\mathcal{NP}$-complete" uses reductions, or transformations, of one problem to another. Suppose we want to solve a problem **P** and we already have an algorithm for another problem **Q**. Suppose we also have a function T that takes an input x for **P** and produces $T(x)$, an input for **Q** such that the correct answer for **P** on x is *yes* if and only if the correct answer for **Q** on $T(x)$ is *yes*. Then, by composing T and the algorithm for **Q**, we have an algorithm for **P**. See Figure 13.2.

Example 13.2 A simple reduction

Let the problem **P** be: Given a sequence of Boolean values, does at least one of them have the value *true*? (In other words, this is a decision-problem version of computing the n-way Boolean *or*, when the string has n values.)

Let **Q** be: Given a sequence of integers, is the maximum of the integers positive?

Let the transformation T be defined by:

$$T(x_1, x_2, \ldots, x_n) = (y_1, y_2, \ldots, y_n)$$

where $y_i = 1$ if $x_i = true$, and $y_i = 0$ if $x_i = false$.

Clearly an algorithm to solve **Q**, when applied to $y_1, y_2, \ldots, y_n$, solves **P** for $x_1, x_2, \ldots, x_n$. ∎

Definition 13.6 Polynomial reduction and reducibility

Let T be a function from the input set for a decision problem **P** into the input set for a decision problem **Q**. T is a *polynomial reduction* (also called a *polynomial transformation*) from **P** to **Q** if all of the following hold:

1. T can be computed in polynomially bounded time.

2. For every string x, if x is a *yes* input for **P**, then $T(x)$ is a *yes* input for **Q**.

3. For every string x, if x is a *no* input for **P**, then $T(x)$ is a *no* input for **Q**.

It is usually easier to prove the contrapositive (Section 1.3.3) of part 3:

3′. For every x, if $T(x)$ is a *yes* input for **Q**, then x is a *yes* input for **P**.

Problem **P** is *polynomially reducible* (also called *polynomially transformable*) to **Q** if there exists a polynomial transformation from **P** to **Q**. (We usually just say **P** is *reducible* to **Q** in this chapter; the polynomial bound is understood.) The notation

$$\mathbf{P} \leq_P \mathbf{Q}$$

is used to indicate that **P** is reducible to **Q**. ■

Notice that parts 2 and 3 (or 3′) in the definition of *reduction* combine to state that $T(x)$ has the *same* answer for problem **Q** as x has for **P**, for every x.

The point of the reducibility of **P** to **Q** is that **Q** is at least as "hard" to solve as **P**. This is made more precise in the following theorem.

Theorem 13.3 If $\mathbf{P} \leq_P \mathbf{Q}$ and **Q** is in $\mathcal{P}$, then **P** is in $\mathcal{P}$.

Proof Let p be a polynomial bound on the computation of T, and let q be a polynomial bound on an algorithm for **Q**. Let x be an input for **P** of size n. Then the size of $T(x)$ is at most $p(n)$ (since, at worst, a program for T writes a symbol at each step). When the algorithm for **Q** is given $T(x)$, it does at most $q(p(n))$ steps. So the total amount of work to transform x to $T(x)$ and then use the **Q** algorithm to get the correct answer for **P** on x is $p(n) + q(p(n))$, a polynomial in n. □

Now we can give the formal definition of $\mathcal{NP}$-complete.

Definition 13.7 $\mathcal{NP}$-hard and $\mathcal{NP}$-complete

A problem **Q** is $\mathcal{NP}$-*hard* if every problem **P** in $\mathcal{NP}$ is reducible to **Q**; that is, $\mathbf{P} \leq_P \mathbf{Q}$. A problem **Q** is $\mathcal{NP}$-*complete* if it is in $\mathcal{NP}$ and is $\mathcal{NP}$-*hard*. ■

It is important to realize that "$\mathcal{NP}$-hard" does *not* mean "in $\mathcal{NP}$ and hard." It means "at least as hard as any problem in $\mathcal{NP}$." Thus a problem can be $\mathcal{NP}$-hard and *not* be in $\mathcal{NP}$.

Being $\mathcal{NP}$-hard constitutes a lower bound on the problem. Being in $\mathcal{NP}$ constitutes an upper bound. Thus the class of $\mathcal{NP}$-complete problems is bounded both from below and from above, although neither boundary is sharply defined with our current state of knowledge. The following theorem follows easily from the definition and Theorem 13.3.

Theorem 13.4 If any $\mathcal{NP}$-complete problem is in $\mathcal{P}$, then $\mathcal{P} = \mathcal{NP}$. □

This theorem indicates, on the one hand, how valuable it would be to find a poly-nomially bounded algorithm for any $\mathcal{NP}$-complete problem and, on the other hand, how unlikely it is that such an algorithm exists because there are so many problems in $\mathcal{NP}$ for which polynomially bounded algorithms have been sought without success.

Although we have seen that many problems are *in* $\mathcal{NP}$, it is not at all clear that any of them are $\mathcal{NP}$-complete. After all, to show that some problem **Q** is $\mathcal{NP}$-hard, the second half of the requirement for $\mathcal{NP}$-completeness, it is necessary to show that *all* problems in $\mathcal{NP}$, even problems we do not know about, are reducible to the specific problem **Q**. How on earth would we even approach such a task? The first proof that a certain problem actually is $\mathcal{NP}$-complete stands as one of the major accomplishments of theoretical computer science and mathematics.

Theorem 13.5 (Cook's theorem)   The satisfiability problem is $\mathcal{NP}$-complete.   □

The proof of this theorem and other theorems stated here without proof can be found in the sources given in Notes and References at the end of the chapter. We will sketch the idea. The proof must show that any problem **P** in $\mathcal{NP}$ is reducible to satisfiability. Steven Cook's proof gives an algorithm to construct a CNF formula for an input x for **P** such that the formula, informally speaking, describes the computation of a nondeterministic algorithm for **P** acting on x. The CNF formula, which is very long but constructed in time bounded by a polynomial function of the length of x, will be satisfiable if and only if the computation produces a *yes* answer for some certificate.

Polynomial reduction is a transitive relation (see Exercise 13.6). Thus if satisfiability can be reduced to some problem **Q**, then **Q** is also $\mathcal{NP}$-hard. If **Q** is also in $\mathcal{NP}$ (which is usually easy to show), then **Q** is $\mathcal{NP}$-complete. Thus reduction provides a tool for showing other problems are $\mathcal{NP}$-complete without having to repeat all the work of Cook's theorem. For example, satisfiability can be reduced to 3-satisfiability (see Exercise 13.7).

Satisfiability (and 3-satisfiability) are logical problems, and have no obvious relationship to the other problems described in Section 13.2.2 or the many other optimization problems that were defying efficient solution, some concerning graphs, others concerning compilers and operating systems. If the only $\mathcal{NP}$-complete problems were problems like satisfiability, then $\mathcal{NP}$-completeness might have remained an interesting curiosity, but nothing more.

The second seminal paper in the field was by Richard Karp, who showed that the decision versions of a large number of optimization problems, including several of the sample problems we described, are also $\mathcal{NP}$-complete. Very ingenious reductions were needed to show that problems could be reduced to apparently unrelated problems. For example, he showed that 3-satisfiability could be reduced (through a chain of reductions in some cases) to apparently unrelated graph problems, such as the Hamiltonian cycle problem and the graph coloring problem. This opened the flood gates. Soon many problems for which polynomially bounded algorithms were being sought unsuccessfully were shown to be $\mathcal{NP}$-complete. In fact, the list of $\mathcal{NP}$-complete problems grew to hundreds in the 1970s.

Theorem 13.6   Graph coloring, Hamiltonian cycle, Hamiltonian path, job scheduling with penalties, bin packing, the subset sum problem, the knapsack problem, and the traveling salesperson problem are all $\mathcal{NP}$-complete.   □

As mentioned, to prove that a problem $\mathbf{Q} \in \mathcal{NP}$ is $\mathcal{NP}$-complete, it suffices to prove that some other $\mathcal{NP}$-complete problem is polynomially reducible to $\mathbf{Q}$, since the reducibility relation is transitive. Hence the various parts of Theorem 13.6 are proved by establishing chains of transformations beginning with the satisfiability problem. We will do a few as examples.

Students often get confused about the direction of the reduction needed to prove that a problem is $\mathcal{NP}$-complete, so we emphasize: To show that the problem $\mathbf{Q}$ is $\mathcal{NP}$-complete, choose some known $\mathcal{NP}$-complete problem $\mathbf{P}$ and reduce $\mathbf{P}$ to $\mathbf{Q}$, not the other way around. The logic is as follows:

1. Since $\mathbf{P}$ is $\mathcal{NP}$-complete, all problems $\mathbf{R} \in \mathcal{NP}$ are reducible to $\mathbf{P}$; that is, $\mathbf{R} \leq_P \mathbf{P}$.
2. Show $\mathbf{P} \leq_P \mathbf{Q}$.
3. Then all problems $\mathbf{R} \in \mathcal{NP}$ satisfy $\mathbf{R} \leq_P \mathbf{Q}$, by transitivity of reductions.
4. Therefore $\mathbf{Q}$ is $\mathcal{NP}$-complete.

Theorem 13.7 The directed Hamiltonian cycle problem is reducible to the undirected Hamiltonian cycle problem. (Thus, if we know that the directed Hamiltonian cycle problem is $\mathcal{NP}$-complete, we can conclude that the undirected Hamiltonian cycle problem is also $\mathcal{NP}$-complete.)

Proof Let $G = (V, E)$ be a directed graph with n vertices. G is transformed into the undirected graph $G' = (V', E')$, where, for each vertex $v \in V$, the transformed vertex set V' contains three vertices named v^1, v^2, and v^3. Also, for each $v \in V$, the transformed edge set E' contains *undirected* edges v^1v^2 and v^2v^3. In addition, for each *directed* edge $vw \in E$, E' contains the *undirected* edge v^3w^1. In other words, each vertex of G is expanded to three vertices connected by two edges, and an edge vw in E becomes an edge from the third vertex for v to the first for w. See Figure 13.3 for an illustration. The transformation

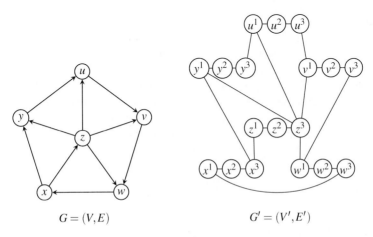

$$G = (V, E) \qquad G' = (V', E')$$

Figure 13.3 Reduction of the directed Hamiltonian cycle problem to the undirected Hamiltonian cycle problem

is straightforward, and G' can certainly be constructed in polynomially bounded time. If $|V| = n$ and $|E| = m$, then G' has $3n$ vertices and $2n + m$ edges.

Now suppose G has a (directed) Hamiltonian cycle $v_1, v_2, \ldots, v_n$. (That is, $v_1, v_2, \ldots, v_n$ are distinct, and there are edges $v_i v_{i+1}$, for $1 \leq i < n$, and $v_n v_1$.) Then $v_1^1, v_1^2, v_1^3, v_2^1, v_2^2, v_2^3, \ldots, v_n^1, v_n^2, v_n^3$ is an undirected Hamiltonian cycle for G'. On the other hand, if G' has an undirected Hamiltonian cycle, the three vertices, say v^1, v^2, and v^3, that correspond to one vertex from G must be traversed consecutively in the order v^1, v^2, v^3 or v^3, v^2, v^1 since v^2 cannot be reached from any other vertex in G'. Since the other edges in G' connect vertices with superscripts 1 and 3, if for any one triple the order of the superscripts is 1, 2, 3, then the order is 1, 2, 3 for all triples. Otherwise, it is 3, 2, 1 for all triples. Since G' is undirected, we may assume its Hamiltonian cycle is $v_{i_1}^1, v_{i_1}^2, v_{i_1}^3, \ldots, v_{i_n}^1, v_{i_n}^2, v_{i_n}^3$. Then $v_{i_1}, v_{i_2}, \ldots, v_{i_n}$ is a directed Hamiltonian cycle for G. Thus G has a directed Hamiltonian cycle if and only if G' has an undirected Hamiltonian cycle. □

It is of course much easier to see that the G' defined in the proof is the proper transformation to use than it is to think up the correct G' in the first place, so we make a few observations to indicate how G' was chosen. To ensure that a cycle in G' corresponds to a cycle in G, we need to simulate the direction of the edges of G. This aim suggests giving G' two vertices, say v^1 and v^3, for each v in G with the interpretation that v^1 is used for edges in G whose head is v and v^3 is used for edges whose tail is v. Then wherever v^1 and v^3 appear consecutively in a cycle for G' they can be replaced by v to get a cycle for G, and vice versa. Unfortunately, there is nothing about G' that forces v^1 and v^3 to appear consecutively in all of its cycles; thus G' could have a Hamiltonian cycle that does not correspond to one in G (see Exercise 13.13). The third vertex, v^2, which can only be reached from v^1 and v^3, is introduced to force the vertices that correspond to v to appear together in any cycle in G'.

Theorem 13.8   The subset sum problem (Problem 13.5) is reducible to the job scheduling problem (Problem 13.2).

Proof   Let $s_1, \ldots, s_n, C$ be an input I for the subset sum problem (which asks if there is a subset of the objects that adds up to exactly C). Let $S = \sum_{i=1}^{n} s_i$. If $S < C$, then the output for I is no, and I may be transformed to any job scheduling input with a no output, for example, $t_i = 2$, $d_i = p_i = 1$, and $k = 0$. If $S \geq C$, then I is transformed into the following input: $t_i = p_i = s_i$ and $d_i = C$ for $1 \leq i \leq n$, and $k = S - C$. Clearly the transformation itself takes little time.

Now suppose the subset sum input produces a yes answer; that is, there is a subset J of $N = \{1, 2, \ldots, n\}$ such that $\sum_{i \in J} s_i = C$. Then let π be any permutation of N that causes all jobs with indexes in J to be done before any jobs with indexes in $N - J$. The first $|J|$ jobs are completed by their deadline since $\sum_{i \in J} t_i = \sum_{i \in J} s_i = C$, and C is the deadline for all jobs. The penalty for the remaining jobs is

$$\sum_{i=|J|+1}^{n} p_{\pi(i)} = \sum_{i=|J|+1}^{n} s_{\pi(i)} = S - \sum_{i \in J} s_i = S - C = k.$$

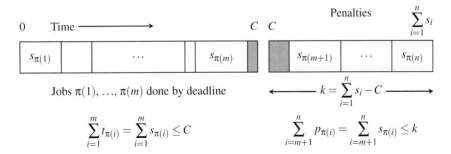

Figure 13.4 A satisfactory job schedule solves the subset sum problem.

Thus the jobs can be done with total penalty of k.

Conversely, let π be any schedule for the jobs with total penalty $\leq k$. Let m be the number of jobs completed by the common deadline C; that is, m is the largest number such that

$$\sum_{i=1}^{m} t_{\pi(i)} \leq C. \tag{13.1}$$

The penalty, then, is

$$\sum_{i=m+1}^{n} p_{\pi(i)} \leq k = S - C. \tag{13.2}$$

See Figure 13.4 for an illustration. Since $t_i = p_i = s_i$ for $1 \leq i \leq n$, we must have

$$\sum_{i=1}^{m} t_{\pi(i)} + \sum_{i=m+1}^{n} p_{\pi(i)} = S,$$

and this can only happen if the inequalities in Equations 13.1 and 13.2 are equalities (i.e., if the shaded areas in Figure 13.4 are zero). Thus $\sum_{i=1}^{m} t_{\pi(i)} = C$, so the objects with indexes $\pi(1), \ldots, \pi(m)$ are a solution for the subset sum problem. $\quad\square$

There are similar reduction problems in the exercises.

13.3.2 Some Known $\mathcal{NP}$-Complete Problems

We collect here several additional $\mathcal{NP}$-complete problems that are discussed in the chapter and in the exercises.

Problem 13.10 Vertex cover

A *vertex cover* for an undirected graph G is a subset C of vertices such that each edge is incident upon some vertex in C. Think of the edges of the graph as an irregular system of corridors that intersect at vertices. What is the minimum number of sentries that can be posted at the intersections such that all corridors are monitored by some sentry?

Optimization Problem: Given an undirected graph G, find a vertex cover for G with as few vertices as possible.

Decision Problem: Given an undirected graph G and an integer k, does G have a vertex cover consisting of k vertices?   ■

Problem 13.11   Clique

A *clique* is a subset K of vertices in an undirected graph G such that every pair of distinct vertices in K is joined by an edge of G. In other words, the subgraph induced by K is complete. A clique with k vertices is called a *k-clique*.

    Notice that a graph with a k-clique requires at least k colors to color it.

Optimization Problem: Given an undirected graph G, find a clique with as many vertices as possible.

Decision Problem: Given an undirected graph G and an integer k, does G have a clique consisting of k vertices?   ■

Problem 13.12   Independent set

An *independent set* is a subset I of vertices in an undirected graph G such that no pair of vertices in I is joined by an edge of G.

Optimization Problem: Given an undirected graph G, find an independent set with as many vertices as possible.

Decision Problem: Given an undirected graph G and an integer k, does G have an independent set consisting of k vertices?   ■

    The three problems, vertex cover, clique, and independent set, are closely related, as suggested by Figure 13.5.

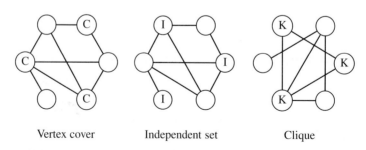

Vertex cover   Independent set   Clique

Figure 13.5   Examples for vertex cover, independent set, and clique

Problem 13.13   Feedback edge set

A *feedback edge set* in a digraph G is a subset F of edges such that every cycle in G has an edge in F.

Optimization Problem: Given a digraph G, find a feedback edge set with as few edges as possible.

Decision Problem: Given a digraph G and an integer k, does G have a feedback edge set consisting of k edges?   ∎

13.3.3   What Makes a Problem Hard?

If the set of inputs for an $\mathcal{NP}$-complete problem is restricted in some way, the problem may be in $\mathcal{P}$; in fact, it may have a very fast solution. Technically, restricting the inputs means changing the question part of the problem so that more input instances have easy (i.e., polynomial-time) *no* answers. This is done by adding a condition to the standard question for that problem, as illustrated with some examples in the discussion below. It is more convenient to think of the added condition as a restriction on the set of inputs.

However, even with restrictions, the problem may still be $\mathcal{NP}$-complete. Knowing the effect on complexity of restricting the set of inputs for a problem is important because, in many applications, the inputs that actually occur have special properties that might allow a polynomially bounded solution. Unfortunately, the results are discouraging; even with quite strong restrictions on the inputs, many $\mathcal{NP}$-complete problems are still $\mathcal{NP}$-complete.

On the other hand, in many engineering situations there is some flexibility in the way a problem is defined and in the precise criterion for optimization. If one criterion produces an $\mathcal{NP}$-complete problem, it is quite possible that an alternative criterion is quite acceptable, and produces a problem in $\mathcal{P}$. Therefore familiarity with the characteristics of hard problems can be very useful in practical situations.

Definition 13.8   Vertex degree

In an undirected or directed graph, the *degree* of a vertex is the number of edges incident upon it. The maximum degree of any vertex in G is denoted $\Delta(G)$. For directed graphs the *indegree* and *outdegree* of a vertex are the number of incoming and outgoing edges, respectively.   ∎

For graph problems we can consider restrictions on $\Delta(G)$. It is easy to test most graph properties on graphs with $\Delta \leq 2$. For such graphs, the Hamiltonian cycle problem can be solved in polynomial time. (That is, the modified question "Is $\Delta(G) \leq 2$ *and* does G have a Hamiltonian cycle?" is easy.) The k-colorability problem can also be solved in polynomial time if $\Delta \leq 3$. (That is, the modified question "Is $\Delta(G) \leq 3$ *and* can G be colored with k colors?" can be solved in polynomial time.) However, even for graphs with $\Delta = 3$, the Hamiltonian cycle problem is $\mathcal{NP}$-complete. For graphs with $\Delta \leq 4$, k-colorability is $\mathcal{NP}$-complete. Thus it is not the presence of vertices with high degree that makes these problems hard.

However, the clique problem (Problem 13.11) is in $\mathcal{P}$ for graphs with $\Delta \leq d$ for any constant d. (A simple algorithm that checks all subsets of $d + 1$ vertices runs in time $O\left(n^{d+1}\right)$.) Therefore it *is* high-degree vertices that make this problem hard.

A *planar* graph is one that can be drawn in a plane such that no two edges intersect. They occur in many applications, so it is well worth knowing how hard various problems are if the inputs are restricted to planar graphs. (Determining if an arbitrary graph is planar is an important problem in itself; fortunately, it is known to be in $\mathcal{P}$. The best algorithms for testing planarity are complicated but run in linear time.) The directed Hamiltonian path problem is $\mathcal{NP}$-complete even when restricted to planar directed graphs.

The vertex cover problem (Problem 13.10) is still $\mathcal{NP}$-complete when restricted to planar graphs. Planarity simplifies the clique problem (Problem 13.11), though. For planar graphs it is in $\mathcal{P}$ because a planar graph cannot have a clique with more than four vertices.

Three-colorability is still $\mathcal{NP}$-complete if the graphs are planar and the maximum degree is 4. However, 4-colorability of planar graphs is polynomial, because *every* planar graph is 4-colorable (this is the famous four-color theorem). That is, the modified question, "Is G a planar graph *and* can G be colored with 4 colors?" always has the same answer as "Is G a planar graph?" It is unnecessary to find a 4-coloring to answer this question.

One of the earliest restrictions to be studied was 3-satisfiability (Problem 13.6), which restricts formulas to have at most three literals per clause. It is $\mathcal{NP}$-complete. The 2-satisfiability problem restricts formulas to at most two literals per clause, and it can be solved in polynomial time.

Another interesting phenomenon, illustrated by some of the following examples, is that two problems that seem to differ only slightly in their statement may differ very much in complexity; one may be in $\mathcal{P}$ while the other is $\mathcal{NP}$-complete.

Although the vertex cover problem (Problem 13.10) is $\mathcal{NP}$-complete, its dual, the edge cover problem—Is there a set of k edges such that each vertex is incident upon at least one of them?—is in $\mathcal{P}$.

In Chapter 7 we saw that there are efficient algorithms for finding the shortest simple path between two specified vertices in a graph. The longest simple path problem is $\mathcal{NP}$-complete. (The decision problem formulation for these two problems includes an integer k as input and asks if there is a path shorter than k, or a path longer than k, respectively.)

Determining if a graph is 2-colorable is easy; determining if it is 3-colorable is $\mathcal{NP}$-complete.

As mentioned, 2-satisfiability can be solved in polynomial time. However, consider this variation of the problem: Given a CNF formula with at most two literals per clause, and given an integer k, is there a truth assignment for the variables that satisfies at least k clauses? This problem is $\mathcal{NP}$-complete.

The feedback edge set problem (Problem 13.13) is $\mathcal{NP}$-complete; however, the same problem for undirected graphs is in $\mathcal{P}$.

The problem of job scheduling with penalties (Problem 13.2) is $\mathcal{NP}$-complete, but if the penalties are omitted and we simply ask if there is a schedule such that at most k jobs miss their deadlines, then the problem is in $\mathcal{P}$. (In other words, if the penalty for each miss is 1, we can minimize this penalty in polynomially bounded time.)

These examples do not yield any nice generalizations about *why* a problem is NP-complete. There are still a great many open questions in this field, the main one being, of course, does $P = NP$?

13.3.4 Optimization Problems and Decision Problems

In our descriptions of sample NP-complete problems in Section 13.2.2, we included two aspects of the optimization problems: We may ask for the optimal solution *value* (e.g., the chromatic number of a graph or the minimum number of bins into which a set of objects fit) or we may ask for an actual solution (a coloring of the graph, a packing of the objects) that achieves the optimal value. Thus we have three kinds of problems:

1. Decision problem: Is there a solution better than some given bound?
2. Optimal value: What is the value of a best possible solution?
3. Optimal solution: Find a solution that achieves the optimal value.

It is easy to see that these are listed in order of increasing difficulty. For example, if we have an optimal coloring for a graph, we need only count the colors to determine the graph's chromatic number, and if we know its chromatic number, it is trivial to determine if the graph is k-colorable for any given k. In real applications we usually want an optimal (or nearly optimal) solution.

It has been easier to work out the theory of NP-completeness for decision problems, and since the optimization problems are at least as hard to solve as the related decision problems, we have not lost anything essential by doing so. That is, our comments about the difficulty of NP-complete decision problems apply to the optimization problems associated with them. These optimization problems are often called NP-hard, although they are not decision problems. In fact, they are harder than the NP-complete decision problems in some sense because they are not known to be in NP. That is, no polynomial verification algorithm is known that can determine if a proposed solution is an *optimal* solution.

But suppose it turns out that $P = NP$. If we had polynomial time algorithms for the decision problems, could we then find the optimal solution value in polynomial time? In many cases it is easy to see that we could. Consider graph coloring. Suppose we have a polynomial time Boolean function subprogram canColor(G, k) which returns **true** if and only if the graph G can be colored with k colors. Then we can write the following program:

```
chromaticNumber(G)
    for (k = 1; k ≤ n; k ++)
        if (canColor(G, k))
            break;
    return k;
```

Since any graph with n vertices can be colored with n colors, we know that canColor(G, k) will be true within at most n iterations of the **for** loop. So if canColor runs in polynomial time, so does the whole program.

The same technique will show that for some other problems as well, if we can solve the decision problem in polynomial time, we can find the optimal solution *value* in polynomial time. However, it is not always this simple. Consider the traveling salesperson problem. We are given a complete graph with an integer cost assigned to each edge, and we want to find the cost of a minimum tour, or Hamiltonian cycle. If tspBound(G, k) is a function with value **true** if and only if there is a tour of cost at most k, then the following program finds the cost of a minimum tour:

```
tspMin(G)
    for (k = 1; k ≤ ∞; k ++)
        if (tspBound(G, k))
            break;
    return k;
```

How many iterations of the loop can there be? Let W be the maximum of the edge weights. Since there are n edges in a Hamiltonian cycle, the weight of a minimum tour is at most nW, and so there will be at most nW iterations. Unfortunately, as the discussion of input size in Section 13.2.5 indicates, this is not good enough to conclude that the program runs in polynomial time. We leave it for the exercises to show that this program can be modified to find the cost of a minimum tour in polynomial time, and, in fact, that an optimal tour can be found in polynomial time—both of course, under the assumption that the decision problem has a polynomial time solution (see Exercise 13.59).

13.4 Approximation Algorithms

Many hundreds of important applications problems are $\mathcal{NP}$-complete. What can we do if we must solve one of these problems? There are several possible approaches. Even though no polynomially bounded algorithm may exist, there may still be significant differences in the complexities of the known algorithms; we can try, as usual, to develop the most efficient one possible. We can concentrate on average rather than worst-case behavior and look for algorithms that are better than others by that criterion, or, more realistically, we can seek algorithms that just seem to work well for the inputs that usually occur; this choice may depend more on empirical tests than on rigorous analysis.

In this section we study a different approach to solving $\mathcal{NP}$-complete optimization problems: the use of fast (i.e., polynomially bounded) algorithms that are not guaranteed to give the best solution but will give one that is close to the optimal. Such algorithms are called *approximation algorithms* or *heuristic algorithms*. A heuristic is a "rule of thumb," usually an idea that seems to make good sense, but might not be provably good.

In many applications an approximate solution is good enough, especially when the time required to find an optimal solution is considered. You do not win by finding an optimal job schedule, for example, if the cost of the computer time needed to find it exceeds the worst penalty you might have paid.

The strategies, or heuristics, as they are often called, used by many of the approximation algorithms are simple and straightforward, yet for some problems they provide surprisingly good results. Many of them are *greedy* heuristics. In Chapter 8 we studied several greedy algorithms that yielded optimal solutions; in this chapter they do not. To make precise statements about the behavior of an approximation algorithm (how good its results are, not how much time it takes), we need several definitions. In the following paragraphs, assume that we are considering a particular optimization problem **P** and a particular input I.

Definition 13.9 Feasible solution set

A *feasible solution* is an object of the right type but not necessarily an optimal one. $FS(I)$ is the set of feasible solutions for I. ■

Example 13.3 Feasible solution sets

For the graph coloring problem and an input graph G, $FS(G)$ is the set of all valid colorings of G using any number of colors.

For the bin packing problem and an input $I = \{s_1, \ldots, s_n\}$, $FS(I)$ is the set of all valid packings using any number of bins (i.e., all partitions of I into disjoint subsets $T_1, \ldots, T_p$, for some p, such that the total of the s_i in any subset is at most 1).

The set of feasible solutions for an input to the job scheduling problem is the set of permutations of the n jobs. ■

Definition 13.10 Value function

The function $val(I, x)$ returns the value of the optimization parameter that is achieved by the feasible solution x, for input instance I. ■

Example 13.4 Value functions

1. For graph colorings, $val(G, C)$ is the number of colors used by the coloring C.
2. For bin packing, if $T_1, \ldots, T_p$ is a feasible partition of the objects for an input I, then $val(I, (T_1, \ldots, T_p)) = p$, the number of bins used.
3. For job scheduling $val(I, \pi) = P_\pi$, the penalty for the schedule π. ■

It should be easy for readers to identify the feasible solution sets and the solution value functions for other optimization problems.

Definition 13.11 Optimum value

Depending on the problem, we want to find a solution that either minimizes or maximizes *val*; let "best" be "min" or "max," respectively. Then $opt(I) = \text{best}\,\{val(I, x) \mid x \in FS(I)\}$. That is, it is the best value achievable by any feasible solution. An *optimal solution for I* is an x in $FS(I)$ such that $val(I, x) = opt(I)$. ■

Definition 13.12 Approximation algorithm

An *approximation algorithm* for a problem is a polynomial-time algorithm that, when given input I, outputs an element of $FS(I)$. ■

There are several ways to describe the quality of an approximation algorithm. Usually it is most useful to look at the ratio between the value of the algorithm's output and the value of an optimal solution (though sometimes we might want to look at the absolute difference between the two). Let **A** be an approximation algorithm. We denote by $\mathbf{A}(I)$ the feasible solution **A** chooses for input I. We define:

$$r_{\mathbf{A}}(I) = \frac{val(I, \mathbf{A}(I))}{opt(I)} \qquad \text{for minimization problems,} \qquad (13.3)$$

$$r_{\mathbf{A}}(I) = \frac{opt(I)}{val(I, \mathbf{A}(I))} \qquad \text{for maximization problems.} \qquad (13.4)$$

In both cases, $r_{\mathbf{A}}(I) \geq 1$. To summarize the behavior of **A**, we would like to consider the worst-case ratio. Again, there are several choices: We could consider the worst-case ratio for all inputs of a certain size, or for all inputs with a certain optimal solution value, or for all inputs. Different approaches are useful for different problems. We define the following functions:

$$R_{\mathbf{A}}(m) = \max \left\{ r_{\mathbf{A}}(I) \mid I \text{ such that } opt(I) = m \right\}, \qquad (13.5)$$

$$S_{\mathbf{A}}(n) = \max \left\{ r_{\mathbf{A}}(I) \mid I \text{ of size } n \right\}. \qquad (13.6)$$

Note that $R_{\mathbf{A}}(m)$ may be infinite for some m. For some problems, the maximum ratio is not well defined; this can occur when the set of inputs being considered is infinite. For some problems there are approximation algorithms for which R and S are arbitrarily close to 1, for others they are bounded by small constants, and for still others no algorithms are known that can guarantee to produce reasonably close solutions. For some problems it can be shown that finding a nearly optimal solution is as hard as finding an optimal solution. We will present some approximation algorithms in the next few sections.

13.5 Bin Packing

The bin packing problem is a simplification of a class of problems that arise frequently in practice: how to pack or store objects of various sizes and shapes with a minimum of wasted space. It is one of the earliest problems for which polynomial algorithms were found that were guaranteed to be within a constant factor of the optimal solution. Since the constant factor is quite small, these approximation algorithms and their variants are quite useful in practice.

Let $S = (s_1, \ldots, s_n)$ where $0 < s_i \leq 1$ for $1 \leq i \leq n$. The problem is to pack $s_1, \ldots, s_n$ into as few bins as possible, where each bin has capacity one. An optimal solution can be found by considering all ways to partition a set of n items into n or fewer subsets, but the number of possible partitions is more than $(n/2)^{n/2}$.

13.5.1 The First Fit Decreasing Strategy

The approximation algorithm we present here uses a very simple heuristic greedy strategy, called *first fit decreasing*; it has worst-case time complexity in $\Theta(n^2)$, and produces good solutions. The simple *first fit* strategy places an object in the first bin in which it fits. The

$S = (0.8, 0.5, 0.4, 0.4, 0.3, 0.2, 0.2, 0.2)$

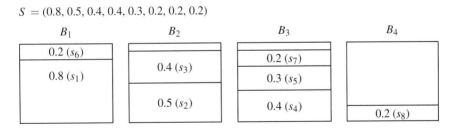

Figure 13.6 Example of *first fit decreasing* heuristic for bin packing: The packing is not optimal.

first fit decreasing (FFD) strategy is a modification that sorts the objects first so that they are considered in order of nonincreasing size. The sizes may not be distinct, so a more accurate name might be "first fit nonincreasing"; however, "first fit decreasing" is the traditional name. There is an example in Figure 13.6.

Algorithm 13.1   Bin Packing—First Fit Decreasing (FFD)

Input: A sequence $S = (s_1, \ldots, s_n)$ of type **float**, where $0 < s_i \leq 1$ for $1 \leq i \leq n$. S represents the sizes of objects $\{1, \ldots, n\}$ to be placed in bins of capacity 1.0 each.

Output: An array bin where for $1 \leq i \leq n$, bin[i] is the number of the bin into which object i is placed. For simplicity, objects are indexed after being sorted in the algorithm. The array is passed in and the algorithm fills it.

```
binpackFFD(S, n, bin)
     float[] used = new float[n+1];
     // used[j] is the amount of space in bin j already used up.
     int i, j;
     Initialize all used entries to 0.0.
     Sort S into descending (nonincreasing) order, giving the sequence
     s₁ ≥ s₂ ≥ ··· ≥ sₙ.

     for (i = 1; i ≤ n; i ++)
          // Look for a bin in which s[i] fits.
          for (j = 1; j ≤ n; j ++)
               if (used[j] + sᵢ ≤ 1.0)
                    bin[i] = j;
                    used[j] += sᵢ;
                    break;  // exit for (j)
          // Continue for (i)
```

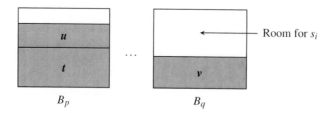

Figure 13.7 First illustration for the proof of Lemma 13.9

The input can be sorted in $\Theta(n \log n)$ time. Index j is incremented while searching for an appropriate bin for s_i at most $n(n-1)/2$ times, totaled over all i. All of the other instructions are executed at most n times so the worst-case time complexity is in $O(n^2)$.

The FFD heuristic does not always give optimal packings; the packing in Figure 13.6 is not optimal. Theorem 13.11, which gives upper bounds on the worst packings produced by FFD, is established via the next two lemmas. After the theorem we will mention some results about how well FFD does on the average.

Lemma 13.9 Let $S = (s_1, \dots, s_n)$ be an input, in nonincreasing order, for the bin packing problem and let $opt(S)$ be the optimal (i.e., minimum) number of bins for S. All of the objects placed by FFD in extra bins (i.e., bins with index larger than $opt(S)$) have size at most $1/3$.

Proof Let i be the index of the first object placed by FFD in bin $opt(S) + 1$. Since S is sorted in nonincreasing order, it suffices to show $s_i \le 1/3$. We examine the contents of the bins at the time s_i is considered by FFD. Suppose $s_i > 1/3$. Then $s_1, \dots, s_{i-1} > 1/3$ so bins B_j for $1 \le j \le opt(S)$ contain at most two objects each. We claim that for some $k \ge 0$ the first k bins contain one object each and the remaining $opt(S) - k$ bins contain two each. Otherwise there would be bins B_p and B_q, as in Figure 13.7, with $p < q$ such that B_p has two objects, say t and u (with $t \ge u$) and B_q only one, v. Since the objects are considered in nonincreasing order, $t \ge v$ and $u \ge s_i$; so $1 \ge t + u \ge v + s_i$, and FFD would have put object i in B_q.

Thus the bins are filled by FFD as in Figure 13.8. Since FFD did not put any of the objects $k+1, \dots, i$ in the first k bins, none of them can fit. Therefore in an optimal solution there will be k bins that do not contain any of the objects $k+1, \dots, i$; without loss of generality, we may assume they are the first k bins. Then, in an optimal solution, although they may not be arranged exactly as in Figure 13.8, objects $k+1, \dots, i-1$ will be in bins $B_{k+1}, \dots, B_{opt}$, and since these objects are all larger than $1/3$, there will be two in each bin and $s_i > 1/3$ cannot fit. But an optimal solution must fit object i in one of the first $opt(S)$ bins; therefore the assumption that $s_i > 1/3$ must be false. $\square$

Lemma 13.10 For any input $S = (s_1, \dots, s_n)$ the number of objects placed by FFD in extra bins is at most $opt(S) - 1$.

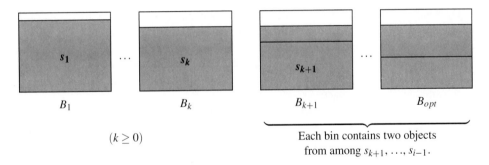

$(k \geq 0)$

Each bin contains two objects
from among $s_{k+1}, \ldots, s_{i-1}$.

Figure 13.8 Second illustration for the proof of Lemma 13.9

Proof   Since all the objects fit in $opt(S)$ bins, $\sum_{i=1}^{n} s_i \leq opt(S)$. Suppose FFD puts $opt(S)$ objects with sizes $t_1, \ldots, t_{opt(S)}$ in extra bins and let b_j be the final contents of bin B_j for $1 \leq j \leq opt(S)$. If $b_j + t_j \leq 1$, FFD could have put t_j in B_j, so

$$\sum_{i=1}^{n} s_i \geq \sum_{j=1}^{opt(S)} b_i + \sum_{j=1}^{opt(S)} t_i = \sum_{j=1}^{opt(S)} (b_i + t_i) > opt(S),$$

which is impossible.   □

Theorem 13.11 $R_{FFD}(m) \leq (4/3) + (1/3m)$. $S_{FFD}(n) \leq 3/2$, and for infinitely many n, $S_{FFD} = 3/2$.

Proof   Let $S = (s_1, \ldots, s_n)$ be an input with $opt(S) = m$. FFD puts at most $m - 1$ objects, each of size at most $1/3$, in extra bins, so FFD uses at most $m + \lceil (m - 1)/3 \rceil$ bins. Thus

$$r_{FFD}(S) \leq \frac{m + \lceil (m-1)/3 \rceil}{m} \leq 1 + \frac{m+1}{3m} \leq \frac{4}{3} + \frac{1}{3m}.$$

Thus $R_{FFD} \leq 4/3 + 1/3m$. For input size n, $r_{FFD}(S)$ is largest for $m = 2$ (if $m = 1$, FFD uses only one bin), so $S_{FFD}(n) \leq 4/3 + 1/6 = 3/2$. Construction of a sequence of examples I_n for arbitrarily large n where $r_{FFD}(I_n) = 3/2$ is left as an exercise.   □

A stronger result than that stated in Theorem 13.11 is known: The number of extra bins used by FFD is bounded by $2\, opt/9 + 4$, about 22 percent of the optimal number. (That is, $R_{FFD}(m) \leq 11/9 + 4/m$.) For arbitrarily large m, there are examples that show $R_{FFD}(m) \geq 11/9$, so we cannot improve the bound on the worst packings produced by FFD.

FFD usually does much better than these worst-case bounds would suggest. To determine the expected (average) number of extra bins used by FFD (i.e., the excess over the optimal number needed), extensive empirical studies have been done on large inputs. The data were randomly generated for various distributions. The alert reader may wonder how extensive studies of the number of extra bins used for large inputs could be done. Don't we have to know the number of optimal bins to determine the number of extra bins used by

FFD? We are developing approximation algorithms because it takes too long to determine the number of optimal bins for large inputs! In fact, the empirical studies did not determine exactly the optimal number of bins; they estimated the number of extra bins by the amount of empty space in the packings produced by FFD. The empty space is the number of bins used by FFD minus $\sum_{i=1}^{n} s_i$. The number of extra bins used in a packing is clearly bounded by the amount of empty space.

For inputs S with $n = 128,000$ and object sizes uniformly distributed between zero and one, FFD produced packings using roughly 64,000 bins. The strongest worst-case bound (mentioned above) guarantees that the number of extra bins is at most $2\,opt(S)/9 + 4 \leq 2 \times 64,000/9 + 4 \approx 14,200$. In fact, there were only about 100 units of empty space in the FFD packings. It has been shown that for n objects with sizes uniformly distributed between zero and one, the expected amount of empty space in packings by FFD is approximately $0.3\sqrt{n}$. Hence the expected number of extra bins is at most roughly $0.3\sqrt{n}$.

13.5.2 Other Heuristics

The first fit strategy (FF) can be used without sorting the objects. The results are not as good as for FFD, but it can be shown that the number of extra bins used by FF is at most about 70 percent more than the optimal (and some examples are that bad). Empirical studies have shown that the expected behavior of FF is not bad. For $n = 128,000$, for example, the number of extra bins used was no more than about 2 percent of the total number of bins used.

Another heuristic greedy strategy is *best fit* (*BF*): An object of size s is placed in a bin B_j, which is the fullest among those bins in which the object fits; that is, used[j] is maximum subject to the requirement used[j] $+ s \leq 1.0$. If the s_i are sorted in nonincreasing order, the best fit strategy works about as well as FFD. If the s_i are not sorted, the results can be worse but the number of bins would still be smaller than twice the optimal.

There is another strategy that is even simpler than FF and BF, and gives an approximation algorithm that is faster and can be used in circumstances where the contents of all the bins cannot be stored but must be output as the packing progresses. The strategy is called *next fit*. The s_i are not sorted. One bin is filled at a time. Objects are put in the current bin until the next one does not fit; then a new bin is started and no more objects are packed in bins considered earlier.

Example 13.5 The next fit strategy

Let $S = (0.2, 0.2, 0.7, 0.8, 0.3, 0.6, 0.3, 0.2, 0.6)$. The objects would be placed in six bins, as in Figure 13.9, although they would fit in four. ∎

Clearly the next fit strategy can be implemented with a linear-time algorithm. It may seem, however, that next fit will use a lot of extra bins. In fact, its worst-case behavior is worse than FFD, but the observation that the sum of the contents of any two consecutive bins must be greater than 1 allows us to conclude that $R_{nextfit}(m) < 2$.

$S = (0.2, 0.2, 0.7, 0.8, 0.3, 0.6, 0.3, 0.2, 0.6)$

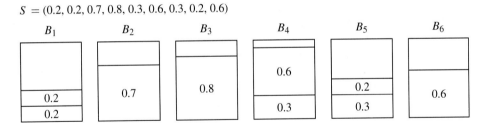

Figure 13.9   Example of *next fit* heuristic for bin packing

For some bin packing strategies, if the s_i are bounded by some number less than 1, better (i.e., lower) bounds on the ratio of actual to optimal output can be proved.

13.6 The Knapsack and Subset Sum Problems

An input for the knapsack problem (Problem 13.4) consists of an integer C and two sequences of integers, $(s_1, \ldots, s_n)$ and $(p_1, \ldots, p_n)$. Let $N = \{1, \ldots, n\}$, which we call the set of indexes. The problem is to find a subset $T \subseteq N$ (T for "take") that maximizes the total profit, $\sum_{i \in T} p_i$, subject to the constraint, $\sum_{i \in T} s_i \le C$; that is, the total size of the taken objects is at most C.

Let I be some particular input to the knapsack problem. Using the terminology and notation of Section 13.4,

$$FS(I) = \left\{ T \mid T \subseteq N \text{ and } \sum_{i \in T} s_i \le C \right\}. \tag{13.7}$$

In other words, an approximation algorithm must output a set of objects that fits in the knapsack, and any such set T is a feasible solution. The value function (Definition 13.10) for the knapsack problem is

$$val(I, T) = \sum_{i \in T} p_i.$$

That is, the total profit of the objects specified by T. (The parameter I will henceforth be omitted from *val*.) An optimal solution can be found by computing $val(T)$ for each $T \subseteq N$, but there are 2^n such subsets.

We will describe some approximation algorithms for a slightly simpler version of the knapsack problem, which is equivalent to the optimization version of the subset sum problem (Problem 13.5). In the *simplified knapsack problem,* the profit for each object is the same as its size. Thus the input is an integer C and a sequence $(s_1, s_2, \ldots, s_n)$. We want to find a subset $T \subseteq N$ to maximize $\sum_{i \in T} s_i$ subject to the requirement that $\sum_{i \in T} s_i \le C$.

The algorithms we will describe can be extended to the general knapsack problem by starting with the list of objects in order by "profit density"; that is, sorting so that $p_1/s_1 \geq p_2/s_2 \geq \cdots \geq p_n/s_n$. There are a few places in the algorithms where references to sizes would have to be replaced by references to profits; these should be obvious. The theorems about the closeness of the approximations can easily be carried over to the general knapsack problem too.

There is a very simple greedy strategy. Let M be the maximum value (profit) of any object in the input. First, go through the sequence of objects and put each one in the knapsack if it fits. Let V be the sum of values of the objects chosen. Now, if $V < M$, dump everything out of the knapsack, and put in an object of value M. It is not hard to show that with this strategy the sum of the objects chosen will be at least half the optimal; that is, the ratio defined in Equation (13.5) satisfies $R_{greedy}(m) \leq 2$ for all $m > 0$. We can do much better.

We will present a sequence of polynomially bounded algorithms sKnap_k for which the ratio of the optimal solution to the algorithm's output is $1 + 1/k$ (sKnap stands for "simplified knapsack"). Hence, we can get as close to optimal as we choose. However, the amount of work done by sKnap_k is in $O(kn^{k+1})$. Thus the closer the approximation, the higher the degree of the polynomial describing the time bound. Using the main idea in these algorithms along with an additional trick, it is possible to get a sequence of algorithms that achieve equally good results but run in time $O(n + k^2 n)$. (See Notes and References at the end of this chapter.)

For $k \geq 0$, the algorithm sKnap_k considers each subset T with at most k elements. If $\sum_{i \in T} s_i \leq C$, it goes through the remaining objects (in some arbitrary order), $\{s_i \mid i \notin T\}$, and greedily adds objects to the knapsack as long as they still fit. The output is the set so obtained that gives the largest sum. An example follows the algorithm.

Algorithm 13.2 Simplified Knapsack Approximation sKnap_k

Input: Integer C and $s_1, s_2, \ldots, s_n$, a sequence of positive integers.

Output: take, a subset of $N = \{1, \ldots, n\}$; an object to hold take is passed in and the algorithm fills its fields. Also, the algorithm returns maxSum, the sum of s_i for $i \in$ take.

Remark: We assume the class IndexSet is available to represent subsets of N and the needed set operations are implemented efficiently in this class. The output parameter take is in this class.

Procedure: See Figure 13.10. ∎

Example 13.6 Simplified knapsack approximation

Suppose the input for the problem is $C = 110$ and the sequence (54, 45, 43, 29, 23, 21, 14, 1). We arranged the sequence in descending order to make it easier to work with; this is not a requirement of the algorithm. Table 13.1 shows the subsets considered by sKnap_0 and sKnap_1. The optimal solution includes the sizes (43, 29, 23, 14, 1) and fills the knapsack completely. This solution would be found by sKnap_2. ∎

sKnap$_k$(C, S, take)
    int maxSum, sum;
    IndexSet T = **new** IndexSet;
    int j;
    take = ∅; maxSum = 0;
    For each subset $T \subseteq N$ with at most k elements:
        sum = $\sum_{i \in T} s_i$;
        if (sum ≤ C)
            // Consider remaining objects.
            For each j not in T:
                if (sum + s_j ≤ C)
                    sum += s_j;
                    T = T ∪ {j};
            // See if T fills the knapsack best so far.
            if (maxSum < sum)
                maxSum = sum;
                Copy fields of T into take.
    // Continue with next subset of at most k indexes.
    return maxSum;

Figure 13.10   Procedure for Algorithm 13.2

	Subsets of size k	Object added by inner **for** loop	sum
$k = 0$	∅	54, 45, 1	100
	Objects taken: {54, 45, 1}	maxSum = 100	
$k = 1$	{54}	45, 1	100
	{45}	54, 1	100
	{43}	54, 1	98
	{29}	54, 23, 1	107
	{23}	54, 29, 1	107
	{21}	54, 29, 1	105
	{14}	54, 29, 1	98
	{1}	54, 45	100
	Objects taken: {29, 54, 23, 1}	maxSum = 107	

Table 13.1   Knapsack example

Theorem 13.12 For $k > 0$, algorithm sKnap_k does $O(kn^{k+1})$ operations; sKnap_0 does $\Theta(n)$. Hence $\mathsf{sKnap}_k \in P$ for $k \geq 0$.

Proof   There are $\binom{n}{j}$ subsets containing j elements of N, so the outer loop is executed $\sum_{j=0}^{k} \binom{n}{j}$ times. Since $\binom{n}{j} \leq n^j$ and $\binom{n}{0} = 1$, $\sum_{j=0}^{k} \binom{n}{j} \leq kn^k + 1$. The amount of work done in one pass through the loop is in $O(n)$ so for all passes it is in $O(kn^{k+1} + n)$. We leave it to you to show that the overhead for systematically generating one subset with at most k elements from the previous one can be done in $O(k)$ time (Exercise 13.37; this is not a trivial problem). Thus the total work done is in $O(kn^{k+1} + n)$ and the theorem follows.
□

Theorem 13.13 For $k > 0$, $R_{\mathsf{sKnap}_k}(m)$ and $S_{\mathsf{sKnap}_k}(n)$, the worst-case ratios of the optimal solution to the value found by sKnap_k (Equations 13.5 and 13.6), are at most $1 + 1/k$ for all m and n.

Proof   Fix k and let C and $s_1, \ldots, s_n$ be a particular input I. Let $opt(I) = m$. Suppose an optimal solution is obtained by filling the knapsack with p objects of values, $s_{i_1}, s_{i_2}, \ldots,$ s_{i_p}. If $p \leq k$, then this subset is explicitly considered by sKnap_k, so $val(\mathsf{sKnap}_k(I)) = m$ and $r_{\mathsf{sKnap}_k}(I) = 1$. Now consider the case when $p > k$. The subset consisting of the largest k objects in the optimal solution will be considered explicitly as T by sKnap_k. Let j be the first index in the optimal solution that is not added to this T by sKnap_k. (If there is no such j, then sKnap_k gives an optimal solution.) The object j is not one of the k largest of the objects in the optimal solution, which has sum m, so $m/(k + 1) \geq s_j$. Since object j was rejected, the unfilled space in the knapsack is less than s_j. Thus $val(\mathsf{sKnap}_k(I)) + s_j > C \geq m$. Combining the last two inequalities gives

$$val(\mathsf{sKnap}_k(I)) > m - \frac{m}{k+1} = \frac{mk}{k+1}.$$

Thus we have

$$r_{\mathsf{sKnap}_k}(I) = \frac{m}{val(\mathsf{sKnap}_k(I))} < (k+1)/k.$$

Since this bound holds for any input I, $R_{\mathsf{sKnap}_k}(m) \leq 1 + 1/k$ and $S_{\mathsf{sKnap}_k}(n) \leq 1 + 1/k$.
□

Corollary 13.14 Given any $\epsilon > 0$, there is a polynomially bounded algorithm $\mathbf{A}(\epsilon)$ for the knapsack problem for which $R_{\mathbf{A}(\epsilon)}(m) \leq 1 + \epsilon$ for all $m > 0$, and $S_{\mathbf{A}(\epsilon)}(n) \leq 1 + \epsilon$ for all n.   □

Even though there are approximation algorithms for which the ratio $r(I)$ can be made arbitrarily close to one, it is very unlikely that any approximation algorithm $\mathbf{A}$ can guarantee an $O(1)$ bound on the absolute error, which is $(opt(I) - val(I, \mathbf{A}(I)))$. It can be proved that if there is such an algorithm, then $\mathcal{P} = \mathcal{NP}$. (The proof is not very hard, and this problem is included in the exercises, but you might find it helpful to read Section 13.7.2 before tackling it.)

13.7 Graph Coloring

For the knapsack and bin packing problems we have found approximation algorithms that give fairly good results; the behavior ratio for any particular optimal value is bounded by a small constant. A number of heuristic algorithms have been developed for the graph coloring problem, but unfortunately they all might produce colorings that are very far from optimal. In fact it has been shown that if there were an approximation algorithm for graph coloring that was guaranteed to use at most roughly twice the optimal number of colors, then it would be possible to obtain an optimal coloring in polynomially bounded time, and that would imply $\mathcal{P} = \mathcal{NP}$. Thus getting near-optimal colorings is as hard as getting optimal ones. (We will prove a slightly weaker version of this statement in Section 13.7.2.)

13.7.1 Some Basic Techniques

In this section we examine an easy heuristic greedy strategy. It can produce poor colorings, but it is useful as a subroutine in more complex algorithms that use fewer colors. In the next section we will present such an algorithm.

Let $G = (V, E)$ where $V = \{v_1, \ldots, v_n\}$, and let the "colors" be positive integers. The *sequential coloring* strategy (*SC* for short) always colors the next vertex, say v_i, with the minimum acceptable color (i.e., the minimum color not already assigned to a vertex adjacent to v_i).

Algorithm 13.3 Sequential Coloring (SC)

Input: $G = (V, E)$, an undirected graph, where $V = \{v_1, \ldots, v_n\}$.

Output: A coloring of G.

```
seqColor(V, E)
    int c, i;
    for (i = 1; i ≤ n; i ++)
        for (c = 1; c ≤ n; c ++)
            If no vertex adjacent to vᵢ has color c:
                Color vᵢ with c.
                break; // exit for (c)
            // Continue for (c)
        // Continue for (i)
```

Algorithm 13.3 can easily be implemented so that its worst-case complexity is in $O(n^3)$.

The behavior of SC on a given graph depends on the ordering of the vertices. For $k \geq 2$, define the sequence of graphs $G_k = (V_k, E_k)$, where $V_k = \{a_i, b_i \mid 1 \leq i \leq k\}$ and $E_k = \{a_i b_j \mid i \neq j\}$. See Figure 13.11 for an illustration. If V is given in the order $a_1, \ldots, a_k, b_1, \ldots, b_k$, then SC will color all the a's with one color and all the b's with another, producing an optimal coloring. However, if the vertices are ordered $a_1, b_1, a_2, b_2, \ldots, a_k, b_k$, then SC needs a new color for each pair a_i and b_i, using a total of k colors. Thus $R_{SC}(2) = \infty$, and if we take $n = |V|$ as the size of a graph, $S_{SC}(n) \geq n/4$ for $n \geq 4$.

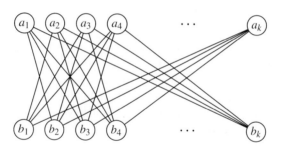

Figure 13.11   The graph G_k

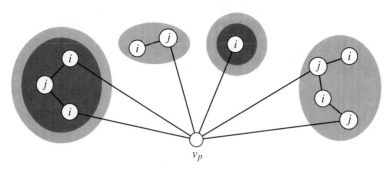

Figure 13.12   Switching colors: G_{ij} consists of the four connected components outlined in lighter gray. S_i consists of the two components also outlined in darker gray.

Recall from Definition 13.8 that $\Delta(G)$ denotes the maximum degree of any vertex in a graph G. The following theorem is easy to prove.

Theorem 13.15   The number of colors used by the sequential coloring scheme is at most $\Delta(G) + 1$.   □

Several more complicated graph coloring algorithms based on sequential coloring have additional features intended to prevent the poor behavior of SC. One such feature is to interchange two colors in the colored portion of the graph when so doing avoids the need for a new color. The interchange rule, formulated as follows, is illustrated in Figure 13.12.

Suppose that $v_1, \ldots, v_{p-1}$ have been colored using colors 1, 2, $\ldots$, c (where $c \geq 2$) and v_p is adjacent to a vertex of each color. For each pair i and j with $1 \leq i < j \leq c$, let G_{ij} be the subgraph consisting of all vertices colored i or j and all edges between these vertices. If there is a pair (i, j) such that in each connected component of G_{ij} the vertices adjacent to v_p are all of the same color, then an interchange will be done. Notice that the subgraph G_{ij} is itself 2-colored, with colors i and j. If these two colors are swapped throughout a connected component of G_{ij}, the result will still be a correct c-coloring of $v_1, \ldots, v_{p-1}$.

Specifically, let S_i be the set of all vertices in connected components of G_{ij} where vertices adjacent to v_p are colored i. Colors i and j are interchanged in S_i. Now v_p is adjacent to vertices colored j in S_i, and v_p was already adjacent to vertices colored j in the rest of G_{ij}. Now v_p is colored with i. The algorithm then goes on to v_{p+1}. This algorithm is called *sequential coloring with interchanges* (abbreviated *SCI*).

The work needed to determine when to interchange colors and to carry out the interchange may add significantly to the time requirement of the algorithm, but doing the interchanges will produce better colorings than SC for many graphs. It will give optimal colorings for the graphs G_k where SC can do poorly (you should check this).

Recall $\chi(G)$, the chromatic number of G, from Definition 13.1. It can be shown that SCI will yield an optimal coloring for any graph G whose $\chi(G)$ is 2. However, for $k \geq 3$, there is a sequence of graphs H_k, with $3k$ vertices, that are 3-colorable, for which SCI uses k colors: $H_k = (V_k, E_k)$ where $V_k = \{a_i, b_i, c_i \mid 1 \leq i \leq k\}$ and $E_k = \{a_i b_j, a_i c_j, b_i c_j \mid i \neq j\}$. Thus $R_{SCI}(3) = \infty$, and $S_{SCI}(n) \geq n/9$ for large enough n.

Readers might observe that, if the vertices in this sequence of graphs H_k are ordered $a_1, \ldots, a_k, b_1, \ldots, b_k, c_1, \ldots, c_k$, then SCI produces an optimal coloring. Thus another approach to the problem of improving the basic sequential-coloring strategy is to order the vertices in a special way before assigning colors. Some such techniques yield improvements in the colorings produced for many graphs, but again, there are cases where they perform about as badly as SC and SCI.

13.7.2 Approximate Graph Coloring Is Hard

No polynomially bounded graph coloring algorithms are known for which the ratio of the number of colors used to the optimal number is bounded by a constant. In fact, guaranteeing a small constant bound on the ratio is $\mathcal{NP}$-hard.

Theorem 13.16 If there were a polynomial-time graph coloring algorithm that colors every graph G with fewer than $(4/3)\chi(G)$ colors, then the 3-colorability problem could be solved in polynomial time (and since 3-colorability is $\mathcal{NP}$-complete, it would follow that $\mathcal{P} = \mathcal{NP}$).

Proof Suppose G is an input for the 3-colorability problem; that is, we want to know if G can be colored with three colors. Let **A** be an approximate graph coloring algorithm described in the theorem. If **A** colors G with three colors, then obviously G is 3-colorable. If **A** colors G with four or more colors, then G is not 3-colorable, because four is not less than $(4/3)3$. Thus **A** uses three colors on G if and only if G is 3-colorable, and we can use **A** to solve the 3-colorability problem in polynomial time. □

All the previous proof really proves is that we cannot approximate 3-coloring with fewer than four colors, which is a rather limited conclusion. However, we can prove a similar theorem even for graphs with large chromatic numbers. The proof uses a construction called the *composition* of two graphs. Informally, in the composition of G_1 and G_2, each

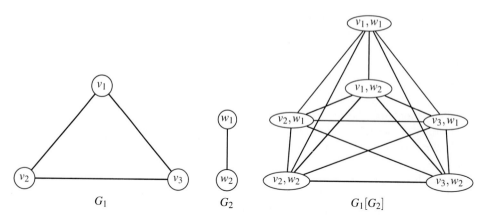

Figure 13.13 The composition of two graphs

vertex of G_1 is replaced by a copy of G_2. An edge xy in G_1 is replaced by edges between each vertex in x's copy of G_2 and each vertex in y's copy of G_2. See Figure 13.13 for an example. The formal definition follows.

Definition 13.13 Composition of graphs

Let $G_1 = (V_1, E_1)$ and $G_2 = (V_2, E_2)$ be two graphs. The *composition* of G_1 and G_2, denoted $G_1[G_2]$, is the graph $G = (V, E)$ where $V = V_1 \times V_2$ (i.e., ordered pairs with the first component from V_1 and the second from V_2). The set of edges is the union of two sets, which we call *local* and *long-distance* edges. A local edge is between two vertices in the same copy of G_2, and is of the form $(x, v)(x, w)$, where $x \in V_1$ and $vw \in E_2$. A long-distance edge is between two vertices in different copies of G_2, where the two copies are "adjacent" in terms of G_1; that is, it has the form $(x, v)(y, w)$, where $xy \in E_1$ and v and w are *any* vertices in V_2, not necessarily different. ∎

It is easy to see that the number of vertices and edges in G is bounded by polynomials in the number of vertices and edges in G_1 and G_2, and G can be constructed in polynomially bounded time.

Theorem 13.17 If there were a polynomial-time graph coloring algorithm that uses fewer than $(4/3)\chi(G)$ colors for every graph G with $\chi(G) \geq k$, for some integer k, then the 3-colorability problem could be solved in polynomial time.

Proof Let **A** be an algorithm as described in the theorem. Let G be an input for the 3-colorability problem. Let K_k be the complete graph with k vertices, and let $H = K_k[G]$. H consists of k copies of G where each vertex in one copy is connected by an edge to each vertex in each other copy. Each copy of G can be colored with $\chi(G)$ colors, but because every vertex in one copy is adjacent to every vertex in each other copy, a new set of k colors is needed for each copy. So $\chi(H) = k\chi(G)$. Since this is at least k, **A**'s performance guarantee holds for H. Now, run $\mathbf{A}$ on H, and let $val(H, \mathbf{A}(H))$ denote the number of colors $\mathbf{A}$ uses. If G is 3-colorable, then

$$val(H, \mathbf{A}(H)) < (4/3)\chi(H) \leq (4/3)3k = 4k.$$

That is, $\mathbf{A}$ uses fewer than $4k$ colors. On the other hand, if G is not 3-colorable, then it needs at least four colors and H needs at least $4k$ colors, so $\mathbf{A}$ uses at least $4k$ colors. Thus we can infer whether G is 3-colorable by running $\mathbf{A}$ on $H = K_k[G]$.

The running time of $\mathbf{A}$ is polynomially bounded in the size of H, and H can be constructed in polynomial time from G. Thus running $\mathbf{A}$ on H and checking whether or not the number of colors used is less than $4k$ answers the 3-colorability question for G in polynomial time. □

13.7.3 Wigderson's Graph Coloring Algorithm

As usual, let $G = (V, E)$, and $n = |V|$. For many graph coloring heuristics, the worst ratio of the number of colors used to the optimal can be as bad as $\Theta(n)$; for some it is in $\Theta(n/\log n)$. For a long time, no better algorithms were known. Now, however, there is one (due to A. Wigderson) that does somewhat better (though still, $R(3) = \infty$). The number of colors it uses is in $O(n^p)$ for $p < 1$ (but p depends on $\chi(G)$). If $\chi(G) = 3$, the algorithm uses at most $3\lceil \sqrt{n} \rceil$ colors.

Let $v \in V$. The *neighborhood* of v, denoted $N(v)$, is the set of vertices adjacent to v. The subgraph induced by $N(v)$ is denoted as $H(v)$; recall that it consists of $N(v)$ and all edges of G between vertices of $N(v)$. Note that v is not in its neighborhood.

A key idea in the algorithm is that neighbors of vertices with high degree are colored first. While there are vertices with high degree, the neighborhood subgraphs are colored recursively (with 2-colorable graphs as an easy boundary case). If all vertices have small degree, the graph is colored directly. The general algorithm and its analysis are not easy to follow, so we present and analyze Wigderson's nonrecursive algorithm for 3-colorable graphs first, and then briefly describe the general algorithm.

Neighborhoods and neighborhood subgraphs, $N(v)$ and $H(v)$, depend on the graph G. The algorithm discards vertices from G as they are colored; as G changes so do the neighborhoods of the vertices. $N(v)$ and $H(v)$ are always defined in terms of the current graph G.

The algorithm uses the following lemma, which is easy to prove.

Lemma 13.18   If G is k-colorable, then for any $v \in V$, $H(v)$ is $(k-1)$-colorable. □

Since 2-colorable graphs can be identified and colored (with only two colors) in polynomial time, the neighborhood of any vertex in a 3-colorable graph can be colored with two colors in polynomial time.

Algorithm 13.4   Approximate Coloring for 3-Colorable Graphs

Input: G, a 3-colorable graph; n, the number of vertices in G.

Output: A coloring of G.

```
color3(G)
    int c;  // the current color
    c = 1;
    while (Δ(G) ≥ √n)
        Let v be a vertex in G of maximum degree.
        Color H(v) with colors c and c + 1.
        Color v with the color c + 2.
        Delete v and N(v) from G, and delete all edges incident upon the
        deleted vertices.
        c += 2;
    // Now Δ(G) < √n.
    Use sequential coloring (SC) to color G, beginning with color c.
```

Example 13.7   color3 in action

Consider the graph in Figure 13.14, in which most of the steps are explained. Note, however, that the sequential coloring step could have used three colors, not two. The coloring produced depends on the order in which the vertices are encountered. If, after coloring the vertex at the top of the graph with 3, the next vertex encountered were the one at the bottom, the latter would have been colored 3 also (because these two vertices are not adjacent); then color 5 would have been needed. ■

Theorem 13.19   If G is 3-colorable, color3 produces a legal coloring.

Proof   By Lemma 13.18, each neighborhood is 2-colorable. The colors used for $N(v)$ are not used again, so they can cause no conflict. The color used for v is used again, but on the graph that remains after $N(v)$ is removed, so no other vertex assigned v's color is adjacent to v. The colors used for the sequential coloring of the graph with $\Delta < \sqrt{n}$ are not used again.   □

Theorem 13.20   If G is 3-colorable, color3 runs in polynomially bounded time and uses at most $3 \lceil \sqrt{n} \rceil$ colors.

Proof   First, the timing. Since each neighborhood is 2-colorable, each can be colored in polynomial time (Exercise 13.3). The algorithm colors neighborhoods while $\Delta(G) \geq \sqrt{n}$. So for each v whose neighborhood is colored, $N(v)$ has at least $\sqrt{n}$ vertices. These vertices are discarded after they are colored, so the number of iterations of the **while** loop is at most $\sqrt{n}$. Sequential coloring is done once after the **while** loop; it (Algorithm 13.3) runs in polynomial time. Hence the total work is polynomially bounded.

Two new colors are used for each neighborhood colored in the **while** loop (note that c is incremented by 2 in this loop.) Hence at most $2\sqrt{n}$ colors are used by the loop for all the neighborhoods.

When sequential coloring is used after the loop, $\Delta(G) < \sqrt{n}$, the number of colors used there is at most $\Delta(G) + 1$ (by Theorem 13.15). Thus sequential coloring uses at most $\lceil \sqrt{n} \rceil$ colors, so the total is at most $3 \lceil \sqrt{n} \rceil$.   □

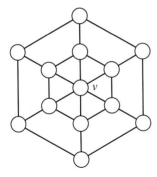

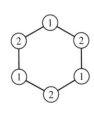

(a) Graph G with $n = 13$ vertices: The degree of v is $6 \geq \sqrt{13}$.

(b) $H(v)$: v is assigned color 3.

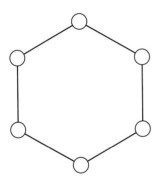

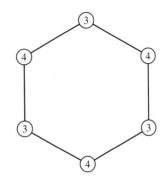

(c) G with $H(v)$ and v removed: $\Delta(G) = 2 < \sqrt{13}$.

(d) Sequential coloring

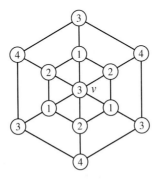

(e) The complete coloring

Figure 13.14   Example for Algorithm 13.4

At this point, readers should be wondering what good this algorithm is, since determining if a graph is 3-colorable is an $\mathcal{NP}$-complete problem. In fact, color3 can produce a legal coloring for input graphs where $\chi(G) > 3$. After all, it can use as many as $3 \lceil \sqrt{n} \rceil$ colors. Algorithm color3 will get stuck if it tries to 2-color a neighborhood graph that is not 2-colorable. Such a failure can be detected and reported easily. So, color3 can easily be modified to return a Boolean variable colored that indicates whether it successfully colored its input graph. Theorems 13.19 and 13.20 can be generalized to state that color3 always runs in polynomial time, and if it succeeds in coloring the input graph (which it is guaranteed to do if the graph is 3-colorable), it will produce a legal coloring using at most $3 \lceil \sqrt{n} \rceil$ colors.

⋆ The General Case

We now consider the general coloring algorithm. Recall that the key idea was to color neighbors of vertices with high degree first. The neighborhood subgraphs are colored recursively. How small should $\Delta(G)$ be before we do a direct coloring rather than use recursion? This cutoff point is chosen to more or less balance the number of colors used by the recursive and nonrecursive parts. The value used is $n^{1-1/(k-1)}$, where k is a parameter to the algorithm which we may think of as a guess at $\chi(G)$. Let $p(k) = 1 - 1/(k-1)$. For a k-colorable graph G with n vertices, the recursive coloring algorithm, which we will call color, runs in polynomial time and produces a legal coloring using at most $2k \lceil n^{p(k)} \rceil$ colors. (The proof is a more general, and harder, argument using the ideas of the proofs of Theorems 13.19 and 13.20.)

Once again we have the problem that we do not know if an arbitrary graph is k-colorable. We want a coloring algorithm that works well for any graph, whether or not we know its chromatic number. color can be used to obtain such an algorithm. If k, the guess at $\chi(G)$, is too small, and color cannot color G, it will fail on one of the "boundary" cases; that is, when it tries to 2-color a graph that is not 2-colorable. So, here too, color can be modified so that it returns a Boolean variable colored that indicates whether it colored its input graph successfully. Now, color is called repeatedly to find the minimum value of k for which it succeeds in coloring G. To find the minimum such k quickly, only powers of 2 are tried first. Then we use a binary-search–like scheme to check the values between two powers of 2. Here is an outline of the scheme.

Algorithm 13.5   Approximate Graph Coloring

```
approxColor(G)
    k = 1;
    colored = false;
    while (colored == false)
        k = 2*k;
        colored = color(G, k);
    // The minimum k0 for which color(G, k0) succeeds is
    // between k/2 and k.
    Do binary search on the integers k/2, . . ., k to find the smallest k0 such that
    color(G, k0) returns true.
    Output the coloring produced by color(G, k0).
```

Theorem 13.21 The approximate graph coloring algorithm, Algorithm 13.5, runs in polynomial time and uses at most $2\chi(G)\left\lceil n^{1-1/(\chi(G)-1)}\right\rceil$ colors.

Proof The number of calls to color in Algorithm 13.5 (not counting the recursive calls from within color itself) is at most $2\lg k_0$, so since color runs in polynomial time, Algorithm 13.5 does also. For all $k \geq \chi(G)$, color(G, k) return **true**, so $k_0 \leq \chi(G)$. So the number of colors used by Algorithm 13.5 is at most

$$2k_0\left\lceil n^{p(k_0)}\right\rceil \leq 2\chi(G)\left\lceil n^{p(\chi(G))}\right\rceil \leq 2\chi(G)\left\lceil n^{1-1/(\chi(G)-1)}\right\rceil. \quad \square$$

13.8 The Traveling Salesperson Problem

For the traveling salesperson problem (TSP), we are given a complete, weighted graph and we want to find a tour (a cycle through all the vertices) of minimum weight. This problem has a large number of applications in routing and scheduling problems. Consequently, this problem has been studied intensely, both by theoreticians and practitioners. This section presents some easy approximation algorithms, and then gives a theorem (without proof) that says provably good approximation algorithms are unlikely to exist. For this section, all edge weights are integers or rational numbers.

13.8.1 Greedy Strategies

In Chapter 8 we studied two greedy algorithms for finding minimum spanning trees in weighted, undirected graphs (Prim's and Kruskal's algorithms). Both of these algorithms have natural, easy variations for the traveling salesperson problem. In this section, we will investigate those methods.

Recall that the greedy method for optimization problems consists of making choices in sequence such that each individual choice is best according to some limited "short term" criterion that is relatively easy to evaluate. Once a choice is made, it cannot be undone, even if it becomes evident later that it was a poor choice. In general, greedy strategies are heuristics: They seem to make good sense, but many of them don't always lead to optimal solutions or aren't always efficient. In Chapter 8, we were able to prove that Prim's and Kruskal's greedy strategies for the minimum spanning tree problem *do* always produce optimum solutions efficiently.

Recall that Prim's algorithm begins at an arbitrary start vertex and grows a tree from there. At each iteration of the main loop it chooses an edge from a tree vertex to a fringe vertex; it "greedily" chooses such an edge with minimum weight.

Kruskal's algorithm, on the other hand, "greedily" grabs the lowest-weighted remaining edge from anywhere in the graph, so long as it does not form a cycle with the edges already chosen. The subgraph consisting of the edges already chosen at any point in Kruskal's algorithm may not be connected; it is a forest, but not necessarily a tree (until the end).

The corresponding strategies for the traveling salesperson problem are called the nearest-neighbor strategy and the shortest-link strategy, respectively.

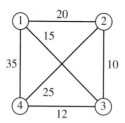

Figure 13.15   An input for the nearest-neighbor and shortest-link algorithms

13.8.2   The Nearest-Neighbor Strategy

The *nearest-neighbor strategy* is quite simple. In Prim's algorithm, when we select a new edge we could be branching out from any vertex in the tree. Here we are constructing a cycle, rather than a tree, so we always branch out from the endpoint of the path constructed so far. At the end, we add the edge from the last vertex back to the start vertex to complete the tour. The nearest-neighbor strategy may be described as follows:

```
nearestTSP(V, E, W)
    Select an arbitrary vertex s to start the cycle C.
    v = s;
    While there are vertices not yet in C:
        Select an edge vw of minimum weight, where w is not in C.
        Add edge vw to C;
        v = w;
    Add the edge vs to C.
    return C;
```

It is easy to implement this algorithm with worst case time in $O(n^2)$ for a graph with n vertices.

When the nearest-neighbor strategy is run on the graph in Figure 13.15 starting at vertex 1, it gives the cycle 1, 3, 2, 4, 1, with total weight 85. Did the algorithm find the minimum tour? No. This is an example of a greedy strategy that does not always give the optimum solution. Let us see if the shortest-link strategy is better.

13.8.3   The Shortest-Link Strategy

We describe the *shortest-link strategy* for undirected graphs. It needs small changes if the graph is directed (Exercise 13.52). At each iteration of its main loop, the shortest-link strategy for TSP (like Kruskal's algorithm for MST) grabs a lowest-weighted edge from among all remaining edges anywhere in the graph. However, the shortest-link strategy must discard an edge if it could not be part of a tour with the other edges already chosen. The subgraph consisting of the edges already chosen at any point in the algorithm forms a collection of simple paths. There must be no cycles (until the end) and no vertices incident with more than two chosen edges. The algorithm terminates when all edges have been processed.

```
shortestLinkTSP(V, E, W)
    R = E;  // R is remaining edges.
    C = Ø;  // C is cycle edges.
    While R is not empty:
        Remove the lightest (shortest) edge, vw, from R.
        If vw does not make a cycle with edges in C
        and vw would not be the third edge in C incident on v or w:
            Add vw to C.
        // Continue loop
    Add the edge connecting the endpoints of the path in C.
    return C;
```

The **while** loop could be made to end when $n - 1$ edges have been chosen. It is easy to maintain a count of selected edges incident with each vertex, so the running time of the shortest-link strategy is about the same as for Kruskal's algorithm.

When the shortest-link strategy is run on the graph in Figure 13.15, it selects the edges (2,3), (3,4), (1,2), and (1,4). The tour consisting of these edges has weight 77. That is better than the tour found by the nearest-neighbor strategy, but it is not optimal. (Find the optimal tour.)

13.8.4   How Good Are the TSP Approximation Algorithms?

It should be no surprise that these simple, polynomial-time strategies for the TSP fail to produce minimum tours. We have already said that TSP is $\mathcal{NP}$-complete, and there is probably no algorithm that solves it in polynomial time. (This does not mean, of course, that the nearest-neighbor and shortest-link strategies always produce a nonoptimum tour; sometimes they happen to find the minimum tour.)

The nearest-neighbor and shortest-link algorithms are approximation algorithms for TSP. Can we establish a bound on how much the weights of the tours found by these algorithms differ from the weight of a minimum tour? Unfortunately, no. Consider the following theorem.

Theorem 13.22   Let **A** be any approximation algorithm for the traveling salesperson problem. If there is any constant c such that $r_\mathbf{A}(I) \leq c$ for all instances I, then $\mathcal{P} = \mathcal{NP}$.

Proof   See Notes and References at the end of the chapter.   □

This theorem says that it is as unlikely that "guaranteed" good approximation algorithms for the TSP exist as it is that any polynomial-time algorithm for the TSP itself exists—even if "good" is defined so loosely as to allow any constant multiple of the weight of a minimum tour. However, if we restrict the inputs to graphs with some special properties, then there are approximation algorithms for the TSP with bounds on the weight of the tours produced. For example, if the weights on the edges of the graph represent distances in a plane, they satisfy the triangle inequality, which in this context is

$$W(u, w) \leq W(u, v) + W(v, w) \qquad \text{for all } u, v, w \text{ in } G. \qquad (13.8)$$

Exercise 13.53 describes an approximation algorithm for the TSP which is guaranteed to produce a tour with weight at most twice the optimal if the graph satisfies the triangle inequality. Algorithms with better bounds than that are known for this special class of graphs.

13.9 Computing with DNA

When we hear the word *computer* we think of modern electronic, digital computers. But the word has had many other meanings. For centuries, a computer was a person who did calculations for a living. Computing technology has evolved from fingers (for counting) to a variety of mechanical devices (the abacus, adding machines, card sorters), then to the electronic computers of the current era (room-sized mainframes to personal computers on a desktop to portables and embedded systems). There is no reason to think the evolution in computing technology will stop here. What is next? Perhaps DNA-based, or biological, computers.

In 1994 Len Adleman, a computer scientist already well-known for his role in developing the public key encryption system called RSA, showed that an instance of an $\mathcal{NP}$-complete problem could be solved using DNA. We have seen that it is unlikely that there will be algorithms, in the usual sense, to solve $\mathcal{NP}$-complete problems feasibly. Biochemical processes work on huge numbers of molecules in parallel, giving the potential for fast solutions. Adleman's method opened a whole new approach to computing. It is now a subject of intense research. In this section we describe Adleman's experiment, then discuss some recent work and the potential and limitations of DNA computing. Our point is to emphasize the algorithmic process, but we very briefly describe the biochemical processes used by Adleman.

13.9.1 The Problem and an Overview of the Algorithm

The problem Adleman tackled is the Hamiltonian path problem in directed graphs with designated start and end vertices. (We will refer to the problem as HP for the rest of this discussion.) The input consists of a directed graph $G = (V, E)$, a vertex $v_{start} \in V$, and a vertex $v_{end} \in V$. The decision problem is to determine if there is a path from v_{start} to v_{end} that passes through each other vertex in G exactly once. In many applications, if there is such a path, we would like to find one.

HP is $\mathcal{NP}$-complete. Thus HP is in $\mathcal{NP}$, and, in the terminology of Section 13.2.4, if we are given an input for the problem and a proposed solution, we can check the validity of the solution in polynomial time. Let (G, v_{start}, v_{end}) be the input. Let $n = |V|$. Let $w_0, w_1, \ldots, w_q$ be any path in G. We can check whether or not this is a Hamiltonian path from v_{start} to v_{end} by determining if it satisfies the following properties:

1. The path begins and ends at the right vertices; that is, $w_0 = v_{start}$ and $w_q = v_{end}$.

2. The path has the correct length; that is, $q = n - 1$.

3. Every vertex of V appears in the path.

These checks can be carried out very quickly (certainly in polynomially bounded time) by a "normal" algorithm. As we saw in Section 13.2.4, the ability to check one proposed path quickly does not give us a polynomially bounded algorithm for the Hamiltonian path problem because the number of distinct paths to check is not, in general, polynomially bounded. However, with the DNA technique, we generate strands of DNA to represent paths and check them in parallel. Here is a high-level summary of the algorithm:

1. Generate DNA strands to represent paths in G.

2. Use biochemical processes to extract strands satisfying properties 1 through 3 above, discarding all others.

    a. Extract strands that start at v_{start} and end at v_{end}. (Discard the rest.)

    b. Extract strands that include n vertices. (Discard the rest.)

    c. Extract strands that contain every vertex. (Discard the rest.)

3. Any strand that remains represents a Hamiltonian path from v_{start} to v_{end}. If no strand remains, G has no such path.

Unfortunately, the biochemical processes are not as exact as digital computers. As we describe the algorithm in more detail, we will mention where problems occur. We will discuss the impact of these problems later. We need to know a little about DNA to understand how the computation works.

13.9.2   DNA Background

DNA is deoxyribonucleic acid, the genetic material that encodes the characteristics of living things. This brief background is intended to be sufficient to understand how DNA can be used to do computation. From the point of view of a biologist, it is somewhat simplified and imprecise.

DNA consists of strings of chemicals called nucleotides. There are four nucleotides in DNA, each denoted by the first letter of its name: adenine (A), cytosine (C), guanine (G), and thymine (T). We can encode any information using this 4-letter alphabet, just as we can encode any information in bits (0 and 1). It is now possible to synthesize strands of DNA containing a specified sequence of nucleotides; that is, to create any desired string of letters to represent data.

John Watson and Francis Crick discovered the double helix structure of DNA (and won a Nobel Prize for their work). The nucleotides form complementary pairs; A and T are complements, and C and G are complements. Two strands of nucleotides will attach to each other (and twist around each other in a double helix) if they have complementary elements in corresponding positions. For example, see Figure 13.16 (where we illustrate the attachment of complementary strands, but not the double helix). The fact that complementary strands attach to each other is used repeatedly in the DNA algorithm for the Hamiltonian

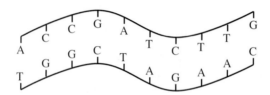

Figure 13.16   Double-stranded DNA, showing complementary pairs

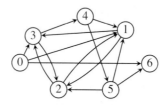

Figure 13.17   The input for the Hamiltonian path problem: $n = 7$, $v_{start} = v_0$, $v_{end} = v_6$

path problem. It can happen that two strands attach even though they do not have complementary elements in some positions; this is one of the properties of DNA processes that can cause problems for the algorithm.

Kary Mullis, a chemist, developed a process called the *polymerase chain reaction* (*PCR*), which duplicates small samples of DNA. (PCR is now widely used in genetics research and in forensics, and Mullis also won a Nobel Prize for his work.) PCR is used in several steps of the algorithm to reproduce strands that satisfy properties we are seeking. The actual biochemical processes used at each step of the algorithm are complex, but we do not have to understand them to follow the logic of the algorithm. Thus this is all the background we need.

13.9.3   Adleman's Directed Graph and the DNA Algorithm

The specific directed graph used by Adleman as the input for the problem is shown in Figure 13.17.

First we associate a string R_i of 20 letters from the alphabet A, C, G, T with each vertex v_i in G. For example, $R_2 = \text{TATCGGATCGGTATATCCGA}$. We denote the letters in the string R_i as $d_{i,1} d_{i,2} \cdots d_{i,20}$. Thus $d_{2,1} = T$, $d_{2,6} = G$, and $d_{2,20} = A$.

Step 1: Generate Paths in G

The "recipe" for generating DNA strands to represent paths in G uses two kinds of ingredients, strands that represent edges of G and strands that represent vertices.

First, we describe the strands that represent edges of G. For each edge $v_i v_j$, such that $v_i \neq v_{start}$ and $v_j \neq v_{end}$, make a strand, denoted $S_{i \to j}$, using the second half of R_i and the first half of R_j. Thus $S_{i \to j} = d_{i,11} d_{i,12} \cdots d_{i,20} d_{j,1} d_{j,2} \cdots d_{j,10}$.

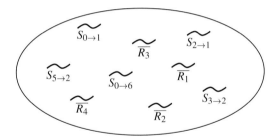

Figure 13.18 The DNA "soup," containing edge strands and vertex strands

Observe that each $S_{i \to j}$ has length 20, and that the orientation of the edges in G is preserved. That is, $S_{i \to j} \neq S_{j \to i}$ (probably).

For edges that leave from the start vertex or enter the end vertex, we create slightly different strands. For these edges we use all of R_{start} or R_{end}. For example, $S_{start \to 3}$ consists of all of R_{start} followed by the first half of R_3; that is,

$$S_{start \to 3} = d_{start,1} d_{start,2} \cdots d_{start,20} d_{3,1} d_{3,2} \cdots d_{3,10}.$$

This strand has length 30.

A large number of the edge strands, about 10^{14} copies of each for the graph with 7 vertices and 14 edges, are synthesized and put into the "pot."

For each vertex v_i, not including v_{start} and v_{end}, create a large quantity (again, about 10^{14} for this size graph) of strands that are the complement of R_i; call them $\overline{R_i}$. That is, the nucleotide (letter) in each position of $\overline{R_i}$ is the complement of the nucleotide (letter) in the corresponding position of R_i. For example, $\overline{R_2}$ is ATAGCCTAGCCATATAGGCT. These go into the "pot" along with the edge strands. (The pot is really a test tube, and the ingredients—the DNA along with some water, salt, and a chemical called a ligase—fill about 1/50-th of a teaspoon, or 1/10-th of a milliliter, for this size graph.) Figure 13.18 shows some of the strands in the mix.

To create long strands that represent paths, we would like, for example, $S_{4 \to 5}$, $S_{5 \to 2}$, and $S_{2 \to 1}$ to join (end to end) to represent the path consisting of the edges $v_4 v_5$, $v_5 v_2$, and $v_2 v_1$. But what would make these strands join? Recall that strands of DNA attach to form double strands if they have complementary elements in corresponding positions. The vertex strands will hold the appropriate edge strands together. Recall, for example, that the last half of $S_{5 \to 2}$ is the first half of R_2, and the first half of $S_{2 \to 1}$ is the last half of R_2. Thus the vertex strand $\overline{R_2}$ in the soup will attach to $S_{5 \to 2}$ and $S_{2 \to 1}$, as shown in Figure 13.19. We now have (double) strands for paths in G. Some of these paths are

$$v_4 v_1 v_2 v_1 \qquad v_3 v_2 v_1 \qquad v_5 v_6 \qquad v_0 v_3 v_4 v_5 v_6 \qquad v_0 v_6$$

$$v_0 v_1 v_2 v_3 v_4 v_5 v_6 \qquad v_4 v_5 v_2 v_1 \qquad v_0 v_3 v_2 v_1 v_2 v_3 v_4 v_5 v_6$$

The ligase in the mix "glues" the edge strands together, so edges that make up a path will remain together when the vertex strands are removed later.

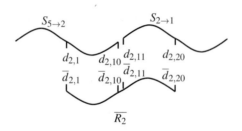

Figure 13.19   Attaching strands to generate paths

At this point, we would like to say that we have strands to represent *all* simple paths in G, but here is one of the problems: We may not get all simple paths. Although the probability is very small (there are only a few hundred simple paths in this graph), it is possible that the necessary strands just may not happen to bump into each other and attach. Let us ignore this problem for now and go on. Next, we must eliminate the strands that do not satisfy the properties 1 through 3 that describe Hamiltonian paths.

Step 2a: Verify Proper Start and End Vertices

The PCR process can be made to duplicate DNA strands that have specific sequences at the ends of the strands. In this case, the strands that begin with R_{start} and end with R_{end} were duplicated. Thus we now consider the mix to contain strands representing paths with the correct starting and ending vertices. Some of these paths are

$$v_0 v_6 \qquad v_0 v_1 v_2 v_3 v_4 v_5 v_6$$

$$v_0 v_3 v_2 v_3 v_4 v_5 v_6 \qquad v_0 v_3 v_2 v_1 v_2 v_3 v_4 v_5 v_6$$

However, although strands for these paths vastly outnumber "bad" strands (i.e., strands for paths that do not have the proper endpoints), some of the latter will remain.

Step 2b: Extract Paths with Correct Length

A DNA molecule representing a path has a complete copy of R_i for each vertex v_i in the path. Each R_i has length 20. Our input graph has seven vertices, so we want to extract DNA strands of length 140. There is a process to do this. DNA is negatively charged. The DNA mixture is put at one end of a block of gel, and the other end is positively charged. The DNA molecules move toward the positive charge, but smaller molecules move faster and the molecules of the desired length can be separated out. Once again, some undesirable strands may be included. The process was repeated several times to reduce the fraction of strands with incorrect lengths.

Now, after stripping off the vertex strands, we have single-strand DNA representing paths such as

$$v_0 v_1 v_2 v_3 v_4 v_5 v_6 \quad \text{and} \quad v_0 v_3 v_2 v_3 v_4 v_5 v_6.$$

This example shows the necessity of the next step. The second path has the correct starting and ending vertices and the correct length, but it passes through v_3 twice and v_1 not at all.

Step 2c: Extract Paths that Pass through Every Vertex

For each vertex v_i in turn (other than v_{start} and v_{end}), we mix in copies of $\overline{R_i}$, extract the strands to which they attach, and discard the others. $\overline{R_i}$ will attach to strands representing paths that pass through v_i. (Adleman attached the $\overline{R_i}$ molecules to microscopic magnetic beads, then used a magnet to separate the desired strands from the others.) Then the $\overline{R_i}$ molecules are separated from the path strands and removed. Now the remaining path strands represent paths that pass through v_i. (Again, some bad strands may slip through.)

When this step is completed for all the vertices (other than v_{start} and v_{end}), the remaining DNA strands, if there are any, represent the desired Hamiltonian paths. The sequence of the path can be read using a device called a sequencer.

13.9.4 Analysis and Evaluation

Correctness

The theoretical algorithm (generate all paths, then check the required properties) is correct, but as we have pointed out, "mistakes" can occur in the biochemical processes of the DNA implementation. Thus the DNA computation is not guaranteed to give the correct answer.

All the algorithms we have studied in this book work correctly for all valid inputs (unless we made a mistake in logic). However, there is a class of algorithms called *probabilistic algorithms* (programmed for ordinary electronic computers) that use randomness at various steps. Such algorithms may give an incorrect answer, or may give no answer at all, or may fail to give an answer within the specified time bound. Probabilistic algorithms that are programmed for computers can be analyzed mathematically. We can calculate the probability with which they return the correct answer. Such algorithms have advantages that make the trade-off of "certainty" worthwhile in some situations. Often they are much faster than usual (deterministic) algorithms for the same problem. For some, we can determine precise trade-offs between more computing time and a higher probability of correct results. Some can be designed so that the probability of a bad outcome is smaller than the probability of a hardware error on a typical computer.

DNA algorithms are like probabilistic algorithms. The obvious potential advantage here is the speed gained from the fact that a huge number of biochemical processes are occurring at the same time, in parallel. Currently, errors are a significant drawback. Adleman found the Hamiltonian path with very careful lab work, repeating some of the processes several times to purify the DNA solution. The practical usefulness of this approach will depend on future work to improve techniques to reduce errors so that correct answers are achieved with high probability.

Analysis of Time and Space

We will summarize the steps performed in Adleman's experiment, keeping in mind that counting steps in the laboratory is somewhat less precise than counting operations performed on a digital computer. Let $G = (V, E)$, $n = |V|$, and $m = |E|$.

1. Synthesis of strands for vertices and edges. The time depends polynomially on the size of the graph.

2. Path generation. This step depends on the volume of DNA, which depends on the problem size. Researchers in the field believe that this can be considered nearly constant time for practical volumes of material. Similarly, the volume of material being processed affects the time for the remaining steps, but there are practical limits on the volume of material, so in a sense the steps are in constant time. However, there is a question of how large a problem can be solved with a practical volume of material. We will return to this question.

3. Amplification and extraction of strands with desired endpoints.

4. Extraction of strands with desired length.

5. For each vertex (other than the endpoints), extraction of strands that include that vertex. The number of steps is proportional to the number of vertices.

6. In the above steps, several applications of PCR, various washes, heating, and other processes.

Thus we have described a solution for an $\mathcal{NP}$-complete problem in a linear number of steps, but the times for the steps depend on the volume of the material needed for the particular input. For a fixed amount of laboratory equipment, some of the steps take time that is at least linear in this volume. Thus understanding how the volume increases with input size is critical to analyzing the complexity of both time and space.

For the seven-vertex graph, the volume is about 1/50-th of a teaspoon. Will volume really be a practical concern for inputs of reasonable size? In the beginning of the chapter we pointed out that algorithms with exponential growth become infeasible for quite modest input sizes. If volume grows exponentially with input size, even a very small constant factor will soon be overcome.

Let's restrict ourselves to graphs with out-degree two. The number of paths of length $n - 1$ that begin at the start vertex is 2^{n-1}. (Remember, paths need not be simple.) Certainly we need enough strands to generate at least that many paths, and actually we need to generate considerably more. With a few rough calculations we can see that if 1/50-th of a teaspoon (1/10-th of a milliliter) is needed to provide enough strands for a seven-vertex graph, then 25 thousand gallons (about 100 thousand liters) would be needed for a 37-vertex graph with out-degree two. Some researchers have estimated that 10^{25} kilograms of nucleotides would be needed for a 70-vertex graph. (This is about the mass of the earth.) Such is the tyranny of exponential growth.

This example shows the value of asymptotic analysis. Without it, people might spend large amounts of time and money trying to build systems to solve larger problems by methods similar to that used by Adleman. However, Adleman and the research community recognize that something more sophisticated is needed before DNA computing can scale up to significantly large problems. The purpose of the initial experiment was to determine if DNA could be harnessed to carry out a significant computation at all, with today's technology.

Future Directions

Research in DNA computation (and more generally, molecular computation) is currently very active. A thorough survey would be far beyond the scope of this book. Interested readers should consult Notes and References at the end of the chapter, and look for recent literature. Some of the research areas are control of errors, improving the constant factors, and improving the asymptotic order.

DNA computation has some advantages over electronic computers. Adleman summarized its potential for being faster, using less energy, and storing data more densely. Computer speeds are constantly improving, so the figures we give may be out of date, but they illustrate the point. At the time Adleman did his experiment (1994), the fastest supercomputers executed approximately 10^{12} operations per second. Taking concatenation of DNA molecules (to generate paths) as a basic operation, Adleman estimated that the DNA method performed approximately 10^{14} operations (over the course of several hours) and that this number could be increased to about 10^{20}. At the higher rate, the number of operations per second would be more than 1000 times as many as executed by a supercomputer. This comparison has to be interpreted carefully, however, because all the computer operations are directed by a program, while the DNA operations are only loosely controlled, and are largely random.

The DNA method uses less energy than a supercomputer. Adleman suggests that the path generation process could (in principle) perform more than 10^{19} operations per joule of energy, whereas a supercomputer performs approximately 10^9 operations per joule. One gram of DNA, which takes up about one cubic centimeter of space, can store as much information as one trillion compact disks.

Counterbalancing the speed and low energy requirements of the molecular operations is the difficulty of obtaining the "output." The actual process took seven days of real time in a laboratory. That is a lot of time to find a Hamiltonian path in a seven-vertex graph. Also, Adleman's experiment required human intervention and control at each step. The process was not automated. There was no "program" submitted to a machine to be run. It remains for researchers to find ways to automate the process.

DNA algorithms seem naturally suited to problems like the Hamiltonian path problem, because it is easy to see how paths can be represented by strands of DNA. Can the techniques used here be applied, in general, to many other kinds of problems? A fundamental theoretical result has been proven about DNA computation: Using a few basic operations to cut and paste DNA strands, DNA computing is a *universal model of computation*. This means that it has all the computational power of a general-purpose computer. Any problem for which we can write an algorithm, in the traditional sense, to run on a computer, can be solved using this model of DNA computation, and programs can be written into the DNA itself.

As we saw, the amount of material needed to generate all certificates of a problem with DNA strands can grow exponentially with input size. Thus the challenge is to find methods whose material requirements (i.e., space requirements) are not so explosive. Newer DNA algorithms being developed use more sophisticated techniques, generating some potential solutions, then eliminating bad ones, then generating more, and so on, to reduce the space requirements.

The technology of DNA computing is very young now and the actual accomplishments so far are small. Laboratory computations have been done for inputs so small that, like Adleman's seven-vertex graph, they could be solved much more quickly without a computer at all. But that is how any new technology starts. The first electronic computers filled large rooms and weighed many tons. They were less powerful than computers we can now carry in our pockets. Research into ways to speed up the DNA chemical processes and make them less error-prone is continuing. It seems likely that DNA computing will prove useful for some kinds of problems, especially those whose solution can take advantage of the massive parallelism of the biochemical processes. At this point we do not know how useful it will be.

Exercises

Section 13.2 $\mathcal{P}$ and $\mathcal{NP}$

13.1   Suppose algorithms A_1 and A_2 have worst-case time bound p and q, respectively. Suppose algorithm A_3 consists of applying A_2 to the output of A_1. (The input for A_3 is the input for A_1.) Give a worst-case time bound for A_3.

13.2   Give a necessary and sufficient condition for a graph to be colorable with one color.

13.3   Write an algorithm to determine whether a graph $G = (V, E)$ is 2-colorable. The algorithm should run in $\Theta(n + m)$ time, where $n = |V|$ and $m = |E|$, and produce a 2-coloring if one exists.

13.4   Show that each of the following decision problems is in $\mathcal{NP}$. To do this, indicate what a "proposed solution" for a problem instance (in the sense of Section 13.2.4) would be, and tell what properties would be checked to determine if a proposed solution justifies a *yes* answer to the problem.

a.   the bin packing problem
b.   the Hamiltonian cycle problem
c.   the satisfiability problem
d.   the vertex cover problem (Problem 13.10 in Section 13.3.2)
e.   The question, "Is integer n nonprime?" Note that you cannot assume arithmetic operations take $O(1)$ when the operands are as big as the input itself.

13.5

★ **a.**   Give a dynamic programming solution for the subset sum problem. (See also Exercise 10.21.) Analyze the asymptotic order of your solution. Explain why this solution does not put the subset sum problem in $\mathcal{P}$.

b.   Example 10.3 gave a dynamic programming procedure to compute the nth Fibonacci number. Explain why this procedure does not run in polynomial time.

★★ **c.**   Give a polynomial-time algorithm to compute the nth Fibonacci number. Analyze the asymptotic order of your algorithm. *Hint*: Consider Exercise 12.17.

Section 13.3   NP-Complete Problems

Note: For the exercises that ask you to show that one problem (**P**) is reducible to another (**Q**), remember that this involves several steps: Define a transformation from **P** to **Q**, and show that the transformation satisfies all three properties in Definition 13.6.

13.6   Show that polynomial reduction is a transitive relation.

⋆ **13.7**   Show that satisfiability is reducible to 3-satisfiability. *Hint*: The clause $C = (x_1 \lor x_2 \lor x_3 \lor \cdots \lor x_k)$, where $k \geq 4$, means "(at least) one of $x_1, \ldots, x_k$ is true." Introduce a new variable γ and write clauses that mean "γ implies $x_1 \lor x_2$" and "$\neg\gamma$ implies $x_3 \lor \cdots \lor x_k$." How many literals does each of your clauses have? What is the relationship between C being true and either or both of these clauses being true?

13.8   The subset sum problem may be stated so that $s_1, \ldots, s_n$ and C are rational numbers. Show that this version of the problem is reducible to the version in the text and vice versa.

13.9   The *set intersection* problem is defined as follows:

Problem 13.14

Given finite sets $A_1, A_2, \ldots, A_m$ and $B_1, B_2, \ldots, B_n$, is there a set T such that

$$|T \cap A_i| \geq 1 \qquad \text{for } i = 1, 2, \ldots, m, \text{ and}$$
$$|T \cap B_j| \leq 1 \qquad \text{for } j = 1, 2, \ldots, n \text{ ?} \quad \blacksquare$$

Show that the set intersection problem is NP-complete by showing it is in NP and that satisfiability is reducible to it.

13.10   Show that the Hamiltonian cycle problem for undirected graphs is reducible to the Hamiltonian cycle problem for directed graphs.

13.11   Show that the Hamiltonian cycle problem is reducible to the traveling salesperson problem. (Choose either directed or undirected graphs for both problems.)

13.12   Show that the traveling salesperson problem is NP-complete even if weights are restricted to the values $\{1, 2\}$. *Hint*: You can do this with a reduction from the Hamiltonian cycle problem for undirected graphs.

13.13   Suppose that we transform a directed graph $G = (V, E)$ into the undirected graph $G' = (V', E')$ where $V' = \{v^i \mid i = 1, 2 \text{ and } v \in V\}$ and $E' = \{v^1v^2 \mid v \in V\} \cup \{v^2w^1 \mid vw \in E\}$. Show by example that there is a directed graph G such that G does not have a Hamiltonian cycle but G' does.

13.14   This problem considers an attempt at a polynomial transformation from one problem to another that *does not work*. Your problem is to find the flaw. A *bipartite graph* is an

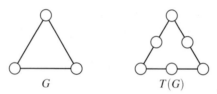

Figure 13.20 Transformation of a graph to a bipartite graph

undirected graph in which every cycle has even length. We attempt to show that the Hamiltonian cycle problem (for undirected graphs) is reducible to the Hamiltonian cycle problem in bipartite graphs. We need a function $T : \{\text{graphs}\} \rightarrow \{\text{bipartite graphs}\}$ such that T can be computed in polynomial time and, for every graph G, G has a Hamiltonian cycle if and only if $T(G)$ has a Hamiltonian cycle. Let $T(G)$ be the bipartite graph obtained by inserting a new vertex in every edge. See Figure 13.20 for an example. What is wrong with this transformation?

13.15 We described a variation of the directed Hamiltonian path problem in which the path must begin and end at specified vertices, say, v_{start} and v_{end}. This exercise shows that this variation is also $\mathcal{NP}$-complete.

a. Show that this problem is in $\mathcal{NP}$ by briefly describing an algorithm to verify a certificate for a given instance of the problem.

★ **b.** Show that the directed Hamiltonian cycle problem is reducible to the directed Hamiltonian path problem with specified start and end vertices.

★ **13.16** Show that the 3-colorability problem is reducible to the satisfiability problem. (This, of course, follows from Cook's theorem; give a direct transformation.)

13.17 Show that the 3-colorability problem is reducible to the 4-colorability problem.

13.18 Show that the clique decision problem (Problem 13.11) is $\mathcal{NP}$-complete by showing that it is in $\mathcal{NP}$ and then using the following polynomial transformation to reduce satisfiability to it. Suppose $C_1, C_2, \ldots, C_p$ are the clauses in a CNF formula and let the literals in the ith clause be denoted $l_{i,1}, l_{i,2}, \ldots, l_{i,q_i}$. The formula is transformed to the graph with $V = \{(i, r) \mid 1 \leq i \leq p, 1 \leq r \leq q_i\}$; that is, V has a vertex representing each occurrence of a literal in a clause, and $E = \left\{(i, r)(j, s) \mid i \neq j \text{ and } l_{ir} \neq \overline{l_{js}}\right\}$. In other words, there is an edge between two vertices representing literals in different clauses so long as it is possible for both of those literals to be assigned the value **true**. Let $k = p$.

13.19 If a graph has a k-clique, it is clear that any coloring must use at least k colors. However, k colors may not be sufficient. Give an example of a graph in which the largest clique size is three, but four colors are needed to color the graph.

13.20 Show that the clique decision problem (Problem 13.11) is reducible to the vertex cover decision problem (Problem 13.10).

13.21 A *feedback vertex set* in a directed graph $G = (V, E)$ is a subset V' of V such that V' contains at least one vertex from each directed cycle in G. The *feedback vertex set problem* is:

Problem 13.15

Given a directed graph G and an integer k, does G have a feedback vertex set with at most k vertices?   ■

Show that the vertex cover decision problem (Problem 13.10) is reducible to the feedback vertex set problem.

13.22 Consider the following problem: An organization has 200 members and 17 committees. Each committee must meet for a full afternoon during the week of the organization's annual meeting. You are given a list of the members of each committee. Your job is to determine whether it is possible to schedule the committee meetings in five afternoons so that each member can attend the meeting of each committee of which he or she is a member. Which of the problems discussed in this chapter most closely resembles this problem? Explain the correspondence.

13.23 Devise an algorithm to determine the chromatic number of graphs with the property that each vertex has degree at most 2 (i.e., is incident with at most two edges). The running time of your algorithm should be linear in the number of vertices in the graph.

13.24 We have stated that the vertex cover problem (Problem 13.10) is $\mathcal{NP}$-complete. Show that if the input is restricted to trees (acyclic, connected, undirected graphs), a minimum vertex cover can be found in polynomial time. (With careful implementation, you can devise a linear algorithm.)

★ **13.25** Devise a polynomially bounded algorithm to determine whether a CNF formula with at most two literals per clause is satisfiable. What is the worst-case complexity of your algorithm? *Hint*: Construct a directed graph associated with the formula; then use an algorithm from Chapter 7.

13.26 Give a polynomially bounded algorithm to determine if a graph has a 4-clique. What is the worst-case complexity of your algorithm?

13.27 Give necessary and sufficient conditions for an undirected graph with maximum degree 2 to have a Hamiltonian cycle. Outline an efficient algorithm to test the conditions.

13.28 Show that if the bin packing decision problem can be solved in polynomial time, then the optimal number of bins can be found in polynomial time.

Section 13.4   Approximation Algorithms

13.29   We may state the satisfiability problem as an optimization problem in the following form:

Problem 13.16

Given a CNF formula F, find a truth assignment for the variables in F to make the maximum possible number of clauses true.   ∎

Describe the set $FS(F)$ and the value $val(F, x)$ for this problem (where x is a feasible solution).

13.30   Let $F = \{S_1, \ldots, S_n\}$ be a set of subsets of a set A such that $\cup_{i=1}^n S_i = A$. A *cover* of A is a subset of F, say $\{S_{i_1}, \ldots, S_{i_k}\}$ such that $\cup_{j=1}^k S_{i_j} = A$. (F itself is a cover of A.) A *minimum cover* is a cover using the smallest possible number of sets. The *set cover* problem is:

Problem 13.17

Given F as described above, find a minimum cover of A.   ∎

What is the set $FS(F)$ and the value $val(F, x)$ for this problem (where x is a feasible solution)?

Section 13.5   Bin Packing

13.31

a.   Construct an example for the bin packing problem where the FFD algorithm uses three bins but the optimal number is two.

b.   Construct an infinite sequence of examples I_t, where I_t has n_t objects for some $n_1 < n_2 < \cdots < n_t$, and $opt(I_t) = 2$ but FFD uses three bins.

13.32   Show that Lemma 13.10 cannot be made stronger by constructing a sequence of examples such that for each $k \geq 2$, there is an input I with $opt(I) = k$ and FFD puts $k - 1$ objects in extra bins.

13.33   Show that, if $2 \leq opt(I) \leq 4$, FFD uses at most $opt(I) + 1$ bins.

13.34   Write a *best fit decreasing* algorithm for bin packing. What is the order of the worst-case running time?

13.35

a.   Give an example in which the *best fit decreasing* (henceforth *BFD*) strategy for bin packing produces a packing that is not optimal.

b.   Give an example in which BFD produces a different packing from FFD.

Section 13.6   The Knapsack and Subset Sum Problems

13.36   Show that the output of the greedy algorithm described in the text for the simplified knapsack problem (i.e., the subset sum problem) is always more than half the optimal. *Hint*: Consider the two cases: the algorithm's result is greater than $C/2$, and the algorithm's result is at most $C/2$.

13.37   Show that if the greedy algorithm described in the text for the simplified knapsack problem (i.e., the subset sum problem) did not explicitly consider the object with the largest size, it could give a result arbitrarily far from the optimal. *Hint*: Construct an example with only two objects.

★ **13.38**   Devise an algorithm that, when given n and k such that $1 \leq k \leq n$, generates all subsets of $N = \{1, 2, \ldots, n\}$ containing at most k elements. The number of operations done between generating one subset and generating the next one should be in $O(k)$ and independent of n.

★ **13.39**   Extend the approximation algorithms for the simplified knapsack problem and Theorems 13.12 and 13.13 to the general formulation of the problem (with profits as well as sizes).

★ **13.40**   The beginning of Section 13.6 stated that there is a sequence of algorithms $\mathbf{A}_k$ that run in time $O(n + k^2 n)$ and find solutions of the simplified knapsack problem that are within a factor of $(1 + 1/k)$ of the optimal.

   a.   For a given input $C, (s_1, s_2, \ldots, s_n)$, explain how to choose k so that solution produced by $\mathbf{A}_k$ is optimal. *Hint*: Remember that all quantities in the input are integers.

   b.   Does your choice of k in part (a) lead to a polynomial time algorithm for the exact solution of the simplified knapsack problem? Explain why or why not.

Section 13.7   Graph Coloring

13.41   Describe data structures for representing the graph and the coloring in Algorithm 13.3 to achieve a fast implementation. What is the complexity of your implementation?

13.42   Prove Theorem 13.15.

13.43   Describe how the SCI strategy behaves on the graphs G_k defined in Section 13.7. In particular, how many times are pairs of colors interchanged?

13.44   Suppose $G_1 = (V_1, E_1)$ and $G_2 = (V_2, E_2)$, where $|V_1| = n_1, |V_2| = n_2, |E_1| = m_1$, and $|E_2| = m_2$. How many vertices and edges are in $G = G_1[G_2]$? (See Definition 13.13.)

13.45   Show that the graph in Figure 13.14 is 3-colorable.

13.46   Prove Lemma 13.18.

13.47   For $k = 3$, Lemma 13.18 says that if a graph is 3-colorable, then the neighborhood graph for each vertex is 2-colorable. The converse says: If the neighborhood of every vertex is 2-colorable, then the graph is 3-colorable. If the converse were true, there would be a polynomial algorithm for the 3-colorability problem (since it is easy to determine if each neighborhood is 2-colorable). Show by constructing an example that the converse of Lemma 13.18 is not true.

13.48   Describe the coloring that would be produced by Wigderson's algorithm (color3, Algorithm 13.4) for the graphs $G_k = (V_k, E_k)$, where $V_k = \{a_i, b_i \mid 1 \le i \le k\}$ and $E_k = \{a_i b_j \mid i \ne j\}$. (In Section 13.7.1 we observed that the sequential coloring algorithm may do a very poor job on these graphs.)

Section 13.8   The Traveling Salesperson Problem

13.49   Make up an example of a complete, weighted graph for which the tour found by the nearest-neighbor strategy has lower weight than the tour found by the shortest-link strategy.

13.50   Make up an example of a complete, weighted graph for which the nearest-neighbor strategy and the shortest-link strategy find optimal tours.

13.51   A simple extension of the nearest-neighbor strategy is to choose an edge of minimum weight that extends *either* end of the path under construction (without making a cycle).

a.   Outline the procedure for this extension.

b.   How good a solution does it find on Figure 13.15, compared to the nearest-neighbor strategy?

c.   Does this extension always find a tour at least as small, and possibly smaller, than that found by the nearest-neighbor strategy? Justify your answer with an argument or a counterexample.

13.52   What changes are needed in shortestLinkTSP for directed graphs?

13.53   Consider the following approximation algorithm for the TSP. The input is a complete, weighted, undirected graph G with n vertices and m edges.

```
mstTSP(V, E, W)
        Find a minimum spanning tree for G; call it T.
        Choose any vertex v₁ as the root.
        List the vertices in the order in which they are visited by a preorder traversal
        of T; say, v₁, . . . , vₙ.
        Output the tour v₁, . . . , vₙ, v₁.
```

a.   Give a good upper bound on the worst-case running time for this algorithm.

★ **b.**   Prove that if G satisfies the triangle inequality, Equation (13.8), the weight of a tour produced by this algorithm is at most twice the weight of an optimal tour.

Section 13.9   Computing with DNA

13.54 Show that if the strings R_i that represent the vertices in Adleman's algorithm are chosen arbitrarily, it is possible that in Step 2c, a DNA vertex strand $\overline{R_i}$ could attach to a complementary segment of a path strand even if the vertex v_i does not appear in the path represented by the path strand. (Make up an example of strings for the vertices where this happens.)

Additional Problems

13.55 For each of the following statements, indicate whether it is true, false, or unknown. ("Unknown" means it is currently not known if the statement is true or false.) Don't be too hasty.

a. The satisfiability problem is reducible to the traveling salesperson problem.

b. If $\mathcal{P} \neq \mathcal{NP}$, then no problem in $\mathcal{NP}$ can be solved in polynomial time.

c. 2-SAT (the satisfiability problem, in which each clause has exactly two literals) is reducible to the satisfiability problem.

d. There cannot exist any (polynomial-time) approximation algorithm for graph coloring that is guaranteed to use fewer than $2\chi(G)$ colors for all graphs G, where $\chi(G)$ is the chromatic number of G, as in Definition 13.1.

13.56 Consider the following optimization problem:

Problem 13.18

Given $t_1, t_2, \ldots, t_n$, where all the t_i are positive integers, find a partition of these integers into two subsets that minimizes the larger sum. ∎

This may be thought of as the problem of scheduling jobs on two processors. Job i takes time t_i. We want to finish the set of jobs at the earliest possible time.

a. Give a reasonable, but fairly simple, polynomial-time approximation algorithm **A** for this problem. (How much time does your algorithm take?)

b. Give an example that shows that your algorithm does not always produce an optimal schedule.

★ **c.** Say as much as you can about the quality of your algorithm's output (i.e., about the functions S_A and R_A).

13.57 Consider the following generalization of the previous problem:

Problem 13.19

You have p bins, each with unbounded capacity, and are given integers $t_1, \ldots, t_n$. Pack the t_i into the bins so as to minimize the maximum bin level. ∎

Think of the bins as processors and the t_i as the time requirements for n independent jobs. The problem is to assign jobs to processors to finish the set of jobs at the earliest possible time.

Give a polynomial-time approximation algorithm **A** for this problem. Say as much as you can about the quality of its output.

13.58   Let $G = (V, E)$ be a graph. Consider the following greedy attempt at an algorithm to find a minimum vertex cover C for G. (See Problem 13.10 for the definition of a vertex cover.)

> Initially all edges are "unmarked" and C is empty;
> **while** (there are unmarked edges left)
>> Choose a vertex v incident with the maximum number of unmarked edges;
>> Put v in C;
>> Mark all edges incident with v.

Find an example in which this algorithm does not produce a minimum vertex cover.

$\star$ **13.59**   Suppose we had a polynomial time subprogram, TSP, to solve the traveling salesperson decision problem (i.e., given a complete weighted graph and an integer k, it determines if there is a tour of total weight at most k).

a.   Show how to use the TSP subprogram to determine the weight of an optimal tour in polynomial time.

b.   Show how to use the TSP subprogram to find an optimal tour in polynomial time.

$\star$ **13.60**   Show that if there were a polynomial-time approximation algorithm for the knapsack problem that was guaranteed to fill the knapsack with objects whose total value differed from the optimal by a constant, then an optimal solution could be found in polynomial time. (In other words, if there is a polynomial-time algorithm **A** and an integer k such that for all inputs I, $opt(I) - val(A, I) \leq k$, then an optimal solution could be found in polynomial time.)

$\star$ **13.61**   Suppose there were a polynomial-time algorithm for the satisfiability problem, say polySatDecision(F), which returns **true** if and only if the CNF formula F is satisfiable. Give a polynomial-time algorithm that, when given a CNF formula, finds a truth assignment for the variables that satisfies the formula, if one exists, or tells that the formula is not satisfiable, if that is the case. Your algorithm may call polySatDecision as a subroutine.

Notes and References

The two papers that began the intensive study of $\mathcal{NP}$-complete problems are Cook (1971) and Karp (1972). The latter outlines proofs of reducibility among many $\mathcal{NP}$-complete problems. Both Stephen Cook and Richard Karp have won the ACM Turing Award, and their Turing Award lectures (1983 and 1986, respectively) present interesting overviews of computational complexity and their own views of the context of their work.

A major source for more detail, formalism, applications, implications, approximation algorithms, and so on, is Garey and Johnson (1979), a whole book on the subject of $\mathcal{NP}$-completeness. The definition of $\mathcal{NP}$ given here uses an informal version of the definition of nondeterministic Turing machines given in Garey and Johnson. The latter also contains a proof of Cook's theorem, a proof of Theorem 13.22, a list of several hundred $\mathcal{NP}$-complete problems, and a long bibliography (so we will not repeat most of the original references here).

The approximation algorithms in Sections 13.5 through 13.7 are from Sahni (1975) (knapsack); Garey, Graham, and Ullman (1972) and Johnson (1972) (bin packing); and Johnson (1974) and Wigderson (1983) (graph coloring). The faster approximation scheme mentioned for the knapsack problem is in Ibarra and Kim (1975). There are more algorithms and references in Garey and Johnson. Empirical studies of the expected behavior of the bin-packing heuristics are in Bentley, Johnson, Leighton, and McGeoch (1983).

Approximation algorithms for scheduling problems are in Sahni (1976). Hochbaum (1997) is a book on approximation algorithms for $\mathcal{NP}$-complete problems. Lawler (1985) is a book entirely about the traveling salesperson problem. Garey and Johnson has more theorems concerning the unlikelihood of obtaining good approximation algorithms for some problems.

Empirical studies of the clique, coloring, and satisfiability problems are collected in Johnson and Trick (1996).

Adleman's DNA algorithm is described in Adleman (1994, 1998). Kaplan, Cecchi, and Libchaber (1995) attempted to repeat the experiment and reported "ambiguous" results. As of late 1998, no other attempts to replicate the experiment are known. The estimate that a 70-vertex graph would require 10^{25} kilograms is from Linial and Linial (1995). One model for universal DNA computing appears in Kari, Păun, Rozenberg, Salomaa, and Yu (1998), and several others have been proposed. Păun, Rozenberg, and Salomaa (1998) is a book about DNA computing. Maley (1998) surveys DNA computing, including other laboratory work, with an extensive bibliography. He provides a good nontechnical introduction, and explains many of the issues and methods.

14

Parallel Algorithms

14.1   Introduction

Our model of computation throughout most of this book has been a general-purpose, deterministic, random access computer that carried out one operation at a time. Several times we used specialized models to establish lower bounds for various problems; these were not general-purpose machines, but they too carried out one operation at a time. We will use the term *sequential algorithm* for the usual one-step-at-a-time algorithms that we have been studying up to now. (They are also sometimes called *serial algorithms*.) In this chapter we will consider *parallel algorithms*, algorithms where several operations can be executed at the same time in parallel, that is, algorithms for machines that have more than one processor working on one problem at the same time.

In recent years, as microprocessors have become cheaper and the technology for interconnecting them has improved, it has become possible and practical to build general-purpose parallel computers containing a very large number of processors. The purpose of this chapter is to introduce some of the concepts, formal models, techniques, and algorithms from the area of parallel computation.

Parallel algorithms are natural for many applications. In image processing (for example, in vision systems for robots) different parts of a scene can be processed simultaneously, that is, in parallel. Parallelism can speed up computation for graphics displays. In search problems (e.g., bibliographic search, scanning news stories, and text editing), different parts of the database or text can be searched in parallel. Simulation programs often do the same computation to update the states of a large number of components in the system being simulated; these can be done in parallel for each simulated time step. Artificial intelligence applications (which include image processing and a lot of searching) can benefit from parallel computing. The fast Fourier transform (Section 12.4) is implemented on specialized parallel hardware. Algorithms for many combinatorial optimization problems (such as the optimization versions of some of the $\mathcal{NP}$-complete problems described in Chapter 13) involve examining a large number of feasible solutions; some of the work can be done in parallel. Parallel computations can also speed up computation easily and substantially in other application areas.

For the examples of parallel applications just mentioned, and for some of the algorithms studied earlier in this book, there seem to be fairly straightforward ways to break up the computation into parallel subcomputations. Many other well-known and widely used algorithms seem inherently sequential. Thus a lot of work has been done both in finding parallel implementations of sequential algorithms where that approach is fruitful, and in developing entirely new techniques for parallel algorithm design.

14.2   Parallelism, the PRAM, and Other Models

If the number of processors in parallel computers were small, say two or six, then there would be a practical advantage to using them for some problems in which computation could be speeded up by some small constant factor. But such machines, and the algorithms for them, wouldn't be very interesting in the context of this book where we often ignore small constants. Parallel algorithms become interesting from a computational complexity point of view when the number of processors is very large, larger than the input size for many of the actual cases for which a program is used. This is where we can get significant speedups and interesting algorithms.

How much can parallelism do for us? Suppose that a sequential algorithm for a problem does $W(n)$ operations in the worst case for input of size n, and we have a machine with p processors. Then the best we can hope for from a parallel implementation of the algorithm is that it runs in $W(n)/p$ time, and we can't necessarily achieve this maximum speedup in every case. Suppose that the problem is putting on socks and shoes, and a processor is a pair of hands. A common sequential algorithm is: put on the right sock, put on the right shoe, put on the left sock, put on the left shoe. If we have two processors we can assign one to each foot and accomplish the task in two time units instead of four. However, if we have four processors, we can't cut the time down to one unit, because the socks must go on before the shoes.

There are several general-purpose and special-purpose formal models of parallel machines that correspond to various (real or theoretical) hardware designs. We will focus on one major class of models for general-purpose parallel computers: the PRAM (pronounced "p ram"), or parallel random access machine. Although the PRAM model has some unrealistic features (which we will mention later), it serves as a good tool for introducing parallel computing.

We will not always give the most efficient algorithm known for a problem; our aim here is to present some techniques and algorithms that can be understood without great difficulty. Since this is a short, introductory chapter, much that is interesting and important in the study of parallel algorithms is left out. Notes and References at the end of the chapter suggest a few additional topics and sources for readers who wish to pursue the subject.

14.2.1   The PRAM

A *parallel random access machine* (*PRAM*, pronounced "p ram") consists of p general-purpose processors, $P_0, P_1, \ldots, P_{p-1}$, all of which are connected to a large shared, random access memory M, which is treated as a (very large) array of integers (see Figure 14.1). The

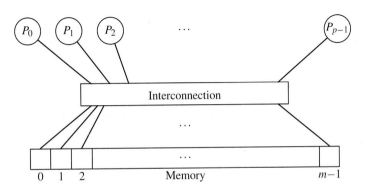

Figure 14.1   A PRAM

processors have a private, or local, memory for their own computation, but all communication among them takes place via the shared memory. Unless we indicate otherwise, the input for an algorithm is assumed to be in the first n memory cells, and the output is to be placed in M[0] (or an initial sequence of cells). All memory cells that do not contain input are assumed to contain zero when a PRAM program starts.

All the processors run the same program, but each processor "knows" its own index (called the *processor id*, or *pid*), and it "knows" the input size, usually designated as n, sometimes as a pair (n, m) or some other small, fixed set of parameters.[1] The program may instruct processors to do different things depending on their pids. Frequently, a processor uses its pid to calculate the index of the memory cell from which to read or into which to write.

PRAM processors are synchronized; that is, they all begin each step at the same time, all read at the same time, and all write at the same time, within each step. Some processors might not read or write in certain steps. Each time step has two phases: the read phase, in which each processor may read from a memory cell, and the write phase, in which each processor may write to a memory cell. Each phase may include some $O(1)$ computation using local variables before and after its read or write. The time allowed for these computations is the same for all processors and all steps so that their reading and writing remain synchronized. The model allows processors to do lengthy (but $O(1)$) computations in one step because for parallel algorithms, communication among processors through the shared memory (i.e., reading and writing) is expected to take considerably longer than local operations within one processor. There are several models with different assumptions about how much information fits in one memory cell and which local operations are available. The algorithms described in this chapter work with the weakest assumptions, so they are robust in this sense.

In the models we consider in this chapter, any number of processors may read the same memory cell concurrently (i.e., at the same step). This is known as the *concurrent read* model. There are also models that prohibit concurrent reads, known as *exclusive read* models. There are several more variations of the PRAM depending on how write conflicts are handled. After looking at a few algorithms in which write conflicts are not a problem in Section 14.3, we will consider the variations in Section 14.4.

Several programming languages for describing parallel algorithms exist, but we will use a mixture of English and our usual pseudocode language. Types are usually omitted from procedure headers because PRAMs only use integers and arrays, and the types are made clear in the context. Several of our algorithms have **for** and **while** loops. Each processor can keep track of the loop index and do the appropriate incrementing and testing during the computation phases of its steps.

Several algorithms use arrays stored in the shared memory. We can assume these are handled just as arrays in high-level languages are handled. That is, a compiler decides on some fixed arrangement of the arrays in memory following the input, and translates

---

[1] We could assume the input size was in a fixed global memory location, but that just adds one read operation per size parameter and does not affect the asymptotic order.

array references to instructions to compute specific memory addresses. For example, if the input occupies n cells, and alpha is the third k-element array, the compiler translates an instruction telling processor P_i to read alpha[j] into PRAM instructions to compute index = n + 2*k + j, and then read M[index]. The address computation is completed within one PRAM step.

14.2.2   Other Models

Although the PRAM provides a good framework for developing and analyzing algorithms for parallel machines, the model would be difficult or expensive to provide in actual hardware. The PRAM assumes a complex communication network that allows all processors to access any memory cell at the same time, in one time step, and to write in any cell in one time step. Thus any processor can communicate with any other in two steps: One processor writes some data in a memory location on one step, and the other processor reads that location on the next step. Other parallel computation models do not have a shared memory, thus restricting communication between processors. A model that more closely resembles some actual hardware is the *hypercube*. A hypercube has 2^d processors for some d (the *dimension*), each connected to its neighbors. Figure 14.2(a) shows a hypercube of dimension 3. Each processor has its own memory and communicates with the other processors by sending messages. At each step each processor may do some computation, then send a message to one of its neighbors. To communicate with a non-neighbor, a processor may send a message that includes routing information indicating the ultimate destination; the message might take as many as d time steps to reach its destination. In a hypercube with p processors, each processor is connected to lg p other processors.

Another class of models, called *bounded-degree networks*, restricts the connections still further. In a bounded-degree network, each processor is directly connected to at most d other processors, for some constant d (the *degree*). There are different designs for bounded-degree networks; an 8×8 network is illustrated in Figure 14.2(b). Hypercubes and bounded-degree networks are more realistic models than the PRAM, but algorithms for them can be harder to specify and analyze. The routing of messages among processors, an interesting problem in itself, is eliminated in the PRAM.

The PRAM, while not very practical, is conceptually easy to work with when developing algorithms. Therefore a lot of effort has gone to finding efficient ways to simulate PRAM computations on other parallel models, particularly models that do not have shared memory. For example, each PRAM step can be simulated in approximately $O(\log p)$ steps on a bounded-degree network. Thus we can develop algorithms for the PRAM, and know that these algorithms can be translated to algorithms for actual machines. The translation may even be done automatically by a translator program.

In Chapter 13, we defined the class of problems $\mathcal{P}$ to help distinguish between tractable and intractable problems. $\mathcal{P}$ consists of problems that can be solved in polynomially bounded time. For parallel computation, too, we classify problems according to their use of resources: time and processors. The class $\mathcal{NC}$ consists of problems that can be solved by a parallel algorithm with p (the number of processors) bounded by a polynomial in the input size, and the number of time steps bounded by a polynomial in the *logarithm* of the input

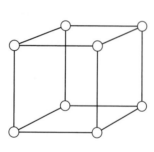

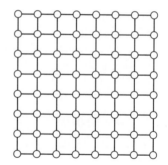

(a) A hypercube (dimension = 3)   (b) A bounded-degree network (degree = 4)

Figure 14.2   Other parallel architectures

size. More succinctly, if the input size is n, then $p(n) \in O\left(n^k\right)$ for some constant k, and the worst-case time, $T(n)$, is in $O\left(\log^m n\right)$ for some constant m. (Recall that $\lg^m n = (\lg n)^m$.) The origin of the name $\mathcal{NC}$ is explained in Notes and References at the end of the chapter.

The time bound for $\mathcal{NC}$, sometimes referred to as "poly-log time" because it is a polynomial in the log of n, is quite small—but we expect parallel algorithms to run very fast. The bound on the number of processors is not so small. Even for $k = 1$, it may not be practical to use n^k processors for moderately large input. The reasons for using a polynomial bound, rather than some specific exponent, in the definition of $\mathcal{NC}$ are similar to the reasons for using a polynomial bound on time to define the class $\mathcal{P}$. For one, the class of problems that can be solved in poly-log time using a polynomially bounded number of processors is independent of the specific parallel computation model used (among a large class of models considered "reasonable"). Thus $\mathcal{NC}$ is independent of whether we are using a PRAM or a bounded-degree network. Second, if a problem *cannot* be solved quickly with a polynomial number of processors, then that is a strong statement about how hard the problem is. In fact, for most of the algorithms we will look at, the number of processors is in $O(n)$.

14.3 Some Simple PRAM Algorithms

In this section we introduce some commonly used techniques for PRAM computation, and develop some simple algorithms that both illustrate the "flavor" of PRAM algorithms and also provide some building blocks or subroutines for later use.

In general, PRAM algorithms are "theoretical" in the sense that they demonstrate that a problem can be solved within time that is in some particular asymptotic order class. There are no real PRAMs that magically have more processors for larger inputs, without limit. Therefore there is little point in trying to optimize constant factors, since the algorithm will not actually be run as is. Instead, the presentation strives for simplicity and clarity.

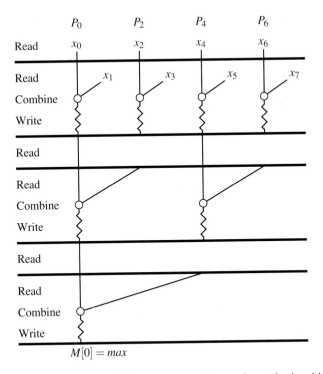

Figure 14.3 A parallel tournament: Write steps are not shown for cycles in which no processor writes.

14.3.1 The Binary Fan-In Technique

Consider the problem of finding the largest key in an array of n keys. We have seen two algorithms for this problem: Algorithm 1.3 and the tournament method described in Section 5.3.2. In Algorithm 1.3, we proceeded sequentially through the array comparing max, the largest key found so far, to each remaining key. After each comparison, max may change; we can't do the next comparison in parallel because we don't know which value to use. In the tournament method, however, elements are paired off and compared in "rounds." In succeeding rounds, the winners from the preceding round are paired off and compared (see Figure 5.1). The largest key is found in $\lceil \lg n \rceil$ rounds. All of the comparisons in one round can be performed at the same time. Thus the tournament method naturally gives us a parallel algorithm.

In a tournament, the number of keys under consideration at each round decreases by half, so the number of processors needed at each round decreases by half. However, to keep the description of the algorithm short and clear, we specify the same instructions for all processors at each time step. The extra work being done may be confusing, so it is helpful to look at Figure 14.3 first. Figure 14.3 shows the work that actually contributes to the answer. A straight line represents a *read* operation. A zigzag line represents a *write* operation; a processor writes (the largest key it has seen) in the memory cell with the same number as the processor (i.e., P_i writes in M[i]). A circle represents a binary operation that "combines" two values; in this case it is a comparison that selects the maximum of two keys. "Bookkeeping" computations fit in around the reads and writes. If a *read* line comes into P_i from the column of P_j, that means P_i reads from M[j], since that is where P_j wrote. Figure 14.4 shows a complete example of the activity of all the processors. The shaded parts correspond to Figure 14.3 and show the computations that affect the answer.

Algorithm 14.1   Parallel Tournament for Maximum

Input: Keys x[0], x[1], . . ., x[n−1], initially in memory cells M[0], M[1], . . ., M[n−1], and integer n.

Output: The largest key will be left in M[0].

Remarks: Each processor carries out the algorithm using its own index number (pid) for a unique offset into M. The variable incr is used to compute the upper cell number to read. Since n may not be a power of 2, the algorithm initializes cells M[n], . . ., M[2∗n−1] with $-\infty$ (some small value), because some of these cells will enter the tournament.

```
parTournamentMax(M, n)
    int  incr;
1.  Write −∞ (some very small value) into M[n+pid].
    incr = 1;
2.  while (incr < n)
        Key  big, temp0, temp1;
        Read M[pid] into temp0.
3.      Read M[pid+incr] into temp1.
        big = max(temp0, temp1);
        Write big into M[pid].
        incr = 2 * incr;
```

Analyzing the algorithm is easy. The initialization before the **while** loop takes one read/write step (Step 1), and each iteration of the **while** loop is two read/write steps (Steps 2 and 3); the total is $2\lceil \lg n \rceil + 1$ steps. So Algorithm 14.1 uses n processors and $\Theta(\log n)$ time. (It actually needs only $n/2$ processors and one read/write step in the body of the **while** loop, but this complicates it slightly; see Exercise 14.3.)

The tournament, or binary fan-in, scheme used by Algorithm 14.1 can be applied to several other problems as well, so it is worth doing a formal proof of the correctness of this algorithm. We want to show (by induction on t) that after the tth iteration of the **while** loop, incr $= 2^t$ and M[i] contains the maximum of x[i], . . ., x[i+incr−1], with the convention that $x[j] = -\infty$ if $j \geq n$. Thus, when the loop terminates after $\lceil \lg n \rceil$ iterations, M[0] will contain the maximum of x[0], . . ., x[n−1]. Notice that we are proving a statement that is more than we really want to prove, to facilitate the use of induction. This is called strengthening the inductive hypothesis.

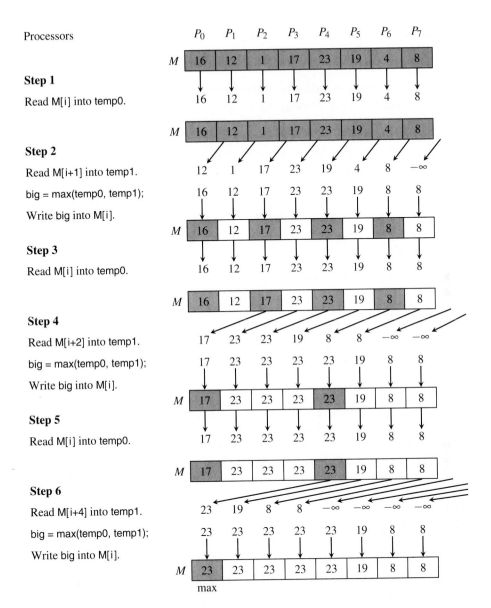

Figure 14.4 A tournament example showing the activity of all the processors

Theorem 14.1   At the end of the tth iteration of the **while** loop, incr $= 2^t$ and each cell M[i], for $0 \le i < 2^{\lceil \lg n \rceil}$, contains the maximum of x[i], ..., x[i+incr−1]. (Thus when $t = \lceil \lg n \rceil$ and $i = 0$, the desired conclusion follows.)

Proof   The proof is by induction on t, the number of iterations completed. Throughout the proof, i is any integer in the range $0 \le i < 2^{\lceil \lg n \rceil}$ unless stated otherwise. For the basis of the induction, let $t = 0$. The theorem claims that before the **while** loop is executed, M[i] contains the maximum of x[i], ..., x[i] (i.e., x[i]), which is true because that is the input, or is the value $-\infty$. Also, from the initialization step, incr $= 1 = 2^0$.

Now let $t > 0$, and we examine the tth iteration of the loop. By the inductive hypothesis, at the end of the $(t-1)$-st iteration, incr $= 2^{t-1}$, M[j] contains the maximum of x[j], ..., x[j+incr−1], for $0 \le j < 2^{\lceil \lg n \rceil}$. The same is true at the beginning of the tth iteration. If $i \ge n$, M[i] is unchanged, and $-\infty$ is the maximum of all x's with indexes greater than i because they are all $-\infty$. For $0 \le i < p$, in the tth iteration, the values of the local variables of P_i just before the write are

$$\text{temp0} = \max(x[i], ..., x[i+2^{t-1}-1])$$

$$\text{temp1} = \max(x[i+2^{t-1}], ..., x[i+2^{t-1}+2^{t-1}-1])$$

$$\text{big} = \max(x[i], ..., x[i+2^t-1])$$

Also the new value of incr is 2^t. The above value of big is written in M[i] during the write step of the tth iteration. This establishes the induction claim for t and completes the proof. $\square$

Note that Algorithm 14.1 overwrites the input data. If this is not desirable, it is a simple matter to copy the input (in one parallel step) to a scratch area in memory and do the computation there.

With only slight modification to Algorithm 14.1, the binary fan-in scheme can be used to find the minimum of n keys, to compute the Boolean *or* or Boolean *and* of n bits, and to compute the sum of n keys, each in $\Theta(\log n)$ steps, without any write conflicts. The common theme of these problems is that an associative binary operator is used to combine all the elements of the input into a single value. The proof of correctness carries over also, as it only used the fact that the binary operation was associative.

14.3.2   Other Easily Parallelizable Algorithms

Numerous algorithms based on arrays or matrices are easily parallelizable because all parts of such structures can be accessed simultaneously—there are no "links" to follow as there are in linked lists and trees.

Problem 14.1   Parallel matrix multiplication

Consider the problem of multiplying two $n \times n$ matrices A and B. Recall the formula for the entries of the product matrix C:

$$c_{ij} = \sum_{k=0}^{n-1} a_{ik}b_{kj} \qquad \text{for } 0 \le i, j < n.$$

We are using indexes starting at 0 for matrices. Of course, for this problem the output does not all go in M[0]; we assume n^2 cells of memory are designated for the elements of C. ∎

The usual matrix multiplication algorithm has a natural parallel version. Since concurrent reads are allowed, we can simply assign one processor to each element of the product, thus using n^2 processors. Notice that n^2 is *linear* in the size of the input. Each processor P_{ij} can compute its c_{ij} in $2n$ steps. (There are n terms to add, and each term needs two reads. The multiplications and additions fit into these steps.) With more processors we can do better.

All the multiplications can be done and stored in two steps using n^3 processors. Clearly, the binary fan-in scheme used in Algorithm 14.1 can be used to add n integers in $\Theta(\log n)$ steps. The work done would "look" the same as in Figure 14.3 with the dots representing additions instead of comparisons. Thus the matrix product can be computed in $O(\log n)$ time with $\Theta(n^3)$ processors.

Problem 14.2   Parallel transitive closure

Recall that the (reflexive) transitive closure of a binary relation A on a set S is the binary relation R (also on set S) that describes reachability in the directed graph $G = (S, A)$ (Definition 9.1). That is, $(u, v) \in R$ if and only if there is a path from u to v in G. Paths of zero edges are allowed, so $(v, v) \in R$ for all $v \in S$, making R reflexive. (Irreflexive transitive closure is sometimes defined, in which paths are required to be nonempty.) The input is the bit matrix representation of A with 1 for **true** and 0 for **false**, one bit per memory cell. The output has the same format. As with parallel matrix multiplication, n^2 output locations are designated. ∎

This problem is one level more complex than matrix multiplication. Although Algorithm 9.1, Transitive Closure by Shortcuts, was not the most efficient sequential algorithm, its regular structure makes it easy to parallelize. Its **while** loop executes about $\lg n$ times in the worst case. The *body* of the **while** loop can be parallelized in a manner very similar to parallel matrix multiplication (see Exercise 14.4) and run in $O(\log n)$ steps. Therefore transitive closure can be computed in $O(\log^2 n)$ steps without write conflicts.

Many dynamic programming algorithms can be speeded up easily (although not to poly-log time, usually) by doing computation in parallel. Recall that dynamic programming solutions usually involve computing elements of a table. Often the elements in one row (or column or diagonal) depend only on entries in earlier rows (or columns or diagonals). Thus with n processors, all elements in one row of an $n \times n$ table can be computed in parallel, cutting the running time of the algorithm by a factor of n.

14.4   Handling Write Conflicts

PRAM models vary according to how they handle write conflicts. The CREW (Concurrent Read, Exclusive Write) PRAM model requires that only one processor write in a particular cell at any one step; an algorithm that would have more than one processor write to one cell at the same time is an illegal algorithm.

There are several ways to relax the CREW restriction, which are collectively called CRCW (Concurrent Read, Concurrent Write) models.[2]

1. In the *Common-Write* model, it is legal for several processors to write in the same cell at the same time if and only if they all write the same value.

2. In the *Arbitrary-Write* model, when several processors try to write in the same memory cell at the same time, an arbitrary one of them succeeds. An algorithm for this model must work correctly no matter which processor "wins" the write conflict.

3. In the *Priority-Write* model, if several processors attempt to write in the same memory cell at the same time, the processor with the smallest index succeeds.

These CRCW models are successively stronger, and all are stronger than CREW: An algorithm that is legal and correct for an earlier model in the list is legal and correct for all later models, but not vice versa.

The models differ in how fast they can solve various problems. To illustrate the difference, we consider the problem of computing the Boolean *or* function on n bits.

14.4.1   Boolean *or* on n Bits

Using the binary fan-in scheme of Algorithm 14.1, each processor performs an *or* operation on a pair of bits at each round, and the problem is solved in $\Theta(\log n)$ time. This method works on all of the models mentioned because there are no write conflicts; the processors write the results of their operations in different memory cells. Can we find an even faster algorithm?

Problem 14.3   Parallel Boolean *or*

Find the *or* of n bits $x_0, \ldots, x_{n-1}$, input as 0's and 1's in M[0], ..., M[n−1].   ■

It has been shown that the lower bound for Problem 14.3 on a CREW PRAM is in $\Omega(\log n)$ time (even if more than n processors are used). However, in all the CRCW models the problem can be solved in constant time.

Algorithm 14.2   Common-Write Boolean *or*

Input: Bits $x_0, \ldots, x_{n-1}$ in M[0], ..., M[n−1].

---

[2] *Warning*: The abbreviations used for the various models in research papers are not consistent. EREW and CREW are used consistently for Exclusive Read, Exclusive Write and Concurrent Read, Exclusive Write, respectively. But CRCW might mean any of several concurrent-write models. To avoid ambiguity, we spell out the rule for write conflicts.

Output: $x_0 \vee \cdots \vee x_{n-1}$ in M[0].

>   commonWriteOr(M, n)
>   1. P_i reads x_i from [i];
>   If x_i is 1, then P_i writes 1 in M[0].

Since all the processors that write into M[0] write the same value, this is a legal program for the Common-Write model, and therefore also for the Arbitrary-Write and Priority-Write models. Thus the *or* of n bits can be computed in one step on these models with n processors. The technique can be used on the transitive closure problem (see Exercise 14.8).

14.4.2   An Algorithm for Finding Maximum in Constant Time

If we use the Common-Write (or stronger) PRAM model we can get an algorithm for finding the maximum of n numbers in less time than the binary fan-in method. This algorithm uses n^2 processors to simplify indexing, although only $n(n-1)/2$ processors do any work. The strategy is to compare all pairs of keys in parallel, then communicate the results through the shared memory. We use an array loser. Recall that this can occupy memory cells M[n], ..., M[2*n−1], or some other segment of global memory chosen by the compiler. Initially, all entries in this array are zero (or can be initialized to zero in one step). If x_i "loses" a comparison, then loser[i] will be assigned the value 1.

Algorithm 14.3   Common-Write Maximum of n Keys

Input: Keys $x_0, x_1, \ldots, x_{n-1}$, initially in memory cells M[0], M[1], ..., M[n−1], and the integer $n > 2$.

Output: The largest key will be left in M[0].

Remarks: For clarity, the processors will be numbered $P_{i,j}$, for $0 \leq i < j \leq n-1$. Each processor computes i and j from its index (pid) by $i = \lfloor \text{pid}/n \rfloor$ and $j = \text{pid} - ni$. If $i \geq j$, the processor does no work. Figure 14.5 illustrates the algorithm.

Procedure: See Figure 14.6.   ∎

This algorithm does only three read/write steps. However, the number of processors is in $\Theta(n^2)$. If the number of processors is limited to n, the largest key can be found in $\Theta(\log \log n)$ time by an algorithm that uses Algorithm 14.3 on small groups of keys repeatedly. (See Notes and References at the end of the chapter.)

This algorithm shows that, if common writes are allowed, the binary fan-in scheme is not the fastest way to find the maximum key. In the matrix multiplication example in Section 14.3, we suggested using binary fan-in to add n integers in $\Theta(\log n)$ time. You may now wonder if addition can also be done in constant time on Common-Write PRAMs. In Section 14.7 we will show that it cannot. Thus adding n integers is a harder problem than finding the maximum of n integers.

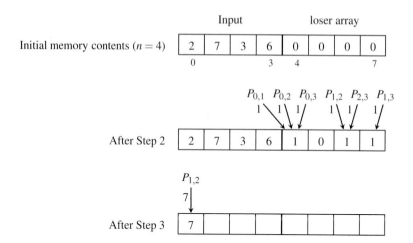

Figure 14.5   The constant-time maximum algorithm

fastMax(M, n)
1. Compute i and j from pid.
    if (i ≥ j) **return**;

    $P_{i,j}$ reads x_i (from M[i]).
2. $P_{i,j}$ reads x_j (from M[j]).
    $P_{i,j}$ compares x_i and x_j.
    Let k be the index of the smaller key (i if tied).
    $P_{i,j}$ writes 1 in loser[k].
    // At this point, every key other than the largest
    // has lost a comparison.
3. $P_{i,i+1}$ reads loser[i] (and $P_{0,n-1}$ reads loser[n−1]).
    The processor that read a 0 writes x_i in M[0]. ($P_{0,n-1}$ would write x_{n-1}.)
    // This processor already has the needed x in its local memory
    // from steps 1 and 2.

Figure 14.6   Procedure for Algorithm 14.3

14.5 Merging and Sorting

It is not difficult to find ways to speed up some of the sorting algorithms in Chapter 4 by doing some of the operations in parallel. You should be able to find parallel implementations of, for example, Insertion Sort and Mergesort that can sort n keys in $\Theta(n)$ time. In this section we present a parallel sorting algorithm based on Mergesort that does roughly $\lg^2(n)/2$ PRAM steps using n processors.

The algorithm presented here gives a dramatic improvement over $\Theta(n \log n)$ sequential sorting. For example, an array of 1000 keys can be sorted in 55 parallel steps; a sequential algorithm does about 10,000 comparisons. It is not the asymptotically fastest parallel sorting algorithm known; parallel sorting can be done in $O(\log n)$ time (in theory—the constants are too large for the method to be practical). The algorithm we describe is very easy to understand, it uses only n processors, and the number of steps is a small multiple of $\lg^2(n)$. As usual, we assume that we wish to sort into nondecreasing order.

14.5.1 Parallel Merging

As shown in Section 4.5, we can merge two sorted sequences, each containing $n/2$ keys, by doing at most $n - 1$ comparisons. The merging algorithm we used there (Algorithm 4.4) seems essentially sequential: the two keys compared at one step depend on the result of the previous comparison. Here we use a different approach to merge in $\lg n$ parallel steps. Since we intend to use the merge algorithm in a Mergesort-style sorting algorithm in which we will always merge two array subranges of equal length, we will write the merge algorithm for subranges of equal length. It is an easy exercise to generalize the algorithm and its analysis to subranges of different sizes. The central idea is the *cross-rank* subroutine.

Definition 14.1 Cross-rank subroutine

Given two sorted arrays, say X and Y, the *cross-rank subroutine* finds the rank in Y for each element of X and the rank in X for each element of Y. Specifically, the *cross-rank* of $x \in X$ is the smallest r such that $x \le y_r$; that is, if x were inserted into Y maintaining sorted order and placing x in the lower position in case of a tie, then x would be placed in $Y[r]$ and its rank in Y would be r. If x is greater than every element of Y, its cross-rank is one greater than the maximum index of Y. Also, the *cross-rank* of $y \in Y$ is the smallest r such that $y < x_r$. Notice the asymmetry of the definition, which causes elements of X to be treated as smaller than elements of Y in case of a tie. ∎

Suppose the two sorted arrays are in the $2k$ memory cells $M[i], \ldots, M[i + k - 1]$ and $M[i + k], \ldots, M[i + 2k - 1]$. For clarity, we refer to the first subrange as $X = (x_0, x_1, \ldots, x_{k-1})$ and the second as $Y = (y_0, y_1, \ldots, y_{k-1})$. To implement cross-ranking in parallel, each of the $2k$ processors, $P_i, \ldots, P_{i+2k-1}$ is assigned to one key and has the task of determining that key's cross-rank. A processor assigned to a key in X, say x_m, does a binary search in Y to determine the cross-rank of x_m, call it $r(x_m)$. Similarly, a processor assigned to a key in Y, say y_m, determines the cross-rank of y_m, call it $r(y_m)$. Each processor remembers the value of r that it computed for its assigned element.

Now we are prepared to merge X and Y. Since x_m follows exactly m keys in X and is greater than $r(x_m)$ keys in Y, its proper position in the merged subrange is in $M[i + m + r(x_m)]$. Similarly, y_m follows exactly m keys in Y and is greater than or equal to $r(y_m)$ keys in X, so its proper position in the merged subrange is in $M[i + m + r(y_m)]$. (In Exercise 14.14 you prove that the positions of an X element and Y element cannot conflict.) After the binary searches are completed, each processor writes its assigned element into the correct position. (See Figure 14.7, which illustrates the case of x_m and processor P_{i+m}.)

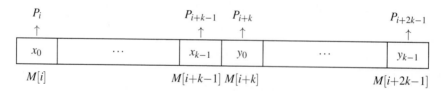

(a) Assignment of processors to keys

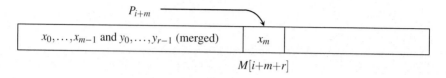

(b) Binary search steps: P_{i+m} finds r such that $y_{r-1} < x_m \le y_r$.

P_{i+m}

| $x_0,\ldots,x_{m-1}$ and $y_0,\ldots,y_{r-1}$ (merged) | x_m | |

$M[i+m+r]$

(c) Output step: P_{i+m} stores x_m.

Figure 14.7   Cross-ranking and parallel merging

Algorithm 14.4   Parallel Merge

Input: Two sorted array subranges of k keys each, in M[i], . . ., M[i+k−1] and M[i+k], . . ., M[i+2∗k−1].

Output: The merged array, M[i], . . ., M[i+2∗k−1].

Remarks: Processors P_i, . . ., P_{i+2k-1} participate. Each processor P_{i+m} has a local variable x (if $0 \le m < k$) or y (if $k \le m < 2k$) and other local variables for conducting its binary search. Each processor has a local variable position that indicates where to write its key.

Procedure: See Figure 14.8.   ∎

Theorem 14.2   The parallel merge algorithm does $\lfloor \lg k \rfloor + 2$ steps to merge two sorted array subranges, with k keys each, using $2k$ processors.

Proof   The initialization is one PRAM step. The binary searches are all done in subranges of k keys, so they take $\lfloor \lg k \rfloor + 1$ read/computation steps. Since the binary searches do not involve any writing to the shared memory, the output can be done in the last binary search step. Thus the total is $\lfloor \lg k \rfloor + 2$.   □

Note that since there are no write conflicts, the merge algorithm works on all the variations of the PRAM we have described.

parMerge(M, i, k)
    int r, position;
    KeyType x, y;
    // *Initialization:*
    If $m < k$, P_{i+m} reads M[i+m] into x.
    If $m \geq k$, P_{i+m} reads M[i+m] into y.

    // *Cross-ranking steps:*
    Processors P_{i+m}, for $0 \leq m < k$, cross-rank x in M[i+k], ..., M[i+2*k−1],
    saving the result locally in r.
    (Simultaneously) processors P_{i+m}, for $k \leq m < 2k$, cross-rank y in
    M[i], ..., M[i+k−1], saving the result locally in r.

    // *Output step:*
    Each P_{i+m} (for $0 \leq m < k$) computes position $= i + m + r$.
    Each P_{i+k+m} (for $0 \leq m < k$) computes position $= i + m + r$.
    Each P_{i+m} (for $0 \leq m < 2k$) writes its key (x or y) in M[position].

Figure 14.8 Procedure for Algorithm 14.4

14.5.2 Sorting

Suppose we have an array of n keys to be sorted. Recall the strategy of Mergesort:

> Break the array into two halves.
> Sort the two halves (recursively).
> Merge the two sorted halves.

If we "unravel" the recursion, we see that the algorithm merges small sorted subranges of the array (one key each) first, then merges slightly larger subranges (two keys each), then larger subranges, and so on until finally it merges two subranges of size (roughly) $n/2$. The recursive algorithm merges some larger subranges before doing all the small subranges (since it completely sorts the first half of the keys before even beginning on the second half). To write a systematic, iterative parallel algorithm, we merge all the pairs of subranges of size 1 in the first pass (in parallel), then merge all the pairs of subranges of size 2 in the next pass, and so on. Clearly we use $\lceil \lg n \rceil$ merge passes. The assignment of processors to their tasks is very easy. Whenever two array subranges occupying, say M[i], ..., M[j] are being merged, processors $P_i, ..., P_j$ do the merge using Algorithm 14.4. Figure 14.9 illustrates one pass.

Algorithm 14.5 Sorting by merging

Input: An array of n keys in M[0], ..., M[n−1].

Output: The n keys sorted in nondecreasing order in M[0], ..., M[n−1].

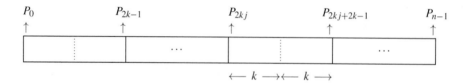

Figure 14.9 Assignment of processors for one merge pass: Processors $P_{2kj}, \ldots, P_{2kj+2k-1}$ merge the jth pair of array subranges of size k.

Remarks: The indexing in the algorithm is easier if the number of keys is a power of 2, so the first step will "pad" the input with large keys at the end. We still use only n processors.

```
parMergeSort(M, n)
    int k; // the size of subranges being merged
    P_i writes ∞ (some large key) in M[n+i].
    for (k = 1; k < n; k = 2 * k)
        For each i = 0, 2k, 4k, 6k, . . ., i < n (simultaneously)
            P_i, . . ., P_{i+2k-1} execute: parMerge(M, i, k).
```

Theorem 14.3   Algorithm 14.5 sorts n keys in $(\lceil \lg n \rceil + 1)(\lceil \lg n \rceil + 2)/2$ steps. Hence parallel sorting can be done in $O(\log^2 n)$ time with n processors.

Proof   At the tth pass through the **for** loop, each subrange being merged has $k = 2^{t-1}$ keys, so, by Theorem 14.2, the tth execution of parMerge does $t + 1$ steps. There are $\lceil \lg n \rceil$ passes because k doubles after each pass. In total, all the passes do

$$\sum_{t=1}^{\lceil \lg n \rceil} (t + 1) = \tfrac{1}{2} \left(\lceil \lg n \rceil + 1 \right) \left(\lceil \lg n \rceil + 2 \right) - 1$$

steps, and there is one initialization step.   □

14.6 Finding Connected Components

In Chapter 7, Algorithm 7.2, we studied a sequential algorithm to find the connected components of an undirected graph (or symmetric digraph) G. It used depth-first search and ran in $\Theta(n + m)$ time. Although depth-first search may seem inherently sequential, there are fast parallel algorithms to construct depth-first search trees. However, it is not necessary to do depth-first search to find connected components. (For example, breadth-first search can be used.) How much can we speed up the solution by "throwing more processors at it"?

For this section $G = (V, E)$ is an undirected graph with $|V| = n$ and $|E| = m$. (As a symmetric digraph, $|E| = 2m$.) To keep the notation simple, let $V = \{1, 2, \ldots, n\}$. The graph is presented in the input as the two size parameters, n and m, and a sequence of $2m$ integers representing the m edges.

It is relatively straightforward to find connected components in $O(\log n)$ time using n^3 processors in the Common-Write model. The idea is to do transitive closure first (see

Exercise 14.8), then in parallel for each vertex v, find an identifier for the connected component of v. The details are addressed in Exercise 14.18. Since a graph has at most $O(n^2)$ edges, the number of processors used grows more than linearly with the input size. But the transitive closure of G contains much more information than we needed. Can we solve the connected components problem with an algorithm that uses a linear number of processors?

In this section we present a parallel algorithm that finds connected components in $O(\log n)$ time using $\max(n + 1, 2m)$ processors. The algorithm has genuine write conflicts: not only are multiple processors trying to write to the same cell, but they may be trying to write different values. Among the variations of the PRAM we have described, the CREW and the Common-Write models cannot be used. Either the Priority-Write PRAM or the weaker Arbitrary-Write PRAM must be used here. Correctness will be shown in the weaker model, from which correctness in the stronger model follows.

14.6.1   Strategy and Techniques

The connected component algorithm is more complicated than any of the other parallel algorithms we have looked at so far. We will give a high-level description of the algorithm, then show how the various parts of the algorithm can be implemented on a PRAM. We introduce some terminology.

Definition 14.2   Supervertex, star

Given a forest of in-trees (edges are directed from vertices to their parents, as in Section 2.3.5), a *supervertex* is the set of vertices in any one tree, and a *star* is a tree of height 0 or 1. See Figure 14.10 for an illustration.   ■

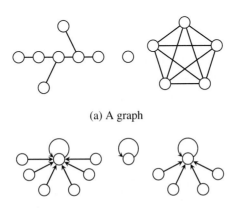

(a) A graph

(b) Its components as stars

Figure 14.10   Connected components turned into stars: Edges from roots to themselves are a bookkeeping convenience.

The algorithm begins with each vertex in a separate in-tree, then repeatedly combines trees that are in the same connected component, forming larger supervertices, and shortens the trees. Ultimately, each connected component is converted to a star. The in-trees are represented by an array parent, such that parent[v] is the parent of vertex v. By convention, the parent of a root is the root itself. Once the connected components have been converted to stars, we can determine if two vertices are in the same component in constant time by comparing their parents.

Readers who have studied dynamic equivalence relations and Union-Find programs in Section 6.6 will notice a lot of similarities to them in the above description. Indeed, connected components do define an equivalence relation on an undirected graph. Recall that cFind (find with path compression) also shortened in-trees, which were formed by union operations. Keeping these similarities in mind will help as we delve into the details of the parallel method.

The algorithm repeatedly uses two basic techniques: *shortcutting* and *hooking*. Short-cutting shortens trees. It is useful in other parallel graph algorithms, too. It is interesting to compare this operation with *path compression*.

Definition 14.3   Shortcutting

Shortcutting (sometimes called *doubling* or *pointer jumping*) simply changes the parent of a vertex v to the current grandparent of v:

parent[v] = parent[parent[v]].   ∎

Shortcutting is applied in parallel to all vertices. To see the speed with which this operation can cut down long paths, consider a simple chain of vertices as in Figure 14.11(a), where parent[v] = $v - 1$ (and parent[1] = 1). Parts (b) and (c) of Figure 14.11 show the parent pointers after the first and second applications of the shortcutting operation. If we start with n vertices in the chain, after $\lceil \lg n \rceil$ applications of shortcutting, all vertices have the same parent.

Remember, the graph $G = (V, E)$ for which the algorithm is finding connected components is an undirected graph, but the forest of in-trees manipulated by the algorithm is directed and has different edges from G. We need to keep track of whether we are talking about an (undirected) edge in G or a directed edge in the forest. The term *parent* only applies in the forest and the directed edges in the forest are $(v, \text{parent}[v])$, provided that parent[v] is distinct from v.

Shortcutting never joins two separate trees. We need the hooking operation to connect trees. This is analogous to the union operation of a Union-Find program.

Definition 14.4   Hooking

The operation hook(i, j) attaches the root of i's in-tree to the parent of j as a new child. We say that i's in-tree is *hooked to* the parent of j. (Note that either i or j may be its own "parent" in the parent array.) The algorithm only applies hook(i, j) when parent[i] is a root (i.e., i is a root or a child of a root). Thus the operation can be implemented by

parent[parent[i]] = parent[j].

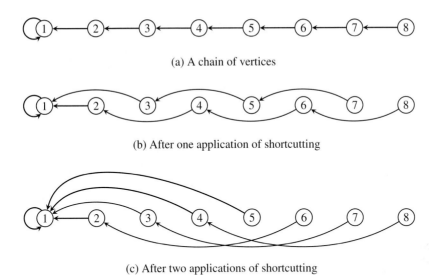

(a) A chain of vertices

(b) After one application of shortcutting

(c) After two applications of shortcutting

Figure 14.11 The effect of shortcutting in a simple example: After a third shortcut operation, all vertices will point to the root.

The algorithm uses certain special cases of hooking:

1. *Conditional star hooking*:
   If i is in a star, j is adjacent to i in G, and j's parent is less than i's parent, then hook(i, j). The requirement that we attach to the smaller of the two parents helps avoid the introduction of cycles. Conditional star hooking is illustrated in Figure 14.12, parts (a) and (b).

2. *Unconditional star hooking*:
   If i is in a star, j is adjacent to i in G, and j is not in i's star, then hook(i, j). Unconditional star hooking is illustrated in Figure 14.12 parts (c) and (d).

Note that the algorithm requires i to be in a star in both cases. ∎

   At any one time, there may be several pairs of vertices, i and j, that satisfy the conditions for hooking, but only one value can be stored as the new parent of i's root. In the parallel algorithm, different processors will be trying the different choices, and several processors may try to write in parent[parent[i]] at the same time. For example, in Figure 14.12, parts (c) and (d), we show the result of hook(8, 10), which changes parent[7]. The requirements for operations hook(7, 11) and hook(8, 11) are satisfied in Figure 14.12(c), so other processors will perform them, also trying to write in parent[7]. Only one processor succeeds in writing, but the algorithm will work properly no matter which one succeeds.

   Notice that two trees are hooked only if there is an edge of G incident upon a vertex in each tree. Thus a supervertex is always a subset of a connected component. By running long

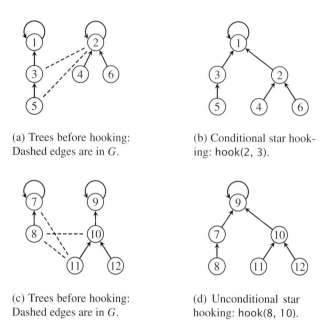

(a) Trees before hooking: Dashed edges are in G.

(b) Conditional star hooking: hook(2, 3).

(c) Trees before hooking: Dashed edges are in G.

(d) Unconditional star hooking: hook(8, 10).

Figure 14.12   Illustrations of hooking

enough, the algorithm eventually hooks together all trees that are part of one connected component.

14.6.2   The Algorithm

The algorithm begins with each vertex of G in a separate tree, so every vertex is a star by itself, initially. The algorithm repeatedly does hooking and shortcutting until the desired structure is achieved. We first give a high-level description.

Drawing on our experience with Union-Find programs in Section 6.6, we might expect that initializing each vertex to be its own tree (i.e., parent[v] = v) would be sufficient to get the algorithm started. Unfortunately, that does not quite work. After presenting the algorithm, we will explain the problem and the solution.

Algorithm 14.6   Parallel Connected Components (Outline)

Input: An undirected graph $G = (V, E)$.

Output: A forest of directed trees of height at most 1, represented by the array parent, indexed by the vertices. Each tree contains the vertices of one connected component.

Remarks: An instruction specified for a vertex v is performed in parallel for all vertices. The hooking steps are performed in parallel for all edges ij in G (and *only* for pairs i and j such that ij is an edge). Each edge, say xy, is processed twice (in parallel), once with x

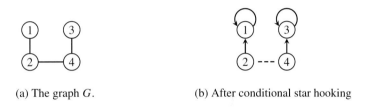

(a) The graph G. (b) After conditional star hooking

(c) After unconditional star hooking: Both
hook(2, 4) and hook(4, 2) were performed.

Figure 14.13 Introduction of a cycle during first pass, after faulty initialization

in the role of i, and once with y in the role of i. The subroutine initParCC is discussed in the text.

```
parConnectedComps(G, n, m)  // OUTLINE
    initParCC(G, n, m);
    While shortcutting produces changes:
        // Conditional star hooking
        If ij ∈ E and i is in a star and parent[i] > parent[j]:
            hook(i, j);
        // Unconditional star hooking
        If ij ∈ E and i is in a star and parent[i] ≠ parent[j]:
            hook(i, j);
        // Shortcutting
        If v is not in a star:
            parent[v] = parent[parent[v]];
```

One of the facts used in the proof that the algorithm works correctly is that conditional and unconditional star hooking do not produce new stars, because the new supervertex forms a tree of height at least 2. But unfortunately, they might do so on the first pass through the loop, if initParCC did nothing more than make each vertex its own star. Single vertices (trees of height 0) may form a tree of height 1 (a star) when they are hooked together. Then, the unconditional star hooking step might hook two stars to each other in both directions, thus creating a cycle. See Figure 14.13 for an illustration. The problem is eliminated by having initParCC ensure that all singletons (trees with only one vertex) are hooked to something or something is hooked to them (unless the vertex is isolated, i.e., is not in any edge of E). Here is the correct initialization.

Algorithm 14.7 Initialize for connected components

Input: Same as for Algorithm 14.6.

Output: The parent array represents a forest of in-trees of height 1, except for isolated nodes. That is, every vertex that is incident upon any edge in G is in a tree of height 1. Also every edge in the forest is between two vertices that are connected in G (by a path of length one or two).

```
initParCC(G, n, m)
    Compute v, i, and j from pid.
    parent[v] = v;
    if (ij ∈ E && i > j)  // Conditional singleton hooking
        hook(i, j);
    if (ij ∈ E && i is a singleton)  // Unconditional singleton hooking
        hook(i, j);
```

Figure 14.14 illustrates the action of the algorithm. The correctness of the algorithm is based on two theorems which in turn are proved in a series of lemmas. The algorithm itself is not very hard to understand if a few examples are worked through, so you should examine Figure 14.14 carefully before proceeding. (Notice how Algorithm 14.7 protects the trees rooted at 5 and 7 from the problem illustrated in Figure 14.13.)

Theorem 14.4 At any time during execution of Algorithm 14.6, the structure defined by the parent pointers is a forest.

Theorem 14.5 When Algorithm 14.6 terminates, the forest defined by the parent pointers consists only of stars, and the vertices in each star are exactly the vertices of a connected component of G.

The proofs of the theorems use the following lemmas.

Lemma 14.6 After the initialization, the structure defined by the parent pointers is a forest. All trees have at least two vertices, except for trees consisting of one vertex that is isolated in G (i.e., is a connected component of G).

Proof Exercise 14.22. □

Lemma 14.7 Conditional and unconditional star hooking never create new stars; that is, the resulting supervertex forms a tree of height at least 2.

Proof Singletons existing after the initialization will never be hooked to anything else. When the root of a tree with at least two nodes is attached to another tree, the new tree will have height at least 2. □

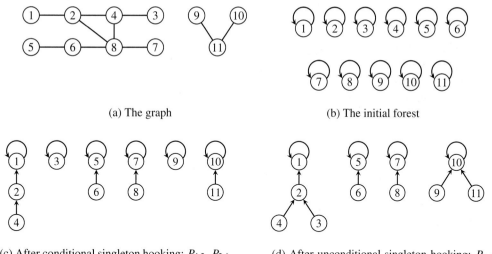

(a) The graph

(b) The initial forest

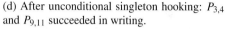

(c) After conditional singleton hooking: $P_{4,2}$, $P_{2,1}$, $P_{6,5}$, $P_{8,7}$, and $P_{11,10}$ succeeded in writing.

(d) After unconditional singleton hooking: $P_{3,4}$ and $P_{9,11}$ succeeded in writing.

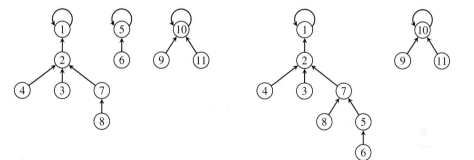

(e) After conditional star hooking: $P_{8,4}$ succeeded in writing.

(f) After unconditional star hooking: $P_{6,8}$ succeeded in writing.

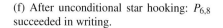

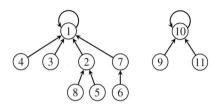

(g) After shortcutting

Figure 14.14   Illustration of the connected component algorithm: After part (g) completes, on the next iteration, no hooking is done. After shortcutting, both components will be stars. On the last iteration there will be no changes, and the algorithm will terminate.

Lemma 14.8   The unconditional star hooking step never hooks a star to another star.

Proof   Suppose it does. Then, at the beginning of the unconditional star hooking step there were two stars, S_1 and S_2, containing vertices i and j, respectively, such that ij is an edge in G. Since conditional star hooking does not create stars (Lemma 14.7), S_1 and S_2 were stars at the beginning of the conditional star hooking step. Either parent[i] > parent[j], in which case i's tree would have been hooked (to something) in the conditional star hooking step, or parent[j] > parent[i], in which case j's tree would have been hooked. Therefore either i or j is no longer in a star.   □

Proof of Theorem 14.4   The loop starts with trees (Lemma 14.6); we have to show that no step in the loop introduces a cycle. It is clear that shortcutting cannot introduce a cycle. In the hooking steps, if a star is hooked to some vertex in a nonstar, no cycle is introduced, because nonstars are not hooked to anything else. Since unconditional star hooking always hooks a star to a vertex in a nonstar (Lemma 14.8), it cannot introduce a cycle.

Conditional star hooking attaches the root of a star only to a smaller numbered vertex. Suppose v is attached to w in this step. If w is not the root of its tree, then w is not in a star, and *no* vertex in w's tree has its parent changed in this step. Therefore, if a cycle is formed in conditional star hooking, it must consist entirely of roots of stars. But conditional star hooking only attaches a root to a smaller numbered vertex, so no such cycle can be formed.   □

Lemma 14.9   Any star that exists at the end of the unconditional star hooking step must be an entire connected component.

Proof   By Lemma 14.8, the star was a star at the beginning of the unconditional star hooking step. But if any vertex in the star were adjacent (in G) to a vertex in any other tree, the unconditional star hooking step would have hooked the star to another tree, and it would no longer be a star.   □

Proof of Theorem 14.5   Since the vertices of G start out in disjoint trees, and two trees are hooked only if they contain vertices i and j that are adjacent, all the vertices in any one tree at any time are in the same connected component. The algorithm stops when shortcutting produces no changes. This can happen only when there are no vertices of distance 2 from their roots; that is, all vertices are in stars at the end of the unconditional star hooking step. By Lemma 14.9, each such star is an entire component.   □

14.6.3   PRAM Implementation of the Algorithm

Some processors have two "names." When we perform an operation for each vertex (say, shortcutting), we will use $P_1, \ldots, P_n$, referring to them as P_v. Because edges are processed in each "direction," it is convenient, for a while, to assume that there are at least $2m$ processors (though only m will be needed). When we perform an operation for each edge, we use the first $2m$ processors, referring to them by the names P_{ij}. Since operations on vertices and operations on edges are done in different instructions, each processor does only one thing at a time.

The PRAM algorithm assumes that the input is in the form of an array of edges in the graph G. Each edge appears as two consecutive array entries: the eth edge is in M[2*e] and M[2*e+1]. Processor P_{2e}, having an even pid, reads M[2*e], then M[2*e+1]. Processor P_{2e+1}, having an odd pid, reads M[2*e+1], then M[2*e]. If a processor reads i, then j, from then on it is the processor for the (oriented) edge (i, j). In the program we refer to this processor as P_{ij}. Thus every edge has two dedicated processors, one for each orientation.

The form of the input is not critical to the speed of the algorithm. If the input were provided as an adjacency matrix, we would have n^2 processors read the matrix entries in the first step. Those that read a zero would do no more work for edges. Other variations of the input format are also acceptable.

We present the algorithm again with more implementation detail. The important observation to make here is that each step of the algorithm can be implemented in a constant number of PRAM steps.

Algorithm 14.8   Parallel Connected Components

Input: An array of edges in the graph, each edge entered in two consecutive locations; n, the number of vertices, and m, the number of edges.

Output: A forest of directed trees of height at most 1, represented by the array parent, indexed by the vertices. Each tree contains the vertices of one connected component.

Remarks:

1. A Boolean array star is used to tell if a vertex is in a star; star[v] is true if and only if v is in a star. The subroutine computeStar is given in Algorithm 14.9.
2. Subroutine initParCC is given in Algorithm 14.7.
3. The hook operation is defined in Definition 14.4.
4. The shared Boolean variable *changed* tells whether or not the shortcutting step has made any changes at each iteration of the loop.

Procedure: See Figure 14.15. ∎

Observe that on every iteration of the loop, a processor P_{ij} tests to determine whether it should hook. Sometimes it may try to hook but fail because another processor succeeds in writing in parent[parent[i]]. Processor P_{ij} actually succeeds in hooking at most one time during the entire course of the algorithm. This observation suggests that it may be possible to speed up the algorithm by organizing the work of the processors in a more efficient way. In any case, as we will see, this algorithm runs in $O(\log n)$ time.

Determining If a Vertex Is in a Star

A vertex is not in a star if and only if one of the following conditions holds:

1. Its parent is not its grandparent,
2. It is the grandparent, but not the parent, of some other vertex,
3. Its parent has a nontrivial grandchild.

```
parConnectedComps(G, n, m)
    // Initialization
    Each processor reads n and m.
    Each processor computes a vertex number v from its pid:
        For P_k such that 1 ≤ k ≤ n, v = k;
        for P_k outside the above range, v = 0.
    Each processor reads a different oriented edge:
        for P_k, 0 ≤ k < 2m:
            If k is even, read M[k] into i and read M[k+1] into j.
            If k is odd, read M[k] into i and read M[k−1] into j.
        (Note that different processors are assigned to (i, j) and (j, i).)

    initParCC(G, n, m);

    changed = true;
    while (changed == true)
        // Conditional star hooking
        P_v executes computeStar(v).
        P_ij does:
        Read parent[i], parent[j], and star[i].
        if (star[i] == true && parent[i] > parent[j])
            hook(i, j).

        // Unconditional star hooking
        P_v executes computeStar(v).
        P_ij does:
        Read parent[i], parent[j], and star[i].
        if (star[i] == true && parent[i] ≠ parent[j])
            // j is not in i's star
            hook(i, j).

        // Shortcutting
        P_v does:
        Write false into changed.
        Read parent[v] and parent[parent[v]].
        if (parent[parent[v]] ≠ parent[v])
            Write parent[parent[v]] into parent[v].
            Write true into changed.
        All processors read changed to determine if they should stop.
```

Figure 14.15   Procedure for Algorithm 14.8

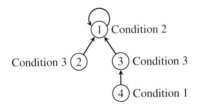

(a) How to tell each vertex is not in a star

Initial values of the star array

$\boxed{T}\boxed{T}\boxed{T}\boxed{T}$

If v's grandparent $\neq$ v's parent, star$[v]$ = F (condition 1).

$\boxed{T}\boxed{T}\boxed{T}\boxed{F}$

If v's grandparent $\neq$ v's parent, star$[v$'s grandparent$]$ = F (condition 2).

$\boxed{F}\boxed{T}\boxed{T}\boxed{F}$

(In general at this point, if the tree is not a star, only children of the root can still have star$[v]$ = T.)

If star$[v$'s parent$]$ is F, then star$[v]$ = F (condition 3).

$\boxed{F}\boxed{F}\boxed{F}\boxed{F}$

(b) The computation for the example in part (a)

Figure 14.16   Computation of the star array

Figure 14.16 illustrates all three cases and the computation of star. The computation is described in the following algorithm which clearly takes constant time.

Algorithm 14.9   Computation of star

Remarks: These steps are carried out by P_v (for $1 \leq v \leq n$).

```
computeStar(v)
     Write true into star[v].
     Read parent[v] and parent[parent[v]].
     if (parent[v] ≠ parent[parent[v]])
          Write false into star[v].
          Write false into star[parent[parent[v]]].
     Read star[parent[v]].
     if (star[parent[v]] == false)
          Write false into star[v].
```

14.6.4   Analysis

Each of the steps in the main loop of Algorithm 14.8 can be carried out in constant time by an Arbitrary-Write PRAM, so the number of iterations of the loop determines the order of the running time. All that remains is to show that the number of iterations is in $O(\log n)$.

Lemma 14.10   Let h be the height of a nonstar tree before the shortcutting step. After shortcutting, its height is at most $\lfloor (h+1)/2 \rfloor$.

Proof   The number of edges in a longest path from a leaf to the root is h. Every sequence of two edges, starting from the leaf, is replaced by one edge during shortcutting. If h is even, the path length after shortcutting will be exactly $h/2$. If h is odd, the path length after shortcutting will be $(h+1)/2$.   □

Definition 14.5

For any connected component C and $t \geq 0$, let $h_C(t)$ be the sum of the heights of all the trees in C at the end of the tth iteration of the **while** loop.   ∎

Lemma 14.11   For any connected component whose vertices do not form a star at the beginning of the tth iteration of the loop (for $t \geq 1$), $h_C(t) \leq (2/3)h_C(t-1)$.

Proof   Consider what happens to the trees of C during the tth iteration. Since a tree is never hooked to a leaf in the loop, the height of a tree that results from hooking is at most the sum of the heights of the two trees that were hooked. After shortcutting, each tree is at most two-thirds as high as it was before, so the sum of the heights is at most two-thirds what it was before.   □

Theorem 14.12   Algorithm 14.8 runs in $O(\log n)$ time in the worst case on an Arbitrary-Write PRAM with $\max(n, m)$ processors.

Proof   From Lemma 14.11, for any connected component C, we have

$$h_C(t-1) \geq \frac{3}{2}h_C(t).$$

Iterating this recurrence gives

$$h_C(0) \geq \left(\frac{3}{2}\right)^t h_C(t).$$

Since there are n vertices in G, $h_C(t) < n$ for all C and t, so $h_C(0) < n$. Let T be the number of the first iteration after which the vertices of C are in one star. Then $h_C(T) = 1$. So

$$n > h_C(0) \geq \left(\frac{3}{2}\right)^T h_C(T) = \left(\frac{3}{2}\right)^T,$$

that is,

$$n > \left(\frac{3}{2}\right)^T.$$

So

$$T < \lg(n)/\lg(3/2).$$

Since T is an integer, we conclude that after $\lfloor \lg(n)/\lg(3/2) \rfloor$ iterations, each component is a star. The algorithm does just one more iteration during which nothing changes, so the total number of iterations, and the running time of the algorithm, is in $O(\log n)$.

With only m processors, we give each processor responsibility for two (oriented) edges. Each hooking step, including the initialization, is performed twice (serially) by each processor, once for each of its edges. This obviously does not change the fact that each step takes constant time.   □

14.7 A Lower Bound for Adding *n* Integers

In this section we present a lower-bound argument for parallel computation. In earlier sections we saw that all variants of the PRAM can add n integers, or find the *or* of n bits, or find the maximum of n keys, in time $O(\log n)$. Some models can compute the *or* or the maximum in constant time, with enough processors. But we have not seen an algorithm to add n integers in $o(\log n)$ in any of these models. We will derive a lower bound that proves that this would be impossible on the Priority-Write PRAM, the strongest of the models we have considered. Let parAdd be some PRAM algorithm to add n integers that are located in M[0], ..., M[n−1], and leave the result in M[0]. We assume that each integer can be as many as n bits.

Several of our earlier lower-bound arguments used decision trees. The idea underlying those arguments was that there had to be enough branching in the tree, enough decisions, to distinguish inputs that should generate different outputs. A similar idea is used here. A PRAM for parAdd must do enough steps to distinguish between all possible outputs, which are all integers in the range 0 through $n(2^{n-1} - 1)$. Since the output is written in M[0], a PRAM must do enough steps so that any of the different values could be written in M[0]. Of course, for one particular input, a PRAM always writes exactly one specific value in M[0] at any step. Here we are considering the space of all inputs; we count all the different values a PRAM could write for all possible inputs.

Actually, to simplify the counting, we severely restrict the space of inputs, without restricting the range of outputs too much. We will consider only inputs in which the ith input integer (in M[i]) is either 2^i or 0. This gives us 2^n possible different inputs (remember, each input is a sequence of n integers), and *each input has a different sum*. That is, the ith bit from the right is 1 in the sum if and only if input M[i] contained 2^i. So there are also 2^n possible different outputs from this restricted space of inputs.

In fact, in many PRAM models one memory cell cannot store an n-bit integer, and the output would need to be written in more than one cell. For purposes of the lower-bound argument, all the cells needed to hold an n-bit integer are treated as a single cell.

The value in a memory cell depends on what the processors write (or do not write). What a processor writes depends on the "state" of the processor at the beginning of a step and what it reads from memory on that step. Think of the state of a processor as everything internal to the processor that affects its action (e.g., the values of all the variables in its local memory and its own index). The proof of the lower bound counts how many different states processors can be in, and how many values could be written in memory cells, after each step.

Theorem 14.13 Any Priority-Write PRAM with p processors that computes parAdd must do at least $\lg(n) + 1 - \lg \lg(4p)$ steps.

Proof We want to find answers to the following two questions:

1. How many different values can be in any particular memory cell M[i] after t steps? (The range of i is not restricted to the input cells).
2. How many different states can any particular processor P_i be in after t steps?

We define two sequences of numbers:

$$r_t = r_{t-1}s_{t-1} \quad \text{for } t > 0, \qquad r_0 = 1,$$
$$s_t = pr_t + s_{t-1} \quad \text{for } t > 0, \qquad s_0 = 2, \qquad (14.1)$$

where r_t and s_t have meanings as defined in the following lemma, and p is the number of processors. Here are the first few values in the sequences:

t	r_t	s_t
0	1	2
1	2	$2p + 2$
2	$2(2p + 2)$	$2p(2p + 2) + 2p + 2$

After proving some lemmas, we return to the proof of the lower-bound theorem.

Lemma 14.14 The number of distinct states a processor can be in after t steps (considering all inputs in the restricted class described above) is at most r_t. The number of distinct values that could be in a memory cell after t steps (considering all inputs in the restricted class) is at most s_t.

Proof We prove the lemma by induction on t. For $t = 0$ (that is, before the PRAM has executed any instructions), each processor can be in only one state, its initial state. Each memory cell M[i] contains one of two possible values: 0 and 2^i. Since $r_0 = 1$ and $s_0 = 2$, the basis for the induction is established.

Now, for $t > 0$, assume that after $t - 1$ steps a processor can be in any one of at most r_{t-1} states, and a memory cell can have one of at most s_{t-1} values. The new state of a processor after step t depends on the old state (the state after step $t - 1$) and the value read from memory by that processor on step t. Thus the number of possible states after step t is at most $r_{t-1}s_{t-1}$, which is r_t. On step t any processor can write in a particular memory cell, and a processor can write a different value for each state it could be in. That gives pr_t possible values, but it is also possible that no processor writes in the cell on this step, so any of the s_{t-1} values that could have been there before, may still be in the cell after step t. Thus the total number of possible values in a memory cell at the end of step t is $pr_t + s_{t-1}$, which is s_t. □

Lemma 14.15   For $t > 1$, $s_t \le s_{t-1}^2$.

Proof   Using Equation (14.1),

$$s_t = pr_t + s_{t-1} = pr_{t-1}s_{t-1} + s_{t-1} = s_{t-1}(pr_{t-1} + 1) \le s_{t-1}(pr_{t-1} + s_{t-2}) = s_{t-1}^2. \quad \square$$

Lemma 14.16   For $t \ge 1$, $s_t \le (4p)^{2^{t-1}}$.

Proof   For $t = 1$, $s_1 = pr_0s_0 + s_0 = 2p + 2 \le 4p$. For $t > 1$,

$$s_t \le s_{t-1}^2 \le \left((4p)^{2^{t-2}}\right)^2 = (4p)^{2^{t-1}}. \quad \square$$

Proof of Theorem 14.13   We observe that if any PRAM algorithm computes parAdd in T steps, then $s_T \ge 2^n$, because there are 2^n distinct outputs that could appear in M[0] when the algorithm terminates. So

$$2^n \le s_T \le (4p)^{2^{T-1}}.$$

Taking logs,

$$n \le 2^{T-1} \lg(4p).$$

Taking logs again,

$$\lg n \le T - 1 + \lg \lg(4p).$$

Therefore

$$T \ge \lg(n) + 1 - \lg \lg(4p). \quad \square$$

Corollary 14.17   Any CREW PRAM, Common-Write PRAM, Arbitrary-Write PRAM, or Priority-Write PRAM that computes parAdd must do at least $\Theta(\log n)$ steps if p is bounded by any polynomial in n.

Proof   Any program for either of these other models is also a valid program for the Priority-Write model, so the lower bound in Theorem 14.13 applies. Such a program does at least $\lg(n) + 1 - \lg \lg(4p)$ steps.

If p is bounded by a polynomial in n, then $\lg \lg(4p)$ is in $\Theta(\log \log n)$, and $\lg n + 1 - \lg \lg(4p)$ is in $\Theta(\log n)$. $\square$

Exercises

Section 14.3   Some Simple PRAM Algorithms

14.1   For Algorithm 14.1, what does P_1 compute in the first three iterations of the loop?

14.2   Modify Algorithm 14.1 so that it outputs an index of the largest key instead of the largest key itself. (The modified algorithm should not have write conflicts, and it should still do $\Theta(\log n)$ steps.)

14.3   Revise Algorithm 14.1 to use only one read/write step inside the loop, and to use only $n/2$ processors.

14.4   Describe a PRAM version of Transitive Closure by Shortcuts, Algorithm 9.1, that has no write conflicts and runs in $\Theta(\log^2 n)$ steps. How many processors does it use? *Hint*: Use the idea for matrix multiplication given after Problem 14.1 in Section 14.3.2.

Section 14.4   Handling Write Conflicts

14.5   Write a CREW PRAM algorithm to compute the sum of n integers in $O(\log n)$ time.

14.6   Show that the Boolean *and* of n bits can be computed in constant time by a Common-Write (or stronger) PRAM.

14.7   Show that the Boolean matrix product of two $n \times n$ Boolean matrices can be computed in constant time by a Common-Write (or stronger) PRAM. (The number of processors should be bounded by a polynomial in n.)

14.8   Describe a PRAM version of Transitive Closure by Shortcuts, Algorithm 9.1, that runs in $\Theta(\log n)$ steps in the Common-Write (or stronger) model. How many processors does it use? *Hint*: Combine the idea for matrix multiplication given after Problem 14.1 in Section 14.3.2 with the ideas of Algorithm 14.2 and Exercise 14.7.

14.9   Using the lower bound stated in Section 14.4 (right after Problem 14.3) for computing the *or* of n bits in the CREW model, show that computing the maximum of n integers requires at least $\Omega(\log n)$ time on a CREW PRAM. *Hint*: Use the *reduction technique*. Show that the known "hard" problem (*or* of n bits) can be transformed into the current problem (maximum of n integers) very quickly (in constant time) in such a way that the answer to the current problem immediately gives the answer to the "hard" problem. Now assume that the current problem can be solved in $o(\log n)$ time on a CREW PRAM, and derive a contradiction to the known lower bound. (The reduction technique was used extensively in Chapter 13 in a different context, but it is a very general technique, and it is not necessary to have read Chapter 13 to use it on this problem.)

14.10   Using the lower bound stated in Section 14.4 (right after Problem 14.3) for computing the *or* of n bits in the CREW model, show that Boolean matrix multiplication requires $\Omega(\log n)$ time on a CREW PRAM. *Hint*: See the hint for Exercise 14.9. In this case you need to be a little more creative with your reduction.

14.11   Would Algorithm 14.3 work correctly if we did not specify how k should be chosen when a processor compares two equal keys? Justify your answer with an argument or a counterexample.

14.12   Modify Algorithm 14.3 so that it outputs an index of the largest key instead of the largest key itself. (The modified algorithm should do only a constant number of steps.)

Section 14.5   Merging and Sorting

14.13   Give a PRAM implementation of Insertion Sort for n keys that runs in $O(n)$ time steps. (You can use any PRAM variation, but specify which one.)

14.14   Show that the position of an X element and a Y element cannot be the same in the output step of Algorithm 14.4.

14.15   Modify the parallel merge algorithm (Algorithm 14.4) to merge two sorted arrays of n and m keys, respectively. The indexing used in Algorithm 14.4 was designed specifically so that parMerge could be used in the recursive sorting algorithm, parMergeSort (Algorithm 14.5). For this exercise, simplify the indexing by writing the merge algorithm for arrays indexed $0, \ldots, n - 1$ and $0, \ldots, m - 1$.
How many steps does the revised algorithm take?

14.16   Describe an algorithm to sort n keys in $O(\log n)$ steps on an CREW PRAM. The number of processors may be greater than n, but it should be bounded by a polynomial in n. *Hint*: Start by finding the ranks of all elements, in parallel. You might find Exercise 14.5 helpful.

⋆ **14.17**   Give an algorithm to merge two sorted arrays of n keys each in constant time on a CREW PRAM. The number of processors may be greater than n, but it should be bounded by a polynomial in n.

Section 14.6   Finding Connected Components

⋆ **14.18**   Describe how to combine the parallel transitive closure algorithm in Exercise 14.4 or 14.8 with other parallel algorithms in the chapter to produce an algorithm for connected components, using n^3 processors on a graph of n vertices. The output should be an array leader[v] that contains the vertex with the least index of any vertex in the connected component. Thus leader[v] = leader[w] if and only if v and w are in the same connected component. (Note that the leader array can also be interpreted as an in-forest of trees with height at most one, just as the parent array is in Algorithm 14.8.)

a.   How fast does your algorithm run in the Common-Write model?

b.   How fast does your algorithm run in the CREW model? Do any different algorithms need to be used as subroutines in the CREW model? Which ones?

14.19   The connected component algorithm (Algorithm 14.8) does not tell us the number of connected components in the input graph G. Write a parallel algorithm to determine how many connected components G has. Your algorithm should run in $O(\log n)$ time.

14.20   Using the trees in Figure 14.12(c), show the result of hook(7, 11) and (separately) show the result of hook(8, 11).

14.21   In the example in Figure 14.14, when more than one processor tried to write in one memory cell at the same time, we made an arbitrary choice as to which one succeeded.

Redo the example making a different valid choice at each step at which there was a write conflict.

14.22   Prove Lemma 14.6.

14.23   Suppose that in the proof of Lemma 14.8 S_1's root is larger than S_2's root. Would S_1 necessarily have been hooked to S_2? Why?

14.24   We showed how to determine if a vertex is in a star. Give a method for determining if a vertex is a singleton (in constant time), for the initialization steps.

14.25   Show that when there are write conflicts, the arbitrary choice of which processor succeeds in writing can have an extreme effect on the number of iterations of the loop in Algorithm 14.8. Specifically, describe a connected graph G with n vertices (for general n) such that it is possible that all the vertices will be in one star after the initialization steps, but it is also possible that the number of iterations of the loop will be in $\Theta(\log n)$ for this graph.

14.26   Let G be the input graph for Algorithm 14.8. Let S be the set of edges (i, j) for which P_{ij} succeeds in performing a hook(i, j) operation. In other words, $(i, j) \in S$ if and only if P_{ij} is the processor that actually writes in parent[i], not simply one of perhaps several processors that try. Prove that S is a spanning tree collection (Definition 8.4) for G.

14.27   Show how to modify Algorithm 14.8 to produce a spanning tree collection for the input graph G. The output may be in the form of a Boolean matrix stc indexed by the pairs (i, j), where stc[i][j] = **true** indicates that the edge ij is in the spanning tree collection. (See Exercise 14.26.)

★ **14.28**   This exercise investigates whether a small change in Algorithm 14.8 produces an algorithm that will find a minimum spanning tree collection for a weighted graph.

   The initialization step of Algorithm 14.8 is modified so that, before each processor reads an edge from the input list, the edges are sorted in nondecreasing order by weight. We assume that each processor reads the edge from the position in the input list that corresponds to its own index. Thus for $k_1 < k_2$, the weight of P_{k_1}'s edge is less than or equal to the weight of P_{k_2}'s edge. The revised algorithm will be run on a Priority-Write PRAM. In this model, as described in Section 14.4, when more than one processor tries to write in the same shared memory location at the same time, the processor with the lowest index wins.

   Assume that the algorithm has been modified as indicated in Exercise 14.27 to produce a spanning tree collection.

   Either prove that the spanning tree collection produced is always a minimum spanning tree collection, or show an example where it is not. In the latter case, try to make whatever further modifications are needed in the algorithm so that it always produces a minimum spanning tree collection.

Additional Problems

14.29 The n-bit unary representation of an integer k is a sequence of k ones followed by $n - k$ zeros. For each of the following problems you should use at most n processors.

a. Show that a PRAM (CREW, Common-Write, or stronger model) can read an integer k between 0 and n from M[0] and convert k to its unary representation in one step. (The output is to go in cells M[0], . . ., M[n−1].)

b. Show that a Priority-Write PRAM with n processors can read the unary representation of an integer k from cells M[0], . . ., M[n−1] and write k in M[0] in one step.

c. Show that a CREW PRAM can solve the problem in part (b) in two steps.

★ **14.30** Suppose you have a sorted array of n keys in memory and p processors, where p is small compared to n. Give a CREW PRAM algorithm for searching the array for a key x. How many steps does your algorithm do? *Hint*: Use a generalization of binary search. You may find Exercise 14.29(c) helpful. Your search algorithm should do $\Theta(\log(n)/\log(p + 1))$ steps in the worst case.

14.31 Go through the earlier chapters of this book and pick out any algorithm that has a natural parallel version. Write the parallel algorithm and tell how many processors and time steps it uses. (Choose an algorithm for which the running time of the parallel version is of lower order than the sequential version.)

14.32 Make a list of the problems covered in this chapter that are in the class $\mathcal{NC}$ (defined in Section 14.2). Are there any algorithms in this chapter that are not $\mathcal{NC}$ algorithms?

Notes and References

The PRAM model was presented (in slightly different forms) in Fortune and Wyllie (1978) and Goldschlager (1978). The class $\mathcal{NC}$ was defined and named by Steven Cook (1985) as an abbreviation for "Nick's class." The name refers to Nick Pippenger (1979). Pippenger studied the same class of problems, but in terms of circuit complexity rather than parallel computation. The class has several other equivalent definitions.

Section 14.5 is based on Shiloach and Vishkin (1981). Their paper gives algorithms for sorting (and several other problems) in which the number of processors is smaller than the number of keys. It also contains the $O(\log \log n)$ algorithm for finding the largest of n keys mentioned in Section 14.4.2 and a solution to Exercise 14.29(c).

The general strategy of the connected component algorithm presented in Section 14.6 is from Hirschberg (1976). The fast version presented here is based on Shiloach and Vishkin (1982) and Awerbuch and Shiloach (1983, 1987). The Awerbuch and Shiloach papers also contain a parallel algorithm for finding a minimum spanning tree collection (Definition 8.4). The lower bound in Section 14.7 is based on Beame (1986), where more general results of a similar nature are derived.

For those who wish to read further, the bibliography includes a sampling of other papers: Cook, Dwork, and Reischuk (1986) on upper and lower bounds for several problems considered in Sections 14.3 and 14.5; Chandra, Stockmeyer, and Vishkin (1984) on a number of interesting problems and the relations between their parallel complexity; Kruskal (1983) and Snir (1985) on parallel searching (including the solution to Exercise 14.30); Batcher (1968) on sorting networks; Landau and Vishkin (1986) on approximate string matching; and Tarjan and Vishkin (1985) on biconnected components of graphs. Akl (1985) is a book on parallel sorting (using various models of parallel computation); Richards (1986), a bibliography on parallel sorting, contains nearly 400 entries. Quinn and Deo (1984) is a survey of parallel graph algorithms. JáJá (1992) is a text on parallel algorithms using the PRAM model.

Greenlaw, Hoover, and Ruzzo (1995) survey known limits to parallel computation, in terms of the class of $\mathcal{P}$-complete problems (not to be confused with $\mathcal{NP}$-complete). The question of whether $\mathcal{P}$-complete problems are separate from $\mathcal{NC}$ is a long-standing open question, and is the parallel analog of the question of whether the $\mathcal{NP}$-complete class is separate from $\mathcal{P}$ for serial computation (see Chapter 13).

Another important model for parallel computation requires processors to be arranged in a plane and only connected to their neighbors; there is no shared memory. This model is considered to be good for studying the capabilities of VLSI (very large scale integration) chips, and is generally considered to be more realistic than the PRAM model. Ullman (1984) surveys theoretical results for this kind of model. Hambrusch and Simon (1985) give some results on the connected component problem in this model. Parberry (1987) surveys several models of parallel computation.

Java Examples and Techniques

A.1 Introduction

The purpose of this appendix is to help readers get Java programs working to implement and test some algorithms. As you read it, you will see that many aspects are not thoroughly explained, the reasons for the choices we made might not be given, and the alternatives are not mentioned. Where we have presented a "cookbook" solution, it can be used intact for its purpose, and does not require modification from one program to another, or the modifications are very straightforward, such as a simple name substitution. Readers wishing to learn about *Java* should plan to consult other sources.

The programming language Java became famous because it was adaptable to the special needs of Internet programming. But Java was designed first as a general-purpose programming language, and that is how we treat it. However, Java is closely linked to the Internet even if you do not plan to use it for an Internet application, because the Internet is the primary source for much of the information about the language. Here are some Internet sites (URLs) for information about Java, release 1.2:

http://java.sun.com/products/jdk/1.2/docs
http://java.sun.com/products/jdk/1.2/docs/api
http://java.sun.com/docs/books/jls/html

There are many books about Java, but they rarely cover the whole language, let alone all the packages that are available. However, the reference manual is Gosling, Joy, and Steele (1996).

All code in this appendix is automatically translated from tested code and is protected under the copyright covering this book. However, this does not ensure that it is free of errors, and the author and publisher make no expressed or implied warranty of any kind and assume no responsiblity for errors or omissions.

Java restores many of the restrictions and checks that are in Pascal, and are omitted from C and C++. Pascal was designed as a teaching language; C and C++ are designed as production languages. To an expert programmer, these restrictions might be an annoyance and the checks might be unnecessary, but for most students learning to program, the restrictions help to avoid errors and the checks help to detect other errors. For example, in Java, if you use an out-of-range index on an array, the system catches it; this is like Pascal and different from C and C++. In Java, you cannot create a pointer to another object, such as an integer, nor can you add to a pointer, nor can you assign an arbitrary value to a pointer. None of these operations are available in Pascal, but all of them are available in C and C++. With currently available compilers, a program written in Java runs much more slowly than a program written in C. For student exercises, this is usually not a big concern. Having a program that runs correctly at any speed is usually the primary goal.

Even if you need "production" software, you may find it beneficial to do the first implementation in Java, because you will have it working much sooner. This is called *rapid prototyping*. The logic and data structures are checked out in the language that provides the most help. Then the working procedures are recoded into a more efficient language.

One purpose of this appendix is to cover enough material on Java so readers can implement the algorithms in the book. There are annoying details like input and output that are necessary for a real program. Many Java packages throw exceptions, which must be handled, whether you are interested in exceptions or not (we're not).

A second purpose is to introduce a few features of Java that we avoided in the book in order not to distract attention from the algorithmic issues. These are features that most programmers will wish to use if they do serious programming in Java. We will stick to simplicity, even so, and avoid many of the more "interesting" features.

A.2 A Java Main Program

We begin by showing a main program in Figure A.1. This program must be in a file named graph.java because main is in a class named graph. The file can be compiled by the command "javac graph.java." The program would be executed by the command "java graph *inputFile*." The commands to compile and execute are based on a Unix[1] environment. Alternatively, invoke the Java debugger with jdb and then type "run graph *inputFile*."

The program reads a file and builds the adjacency list representation (see Section 7.2.3) of the graph defined in the file. The file is expected to have the number of vertices on the first line and to have one edge per line after that. Each edge is specified by the two vertices, from and to, and possibly followed by a weight, which is floating point. The input format is flexible in that there may be extra spaces or tabs. After the data structure is built, its contents are printed; this would not be practical for a large graph.

This is a typical main procedure. It calls subroutines in the LoadGraph and InputLib classes, which are shown in this appendix. It first checks if the parameter *inputFile* is present, and if not, it issues a usage message and exits. Otherwise, it uses the facilities of InputLib (Appendix A.3) to obtain a BufferedReader object, inbuf, for the input file. The BufferedReader class is a standard Java class. The InputLib class conceals several technicalities that are needed for accessing the input file, and provides procedures for opening, closing, and reading lines of a file. Next, the first line of the input file is read, using getLine, but this only returns a **String**, so another procedure, parseN, is needed to extract the integer from the string. This integer is the number of vertices in the graph represented in the input file. Most of the real work is accomplished by calling the subroutines initEdges and loadEdges.

Output is accomplished with the standard Java procedures System.out.println and System.err.println (used in some subroutines for error output). Most details of standard Java procedures and classes are omitted from this appendix; see the Internet sites mentioned for complete information, or a book on Java. The println procedure simply prints a **String**, followed by a newline (print would print the string only). It is the programmer's job to assemble the information into a string, but this is made fairly easy by the use of "+" to concatenate strings, and the fact that Java automatically converts numbers into type **String** when they appear in an expression that requires that type. It is normally necessary to write a toString procedure to convert objects in programmer-defined classes into strings, because the Java default is not very meaningful. But Java finds the toString for the class

---

[1] Unix is a trademark of AT&T Bell Laboratories.

```java
import java.io.*;

class graph
    {
    public static
    void main(String[] argv)
        {
        int m, n;
        IntList[] adjVertices;

        if (argv.length == 0)
            {
            System.out.println("Usage: java graph input.data");
            System.exit(0);
            }
        String infile = argv[0];
        BufferedReader inbuf = InputLib.fopen(infile);
        System.out.println("Opened " + infile + " for input.");
        String line = InputLib.getLine(inbuf);
        n = LoadGraph.parseN(line);
        System.out.println("n = " + n);

        adjVertices = LoadGraph.initEdges(n);
        m = LoadGraph.loadEdges(inbuf, adjVertices);
        InputLib.fclose(inbuf);
        System.out.println("m = " + m);

        for (int i = 1; i <= n; i ++)
            System.out.println(i + "\t" + adjVertices[i]);
        return;
        }
    }
```

Figure A.1 Java program graph.java: See Figures A.2–A.4 for the LoadGraph class. See Figures A.5 and A.6 for the InputLib class.

automatically through inheritance mechanisms; even though the type of adjVertices[i] is IntList in the last println, it is printed intelligibly because the IntList class has a toString method. See Section A.6 for more details.

The LoadGraph class has several procedures. The main subroutines are initEdges and loadEdges, shown in Figure A.2. The latter builds adjacency lists in a simple loop, but some not so trivial details of getting the numbers out of the input line are relegated to the subroutine parseEdge. An organizer class Edge is defined to communicate between loadEdges and parseEdge; it will be discussed shortly. In the loadEdges loop, the cons

```
import java.io.*;
import java.util.*;

public class LoadGraph
    {
    public static
    IntList[] initEdges(int n)
        {
        IntList[] adjVertices = new IntList[n+1];
        for (int i = 1; i <= n; i ++)
            adjVertices[i] = IntList.nil;
        return adjVertices;
        }

    public static
    int loadEdges(BufferedReader inbuf, IntList[] adjVertices)
        {
        int num;
        String line;

        num = 0;
        line = InputLib.getLine(inbuf);
        while (line != null)
            {
            Edge e = parseEdge(line);
            adjVertices[e.from] = IntList.cons(e.to, adjVertices[e.from]);
            num ++;
            line = InputLib.getLine(inbuf);
            }
        return num;
        }
```

Figure A.2 The LoadGraph class, part 1

function makes a new list by attaching e.to to the front of the old adjacency list of e.from; the new list is then assigned as the adjacency list of e.from.

The procedures parseEdge in Figure A.3 and parseN in Figure A.4 demonstrate the use of several Java features. Let's step through the process in parseEdge. It needs to extract information from line, construct an Edge, newE, and return it. The Edge organizer class has three instance fields (see Figure A.4). Notice that we use **double** rather than **float**; the text uses **float** for readability, but **double** is usually preferred unless space is really an issue, because of its greater precision.

First we construct sTok, giving it the line we want to parse, getting an object in the stringTokenizer class. Now we can apply methods of that class to get the words (tokens)

```
static
Edge  parseEdge(String line)
    {
    StringTokenizer  sTok = new StringTokenizer(line);
    int  numWords = sTok.countTokens();
    if (numWords < 2 || numWords > 3)
        {
        System.err.println("Bad edge: " + line);
        System.exit(1);
        }

    Edge  newE = new Edge();
    newE.from = Integer.parseInt(sTok.nextToken());
    newE.to = Integer.parseInt(sTok.nextToken());
    if (numWords == 3)
        newE.weight = Double.parseDouble(sTok.nextToken());
    else
        newE.weight = 0.0;
    return newE;
    }
```

Figure A.3   The LoadGraph class continued, part 2: Note that Edge is an inner class.

on line, and other information. We check that the line has the required number of words with the countTokens method. Then the nextToken method repeatedly extracts the next word, skipping over spaces and tabs as necessary. But nextToken returns a string and we need integers and doubles.

The primitive types **int** and **double** are not classes, but Java provides classes **Integer** and **Double** (and several others) to allow integers and doubles to enjoy the facilities of objects. The **Integer** class provides the static method parseInt to convert a string into an **int**. Similarly, **Double** provides parseDouble to convert a string into a **double**. Other primitive types can be converted from strings also.

The organizer class Edge is defined in Figure A.4 as a subclass of Organizer so it can inherit the copy1level function, which is explained in Appendix A.7. We follow the rule that any *inner* class should be declared static (Section 1.2.1); the reasons are too technical for this appendix.

A Word about Visibility

As we mentioned in the early chapters, Java gives programmers a lot of control over *visibility*: which program elements are accessible from others. For getting a program working to implement or test algorithms, you probably do not want to worry about this any more than is necessary. If all your code is assembled in one directory, and you do not use any **package** declarations, then all this code is in something called the "unnamed package,"

```
public static class Edge extends Organizer
    {
    int from, to;
    double weight;

    public static Edge copy(Edge oldE)
        { return (Edge) copy1level(oldE); }
    }

public static
int parseN(String line)
    {
    StringTokenizer sTok = new StringTokenizer(line);
    if (sTok.countTokens() != 1)
        {
        System.err.println("Bad line 1: " + line);
        System.exit(1);
        }

    int n = Integer.parseInt(sTok.nextToken());
    return n;
    }
}
```

Figure A.4 The LoadGraph class continued, part 3

and all classes and members of classes are accessible from each other by default, without needing to declare them public.

To use classes defined in a different package, you need to **import** them (except for the package java.lang, which is considered so fundamental that its import is not required). The various figures show that we have imported the Java packages io and util in files where one or more of their classes are used.

In this appendix we have declared classes **public** where they are of general use, and we have declared members **public** where they are intended to be accessed from other classes. We have declared members **protected** where they are intended to be accessed from subclasses only. However, a **protected** member is still accessible everywhere in its own package. We could have declared members **private** (the third visibility category) to prevent their access outside of the class, but did not. These examples illustrate the appropriate declarations for breaking the files up into various packages. However, anyone wishing to develop packages should consult other sources for details. All **public** and **protected** declarations can be omitted if all files are in the same directory. The **static** declarations are necessary, though.

```java
import java.io.*;
import java.util.*;

public class InputLib
    {
    static class InputError extends Error   // or extends RuntimeException
        {
        public InputError(String s) { super(s); }
        }

    /** fopen opens infile or System.in if infile == "-". */
    public static
    BufferedReader fopen(String infile)
        {
        BufferedReader inbuf;
        try
            {
            InputStream instream;
            if (infile.equals("-"))
                instream = System.in;
            else
                instream = new FileInputStream(infile);

            InputStreamReader in = new InputStreamReader(instream);
            inbuf = new BufferedReader(in);
            }
        catch (java.io.IOException e)
            {
            throw new InputError(e.getMessage());
            }

        return inbuf;
        }
```

Figure A.5   The InputLib class, part 1

A.3   A Simple Input Library

The InputLib class (see Figures A.5 and A.6) is a technical class that we want to use often and think about seldom. Readers will have to consult other sources to get explanations of most of the internals. However, using it is straightforward. We call fopen with the name of the input file, or the string "-" to read standard input. It returns a BufferedReader object for that file. This is something we don't want to look at too closely, so we just pass it to another

```
/** fclose closes inbuf, which fopen returned earlier. */
public  static
void  fclose(BufferedReader inbuf)
    {
    try
        {
        inbuf.close();
        }
    catch (java.io.IOException e)
        {
        throw new InputError(e.getMessage());
        }
    }


/** getLine reads and returns the next line from inbuf.
 * It returns null on EOF; it's OK to keep calling
 * after EOF was reached.
 * Note that getLine returns a String with no CR, whether
 * the line ends with a CR or ends via EOF.
 * Thus it is not quite like fgets() in C.
 */
public  static
String  getLine(BufferedReader inbuf)
    {
    String line;
    try
        {
        line = inbuf.readLine();
        }
    catch (java.io.IOException e)
        {
        throw new InputError(e.getMessage());
        }

    return line;
    }

}
```

Figure A.6 The InputLib class, part 2

function, getLine, to read a line of data from the file. We saw an example in Figure A.2. Refer to the discussion of parseEdge in Appendix A.2 for information on extracting data fields from this line. If there is nothing to read, getLine returns **null**; otherwise it returns the next line as one string. Finally, fclose closes the file.

A line-oriented format is most common for data, and we recommend it because it helps to verify that the data has the correct format. Frustrating hours can be spent looking for a program bug that is really just a missing or extra field in the input data. However, text input (like program code) is usually *not* line oriented, and getLine would usually not be the best choice for reading such input.

There is one technique that we want to look at in some detail. Java provides for *exceptions* and *errors*. If a class "throws an exception" and you want to use this class, you are required to "handle" the exception. Usually you don't want to bother. In that case, what most sources recommend is that you just throw it to your caller. But then that caller has to handle it, or throw it, and so on.

The interesting fact is that you *are not* required to "handle" an *error*. So our recommendation for situations where you want to use a standard Java package, and it throws an exception that you do not want to worry about, is to convert the *exception* to an *error* at the lowest level possible, so it doesn't clutter up your higher level code. This technique is demonstrated in Figures A.5 and A.6, using **try** and **catch**. Procedures are *allowed* to handle errors (also with **try** and **catch**); they just aren't *required* to do so. The system will catch the error if no other procedure does; your program will not sail on into oblivion. So these procedures catch the exceptions thrown by BufferedReader, and convert them into errors, so their clients can either ignore them or catch them, as they please.

RuntimeException may be used instead of Error.

A.4 Documenting Java Classes

Java provides a special comment format for the documentation of a class, including the preconditions and postconditions of its methods. Comments beginning with "/**" begin a javadoc comment. Readers may look through the figures of this appendix and see several examples. This facility is particularly useful for documenting an abstract data type (ADT), because one of the features of ADT design is that the implementation should be encapsulated and should *not* be examined to determine how the ADT works.

The javadoc program extracts these comments, as well as prototypes of the public functions and procedures, from the java file in which the ADT class is implemented, and formats this information in html. It can then be read with a Web browser or other html reader. If the class has public instance fields, declarative information about these is also extracted. There are conventions for special formating of parameters, and other ways to dress up the output; refer to javadoc documentation for details. Since there are no header files in Java, as there are in C and C++, the best way for a person to get information about a class is often to read the files produced by javadoc on that class.

The placement of comments relative to the material that they are documenting may be somewhat unintuitive. The comment must *precede* whatever it is related to. Thus a comment about a procedure must be placed before the procedure header, or javadoc will not associate it with that procedure. You might want to repeat the name of the procedure or data field at the beginning of a long comment, so the reader of the code knows what the comment is about without trying to skip to the end of it and see what's there. There is no problem after it has been processed through javadoc; then the procedure name appears first and the comments follow.

A.5 Generic Order and the "Comparable" Interface

Wouldn't it be nice if we could write one sorting procedure and it could sort a set of objects from any class? Well, we can go a long way in that direction by using the **Comparable** interface. We can think of an "interface" as a sort of generic class name. Various classes may "implement" an interface by supplying methods with the names and type signatures required for that interface. Other procedures, unrelated to that class, can invoke the methods in the interface, and get whatever method each class implements. We use the important **Comparable** interface as an example. Many standard Java classes implement the **Comparable** interface, such as **Integer**, **Double**, **Float**, and **String**. First we show an example class that *uses* the **Comparable** interface as though it were a class, to provide a generic capability. Then we show another class that *implements* the **Comparable** interface. A test program is included.

Figures A.7 and A.8 show a class named Sort. This class defines five **boolean** functions for generic comparisons, named less, lessEq, eq, greater, and greaterEq. It also defines a function insert1 that uses lessEq to insert a new element into a List in sorted order, without knowing anything about the class of the element. This will only work if the elements already in the list are of the same class as the new element being inserted, and that class implements the **Comparable** interface. In this context we see that the word **Comparable** is used as though it were a class name. The method compareTo returns an **int**, and appears to be a method in a class named **Comparable**.

The code for the List class is not shown, but it is similar to that for the IntList class, which is given in Section A.6. The logic of the insert1 method was discussed in Example 2.1.

If you would like procedures to be able to use the facilities of the Sort class on a class that you are defining, then you should specify that your class implements the **Comparable** interface. We show an example in Figure A.9, where the WgtEdge class is defined. Notice that the **class** statement includes the phrase "**implements Comparable**," indicating that this class intends to participate in that interface.

The WgtEdge class has some similarities to the Edge class in Figure A.4, but it is considerably richer, and therefore is not an organizer class. We have not emphasized nondefault constructors, but that is what the two methods named WgtEdge (the same as the class name) are. Notice that there is no return type and no return statement, but a new WgtEdge object is returned implicitly. The *use* of a Java constructor is always preceded by the **new** operator, as illustrated in Figure A.10. Defining two methods with the same name and the same return type, but different parameter type signatures is called *overloading*. It can be convenient, but indiscriminate overloading can defeat error detection through type

```java
public class Sort
    {
    public  static
    boolean  less(Comparable x, Comparable y)
        { return (x.compareTo(y) < 0); }

    public  static
    boolean  lessEq(Comparable x, Comparable y)
        { return (x.compareTo(y) <= 0); }

    public  static
    boolean  eq(Comparable x, Comparable y)
        { return (x.compareTo(y) == 0); }

    public  static
    boolean  greater(Comparable x, Comparable y)
        { return (x.compareTo(y) > 0); }

    public  static
    boolean  greaterEq(Comparable x, Comparable y)
        { return (x.compareTo(y) >= 0); }
```

Figure A.7   The Sort class illustrates use of the Comparable interface as though it were a class. This figure contains part 1.

checking—although the programmer wrote something that was not intended, it matches *some* version of the method and the semantic error goes undetected.

The crux of implementing the **Comparable** interface is to provide the compareTo method. The expression x.compareTo(y) performs a three-way comparison between x and y and returns a negative integer if $x < y$, a positive integer if $x > y$, and 0 if $x = y$. (See the methods less, lessEq, and so on, in Figure A.7, which interpret the return values.) The comparison is based on whatever order the programmer wants to define on objects in this class. There are some technicalities involved. First, we need to typecast the parameter e2 from **Object** into WgtEdge, so we can access its WgtEdge fields. That is what the expression "((WgtEdge)e2)" is doing. Notice that the outer parentheses are needed to get the correct precedence with respect to the following dot operator. (Suppose the object is not really a WgtEdge and does not have those fields? That would be a run-time error, and Java would stop execution.)

Now we want to delegate the decision to the compareTo method of the **Double** class, rather than figure it out independently. Keep in mind that **Double** is a class, while **double** is a primitive type. Primitive types do not have methods, so the **Double** class provides methods and other object-oriented facilities for objects that are surrogates for doubles; this

```
/** Return new List with newElement inserted in order. */

public static
List insert1(Comparable newElement, List oldList)
    {
    List ans;

    if (oldList == List.nil)
        ans = List.cons(newElement, oldList);
    else
        {
        Comparable oldFirst = (Comparable)List.first(oldList);

        if (lessEq(newElement, oldFirst))
            ans = List.cons(newElement, oldList);
        else
            {
            List oldRest = List.rest(oldList);
            List newRest = insert1(newElement, oldRest);
            ans = List.cons(oldFirst, newRest);
            }
        }
    return ans;
    }
}
```

Figure A.8   The Sort class illustrates use of the Comparable interface as though it were a class. This figure contains part 2, the final part.

is often called a *wrapper* class. So we create two wrapper objects in the **Double** class, using the weights of the edges to be compared. Ultimately, our compareTo on objects of type WgtEdge simply runs compareTo for **Double** on the weight fields, and returns that result.

Our implementation allows ties—two objects compare as equal if they have equal weights, although their other fields might differ. The Java documentation recommends, but does not require, that such ties be broken. For simplicity we have not broken the ties.

A test program to exercise the Sort and WgtEdge classes is shown in Figure A.10. It calls methods in the Sort class with three different classes of parameter, requiring three different comparison methods, but they all fall under the umbrella of **Comparable**, so only one greater method, for example, is sufficient. Without the interface, the Sort class would need three greater methods with different type signatures, and each would require its own code. Moreover, the support would be limited to those three types; if any new class were to be supported, another procedure with a new type signature would need to be added.

```java
public class WgtEdge implements Comparable
    {
    public int from, to;
    public double weight;

    public
    WgtEdge(int f, int t, double w)
        { from = f; to = t; weight = w; }
    public
    WgtEdge(int f, int t)
        { from = f; to = t; weight = 0.0; }
    public
    int compareTo(Object e2)
        {
        Double e1wgt = new Double(weight);
        Double e2wgt = new Double( ((WgtEdge)e2).weight );
        return e1wgt.compareTo(e2wgt);
        }
    public
    String toString()
        { return "(" + from + ", " + to + ", " + weight + ")" ; }
    }
```

Figure A.9 The WgtEdge class implements the **Comparable** interface and supplies the required compareTo method for that interface. It also has two nondefault constructors and a toString method.

```
public class testSort
    {
    public static void main(String argv[])
        {
        Integer  i88 = new Integer(88), i66 = new Integer(66);
        WgtEdge  e88 = new WgtEdge(1, 2, 88.0);
        WgtEdge  e66 = new WgtEdge(2, 3, 66.0);
        WgtEdge  e54 = new WgtEdge(1, 4, −54.0);
        WgtEdge  e33 = new WgtEdge(4, 2, 33.0);
        List  x1;

        x1 = List.cons(e88, List.nil);
        x1 = List.cons(e66, x1);
        x1 = List.cons(e54, x1);
        System.out.println(x1);
        System.out.println(e33);
        List x2 = Sort.insert1(e33, x1);
        System.out.println(x2);
        System.out.println(Sort.greater("abc", "ab"));
        System.out.println(Sort.greater(i66, i88));
        }
    }
```

Figure A.10   The file testSort.java tests the functions of the Sort class that use the **Comparable** interface.

A.6   Subclasses Extend the Capability of Their Superclass

This section demonstrates some Java features involving subclasses and inheritance. The explanations are brief, and these are involved subjects. We will show a dynamic (opposite of static) method, toString, which is useful for printing lists, and we will define an extended class, or subclass, of IntList that has a new list operation. A short test program is included.

One aspect of subclasses that seems backwards at first is that a subclass has *more* capabilities than its superclass, which is the class from which it is derived, or which it extends. To see why this really makes sense, let's think of the classes *person*, *athlete*, and *star athlete*. Athletes are a subclass of people, because some people are not athletes, while all athletes are people. However, athletes have capabilities that not every person has. Similarly, star athletes are a subclass of athletes, but have more capabilities. This is not to say that some individual person does not have capabilities that star athletes do not have; it only means that any capability present in *every* person is present in every star athlete.

Figure A.11 repeats the class definitions for IntList as they were given in Section 2.3.2, but with comments removed. There is one change: The instance fields are declared **protected**, so they can be accessed by subclasses. The toString method is defined next, to convert an IntList object to a **String**. Java converts any object into a **String** if it appears in a context that requires that type. Java supplies a default method named toString that is inherited by every class. A class may *override* the default by defining its own toString method, and that is what we do in Figure A.11. A method in a subclass *overrides* a method in a superclass when it has the same name, the same return type, and the same parameter type signature.

Notice that toString is a "wrapper" for the recursive function toStringR. Java automatically converts the elements of the list (returned by first) into strings using the toString method for that object's class, so this technique works for lists of other types of elements; it is not specialized for integers.

Now let's say we want to add a new list operation, but want to leave IntList intact. We can *extend* IntList instead, to a subclass that we'll call IntListA, and define the new operation in IntListA. Then IntList is called the *superclass* of IntListA. The new operation is a manipulation procedure, append1, so IntListA is no longer a nondestructive class. The intent is that append1 puts a new element at the *end* of an existing nonempty list. In terms of the implementation, the list object whose next field is nil is modified. The new next field is a list of one element, the new element. However, the next field is not part of the ADT interface, and so the logical specification of what append1 does is stated in terms of the access functions, which *are* in the interface. Figure A.12 shows the specifications as javadoc comments, and shows the necessary code.

Unfortunately, it is necessary to redefine **static** members of IntList if we want their result type to be IntListA. The result type is the type of a field or the return type of a function. This applies to nil, rest, and cons in this case. Notice, for nil and rest, the expression "(IntListA)." This is called a *type cast*, or simply a *cast*. In our examples it changes the type from the superclass IntList to the subclass IntListA. The situation for cons is more involved because it needs to construct an instance of the subclass, not just process an existing instance. So cons invokes the class constructor IntListA using the **new** operator. We see that this is similar to IntList. However, the IntListA constructor does not want to invent a completely new kind of object; it wants to create an object that is like the superclass object. Java has a special method for this purpose, called **super**. In our example, using **super** is all that is necessary. When the subclass has additional instance fields, compared to the superclass, the constructor might have additional statements to initialize these fields.

Figure A.13 shows a program that tests the IntListA class. Notice that it is able to print objects in the IntListA class simply by passing them to println. This program does not even need to know that the IntList class exists—it only deals directly with IntListA. However, the toString method in IntList is inherited by IntListA and becomes available for use by any method that processes an IntListA object.

Notice that length is followed by parentheses in one case and not in the other in main. This is because argv is an *array* (of strings), so its length is an instance field, while argv[0] is a **String** object, so *its* length is a method call.

We leave it to readers to decipher what testA.java "does." As a hint, it is related to a FIFO queue (see Section 2.4.2). Suppose the command "java testA *word*" is issued. The value of n is the length of *word*. If *word* is omitted, n = 0. What do you think the asymptotic order of this program's time is, as a function of n?

```java
public class IntList
    {
    protected int element;
    protected IntList next;
    public static final IntList  nil = null;
    public static int  first(IntList aList)
        { return aList.element; }
    public static IntList  rest(IntList aList)
        { return aList.next; }
    public static IntList  cons(int newElement, IntList oldList)
        { return new IntList(newElement, oldList); }
    // the real constructor, but we want cons for interface.
    protected  IntList(int newElement, IntList oldList)
        {
        element = newElement;
        next = oldList;
        }

    /** Convert IntList to String, similar to prolog, ML style. */
    public
    String  toString()
        { return "[" + toStringR("", this); }

    static
    String toStringR(String prefix, IntList L)
        {
        String s;

        if (L == nil)
            s = "]";
        else
            s = prefix + first(L) + toStringR(", ", rest(L));
        return s;
        }
    }
```

Figure A.11   The file IntList.java gives the definition of toString, as well as the basic IntList ADT operations. Some members are **protected** so they can be accessed from subclasses.

Pros and Cons of Subclasses

For a small class like IntList, not much is accomplished by making a subclass; that is, the subclass does not inherit much. Seeing all the complications of defining the subclass, it is reasonable to ask whether it is all worthwhile. However, in other cases there is more

```
public class IntListA  extends IntList
    {
    // Redefine all members whose result type becomes IntListA.
    public static final IntListA  nil = (IntListA) IntList.nil;
    public static IntListA  rest(IntListA aList)
        { return (IntListA) IntList.rest(aList); }
    public static IntListA  cons(int newElement, IntListA oldList)
        { return new IntListA(newElement, oldList); }
    // the real constructor, but we want cons for interface.
    protected  IntListA(int newElement, IntListA oldList)
        { super(newElement, oldList); }


    /** append1 is new in the extended class.
     * Precondition: aList != nil.
     * Postcondition: aList has newE as additional element at
     * the end, after the previous last element.
     * That is, suppose previously endL was the suffix of aList
     * for which rest(endL) == nil. Now first(rest(endL)) == newE
     * and rest(rest(endL)) == nil.
     */
    public static
    void  append1(IntListA aList, int newE)
        {
        if (rest(aList) == nil)
            {
            IntListA  newLast = cons(newE, nil);
            aList.next = newLast;
            }
        else
            {
            append1(rest(aList), newE);
            }
        }
    }
```

Figure A.12 The file IntListA.java gives the definition of IntListA. The **extends** keyword states that this is a subclass of IntList.

functionality to inherit. Reusing code helps ensure consistency. We saw IntListA inherit the functionality of toString, and it was able to reuse the method first.

On the negative side, use of subclasses can make things very confusing. There may be several versions of a method with the same name, and it is often unclear which one will be applied unless you have a thorough understanding of the language. Type casting is

```
public class testA
{
    public static void main(String argv[])
        {
        int  n;
        if (argv.length > 0)
            n = argv[0].length();
        else
            n = 0;
        IntListA  a = IntListA.cons(1, IntListA.nil);
        IntListA  end = a;
        for (int i = 0; i < n; i++)
            {
            IntListA.append1(end, i+2);
            end = IntListA.rest(end);
            }
        System.out.println(a);
        System.out.println(IntListA.first(a));
        System.out.println(IntListA.rest(a));
        }
    }
```

Figure A.13   The file testA.java contains a main procedure that exercises the IntListA class.

frequently necessary. Implementing and testing algorithms does not require programmer-defined subclass structures, so if that is your main goal, we suggest that you avoid them.

A.7 Copy via the "Cloneable" Interface

Java provides an interface called **Cloneable** that requires the method clone for copying objects. The class **Object** implements clone as a one-level copy of the members of the object. That is, any members that are themselves objects simply have their *references* copied; they are not cloned recursively. We have assembled the ugly technical code in a class named Organizer, as shown in Figure A.14. The **catch** statement simply suppresses the exception, which we don't expect ever to occur. If you'd rather throw an error, see Appendix A.3.

Programmer-defined organizer classes can be declared as subclasses of Organizer, inherit copy1level, and use that to implement their own copy functions. The simple case is shown for the Edge class in Figure A.4. If the organizer class contains an instance field in another organizer class, that instance field must be copied explicitly, to conform to the conventions for organizer classes set forth in Section 1.2.2. Using the Date example from

```
public class Organizer implements Cloneable
    {
    protected static
    Organizer copy1level(Organizer obj)
        {
        Organizer objCopy;
        objCopy = null; // needed because of try/catch
        try{ objCopy = (Organizer)obj.clone(); }
        catch(CloneNotSupportedException e) { }
        return objCopy;
        }
    }
```

Figure A.14   The file Organizer.java

that section (Date would be declared with "**extends** Organizer," like edge), the copy function for date becomes:

```
class Date extends Organizer
    ⋮
    public static Date  copy(Date d)
        { Date  d2 = (Date) copy1level(d);
          d2.year = Year.copy(d.year);  // organizer class
          return d2;
        }
```

Notice that the type cast "(Date)" is necessary. The type returned by copy1level is **Object**.

Bibliography

Adleman, L. M. (1994). Molecular Computation of Solutions to Combinatorial Problems. *Science*, 266:1021–1024.

Adleman, L. M. (1998). Computing with DNA. *Scientific American*, pages 54–61.

Aho, A. V. and Corasick, M. J. (1975). Efficient String Matching: An Aid to Bibliographic Search. *Communications of the ACM*, 18(6):333–340.

Aho, A. V., Hopcroft, J. E., and Ullman, J. D. (1974). *The Design and Analysis of Computer Algorithms*. Addison-Wesley, Reading, MA.

Aho, A. V., Hopcroft, J. E., and Ullman, J. D. (1983). *Data Structures and Algorithms*. Addison-Wesley, Reading, MA.

Akl, S. (1985). *Parallel Sorting*. Academic Press, Orlando, FL.

Angluin, D. (1976). The Four Russians' Algorithm for Boolean Matrix Multiplication Is Optimal in its Class. *SIGACT News*, 8(1):29–33.

Apostolico, A. and Giancarlo, R. (1986). The Boyer-Moore-Galil String Searching Strategies Revisited. *SIAM Journal on Computing*, 15(1):98–105.

Arlazarov, V. L., Dinic, E. A., Kronrod, M. A., and Faradzev, I. A. (1970). On Economical Construction of the Transitive Closure of a Directed Graph. *Soviet Mathematics, Doklady*, 11(5):1209–1210.

Awerbuch, B. and Shiloach, Y. (1983). New Connectivity and MSF Algorithms for Ultracomputer and PRAM. In *Proceedings of the IEEE International Conference on Parallel Processing*, pages 175–179.

Awerbuch, B. and Shiloach, Y. (1987). New Connectivity and MSF Algorithms for Shuffle-Exchange Network and PRAM. *IEEE Transactions on Computers*, C-36(10):1258–1263.

Batcher, K. E. (1968). Sorting Networks and Their Applications. In *Proceedings of the AFIPS Spring Joint Computer Conference*, pages 307–314.

Bayer, R. (1972). Symmetric Binary B-Trees: Data Structure and Maintenance Algorithms. *Acta Informatica*, 1(4):290–306.

Beame, P. (1986). Limits on the Power of Concurrent-Write Parallel Machines. In *Proceedings of the Eighteenth Annual ACM Symposium on Theory of Computing*, pages 169–176.

Bellman, R. E. (1957). *Dynamic Programming*. Princeton University Press, Princeton, NJ.

Bellman, R. E. and Dreyfus, S. E. (1962). *Applied Dynamic Programming*. Princeton University Press, Princeton, NJ.

Bentley, J. L. (1982). *Writing Efficient Programs*. Prentice-Hall, Englewood Cliffs, NJ.

Bentley, J. L. (1986). *Programming Pearls*. Addison-Wesley, Reading, MA.

Bentley, J. L. (column). Programming Pearls. *Communications of the ACM*.

Bentley, J. L., Johnson, D., Leighton, F. T., and McGeoch, C. C. (1983). An Experimental Study of Bin packing. In *Proceedings of the 21st Annual Allerton Conference on Communication, Control, and Computing*, pages 51–60.

Blum, M., Floyd, R. W., Pratt, V., Rivest, R. L., and Tarjan, R. E. (1973). Time Bounds for Selection. *Journal of Computer and System Sciences*, 7:448–461.

Borodin, A. and Munro, I. (1975). *Computational Complexity of Algebraic and Numeric Problems*. American Elsevier, New York.

Boyer, R. S. and Moore, J. S. (1977). A Fast String Searching Algorithm. *Communications of the ACM*, 20(10):762–772.

Brassard, G. (1985). Crusade for a Better Notation. *SIGACT News*, 17(1):60–64.

Brigham, E. O. (1974). *The Fast Fourier Transform*. Prentice-Hall, Englewood Cliffs, NJ.

Carlsson, S. (1987). A Variant of Heapsort with Almost Optimal Number of Comparisons. *Information Processing Letters*, 24(4):247–250.

Chandra, A. K., Stockmeyer, L. J., and Vishkin, U. (1984). Constant Depth Reducibility. *SIAM Journal on Computing*, 13(2):423–439.

Cook, S. A. (1971). The Complexity of Theorem Proving Procedures. In *Proceedings of the Third Annual ACM Symposium on Theory of Computing*, pages 151–158.

Cook, S. A. (1983). An Overview of Computational Complexity. *Communications of the ACM*, 26(6):400–408.

Cook, S. A. (1985). A Taxonomy of Problems with Fast Parallel Algorithms. *Information and Control*, 64(1–3):2–22.

Cook, S. A., Dwork, C., and Reischuk, R. (1986). Upper and Lower Time Bounds for Parallel Random Access Machines without Simultaneous Writes. *SIAM Journal on Computing*, 15(1):87–97.

Cooley, J. W. and Tukey, J. W. (1965). An Algorithm for the Machine Calculation of Complex Fourier Series. *Mathematics of Computation*, 19:297–301.

Coppersmith, D. and Winograd, S. (1987). Matrix Multiplication via Arithmetic Progressions. In *Proceedings of the 19th Annual ACM Symposium on Theory of Computing*, pages 1–6.

Cormen, T. H., Leiserson, C. E., and Rivest, R. L. (1990). *Introduction to Algorithms*. McGraw-Hill, New York.

Crochemore, M. and Rytter, W. (1994). *Text Algorithms*. Oxford University Press, New York.

Cytron, R., Ferrante, J., Rosen, B. K., Wegman, M. N., and Zadeck, F. K. (1991). Efficiently Computing Static Single-Assignment Form and the Control Dependence Graph. *ACM Transactions on Programming Languages and Systems*, 13(4):451–490.

De Millo, R. A., Lipton, R. J., and Perlis, A. J. (1979). Social Processes and Proofs of Theorems and Programs. *Communications of the ACM*, 22(5):271–280.

Deo, N. (1974). *Graph Theory with Applications to Engineering and Computer Science*. Prentice-Hall, Englewood Cliffs, NJ.

Dijkstra, E. W. (1959). A Note on Two Problems in Connexion with Graphs. *Numerische Mathematik*, 1:269–271.

Dijkstra, E. W. (1976). *A Discipline of Programming*. Prentice-Hall, Englewood Cliffs, NJ.

Dor, D. and Zwick, U. (1995). Selecting the Median. In *Proceedings of the Sixth Annual ACM-SIAM Symposium on Discrete Algorithms*, pages 28–37.

Dor, D. and Zwick, U. (1996a). Finding the αn-th Largest Element. *Combinatorica*, 16(1):41–58.

Dor, D. and Zwick, U. (1996b). Median Selection Requires $(2 + \epsilon)n$ Comparisons. In *Proceedings of the 37th Annual Symposium on Foundations of Computer Science*, pages 125–134.

Estivill-Castro, V. and Wood, D. (1996). An Adaptive Generic Sorting Algorithm that Uses Variable Partitioning. *International Journal of Computer Mathematics*, 61(3–4):181–94.

Even, S. (1973). *Algorithmic Combinatorics*. Macmillan, New York.

Even, S. (1979). *Graph Algorithms*. Computer Science Press, Inc., Rockville, MD.

Fischer, M. J. (1972). Efficiency of Equivalence Algorithms. In Miller, R. and Thatcher, J., editors, *Complexity of Computer Computations*, pages 153–167. Plenum Press, New York.

Fischer, M. J. and Meyer, A. R. (1971). Boolean Matrix Multiplication and Transitive Closure. In *Conference Record, IEEE 12th Annual Symposium on Switching and Automata Theory*, pages 129–131.

Floyd, R. W. (1962). Algorithm 97: Shortest Path. *Communications of the ACM*, 5(6):345.

Floyd, R. W. (1964). Algorithm 245: Treesort 3. *Communications of the ACM*, 7(12):701.

Ford, Jr., L. R. and Fulkerson, D. R. (1962). *Flows in Networks*. Princeton University Press, Princeton, NJ.

Fortune, S. and Wyllie, J. (1978). Parallelism in Random Access Machines. In *Proceedings of the Tenth Annual ACM Symposium on Theory of Computing*, pages 114–118.

Fredman, M. L. (1999). On the Efficiency of Pairing Heaps and Related Data Structures. *Journal of the ACM*, 46. (to appear).

Fredman, M. L. and Saks, M. E. (1989). The Cell Probe Complexity of Dynamic Data Structures. In *Proceedings of the Twenty-First Annual ACM Symposium on Theory of Computing*, pages 345–354.

Fredman, M. L., Sedgewick, R., Sleator, D. D., and Tarjan, R. E. (1986). The Pairing Heap: A New Form of Self-Adjusting Heap. *Algorithmica*, 1(1):111–129.

Fredman, M. L. and Tarjan, R. E. (1987). Fibonacci Heaps and Their Uses in Improved Network Optimization Algorithms. *Journal of the ACM*, 34(3):596–615.

Gabow, H. N. (1977). Two Algorithms for Generating Weighted Spanning Trees in Order. *SIAM Journal on Computing*, 6(1):139–150.

Galil, Z. (1976). Real-Time Algorithms for String-Matching and Palindrome Recognition. In *Proceedings of the Eighth Annual ACM Symposium on Theory of Computing*, pages 161–173.

Galil, Z. (1979). On Improving the Worst Case Running Time of the Boyer-Moore String Matching Algorithm. *Communications of the ACM*, 22(9):505–508.

Galler, B. A. and Fischer, M. J. (1964). An Improved Equivalence Algorithm. *Communications of the ACM*, 7(5):301–303.

Gardner, M. (1983). *Wheels, Life, and Other Mathematical Amusements*. W. H. Freeman, San Francisco.

Garey, M. R., Graham, R. L., and Ullman, J. D. (1972). Worst-Case Analysis of Memory Allocation Algorithms. In *Proceedings of the Fourth Annual ACM Symposium on Theory of Computing*, pages 143–150.

Garey, M. R. and Johnson, D. S. (1976). The Complexity of Near-Optimal Graph Coloring. *Journal of the ACM*, 23(1):43–49.

Garey, M. R. and Johnson, D. S. (1979). *Computers and Intractability: A Guide to the Theory of NP-Completeness*. W. H. Freeman, San Francisco.

Gehani, N. (1988). *C: An Advanced Introduction, ANSI C Edition*. Computer Science Press, Rockville, MD.

Gibbons, A. (1985). *Algorithmic Graph Theory*. Cambridge University Press, Cambridge, England.

Goldschlager, L. M. (1978). A Unified Approach to Models of Synchronous Parallel Machines. In *Proceedings of the Tenth Annual ACM Symposium on Theory of Computing*, pages 89–94.

Gonnet, G. H. and Baeza-Yates, R. (1991). *Handbook of Algorithms and Data Structures*. Addison-Wesley, Reading, MA, second edition.

Gosling, J., Joy, B., and Steele, G. (1996). *The Java Language Specification*. Addison-Wesley, Reading, MA.

Graham, R. L., Knuth, D. E., and Patashnik, O. (1994). *Concrete Mathematics: A Foundation for Computer Science*. Addison-Wesley, Reading, MA, second edition.

Grassmann, W. K. and Tremblay, J. P. (1996). *Logic and Discrete Mathematics: A Computer Science Perspective*. Prentice-Hall, Upper Saddle River, NJ.

Greene, D. H. and Knuth, D. E. (1990). *Mathematics for the Analysis of Algorithms*. Birkhauser, Boston, third edition.

Greenlaw, R., Hoover, H. J., and Ruzzo, W. L. (1995). *Limits to Parallel Computation: P-Completeness Theory*. Oxford University Press, New York.

Gries, D. (1981). *The Science of Programming*. Springer-Verlag, New York.

Guibas, L. J. and Odlyzko, A. M. (1977). A New Proof of the Linearity of the Boyer-Moore String Searching Algorithms. In *Proceedings of the 18th Annual IEEE Symposium on Foundations of Computer Science*, pages 189–195.

Guibas, L. J. and Sedgewick, R. (1978). A Dichromatic Framework for Balanced Trees. In *Proceedings of the 19th Annual IEEE Symposium on Foundations of Computer Science*, pages 8–21.

Hall, P. A. V. and Dowling, G. R. (1980). Approximate String Matching. *Computing Surveys*, 12(4):381–402.

Hambrusch, S. E. and Simon, J. (1985). Solving Undirected Graph Problems on VLSI. *SIAM Journal on Computing*, 14(3):527–544.

Hantler, S. L. and King, J. C. (1976). An Introduction to Proving the Correctness of Programs. *ACM Computing Surveys*, 8(3):331–353.

Hirschberg, D. S. (1976). Parallel Algorithms for the Transitive Closure and the Connected Component Problems. In *Proceedings of the 8th Annual ACM Symposium on Theory of Computing*, pages 55–57.

Hoare, C. A. R. (1962). Quicksort. *Computer Journal*, 5(1):10–15.

Hochbaum, D. S., editor (1997). *Approximation Algorithms for NP-Hard Problems*. PWS Publishing Co., Boston, MA.

Hopcroft, J. E. and Tarjan, R. E. (1973a). Dividing a Graph into Triconnected Components. *SIAM Journal on Computing*, 2(3):135–157.

Hopcroft, J. E. and Tarjan, R. E. (1973b). Algorithm 447: Efficient Algorithms for Graph Manipulation. *Communications of the ACM*, 16(6):372–378.

Hopcroft, J. E. and Tarjan, R. E. (1974). Efficient Planarity Testing. *Journal of the ACM*, 21(4):549–568.

Hopcroft, J. E. and Ullman, J. D. (1973). Set Merging Algorithms. *SIAM Journal on Computing*, 2(4):294–303.

Hyafil, L. (1976). Bounds for Selection. *SIAM Journal on Computing*, 5(1):109–114.

Ibarra, O. H. and Kim, C. E. (1975). Fast Approximation Algorithms for the Knapsack and Sum of Subset Problems. *Journal of the ACM*, 22(4):463–468.

JáJá, J. (1992). *An Introduction to Parallel Algorithms*. Addison-Wesley, Reading, MA.

Johnson, D. S. (1972). Fast Allocation Algorithms. In *Proceedings of the Thirteenth Annual Symposium on Switching and Automata Theory*, pages 144–154.

Johnson, D. S. (1973). Approximation Algorithms for Combinatorial Problems. In *Proceedings of the Fifth Annual ACM Symposium on Theory of Computing*, pages 38–49.

Johnson, D. S. (1974). Worst-Case Behavior of Graph Coloring Algorithms. In *Proceedings of the Fifth Southeastern Conference on Combinatorics, Graph Theory, and Computing*, pages 513–528. Utilitas Mathematica Publishing, Winnipeg, Canada.

Johnson, D. S. and Trick, M. A., editors (1996). *Cliques, Coloring, and Satisfiability: Second DIMACS Implementation Challenge.*, volume 26 of *DIMACS Series in Discrete Mathematics and Theoretical Computer Science*. American Mathematical Society, Providence, RI.

Jones, D. W. (1986). An Empirical Comparison of Priority-Queue and Event-Set Implementations. *Communications of the ACM*, 29(4):300–311.

Kaplan, P. D., Cecchi, G., and Libchaber, A. (1995). Molecular Computation: Adlemen's Experiment Repeated. Technical report, NEC Research Institute, Princeton, NJ.

Kari, L., Păun, G., Rozenberg, G., Salomaa, A., and Yu, S. (1998). DNA Computing, Sticker Systems, and Universality. *Acta Informatica*, 35(5):401–420.

Karp, R. M. (1972). Reducibility Among Combinatorial Problems. In Miller, R. and Thatcher, J., editors, *Complexity of Computer Computations*, pages 85–104. Plenum Press, New York.

Karp, R. M. (1986). Combinatorics, Complexity, and Randomness. *Communications of the ACM*, 29(2):98–109.

King, K. N. and Smith-Thomas, B. (1982). An Optimal Algorithm for Sink-Finding. *Information Processing Letters*, 14(3):109–111.

Kingston, J. H. (1997). *Algorithms and Data Structures: Design, Correctness, Analysis*. Addison-Wesley, Reading, MA.

Kleene, S. C. (1956). Representation of Events in Nerve Nets and Finite Automata. In Shannon, C. E. and McCarthy, J., editors, *Automata Studies*, pages 3–40. Princeton University Press, Princeton, NJ.

Knuth, D. E. (1968). *The Art of Computer Programming,* volume 1: *Fundamental Algorithms*. Addison-Wesley, Reading, MA.

Knuth, D. E. (1976). Big Omicron and Big Omega and Big Theta. *SIGACT News*, 8(2):18–24.

Knuth, D. E. (1984). The Complexity of Songs. *Communications of the ACM*, 27(4):344–346.

Knuth, D. E. (1997). *The Art of Computer Programming,* volume 1: *Fundamental Algorithms*. Addison-Wesley, Reading, MA, third edition.

Knuth, D. E. (1998). *The Art of Computer Programming,* volume 3: *Sorting and Searching*. Addison-Wesley, Reading, MA, second edition.

Knuth, D. E., Morris, Jr., J. H., and Pratt, V. R. (1977). Fast Pattern Matching in Strings. *SIAM Journal on Computing*, 6(2):323–350.

Kronsjo, L. (1985). *Computational Complexity of Sequential and Parallel Algorithms*. Wiley, New York.

Kruse, R. L., Tondo, C. L., and Leung, B. P. (1997). *Data Structures and Program Design in C*. Prentice-Hall, Upper Saddle River, NJ, second edition.

Kruskal, C. P. (1983). Searching, Merging, and Sorting in Parallel Computation. *IEEE Transactions on Computers*, C-32(10):942–946.

Kruskal, Jr., J. B. (1956). On the Shortest Spanning Subtree of a Graph and the Traveling Salesman Problem. *Proceedings of the AMS*, 7(1):48–50.

Landau, G. M. and Vishkin, U. (1986). Introducing Efficient Parallelism into Approximate String Matching and a New Serial Algorithm. In *Proceedings of the 18th Annual ACM Symposium on Theory of Computing*, pages 220–230.

Lawler, E. L., Lenstra, J. K., Kan, A. H. G. R., and Schmoys, D. B., editors (1985). *The Traveling Salesman Problem*. Wiley, New York.

Linial, M. and Linial, N. (1995). Letters to *Science*. *Science*, 268:481.

Lueker, G. S. (1980). Some Techniques for Solving Recurrences. *Computing Surveys*, 12(4):419–436.

Maley, C. C. (1998). DNA Computation: Theory, Practice, and Prospects. *Evolutionary Computation*, 6(3):201–229.

Munro, I. (1971). Efficient Determination of the Transitive Closure of a Directed Graph. *Information Processing Letters*, 1(2):56–58.

Oldehoeft, R. R., Cann, D. C., and Allan, S. J. (1986). SISAL: Initial MIMD Performance Results. In Handler, W., Haupt, D., et al., editors, *Conference on Algorithms and Hardware for Parallel Processing*, pages 120–127. Springer-Verlag, New York.

Pan, V. (1966). On Means of Calculating Values of Polynomials. *Russian Mathematical Surveys*, 21(1):105–136.

Parberry, I. (1987). *Parallel Complexity Theory*. Wiley, New York.

Parnas, D. L. (1972). A Technique for Software Module Specification with Examples. *Communications of the ACM*, 15(5):330–36.

Pǎun, G., Rozenberg, G., and Salomaa, A. (1998). *DNA Computing: New Computing Paradigms*. Springer-Verlag, New York.

Perlis, A. J. (1978). The American Side of the Development of ALGOL. *SIGPLAN Notices*, 13(8):3–14.

Pippenger, N. (1979). On Simultaneous Resource Bounds. In *Proceedings of the 20th Annual Symposium of Foundations of Computer Science*, pages 307–311. IEEE, New York.

Press, W., Flannery, B., Teukolsky, S., and Vettering, W. (1988). *Numerical Recipes in C: The Art of Scientific Computing*. Cambridge University Press.

Prim, R. C. (1957). Shortest Connection Networks and Some Generalizations. *Bell System Technical Journal*, 36:1389–1401.

Purdom, Jr., P. W. and Brown, C. A. (1985). *The Analysis of Algorithms*. Holt, Rinehart and Winston, New York.

Quinn, M. J. (1987). *Designing Efficient Algorithms for Parallel Computers*. McGraw-Hill, New York.

Quinn, M. J. and Deo, N. (1984). Parallel Graph Algorithms. *ACM Computing Surveys*, 16(3):319–348.

Rabin, M. O. (1977). Complexity of Computations. *Communications of the ACM*, 20(9):625–633.

Reingold, E. M. (1972). On the Optimality of Some Set Merging Algorithms. *Journal of the ACM*, 19(4):649–659.

Reingold, E. M., Nievergelt, J., and Deo, N. (1977). *Combinatorial Algorithms: Theory and Practice*. Prentice-Hall, Englewood Cliffs, NJ.

Reingold, E. M. and Stocks, A. I. (1972). Simple Proofs of Lower Bounds for Polynomial Evaluation. In Miller, R. and Thatcher, J., editors, *Complexity of Computer Computations*, pages 21–30. Plenum Press, New York.

Richards, D. (1986). Parallel Sorting—A Bibliography. *SIGACT News*, 18(1):28–48.

Roberts, E. (1995). *The Art and Science of C: A Library-Based Introduction to Computer Science*. Addison-Wesley, Reading, MA.

Roberts, E. (1997). *Programming Abstractions in C: A Second Course in Computer Science*. Addison-Wesley, Reading, MA.

Sahni, S. K. (1975). Approximate Algorithms for the 0/1 Knapsack Problem. *Journal of the ACM*, 22(1):115–124.

Sahni, S. K. (1976). Algorithms for Scheduling Independent Tasks. *Journal of the ACM*, 23(1):116–127.

Savage, J. E. (1974). An Algorithm for the Computation of Linear Forms. *SIAM Journal on Computing*, 3:150–158.

Schönhage, A., Paterson, M., and Pippenger, N. (1976). Finding the Median. *Journal of Computer and System Sciences*, 13:184–199.

Sedgewick, R. (1977). Quicksort with Equal Keys. *SIAM Journal on Computing*, 6(2):240–267.

Sedgewick, R. (1978). Implementing Quicksort Programs. *Communications of the ACM*, 21(10):847–857.

Sedgewick, R. (1988). *Algorithms*. Addison-Wesley, Reading, MA, second edition.

Sethi, R. (1996). *Programming Languages: Concepts and Constructs*. Addison-Wesley, Reading, MA, second edition.

Sharir, M. (1981). A Strong-Connectivity Algorithm and its Application in Data Flow Analysis. *Computers and Mathematics with Applications*, 7(1):67–72.

Shell, D. L. (1959). A High-Speed Sorting Procedure. *Communications of the ACM*, 2(7):30–32.

Shiloach, Y. and Vishkin, U. (1981). Finding the Maximum, Merging and Sorting in a Parallel Computation Model. *Journal of Algorithms*, 2:88–102.

Shiloach, Y. and Vishkin, U. (1982). An $O(\log n)$ Parallel Connectivity Algorithm. *Journal of Algorithms*, 3:57–67.

Sleator, D. D. and Tarjan, R. E. (1985). Self-Adjusting Binary Search Trees. *Journal of the ACM*, 32(3):652–686.

Smit, G. de V. (1982). A Comparison of Three String Matching Algorithms. *Software: Practice and Experience*, 12:57–66.

Snir, M. (1985). On Parallel Searching. *SIAM Journal on Computing*, 14(3):688–708.

Stasko, J. T. and Vitter, J. S. (1987). Pairing Heaps: Experiments and Analysis. *Communications of the ACM*, 30(3):234–249.

Strassen, V. (1969). Gaussian Elimination Is Not Optimal. *Numerische Mathematik*, 13:354–356.

Tarjan, R. E. (1972). Depth-First Search and Linear Graph Algorithms. *SIAM Journal on Computing*, 1(2):146–160.

Tarjan, R. E. (1975). On the Efficiency of a Good but Not Linear Set Union Algorithm. *Journal of the ACM*, 22(2):215–225.

Tarjan, R. E. (1983a). *Data Structures and Network Algorithms*. Society for Industrial and Applied Mathematics, Philadelphia.

Tarjan, R. E. (1983b). Updating a Balanced Search Tree in $O(1)$ Rotations. *Information Processing Letters*, 16(5):253–257.

Tarjan, R. E. and Vishkin, U. (1985). An Efficient Parallel Biconnectivity Algorithm. *SIAM Journal on Computing*, 14(4):862–874.

Thompson, K. (1986). Retrograde Analysis of Certain Endgames. *ICCA Journal*, 9(3):131–139. (request paper from author).

Thompson, K. (1990). KQPKQ and KRPKR Endings. *ICCA Journal*, 13(4):196–199. (request paper from author).

Thompson, K. (1991). New Results for KNPKB and KNPKN Endgames. *ICCA Journal*, 14(1):17. (request paper from author).

Thompson, K. (1996). 6-Piece Endgames. *ICCA Journal*, 19(4):215–226. (request paper from author).

Ullman, J. D. (1984). *Computational Aspects of VLSI*. Computer Science Press, Rockville, MD.

van Leeuwen, J. and Tarjan, R. E. (1984). Worst-Case Analysis of Set Union Algorithms. *Journal of the ACM*, 31(2):245–281.

Wagner, R. A. and Fischer, M. J. (1974). The String-to-String Correction Problem. *Journal of the ACM*, 21(1):168–178.

Wainwright, R. L. (1985). A Class of Sorting Algorithms Based on Quicksort. *Communications of the ACM*, 28(4):396–403.

Warshall, S. (1962). A Theorem on Boolean Matrices. *Journal of the ACM*, 9(1):11–12.

Wegner, P. (1974). Modification of Aho and Ullman's Correctness Proof of Warshall's Algorithm. *SIGACT News*, 6(1):32–35.

Weiss, M. A. (1998). *Data Structures and Problem Solving Using Java*. Addison-Wesley, Reading, MA.

Wigderson, A. (1983). Improving the Performance Guarantee for Approximate Graph Coloring. *Journal of the ACM*, 30(4):729–735.

Wilf, H. S. (1986). *Algorithms and Complexity*. Prentice-Hall, Englewood Cliffs, NJ.

Williams, J. W. J. (1964). Algorithm 232: Heapsort. *Communications of the ACM*, 7(6):347–348.

Winograd, S. (1970). On the Number of Multiplications Necessary to Compute Certain Functions. *Journal of Pure and Applied Mathematics*, 23:165–179.

Yao, F. (1982). Speed-Up in Dynamic Programming. *SIAM Journal on Algebraic and Discrete Methods*, 3(4):532–540.

Index